W9-CSJ-430

Real Estate Law in California

THIRD EDITION

ARTHUR G. BOWMAN, A.B., J.D.

Member State Bar of California and Hawaii

PRENTICE HALL, INC., ENGLEWOOD CLIFFS, N.J.

PRENTICE-HALL SERIES IN REAL ESTATE

13-763995-3
Library of Congress Catalog Card Number: 70-102713

current printing (last digit):
10 9 8 7 6 5

PRENTICE-HALL INTERNATIONAL, INC., *London*
PRENTICE-HALL OF AUSTRALIA, PTY LTD, *Sydney*
PRENTICE-HALL OF CANADA, LTD., *Toronto*
PRENTICE-HALL OF INDIA PRIVATE LTD., *New Delhi*
PRENTICE-HALL OF JAPAN, INC., *Tokyo*

Printed in the United States of America

Preface

The broad expanse of California real property law, with its many special features, has given rise to a need for a book devoted exclusively to the real estate law of the state. This need was filled by the publication of the first edition of this book in 1958 which sought to present a complete and well-organized coverage of all aspects of the California law.

The second edition of this book included changes and additions to the law through September, 1964. Since then there have been many more statutory changes and court decisions, including recent decisions of the United States Supreme Court, of vital importance in the field of real estate. The California legislature now meets annually in a general session, and it is anticipated that each year will see further changes in the real estate law.

This new edition includes changes and additions in the law through July, 1969. In order to present the material in the most effective manner, the chapters of the previous edition were revised after considerable testing. In this new edition only minor chapter revision has been necessary.

The objective of this book is to acquaint all persons interested in real estate with the facts of California real estate law. The book deals with California law only—with the practical aspects of that law, not with theory alone. It will be helpful to anyone concerned with real estate: brokers, salesmen, college students majoring in real estate, and the California real property owner. It will give them a better understanding and a thorough acquaintance with the principles of real estate law in this state. The newer attorney and others will also find valuable the discussions of practical aspects of real estate transactions.

Because of the scope of coverage and its authoritative treatment, the previous editions have had many users. Most adults in California have a vital and abiding interest in the subject of real estate. As is apparent from the many changes in the law since this book was first published, the law is a dynamic source, constantly being extended to meet the needs and requirements of modern developments and trends in the real estate field. An understanding of the laws pertaining to real estate is, of course, essential to those engaged in some phase of real estate, and a basic understanding on the part of other members of the public is also desirable because it increases their awareness of the implications of our legal system in regard to rights, duties, and obligations pertaining to real property. The present book has been an important contribution in this respect.

Contents

MAP OF CALIFORNIA

Showing County Lines

Table of Abbreviations

A.C. Advance California Reports. (Official advance sheets containing the latest decisions of the California Supreme Court.)

A.C.A. Advance California Appellate Reports. (Official advance sheets containing the latest decisions of the California District Courts of Appeal.)

Agr. C. Agricultural Code.

Bus. & Prof. C. Business and Professions Code.

C.A. California Appellate Reports. (Bound volumes containing decisions of the California District Courts of Appeal.)

C.A.2d California Appellate Reports, second series.

C.A.2d Supp. California Appellate Reports, second series, Supplement. (Cases determined in the Appellate Departments of the Superior Court.)

Cal. California Reports. (Bound volumes containing decisions of the California Supreme Court.)

Cal.2d California Reports, second series.

Cal. Const. California Constitution.

C.C. Civil Code.

C.C.P. Code of Civil Procedure.

Corp. C. Corporations Code.

Evid. C. Evidence Code.

Fed. Federal Reporter. (Bound volumes containing decisions of the Federal Courts of Appeal.)

Fed.2d Federal Reporter, second series.

Fed. Supp. Federal Supplement. (Bound volumes containing decisions of the U. S. District Courts.)

Fin. C. Financial Code.

Govt. C. Government Code.

H. & S. C. Health and Safety Code.

Ins. C. Insurance Code.

Int. Rev. C. Internal Revenue Code.

L.Ed.2d. United States Supreme Court Reports, Lawyers' Edition, Second Series.

Ops. Cal. Atty. Gen. Opinions of the Attorney General of California.

Pen. C. Penal Code.

Pro. C. Probate Code.

Pub. Res. C. Public Resources Code.

Rev. & Tax. C. Revenue and Taxation Code.

Sec. Section.

Sts. & Hy. C. Streets and Highways Code.

U.C.C. Uniform Commercial Code.

U.S. United States Reports. (Bound volumes containing the decisions of the Supreme Court of the United States.)

U.S.C. United States Code.

U.S.C.A. United States Code Annotated.

U. S. Const. United States Constitution.

Definition of Words and Phrases

Abatement of nuisance. Extinction or termination of a nuisance.

Abstract. An abridgement; a brief summary.

Abstract of judgment. A condensation of the essential provisions of a court judgment.

Abstract of title. A summary of the condition of title based on an examination of public records.

Abutting owner. Owner whose land touches a highway or other public place.

Acceleration clause. A clause in a note or trust deed permitting the payee or beneficiary to declare the entire unpaid balance immediately due and payable upon the happening of a stated event, such as the failure to pay an installment when due.

Accession. Acquisition of property by its incorporation or union with other property.

Accommodation party. A person who, for the purpose of permitting another person to obtain credit, signs a note without receiving value.

Accretion. Increase of land on a shore or bank of a river by the gradual action of the water.

Acknowledgment. A form for authenticating instruments conveying property or otherwise conferring rights; a declaration by the party executing an instrument that it is his act and deed.

Action in personam. A court action which seeks a judgment against the person as distinguished from a judgment against property.

Action in rem. A court action which seeks a judgment against property.

Adjudication. Judicial determination of a case or controversy.

Administrator. A person appointed by a probate court as the representative of a decedent's estate where the decedent left no will.

Administrator C. T. A. Administrator with the will annexed; the representative of a decedent's estate where no one is named as executor, or where the named person is unable or unwilling to act.

Ad valorem. According to the value.

Adverse possession. A method of acquisition of property based on continued use and payment of taxes.

Affiant. A person who makes an affidavit.

Affidavit. A sworn statement in writing, made before an authorized official.

Agent. A person who acts for another, called a principal.

Alienation. The voluntary parting with the ownership of real property.

Alien. An unnaturalized foreign resident.

Alluvion. Soil deposited by accretion.

Amortization. Provision for the payment of a debt or obligation by creating a sinking fund, or paying on an installment basis.

Ancillary administrator. An administrator appointed in a place other than the decedent's domicile.

Antenuptial agreement. A contract made by a man and a woman in contemplation of their marriage.

Appraisal. An opinion as to the fair market value of property.

Appurtenant. Belonging to.

Assessed value. Value placed on property as a basis for taxation.

Assessments. Special and local impositions upon property in the immediate vicinity of an improvement.

Assignment. A transfer by writing of a person's interest in property, usually of a chose in action.

Assumption agreement. An undertaking or adoption of a debt or obligation primarily resting upon another person.

Attachment. A seizure of property by judicial process during the pendency of an action.

Attestation clause. A clause in an instrument denoting that the persons therein named have affixed their names as witnesses.

Attorney-in-fact. An agent authorized to act for another under a power of attorney.

Avulsion. The sudden tearing away of land by the violent action of a river or other water course.

Base lines. Imaginary east-west lines which intersect meridians to form a starting point for the measurement of land.

Beneficiary. As used in a trust deed, the lender is designated as the beneficiary, *i.e.*, obtains the benefit of the security.

Benevolent associations. Voluntary groups which are formed, not for profit, but to render financial or other aid to their members.

Bequest. A gift of personal property by will.

Bill of sale. A written instrument evidencing the transfer of title to personal property.

Bona fide purchaser. One who buys property, in good faith, for a fair value, and without notice of any adverse claims or rights of third parties.

Breach The violation of an obligation.

Caveat emptor. Let the buyer beware.

Certificate of sale. A certificate issued to the purchaser at a judicial sale.

Certificate of title. A certification of the ownership of land, based on an examination of the record title.

Cestui que trust. The person for whose benefit property is held in trust.

Chain of title. A chronological list of recorded instruments affecting the title to land.

Chattel. Personal property.

Chattel real. Interest in real estate less than freehold, such as an estate for years.

Chose in action. A personal right not reduced to possession, but recoverable by an action at law.

Civil law. Law of the Roman empire, based on the code of the Emperor Justinian.

Cloud on title. A semblance of title or a claim appearing in some legal form but which is in fact invalid.

Color of title. That which gives the appearance of title, but is not title in fact.

Common law. Body of unwritten law, founded upon general custom, usage, or common consent; prevails in England and most of the United States.

Community property. Property acquired by husband and wife during marriage when not acquired as separate property.

Competent. Legally qualified.

Conclusive presumption. An inference the law makes that cannot be contradicted.

Condemnation. The exercise of the power of eminent domain, *i.e.*, the taking of property for a public use.

Condition precedent. A condition which must be fulfilled before an estate can vest.

Condition subsequent. A condition by the failure or nonperformance of which an estate already vested may be defeated.

Conditional sale contract. A contract of sale where title remains in the seller until the conditions of the contract have been performed.

Condominium. Ownership of a divided interest, *i.e.*, an individually owned unit, in a multi-family or other structure.

Confirmation of sale. Court approval of the sale of property by an executor, administrator, guardian or conservator.

Conservator. A person appointed by the probate court to take care of the person or property of an adult person needing such care.

Consideration. The inducement for entering into a contract; it consists of either a benefit to the promisor, or a loss or detriment to the promisee.

Constructive eviction. Any disturbance of a tenant's possession by the landlord whereby the premises are rendered unfit or the tenant is deprived of the benefit of the premises.

Constructive notice Notice given by the public records.

Constructive trust. A trust imposed by law to redress a wrong or to prevent unjust enrichment.

Contiguous. In actual or close contact; near.

Contingent. Dependent upon an uncertain future event.

Contract. An agreement by which a person undertakes to do or not to do a certain thing.

Conveyance. A written instrument transferring the title to land or an interest therein from one person to another.

Corporation. An artificial being, created by law; and possessing certain rights, privileges, and duties of natural persons.

Covenants. Agreements contained in deeds and other instruments for the performance or nonperformance of certain acts, or the use or nonuse of property in a certain manner.

Dedication. An appropriation of land by the owner for a public use.

Deed. Written instrument by which the ownership of land is transferred from one person to another.

Deed of trust. Written instrument by which title to land is transferred to a trustee as security for a debt or other obligation.

Default. Failure to perform a duty or to discharge an obligation.

Defendant. A party against whom an action is brought.

Deficiency judgment. A personal judgment in a foreclosure action for the amount remaining due after a sale of the security.

Demise. A transfer to another of an estate for years, for life, or at will.

Deponent. A person who gives testimony under oath or affirmation.

Deposit receipt. Used when accepting "earnest money" to bind an offer for property by a prospective purchaser; also includes terms of a contract.

Deraign. To trace or prove.

Descent. Succession to property by an heir.

Devise. A gift of real property by will.

Devisee. One who receives property by will.

Divest. To deprive of a right or title.

Document. An original or official paper relied upon as the basis, proof, or support of anything else. A more comprehensive word than "instrument."

Domicile. A person's legal residence.

Domiciliary administrator. The administrator of a decedent's estate appointed at the place of decedent's domicile.

Dominant tenement. The tenement obtaining the benefit of an easement appurtenant.

Donee. A person to whom a gift is made.

Donor. A person who makes a gift.

Earnest money. Something given as a part of the purchase price to bind a bargain.

Easement. A right or interest in the land of another existing apart from the ownership of the land.

Eleemosynary. Charitable.

Eminent domain. The right or power of the government to take property for a public purpose upon payment of just compensation.

Encroachment. The extension of an improvement onto the property of another.

Encumbrance. A lien or charge on land.

Equitable lien. A lien recognized only in a court of equity.

Equitable title. Title of the purchaser under a contract of sale.

Equity of redemption. Right to redeem property from a foreclosure sale.

Equity in property. The monetary value of the owner's interest; the difference between the market value of the property and the amount of liens and encumbrances against it.

Erosion. Gradual eating away of the soil by the operation of currents or tides.

Escheat. The reverting of land to the State in cases where there are no heirs, devisees, or legatees.

Escrow. A deposit of a deed or other instrument with a third party for delivery upon performance of a condition.

Estate. The degree, quantity, nature, and extent of the interest a person has in real property.

Estoppel. A doctrine which bars one from asserting rights which are inconsistent with a previous position or representation.

Exception. Some part of a thing granted which is excluded from the conveyance and remains in the grantor.

Exclusive agency. A listing giving one agent the right to sell property during a specified time but reserving to the owner the right to sell the property himself.

Exclusive right to sell. A listing giving the agent the right to sell property during a specified time and to collect a commission if the property is sold by anyone during such period.

Executor. A person who is designated in a will as the representative of a decedent's estate.

Executrix. Feminine of executor.

Exemption. An immunity from some burden or obligation.

Extension agreement. A grant of further time within which to pay an obligation.

Fee. An estate of inheritance.

Fiduciary. One who holds a thing in trust for another.

Fixture. A thing which was originally personal property but which has become attached to and is considered as part of the real property.

Foreclosure. A proceeding to enforce a lien.

Forfeiture. A loss of some right, title, estate, or interest in consequence of a default.

Franchise. A right or privilege conferred by law.

Freehold. An estate of inheritance or for life.

Garnishment. A statutory proceeding whereby property, money, or credits of a debtor in possession of another are seized and applied to payment of the debt.

General plan restrictions. Restrictions on the use of property imposed for the benefit of several parcels of property, usually a tract.

Grant. A transfer of real property.

Grantee. The person to whom a grant is made.

Grantor. The person who makes a grant.

Guardian. A person appointed by the probate court to care for the person or estate of a minor or incompetent person.

Habendum. The clause in a deed which repeats the name of the grantee, describes the estate conveyed, and to what use, as "to have and to hold unto the said ____________."

Heirs. The persons designated by law to succeed to the estate of a decedent who leaves no will.

Hereditaments. Anything capable of being inherited.

Holographic will. A will entirely written, dated and signed by the testator in his own handwriting.

Homestead. A home upon which the owner has recorded a declaration of homestead under California law.

Hypothecate. To give a thing as security without parting with possession.

Implied. Presumed or inferred, rather than expressed.

Inchoate. Incomplete; not perfected.

Incompetent. Incapable of managing one's affairs.

Incorporeal. Intangible; without physical existence.

Indenture. Deeds or other instruments executed by both parties.

Injunction. An order of a court of equity prohibiting some act, or compelling an act to be done.

Installment note. A promissory note providing for payment of the principal in two or more certain amounts at different stated times.

Instrument. A writing, such as a deed, made and executed as the expression of some act, contract, or proceeding.

Interlocutory decree. A decree that does not finally dispose of a cause but requires that some further steps be taken.

Inter vivos. Between living persons.

Intestate. A person who dies without leaving a will.

Inure. To accrue to the benefit of a person.

Involuntary lien. A lien not voluntarily created.

Irrevocable. Not to be revoked or withdrawn.

Joint tenancy. Title held by two or more persons in equal shares with right of survivorship.

Judgment lien. A statutory lien created by recording an abstract of judgment.

Junior lien. A subordinate lien.

Jurat. A certificate evidencing the fact that an affidavit was properly made before an authorized officer.

Jurisdiction. The power to hear and determine a matter.

Laches. Inexcusable delay in asserting a right.

Lands, tenements, and hereditaments. Inheritable lands or interests therein.

Landowner's royalty. Interest in oil and gas which is retained or reserved to the landowner on a transfer of an interest in the real property.

Latent. Hidden from view; concealed.

Lateral support. The support which the soil of an adjoining owner gives to his neighbor's land.

Lease. A contract for the possession of land in consideration of payment of rent.

Legacy. A gift of personal property by will, usually money.

Legatee. One to whom personal property is given by will.

Lessee. The tenant under a lease.

Lessor. The landlord under a lease.

Levy. A seizure of property by judicial process.

License. A personal privilege to do some act on the land of another.

Lien. A charge upon property for the payment of a debt or performance of an obligation.

Life estate. An estate measured by the life of a natural person.

Limited partnership. A partnership composed of some partners whose contribution and liability are limited.

Lis pendens. A notice of the filing of an action.

Listing. An employment contract between a broker and his client.

Littoral. Pertaining to the shore.

L. S. *Locus sigilli,* the place of a seal; often appears in an instrument instead of an actual seal.

Marketable title. A title free from reasonable doubt in law and in fact.

Market value. The price at which a thing may be sold.

Meander. To follow a winding course.

Mechanic's lien. A statutory lien in favor of laborers and materialmen who have contributed to a work of improvement.

Merger of title. The absorption of one estate in another.

Meridians. Imaginary north-south lines which intersect base lines to form a starting point for the measurement of land.

Mesne. Intermediate; intervening.

Metes and bounds. Measurements and boundaries.

Minor. A person under 21 years of age (although a married person 18 years or older is deemed an adult for purposes of property transactions).

Monuments. Objects or marks used to fix or establish a boundary.

Moratorium. Temporary suspension by statute of the enforcement of liability for a debt.

Mortgage. A written document by which land is given as security for the payment of a debt.

Mortgagee. The party who obtains the benefit of a mortgage.

Mortgagor. The party who executes a mortgage.

Multiple listing. An organized real estate listing service under which brokers pool their listings.

Muniments of title. Deeds and other original documents showing a chain of title.

Naturalization. The conferring of the rights of citizenship upon a person who has been an alien.

Net listing. A listing under which the broker is entitled to all proceeds of a sale in excess of a designated selling price.

Notice of completion. Notice recorded within 10 days after completion

Power of attorney. A written authorization to an agent to perform specified acts on behalf of his principal.

Prescription. Title obtained by possession for a prescribed period.

Notice of default. Recorded notice that a default has occurred under a deed of trust.

Notice of nonresponsibility. Notice recorded by an owner to relieve the land from mechanics' liens under prescribed conditions.

Notice to quit. Notice to a tenant to vacate.

Nuisance. Anything that is offensive and works an injury or harm to a person or property.

Nuncupative will. An oral will.

Offset statement. Statement furnished to an escrow from a tenant regarding his rights of possession; also, by an owner of land subject to an encumbrance as to the amount due.

Omnibus clause. A clause in a decree of distribution by which property passes to the distributees without specific description.

Open end mortgage. A mortgage which secures additional advances which a lender may advance to the mortgagor.

Open listing. A non-exclusive listing.

Option. A right to require an act to be done in the future.

Option listing. A listing which gives the broker an option to buy the property.

Oral. Spoken.

Oral contract. One not in writing.

Ordinance. A legislative enactment of a city or county.

Ownership. The right to the use and enjoyment of property to the exclusion of others.

Overriding royalty. The interest in oil and gas that a lessee may retain when executing a sublease or assignment of an oil and gas lease.

Parol. Oral; verbal.

Parol evidence. Oral or verbal testimony of a witness.

Partition action. A court proceedings by which co-owners seek to sever their joint ownership.

Partnership. A voluntary association of two or more persons to carry on as co-owners a business for profit.

Party wall. A wall for the common benefit of adjoining owners.

Patent. A conveyance of the title to government lands by the government.

Personal property. Movable property; all property which is not real property.

Plaintiff. The party who brings a court action.

Police power. The power to enact laws and regulations necessary for the common welfare.

Presumption. That which may be assumed without proof.

Prima facie. Assumed correct until overcome by further proof.

Principal. One who employs an agent to act on his behalf.

Priority. That which is earlier or previous in point of time or right.

Privity. Closeness or mutuality of relationship.

Procuring cause. The cause of originating a series of events that leads to the consummation of a sale.

Profit à prendre. The right to take part of the soil or produce of land.

Property. Anything of which there may be ownership.

Pro tanto. As far as it goes.

Quasi contract. A contract implied by law.

Quiet title. An action to establish title to real property.

Quitclaim deed. A deed which conveys whatever present right, title, or interest the grantor may have.

Range. One of a series of tier of townships in a row parallel to, and east or west of, a given prime meridian.

Ratification. The adoption or approval of an act performed on behalf of a person without previous authorization.

Rebuttable presumption. A presumption which is not conclusive and which may be contradicted by evidence.

Reconveyance. A conveyance to the land owner of the title held by a trustee under a deed of trust.

Recordation. Filing for record in the office of the county recorder.

Redemption. Buying back one's property after a judicial sale.

Reformation. An action to correct a mistake in a deed or other document.

Release clause. A clause in a deed of trust providing for release of specified portions of the property upon compliance with certain conditions.

Reliction. Gradual recession of water from the usual watermark.

Remainder. An estate limited by the grantor to take effect in a third person upon the termination of a preceding estate.

Rescission. An action to annul the effect of executing a contract or other document.

Reservation. The creation on behalf of the grantor of a new right issuing out of the thing granted.

Residue. That portion of a decedent's estate which has not been specifically devised.

Restrictions. Limitations on the use and enjoyment of property.
of a work of improvement to shorten time for filing mechanics' liens.

Resulting trust. A trust which is implied by law from the acts of the parties.

Reversion. The residue of an estate remaining in the grantor after the determination of a lesser estate granted by him.

Right of way. A right to cross over a parcel of land.

Riparian. Pertaining to the bank of a river.

Satisfaction. Performance of the terms of an obligation.

Seal. An impression upon a document which lends authenticity to its execution.

Section. One of the divisions employed in a government survey; measures one mile on each side and contains 640 acres of land.

Security deposit. A deposit made to assure performance of an obligation, usually by a lessee.

Seizin. The possession of land under a claim of freehold.

Separate property. Property acquired before marriage, and property acquired during marriage by gift, devise, descent, or bequest.

Servient tenement. An estate burdened by an easement.

Servitude. A right in the nature of an easement.

Situs. Location.

Special assessments. Charge on property for its share of special levies, as distinguished from taxes levied for the general support of government.

Specific performance. An action to compel performance of an agreement for the sale of land.

Spouse. A husband or wife.

Sublease. A grant of an interest in demised premises by a tenant for a term less than his own, the tenant retaining a reversion.

Subordination agreement. An agreement under which a prior lien is made inferior to an otherwise junior lien.

Subrogate. To substitute one person in the place of another with reference to an obligation.

Succession. The taking of property by inheritance.

Surety. A person who binds himself with another, called the principal, for the performance of an obligation.

Survey. A map or plat containing a statement of courses, distances and quantity of land and showing lines of possession.

Tax deed. A deed issued to the purchaser at a tax sale.

Tenancy in common. Ownership of property by two or more persons in undivided interests without right of survivorship.

Tender. An unconditional offer of payment of a debt.

Tenements. All rights in land which pass with a conveyance of the land.

Tenure. The manner in which land is held.

Testament. The written declaration of one's last will.

Testamentary trust. A trust created by will.

Testator. One who makes a will.

Testatrix. Feminine of testator.

Title. Evidence of a person's right or the extent of his interest in property.

Toll. To bar; defeat.

Township. Subdivision of the public lands of the United States; each township contains 36 sections.

Trade fixture. Articles of personal property annexed to real property but which are necessary to the carrying on of a trade and are removable by the owner.

Trespass. An invasion of an owner's rights in his property.

Trust deed. Same as deed of trust.

Trustee. The person to whom property is conveyed in trust.

Trustor. The person who conveys property in trust.

Unlawful detainer. An action to recover possession of real property.

Usury. Taking more interest than the law allows on a loan.

Valid. Sufficient in law; effective.

Variance. A departure from the general rule.

Vendee. Purchaser.

Vendor. Seller.

Verification. An affidavit attached to a pleading or other document which states that the matters set forth are true.

Versus. Against (abbreviated vs. or v.).

Vested interest. An interest that is fixed or determined.

Void. Having no legal effect; null.

Voidable. An instrument that appears to be valid, but is in fact lacking in some essential requirement.

Waiver. A relinquishment or abandonment of a right.

Warranty. An assurance or undertaking that certain defects do not exist.

Waste. The destruction or material alteration of or injury to premises by a tenant for life or years.

Will. A disposition of property effective upon the maker's death.

Writ. A process of the court under which property may be seized and sold.

Zoning. Governmental regulations relating to the use of property.

1

Origin and History of Land Titles in California

Summary

I. Introductory

California, long noted for its many natural splendors, has as unique and picturesque a history as any of the states of the Union. Much of this history can be told in terms of its land and the people claiming the land.

Heading the procession that begins in prehistory are the American Indians, stemming out of a mysterious past, and laying claims to certain hunting, fishing, and acorn-gathering areas before the coming of the white man.

The year 1542, just fifty years after the discovery of the Americas by Columbus, marks the first important date in the history of land titles in California. Following the conquest of Mexico by Cortés in the early part of the sixteenth century, expeditions reached the west coast of Mexico and established bases for maritime exploration, both along the coastal areas and into the vast reaches of the Pacific Ocean. In 1532 a Spanish adventurer named Fortún Jiménez crossed the Gulf and discovered what is now known as Baja California. Ten years later Alta California, which is the state of California as we know it today, was discovered by Juan Rodríguez Cabrillo, a Portuguese navigator in the service of Spain.

Cabrillo's "fleet" of two small ships, called the *San Salvador* and the *Victoria,* sailed from Navidad on the west coast of Mexico on June 27, 1542. After working northward along the coast of Baja California, the two ships arrived on September 28, 1542, at what was described as a "very large" bay. Cabrillo named this bay San Miguel; the name was later changed to the present one, San Diego. Cabrillo and his sailors went ashore, took possession in the name of the King of Spain, and thus became the first white men to set foot on the coast of Alta California.

Alarcón also discovers California. Although 1542 is the widely accepted date of discovery of California, the champions of another explorer, Hernando de Alarcón, claim it to be 1540 when Alarcón sailed up the Gulf of California, reached the mouth of the Colorado River, and managed to work his way upstream with the help of the Cocopah Indians, who thought he was a sun god, and who towed his ship from the river banks, canal fashion. It is generally accepted that Alarcón induced the Indians to pull the ship beyond what is now Yuma, Arizona, and even some distance north of the confluence of the Colorado and the Gila rivers. Doubtless Alarcón and his crew went ashore numerous times, and if they went ashore on the California side, as seems probable, they became the first white men to set foot on what is now the state of California. However, Cabrillo is generally given credit as the discoverer of California, and in any event he is the first discoverer and explorer of the California coast.

California as an island. California was first thought to be an island, and for a century after Cabrillo's voyage mapmakers showed it as an island. This "Island of California" was shaped like a lopsided cornucopia, with the wide end to the north. Between California and the mainland a sea, called the Vermilion Sea, dotted with islands, occupied the space that is now Arizona and Nevada. The island theory was not universally accepted, and in the year 1698 a Jesuit priest, Father Kino, in his explorations of the southwest area ascertained to his satisfaction that the island idea was a fallacy. When a map thereafter appeared showing California as part of the mainland, it aroused a storm of protest. But fifty years later definite proof was established that California was not an island, and to eliminate any doubt, the King of Spain issued a Royal Decree reciting that "California no es Isla," which decree is now in the Bancroft Library at the University of California.

II. The Spanish period

Although discovered in 1542, it was not until 1769, starting with Gaspar de Portola, that the actual occupation of California commenced. The occupation by the Spaniards embraced a threefold plan of colonization, calling for (1) missionaries to establish missions in the interior and to civilize the Indians; (2) soldiers to found frontier outposts, or *presidios,* at strategic points along the coast; and (3) settlers to start farming communities, or *pueblos,* to provide food for the soldier garrisons. Between the years 1769 and 1822 a chain of twenty-one missions was established, extending from San Diego in the south to Sonoma in the north, and by 1822 there were four presidios (at San Diego, Santa Barbara, Monterey and San Francisco), and three pueblos (Los Angeles, San Jose, and Branciforte near Santa Cruz).

LAW OF THE INDIES APPLIED TO LAND IN CALIFORNIA

The law governing colonization and ownership of land was the Law of the Indies. All land was held in the name of, and belonged to, the King of Spain. The ownership and transfer of land was based on the civil law prevailing in Spain, which was based on the old Justinian Code, dating back to the Roman Empire.

Ownership by the King of Spain. Under the application of the law prevailing during the Spanish period absolute ownership of land by individuals was unknown, but the use of the land might be acquired through military or political agencies of the King. Thus, concessions of the land outside the pueblos could be granted by the governors for farms and cattle grazing. At least thirty of these rancho concessions were made during the Spanish period, mostly to soldiers as a reward for their services. Within the pueblos and presidios, the local authorities could grant house lots and other land to the inhabitants. The missions were permitted to occupy and use certain lands for the benefit of the Indians, but were not granted ownership of such lands. The missions were not intended to be permanent and were subject to secularization, that is, being turned over to lay administration and having their lands ultimately disposed of as part of the public domain.

SPANISH OWNERSHIP CONTRASTED WITH OWNERSHIP IN OTHER AREAS OF AMERICA

As contrasted with the ownership of land in California during the Spanish period, what was the status of ownership in other areas of America? The basis of the land law in a large part of the United States today is the feudal system of England, which system was established after the year 1066 and marks the beginning of the law of real property. Under this system, land was not the subject of private ownership; it was merely the subject of *tenure,* which gave a right of occupancy subject to various types of services owed by the tenant or by the land, such as military service or agricultural service.

Tenure under the feudal system. Under the feudal system, the king was the lord paramount. No ordinary person could own land as he could own chattels; all he could own was an interest in land under some form of tenure. His occupancy was "under" someone. Feudalism consisted, in general, of a relationship between a monarchial chieftain and his followers, and resulted from a land grant by the chieftain. In time, ownership rights were considerably enlarged, but to this day, in theory, no one owns land in England; he merely holds it as a tenant. If he has no other lord, the king is his lord. Hence, if a freeholder dies without a will and without heirs, his freehold falls to the Crown.

Ownership in the colonies. In colonial times in America, colonial land grants from the Crown usually called for payment of a nominal rental, and the land was held under a form of tenure that imposed an obligation to perform, upon the land of the overlord, agricultural duties of a fixed nature. After the Revolution the states succeeded to the rights formerly held by the Crown as overlord. Statutes were thereafter enacted in many of the states disclaiming the fact that the state occupied the position of an overlord, and declaring that land might be held in absolute ownership. Thus, absolute ownership of land by individuals was realized in other parts of the American continent during the period of Spanish occupancy of California.

III. The Mexican period

The next important date in the history of land titles in California is April 9, 1822. On that date California, which had been a Spanish possession since its discovery in 1542, became a Mexican province, Mexico having established her independence from Spain. The Mexican empire, newly established, lasted only a few months, and thereafter gave way to the Mexican national government.

GRANTS OF LAND BY MEXICAN AUTHORITIES

Between 1822 and 1846 the Mexican government granted many ranch titles, some of the grants being confirmatory of Spanish concessions. In order to encourage colonization, liberal laws authorizing grants of land were enacted. Governors were given authority to grant lands outside the pueblos in accordance with a specified procedure, and had the absolute discretion in the selection of persons who could receive grants. The procedure included the filing of a petition to the governor for the grant, accompanied by a map of the land sought; the issuance of a formal grant by the governor; the filing of a copy of the grant and other papers constituting the evidence of title, called an *expediente,* in official archives; and approval of the grant by the legislative body.

Era of the ranchos. The grants of ranchos were stimulated by the secularization of the missions in the year 1834, and by 1846 more than five hundred rancho grants had been made, embracing most of the good grazing and farming areas in what was later to become the state of California. Ranchos had their flowering during California's Mexican regime.

INFLUX OF AMERICANS

The early 1800's saw a great number of Americans settling in the Far West, and it became increasingly apparent that Mexico could not maintain her sovereignty over California. Conditions in California became somewhat chaotic. After a period of turmoil and disorder the Bear Flag Republic emerged; this event was followed by the Mexican War and the loss of California to the United States in 1848.

IV. California a part of United States

February 2, 1848 is a very important date in the history of land titles in California, for on that date the Treaty of Guadalupe Hidalgo was signed, by which California became a part of the United States. Full protection of all property rights of Mexicans was promised by this treaty. With this end in view a Board of Land Commissioners was set up, to which all claims to private lands were to be submitted. In the meantime, California was admitted as a state by act of Congress on September 9, 1850, another important date in the history of land titles in California.

V. Property rights under the Treaty of Guadalupe Hidalgo

The treaty of Guadalupe Hidalgo provided that property rights of Mexicans should be "inviolably respected." The problem, then, was to determine the validity and extent of the Spanish and Mexican grants. Titles acquired under such grants varied from complete legal and equitable estates to mere possessory rights. Some were so-called "perfect" titles requiring no further acts under Mexican law, whereas others were "imperfect" titles, dependent upon further acts to be performed. The question of boundaries also presented a problem; in many cases it was almost impossible to identify the land from the boundaries given in the grant.

LAND COMMISSION CREATED IN 1851

In fulfillment of its obligations under the Treaty, Congress in 1851 passed an act providing for the appointment of a Land Commission, consisting of three members. All persons claiming title under Spanish and Mexican grants were required to present their claims and proofs to the Commissioners within two years. This Commission was a judicial body with jurisdiction to confirm or reject claims, subject to a right of appeal to the federal courts. Following a decree of confirmation of a grant, the land was surveyed by the Surveyor General and a map of the survey prepared. Thereafter, upon proof to the General Land Office of the confirmation and approved survey, a *patent* was issued by the United States to the claimant. All lands for which the claims were rejected, or for which no claims were presented within the prescribed time, became a part of the *public domain* of the United States. The total number of private land grant cases in California was in excess of 800, one report listing 813 cases, of which 604 were finally confirmed, 190 were finally rejected, and 19 were withdrawn. This means claims filed; it does not mean the number of grants or granted pieces of land. About one-twelfth of the state's total area was included in the claims that were approved.

Pueblo lands. Pueblo claims to land were also protected by the Treaty. The act passed in 1851 authorized the filing of claims to pueblo lands, and upon confirmation of the claim, a patent was issued to the municipality. A patent to such former pueblo lands issued by the United States is conclusive evidence of the title in a city to such lands. The number of pueblos whose claims were filed and confirmed totaled seven.

The history of pueblo lands, the manner in which they were held, and the nature of the title thereto have been treated at length in many of the earlier court decisions in this state. These cases relate how such lands were granted to the pueblos for the benefit of its inhabitants and the various ways in which the lands were to be used and treated. Some of the lands were set apart for the common use of all; the income from another part was to be used to defray the expense of municipal administration, while other portions were to be conveyed to individuals to be held in private ownership. (*Dunlop* v. *O'Donnell*, 6 C.A.2d 1.)

VI. Disposition of Indian land claims

Indian tribes originally occupied or claimed most of the lands encompassed in the treaties and purchases of the United States, including California. When California became a part of the United States, the California Indians, numbering about 110,000, became subject to its jurisdiction. The United States admitted the Indians' right to occupy land possessed by them, but the absolute title to the land was deemed to be vested in the United States, and the courts so held. (*Thompson* v. *Doaksum*, 68 C.A. 593, citing *Mintum* v. *Brower*, 24 Cal. 644.)

A policy was adopted that recognized the tribes as nations and the power to enter into treaties with them as such. By these treaties specified lands were agreed upon as tribal, with a cession to the United States, for compensation, of outside areas. Several hundred thousand acres of land in California became embraced in Indian reservations.

In recent years numerous Indian land claims have arisen, the Indians asserting that the taking of the lands by the United States had been involuntary and uncompensated. In 1946 Congress set up the Indian Claims Commission to act as a court, with a mandate to settle "all just and equitable Indian tribal claims against the United States." Before the filing deadline five years later, the Indian tribes made claims to the Commission in which they asked compensation for approximately 75 per cent of the nation's land area, including all of California. In 1959 a ruling was made by the Commission that California's Indians were entitled to be paid for the land the government took from their ancestors in 1851, consisting of about 75 per cent of California, at its 1853 value. The exact amount awarded is to be measured by the then appraised value of the lands, plus reasonable interest, offset by the value of the tribe's interests in the reservation lands allotted to them as of the date the lands were taken, and less the equivalent of gratuities from the United States to the tribes over the years to the latest date of accounting.

VII. Classification of land based on origin of title

All land in California may be classified according to origin of title as follows:

First: lands—mostly rancho and pueblo—the titles to which were granted by, or derived from, Spanish or Mexican authority before California became a part of the United States, and which titles were later confirmed by the United States in accordance with the procedure described previously.

Second: public lands of the United States. This category includes lands that were unconveyed under Spanish or Mexican authority and that were outside rancho and original pueblo areas, though once a part of the land vested in the King of Spain and later the Mexican nation. These lands passed directly to the United States with the cession of California by Mexico. Much of the public domain in California has since been conveyed by the United States to individuals or to governing bodies, or has been reserved. Conveyances of "public lands" have been made under the laws of the United States governing preemption, homestead, desert, timber culture, timber and stone entries, military bounty warrants and scrip, mining claims, federal townsites, railroad titles, and Indian reservations. Some of the public lands are now within national forests or national parks set apart for the benefit of the people in perpetuity. Nearly one half of California, including national forests, national parks and monuments, military installations, and desert holdings is still owned by the United States.

Third: state lands, which embrace lands granted by Congress to the state of California out of the public domain to furnish the state with funds for education, reclamation, and other purposes. Swamp and overflowed lands are also included within state lands.

Fourth: tidelands and submerged lands, which are also state-owned lands, but which are classified separately because of the special nature of their ownership.[1]

Questions

1. What event makes the year 1542 an important one in the history of California?
2. When did the Spanish occupation of California commence?
3. Explain briefly the threefold plan of colonization embraced by the Spanish occupation.
4. Describe the ownership of land during the Spanish period.
5. Why is the year 1822 significant in the history of California?
6. Describe briefly the ownership and disposition of lands during the Mexican period.
7. When did California become a part of the United States?
8. What disposition of Mexican land grants was made after California became a part of the United States?
9. When did California become a state?
10. Describe briefly the disposition of pueblo lands after California became a state.
11. Explain the basis for Indian claims to land in California.
12. What is embraced by the term "public lands of the United States"?
13. What is embraced by the term "state lands"?

---

[1] The coverage of this book does not permit a more detailed discussion of the law as it relates to public lands and state lands, since primary consideration is given to private ownership. Consult Ogden's *California Real Property Law,* pages 136–88, for an excellent discussion of the subject of public and state lands; and see W. W. Robinson, *Land in California,* for a complete and authentic story of early land ownership in California.

2

Sources of Real Estate Law

Summary

I. Introductory

In each of the states of this country there are two separate systems of law in force, namely, state law and federal law. Federal law operates uniformly throughout the United States, with few exceptions. State law, however, may vary considerably from state to state. Each state has its own constitution, statutes, and court decisions, and it is primarily to these that we must look in determining the law that is applicable to a real estate transaction. Real property, unlike personal property, is subject to the laws of the state within which it is located, and not to the laws of the domicile of the owner.

COMMON LAW OF ENGLAND IN CALIFORNIA

When California was admitted as a state, it adopted by statute the common law of England, not the laws of Mexico, as the law of the land. The law of real estate in the United States is based largely on the common law of England rather than the civil law. The term "civil law" refers to the system of law prevailing in the countries that modeled their law after the Roman civil law, as distinguished from the common law of England. The method of the civil law, basically, is to attempt to set down at one time, by appropriate rules, just relations between all persons in all possible situations. The method of the common law, on the other hand, is to decide just relations between persons, case by case, as conflicts and disputes arise. In its earliest inception, it consisted of customs and usages, and afterward of principles defined by the courts in the trial of causes that came before them. Precedent has played a basic role in the development of the common law.

SPANISH INFLUENCE ON CALIFORNIA LAW

The laws of Spain and Mexico were based on the civil law. Although the common law applies generally in California today, some Mexican law, which was based on Spanish law, was made the statutory law of California. This includes the community property law, a very important part of California real property law.

II. Principal sources

Consideration will be given to many rules of law applicable to the ownership and transfer of real property in California, and it is important to ascertain the basis for these rules. To know the law applicable to real estate in California, we must look to the following principal sources: (1) the Constitution of the United States; (2) treaties; (3) laws passed by Congress; (4) federal regulations; (5) the Constitution of the State of California; (6) laws passed by the state legislature; (7) rules and regulations of state and local agencies; (8) ordinances; and (9) court decisions.

SEPARATION OF POWERS

The powers of the government, both federal and state, are divided into three separate departments—the legislative, executive, and judicial—and generally speaking, one department cannot exercise the functions of the others. The power to make laws is vested in the *legislative* department.

The *executive* department is responsible for the administration of the laws. The *judicial* function is to declare the law and determine the rights of parties to a controversy before the court. Since the courts are empowered to determine whether or not the legislature has exceeded its authority in enacting legislation, a measure of judicial control is placed upon the powers of the legislature.

DELEGATION OF JUDICIAL POWERS

The growth of administrative law in recent years has resulted in a modification of the strict doctrine that judicial powers cannot be delegated to a nonjudicial board or officer. Such a board or officer may be invested with power to determine facts and exercise discretion; this power is judicial in nature and is termed "quasi-judicial." The Real Estate Commissioner, for instance, is empowered to hold hearings and revoke licenses for causes defined by law. (*Brecheen* v. *Riley,* 187 Cal. 121.)

ADMINISTRATIVE LAW

The prohibition against delegation of legislative power, like the companion rule that judicial power cannot be delegated, is in conflict with the growing tendency to delegate to boards and officers a large measure of discretionary power that is ordinarily legislative in character. Although the delegation of an uncontrolled discretion is invalid, it is now generally established, both on the federal and state levels, that where the legislature lays down a sufficiently clear test or standard, the discretion to carry out the legislative purpose by rules and regulations may be given to a board or officer.

CONSTITUTIONAL CONTROLS

Both the national and state governments are controlled in what they can do by provisions in their respective constitutions. The fundamental difference between the two constitutions is that the Constitution of the United States is a *grant of power* to Congress, i.e., Congress has such power as has been expressly conferred upon it, whereas the state constitution is a *limitation* upon the power of the legislature, i.e., the legislature has such powers as have not been denied to it. Thus, unless restricted by the federal or state constitution, the state legislature has any power it chooses to exercise. This rule is emphasized in the case of *Fitts* v. *Superior Court,* 6 Cal.2d 230, where the court stated that "we do not look to the Constitution to determine whether the legislature is authorized to do an act, but only to see if it is prohibited."

THE CONSTITUTION OF THE UNITED STATES

The Constitution of the United States is the supreme law of the land. Many rules of law pertaining to real property are based upon provisions of the Constitution and the Amendments thereto. The case of *Shelley* v. *Kraemer*, 334 U.S. 1, is illustrative of this principle. In that case, decided by the United States Supreme Court in 1948, the judicial enforcement by state courts of covenants restricting the use or occupancy of real property to persons of the Caucasian race was held to violate the equal protection clause of the Fourteenth Amendment.

The exercise of the power of eminent domain is another example. If the federal government requires a parcel of land for one of its many functions, it cannot take the land from the owner without the payment of the market value thereof, since the Fifth Amendment forbids the taking of private property for public use without the payment of just compensation.

TREATIES

The federal Constitution provides that treaties made under the authority of the United States are part of the supreme law of the land. A treaty, however, does not automatically supersede local laws that are inconsistent with it unless the treaty provisions are self-executing. In order for a treaty provision to be operative without the aid of implementing legislation and to have the force and effect of a statute, it must appear that the framers of the treaty intended to prescribe a rule that, standing alone, would be enforceable by the courts. Thus, it was held that California's Alien Land Law was not invalidated by the United Nations Charter. (*Sei Fujii* v. *State of California,* 38 Cal.2d 718.) However, as noted later, the law was invalidated on other grounds as violative of the constitution.

LAWS PASSED BY CONGRESS

Although most of the laws pertaining to real property are state laws, many federal laws are applicable to the ownership of real property. The bankruptcy law is an example of this rule. Full power to enact bankruptcy legislation was granted to Congress by the federal Constitution. Pursuant to this grant, Congress has from time to time enacted various bankruptcy laws. Under the provisions of the Bankruptcy Act, when a landowner is declared a bankrupt, title to his land automatically vests in the trustee in bankruptcy, who may sell the land for the purpose of obtaining funds to pay off the bankrupt's debts.

Another illustration of federal statutes affecting real property is the

Internal Revenue Code, various provisions of which create tax liens on property and rights to property of the person liable for the tax. Federal rent control laws enacted as a result of the housing problems created by World War II are further illustrations.

FEDERAL REGULATIONS ADOPTED BY VARIOUS BOARDS AND COMMISSIONS

Many federal agencies are empowered to prescribe rules and regulations that have the force and effect of law. Under the provisions of the National Housing Act, for example, the Federal Housing Commissioner is authorized and directed to make such rules and regulations as may be necessary to carry out the provisions of the Act. Regulations have been adopted that prohibit secondary financing in connection with FHA loans. A second mortgage or deed of trust executed by the borrower as of or about the time of the execution of the FHA first deed of trust would be a violation of such regulations.

Rules and regulations of the Federal Home Loan Bank Board are also illustrative of this principle. Federal savings and loan associations are chartered by the Board as provided by federal law. With respect to such associations, Congress has empowered the Board to organize, incorporate, supervise, and regulate. Rules and regulations having the force and effect of law have been adopted by the Board and they govern the operation of federal savings and loan associations from their inception to their dissolution.

The rent regulations issued under the federal rent control laws are another and very familiar illustration.

THE CONSTITUTION OF THE STATE OF CALIFORNIA

Many basic rights with respect to property are contained in the Constitution of the State of California. The state constitution that governs California's citizens today was adopted in convention at Sacramento on March 3, 1879, and ratified by the people on May 7, 1879. It has since been amended many times. The constitution of today, by reason of its many amendments, has been considerably changed from the original; however, the changes have served to keep the constitution in harmony with the demands of the constant growth and development of the state.

The constitution provides at the outset that all men have certain inalienable rights, among which are those of acquiring, possessing, and protecting property. The statutes pertaining to homesteads are based upon a constitutional provision to the effect that the legislature shall, by law, protect from forced sale a certain portion of the homestead and other property of heads of families. The mechanic's lien law has as its basis a constitutional provision. Many other laws relating to property are based on provisions of the state constitution.

STATE LAWS

A major part of the law relating to real property is contained in statutes enacted by the state legislature. Most of these statutes are now contained in numerous codes, including the Civil Code, the Probate Code, the Corporations Code, the Public Resources Code, and the Government Code, to name a few. There is a total of twenty-seven codes, with some of the statutes still to be found in the general laws, uncodified. The usury law, for instance, is a part of the general laws.

RULES AND REGULATIONS OF STATE AND LOCAL AGENCIES

As in the case of federal agencies, many state and local agencies are empowered to enact rules and regulations that have the force and effect of law. Thus, under the provisions of Section 10080 of the Business and Professions Code, the Real Estate Commissioner may from time to time promulgate necessary rules and regulations for the conduct of his office and the administration and enforcement of the provisions of the Real Estate Law.

Also illustrative of this principle are the rules and regulations of the Air Pollution Control District of the County of Los Angeles, which are of vital concern where, for instance, a transaction affecting a business establishment involves equipment the use of which may cause the issuance of air contaminants in violation of Section 24242 or 24243 of the Health and Safety Code.

Under the provisions of Section 11502, Agricultural Code, rules and regulations may be prescribed by the Director of Agriculture governing the conduct of the business of pest control. The commissioner of any county may adopt additional rules and regulations governing the application of methods of pest control under local conditions.

The Department of Veterans Affairs may make rules and regulations to carry out the provisions of Division 4 of the Military and Veterans Code relating to Veterans' Aid and Welfare, including farm and home purchases by veterans.

CITY AND COUNTY ORDINANCES

Many ordinances affect real property, particularly in the *use* that may be made of property. Zoning ordinances are typical examples. Also, ordinances may be enacted regulating the construction, erection, or alteration of buildings. A municipality may make and enforce reasonable regulations with reference to the location of gas tanks and the storage and use of explosive substances. Ordinances have been adopted that provide for the creation of a lien in connection with the cost of removal of a substandard or unsafe structure. These are but a few of the many types of ordinances that affect the ownership and use of real property.

COURT DECISIONS

A considerable portion of the law relating to real property is contained in the decisions of the California appellate courts. Although the courts do not make the law—this is a function of the legislature—they do interpret the law, and it is quite often necessary to examine the decisions of the appellate courts to determine the meaning and effect of a law pertaining to real property. For example, the courts have frequently imposed limitations on the right of a governmental agency to acquire property by condemnation. In the case of *City and County of San Francisco* v. *Ross*, 44 Cal.2d 52, involving the acquisition of land for use as parking facilities, it was held that a city cannot condemn private property to be immediately leased to private parties for use as a private venture. The court pointed out that the statutes authorizing the acquisition of land by governing bodies for use as parking facilities indicate a clear legislative policy requiring governmental control of rates and charges to assure fulfilling the public need.

The courts are also frequently called upon to interpret provisions of the homestead law. In the case of *Porter* v. *Chapman*, 65 Cal. 365, a question was raised as to whether or not a homestead was abandoned by the removal of the husband from the premises and residing elsewhere. The court held that this did not constitute an abandonment of the homestead, stating as follows: "Under our law we know of no abandonment of the homestead except in the statutory mode. The homestead having once been regularly created out of a parcel of land, in accordance with the statute, the estate so created continues to exist until put an end to in the mode pointed out by the statute."

Enactments of the legislative body may be declared to be invalid by the courts as violative of constitutional provisions. An outstanding example is the decision of the California Supreme Court in the case of *Sei Fujii* v. *State of California*, cited on p. 12, holding that the California Alien Land Law is unconstitutional. A case involving the constitutionality of a statute is that of *Mendoza* v. *Small Claims Court*, 49 Cal.2d 668, where it was held that an amendment to Section 117 of the Code of Civil Procedure was void insofar as it purported to give jurisdiction to Small Claims Courts in unlawful detainer proceedings.

III. The court structure in California

As pointed out, there are two separate systems of law in force, namely, federal law and state law. In certain types of proceedings the federal courts have exclusive jurisdiction; however, in the most frequent situations where parties become involved in court action, the state courts have jurisdiction. Since decisions of the appellate courts are an important source of the law, an understanding of the court structure and the nature of judicial proceedings is essential.

RESORT TO THE COURTS

When parties become involved in a dispute regarding property or other rights which they can not settle amicably, it is often necessary to take the matter to court. The court's job is to hear all of the pertinent facts in the case, apply the law, and then decide in favor of one party or the other. If the losing party feels that the decision is wrong, he has the right of appeal to a higher court. These higher courts, in announcing a decision, state the reasons for their decisions and discuss the legal principles involved, often at length. Such a decision is called an *opinion,* and these opinions are published in bound volumes called *reports,* which serve as a guide in the decision of similar cases in the future. The case is said to set a precedent, and as noted above, these court decisions constitute one of the chief sources of real estate law.

BASIS OF COURTS DECISION

Since California real property law stems in large part from the real estate law of England, it is not uncommon, especially in the earlier cases, for the courts to base their decisions on cases that arose many years ago in England. In dealing with present-day problems, however, the courts must often evoke new rules without the benefit of the past. In some instances, there may not be a California case in point, but a similar case may have been decided in another state, which decision, although not binding on the California court, may have sufficient persuasive effect to be adopted and become a rule of property law in this state. What the courts attempt to do is expressed in Samuel Johnson's remark that "the law is the last result of human wisdom acting upon human experience for the benefit of the public."

CALIFORNIA JUDICIAL SYSTEM

The foregoing brief summary of the main function of the courts leads to a consideration of the court structure in this state. As noted above, there are two classes of courts, state courts and federal courts. The state courts in California consist of the Supreme Court, five District Courts of Appeal, a Superior Court in each county, and either a Municipal Court or a Justice Court in each judicial district.

Municipal and Justice Courts. The state constitution requires that there be a Municipal Court established in a judicial district when the population of the district exceeds forty thousand. A district of lesser population has a Justice Court. The Municipal and Justice Courts are courts of limited jurisdiction; they can hear only certain types of cases where the amount involved is relatively small. Most of the civil cases tried in these courts are actions for money. Actions to foreclose a mechanic's lien where the claim does not exceed $5,000 may be brought in the Municipal Court, but other types of foreclosure actions must be brought in the Superior Court. Execution sales involving real property may be had on judgments obtained in the Municipal or Justice Courts. Thus, proceedings in these courts can affect title to real property, although questions of title to real property are otherwise beyond the jurisdiction of these lower courts.

Superior Courts. The Superior Courts are courts of general jurisdiction, and most cases involving real property have their origin in these courts. Actions to quiet title, actions for specific performance of a real estate contract, actions to foreclose a deed of trust or mortgage, actions to enjoin the breach of a deed restriction, actions for divorce, and probate proceedings are types of cases which must be brought in the Superior Court. The Superior Courts also have jurisdiction to hear appeals from cases arising in municipal and in justice courts in their respective counties.

Appellate Courts. Judgments, orders, and decrees of the Superior Court are appealable to the District Courts of Appeal or to the Supreme Court of the State of California. There are five appellate districts in the state where the District Courts of Appeal meet—in San Francisco (first district); in Los Angeles (second district); in Sacramento (third district); in San Diego and San Bernardino (fourth district), and in Fresno (fifth district). The first and second districts are further subdivided. Each district or division of a district has a presiding justice and two associate justices. A chief justice and six associate justices make up the California Supreme Court. All opinions of the Supreme Court are published, but starting in 1964, the opinions of the District Courts of Appeal and Superior Court Appellate opinions will be published only if they involve a new and important issue of law, a change in an established principle of law, or a matter of general public interest.

JURISDICTION OF FEDERAL COURTS

In several types of cases the federal courts have exclusive jurisdiction, and these proceedings often affect title to real property. The federal courts have exclusive jurisdiction, for instance, over all bankruptcy cases, and over all civil actions in which the United States is a party, such as a condemnation action brought by the United States.

FEDERAL JUDICIAL SYSTEM

Considered generally, the court structure of the federal system is comparable to that of the state, and consists of trial courts, intermediate courts of appeal, and the Supreme Court. Federal cases are commenced in the local United States District Court. The United States is now divided into ninety-eight districts, each with a district court. In California there were formerly two districts, but California is now divided into four judicial districts known as the Northern, Eastern, Central, and Southern Districts of California. In the Northern District court sessions are held at Eureka, Oakland, San Francisco, and San Jose; in the Eastern District court sessions are held in Fresno, Redding, and Sacramento; in the Central District court sessions are held at Los Angeles; and in the Southern District court sessions are held at San Diego. Appeals from the District Courts go to the next highest court, the Court of Appeals (formerly designated as Circuit Court of Appeal). Fewer of these courts exist—just eleven in the whole country—with California being in the 9th Circuit.

UNITED STATES SUPREME COURT

The highest court is the Supreme Court of the United States. This court is made up of nine judges, appointed for life by the President with the advice and consent of the Senate. One of the judges is designated as the Chief Justice, who presides over sessions of the court.

Power of judicial review. Most cases reach the Supreme Court on appeal from a lower federal court, or from a state supreme court where a question of federal law is involved. The Supreme Court has what is called "discretionary jurisdiction," that is, it can usually decide which cases to hear and which not to hear. If the court is of the opinion that the case at hand is of broad and general interest to the nation's welfare as a whole, it will usually grant a hearing to the parties. One of the most important functions of the court is to decide whether a state or federal law conflicts with the federal Constitution and is therefore invalid. This is known as "the power of judicial review."

How the court chooses. It is the established policy of the Supreme Court to choose "in the interest of the law, its appropriate exposition and enforcement, not in the mere interest of the litigants." If review of a case is to be had by the Supreme Court it must be because of the public interest in the questions involved.

IV. Some applicable legal principles

JURISDICTION

Jurisdiction is essential to the validity of a judgment, order, or decree of a court. Generally, it may be said that the following are the jurisdictional requirements: (1) legal organization of the tribunal; (2) jurisdiction over the person; (3) jurisdiction over the subject matter of the action; and (4) power to grant the judgment.

A judgment, although entered in a case over which the court had jurisdiction over the parties and the subject matter, may be void in whole or in part because it granted some relief that the court had no power to grant. Thus, a judgment of foreclosure without giving the right of redemption is void and subject to collateral attack insofar as it bars the right of redemption. (*Tonningsen* v. *Odd Fellows' Cemetery Assn.*, 60 C.A. 568.) And a judgment assigning all community property to a spouse obtaining a divorce on the sole ground of desertion is in excess of the court's jurisdiction and to that extent is void. (*Vasquez* v. *Vasquez*, 109 C.A.2d 280.)

VENUE

Venue is distinguished from jurisdiction in that the latter, in a strict sense, is judicial power to hear and determine a cause, whereas venue is synonymous with "place of trial" and has reference to the proper place of trial from among the courts having jurisdiction of the subject matter of an action, whether a particular county or judicial district. Section 392 of the Code of Civil Procedure provides that the county in which the real property which is the subject of the action is situated is the proper county for the trial of certain types of actions, such as actions for recovery of real property, partition of real property, and foreclosure of liens on real property. However, such actions may be transferred to another county for purposes of trial when, for instance, the convenience of witnesses and the ends of justice would be promoted by the change. (C.C.P., Sec. 397.)

EQUITY

The words "equity" and "equitable rights" are frequently encountered in the field of real property law. What are their origin? In the early days of the development of the common law, there was a tendency on the part of the courts to make the system rigid and formal. If a litigant could not bring his plea for relief within the four corners of an existing remedy, he was denied relief. He would then turn to the king as the fountain of justice, and if the case was meritorious, the king would intervene, through the chancellor, and give the necessary relief despite the fact that no legal remedy was available. In time this became a common procedure, and the chancellor developed a set of rules for the administration of remedies based on principle of right and justice. This system became known as equity and the remedies as equitable remedies. Two classes of courts thus developed, law courts and equity courts. This system was brought over to colonial America, and the principles of equity are still applicable, although only a few of the states still have separate courts for the administration of law and equity. In most of them, as in California, law and equity are administered by the same court.

STATUTES OF LIMITATIONS

A statute of limitations prescribes a time within which an action must be filed. The time varies, depending upon the nature of the action. For instance, an action to recover possession of real property must be commenced within five years from the time the cause of action arose, whereas a personal injury suit, such as an automobile accident case, must be brought within one year. What is the purpose of a statute of limitations? It is based upon the premise that if a person has a just claim, he should assert it within a reasonable time. Stale claims are hard to prove, and defenses against them may even be harder to establish. Witnesses die, move away, forget, or evidence otherwise becomes unavailable.

THE DOCTRINE OF LACHES

An unreasonable delay in asserting a claim may also be barred under the doctrine of laches. This is an equitable defense, and a court of equity will refuse relief to a party who has delayed the assertion of his claim so that granting the relief requested would work an injustice upon the other party. Three elements must be present to constitute this equitable defense, i.e., (1) knowledge by the party of his right; (2) unjustified delay in asserting that right; and (3) some circumstances, such as change of position by the other party, which would make it inequitable to grant the relief requested.

Aside from these general principles, there are no hard and fast rules, and the application of the doctrine depends upon the facts and circumstances of each particular case. It has been said in regard to laches that each case is a law unto itself. (*Esau* v. *Briggs*, 89 C.A.2d 427.)

ESTOPPEL

Another doctrine that applies in the field of real estate law is that of estoppel. An estoppel arises where a party, by his own declaration, act, or omission, has intentionally led another to believe a particular thing to be true and to act on such belief. (Evid. C., Sec. 623.) Although waiver and estoppel are sometimes used indiscriminately, as though possessing common elements, they rest upon different legal principles. Waiver imports a unilateral act and its legal consequences. Estoppel, on the other hand, carries a bilateral connotation: the justifiable reliance by one party upon the intentional act or omission of another. (*Altman* v. *McCollum,* 107 C.A.2d Supp. 847.)

Questions

1. What law governs land titles in California?
2. Is the common law of England applicable in California?
3. Did any Mexican or Spanish law become a part of California law?
4. Discuss the main sources of the law of real property.
5. What is regarded as the supreme law of the land?
6. Which court is the highest court in the country?
7. Distinguish the two court systems having jurisdiction in California.
8. What is the main function of the courts?
9. Describe briefly the principal state courts.
10. Describe briefly the principal federal courts.
11. Define the power of judical review.
12. Explain the reason for a statute of limitations.

3

Nature and Classes of Property

Summary

I. Nature of property

Property is defined in the Civil Code as "the thing of which there may be ownership." Ownership is defined as "the right of one or more persons to possess and use it [property] to the exclusion of others." (C.C., Sec. 654.)

PROPERTY AS A "BUNDLE OF RIGHTS"

When we think of property, we generally think of the thing itself, such as an automobile, a piece of furniture, a promissory note, or a parcel of land. In a strict legal sense, however, the word does not mean the thing itself that is owned, but refers to the rights or interests that a person has in a thing, often referred to as a "bundle of rights." This "bundle of rights" is the exclusive right of a person to own, possess, use, enjoy, and dispose of a determinate thing, either real property or personal property, consistent with the law. This "bundle of rights" is called property.

RIGHT OF DISPOSITION

The owner of property is the one who has complete dominion over it, with rights of disposition, exclusion, and use. These rights are the chief incidents of ownership. The owner may keep the land as long as he wishes (subject, however, to the government's power of eminent domain), or he may sell all or any part of it, or he may give it away. If he decides to sell the land, he may choose the manner of its disposition and the terms of sale, since this is the exclusive right of an owner. He may devise it to a particular person or persons by will, which transfer becomes effective upon his death. He may create a life estate in the land or some lesser estate. He may choose to do nothing with the land during his lifetime, and upon his death his property rights will pass by operation of law to other persons in accordance with the laws of succession in effect at the time of his death. Prior to 1963, an owner in California was free to dispose of the land to whom and as he wished, subject to only one important limitation, i.e., in any disposition of the land he must comply with certain requirements of the law as to the form and manner of execution of the particular instrument. In 1963 the California Fair Housing Act, also known as the Rumford Act, was passed by the State legislature, under which certain penalties can be invoked when dwellings of the type described in the Act are placed for sale or lease, if the owner or agent refuses to sell or lease to a qualified buyer solely because of the buyer's race, color, religion, national origin, or ancestry. The owner is specifically authorized, however, to use all his other usual bases for selection.

In 1964, the State Constitution (Art. I, Sec. 26) was amended by the approval of Proposition 14 by the voters in the November 3 election. This prohibited the state from interfering with a person's absolute right to decline to sell or lease real property to whomever he chooses, and overturned the Rumford Act. Then in 1966 the California Supreme Court held that the 1964 constitutional amendment was violative of the equal protection of the laws as guaranteed by the Fourteenth Amendment to the federal Constitution and was therefore void. (*Mulkey* v. *Reitman*, 64 Cal.2d 529.)

Federal laws and regulations also relate to antidiscrimination in the field of real estate; they are discussed in Chapter 17.

RIGHT OF EXCLUSION

The owner of the land has the right to exclude others from his land. No one has the right to enter upon another person's land without the permission of the owner, and if he does, he may be liable to the owner for trespass. The owner, however, may give permission to others to enter upon his land. He may enter into a written lease with another person for a term of years, under which the lessee would have the right to enter and take over complete possession of the property for the stated period. The owner may rent a portion of the premises to a tenant, or he may give permission to another person, either by the grant of an easement or a license, to use a portion of the land for a particular purpose, such as a right of way for driveway purposes. Other persons may thus receive specific, distinct, and separate rights in relation to the land of another. Although the owner still retains the most important proprietary rights in the land, his bundle of rights is not as large as it was originally, since other persons have acquired rights of possession in the land.

RIGHT OF USE AND ENJOYMENT

The owner has the exclusive right to use and enjoy the land, and while he is the owner may use it as he pleases, subject, however, to the control exercised by the government over the use of the land through its power of taxation and under the police power. The owner may leave the land unimproved or he may improve it. He may grow crops on the land if he chooses; he may clear the land of timber; he may change the contour of the land; or he may dig all the gravel from his land and give it away, and no one can hold him liable for waste and destruction of the land. The land is his to use and enjoy to the exclusion of others.

LIMITATIONS ON RIGHT OF USE

Various obligations and duties are imposed by law on a landowner that restrict to a certain extent the use he may make of his land, and the law in some instances may impose an affirmative duty of care. The law may require him to control weed growth, insects, and other pests. If the owner chooses to improve his land, he must comply with the provisions of zoning ordinances and building and safety codes. Although the owner does have the exclusive right of use, he does not have the right to an unlimited use and freedom of enjoyment. His right is subject to the paramount right of the state to control the use of land in the interest of public health, safety, morals, and welfare.

II. Classes of property

The Civil Code divides property into two classes, namely, *real or immovable property,* and *personal or movable property.*

REAL PROPERTY

Real property, as defined in the Civil Code, consists of the land, that which is affixed to land, that which is incidental or appurtenant to land, and that which is immovable by law. (C.C., Sec. 658.) This is the definition applicable in connection with the transfer of real property. However, for purposes of taxation the definitions in the revenue and taxation laws of the state control whether they conform to definitions used for other purposes or not. (*Atlantic Oil Co.* v. *County of Los Angeles,* 69 A.C. 610.)

PERSONAL PROPERTY

Under the Civil Code, personal property is defined in a negative way; every kind of property that is not real property is personal property.

REAL PROPERTY AS LANDS, TENEMENTS, AND HEREDITAMENTS

Real property is described in another section of the Civil Code (Sec. 14) as "coextensive with lands, tenements and hereditaments." As defined in English law, "tenement" was a broad term embracing not only the land itself, but also incorporeal rights, i.e., rights connected with and arising out of the ownership of the land, such as rents. "Hereditament," the broadest expression for real property of all kinds, included not only land and tenements, but also whatever rights, corporeal or incorporeal, passed to the heirs at law upon the owner's death, rather than to the personal representative of a decedent's estate. Rights of this sort that are recognized generally under present law are *rents, easements,* and *profits à prendre,* i.e., the right to take something, such as oil and gas, from the land.

USE OF WORDS "REAL PROPERTY" IN DEEDS

The words "tenements" and "hereditament" are sometimes used today, but are regarded as obsolete terms in modern conveyancing. The form of deed usually employed conveys "the real property situated in ______ county, state of California, described as [legal description]," without using the phrase "lands, tenements and hereditaments." By the use of the words "real property" there is conveyed the land, together with improvements and fixtures regarded as part of the land, and those incidental rights connected with the land that are the incorporeal hereditaments as recognized today.

REAL PROPERTY DENOTES CERTAIN RIGHTS

The term "real property," used in a technical sense not reflected in the Civil Code definition, is applied not to the land itself but to certain rights or interests that an owner has in land, more specifically to those interests in land that are *estates in fee* or *for life*. All lesser estates in land, such as an estate for years, are regarded as personal property. This limitation of the term "real property" to an estate in fee or for life, which were the types of estates known as "freehold estates" in common law, is the result of the early English rule that the owner of a freehold estate in land, if wrongfully deprived of it, could recover the land itself, i.e., the real thing, in a "real" action, and hence his interest was referred to as "real property" or "real estate." The only remedy available to the owner of a lesser estate was a "personal" action for damages, so his interest in the land was called "personal property."

PROPERTY MAY UNDERGO A CHANGE IN CLASS

Under the proper circumstances, real property or personal property may undergo a transformation and be changed into the other class of property. Land in place is immovable and hence is real property, but when it is severed from the earth, as, for instance, when a load of gravel or topsoil is removed from a plot of ground, it becomes movable and therefore personal property. Similarly, personal property becomes a part of the land when it is attached thereto with the intention of making it a permanent part of the land.

III. The elements of real property

Under the definition contained in Section 658 of the Civil Code, real property includes not only the ground or soil, but also things that are attached to the earth, whether by course of nature, such as trees and other vegetation, or by the hand of man, such as a house or other structure. It also includes things that are incidental to the use of land, such as an easement or right of way. It includes not only the surface of the earth, but everything under it and above it. A tract of land, in legal theory, consists not only of the portion on the earth's surface, but also is like an inverted pyramid having its apex at the center of the earth, and further, extends outward from the surface of the earth at its boundary lines to the periphery of the universe.

OWNERSHIP ABOVE THE SURFACE

The doctrine of ownership of airspace is expressed in Section 829 of the Civil Code, which provides that "The owner of land in fee has the right to the surface and to everything permanently situated beneath or above it." This doctrine, of common-law origin, has been modified to meet the development and needs of air navigation. As stated in the case of *United States* v. *Causby,* 328 U.S. 256, "It is ancient doctrine that at common law ownership of the land extended to the periphery of the universe—*Cujus est solum ejus est usque ad coelum.* But that doctrine has no place in the modern world."

Ownership of airspace today. Modern theories as to ownership of airspace are not uniform, but a rational view, based upon the decision in the above-mentioned case, may be expressed as follows: The airspace is a public highway, but the landowner owns at least as much of the space above the surface as he can use and occupy in connection with his land, even though he does not occupy it in a physical sense by buildings and the like, and he has the right to prevent a use of the space by others that would interfere with his use of the land. Thus, in the case of *Griggs* v. *County of Allegheny,* 369 U.S. 84, the United States Supreme Court held that the noise, vibrations, and fear caused to the occupants of a house located near a county airport by constant and extremely low overflights interfered with the use of the owner's property so as to amount to a "taking," in the constitutional sense, of an air easement for which compensation must be paid.

Use of airspace by landowner. In the case of *Strother* v. *Pacific Gas & Electric Co.,* 94 C.A.2d 525, it was indicated that a proper and beneficial use of the airspace above an owner's land cannot be interfered with, except for necessary police regulation for the safety and protection of the public. In the case of *La Com* v. *Pacific Gas & Electric Co.,* 132 C.A.2d 114, it was stated that a temporary invasion of airspace by aircraft is a privilege so long as it does not interfere unreasonably with persons or property lawfully on the land beneath. The launching of space satellites by Russia and the United States poses new problems, but these are international in scope rather than local, including the problem of defining the boundary between "airspace" and "outer space."

Division of airspace into strata. The division of airspace above the land into strata for purposes of ownership or use apart from the surface of the land is not uncommon in many large cities, and such division has been expressly sanctioned in several jurisdictions. Although such division was recognized in California under its then law, specific recognition was given to the division of airspace in California in 1963 by the adoption of the Condominium Law (see Chapter 8).

WHAT "LAND" CONSISTS OF

Prior to 1963, the word "land" was defined in the Civil Code as "the solid materials of the earth, whatever may be the ingredients of which it is composed, whether soil, rock or other substance." (C.C., Sec. 659.) It was primarily thought of as the ground or soil or earth that we walk upon or place structures upon. In 1963 the Section was amended as part of the Condominium Act to include "free or occupied space for an indefinite distance upwards as well as downwards, subject to limitations upon the use of airspace imposed, and rights in the use of airspace granted, by law."

MINERALS

Land includes all ores, metals, coal, and other minerals in or on the land to the center of the earth. Although in recent times there has been a modification of the doctrine of ownership above the surface, the rule of ownership to the center of the earth still applies. Minerals while they remain in place are real property; when severed from the earth, they become personal property.

Separate ownership of minerals. For purposes of ownership, land may be divided horizontally as well as vertically. For example, the owner of the land may convey the minerals to another person and retain ownership of the land, or he may convey the land with an exception of the minerals, thus retaining the minerals owned by him. The minerals can be conveyed at different levels or strata beneath the surface, and the practice is not uncommon of designating horizontal spheres in mineral leases, including oil and gas leases. The grant or reservation of the minerals carries with it an implied right of entry for the purpose of extracting the minerals. In order to eliminate a right of entry upon the surface of the land, it is common practice to convey the minerals below 500 feet beneath the surface, and to specifically exclude right of entry from the surface. The owner of the minerals will then have to enter from adjoining areas if he wishes to remove the minerals.

Oil and gas. Oil and gas are classified as minerals, but fall in a special category. Unlike solid minerals which are stationary, oil and gas are shifting, migratory substances which are incapable of absolute ownership as a thing in place, and must be reduced to possession before ownership becomes complete. However, the landowner owning the minerals does have an exclusive right to drill for and produce oil and gas, and to retain as his property all such substances brought to the surface. This right may be granted by the owner separate from a grant of the surface, or may be excepted in a conveyance of the surface, and when so granted or excepted is known as a *profit a prendre,* which is an interest in real property in the nature of an incorporeal hereditament.

WATER RIGHTS

General considerations. In its natural state, water is real property; when severed from the realty and reduced to possession by putting it in containers, it becomes personal property. The subject of water rights is complex, with many rules applying. Some of these rights are discussed briefly below.

Riparian water rights. The owner of land bordering upon a river or other water course has no absolute ownership of the waters, but has a right, in common with others, to the reasonable use of waters flowing past his land. This, in brief, is what is designated as riparian water rights.

Underground waters. Underground waters, such as percolating waters, were formerly regarded as part of the soil and owned absolutely by the owner of the land. In California the rule has been modified; the landowner now has only a right in common with other owners to take his share of the water for beneficial use. The right of the overlying landowner to the percolating waters beneath his lands is analogous to riparian rights. In the case of *Trussell* v. *City of San Diego,* 172 C.A.2d 593, it was stated that owners of land have a right to the use of underground waters as a supporting underground water supply available to, and for the benefit of, farming operations, and such use is a beneficial use of the underground waters. In addition to overlying use, rights in an underground basin may also be appropriative. Public interest requires that there be the greatest number of beneficial uses that the water supply can yield, and surplus water may be appropriated for beneficial use subject to the rights of those who have a lawful priority. Any water not needed for the reasonable beneficial use of those having prior rights is excess or surplus water and may rightly be appropriated on privately owned land for nonoverlying use, such as devotion to public use or exportation beyond the basin watershed. As between overlying owners, their rights, like those of riparians, are correlative; each may use only his reasonable share when the water is insufficient to meet the needs of all. (*California Water Service Co.* v. *Sidebotham & Son, Inc.*, 224 C.A.2d 715.)

"LAND" AS INCLUDING IMPROVEMENTS

The statutory definition of land as set forth in the Civil Code (Sec.

659) appears to exclude improvements and other fixtures on the land and appurtenant rights, thereby making land but one of the elements of real property. In some cases, however, the courts have construed the word "land" alone as including improvements, and have declared that the use of the word "land" as synonymous with real property has become its historical, ordinary, and accepted meaning in connection with title, ownership, conveyance, or transfer by deed or inheritance, or with the exercise of the right of eminent domain, or with execution sales and redemption and similar evidences of ownership or modes of transfer. (*Krouser* v. *County of San Bernardino,* 29 Cal.2d 766.) Moreover, regardless of the limited statutory definition, it has been held that a conveyance of "land" transfers the land itself and all that is annexed, incidental, or appurtenant thereto. (*Trask* v. *Moore,* 24 Cal.2d 365.)

"LAND" AS USED IN A TITLE POLICY

"Land" is used in a limited sense in a policy of title insurance. Policies of title insurance insure title to the "land" therein described, and define the word "land" as including improvements affixed thereto that by law constitute real property. Rights in other lands, such as an appurtenant easement over land adjoining that described in the title policy, although embraced as a matter of law in the term "real property," are not included in the coverage of the title policy unless expressly described and insured.

THINGS DEEMED AFFIXED TO LAND

The term "real property" includes, in addition to the land itself, that which is affixed to land. Section 660 of the Civil Code provides that a thing is deemed to be affixed to land when it is attached to it by roots, as in the case of trees, vines, or shrubs; or embedded in it, as in the case of walls; or permanently resting upon it, as in the case of buildings; or permanently attached to what is thus permanent, as by means of cement, plaster, nails, bolts, or screws.

"FRUCTUS NATURALES"

Trees, shrubs, vines, and crops that are a product of nature alone, termed "*fructus naturales,*" are generally regarded as part of the land to which they are attached by roots, and they continue to be real property until severed, actually or constructively, at which time they become personal property. *Fructus naturales* may be owned separately from the land. As an example, standing timber may be conveyed, or may be reserved in a conveyance, apart from the land, and the owner of the timber would have a right of removal, if not limited by the terms of the conveyance.

Transfer of "fructus naturales." An effective conveyance of growing trees and other *fructus naturales* apart from the land should, it would seem, require a writing and other formalities for the transfer of real property. However, the Civil Code provides that for purposes of sale, things attached to the land, that are agreed to be severed before sale or under contract of sale, shall be treated as goods, and governed by the rules regulating the sale of goods. (C.C., Secs. 658 and 660.) Whether an oral sale of timber would be binding on a subsequent purchaser of the land without notice of the constructive severance appears to be doubtful.

"FRUCTUS INDUSTRIALES"

Grain, garden vegetables, and other growing crops that are the result of annual labor, classified as "*fructus industriales,*" i.e., industrial crops, may be either real property or personal property, depending upon the circumstances. A growing crop of fruit upon trees or vines is classed as *fructus industriales.* As between a seller and buyer of land, growing crops are a part of the land until severed or agreed to be severed, and pass to the grantee by a conveyance of the land, unless reserved in writing. As in the case of trees, a sale of growing crops may be made apart from the land, and the crops are treated as goods and governed by the code provisions regulating the sale of goods.

PERSONAL PROPERTY SECURITY AGREEMENTS

The Uniform Commercial Code enacted by the 1963 California legislature became effective on January 1, 1965. It repealed or amended the laws relating to the filing or recording of chattel mortgages, assignments of accounts receivable, conditional sales contracts, pledges, and similar documents used in personal property security transactions. It established in lieu thereof a uniform procedure for perfecting a security interest in personal property. New terms will be encountered, such as Security Agreement, Security Interest, and Financing Statements.

Among the items excluded from the operation of the Code are fixtures, oil and minerals in place, and the creation or transfer of an interest in or lien on real estate. The law has only a limited effect on land titles.

FINANCING STATEMENTS

Under the provisions of Division 9 (Sec. 9101–9507) of the Uniform Commercial Code, a security interest in personal property is perfected by the filing of a "financing statement" as follows:

1. When the collateral is equipment used in farming operations, or farm products other than crops, or accounts or contract rights arising from or relating to the sale of farm products by a farmer, or consumer goods, then the proper place to file is the office of the county recorder in the county of the debtor's residence or, if the debtor is not a resident of this State, then in the office of the county recorder where the goods are kept.
2. When the collateral is crops or timber to be cut, then the proper place to file is in the office of the county recorder in the county where the land on which the crops are growing or to be grown or on which the timber is standing is located.
3. In all other cases the proper place to file is in the office of the Secretary of State in Sacramento.

The only requirement that the description of real property appear in the financing statement is when the collateral consists of crops growing or to be grown, or timber to be cut.

EFFECT OF FILING

The filing of a financing statement is effective for five years and then expires unless a continuation statement is filed within six months prior to the end of the five-year period. This procedure may be repeated indefinitely.

The statement must be indexed by the filing office according to the name of the debtor. In the case of a financing statement relating to crops or timber, the statement must also be indexed in the real property index of grantors under the name of the debtor. The debtor may not necessarily be the owner of the land. He could be a lessee or a contract purchaser. If a statement relating to crops or timber is properly indexed in the office of the county recorder, and if a description of the land is included, the financing statement constitutes constructive notice thereof to any purchaser or encumbrancer of the land. Financing statements under the new law may thus have a greater effect on the title to real property than crop mortgages did under the law prior to January 1, 1965.

IV. Importance of the distinctions between real and personal property

The distinction between real and personal property is an important one in considering the legal aspects. As mentioned previously, real property is a fixed, immovable, and permanent thing, whereas personal property is readily movable from place to place, is often easily consumed or destroyed, and is regarded as something impermanent or transient. These physical contrasts in the two classes of property have resulted in different rules of law regulating their ownership.

REAL PROPERTY SUBJECT TO LAWS OF STATE WHERE LOCATED

Real property is exclusively subject to the laws and jurisdiction of the state within which it is located. The acquisition, disposition, and devolution of title to land in California is governed by the laws of the state of California, except in those instances where title is in the United States, or where the Constitution of the United States has granted jurisdiction to the federal government, as in the case of bankruptcy. California law controls as to form, execution, validity, and effect of instruments relating to land in this state, and determines the descent of such land to heirs or devisees of a deceased owner. Courts of the other states do not have the power to render decrees that directly affect title to land in California. A decree of distribution of real property in California made by the probate court of another state having jurisdiction of the decedent's estate by virtue of domicile of the decedent would be ineffective in California. Personal property, on the other hand, is usually regarded as situated at the domicile of its owner, regardless of the actual situs of the property, and is governed by the law of the owner's domicile.

METHOD OF TRANSFER

The distinction between real and personal property is also of importance as to method of transfer. A voluntary transfer of title to real property can be made only by an instrument in writing, whereas title to personal property generally passes by delivery of possession. A written instrument may be used in connection with the transfer of personal property, such as an assignment of a claim, or a bill of sale of a chattel, but is not necessary to its validity unless required by statute.

REQUIREMENTS AS TO RECORDING

The requirements as to recording are another important distinction between real and personal property. The law contemplates that instruments affecting title to real property will be recorded in a public office, in order that purchasers and other persons dealing with the property may ascertain and rely upon the ownership of the property as evidenced by the public records. In the case of personal property, there are relatively few instruments that may be recorded or that give notice when recorded. Accordingly, the ownership or condition of title to personal property cannot, for the most part, be determined from the public records. Personal property security agreements are, of course, a main exception to this rule.

TAXATION

Several cases have arisen involving the question as to whether or not vaults and vault doors and other equipment of a bank are part of the real property and assessed as real property for tax purposes. If not real property, then such equipment would be tax exempt, since the franchise tax imposed on banks is in lieu of any tax on personal property. In the case of *San Diego Trust & Savings Co.* v. *San Diego County,* 16 Cal.2d 142, it was held that vaults and vault doors constituted a unit for use together and that the vault doors were therefore to be considered improvements to the realty and taxable as such. This view was followed in the case of *Trabue Pittman Corp.* v. *County of Los Angeles,* 29 Cal.2d 385, even though under the terms of a lease between the landowner and the bank as lessee, the items were regarded as trade fixtures and removable by the lessee at the termination of the lease. In a later case, that of *Pajaro Valley Bank* v. *County of Santa Cruz,* 207 C.A.2d 621, heavy metal safe deposit boxes were held to be personalty and not taxable. Although there was an appearance of solidity and permanence, the boxes were in fact readily movable. Then in the case of *Bank of America* v. *County of Los Angeles,* 224 C.A.2d 108, it was held that an electronic computer system installed in a bank was taxable as a fixture.

In a reverse situation, it has been held that rose bushes planted by a nursery company and raised to sell as plants rather than seeking profit from the product of the plants, were not "growing crops" within the provision of the state constitution exempting growing crops from taxation, and were properly taxed as personal property. (*Jackson & Perkins Co. of California* v. *Stanislaus County,* 168 C.A.2d 559.)

CONDEMNATION ACTIONS

Where land is condemned for public use, the value of the buildings or other improvements and fixtures on the land must be considered in determining the owner's compensation. (*City of Los Angeles* v. *Klinker,* 219 Cal. 198.) As stated in the case of *City of Beverly Hills* v. *Albright,* 184 C.A.2d 562, if equipment is affixed to the land that is condemned, compensation for its loss will be included in the value of the property taken. Prior to 1957, the courts applied the traditional tests to determine whether particular articles of personal property had become part of the land for which compensation had to be paid, and in some instances this worked a hardship on owners of manufacturing plants containing pieces of heavy equipment which had not been bolted to the floor. In 1957, section 1248b was added to the Code of Civil Procedure, providing that equipment designed for manufacturing or industrial purposes and installed for use in a fixed location shall be deemed a part of the realty for the purposes of condemnation, regardless of the method of instal-

JUDGMENT LIENS

The distinction between real and personal property is also of importance in the case of judgment liens. The term "real property" as used in connection with the lien of a judgment is taken in its technical sense, which excludes all estates that are chattels real and therefore personalty, such as an estate for years. Thus, a mere leasehold estate is not subject to such a lien. (*Summerville* v. *Stockton Mill Co.*, 142 Cal. 529.)

JUDICIAL SALES

The procedures for levy upon and sale of property through court proceedings differs for real and personal property, hence it is important to know the character of the property before starting any such action or proceeding.

Questions

1. How is property defined?
2. Define "ownership."
3. Explain briefly the various incidents of ownership.
4. Property is divided into how many classes?
5. In what two ways is real property defined in the Civil Code?
6. How is personal property defined?
7. Discuss briefly the constituents or elements of real property.
8. May land be divided horizontally as well as vertically? Explain.
9. Is there any distinction between the ownership of ores and the ownership of oil and gas?
10. Is any limitation placed on the ownership of airspace?
11. Describe briefly the rights of the holder of a personal property security agreement.
12. Discuss the distinctions between real and personal property, and explain their importance.

4

Fixtures

Summary

I. Fixtures defined

Real property includes not only the land itself, but also those things that are affixed to the land. A *fixture* may be defined as a thing that was originally a chattel, but that has been attached to land in a manner to be considered in law as making it a part of the land; thus it becomes real property. (Sec. 660, C.C.) For example, lumber at a lumber yard is personal property; when it is used in the construction of a residence on a parcel of land, it becomes a part of the real property. It is not essential that the article be in actual contact with the soil itself. It may be attached to a building that itself, under the law of fixtures, is considered part of the land. A piece of plumbing, as an example, may fall in this category.

The definition of a fixture as contained in the Civil Code is adapted primarily for determining what passes under a conveyance or mortgage of real property.

II. Applicable rules

Common law rule. The general rule of the common law with respect to fixtures is that whatever is once annexed to the freehold becomes a part of it, and cannot thereafter be removed except by him who is entitled to the inheritance.

California rule. The law of fixtures in California is essentially the same as the common law on the subject and the law prevailing generally throughout the United States.

Controlling factors. There are so many various relations under which the question whether an article constitutes a fixture may arise that the same rule cannot apply to all. A tendency to apply to the question arising in one situation the rule established in another has caused confusion. The subject of fixtures particularly illustrates the importance of a determination of all of the facts and circumstances before reaching a decision in a given case as to whether or not a liability exists.

III. Tests to determine whether or not a thing is a fixture

In determining whether or not an article is a fixture, five generally recognized tests are applied, with the ultimate decision being dependent, of course, upon all of the facts and circumstances of the particular case. These five tests are (1) manner of annexation; (2) character of article and adaptation to use; (3) intention of the parties; (4) relationship of the parties; and (5) agreement of the parties.

MANNER OF ANNEXATION, INCLUDING MOBILITY

The first test is the manner of the article's annexation. Section 660 of the Civil Code provides that a thing is deemed affixed to land when it is "permanently resting" upon the land or "permanently attached to what is thus permanent, as by means of cement, plaster, nails, bolts or screws." This code provision is merely a rule of general guidance. A thing may be attached by means of screws, but not be a fixture. Conversely, a thing may be easily removable or otherwise not attached as specified in the code and yet be a fixture, if it was intended that it remain where fastened until worn out or superseded by another article. The case of *Frick* v. *Frigidaire Corp.*, 119 C.A. 707, is illustrative. In that case it was held that refrigeration equipment securely fastened to a building by bolts, nuts, and screws, with conduits and tubing interwoven in the walls, was a fixture.

A building need not be physically anchored to the land to be considered realty; it may be a fixture even though it is secured to the realty by force of gravity alone. (*Rinaldi* v. *Goller,* 48 Cal.2d 276.)

CHARACTER OF ARTICLE AND ADAPTATION TO USE

The second test is the character of the article and its adaptation to the use and purpose for which the realty is used. It must appear that the article would be essential to the ordinary and convenient use of the property to which it is annexed. An important question is whether or not it can be used elsewhere, or whether it was custom made for the particular building. In the case of *M.P. Moller, Inc.* v. *Wilson,* 8 Cal.2d 31, a pipe organ, although specially installed in a residence, was held not to be a fixture.

INTENTION OF THE PARTIES

The third and often the most important test is the intention of the parties making the annexation. Was the article attached, the courts ask, with the intention of making it a permanent part of the structure? The other tests are helpful in determining the intention of the parties, and once that intention is determined, it ordinarily must govern. However, it is not the secret intention of the person installing the article that controls. The test is an objective one, and the intention may be ascertainable from the nature of the article, the relation of the parties, the adaptation of the article and mode of annexation, and all of the surrounding circumstances.

The case of *Larkin* v. *Cowert*, 263 A.C.A. 29, is illustrative. In that case, decided in June 1968, carpets and drapes in an apartment building were held to be part of the realty. The manner in which the carpets were put in place was held not to be controlling, the court stating that where there is no agreement, no representation, and no basis for an estoppel as to ownership, the controlling factor should be the intention with which the installation is made. The court regarded as significant the fact that the installation was in a rental unit rather than in a private home. In an earlier case (*Plough* v. *Petersen*, 140 C.A.2d 595) the court held that carpeting was not a fixture where the carpets were in a private home.

RELATIONSHIP OF THE PARTIES

Other things being equal, the relationship of the parties may be the decisive factor when a dispute arises between the owner of the land and the owner of the article that has been attached to realty.

Buyer and seller. Where a landowner sells his land, the law favors the buyer, and articles installed on the land will usually be regarded as fixtures and will pass to the purchaser as part of the realty. The purchaser is favored by the rule that whatever is essential for the use of the buildings will be considered a fixture, even though it may be severed without injury to the realty or to the article.

Mortgagor and mortgagee. As between a mortgagor and a mortgagee of real property, the liberal rule as to what passes by deed is also applied. Moreover, if a mortgagor annexes fixtures to the land after the execution of the mortgage, the lien of the mortgage attaches to the fixtures as part of the land, subject, however, to intermediate rights or liens of third persons.

Landlord and tenant. Where a dispute as to the ownership of articles affixed to a structure is between a landlord and tenant, the law favors the tenant and allows him to remove almost any article he has installed in the building, in the absence of an agreement to the contrary.

AGREEMENTS REGARDING FIXTURES

An agreement as to the character of the thing to be affixed may be entered into permitting an article that otherwise would be a fixture to nonetheless remain personal property. An example of such an agreement is a lease giving the lessee the right, at the termination of the lease, to remove buildings and equipment installed by the lessee. Agreements may also be entered into between the landowner and the owner of the article to be affixed, such as a conditional sales agreement, under which the vendor reserves title to the article as personal property, and retains the right to remove it from the land upon default in payment. Such an understanding may also be evidenced by the execution by the landowner of a security agreement to secure the purchase price of an article to be annexed to the land.

Rights of third parties. Agreements that an article shall retain its personal character are valid between the parties and as to other parties with notice. Such agreements are not effective, however, after annexation has taken place, as against the rights of subsequent purchasers or mortgagees of the land for value, in good faith, and without notice of the agreement. Although the land mortgagee may prevail against the conditional sales vendor as to an article affixed *before* the mortgage is recorded, the rule is otherwise where the article is affixed to the land *after* the mortgage is recorded. In the latter case, the conditional sales vendor may exercise his right to remove the fixture unless such removal will substantially injure or diminish the value of the security.

Character of articles may be changed by agreement. The character of articles that have already been affixed to real property may also be determined by an agreement between the landowner and another party. Thus, the vendor and vendee of real property may agree that articles not so annexed as to be fixtures in the eyes of the law will nevertheless pass as fixtures under a conveyance of the land. Conversely, they may agree that articles that otherwise would be fixtures are to be considered as personal property, with title to such articles remaining in the vendor of the realty.

FIXTURES UNDER UNIFORM COMMERCIAL CODE

The Uniform Commercial Code as a general rule retains the existing legal rules pertaining to fixtures. The filing of a financing statement with the Secretary of State would not constitute notice under a policy of title insurance. Land is defined in a policy as the land described therein and improvement affixed thereto which by law constitute real property. Assurances are not given that any specific property is or is not a fixture. A chattel mortgage heretofore has not been recognized by a title insurer as constituting constructive notice, and a financing statement is treated the same way, except those describing timber or crops. The latter, if properly recorded, would be considered as affecting the land.

IV. Trade fixtures

In order to encourage a tenant to equip himself with the tools and implements of his trade, articles installed by the tenant for the purpose of his trade or business are classed as trade fixtures, and may be removed by the tenant anytime during the continuance of his term. This rule has been codified and extended in Section 1019 of the Civil Code, under which articles affixed by a tenant "for purposes of trade, manufacture, ornament, or domestic use" may be removed, if the removal can be effected without injury to the premises, unless they have become an integral part of the premises.

ILLUSTRATIONS

The following are illustrative of the inclusive nature of trade fixtures: gasoline pumps and tanks sunk into the ground by the lessee of a service station; fixtures installed in a market for the purpose of conducting a soft drink stand; a shampoo bowl, dresserettes and mirrors attached to the walls of a hotel room by the operator of a beauty parlor; a basement hardwood floor, mirrors, the woodwork of a grill room and large plaster ornaments, all built for restaurant and café purposes and installed in a tavern; and an electric sign set in a portable frame and fastened by bolts to a fabricated steel tower on a theater.

V. Conflicting claims between owner or mortgagee of chattel and subsequent vendee or mortgagee of realty

As noted above, agreements that articles affixed to land shall retain their character as personalty are not effective as against subsequent purchasers or mortgagees of the land for value and without notice of such agreement. It has been held that the recording of the chattel mortgage is not alone sufficient to charge the subsequent purchaser or mortgagee of the land with notice of the rights of the chattel mortgagee. (*Elliott* v. *Hudson*, 18 C.A. 642.) Whether the recording of a conditional sales contract would impart notice to a subsequent purchaser or encumbrancer of the land is uncertain in this state, as there is no decision of the appellate courts directly in point. However, even though recording may not impart notice, and the purchaser or mortgagee of the land may have no actual notice of the agreement, the physical facts as to the nature of the article or the manner of its attachment may be sufficient to charge him with notice of the possible character of the articles as personalty. Attaching a metal tag to an article, such as a chain link fence or a water heater, in a conspicuous place, disclosing the interest of the conditional vendor, has proven effective in many cases.

MORTGAGES OR DEEDS OF TRUST DESCRIBING PERSONALTY

Another problem sometimes arises where mortgage or deed of trust upon land provides that various items, such as refrigeration equipment, water heaters, stoves, carpets, and other types of appliances or equipment used or installed in buildings on the land, are declared to be fixtures and an integral part of the realty covered by the mortgage or deed of trust. Cases may arise where some of these items are not affixed to the realty in such a manner as to be deemed fixtures in the eyes of the law. As between the parties to the mortgage or deed of trust, such articles will be determined to be fixtures and subject to the lien of the mortgage or deed of trust. However, subsequent purchasers or the holder of a personal property security agreement acquiring interests in these articles, which have the appearance of unattached property, will take free from the real property mortgage or deed of trust, unless such persons have actual notice of such mortgage or deed of trust. The real property mortgage or deed of trust, if not executed in form sufficient as a personal property security agreement, does not impart constructive notice. If the real property mortgage or deed of trust is also executed and recorded as a personal property security agreement, it will then give notice of a lien on the chattel items during the statutory period of such a lien.

ILLUSTRATIVE CASE—RIGHTS UNDER A DEED OF TRUST

The case of *Pacific Mortgage Guaranty Co.* v. *Rosoff*, 20 C.A.2d 383, is illustrative of some of the principles discussed above. In that case an action was brought against a building contractor to enjoin the removal by the latter of wall beds, linoleum, and curtain rods from an apartment building on which the plaintiff held a deed of trust. The contractor claimed that he could remove those articles by virtue of an agreement with the owner of the building reserving title in himself. The court enjoined the removal of the articles, stating that under the facts of this case it could not be concluded that the articles were not fixtures. As a basis for its decision, the court pointed out that the articles were called for as a part of the construction of the building according to the plans and specifications, and constituted a part of the consideration for plaintiff making the loan, and the removal of the articles would impair plaintiff's security.

SINK UNITS

The case of *Daniger* v. *Hunter*, 114 C.A.2d 796, involved an action to foreclose a mechanic's lien and to recover judgment for the purchase price of three sink units installed on defendant's premises in connection with the remodeling of defendant's house and garage into four apartments. The sink units consisted of a gas stove, a sink, and a refrigerator, fitting together as a unit. The trial court held that the sink units, after being installed, became an actual part of the building, and concluded that plaintiff had a lien on the real property. Defendant owner appealed, contending that appliances such as kitchen ranges, refrigerators, and sinks not attached to the dwelling are not materials furnished within the meaning of the mechanic's lien law, and that plaintiff was not entitled to a lien. The appellate court held that the trial court was wrong in impressing a lien on the realty, since the sink units were not to be considered as fixtures. The court in reaching its decision stated as follows:

> It seems quite clear that electrical appliances such as refrigerators and stoves are personal property, and do not become a part of the realty where, as here, they are movable and can be disconnected by merely pulling a plug or unscrewing a gas connection. In the instant case the units sold were of three items: a stove, a sink, and a refrigerator, so constructed as to form one unit, conserving floor space. While ordinarily a sink is "built in" and made a part of the building, in the instant case it is a part of a unit which is so constructed as to be easily disconnected and removed without damage to the realty or the article itself. Under such circumstances we conclude that these units were chattels and not fixtures.

OTHER FIXTURE CASES

In the case of *Story* v. *Christin,* 14 Cal.2d 592, nursery trees planted in a nursery business for the purpose of being transplanted were held not to be affixed, and were considered to be personal property. A trailer used as an office at a trailer court has been held not to be a fixture. (*Clifford* v. *Epsten,* 106 C.A.2d 221.)

Questions

1. Define a fixture.
2. Explain manner of annexation as a test in determining whether or not a thing is a fixture.
3. Discuss other factors of importance in determining whether or not a thing is a fixture.
4. Where a dispute arises as to the ownership of an article, which party does the law favor in the following situations:
   a. Vendor-vendee relationship?
   b. Mortgagor-mortgagee relationship?
   c. Landlord-tenant relationship?
5. Are trade fixtures placed in a special category? If so, what is the reason?
6. To what extent are agreements regarding fixtures binding on subsequent parties?

5

Easements

I. Definition and nature of easements
Characteristics of an easement; Easements include "profits"

II. Classes of easements
Easements appurtenant; Easement in gross; English law distinguished; Determining the classification of an easement; Easements in favor of after-acquired property

III. Purposes for which easements may be created
Statutory rights in gross; Additional rights may be created; Right of way; Purpose should be stated; Illustrative case—right to take water; Light and air; Support of land

IV. Easement and license distinguished
Characteristics of a license; License may give rise to an easement

V. Creation of easements
Express grant or reservation; Implied grant or reservation; Easement by necessity; Easement by prescription; Easement by condemnation; Easement by dedication; Easement by estoppel; Easement created by reference to maps

VI. Extent of use
Lands to be acquired in the future; Right of way; Reasonable use; Incidental rights; Use by owner of servient tenement; Exclusive and nonexclusive easements

VII. Transfer of easement
Limitation on right of transfer; Effect of transfer of dominant tenement; Transfer of servient tenement

VIII. Termination or extinguishment of easements
Statutory provisions; Express release; Legal proceedings; Merger of estates; Nonuse for five years; Abandonment; Adverse possession; Destruction of servient tenement; Excessive use; Illustrative cases

I. Definition and nature of easements

An easement is described as an interest in the land of another person that entitles the owner of such interest to a limited use of enjoyment of the land. It may be either an affirmative easement, involving the doing of some act on the land of another person, such as the right to cross over the other person's land, or it may be a negative easement, involving a right against another person that he refrain from doing certain things with his land, such as the right to preclude the owner of adjoining land from constructing a building on his land that would obstruct light and air. Most parcels of real property are affected by easements, either as a benefit or a burden.

CHARACTERISTICS OF AN EASEMENT

The essential qualities and characteristics of an easement include the following:

First: It is an *interest in land,* being one of the elements of real property, and generally must be transferred and used subject to the rules governing real property.

Second: It is an interest in the *land of another person;* an owner of land cannot, as a rule, have an easement in his own land.

Third: It is considered as a *nonpossessory interest.* The owner of the easement is not entitled to the same benefits that are given to those having possessory interests, such as a tenant under a lease. The latter may exclude other persons from the use or possession of the land, including the landowner, but the holder of an easement, such as a right of way, has only such control of the land as is necessary for the purpose of using the easement, and ordinarily he does not have such control as to enable him to exclude others from using the land as long as such use does not interfere with the enjoyment of the easement.

Fourth: Ordinarily it is essential that the privilege to use land, to be considered an easement rather than some lesser interest, must be one that, in accordance with common understanding, is capable of creation by a *conveyance.*

EASEMENTS INCLUDE "PROFITS"

Easements also include "profits." A *profit à prendre* is a right to take something from the land of another, either a part of the soil or something subsisting in the soil. A familiar example of a profit is the right to take minerals, including oil and gas, from the land of another person.

II. Classes of easements

EASEMENTS APPURTENANT

Easements are divided into two classes, namely, *easements appurtenant,* and *easements in gross.*

"Appurtenant" means *belonging to.* An easement appurtenant is created for the benefit of and belongs to another tract of land. Consequently, for such an easement to exist, there must be at least two tracts of land in separate ownerships. One tract, called the *dominant tenement,* obtains the benefit of the easement, and the other tract, called the *servient tenement,* is subject to (or burdened by) the easement. The dominant tenement does not have to adjoin the servient tenement, although it usually does. An easement appurtenant attaches to the land of the owner of the easement, and passes with a transfer of the land as an incident or appurtenance thereto, even though not specifically mentioned. It cannot exist separate and apart from such land. Such an easement is said to "run with the land."

Example of easement appurtenant. The following is a typical example of an easement appurtenant: *A,* as the owner of Blackacre, grants to *B,* as the owner of Whiteacre, the right to use a private road over a portion of Blackacre for the purpose of getting to and from Whiteacre. Such an easement is appurtenant to Whiteacre, the dominant tenement, and burdens Blackacre, the servient tenement.

EASEMENT IN GROSS

Although an easement in gross is a right in another person's land, it is not created for the benefit of land owned by the easement holder, but rather, is a *personal right.* It is a right attached to the person of the easement holder, and is not attached to any land owned by the easement holder. It is, however, as much an interest in the land of another person as an easement appurtenant. Since an easement in gross exists without a dominant tenement and cannot pass as an appurtenance to land, it must be expressly transferred.

Example of easement in gross. Typical examples of easements in gross are public utility easements, such as a right granted to a telephone company or other utility company to install and maintain poles and wires on, across, or over the grantor's land. Another example is an easement for pipe lines in favor of an oil company.

ENGLISH LAW DISTINGUISHED

Under English law an easement was always appurtenant. Rights to the use of land in gross, usually called "servitudes in gross," existed, but they were not regarded as property interests, and were not assignable or inheritable. In California, however, although early decisions of the courts sometimes stated that an easement must always be for the benefit of other land, rights or servitudes in gross are now commonly referred to as easements, and regardless of technical terminology, are assignable and inheritable property interests.

DETERMINING THE CLASSIFICATION OF AN EASEMENT

A determination as to whether or not an easement is appurtenant or in gross frequently presents a problem. This is true where the instrument creating the easement fails to state that the easement is one appurtenant or one in gross, or where the dominant tenement is not identified. The following case is illustrative of this problem: *A*, the owner of Blackacre, conveys to *B* an easement for road purposes over the south 20 feet of Blackacre. A dominant tenement is not described, and nothing further is said as to the character or purpose of the easement. Thereafter *B* executes a deed purporting to convey the easement to *C*. At the time of the creation of the easement, *B* was the owner of Whiteacre, an adjoining parcel of land, and it is ascertained that the easement was in fact created for the benefit of *B* in his use of Whiteacre. If *B* conveyed Whiteacre to *D* by a deed that did not expressly mention the easement, but that was executed prior to the deed to *C*, would *C* or *D* be determined to be the owner of the easement? Under the principles set forth above, *D* would prevail over *C*.

Rules of interpretation. In determining whether an easement is one appurtenant or one in gross, the following rules are applicable:

First: The nature of the right and the intention of the parties creating it are of primary importance.

Second: An easement will not be presumed to attach to the person of the grantee if it can be construed fairly to be appurtenant to land.

Third: When it cannot be determined from the instrument creating the easement whether the easement was intended to be in gross or appurtenant to land, evidence outside of the instrument of creation is admissible to determine the nature of an easement and to establish a dominant tenement.

EASEMENTS IN FAVOR OF AFTER-ACQUIRED PROPERTY

An easement may be created to benefit and to become appurtenant to a dominant tenement to be acquired by the easement holder in the future, provided the parties express their intention that the easement is to be appurtenant to such after-acquired property. (*Wright* v. *Best*, 19 Cal.2d 368.) In such instance, the easement is apparently in gross when created and appurtenant when the dominant tenement is acquired. This is one of the few cases where an easement changes its character after creation; ordinarily an easement retains the character given to it as appurtenant or in gross according to the time of creation, in the absence of special controlling provisions in the instrument of creation.

III. Purposes for which easements may be created

Section 801 of the Civil Code lists seventeen different land burdens, or servitudes upon land, that may be attached to other land as incidents or appurtenances, including the following: the right of pasture; the right of fishing; the right of taking game; the right of way; the right of taking water, wood, minerals, and other things; the right of transacting business upon land; the right of conducting lawful sports upon land; the right of receiving air, light, or heat from or over, or discharging the same upon or over land; the right of receiving water from or discharging the same upon land; the right of flooding land; the right of having water flow without diminution or disturbance of any kind; the right of using a wall as a party wall; the right of receiving more than natural support from adjoining land or things affixed thereto; the right of having the whole of a division fence maintained by a coterminous owner; the right of having public conveyances stopped, or of stopping the same on land; the right of a seat in church; and the right of burial.

STATUTORY RIGHTS IN GROSS

Section 802 of the Civil Code designates several types of land burdens that may be granted and held, though not attached to land, including the following: the right to pasture, and of fishing and taking game; the right of a seat in church; the right of burial; the right of taking rents and tolls; the right of way; and the right of taking water, wood, minerals, or other things.

ADDITIONAL RIGHTS MAY BE CREATED

The foregoing lists of servitudes upon land are not necessarily exclusive; other rights may also be created. As stated in the case of *Wright* v. *Best*, cited above, although the law may hesitate to increase the range of possible burdens on land by recognizing new easements, still it is said that the novelty of the incident is no bar to its recognition if its creation violates no principles of public policy. Thus, easements for the purpose of retrieving errant golf balls or permitting the flight of golf balls have been created; also vibration, noise, shadow, and avigation easements.

RIGHT OF WAY

A right of way is one of the most common types of easement, and consists of a privilege to pass over another person's land. The means of passage depends upon the purpose and terms of the instrument of creation; it may be by foot, or by motor vehicle, or by a railroad, or by pipe lines, or by whatever other method is intended. A right of way may be private, i.e., one that exists for the benefit of a particular person or persons; or it may be public, i.e., one that exists for all members of the general public.

PURPOSE SHOULD BE STATED

In creating a right of way, it is usual to express the mode of passage, e.g., "right of way for railroad purposes"; "an easement for driveway purposes." Other rights also should be designated with particularity. In the creation of a party wall easement, for example, the following would sufficiently express the purpose:

> *A*, owner of Lot 1, conveys the north half of Lot 1 to *B*, together with an easement consisting of the privilege of utilizing a division wall located equally on the north half and on the south half of said Lot 1, reserving to *A*, for the benefit of the south half of said Lot 1, an easement for party wall purposes over the portion of the wall located on the north half of said Lot 1.

ILLUSTRATIVE CASE—RIGHT TO TAKE WATER

In the case of *Relovich* v. *Stuart,* 211 Cal. 422, a question arose with respect to the nature of the right to take water from the land of another person. The owner of a parcel of land conveyed a portion to *X* and at the same time agreed in writing to furnish *X* with water for his land from the water system on the land retained by the seller. Thereafter the seller conveyed his remaining land to *Y*, who refused to furnish water to *X*, asserting that the water agreement was merely a contract to sell water as personal property, and consequently was not enforceable as against him. The court held, however, than an easement appurtenant to *X's* land was created that constituted a burden on the seller's land, and was binding on subsequent purchasers of the land with notice of the agreement.

LIGHT AND AIR

Regarding light and air, an owner of land has no "natural right" thereto, and cannot complain because the owner of adjoining land erects a building or other obstruction on his land that cuts off light and air. An easement for light and air may be created, however, but only by express grant or words of covenant, and cannot be acquired by use or by implication.

SUPPORT OF LAND

Certain natural rights are incident to the ownership of land, such as support for land, and these rights may be extended or diminished by agreements creating easements between the adjoining landowners. Generally, a landowner is entitled to have his soil remain in a natural position, and an adjoining owner cannot cause it to fall away by reason of excavation or other improvements on adjoining property. However, the right is that of support of the land in its *natural state,* without the added weight of a building upon it. Although a prescriptive right or easement cannot be acquired for the support of buildings, an easement consisting of the right to receive the support of land together with the buildings thereon from adjoining land may be created by express grant.

IV. Easement and license distinguished

A *license* is defined as a personal, revocable, and nonassignable permission or authority to enter upon the land of another person for a particular purpose, but without possessing any interest in the land. An example is a theater ticket or a ticket to a sports event, which authorizes the purchaser of the ticket to enter the theater or sports arena solely for the purpose of viewing the performance.

CHARACTERISTICS OF A LICENSE

It is often difficult to distinguish an easement from a license, but the following are the usual distinguishing characteristics of a license: it may be created by an oral agreement; being personal, it is usually incapable of assignment by the licensee and does not pass to his heirs upon his death; it does not give the licensee a right to sue third persons for interference with the exercise of the privilege given by the license; it is of a temporary nature, and is revocable at any time at the will of the licensor.

LICENSE MAY GIVE RISE TO AN EASEMENT

It has been held that a privilege to use another person's land is a license and not an easement if its creation lacks the formal requirements necessary to the creation of an easement, or if it is created to endure at the will of the owner of the land subject to the privilege. (*County of Alameda* v. *Ross,* 32 C.A.2d 135.) However, there is an exception to this rule in cases where a licensee, in reliance upon a license, has made expenditures of capital or labor in the exercise of his license under such circumstances that its termination would be inequitable. The licensor may be estopped to revoke the license, and in such case the privilege becomes, it is said, "in all essentials an easement." This principle was recognized in the following cases: *Stoner* v. *Zucker,* 148 Cal. 516; *Cooke* v. *Ramponi,* 38 Cal.2d 282.

V. Creation of easements

Easements may be created in a number of different ways, including the following: express grant, express reservation, implied grant, implied reservation, agreement, necessity, prescription, condemnation, dedication, estoppel, and sale of land by reference to a plat.

EXPRESS GRANT OR RESERVATION

An express grant or an express reservation in a deed is one of the most common means of creating an easement, although agreements between adjoining owners are often employed in lieu of deeds. Since an easement is an interest in land, the instrument creating the easement must contain the essential requirements of a voluntary conveyance of land, i.e., the names of the grantor and grantee, operative words of conveyance or the equivalent, and a description of the easement and of the land that is subject to the easement with sufficient clearness to locate it. Execution of the instrument by the grantor, and delivery of the instrument to the grantee are also essential to make it effective. An important distinction applies, however, with respect to the description contained in an easement and a description contained in a deed. A deed conveying the fee title to an indefinite strip of land would be void for uncertainty, but a deed to an unlocated easement is valid. For example, an easement for a roadway over and across Lot 1, without specifying the particular portion of Lot 1 affected, would be good. The exact location of the roadway may be determined subsequently, either by agreement of the parties or by use.

Reservation of easement by deed. Where a landowner sells a part of his land only, e.g., the portion fronting on a street, he may desire to reserve in the deed an easement in favor of the portion retained by him. This can be accomplished by inserting, after the description of the land sold, a clause such as the following, (where, for instance, the deed describes the east half of Lot 1 as the portion sold): "The grantor reserves to himself and his heirs and assigns, as an easement appurtenant to the west half of said Lot 1, an easement for ingress and egress over and across the north 15 feet of the premises hereby conveyed."

Who may create an easement. The only person who can grant a permanent easement is the fee owner of the servient tenement, or a person with the power of disposal of the fee (a life tenant with power of sale). The holder of an estate less than the fee may, however, grant an easement within the terms of his estate, but the easement ceases upon the termination of such estate. For example, a lessee of land for a term of ten years may create an easement in favor of a third party, but the easement would be terminated with the expiration of the lease.

Easements created by mortgage or deed of trust. An easement may be created under a mortgage or deed of trust, and upon a foreclosure, the easement would be as effective as one created by a deed from the owner of the servient tenement. As an illustration, assume that *A*, the owner of Lots 1 and 2, executes a deed of trust on Lot 1, together with an easement for a driveway over a designated portion of Lot 2. If the deed of trust is foreclosed, the purchaser at the foreclosure sale acquires title to Lot 1 and the easement over Lot 2. If, however, the deed of trust is reconveyed, the lien on the easement ceases, and the easement will no longer exist.

IMPLIED GRANT OR RESERVATION

An implied grant of an easement is created in a situation as follows: *A*, the owner of Lots 1 and 2, conveys Lot 1 to *B*. At the time the deed is excuted and delivered, a driveway over a portion of Lot 2 is openly used and is reasonably necessary to the beneficial use of Lot 1. An easement for driveway purposes over Lot 2 would ordinarily pass by implication with the deed of Lot 1.

Statutory rule. The rule as to implied grants of easement is contained in Section 1104 of the Civil Code, which provides:

> A transfer of real property passes all easements attached thereto, and creates in favor thereof an easement to use other real property of the person whose estate is transferred in the same manner and to the same extent as such property was obviously and permanently used by the person whose estate is transferred, for the benefit thereof, at the time when the transfer was agreed upon or completed.

Certain conditions must exist. The courts have ruled that certain conditions must exist at the time of the conveyance before an easement by implied grant will be given effect. These conditions are as follows: (1) a separation of titles; (2) the use that gives rise to the easement must have been so long continued and so obvious as to show that it was intended to be permanent, and (3) the easement must be reasonably necessary to the beneficial use of the land granted. (*Piazza* v. *Schaefer*, 255 C.A.2d 328.)

Use must be apparent. The requirement that the use that gives rise to an implied easement be obvious or apparent does not necessarily mean that the use must be visible upon inspection of the surface of the ground. For example, the use may consist of underground drains or sewers. If such use was known to the parties at the time of the conveyance, or could have been discovered by a reasonably prudent investigation, it is regarded as obvious or apparent.

Implied reservation. Implied easements by reservation are also recognized in California. If an owner conveys the portion of his land that is burdened by a use for the benefit of the land retained by him, an easement by implied reservation arises in favor of the grantor if all conditions that are indispensable to the creation of an implied easement are met.

Implied right of entry. A conveyance or reservation of the minerals carries with it an implied easement to enter and use the surface of the land for the purpose of extracting the minerals. This is known as the implied right of surface entry.

EASEMENT BY NECESSITY

An easement by necessity arises when a grantor conveys a part of his land that is entirely surrounded by the grantor's remaining lands, or by the land of the grantor and of third parties, and that has no means of access to a road. The following is an example: *A*, the owner of Lot 1, which consists of ten acres, conveys the north two acres thereof to *B*. The land conveyed has no access to a public road except over the remaining portion of Lot 1. *B* would have an easement of necessity over the land retained by *A*. Based on considerations of public policy favoring the full utilization of land, and on the presumed intention of the parties that the grantee would have a means of access to his land, the courts have held in such case that an implied way of necessity passes to the grantee as appurtenant to his land. (*Taylor* v. *Warnaky*, 55 C. 350.)

Easement in favor of grantor. A way of necessity may also arise by implied reservation in favor of a grantor who conveys a part of his land in such manner as to leave the land retained by him inaccessible except over the land conveyed, but the courts might be less inclined to apply the doctrine in such a situation.

Distinguishing characteristic of easement by necessity. Although a way of necessity is considered as an easement by implication, the requirements for its creation differ from those of the implied easements already mentioned, primarily for the reason that the way of necessity does not depend upon the existence, at the time of severance, of a way obviously and permanently in use over the servient tenement.

Strict necessity must exist. A way of necessity exists only in cases of strict necessity, that is, where the property would otherwise be landlocked, having no means whatsoever for passage to a public road. The doctrine does not apply where the grantee has another means of access, even though it may be extremely inconvenient. The way of necessity ceases when the necessity ends, where, for instance, the grantor dedicates another road for the grantee's use, or where the grantee acquires other land that gives him a means of access.

Creation by judicial proceedings. A way of necessity may occur not only as the result of a voluntary conveyance, but also may arise where there is a severance of the land by judicial proceedings, such as a partition action in which an allotment of land is made and a portion is allotted without access, or where there is a sale upon foreclosure of a mortgage or deed of trust covering a parcel of inaccessible land.

Common ownership must have existed. A way of necessity does not arise indiscriminately over any land surrounding the grantee's land; it can be claimed only over other land owned by the grantor at the time of the conveyance, and not over land owned by strangers. To establish such a way, the grantee must show that at some time in the past the land for which the benefit of the way is claimed, and the land in which the way is claimed, belonged to the same person. This unity of ownership must be shown to have existed at some previous time.

EASEMENT BY PRESCRIPTION

An easement by prescription may be acquired in California by adverse use for a continuous period of five years. The interest so acquired is as effectual as one obtained by conveyance, but it is not a marketable title until established of record by appropriate court proceedings against the owner of the record title. An interesting case is that of *Costa* v. *Fawcett*, 202 C.A.2d 695, where a *profit à prendre* in growing nut trees was obtained by prescription. In determining the rights of the parties, the court held that the easement holder had the basic right to harvest and retain the annual crops from the trees and, as secondary easements, the right to go on the land at appropriate times to care for the trees during their life span, but not the right to replant any that might die.

Elements of prescriptive easement. The essential elements that must be shown in order to establish an easement by prescription are as follows: open and notorious use, continuous and uninterrupted for a period of five years, hostile to the true owner, exclusive, and under some claim of right. Payment of taxes is not required to obtain an easement by prescription. A use cannot be the basis of a prescriptive easement if it is permissive. Thus, posted notices on land to the effect that the same is "private property" and "permission to pass is revocable at any time" have been held to be sufficient to rebut a claim of adverse use. (*Jones* v. *Tierney-Sinclair*, 71 C.A.2d 366.) However, it has also been held that this is not conclusive, for signs are only one of the many factors to be considered. (*Pratt* v. *Hodgson*, 91 C.A.2d 401.)

Recording notice of consent. In 1963, Section 813 was added to the Civil Code to provide that the holder of record title to land may record a notice of consent to use his land for certain purposes. Such notice of consent is evidence that the subsequent use of the land for such purposes is permissive and not adverse. Notice may be revoked by recording a notice of revocation. The advantage of the recorded notice is that it gives undisputed evidence of the date and scope of the permission.

Posting signs. In 1965, Section 1008 was added to the Civil Code to provide that no use shall ripen into an easement by prescription when the property owner posts signs, as required, stating in substance: Right to pass by permission, and subject to control of, owner.

EASEMENT BY CONDEMNATION

Another method of creating an easement is by condemnation. Although the fee title to land may be acquired for street and highway purposes by condemnation proceedings in the instances authorized by statutes, such as the taking of the fee title by the state of California for state highway purposes, the usual result where land is taken by condemnation for a street, a highway, a railroad right of way, or a telephone or power line, is that the taker acquires only an easement. Most city streets are owned by adjoining lot owners, subject to an easement in favor of the public, and many of these easement rights were obtained through condemnation proceedings.

EASEMENT BY DEDICATION

An easement may also be created by dedication, which may be either a statutory or a common-law dedication. A statutory dedication in California is effected when, in accordance with a map act then in force, a map is recorded expressly dedicating areas shown thereon to public use. The present Subdivision Map Act requires that the map bear a certificate signed and acknowledged by all parties having a record interest in the land, offering certain parcels of land for dedication for the specified public uses. The map must also bear a certificate evidencing acceptance by the governing body of such offer of dedication.

Common-law dedication. A common-law dedication, which embraces all forms of dedication other than statutory, requires no written conveyance or particular form; it results from an intention of the owner, clearly indicated by his words or acts, to dedicate his land to public use, and an acceptance of the offer by the public, either by formal act of the proper authorities (a resolution of acceptance by the city council, for instance), or by public use. As an illustration, the owner of land conveys portions thereof by deeds that reserve connecting strips of land "for road purposes," such strips at the time being used by the public as a street. It has been held that such reservations constitute a dedication of the street. (*City of Santa Ana* v. *Santa Ana Valley Irrigation Co.*, 163 Cal. 211.)

A common-law dedication is generally regarded as conveying merely an easement to the public, with the fee title remaining in the original owner or his successors in interest. This rule has been clearly established in California as to dedicated streets and highways.

EASEMENT BY ESTOPPEL

The creation of an easement by estoppel has been recognized by the courts in this state. For instance, where an owner, in conveying land, describes it as bounded on a street or way that he owns, but that is in fact not dedicated as a street or way, he is estopped to deny the existence of the way for the benefit of the grantee. In effect, he thereby grants an easement for ingress and egress over the supposed street. Also, in the case of an attempted oral grant of an easement, where the grantee makes improvements for the purpose of exercising the easement right, the courts have recognized and enforced the easement on the theory of estoppel.

EASEMENT CREATED BY REFERENCE TO MAPS

Still another method of creating an easement is by the sale of property by reference to a map or plat. Where a landowner subdivides his land into lots, blocks, streets, and alleys, and thereafter sells lots in the subdivision, each purchaser of a lot automatically acquires an easement of passage over the streets and alleys shown on the plat or map of the subdivision, even though the deed to the lot makes no mention whatever of such right. This principle is well illustrated in the case of *Bradley* v.

Frazier Park Playgrounds, 110 C.A.2d 436, where property owners in a subdivision located in a mountainous area just south of Lebec, in Kern County, were held to be entitled to a so-called "equitable easement" for the use of recreational facilities in a portion of the subdivision.

VI. Extent of use

An easement appurtenant can be used only for the benefit of the dominant tenement. It may not be used for the benefit of any other parcel of land without the consent of the owner of the servient tenement. Because of this rule, it is advisable to include a description of the dominant tenement in the instrument creating the easement. This may avoid a claim by the owner of the servient tenement that the easement was not intended to benefit all portions of the land allegedly included in the dominant tenement.

LANDS TO BE ACQUIRED IN THE FUTURE

Where there is the possibility of the owner of the dominant tenement acquiring other lands in the vicinity that may need the benefit of the easement, such as commercial property where it is anticipated there will be an expansion of plant facilities in the future, the instrument creating the easement should provide that such subsequently acquired property shall enjoy the benefit of the easement.

RIGHT OF WAY

It is not essential that a right of way be described by metes and bounds or otherwise specifically located, as long as the description of the servient tenement is sufficient. Where a general right of way is granted or reserved, the owner of the servient tenement may in the first instance designate a suitable way, and if he fails to do so, the owner of the dominant tenement may designate it. If the parties are unable to agree, a court of equity has the power to fix a location.

Location of right of way. If the location of a right of way is not defined by the grant, a reasonably convenient and suitable way is presumed to be intended, and the right cannot be exercised over the whole of the land. Once the location of an easement has been established, whether by express terms of the grant or by use and acquiescence, it cannot be substantially changed without the consent of both parties. In the case of *Youngstown Steel Products Co.* v. *City of Los Angeles,* 38 Cal.2d 407, it was held that the grant of an easement for aerial wires was fixed as to location by wires installed for seventeen years at a height of 51½ feet from the ground, precluding a later increase in the height of the wires without the consent of both parties.

Change in use. The case of *Faus* v. *City of Los Angeles*, 67 Cal.2d 350, raised a question as to whether or not the adoption of a different method of transportation over rights of way would result in a loss of the easement. It was held that the paving and use, for motor coach transportation, of rights of way originally granted and used for electric railway services sufficiently complied with the purpose of the grantor to permit survival of the easement.

REASONABLE USE

Where an easement for ingress and egress is created by grant, it may be used for all reasonable purposes, and the use is not necessarily restricted to such purposes as were reasonable at the date of the grant. Accordingly, the use of an easement by motor vehicles will be permitted even though the easement was created at a time when horse-drawn vehicles were in use. However, when an easement is acquired by prescription, the extent of the right is fixed and determined by the use in which it originates, and it cannot be extended or increased so as to enlarge the burden. Under this rule it was held in the case of *Bartholomew* v. *Staheli*, 86 C.A.2d 844, that a prescriptive easement acquired for access to a farm and house could not be used to reach a pleasure resort thereafter established on the farm.

INCIDENTAL RIGHTS

A grant of an easement carries with it by implication certain secondary rights essential to its enjoyment, such as the right to make repairs, renewals, and replacements. Such incidental rights may be exercised so long as the easement holder uses reasonable care, and does not increase the burden on, or go beyond the boundaries of, the servient estate, or make any material changes therein.

USE BY OWNER OF SERVIENT TENEMENT

The owner of the land subject to the easement has every right or incident of ownership not inconsistent with the easement and enjoyment and use of the same. The servient owner has been permitted, for instance, to make use of his land beneath a power line; to maintain a fence across a drainage canal where no interference with the use of the canal resulted; and to grant another easement over land subject to a previous grant of a similar easement, such as a pipe line easement.

EXCLUSIVE AND NONEXCLUSIVE EASEMENTS

Where an owner has granted an easement for a roadway across a portion of his land, he may use the road himself or grant the right of use to others if the easement owner's use is not interfered with. These rights of the servient owner may be restricted, however, by the terms of the instrument creating the easement, as in a case where the easement is expressly stated to be exclusive, or where the nature of the easement is such as to make it obvious that an exclusive easement was intended. Where it is intended that the easement be nonexclusive, it is customary to specifically so recite in the instrument creating the easement.

VII. Transfer of easement

Easements are property rights, and as such are transferable and inheritable in the same manner, and subject to the same requirements, as other interests in real property. Under California law an easement in gross is assignable unless expressly or by necessary implication made personal to a particular individual. Such an easement cannot, of course, pass as an incident or appurtenance to a dominant tenement, but must be expressly conveyed.

LIMITATION ON RIGHT OF TRANSFER

An important limitation upon the transfer of an easement in gross exists, namely, that it cannot be apportioned so as to increase the burden on the servient tenement. In the case of easements appurtenant, this rule has been codified, Section 807 of the Civil Code providing that the dominant tenement cannot be partitioned in such a way as to increase the burden on the servient tenement.

EFFECT OF TRANSFER OF DOMINANT TENEMENT

In the case of easements appurtenant, the easement passes as an incident of the transfer of the dominant tenement, even though the easement is not expressly mentioned, and the conveyance does not expressly purport to transfer the appurtenances. The type of transfer that will pass an appurtenant easement is not restricted to a deed; it can be a contract of sale of the dominant tenement, or a mortgage or deed of trust on the dominant tenement, or a transfer by operation of law, such as an execution sale.

TRANSFER OF SERVIENT TENEMENT

Insofar as a transfer of the servient tenement is concerned, the owner of the land subject to the easement may, of course, convey his interest in the land, and the grantee takes title to the servient tenement subject to the easement. If the grantee is a purchaser for value, this rule is modified by the further requirement that the purchaser have actual or constructive notice of the easement. If the easement has been recorded, the purchaser is deemed to have constructive notice. If there is an unrecorded easement affecting the land, the purchaser will take subject to such an easement only if he has actual notice, or the easement is indicated by something visible or apparent from an inspection of the land.

VIII. Termination or extinguishment of easements

Easements may be terminated or extinguished in several ways, including the following: by express release; by legal proceedings; by merger of the servient tenement and the easement in the same person; by nonuse for five years of an easement by prescription; by abandonment; by the destruction of the servient tenement; by adverse possession by the owner of the servient tenement; or in some cases by excessive use.

STATUTORY PROVISIONS

Section 811 of the Civil Code expressly provides for the extinguishment of an easement in the following ways: (1) by the vesting of the right to the servitude and the right to the servient tenement in the same person; (2) by the destruction of the servient tenement; (3) by the performance of any act upon either tenement, by the owner of the servitude, or with his assent, that is incompatible with its nature or exercise; and (4) when the servitude was acquired by enjoyment, by disuse thereof by the owner of the servitude for the period prescribed for acquiring title by enjoyment. These methods as described in the Civil Code are not exclusive, however, as easements may be terminated by additional means as set forth above.

EXPRESS RELEASE

An easement, whether appurtenant or in gross, may be extinguished by an express release in favor of the owner of the servient tenement. The customary method of such express release is a quitclaim deed from the easement holder to the owner of the servient tenement.

LEGAL PROCEEDINGS

An easement may be extinguished by appropriate legal proceedings against the easement holder, such as a decree in a quiet title action against the easement holder in favor of the owner of the servient tenement.

MERGER OF ESTATES

An easement is extinguished by merger where the same person becomes the owner of the easement and the owner of the fee title to the servient tenement. The rule is fundamental that a person cannot have an easement over his own property.

NONUSE FOR FIVE YEARS

An easement acquired by prescription is extinguished by nonuse for a period of five years. But an easement founded on a grant or an agreement is not lost by mere nonuse for any length of time. At the most, such nonuse would be one of the facts from which an intention to abandon the easement might be inferred.

ABANDONMENT

An easement may be extinguished by abandonment, which means an intentional relinquishment of the easement as indicated by conduct inconsistent with a continuance of the use. *Intent* to abandon is the essential factor in such cases.

ADVERSE POSSESION

An easement may also be extinguished by the use of the servient tenement by the owner thereof in a manner adverse to the exercise of the easement, for a continuous period of five years or more. The case of *Glatts* v. *Henson,* 31 Cal.2d 368, is illustrative of this rule. In that case it was held that a 30-foot easement for a private road was extinguished as to a portion of the road on which the owner of the servient tenement maintained buildings for over five years with the knowledge of the owner of the easement.

DESTRUCTION OF SERVIENT TENEMENT

An easement is extinguished by the destruction of the servient tenement. The application of this rule usually occurs in connection with easements in buildings that are destroyed. In the case of *Rothschild* v. *Wolf,* 20 Cal.2d 17, involving the destruction of a building without fault of the owner, it was held that the previous grant of the right to use a hall or stairway of the building, although constituting an easement, conferred no interest in the soil and did not survive the destruction of the building.

EXCESSIVE USE

In the case of *Crimmins* v. *Gould,* 149 C.A.2d 383, it was held that an easement by grant for ingress and egress over a private lane became subject to extinguishment for misuser when the owner of the servitude greatly increased the servient burden by extending and connecting the lane with two public roads, making its use available not only to non-dominant property owners but to the general public. In holding that the easement was extinguished the court stated:

> The general rule is that misuse or excessive use is not sufficient for abandonment or forfeiture, but an injunction is the proper remedy. But where the burden of the servient estate is increased through changes in the dominant estate which increase the use and subject it to use of non-dominant property, a forfeiture will be justified if the unauthorized use may not be severed and prohibited.

ILLUSTRATIVE CASES

Controversies regarding easements frequently arise, and many cases on easements are included in the appellate court reports. A reference to two landmark cases will serve to emphasize the rules discussed above.

The case of *Elliott* v. *McCombs,* 17 Cal.2d 23, involved adjoining properties as pictured in Fig. 5-1.

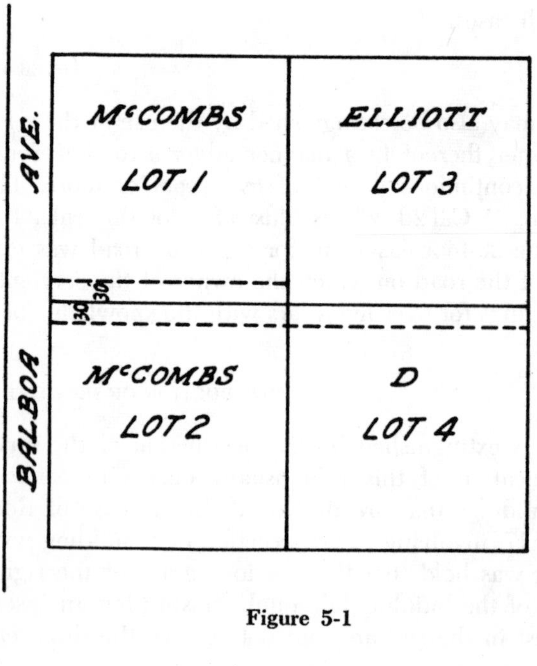

Figure 5-1

These were the facts: *A*, the owner of all four lots, conveyed Lot 1 to *B*, reserving an easement for road purposes over the south 30 feet of Lot 1. *A* also conveyed Lot 2 to *B*, reserving an easement for road purposes over the north 30 feet of Lot 2. *A* then conveyed Lot 3 to *C* by a deed that did not expressly grant or reserve an easement. *C* thereafter conveyed Lot 3 to Elliott by a deed that did not mention an easement. *A* then conveyed Lot 4, the last lot in the tract, to *D*, reserving an easement for road purposes over the north 30 feet of Lot 4. *A* then conveyed the reserved easement over the north 30 feet of Lot 4 to Elliott. *B* brought an action and obtained a decree quieting title as to Lots 1 and 2 against *A*, and then conveyed Lots 1 and 2 to McCombs.

Elliott thereafter brought an action against McCombs and *D* to quiet title to an easement for road purposes over the south 30 feet of Lot 1 and the north 30 feet of Lots 2 and 4. McCombs' defense to the action was that he was an innocent purchaser of Lots 1 and 2 without knowledge that the easement reserved for road purposes was created for the benefit of other lands, i.e., Lot 3; that the road was not in use at the time of his purchase; that the easement, being in gross, was extinguished by the quiet title decree against *A*, the record owner of such easement.

The court gave judgment for Elliott, however, holding that (1) the easement reserved in the deeds of Lots 1 and 2 was presumed to be appurtenant to land retained by the grantor, and McCombs was charged with notice thereof; (2) the easement so reserved passed to the grantees of Lot 3 as an appurtenance, though not expressly described; and (3) as to Lot 4 the easement reserved by *A* was in gross because *A* at the time had no land left to which the easement could be appurtenant, but Elliott's right to this easement was founded on the conveyance of the easement from *A* to Elliott.

The case of *Eastman* v. *Piper*, 68 C.A. 554, also presents an interesting problem. A, the owner of Blackacre, executed an instrument in which he granted to *B*, his heirs or assigns, "the privilege of a temporary roadway 10 feet wide" over Blackacre, until such time as the extension of Alta Vista Street (in the town of Monrovia) was completed past Whiteacre, owned by *B* and adjoining Blackacre. This roadway served to connect Whiteacre with a public highway. *B* conveyed Whiteacre to *C* without mentioning the easement. A dispute arose as to the use of the easement, and *C* brought an action against *A* to quiet *C*'s title to the easement and to restrain *A* from interfering with *C*'s use.

The court in the above case decided in favor of *C*, stating that the privilege granted was an easement and not a mere license, and that the easement was appurtenant to Whiteacre and passed with the deed to Whiteacre. The court stated that the interest of an owner in an easement may vary as to duration in like manner as other estates in real property. Thus, the interest of an easement may be owned (1) in fee, i.e., perpetual enjoyment; or (2) in fee determinable, e.g., to endure until the happening of some event or contingency; or (3) for life; or (4) even for a term of years.

Questions

1. Define an easement, and describe the essential characteristics of an easement.
2. What are the two classes of easements?
3. Indicate the significance of the terms "dominant tenement" and "servient tenement."
4. List some of the purposes for which an easement may be created.
5. How does an easement differ from a license?
6. In what ways may easements be created?
7. May an easement be created by a deed of trust?
8. If an owner grants an easement over his land without locating the easement, can the easement holder change the location from time to time?
9. May an easement appurtenant be used by persons other than the owner of the dominant tenement?
10. Can the owner of the servient tenement use the same right of way he has granted?
11. Is an easement in gross transferable?
12. In what ways may an easement be terminated?

6

Estates or Interests in Real Property

Summary

I. Nature and classification of estates

The ownership interest that a person has in land is called an *estate.* This may vary in size from absolute ownership, called a "fee simple absolute" to a mere tolerated possession, called an "estate at sufferance." An estate in land gives the owner of such interest the right to enjoy and possess the land—presently or in the future—for a period of time that may be long or short, definite or indefinite, depending upon the particular interest owned.

NOT ALL INTERESTS ARE ESTATES

Not all interests in land constitute "estates." For instance, the interest of a mortgagee is not an estate; it is a lien or charge on the land, but it is not considered as a segment of ownership.

CLASSIFICATION BASED ON DURATION OF ENJOYMENT

The word "estate" is used to express the degree, quantity, nature, duration, or extent of an interest in land. The primary classification of estates is with reference to their *duration of enjoyment.* Section 761 of the Civil Code classifies estates as follows: (1) estates of inheritance or perpetual estates, called estates in fee; (2) estates for life (commonly referred to as life estates); (3) estates for years (leasehold estates); or (4) estates at will. Estates in fee and life estates are referred to as "freehold estates," since they are characteristic of the holding of a freeman under the feudal system, with the exact time of termination of the estate being unknown.

FREEHOLD ESTATES

The uncertain duration of its existence is the characteristic that distinguishes a freehold from a nonfreehold estate. No one knows how long a fee simple estate will last, because the holder may dispose of it whenever he pleases. Since a life estate depends upon the duration of a natural person's life, and is terminated only upon the death of the person upon whose life the estate depends—an event that is uncertain as to time—it, too, is an estate of uncertain duration. A nonfreehold estate has a certainty of duration, even though this certainty may not always be expressed in terms of a specified period of time. Because of this certainty of duration, it is a lesser estate than a fee or life estate.

OTHER CLASSIFICATIONS

Estates are also classified in the Civil Code in the following manner: (1) according to *quality,* i.e., they may be either absolute or subject to contingencies, and may be either legal or equitable; (2) according to their *time of enjoyment,* i.e., they may be estates entitling the holder to possession either immediately or at sometime in the future, called "present and future interests"; or (3) with respect to the *number of owners,* i.e., they may be either estates in severalty or joint estates, tenancies in common, partnership interests, or the community interests of husband and wife. (C.C., Secs. 678, 682, 688.) This latter classification of estates is considered at length in the chapter on methods of ownership of real property (Chapter 8).

Another distinction is made between *possessory* and *nonpossessory* interests. The first category includes all those interests or estates in which the holder is entitled to present possession of the property. The nonpossessory type includes those interests in which the holder's right of use of the property is postponed to some future date, or the right of use is limited in nature or extent.

The chart on page 68 will aid in understanding the various types of estates and interests that are being discussed.

II. Estates in fee

An estate in fee simple, also designated as an "estate in fee," or merely a "fee," is the highest type of interest a person can have in land. It is potentially of indefinite duration, and is freely transferable and inheritable. Where we speak of *A* as being the owner of a parcel of land, it is generally understood that he is the fee owner, i.e., he owns the land in fee, or in fee simple, or in fee absolute. His is an absolute ownership, and as long as he obeys the law, he may do as he chooses with his land, either dispose of it during his lifetime, or devise it by his last will and testament, effective upon his death, or do nothing with it and have it pass on to his heirs at law. In California, a fee simple estate is presumed to pass by a grant of real property. (C.C., Sec. 1105.)

SEPARATION OF FEE OWNERSHIP

In a given parcel of land there may be more than one estate in fee. This occurs if part of the land consisting of the minerals is owned in fee by *A,* and the land with the exception of the minerals is owned by *B.*

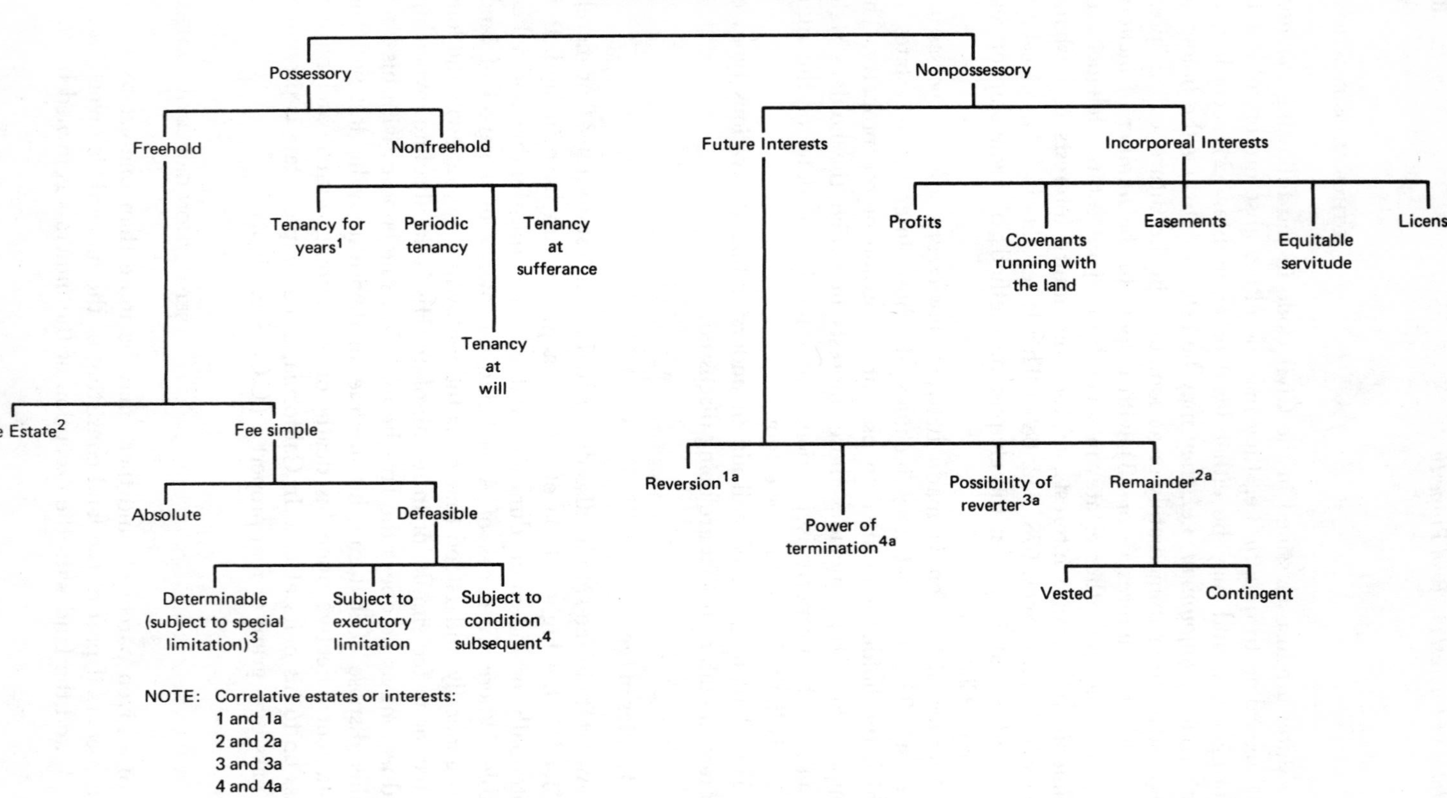
CHART SHOWING
REAL PROPERTY INTERESTS
Possessory
Nonpossessory
Freehold
Nonfreehold
Future Interests
Incorporeal Interests
Tenancy for years[1]
Periodic tenancy
Tenancy at sufferance
Tenancy at will
Profits
Covenants running with the land
Easements
Equitable servitude
License
Life Estate[2]
Fee simple
Absolute
Defeasible
Determinable (subject to special limitation)[3]
Subject to executory limitation
Subject to condition subsequent[4]
Reversion[1a]
Power of termination[4a]
Possibility of reverter[3a]
Remainder[2a]
Vested
Contingent
NOTE: Correlative estates or interests:
1 and 1a
2 and 2a
3 and 3a
4 and 4a

DEFEASIBLE ESTATES

An estate in fee simple is a generic term, and includes an estate "in fee simple absolute," and an estate "in fee simple defeasible." The latter type, sometimes referred to as a qualified fee, creates in the grantee and his heirs an estate that can be lost or defeated by the happening of some event subsequent to the initial grant. The types that are frequently encountered are estates subject to a condition subsequent, determinable fees, and estates subject to executory limitation.

ESTATE ON CONDITION PRECEDENT

An estate on condition may be either *on condition precedent* or on *condition subsequent.* An estate on condition precedent is one that does not vest or commence until the occurrence of some contingent event. For instance, a conveyance may be made to a city provided the city obtains the necessary authority from the legislature and performs certain acts within a period of twelve months from a specified date. Title does not pass until the condition precedent has been performed. (*City of Stockton* v. *Weber,* 98 Cal. 433.)

ESTATE ON CONDITION SUBSEQUENT

An estate on condition subsequent is created where a parcel of land is granted in fee, but subject to termination upon the occurrence of a stated event. As an example, a conveyance may be made upon condition that the land shall not be used for certain purposes, such as the sale of intoxicating liquors, and further providing that title shall revert upon breach of such condition. If there is a violation of the condition, the grantor has the right to terminate the estate granted. However, the estate is divested if, and only if, the grantor exercises his right or power of termination. The future interest here is sometimes defined as a right of reentry.

DETERMINABLE FEE

A determinable fee, sometimes referred to as an estate on special limitation, is one that, by its terms, is to expire automatically upon the occurrence of a stated event. As an example, if *A* conveys land to *B* "as long as *B* remains unmarried," the grantee has an estate on special limitation, and if he marries, his estate automatically terminates. No act is required on the part of the grantor to accomplish the termination. Determinable fees are usually characterized by such words as "until a certain event occurs," or "while," or "so long as" an existing state of things endures. A familiar example of such an estate is that of a lessee under an oil and gas lease for a specified term and "so long thereafter as oil and gas are produced." (*Dabney* v. *Edwards*, 5 Cal.2d 1.) The future interest here is called the possibility of reverter.

The case of *People* v. *City of Fresno*, 210 C.A.2d 500, contains a discussion of a determinable fee as compared with an estate on condition. The court pointed out that a determinable fee in real property is one subject to a contingency on the happening of which the fee terminates ipso facto and title to the property reverts to the grantor. The following words would create such an estate "To A and his heirs so long as Blackacre is used for school purposes."

By comparison, a fee simple subject to condition subsequent would be created by a conveyance such as the following: "To A and his heirs, but if the property is used for the sale of alcoholic beverages, then the grantor has the right to reenter and repossess the land."

The characteristic that distinguishes a determinable fee from a fee subject to condition subsequent is that in the latter case when the named condition occurs, some type of action on the part of the grantor or his heirs must be taken in order to recover the property; there is no automatic reversion.

ESTATE ON EXECUTORY LIMITATION

An estate on executory limitation is one that is created by the transfer of an estate in fee, but subject to a provision that upon the occurrence of a stated event, the estate is divested in favor of some person other than the grantor. To illustrate, *A* conveys a parcel of real property "to *B* and his heirs, but if *B* dies without issue surviving him, then to *C* and his heirs." In this case *B* has an estate in fee simple subject to an executory limitation.

III. Life estates

A life estate is an estate that is measured by the life of a person. The duration of the estate may be limited to the life of the person holding it, or to the life or lives of one or more other persons. Thus, a conveyance to "*A* for the term of his natural life," or to "*A* for life," creates a life estate measured by the life of the life tenant. A conveyance to "*A* for the life of *X*" is a life estate measured by the life of a third person, often referred to as an "estate *pur autre vie.*" If *A* dies before *X*, the life estate vests in the heirs or devisees of *A* during the life of *X*.

As discussed above, a life estate is a "freehold" estate, as distinguished from a nonfreehold estate.

CREATION OF LIFE ESTATE

A life estate may be created by a conveyance to the life tenant, with *remainder* over to some other person; or by a conveyance of a life estate only, leaving the residue of the fee estate, called a *reversion,* in the grantor; or by a conveyance of the fee, reserving a life estate to the grantor. A life estate may be created either by will or by deed.

LIFE ESTATE IN FAVOR OF TWO OR MORE PERSONS

The case of *Green* v. *Brown,* 37 Cal.2d 391, presented an interesting problem where there was a *reservation* of a life estate in favor of two persons. Upon the death of one of the life tenants, the grantee in the deed contended that the life estate was terminated in an undivided half interest in the property, and the surviving life tenant had an estate for life in an undivided one-half interest only and not in the entire property. The trial court so determined, but the Supreme Court rejected this view, holding that where the reservation of a life estate is in favor of two persons, the lives of both of them must have expired before any part of the use of the property is lost to either of them. The reservation clause in that case read as follows: "Reserving and excepting, however, a life estate in the grantors above named in all of the above described property, and the right to use, occupy and enjoy the same and to receive the rents, issues, and profits therefrom during the term of their natural lives." The court stated that these words are equivalent to the phrases "joint tenancy," or "to the survivor of them." Such construction is fortified by the statutory provision that reservations are to be interpreted in favor of the grantor.

GRANT OF A LIFE ESTATE IN FAVOR OF TWO OR MORE PERSONS

Where it is intended to create a life estate in favor of two persons for their joint lives by a *grant* rather than by a reservation, the use of specific language to accomplish that effect is considered advisable. This can be done by the use of the words "as joint tenants," or by the use of a clause such as the following: "To *H* and *W* jointly, a life estate during their joint lifetimes, and to the survivor of them during the period of the balance of the life of such survivor."

LIFE TENANT'S POWER OF DISPOSITION

The instrument creating the life estate may give the owner of the life estate the power to sell or otherwise dispose of the fee. This power may be expressly stated, or it may be inferred from the language used in the instrument of creation. The following language is illustrative: "To *A* for his use, during his natural life, and on his death the unused portion shall go to *B, C,* and *D.*" Such language has been held to create a life estate with the power of disposition of the property, even to the extent of entirely consuming it, providing the consumption is consistent with the life tenant's personal use. (*Hardy* v. *Mayhew,* 158 Cal. 95.) The words "support and maintenance" have a more restricted meaning than "comfort and support" when used in the creation of a life estate.

RESERVATION OF POWER TO REVOKE A DEED

The case of *Tennant* v. *John Tennant Memorial Home,* 167 Cal. 570, is an interesting one involving the reservation of a life estate with the added power to revoke the conveyance. It was held that the reservation of the power to revoke the deed was valid. The deed included a provision in the granting clause as follows: ". . . subject to the reservation hereinafter set forth," and the following language was employed after the description:

> Excepting, however, and reserving to said grantor the exclusive possession and the use and enjoyment in her own right, of the rents, issues and profits of said lots and each of them for and during the term of her natural life.
>
> And further reserving to the said grantor the right to revoke this deed as to the said property above described or as to any portion thereof, and further reserving to her, the said grantor, the right during her natural life to sell any of the above described property, and to sign and execute deeds therefor in her own individual name and to convey by any such deed a full, perfect and absolute title thereto to the purchaser thereof, and with right to use the proceeds arising from such sale or sales to her own use, without any liability for her or her estate to account therefor. In case of such revocation being made, it shall be made and can only be made in writing, duly acknowledged and recorded.

In drafting conveyances reserving life estates with power of disposal, similar language to that used in the last-mentioned case is usually employed.

NATURE OF INTEREST OF LIFE TENANT

A life tenant, unless expressly restrained, may sell, lease, encumber, or otherwise dispose of his interest, but obviously cannot create an estate that will extend beyond the duration of his life estate, unless he has been given added power to that effect. The owner of the life estate has the same right of possession as an owner in fee simple, and has the right to all the rents, issues, and profits of the land accruing during the term of his life estate. He also has certain duties and obligations, which include

(1) keeping the buildings in repair; (2) paying taxes and other annual charges; (3) paying a just proportion of extraordinary assessments; and (4) payment of interest, but not principal, on encumbrances on the land. Also, he must act reasonably with reference to the use of the land so as not to cause harm to the owners of succeeding interests.

IV. Estates for years

An estate for years is an interest or estate in land for a certain period of time, e.g., a year, a month, or any greater or lesser period of fixed duration. Such an estate is often created by a *lease,* whereby the owner of an estate in land conveys the land to another person for some definite and specified period of time, usually in consideration of the payment of rent.

RIGHTS ACQUIRED UNDER A LEASE

By way of illustration, if *A* as the owner in fee simple of a parcel of land executes a 10-year lease to *B, A* has parted with a portion of his rights. He has given up for a 10-year period his right to occupy the land, and in return has received *B*'s promise to pay rent for those 10 years. *B,* of course, has not become the owner in fee simple, but has acquired the right to occupy the land in accordance with the provisions of the lease. *B* has acquired a *leasehold estate* in the land.

NATURE OF A LEASEHOLD ESTATE

The leasehold estate is an interest in land, but it is personal property and not real property. It is referred to as a "chattel real." The interest or estate remaining in the lessor is an estate in reversion, or simply a "reversion." The lessor is still the owner, but his estate is not possessory until the possession of the land reverts to him upon termination of the leasehold estate.

V. Estates at will

A tenancy at will is defined as a tenancy created with the consent of the landlord that is to exist or continue for an indefinite period of time. It may be created by express words, or it may arise by operation of law. The case of *National Bellas Hess* v. *Kalis,* 191 Fed.2d 739, is illustrative of a tenancy at will created by express agreement. In that case, it was held that a lease commencing October 1, 1943, and ending sixty days after signature of the treaty of peace on the close of the war with Germany or Japan, whichever treaty was the later, created a tenancy at will and not a tenancy for years.

PERIODIC TENANCIES

Periodic tenancies, created by the parties to continue for successive periods of the same length, unless sooner terminated by notice, are not expressly recognized by the California codes as a class. However, case law recognizes them as being a form of tenancy at will.

CREATION OF TENANCY AT WILL BY IMPLICATION

A tenancy at will is created by implication of law where a tenant enters into possession under an agreement for the execution of a lease for a specific term, but the lease is never executed. In the case of *Linnard* v. *Sonnenschein,* 94 C.A. 729, the tenant went into possession of a store under a lease for five years but the lease was never reduced to writing. In deciding that this created only a tenancy at will, the court said: "When a tenant enters upon real property, pending a completion of negotiations for a lease, he enters at his peril. True, the entry with the consent of the lessor creates the relation of landlord and tenant, but the tenancy is merely a tenancy at will. Thereafter if the proposed lease is completed, the tenant holds under the lease, but if the lease is not accomplished, the holding is at will, which by the acceptance of rent may become a tenancy from month to month or from year to year."

VI. Future interests

An estate or interest in land, with reference to its time of enjoyment, is either a present interest or a future interest. A present interest entitles the owner to immediate possession, whereas a future interest, as the name implies, is one that entitles the owner to possession of the property only at a time commencing in the future. Thus, a future interest is classified as a nonpossessory interest.

As the chart illustrates, an interest in real property may be nonpossessory for one of two reasons. It may be an incorporeal interest which gives the holder certain present rights in the property which do not include the right to actual possession of the land to the exclusion of others. These interests include easements, profits, covenants running with the land, equitable servitudes, and licenses.

The other type of nonpossessory interest is known as a future interest. The classes of future interests include reversions, remainders, possibilities of reverter, and powers of termination (or right of reentry for condition broken).

REVERSIONS

A reversion is defined in Section 768 of the Civil Code as "the residue of an estate left by operation of law in the grantor or his successors, or in the successors of a testator, commencing in possession on the determination of a particular estate granted or devised." Thus, if *A*, owning an estate in fee simple, conveys a life estate to *B*, the residue of the fee simple estate that is left in *A* is called a reversion, so called because possession reverts to *A* upon termination of *B*'s lesser estate. The estate of the lessor under a lease for a term of years is also referred to as a reversion.

Rights vesting in grantor where estate is conveyed on condition. The term "reversion" is sometimes used to describe the rights that vest in a grantor who has conveyed an estate upon condition, although technically this is an inaccurate designation. If *A*, the owner of land in fee simple, conveys the land to *B* upon a condition subsequent, e.g., on a condition "that the land shall be used for residence purposes only," the right of *A* to terminate the estate of *B* if there is a breach of the condition is not actually an estate in reversion or an estate of any kind. Although this right is sometimes called a "possibility of reverter," it is more aptly defined as a "right of reentry," or as a "power of termination." Such right or power is transferable to the same extent and in the same manner as any estate in land.

REMAINDERS

When a future estate or interest in land, other than a reversion, is dependent on a precedent estate, it is called a "remainder," and it may be created and transferred by that name. (C.C., Sec. 769.) Unlike a reversion, which is an interest left by operation of law in a grantor who conveys a lesser estate, a remainder is an estate created by act of the grantor in favor of some person other than the grantor.

A remainder is so called because, when the prior estate terminates, it (the remainder) "remains" away from rather than reverting to the conveyor. Following is an example: A executes a deed "to B for life and upon B's death to C or his heirs."

In order that there can be an interest to pass in remainder, it is obvious that the particular estate which precedes the remainder must be of a lesser duration than the interest of the conveyor at the time of conveyance. Remainders are classified as *vested remainders* and *contingent remainders*.

Vested remainder. A remainder was vested, as provided in former Section 694 of the Civil Code, "when there is a person in being who would have a right, defeasible or indefeasible, to the immediate possession of the property, upon the ceasing of the intermediate or precedent interest." Under a conveyance of land "to *A* for life, and upon his death the remainder to *B*," the interest of *B* is a vested remainder.

Contingent remainder. A remainder was contingent, in the language of former Section 695 of the Civil Code, "whilst the person in whom, or the event upon which, it is limited to take effect remains uncertain." Thus, where land is conveyed "to *A* for life, and the remainder to *B* provided *B* survives *A*," the remainder is contingent because it is dependent upon an event that is uncertain, namely, the death of *A* during the lifetime of *B*.

Sections 694 and 695 were repealed in 1963 because their definitions conflicted with the definition of a vested interest in new Section 718.5, added to the Civil Code in 1963, which, together with other sections, liberalize the application of the rule against perpetuities. Section 715.8 of the Civil Code now defines an interest as vested if there are persons in being who together could convey a fee simple title.

POSSIBILITY OF REVERTER

A possibility of reverter is the interest remaining in the grantor who conveys a fee simple determinable. A possibility of reverter is always in favor of the conveyor or his successors in interest. The main distinction between a possibility of reverter and a reversion is that a reversion cannot follow the conveyance of a fee simple, whereas a possibility of reverter can.

POWER OF TERMINATION

A power of termination (or right of reentry for condition broken) is the interest retained by the conveyor who conveys an estate subject to a condition subsequent. Like a possibility of reverter, a power of termination is always in favor of the conveyor and his heirs.

TRANSFER OF REMAINDER INTERESTS

Where there is a contemplated transfer of an estate in remainder, a determination as to whether or not the estate is vested or contingent is essential. Remainders, contingent as well as vested, are estates in land, and pass by succession, will, or transfer, in the same manner as present interests, but the successor to a remainderman can, of course, acquire no greater interest than the remainderman had. The problem frequently arises where title is vested in a life tenant with remainder over, and a question is presented whether there are parties who presently can unite in conveying an absolute and marketable title to a purchaser. The following situations are illustrative of this problem:

First: Where title is vested in "*A*, a life estate, remainder upon his death to *B*," the interest of *B* is a remainder indefeasible vested, and *A* and *B* can join in conveying an absolute estate to a third party.

Second: Where title is vested in "*A* for life, remainder in *A*'s children," and *A* presently has one child, namely, *B*, the interest of *B* is a remainder vested subject to being opened, i.e., if *A* has other children, the class "opens up" to let in other children as remaindermen, thus decreasing *B*'s interest to the extent necessary to allow all children of *A* to share equally in the remainder. A present transfer from the life tenant and *B* would not be sufficient to vest a marketable title in their grantee, since there is the possibility of other remaindermen.

Third: Where title is vested in "*A* for life, remainder in *B*, but if *B* dies without issue before *A*, then to *C*," the interest of *B* is a remainder that is presently vested but subject to complete defeasance. Here again, a marketable title would not be conveyed by a transfer from *A* and *B* alone.

Fourth: Where title is conveyed by *X*, the fee owner, to "*A* for life, remainder in the heirs of *A*'s body," and *A* presently has one child, namely, *B*, who would be an heir when *A* died, provided he survived *A*, the remainder is contingent. The persons who are to take upon *A*'s death cannot be ascertained until *A* dies, for the reason that a living person does not have heirs; he has potential heirs. *B*'s contingent interest could be transferred by him, but the interest would lapse and his grantee would take nothing if *B* predeceased *A*. If *A* dies without heirs, the title reverts to *X*, the original grantor.

DOCTRINE OF VIRTUAL REPRESENTATION

Where title to property cannot be effectively transferred by a voluntary conveyance because of the interests of unborn or unascertained remaindermen, and it becomes necessary for the preservation of the interests of all parties that the land be sold, it has been held that the courts have inherent jurisdiction to order such sale in proceedings in which the life tenant and all living remaindermen are joined, and the unborn or unascertained interests are made parties and appear through a guardian *ad litem* under the doctrine of *virtual representation.* (*County of Los Angeles* v. *Winans,* 13 C.A. 234.) A mortgage, exchange, or lease may also be ordered by the court under proper circumstances. A sale in a partition action may also be effected, since jurisdiction over the interests of unborn or unascertained remaindermen can be obtained under the doctrine of virtual representation.

VII. Trusts

Estates in real property may be classified as either *legal estates* or *equitable estates,* the distinction between them arising from the historical circumstances that these two kinds of interests or estates were originally enforced in different courts and by different forms of procedure. As a device to evade certain burdens incident to feudal tenure, it became a practice in England after the Norman Conquest for an owner to convey land to *A* for the "use" of *B*, or for the use of some religious order forbidden by law to hold title to real property. *A*, as the holder of the legal estate, was regarded as the sole owner of the property by the courts of law. *B*, the beneficiary of the use (who was called the *cestui que use*), had no remedy in the courts of law to compel the holder of the legal title to carry out the terms of the conveyance. In time, however, the rights of the beneficiary were recognized and protected by the courts of chancery, or equity, and the beneficiary's equitable interest or estate came to be considered as the real ownership of the property.

Equitable estate under a land contract. Another familiar form of equitable estate arose where an owner of land agreed to sell and convey the land to a purchaser, but a conveyance was not made. In such a case where the purchaser was entitled to a conveyance the courts of equity regarded the seller as holding the legal estate for the use and benefit of the purchaser, in accordance with the terms of the agreement.

Equitable principles applicable. Although the separation between courts of law and courts of equity does not exist in California, legal and equitable estates in land still retain many of the characteristic differences, and the equitable principles as developed in the English courts are still applied. This is particularly true in the field of trusts.

CLASSIFICATION OF TRUSTS

The Civil Code divides trusts into two classes: (1) *voluntary trusts,* or those which arise out of a personal confidence reposed in, and voluntarily accepted by, one person for the benefit of another; and (2) *involuntary trusts,* which are trusts created by operation of law. (C.C., Secs. 2216 and 2217.)

Another classification of trusts regards them as (1) *express trusts,* which arise as the result of an express declaration of trust or some other external expression of intent to create the trust; (2) *resulting trusts,* where the intention to create a trust is implied by law from certain acts of the parties; and (3) *constructive trusts,* where a trust is imposed by law, not to effectuate intention, but to redress wrong or prevent unjust enrichment.

EXPRESS TRUSTS

An express trust in land must be evidenced by a writing that indicates with reasonable certainty the intention of the trustor to create a trust, as well as the subject matter, purpose, and beneficiary of the trust. An express trust is usually created by a formal declaration of trust, or by a deed reciting that title is to be held in trust. Trusts may also be created by last will and testament, which trusts are known as testamentary trusts, as distinguished from living trusts, which are called "*inter vivos* trusts."

Validity of trust. Of primary concern in title examination is the question of the validity of a trust affecting title to real property. In the case of testamentary trusts the problem is only of temporary concern, since the validity of the testamentary trust will be passed upon by a decree of distribution in the probate proceedings, which decree, when it becomes final, i.e., beyond attack in the proceedings, is deemed to be conclusive.

Essential requirements of a valid trust. Before passing on the acts of the trustee under other trusts, however, the first step is to determine whether or not the trust in question is valid. To constitute a valid express trust, it is essential that there be the following: (1) a trustee; (2) an estate conveyed to him; (3) a beneficiary; (4) a lawful purpose; and (5) a valid term. It has been held that while a court of equity will in certain instances make good the absence of the first requisite, if the second or third be lacking, or if the fourth or fifth is illegal, the trust itself must fail. (*In re Walkerly,* 108 Cal. 627.) An exception is made in the case of gifts for charitable purposes. Such trusts are usually created by will, and the courts sometimes sustain the validity of such a trust even though all of the requisites of a valid private trust are lacking.

Who may act as trustee. Any person, including a corporation, having capacity to take and hold property may be the trustee. The trustor may be the trustee, or one of several beneficiaries may be the trustee. A sole beneficiary can be one of several trustees, but ordinarily the sole beneficiary cannot be the sole trustee, since the trust would be extinguished by merger of the legal and equitable estates.

Appointment of trustee by the court. A trust will not be allowed to fail for want of a trustee. Under the provisions of Section 2289 of the Civil Code, when there is no appointed trustee, or where all of the trustees are deceased, renounce the trust, or are discharged, the court may appoint one or more successor trustees. The court may also appoint a trustee to fill a vacancy where the trust instrument does not provide a method of appointment. (C.C., Sec. 2287.)

Who may be a beneficiary. Anyone capable of taking an interest in property, including a minor or an incompetent person, may be a beneficiary. The trustor himself may be a beneficiary under any trust other than a spendthrift trust. (*Bixby* v. *Hotchkis,* 58 C.A.2d 445.)

Term of trust. A trust must be for a lawful term. Since 1849 the California Constitution has provided: "No perpetuity shall be allowed except for eleemosynary purposes." Case law has interpreted this as referring to the common-law rule against perpetuities, which is concerned with remoteness of vesting. The permitted term has been lives in being plus twenty-one years. Heretofore a private trust was void in its inception if by any possibility it could endure beyond the express limitations prescribed by the state constitution and statutes. In 1963 the Civil Code was extensively amended whereby interests that fall within the rule against perpetuities are to be liberally construed to give effect to the general intent of the creator in favor of not finding any interest void or voidable.

Trust purpose. The purpose of the trust must be legal, and it must be definite. Under the provisions of Section 2220 of the Civil Code, a trust can be created for any purpose for which persons may lawfully contract.

Trusts other than express trusts recognized. In addition to express trusts, other types are recognized in California, namely *resulting trusts* and *constructive trusts.*

RESULTING TRUSTS

A resulting trust arises where a transfer of property is made under circumstances that raise an inference that the transferee was not intended to have the beneficial interest in the property. Where *A* conveys land to *B* in trust, but the trust is void for lack of a valid purpose or for some other reason, *B* will be deemed to hold the legal title under a resulting trust in favor of *A* or *A*'s successors. Another example is where *A* pays the consideration for the purchase of a parcel of land and has the title taken in the name of *B*, without any intention that *B* have the beneficial interest.

CONSTRUCTIVE TRUSTS

Constructive trusts are imposed by law where a person holding title is under an equitable duty to convey it to another person because his retention of title is wrongful. Fraud, mistake, undue influence, duress, or breach of a confidential relationship are wrongful acts that may raise a constructive trust. In the case of *Allen* v. *Meyers,* 5 Cal.2d 311, involving a situation where a wife had conveyed property to her husband upon his representations that upon her death he would convey the property to her children by a previous marriage, it was held that a constructive trust could be enforced in favor of the children.

POWERS OF THE TRUSTEE

Where the ownership of real property is vested in a trustee, the powers of the trustee to deal with the property are of vital concern. A trustee has only such powers as are expressly given him under the terms of the trust, and such as are necessarily implied to enable him to carry out the objects and purposes of the trust.

TRUSTEE AS AN AGENT

Under the provisions of Section 2267 of the Civil Code, a trustee is declared to be a general agent for the trust property. His authority is such as is conferred upon him by the declaration of trust and by the code, and none other. His acts, within the scope of his authority, bind the trust property to the same extent as the acts of an agent bind his principal.

UNAUTHORIZED ACTS ARE VOID

Section 870 of the Civil Code provides that where a trust in relation to real property is expressed in the instrument creating the estate, every transfer or other act of the trustees, in contravention of the trust, is void.

ACTS THAT MAY BE AUTHORIZED

For title purposes, the terms of the trust are strictly construed. If the act to be insured is not expressly authorized, or would not be supported by implied powers, special proceedings to raise a new or additional power may be appropriate. A court of equity has power to direct or permit a trustee to deviate from the terms of the trust for the purpose of saving the estate from serious loss or destruction and carrying out the purposes of the trust.

Power of sale. With respect to the power of sale, a trustee can sell property if a power of sale is conferred in specific words, or if such sale is necessary or appropriate to enable the trustee to carry out the purposes of the trust unless such sale is forbidden under the terms of the trust or it appears therefrom that the property was to be retained *in specie* in the trust. An authorization to the trustee to "dispose of" property, or to "invest and reinvest" may confer a power of sale. Power to sell does not authorize a sale on credit as a general rule, but the taking of a purchase money encumbrance may be justified under proper circumstances.

Power to exchange property. A power of sale does not authorize an exchange of the trust property for other property, unless the trustee could properly purchase the property taken in exchange. A power to "sell and dispose" of property, however, may include power to exchange.

Encumbrances by trustee. Although a power to mortgage may be implied from the terms of the trust or as necessary to carry out the purposes of the trust, it is not assumed, at least for title insurance purposes, that a trustee has power to mortgage unless such power is expressly conferred by the terms of the trust. Power to "mortgage or otherwise encumber," or to "mortgage and hypothecate" is regarded as sufficient to give the trustee power to execute a deed of trust.

Power to lease. Power to lease is not necessarily implied from the power to sell or power to dispose of land. However, even though the trust instrument does not expressly authorize a lease, such power is sometimes regarded as implied from the purposes of the trust, or as justified by the trustee's duty to keep the land productive.

WHEN INDIVIDUAL OWNERSHIP IS PRESUMED

Sometimes an instrument runs in favor of a person "as trustee" without designating a trust or disclosing any beneficiaries. In such cases there is a presumption that the title held is free from trust by virtue of the provisions of Section 869a of the Civil Code. Under this section, if an interest in real property is conveyed by an instrument in writing to a person in trust, or where such person is designated "trustee" or "as trustee," and no beneficiary is indicated or named in the instrument, it is presumed that such person holds the interest in his individual right and free from any trust. Any instrument executed by such person, whether individually or as trustee, shall prima facie affect the interest according to the tenor of such instrument. Such presumption is conclusive as to any undisclosed beneficiary and the original grantor or trustor and anyone claiming under them in favor of a purchaser or encumbrancer in good faith and for a valuable consideration when the instrument last mentioned is recorded in the office of the county recorder where the land is situated.

OTHER CONSIDERATIONS

The field of trusts is complex and involves a consideration of many other factors. The subject is discussed further in the chapter on probate proceedings (Chapter 23) as it relates to testamentary trusts.

Questions

1. Describe the principal classes of estates or interests in land in California.
2. Define an estate in fee simple.
3. Distinguish an estate on condition and an estate on limitation.
4. What is the nature of a life estate?
5. How are life estates created?
6. Under what conditions can an effective conveyance of title be made where a life estate exists?
7. Describe the two classes of remainder interests.
8. Distinguish a reversion and a remainder.
9. Define a leasehold estate.
10. What is an estate at will?
11. How are trusts classified?
12. Discuss the essential requirements of a valid express trust.
13. Distinguish a resulting trust and a constructive trust.
14. Do trustees under voluntary trusts have unlimited authority to transfer property?
15. Discuss the effect of a conveyance to a grantee "as trustee," where no trust is disclosed.

7

Acquisition and Transfer of Property

Summary

I. Introductory
Transfer at common law; Methods of acquisition and transfer

II. Deeds
Definition of a deed; Types of deeds; Form of deed; Distinction between grant deed and quitclaim deed; Implied warranties; Doctrine of after-acquired title; Requisites of a deed; What interests may be conveyed by deed; Effect of lack of consideration; When consideration is required; Date is desirable; Designation of grantor; Name variance; Title taken under an assumed name; Change of name of owner; Designation of grantee; Void deeds; Certainty as to grantee; Deeds to heirs; Deeds to organizations; Sufficient description essential; Execution of deed; Signature by mark; Signature in foreign language; Acknowledgments; Delivery of a deed; Conditions in deeds; Acceptance of the deed; Effect of lack of acceptance; Internal Revenue Stamps; Recitals in deeds; Exceptions and reservations; Status of the parties; Conveyance in favor of decedent's estate; Transfers to a minor or incompetent person; Tenancy of title; Effect of apparent invalidity; Types of void deeds; Voidable deeds

III. Acquisition as affected by status
Aliens; Convicts; American Indians

IV. Transfers by attorneys-in-fact
Special or general powers; Limitation of general words; Who may act under a power of attorney; Recordation of power of attorney; Execution of instruments; Restrictions on authority; Termination of power of attorney

V. Adverse possession
Necessity for quiet title decree; Elements of adverse possession; Occupancy of land; Claim of right and color of title; Acts breaking continuity of possession; "Tacking on" possession; Payment of taxes; Limitations on doctrine of adverse possession

VI. Condemnation
Statutory provisions; The United States may also condemn land; Conditions for exercise of right; Condemnation by private individual; Replacement housing; Whether fee or easement condemned; Inverse condemnation

VII. Dedication
Nature of interest created—whether fee or easement; Limitation on use of land acquired by dedication; Dedication of public lands; Subsurface use of park property

VIII. Accession
Annexation; Innocent improver of land; Accretion and reliction; Accretion distinguished from avulsion; Alluvion must be created by natural causes; Waterline boundary descriptions

IX. Escheat
Escheats are not favored

X. Involuntary alienation
Bankruptcy proceedings

XI. Title by estoppel
After-acquired title; Types of deeds sufficient to raise an estoppel; Limitation on after-acquired title doctrine

XII. Abandonment
Nature of abandonment; Property subject to abandonment; Land contract

XIII. Forfeiture
Nature of forfeiture; Property subject to forfeiture

I. Introductory

The word "title" has been defined as the *evidence of ownership,* i.e., the method by which an owner's right to property is established or evidenced. It is in this sense that one speaks of "examining the title," which consists of examining the instruments and acts of record that evidence the ownership of real property. In another sense, the word "title" denotes the result of operative facts and not the facts themselves, and in this sense the word "title" means simply *ownership.*

TRANSFER AT COMMON LAW

Under the early English common law, ownership of real property was transferred by delivery of possession, called "livery of seizin." This transfer was effected by a delivery of the land itself or something symbolical of the land, either a twig, a stone, or a handful of dirt. Another method of transfer was by a statement, usually made before witnesses in view of the land, to the effect that possession was transferred, followed by entry by the new owner. No written instrument was required in these early transfers, hence there was no recording system. The mode of transferring land was sufficient for the needs during those times, since ownership was notorious, and transfer was seldom made except in descent from father to son.

METHODS OF ACQUISITION AND TRANSFER

Today there are many different ways of acquisition and transfer of title to real property. Section 1000 of the Civil Code provides that property may be acquired in the following ways: (1) by occupancy, (2) by accession, (3) by transfer, (4) by will, or (5) by succession. This listing is not exclusive, however. The following specific methods by which title may be acquired or transferred will be considered without reference to the code classification: (1) wills and succession (considered at length in Chapter 23 on probate proceedings), (2) deeds of conveyance, (3) adverse possession, (4) condemnation, (5) dedication, (6) accession, (7) escheat, (8) involuntary alienation, (9) title by estoppel, (10) abandonment, and (11) forfeiture. Additionally, acquisitions as affected by status, and transfers by attorneys-in-fact will be considered in connection with deeds of conveyance.

II. Deeds

The most familiar method of transfer of title to real property is by deed. The word "transfer" is defined in Section 1039 of the Civil Code as an act of the parties, or of the law, by which title to property is conveyed from one living person to another. The term includes *voluntary transfers,* i.e., by act of the parties, and *involuntary transfers,* i.e., by act of the law. A voluntary transfer is in the type primarily considered in a discussion of deeds, although an involuntary transfer, such as an execution sale or a foreclosure sale, involves the execution of a deed.

DEFINITION OF A DEED

A deed is described briefly as a written instrument, executed and delivered, by which the title to real property is transferred from one person, called the grantor, to another person, called the grantee.

TYPES OF DEEDS

The two types of deeds in general use in California are the *grant deed* and the *quitclaim deed.* Warranty deeds are rarely used in California, although such deeds are permissible. Other designations are given to deeds, usually in connection with court proceedings, such as a sheriff's deed, a marshal's deed, a commissioner's deed, an executor's deed, a guardian's deed, a trustee's deed, or a tax deed. Trust deeds are commonly used in California, but these are not primarily for the purpose of conveying title from one person to another; they are used to create a lien on real property. A form of deed, called a reconveyance deed, may be used to convey the title from the trustee to the trustor when the debt secured by the trust deed has been paid.

FORM OF DEED

Any form of written instrument, otherwise sufficient, that contains apt words of conveyance, such as "grant," "transfer," or "convey," is sufficient to pass title to land in California. There is no fixed and absolute form. Statutory provisions authorize the conveyance of real property by means of a simple form deed, providing as follows:

> I, *A.B.*, grant to *C.D.* all that real property situate in the county of ...., state of California, described as follows: ....
> ....
> Witness my hand this _____ day of ______________, 19_____.

This statutory form of grant deed is characterized by the word "grant" in its operative words of conveyance. For a quitclaim deed, the operative words "remise, release, and quitclaim," or merely "quitclaim," are substituted for the word "grant."

DISTINCTION BETWEEN GRANT DEED AND QUITCLAIM DEED

There are two main distinctions between a grant deed and a quitclaim deed: (1) a grant deed contains *implied covenants or warranties*, and (2) the doctrine of *after-acquired title* applies where a grant deed is issued.

IMPLIED WARRANTIES

Section 1113 of the Civil Code provides that from the use of the word "grant" in any conveyance by which a fee estate is passed, the following covenants and none other, on the part of the grantor and his heirs, are implied, unless restrained by express terms in the conveyance: "1. That previous to the time of the execution of such conveyance, the grantor has not conveyed the same estate, or any right, title or interest therein, to any person other than the grantee; 2. That such estate is at the time of the execution of such conveyance free from encumbrances done, made, or suffered by the grantor, or any person claiming under him."

This simply means that the grantor warrants that *he* has not previously conveyed or encumbered the property; it is not a warranty that he is the owner of the property, or that it is not encumbered.

DOCTRINE OF AFTER-ACQUIRED TITLE

A grant deed also conveys any after-acquired title of the grantor, unless a different intent is expressed. (C.C., Sec. 1106.) A quitclaim deed, however, transfers only such interest as the grantor may have at the time the conveyance is executed.

REQUISITES OF A DEED

The requisites of a valid deed in California are as follows: (1) a competent grantor, (2) a grantee capable of holding title, (3) a sufficient description of the property, (4) operative words of conveyance, (5) due execution by the grantor, (6) delivery, and (7) acceptance.

Nonessential matters. Generally, a *consideration* is not necessary to the validity of a voluntary transfer. A *date* is not essential, nor is an *acknowledgment* essential to the validity of the deed, although acknowledgment is a prerequisite to the recording of a deed. A deed *need not be recorded* to be valid as between the parties and as against third parties having notice of the conveyance. It is a common practice to record deeds, and recordation of a deed is essential, of course, for title insurance purposes. Since 1965 the name and address where the tax statement is to be mailed must be disclosed on the deed as a condition for recording. However, the failure to so note any such name and address does not affect the notice otherwise imparted by recording.

WHAT INTERESTS MAY BE CONVEYED BY DEED

As a general rule, any interest in real property, whether present or future, vested or contingent, may be conveyed by deed. However, under the provisions of Section 1045 of the Civil Code, a mere possibility, not coupled with an interest, cannot be transferred. This exception is declaratory of the common-law rule that a mere possibility of an interest, such as the expectancy of an heir apparent in the estate of a living ancestor, was not an interest capable of passing by conveyance or assignment. The rule in equity was different, though, and in California the courts have often enforced conveyances of the prospective interest of an heir against his share of the estate *after* it devolved upon him, and have recognized other transfers of expectations or interests to be acquired in the future, provided they were fairly made and for an adequate consideration, and not contrary to public policy.

EFFECT OF LACK OF CONSIDERATION

Although consideration is not essential to the validity of a deed as between the parties, lack of consideration is of material concern where rights of third persons may be adversely affected by the conveyance. A conveyance by a grantor who is or will be rendered insolvent by such a conveyance is fraudulent as to creditors, without regard to the grantor's actual intent, if the conveyance is made without a fair consideration. Such a conveyance may be set aside by a creditor in an appropriate proceeding. The rights of a grantee under a deed from a married person holding record title are also dependent in part upon the payment of a valuable consideration, where the spouse of the grantor brings an action to set the conveyance aside. Also, priorities between conflicting grants are determined under the recording laws by whether or not a valuable consideration was paid.

WHEN CONSIDERATION IS REQUIRED

The general rule that consideration is not essential to the validity of a deed applies only to voluntary conveyance by private individuals; it does not apply in the case of conveyances by public officials of government-owned property, nor does it apply in the case of deeds by administrators, executors, guardians, trustees, receivers, and similar representatives, or in the case of a deed by an attorney-in-fact under a power of attorney. Also, under title company rules, a deed in lieu of foreclosure of a deed of trust must be evidenced by a consideration, either the cancellation of the debt if the grantor is personally liable, or by a monetary consideration paid to the grantor if he is not personally liable for the debt.

DATE IS DESIRABLE

Although a date is not essential, it is customary and desirable for a deed to recite the date of its execution. Under the provisions of Section 1055 of the Civil Code, a deed is presumed to have been delivered at its date. The date of a conveyance may be of evidentiary value in determining priority between conflicting grants, or where rights of third persons, such as a creditor levying a writ of attachment or execution, are involved.

DESIGNATION OF GRANTOR

The deed must designate a grantor, whose name must appear in the body of the deed, or he must be otherwise so described as to be identified, e.g., "*I, the undersigned,* do hereby grant ...." A deed signed and acknowledged by persons named in the body of the deed as grantors, and by other persons as well, is not the deed of those not named as grantors. This rule has its origin in the fact that deeds in earlier periods of time were not signed but were sealed, and identification of the grantor was therefore required in the body of the deed. An exception to this rule has been applied in the case of a wife who signs her husband's deed conveying community property acquired in his name prior to 1927. (*Strong* v. *Strong*, 22 Cal.2d 540.)

NAME VARIANCE

As between the grantor and grantee, a conveyance executed by the true owner under any name may be sufficient. However, a conveyance in which the name of the grantor materially differs from the name under which he holds the record title does not impart constructive notice to subsequent purchasers or encumbrancers. Accordingly, substantial identity between the name of the grantor in the deed and the record owner should be insisted upon by the grantee. Identity problems often arise in connection with the use of initials, or the use of abbreviations, derivations, and nicknames, and special rules apply in determining whether or not a name variance will affect marketability of title, or prevent the recorded instrument from imparting constructive notice.

TITLE TAKEN UNDER AN ASSUMED NAME

A person may assume any name he chooses when he obtains title to property, and if he assumes a name other than his legal name, a conveyance by him under such assumed name will pass good title. For purposes of giving good notice on the records, his conveyance must be made in the assumed name. A difficulty is sometimes encountered in connection with the statement of identity required by a title company where the person taking title under an assumed name has insufficient proof that he is in fact one and the same person.

CHANGE OF NAME OF OWNER

The phrase "who acquired title as" immediately following the name of the grantor is often noted in deeds. This expression results from the rule that where the grantor has had a change of name, both names must appear in the caption of the deed. Section 1096 of the Civil Code provides that any person in whom the title to real property is vested, who shall afterward, from any cause, have his or her name changed, must, in any conveyance of real property so held, set forth the name in which he or she derived title to said real property. Any conveyance, though recorded, that does not comply with the foregoing requirement does not impart constructive notice to subsequent purchasers and encumbrancers, although it is valid as between parties and those having notice.

When change of name occurs. A change of name may result in various ways and is frequently encountered in title work. A person may change his name by court proceedings, or by the assumption of a new name without resort to legal proceedings, or, in the case of a woman, by marriage. A corporation may change its name by amendment of its articles of incorporation. Whether the change of name is by court proceedings or otherwise, or whether the owner is a natural person or a corporation, the requirement that reference in a conveyance be made to the name under which title was acquired is considered mandatory.

DESIGNATION OF GRANTEE

A deed must designate a grantee to whom the title passes, which grantee must be named or designated in such a way as to be ascertainable, and must be a person in being, either natural or artificial, capable of taking title. It has been held that a deed to a dead person is void. However, an exception to this rule is made in the case of a government patent in favor of a deceased patentee, under which title inures to his grantee, assigns, or heirs. Infants and insane or incompetent persons may be grantees.

VOID DEEDS

If the grantee's name is inserted in a deed executed in blank by the grantor, without proper authorization, the deed is void and conveys no title. A deed to a fictious person is also void. But, as mentioned above, a deed to an actual person by a name that he has assumed for the purpose of taking title is valid. A distinction is thus made between a fictitious person and a fictitious name.

CERTAINTY AS TO GRANTEE

A grantee must be named or designated in such a way that it can be ascertained with certainty who the grantee is. For instance, a deed to "*A* or *B*" has been held to be void for uncertainty. (*Schade* v. *Stewart*, 205 Cal. 658.) However, under some circumstances such a deed might be considered sufficient to convey the grantor's interest on the theory that such designation of the grantees was ineffective to create an intended joint tenancy but nonetheless transferred the grantor's interest.

A deed to a vague group, such as the "inhabitants" of a town, is usually considered insufficient, except in the case of the dedication of an easement for a public purpose. Sometimes it is desired to have a deed made in favor of a large number of grantees without naming them, for reasons of expediency, as in the case of a quitclaim deed to "all of the owners of lots in a specified tract" for the purpose of relinquishing a general easement where time does not permit a search of the records to ascertain the identity of all of the owners. Such a quitclaim deed usually designates the grantees as "the record owners of all lots of Tract ________ in severalty and upon the same tenure as their respective interests appear of record." The designation of the grantees in this manner is sufficient, since a means of identifying them is given, i.e., by an examination of the records.

DEEDS TO HEIRS

A deed that purports to convey a present interest to the "heirs" of a living person is void for uncertainty, since living persons do not have heirs. However, such a deed might be sustained upon proof that the grantor intended to convey title to the children of the person named. A deed to the "heirs of John Doe, deceased" is sufficient, since the persons who are to take title can be ascertained with certainty by the probate court in appropriate proceedings.

DEEDS TO ORGANIZATIONS

Generally, a grantee, if not a natural person, must be a legal entity capable of holding title, such as a corporation or a partnership. A conveyance to an unincorporated body, such as a fictitious firm, is considered void, unless by statute the unincorporated association is permitted to acquire property in its name. The Corporations Code now provides that benevolent or fraternal societies or associations, labor organizations, and certain medical associations may, without incorporation, acquire property in the name of the society or association. Where an unincorporated association does not have capacity to take title, a valid deed may be made to named individuals as trustees for the association.

SUFFICIENT DESCRIPTION ESSENTIAL

As mentioned previously, a deed must contain a description sufficient to identify the land conveyed. The description is considered adequate if a competent surveyor can take the deed and locate the land on the ground from the description contained therein.

EXECUTION OF DEED

A deed must be executed (signed) by the grantor, or by his attorney-in-fact acting pursuant to written authorization. Usually a grantor writes his name in ink in longhand. However, signatures in pencil or typed or by hand printing have been held to be sufficient, although such methods are not recommended. Signatures by mark are valid. Also, the grantor's name may be written for him by another person at the grantor's request and in his presence. The grantor may also adopt and ratify a signature made by another person without previous authority.

SIGNATURE BY MARK

The Civil Code provides that signature includes mark, when the person cannot write, his name being written near the mark, by a person who writes his own name as witness, with two witnesses necessary in order to have the document acknowledged. (C.C., Sec. 14.) Physical weakness, preventing a person from writing his name, or inability to write legibly, is sufficient reason for execution by mark. An instrument executed by mark need not affirmatively state that one of the witnesses wrote the person's name; it is sufficient if it can be established that such is the fact. However, it is the usual practice to include such a statement.

Procedure for executing deed by mark. Execution of a deed by mark is done in the following manner: the grantor makes his mark before two witnesses, one of whom writes the grantor's name near the mark. The witnesses then sign as such, and the grantor acknowledges execution. The standard form for such execution is as follows:

	John Doe, being unable to write, made his mark in my presence, and I signed his name at his request and in his presence.	John × Doe
	______________________	
Additional Witness:	______________________	

Persons who may witness signature by mark. If one spouse signs by mark, the other spouse may act as a witness, but it is preferable to have a disinterested party as a witness. The notary who takes the acknowledgment may be the additional witness.

SIGNATURE IN FOREIGN LANGUAGE

Persons who cannot write their names in English may either sign by mark, or sign in a foreign language. If the signature is in a foreign language, it should be witnessed, and the witness should sign a statement as follows: "Witness to the signature of *A.B.*, whose name is written in Arabic."

ACKNOWLEDGMENTS

Before a deed (or most other instruments) can be recorded, its execution must be acknowledged by the person executing it, or proved by a subscribing witness or by proof of the handwriting (C.C., Secs. 1198 and 1199), and the acknowledgment or proof certified as provided by law (Govt. C., Sec. 27287). An acknowledgment is a formal declaration, made before an officer designated by statute, by the person who has executed an instrument, that he did in fact execute the instrument. Proof of an acknowledgment is evidenced by a certificate made by the officer before whom the acknowledgment is made.

Purpose of an acknowledgment. The main purposes of an acknowledgment are to entitle the instrument to be recorded and thus impart constructive notice of its contents, and to obviate proof of execution of the instrument if it is to be offered in evidence in judicial proceedings.

Who may acknowledge. Under recording laws, the phrase "person executing the instrument" means the person whose property rights are transferred, encumbered, or otherwise affected, such as the grantor in a deed, the vendor in a contract of sale, or the lessor in a lease. Where two or more persons execute an instrument by which property rights are affected, such instrument is entitled to be recorded if acknowledged by any one of such persons.

Persons authorized to take acknowledgments. The Civil Code (Secs. 1180 *et seq.*) designates the persons who are authorized to take acknowledgments, classifying them as to acknowledgments taken within the State of California, outside the state but within the United States, outside the United States, and by officers of the United States Armed Services. Most acknowledgments are taken before a notary public, who must affix his seal to the certificate of acknowledgment.

Notary public seals. Notaries public in this state are required to have a seal on which must appear the name of the notary, the words "Notary Public," the State Seal, and the county in which the notary has his principal place of business. If he transfers his principal place of business to a different county than that shown on the seal, he must have the seal altered to indicate such change. Effective September 20, 1963, notaries may use a rubber-stamp seal. All notaries who are appointed or reappointed on or after January 1, 1964 must use a seal that legibly reproduces under photographic methods the required elements of a notarial seal. In 1967 the law was amended to require that the seal of every notary public whose commission is issued on or after January 1, 1968 (including renewals) show the date his commission expires.

Statewide jurisdiction of notaries. Prior to 1957, notaries public in this state could act only within the county of their appointment, but in 1957 statewide jurisdiction was given to notaries by amendments to the Government Code. In 1959, Section 1181 of the Civil Code was also amended to extend the jurisdiction of notaries statewide and to make the two codes consistent.

Form of certificate of acknowledgment. The Civil Code prescribes various forms of the certificate of acknowledgment for use by individuals, corporations, partnerships, attorneys-in-fact, and so one. The following is the form used where an instrument is executed by an individual:

State of ____________ }
County of ____________ } ss
On this ____ day of ________, 19____, before me [*here insert the name and quality of officer*], personally appeared ____________, known to me (or proved to me on the oath of ____________), to be the person whose name is subscribed to the within instrument, and acknowledged that he executed the same.

The person taking the acknowledgments must then sign his name, recite his office, and affix his seal.

Acknowledgmeents taken outside the state. The form of the certificate of acknowledgment taken in a state other than California where the instrument is to be recorded in California may be either (1) the form prescribed in the Civil Code of California; or (2) the form prescribed for a certificate of acknowledgment by the laws of the state where taken. In the latter case there should be appended a certificate of the clerk of the court of record of the county or district where the acknowledgment is taken to the effect that the certificate of acknowledgment conforms to the laws of the state where taken, and that the officer taking the same was authorized by law to do so, and that the officer's signature is true and genuine. The certificate of the clerk is known as a certificate of authenticity and conformity.

Acknowledgments by a party in interest invalid. An acknowledgment taken by a party directly interested, such as the grantee in the deed or the mortgagee in a mortgage, is void. Where a corporation executes an instrument, an employee or officer of the corporation may take the acknowledgment if he is not personally interested and if he does not execute the instrument as an officer of the corporation. As a general rule, a husband or wife should not take the other's acknowledgment of a deed or other instrument.

Responsibility of person taking an acknowledgment. The person taking an acknowledgment assumes considerable responsibility for his act. He must know, or have satisfactory proof on the oath or affirmation of a credible witness known to him, that the person making the acknowledgment is in fact the individual who is described and who executed the instrument. Both the notary public and the surety on his bond are liable for the notary's misconduct or his negligence, as where the notary acknowledges the signature on a forged instrument. (Govt. C., Sec. 8214.)

Effect of lack of acknowledgment. Failure to acknowledge an instrument does not necessarily prevent its recordation or admissibility in evidence. The Civil Code specifies several alternative methods of proving the execution of instruments, each of these methods has the same effect as acknowledgment unless acknowledgment is an essential requirement to the validity of an instrument, such as a declaration of homestead.

Proof of the execution of an instrument, including a deed, may be made either: (1) by a subscribing witness, i.e., a witness whose name is subscribed to an instrument as a witness and who states under oath the facts of execution and identity (C.C., Secs. 1195 *et seq.*); or (2) by proof of handwriting, i.e., proof by a person who is well acquainted with the grantor's signature where the grantor and the subscribing witness, if any, are nonresident, or are dead, or cannot be located (C.C., Secs. 1195 and 1198 *et seq.*); or (3) by court decree, i.e., any person interested under an instrument may bring an action in court to have it proved.

Curative acts. If defects occur in the certificate of acknowledgment, they are deemed to be cured after one year from date of recordation, under Section 1207 of the Civil Code, which provides that all instruments impart constructive notice after one year from the time they have been recorded, notwithstanding any defect or omission in the certificate or the absence of such certificate. This is known as a "Curative Act," and although it does not cure the absence of acknowledgment of an instrument whose validity depends upon acknowledgment, it apparently will cure any defect in the form of the certificate of acknowledgment where the instrument has been acknowledged before a proper officer.

DELIVERY OF A DEED

A deed is not effective as a transfer of real property until it has been *delivered.* Delivery is the act, however evidenced, by which the deed takes effect and passes title. Delivery is not merely a transfer of the physical possession of the deed, such as the act of handing a deed to the grantee; whether there has been a delivery is a question of intention. The grantor must intend that title pass before there is a legal delivery. Anything that clearly manifests the intention of the grantor that his deed shall presently become operative and effectual, that he divests control over it, and that the grantee has become the owner, constitutes sufficient delivery.

Presumptions as to delivery. Certain presumptions apply in California which are of evidentiary value in determining whether there has been a delivery, but these presumptions are rebuttable, i.e., they are not conclusive. If a deed is found in the possession of the grantee, there is a presumption of delivery, whereas finding the deed in the possession of the grantor raises a presumption of nondelivery. Recordation of a deed raises a presumption of delivery, unless the deed is not recorded until after the death of the grantor.

Evidence of delivery. The best evidence of delivery is the act of handing the deed to the grantee, but manual delivery is not essential. Even though the deed is not handed to the grantee, it is deemed to be constructively delivered to him where, by agreement of the parties, it is understood to be delivered and the grantee is entitled to immediate delivery, or where it is delivered by the grantor to a third party for the benefit of the grantee and the latter's assent is shown or may be presumed. The case of *Goodman* v. *Goodman,* 212 Cal. 730, is illustrative of the first situation. There the grantor executed a deed in favor of the grantee with interest to pass title, but retained possession of the deed for safekeeping. Delivery was held to be sufficient under these facts.

Manual delivery. Manual delivery does not in and of itself prove legal delivery. Thus, where *A* hands a deed to *B* with the request not to record the deed until *A's* death and with the understanding that it is to be returned to *A* if *B* dies first, *A* and *B* both believing that a deed is not effective until recorded, there is no delivery. However, where *A* hands a deed to *B* with the intent to pass title, but with an oral request not to record the deed until after *A's* death, valid delivery has occurred.

Manual delivery not always legal delivery. Another case involving manual delivery without legal delivery is that of *Kimbro* v. *Kimbro,* 199 Cal. 344. There a husband, under pressure from his wife to execute a deed, signed and handed a deed to his wife, saying: "I will sign the deed, but it won't benefit you any, for it is not acknowledged." The husband's belief that the deed would be of no effect unless acknowledged, although erroneous, evidenced his lack of intention to pass title, and it was held that valid delivery had not occurred.

Time of delivery. To be effective, a deed must be delivered to the grantee during the grantor's lifetime. A deed cannot be used to take the place of a will. The case of *Miller* v. *Brode,* 186 Cal. 409, involved the following situation: Husband and wife each signed a deed in favor of the other, and placed the two deeds in a safe deposit box with the understanding that upon the death of one, the survivor would record the deed in his or her favor and destroy the other deed. It was held that the survivor would not take title, since there was no effective delivery during the grantor's lifetime. In the case of *Johns* v. *Scobie,* 12 Cal.2d 618, it was held that the inclusion of a deed in a trunk to which both the grantor and grantee had access was not a valid delivery.

Conditional delivery. A deed cannot be effectively delivered to a grantee conditionally. If a grantor makes a deed, intending to divest himself of the title, and delivers it to the grantee upon an oral condition that the grantee perform some act, such as the payment of money, the grantee will take title absolutely. (C.C., Sec. 1056.) However, oral conditions on delivery should be carefully considered as bearing upon lack of intent to deliver, or upon possible fraud which may result in an action to avoid the deed. A deed may be handed to a third party for delivery to the grantee upon performance of some act or the occurrence of some event. The usual escrow is an example of delivery to a third party upon condition.

Effect of redelivery. When a deed has been delivered with intent to pass title, a subsequent redelivery of the deed to the grantor, or the destruction or cancellation of the deed, does not operate to retransfer the title to the grantor. (C.C., Sec. 1058; *Chaffee* v. *Sorensen,* 107 C.A.2d 284.)

CONDITIONS IN DEEDS

Conditions affecting use or transfer are sometimes imposed in deeds. These conditions will be deemed void if violative of Section 711 of the Civil Code, providing that "conditions restraining alienation, when repugnant to the interest created, are void." This section invalidates any restraint, however short, if it is repugnant to the grant. A conveyance of the fee with the condition that the grantee cannot sell or dispose of the property to specified persons, or for a specified period of time is regarded as void in its inception. In such a case, the grant is valid, but the condition is void and of no effect.

ACCEPTANCE OF THE DEED

Ordinarily a deed cannot be given effect unless there is an acceptance by the grantee. In some cases, acceptance is presumed, as in the case of a beneficial conveyance to a person incapable of consenting—a deed to an infant or an incompetent person, for instance. Acceptance may be presumed where a beneficial conveyance is irrevocably delivered to a custodian for delivery to the grantee upon the grantor's death, even though the grantee has no knowledge of the deed until after the death of the grantor. However, this doctrine will not be applied where intervening rights of third parties are involved.

EFFECT OF LACK OF ACCEPTANCE

In the case of *Green* v. *Skinner,* 185 Cal. 435, where *A* and *B* were joint tenants, and *A* executed a deed of his interest to his grandson, to be delivered by *A*'s son to the grantee upon the death of *A,* the grandson having no knowledge of the deed until it was delivered to him after *A*'s death, it was held that the deed was not effective because there was no acceptance by the grantee during the grantor's lifetime, and title therefore vested in *B* as surviving joint tenant.

What constitutes acceptance. Acceptance of a deed may be shown by acts, words, or conduct of the grantee, indicating an intention to accept, such as the retention of the deed, execution of an encumbrance on the property, or by other acts of ownership.

Acceptance by governmental agency. Deeds or grants conveying real property or any interest therein to a political corporation or government agency, for public purposes, are not entitled to be recorded unless the consent of the grantee is evidenced therein by a resolution or certificate of acceptance. (Govt. C., Sec. 27281.)

INTERNAL REVENUE STAMPS

With few exceptions, Internal Revenue stamps for a long time were required on a deed if the consideration or value of the interest or property conveyed, exclusive of the value of any lien or encumbrance remaining thereon at the time of sale, exceeded $100. (26 U.S.C.A., Sec. 4361.) The federal law was repealed effective January 1, 1968. California, as did other states, enacted a new law effective January 1, 1968, which provided for a documentary stamp tax on conveyances at the rate of 55 cents for each $500 consideration or fractional part thereof. Thereafter the California law was amended to eliminate the need for stamps, with payment of the tax to be made at the time of recording. The new law, effective July 1, 1968, requires that every document subject to tax that is submitted for recordation show on its face the amount of tax due and the incorporated or unincorporated location of the real property described in the document, provided that, if requested, the amount of tax due may be shown on a separate paper instead of the document itself. The new law is known as the Documentary Transfer Tax Act.

RECITALS IN DEEDS

It is not uncommon for deeds to specify with particularity the matters that the grantee is to take subject to, such as easements, covenants, conditions and restrictions, taxes, and assessments. Also, various special recitals may be incorporated in a deed to explain its purpose, or the interest of the parties and their intent, or to incorporate therein portions of other documents of record.

EXCEPTIONS AND RESERVATIONS

Exceptions and reservations are also not uncommon in deeds. Technically, an *exception* withdraws a part of the thing described as granted (e.g., *A* grants to *B* lot 1 of tract *X*, except the south half thereof), whereas a *reservation* creates some right or privilege for the benefit of the grantor in the land described that did not exist independently before the grant (e.g., *A* grants Blackacre, reserving an easement over the west 20 feet thereof). However, the terms are used interchangeably in conveyancing today

Reservations or exceptions in favor of a third party. As a general rule, reservations or exceptions in a deed in favor of a stranger are invalid. In the case of *Fleming* v. *State Bar*, 38 Cal.2d 341, the court raised a question as to the effect of the phrase in a deed from *A* to *B*, "subject to a life estate in favor of *C*," and stated that it is not altogether clear what the effect of such a phrase would be. It was pointed out that the courts of this state, like those of other jurisdictions, have adhered to the feudal rule that an exception or reservation in favor of a stranger to a deed can create no interest in the stranger. But where the reservation or exception is in favor of a spouse, the courts have not applied the general rule, and have effected the manifest interest of the parties to the deed. (*Boyer* v. *Murphy*, 202 Cal. 23.)

STATUS OF THE PARTIES

Although showing the status of the grantor or grantee in a deed is not essential to the validity of the deed, it is desirable, and it is usually done. The status of the parties to a conveyance is given to indicate marriage, age, competency to deal with the property, or relation with others. Where the parties are acting in a fiduciary capacity, status should always be shown, thusly; "as executor," or "as administrator," or "as trustee," and so on.

CONVEYANCE IN FAVOR OF DECEDENT'S ESTATE

Where it is necessary to prepare instruments to vest real or personal property in a decedent's estate subject to administration, the following designations are used: (1) for real property, the deed is in favor of "the heirs or devisees of John Doe, deceased, subject to administration of his estate"; (2) for personal property, such as a note secured by a deed of trust, the transfer is made "to *A*, as executor of the will of John Doe, deceased, subject to administration of his estate," or to "*A*, as administrator of the estate of John Doe, deceased, subject to administration of his estate." A deed should not be made in favor of "the estate of" a deceased person, since an estate is not an entity capable of holding title.

TRANSFER TO A MINOR OR INCOMPETENT PERSON

Minors and incompetent persons may acquire title to real property, and ownership by such persons is not uncommon. Guardianship proceedings are not essential for the purpose of acquiring title but are necessary for the purpose of conveying, encumbering, leasing, or otherwise dealing with the ward's property. Where guardianship proceedings are in effect, a transfer should not be made to the guardian, but should be made to the minor or to the incompetent person, with the status disclosed, as follows: "to Jane Doe, an incompetent person," or "to Jane Doe, a minor." These matters are considered further in Chapter 23 on probate proceedings.

TENANCY OF TITLE

The tenancy of title of the grantee or grantees should also be set forth in the deed, although a failure to disclose the tenancy will not invalidate the deed. Tenancy of title refers to the manner of holding title. It is shown immediately after the status of the grantee, and is designated in the following manner: "as his (or her) separate property"; "as joint tenants"; "as community property"; or "as tenants in common.

EFFECT OF APPARENT INVALIDITY

As noted above, conveyances are considered void if deficient in certain respects, but even though the defects appear on the face of the instrument, this does not mean that the instrument can be disregarded in title work. As a general rule of title practice, all instruments of record are reflected in title reports and policies unless they have been judicially construed to be invalid in proceedings binding on all the parties. An instrument apparently void on its face may be given some effect by the courts on the basis of intention of the parties, or on equitable principles. A deed executed by an attorney-in-fact in his own name instead of in the name of his principal is said to be void, but such a deed has been sustained in equity as an agreement to convey by the principal. (*Salmon* v. *Hoffman*, 2 Cal. 138.) Under other circumstances, a party may be estopped to assert the invalidity of a deed.

TYPES OF VOID DEEDS

The following deeds have been held to be void and pass no title even in favor of innocent purchasers: (1) a forged deed; (2) a deed from a person whose incapacity has been judicially determined; (3) a deed from a person entirely without understanding; (4) a deed from a minor under 18 years of age; (5) a deed executed in blank, where the grantee's name is inserted without the grantor's authorization or consent; (6) a deed materially altered in escrow without the knowledge or consent of the grantor; and (7) an undelivered deed, such as a deed stolen from the grantor, or a deed delivered by an escrow holder in violation of the grantor's instructions.

VOIDABLE DEEDS

The following types of deeds are not considered to be void, but are voidable, and pass title subject to being set aside in appropriate proceedings: (1) a deed procured through fraud, mistake, undue influence, duress, or menace; (2) a deed by a person of unsound mind whose incapacity has not been judicially determined; and (3) a deed by a minor of the age of 18 years or older. As a general rule, a bona fide purchaser for value from the grantee in the voidable deed obtains title good as against the original grantor.

III. Acquisition as affected by status

The right to acquire or transfer property is subject to limitations in some instances, based upon the status of the person giving rise to a legal disability.

ALIENS

Formerly there was an alien land law in California prohibiting aliens ineligible to citizenship from acquiring real property, and providing for *escheat* to the state for violations of the law. (Alien Property Initiative Act of 1920.) The alien land law was held unconstitutional by the California Supreme Court in 1952 in the case of *Sei Fujii* v. *State of California,* cited on p. 12. In 1953 the legislature, recognizing the unconstitutionality of the Act, added a section providing for reimbursement of persons whose property was escheated pursuant to the Act. In 1955 the legislature passed another act providing for the submission to the electors at the general election on November 4, 1956, the proposed repeal of the Alien Land Law, and on the latter date the law was officially repealed.

Enemy aliens. Property rights of enemy aliens are in another category. During World War I the "Trading with the Enemy Act" was enacted to enable the President of the United States to regulate, or cause to be regulated, the transfer of property and credit of persons falling within the meaning of the term "enemy." This legislation provided for an Alien Property Custodian, with authority to seize property in the United States belonging to persons in enemy countries, and to take over, administer, and dispose of such property. Prior to 1941 the United States exercised emergency controls over transactions affecting property owned by nationals of the Axis countries and Axis-occupied countries. When war was declared against Germany, Italy, and Japan in 1941, the wartime controls contained in the Trading with the Enemy Act, as amended, became operative and were enlarged by additional legislation.

Office of Alien Property Custodian. The office of Alien Property Custodian was thereafter established, and by virtue of vesting orders, there was transferred to the Custodian all right, title, or interest in property held by the designated enemy country or national. The "Office of Alien Property" in the Department of Justice subsequently became the successor to the Alien Property Custodian. Dispositions of property by the Director of the Office of Alien Property are considered insurable when evidenced by a deed signed by him or on his behalf, if the procedures prescribed for such disposition have been duly complied with, and if there are no pending judicial proceedings raising a question as to the validity of the vesting of the property in the Alien Property Custodian.

CONVICTS

Another class of persons whose property ownership requires special consideration is that of persons deprived of civil rights, i.e., convicts. Such persons are subject to various disabilities with respect to dealing with property. At common law, conviction of a felony created an attainder in the felon. He suffered a forfeiture of all property and lost all of his civil rights, which loss was referred to as "civil death." Such broad penalties generally do not apply in the United States, although by statute some states, including California, impose civil death as part of the punishment for conviction of a felony. However, these states have given a narrow application to statutes suspending civil rights.

Property rights of convicts. In California, forfeiture of property by reason of conviction of a crime is prohibited, except in cases in which a forfeiture is expressly imposed by law. (Pen. C., Sec. 2604.) Under the provisions of Section 2600 of the Penal Code, a sentence of imprisonment in a state prison for any term less than life sentence suspends all the civil rights of the person so sentenced, and forfeits all public offices and all private trusts, authority, or power during such imprisonment. Under the provisions of Section 2601 of the Penal Code, a person sentenced to imprisonment in a state prison for life is thereafter deemed civilly dead. However, such person is not deprived of his right to inherit property, and certain civil rights may be restored during a person's imprisonment. Such provisions of the Civil Code do not render the persons imprisoned incompetent as witnesses, or incapable of making a will or of making and acknowledging a sale or conveyance of property. Earlier cases indicated that a life convict's estate should be probated just as though he were physically dead, but later cases establish that such a procedure would involve an unlawful forfeiture of property. (*Estate of Donnelly,* 125 Cal. 417.)

Purchase of property by convict. The purchase of property by a convict appears to be within the purview of the suspension of civil rights and civil death, and the courts doubtless would refuse the convict the right to enforce a contract made while the purchaser was under such a disability. However, if a purchase is fully consummated, it appears that no one but the state could question it, and such contract would not be considered void. (*Hall* v. *Hall,* 98 C.A.2d 209.)

Effect of parole or pardon. A person released from a state prison on parole still retains the disabilities of a convict. However, a pardon has the effect of wiping out the conviction and restoring all the rights and privileges of which the person has been deprived. (Pen. C., Sec. 4853.)

AMERICAN INDIANS

Limitations have been imposed on the right of Indians to deal with real property. Under various acts of Congress or treaties, numerous allotments were made to Indians, some allotments providing that the lands should be held by the United States Government in trust for the Indians for a specified period of years, usually twenty-one or twenty-five, and such lands could not be encumbered or alienated during such trust period. In the case of *Spector* v. *Pete,* 157 C.A.2d 432, it was held that an agreement for the sale of real property by a noncompetent Indian, prior to the expiration of the trust period prescribed by federal law, which did not have the approval of the Secretary of the Interior, is void *ab initio* and cannot be the subject of an action for specific performance.

IV. Transfers by attorneys-in-fact

An attorney-in-fact may be vested with certain powers of an owner, including authority to sell and convey real property, and conveyances by an attorney-in-fact are not uncommon. A power of attorney is defined as an instrument in writing whereby one person, designated as the principal, authorizes another person, designated as the attorney-in-fact, to act for him as his agent. The powers granted are determined by the express terms of the instrument itself; they are not implied, except as may be necessary to carry out the powers expressly granted.

SPECIAL OR GENERAL POWERS

The power may be special, limiting the agent to a particular or specific act, such as a power of attorney to convey a particular parcel of real property; or the power may be general, authorizing the agent to transact all business on behalf of the principal. Under the provisions of a general power of attorney, the agent may transfer and convey any property of the principal.

LIMITATIONS OF GENERAL WORDS

General words in a power of attorney are limited and controlled by particular terms. Thus, where the authority to perform specific acts is given, and general words are also employed, the latter are limited to the particular acts authorized.

WHO MAY ACT UNDER A POWER OF ATTORNEY

As a general rule, any person who is competent to contract may execute or act under a power of attorney. However, a person who has interests adverse to those of the principal cannot act as an agent where the principal is without knowledge of such adverse interests.

RECORDATION OF POWER OF ATTORNEY

For the purpose of dealing with real property, the power of attorney must be acknowledged and recorded. When a power of attorney is once recorded, a certified copy may be recorded in other counties with like effect as if the original were recorded.

EXECUTION OF INSTRUMENTS

Where a deed or other instrument is executed by an attorney-in-fact pursuant to a power of attorney, the attorney-in-fact must sign the name of his principal, followed by his own name as attorney-in-fact. (C.C., Sec. 1095.) The principal's name alone should appear in the body of the deed, and the deed then should be executed as follows: "*A.B.* by *C.D.*, his attorney-in-fact." A signature in the following manner is not sufficient: "*C.D.*, attorney-in-fact for *A.B.*"

RESTRICTIONS ON AUTHORITY

Several restrictions on the authority of an attorney-in-fact apply. An attorney-in-fact is prohibited from making a gift deed; or making a deed, mortgage, or release without a valuable consideration; or conveying or mortgaging property on which a declaration of homestead has been filed; or dealing with his principal's property for his own benefit; or deeding his principal's property to himself, or releasing a mortgage made by himself to his principal, or mortgaging his principal's property to himself; or delegating his authority, unless properly authorized.

TERMINATION OF POWER OF ATTORNEY

A power of attorney may be terminated by an express revocation by the principal. The instrument of revocation must be recorded in the same office as the power of attorney. A power of attorney is also terminated by the death of the principal or incapacity of the principal to contract. However, under the provisions of Section 2356 of the Civil Code the authority of an attorney-in-fact is not terminated as to any person entering into any bona fide transaction without actual knowledge of the death or incapacity of the principal.

V. Adverse possession

Adverse possession is a means of acquiring title to real property, after a lapse of time, based on continued possession. In California the occupancy of land for any period of time confers a title which prevails against all except the state and persons having a better title. (C.C., Sec. 1006.) If the occupant maintains adverse possession of the land for the period of time that the owner is given to bring an action for recovery of the land, namely five years, the occupant acquires "title by adverse possession," which title is declared by Section 1007 of the Civil Code to be "sufficient against all" except that property interests dedicated to a public use by a public utility, or dedicated to or owned by the state or any public entity are not subject to adverse possessions (see also p. 108). A new title is created in the adverse possessor, and the title of the record owner is lost.

NECESSITY FOR QUIET TITLE DECREE

Although it has been said that "no title can be better or more absolute" than that acquired by adverse possession (*Woodward* v. *Faris,* 109 Cal. 12), such a title is not considered to be a marketable title (i.e., a title free from reasonable doubt and fairly deducible from the record), which a purchaser can be compelled to accept, until the title is established by judicial proceedings against the record owner. An action to quiet title is the type of proceeding undertaken to establish the title. Upon the recordation of a certified copy of a decree quieting title, the adverse possessor's title becomes a matter of public record.

ELEMENTS OF ADVERSE POSSESSION

The essential elements of adverse possession are set forth in the case of *West* v. *Evans,* 29 Cal.2d 414, as follows: (1) the possession must be by actual occupation and must be open and notorious, i.e., the circumstances of possession must be such as to constitute reasonable notice to the record owner; (2) possession must be hostile to the true owner's title, i.e., not permissive, and must be exclusive; (3) possession must be held under either a claim or right, or a color of title; (4) possession must be continuous and uninterrupted for a minimum period of five years; and (5) the claimant must have paid all taxes levied and assessed during such five-year period.

OCCUPANCY OF LAND

The person taking possession does not have to actually reside on the property; under specified conditions it is possible to acquire title to vacant land by adverse possession. Use of the land for the ordinary purposes for which it is adapted is sufficient, such as its use for agricultural purposes. Personal occupation is not essential; possession may be by a tenant of the one claiming by adverse possession. Actual possession of all of the land claimed is not mandatory if part of the land is occupied under such circumstances as to constitute "constructive possession" of the whole area.

CLAIM OF RIGHT AND COLOR OF TITLE

Adverse possession may be based upon either a *claim of right* or *color of title.* Under a claim of right, the claimant enters as an intruder and remains such as against the true owner, without any bona fide belief, necessarily, in his title. Possession under color of title is based upon some written instrument, judgment, or decree of court that gives an appearance of title, but that is not good title in fact. An example is a deed that describes the land and on its face purports to pass the title, but fails to do so because of a want of title in the person executing the deed, or because the deed is voidable.

Advantage of color of title. If a claim is supported by color of title, there is a marked difference in the extent and character of the possession that will establish an adverse title. Unless the claim is based on color of title, the land is deemed to have been possessed and occupied only where it has been "protected by a substantial enclosure" or where it has been "usually cultivated or improved," and only the land so actually occupied is deemed to have been held and claimed adversely. However, where the claim is supported by color of title, the showing required of actual occupation is less exacting, and the land is deemed to have been actually occupied not only where it has been cultivated, improved, or enclosed, but also where it has been used for other purposes, such as for pasturage or for any ordinary use of the occupant. Furthermore, if some part of the tract of land claimed under color of title is actually occupied in good faith by the claimant, his possession is considered to extend to the whole tract. Thus, the claimant is deemed to be in constructive possession of the entire land described in the color of title, although it is not in his actual possession.

ACTS BREAKING CONTINUITY OF POSSESSION

The requisite continuity of possession by the adverse claimant may be broken at any time during the five-year period by such acts as a reentry into possession by the true owner, or by the commencement of an action of ejectment or to quiet title by the true owner, or by acts on the part of the occupant that recognize the superior title of the true owner, such as the adverse claimant's taking a lease from the true owner.

"TACKING ON" POSSESSION

An adverse claimant does not have to depend solely upon his own possession to establish title by adverse possession; he may "tack on" or add his possession to that of a prior adverse holder to complete the adverse period where there is privity of estate between the two persons, as in the case of a claimant who enters into possession under a conveyance from a prior adverse possessor.

PAYMENT OF TAXES

Regarding payment of taxes, it is not essential that the taxes be paid on time by the adverse claimant. It has been held that a redemption of land sold for delinquent taxes, made in good faith by an adverse claimant while in possession, is a payment of taxes that satisfies the rule. (*Warden* v. *Bailey*, 133 C.A. 383.)

LIMITATIONS ON DOCTRINE OF ADVERSE POSSESSION

There are various exceptions and limitations placed on the doctrine of title by adverse possession. Title by adverse possession cannot be acquired to property devoted to public use, and this rule has been extended by statute to include property owned by certain governmental bodies and agencies in a proprietary capacity. Until the 1935 amendment of Section 1007 of the Civil Code, title to real property held by the state or any of its subdivisions could be lost by adverse possession where the property was held in a proprietary capacity and not reserved for or dedicated to some public use. Effective in 1935, title to real property held by governmental agencies therein described was not subject to adverse possession, regardless of the character of the property or how held. The section was expanded in 1968 to provide that property interests dedicated to a public use by a public utility, or dedicated to or owned by the state or any public entity are not subject to adverse possession.

Torrens title. Under the Land Title Act (Torrens Act), originally adopted in 1914 to provide a special system of land registration, but which was repealed in 1955, title to registered land could not be acquired by adverse possession.

Owner under disability. Owners under certain disabilities, such as minority or insanity, are protected from claims of adverse title by statutory provisions to the effect that the duration of the disability, not to exceed twenty years, is not computed as part of the period prescribed for acquiring adverse title. (C.C.P., Sec. 328.) Under this provision, title by adverse possession cannot be established against an owner who is a minor unless the adverse possession continues until the expiration of five years after the minor attains his majority. The exemption applies, however, only to disabilities existing at the inception of adverse possession. Accordingly, where adverse possession commences against a legal owner not under a disability, the running of the statute is not interrupted by the subsequent adjudication of insanity of the legal owner, or by the death of the legal owner and the descent of the land to a person under a disability.

Limitation based on extent of title claimed. Another limitation arises from the general rule that the extent of the title acquired by adverse possession depends upon the extent of the denial of title in the legal owner. Where a separation of the ownership of the land and the ownership of the minerals has occurred, the possession by the owner of the surface is not considered adverse to the owner of the minerals, and cannot be the basis of an adverse title to the mineral interest. (*Foss* v. *Central Pacific Railroad Co.*, 9 C.A.2d 117.) In the case of *Thompson* v. *Pacific Electric Railway Co.*, 203 Cal. 578, it was held that adverse possession against a life tenant is not adverse to the remaindermen, who do not have a right of possession until the termination of the life estate, at which time the statute begins to run against them.

VI. Condemnation

Land may be acquired in condemnation proceedings through the exercise of the power of eminent domain, which is the sovereign right of the state to take private property for public use upon the payment of just compensation.

STATUTORY PROVISIONS

Various statutes have been enacted in this state authorizing the exercise of the power of eminent domain through special proceedings in a Superior Court. These statutes prescribe (1) who may exercise the right, i.e., cities, counties, the state, and other governmental agencies, as well as corporations and individuals in charge of a public use, such as a public utility or a privately owned school; (2) the purposes for which land may be condemned, i.e., for streets, railroads, drainage, water supply and irrigation, utilities, off-street parking, airports, schools, public buildings and grounds, and the like; (3) the nature of the right or interest acquired, i.e., whether fee or easement; (4) the property that may be taken, i.e., either private property, or public property to be taken for a more necessary public use than that to which the property is already dedicated; and (5) the requisite steps in the proceedings, i.e., the filing of a complaint, issuance of summons, and so on. Under prescribed conditions, an order for immediate possession may be obtained.

In 1965 a new section was added to the Code of Civil Procedure (Sec. 1239.3) whereby counties, cities, port districts and airport districts are permitted to acquire air space or air easements where the taking is necessary to protect the public entity against damage claims arising from the operation of aircraft to and from an airport.

THE UNITED STATES MAY ALSO CONDEMN LAND

The power of eminent domain may also be exercised by the federal government, and various federal statutes authorize agencies of the government to acquire property for the United States by condemnation proceedings brought in the local United States District Court.

CONDITIONS FOR EXERCISE OF RIGHT

Whether the land is taken by an instrumentality of the state or by the United States, two conditions must apply: first, the taking must be for a public use, and second, just compensation, measured by the fair market value of the property, must be paid to the property owner. Also, where the taking is a portion only of the owner's land, the owner may be entitled to damages for loss of value of the portion not taken. This is referred to as "severance damages." In 1965 Section 1248(3) of the Code of Civil Procedure was amended to make it clear that in a partial taking in eminent domain, the value of the benefit conferred upon the portion not taken shall be offset against or deducted from severance damages. However, if the benefit is greater than the severance damages, the benefit shall not be deducted from the value of the portion taken.

The case of *People ex rel. Dept of Public Works* v. *Superior Court*, 68 A.C. 206, decided by the California Supreme Court in February, 1968, presented an unusual situation involving severance damages. The state needed only .65 acre of farm land, but was permitted to condemn an additional 54 acres that would be landlocked in order to avoid payment of excessive severance damages.

Condemnation by private school. The case of *University of Southern California* v. *Robbins*, 1 C.A.2d 523, raised a question as to whether or not the taking of property by a private school for school purposes constituted a public use. The court held that it did.

CONDEMNATION BY PRIVATE INDIVIDUAL

Section 1001 of the Civil Code provides that any person may maintain an action to acquire property by eminent domain; thus a private individual may maintain such an action. This right was recognized in the case of *Linggi* v. *Garovotti,* 45 Cal.2d 20, which was an action to condemn a right of way for a sewer line over adjoining land used for residence purposes.

REPLACEMENT HOUSING

In 1968 new sections were added to the Street and Highways Code (Secs. 135.3-135.7) and to the Health and Safety Code (Sec. 37110.5) to provide for relocation assistance, and to authorize the Department of Public Works to acquire, either in fee or in a lesser estate or interest, real property to provide replacement housing, for low-income people who reside in economically depressed areas and are displaced by acquisition for a project on the state highway system. Such acquisition is called a public purpose and use. With respect to "any unimproved or unoccupied real property, or real property not devoted primarily to residential use," no restriction is made upon the mode of acquisition, but all other property acquired for such purpose shall be acquired by means other than condemnation.

WHETHER FEE OR EASEMENT CONDEMNED

Where the *fee title* to land is condemned for a particular public use, the general rule is that the former owner retains no reversionary or other interest, and such use may be changed or abandoned. Following proper abandonment, the land can be disposed of by the government agency in any manner provided by law, without limitation as to any rights of the former owner. However, where an *easement* only is condemned, the title to the underlying fee remains in the land owner, and upon abandonment of the public use, the original owner or his successor owns the land, free of public use.

INVERSE CONDEMNATION

Sometimes public works are undertaken with resulting damage to private property but no condemnation action is filed by the public body. In such a situation the property owner may initiate an action himself to recover damages. Such an action is referred to as an "inverse" condemnation action.

VII. Dedication

Easements may be acquired by dedication, and the fee title may also be acquired in such manner. *Dedication* is defined as the devotion of land to a public use by an unequivocal act of the fee owner manifesting an intention that the land shall be accepted and used for such public purpose. A conveyance of land to a city "for park purposes" is an example. A dedication may be either a *statutory* or a *common-law* dedication, the distinction being explained in the chapter on easements (Chapter 5).

NATURE OF INTEREST CREATED—WHETHER FEE OR EASEMENT

The nature of the interest created in the public by statutory dedication is usually specified by the statute, the Subdivision Map Act of 1929 providing, for instance, that a dedication "shall convey an easement when a public body can condemn for such purpose only an easement, but in all other cases said dedication shall convey a fee simple estate subject to the terms of the dedication." Other map acts, including the present Subdivision Map Act, do not specify which particular interest is conferred by dedication. It has been stated, however, that "the public acquires the same rights in property by dedication as by condemnation." (*Washington Boulevard Beach Co.* v. *City of Los Angeles,* 38 C.A.2d 135.) In applying this rule, it has been held that the dedication of a park vested the fee title in the government agency. It is doubtful, though, that in all cases the fee title acquired by dedication, which normally is a donation, is the same as the fee title acquired by condemnation, which requires the payment of compensation for the value of the land taken.

LIMITATION ON USE OF LAND ACQUIRED BY DEDICATION

Where the fee title to land is condemned for a public use, the public body may, as a rule, thereafter abandon such use and devote the land to another use. But the fee acquired by dedication may be considered to be a qualified or determinable fee, with the original owner retaining an interest in the nature of a possibility of reverter upon abandonment of the dedicated public use. This would appear to preclude the public body from diverting such use, or from leasing or otherwise disposing of the land for purposes inconsistent with the dedicated use. (*Hall* v. *Fairchild-Gilmore-Wilton Co.,* 66 C.A. 615.)

DEDICATION OF PUBLIC LANDS

A public body, as well as a private owner, may dedicate its land for a particular use. Thus, a city council may pass a resolution declaring a certain area of city-owned lands to be a public park. By dedicating lands owned in fee to a park use, a city does not purport to deprive itself of the power to change the use and devote the land to another purpose. (*Spinks* v. *City of Los Angeles,* 220 Cal. 366.)

Change in use of dedicated lands. The latter case involved the right or power of the city to extend a street through West Lake Park, the land having been owned in fee by the city and dedicated as a public park. The court pointed out the distinction between cases where land has been donated for park purposes, and cases where land owned in fee has been dedicated to such uses, and stated that the city is only dedicating its own property to a different public use than that to which it had been previously subjected. The court upheld the right of a municipality to thus meet changing conditions, and the right of the city to use a portion of the park lands for street purposes.

SUBSURFACE USE OF PARK PROPERTY

The case of *City and County of San Francisco* v. *Linares,* 16 Cal. 2d 441, involved the subsurface use of Union Square Park as a public automobile garage and parking station. In upholding the right of the city to make such use of the park, the court stated that there was nothing in the terms of the original grant of Union Square that would deprive the City and County of San Francisco of the right to change the character of the use of the land so long as the contemplated use was not inconsistent with enjoyment by the public of the land for park purposes.

VIII. Accession

Accession as a method of acquisition of title may occur by annexation, by accretion, or by reliction.

ANNEXATION

Annexation occurs when a person affixes his property to the land of another, without an agreement permitting him to remove it. The thing so affixed belongs to the owner of the land, unless the land owner requires its removal.

INNOCENT IMPROVER OF LAND

What is the rule where a fixture may have been installed by a stranger or a trespasser? Prior to 1953, California followed the common-law rule under which things affixed to land by a stranger or trespasser, without an agreement permitting removal, belonged to the owner of the land. Under this rule, the intention of the person making the improvement did not control, and many persons, under a mistake as to the location of their property, materially improved another person's land without any recourse when the mistake was ascertained. This harsh rule, however, was held inapplicable in cases where the improvements were made by a public service corporation or a public agency, or where the improvements were made by a person under a mistaken belief of ownership and the real owner, having notice of the error and the work, made no effort to prevent continuance of the work. Under this latter principle, an innocent improver of another person's land has been allowed restitution for the value of the labor and materials. (*Burrow* v. *Carley,* 210 Cal. 95.)

Statutory rule. The strict rule as to ownership of things mistakenly affixed to another person's land was modified by statutory enactment in 1953. Section 1013.5 of the Civil Code, added in 1953, provides that a person who affixes improvements to the land of another, in good faith and erroneously believing, because of a mistake of law or fact, that he has a right to do so, may remove the improvements upon payment of all damages proximately resulting from the affixing and removal of such improvements. Such payment is required to be made to the owner of the land and to any other person having an interest in the land who acquired such interest for value in reliance on such improvements.

In 1968 the Code of Civil Procedure was amended to define a "good faith improver" and giving such person, where existing forms of relief are inadequate, relief for improvements made on the land of another in the mistaken belief that the improver owns the land. It is provided that in any action brought pursuant to the new law, the court may adjust the rights, equities, and interests of the good faith improver, the owner of the land and other interested parties, including but not limited to lessees, lienholders, and encumbrancers.

ACCRETION AND RELICTION

Acquisition of title by accession may also be in the form of accretion, which is defined as the process of gradual and imperceptible addition to land bordering on a river or stream, caused by the action of the water in washing up sand, earth, and other materials. (C.C., Sec. 1014.) The land formed as the result of accretion is called *alluvion.* It also includes land that has been covered by water, but that has become uncovered by the gradual recession of the water. This latter process is known as *reliction.* The added land becomes the property of the owner of the land to which it is added. The same rule applies to land fronting on the ocean.

ACCRETION DISTINGUISHED FROM AVULSION

Accretion is to be distinguished from *avulsion,* which occurs when a river or stream, navigable or nonnavigable, by sudden violence carries away a part of the bank of the river or stream, and bears it to the opposite bank or to another part of the same bank. In such case the owner of the part carried away may reclaim it within one year after the owner of the land to which it has been united takes possession thereof.

ALLUVION MUST BE CREATED BY NATURAL CAUSES

For land to be alluvion it must be created by natural causes. It has been held that land created by an addition resulting from any cause whatsoever other than natural causes is not the property of the adjoining or upland owner. (*Carpenter* v. *City of Santa Monica,* 63 C.A.2d 772; *Los Angeles Athletic Club* v. *City of Santa Monica,* 63 C.A.2d 795.) In a controversy between the state or its grantees and the upland owner, artificial accretions (so-called) belong to the state or its grantees as the owner of the tidelands.

WATERLINE BOUNDARY DESCRIPTIONS

Under the doctrine that alluvion formed by accretion to land having a waterline boundary belongs to the owner as part of his land, a conveyance of the land by a description calling for a waterline boundary will ordinarily carry title to any alluvion formed prior to the conveyance, unless a different intent is expressed in the grant. This conclusion results from the rule that where a waterline is the boundary of a given parcel, that line, no matter how it shifts, remains the boundary.

IX. Escheat

Title by escheat is the method by which title to property reverts to the state as the original owner. If a person owning property dies without leaving a will and without heirs, title to the property escheats to the state of California. (Pro. C., Sec. 231.) The estate of a decedent may also escheat to the state where the heirs are nonresident aliens and reciprocal rights do not exist. (Pro. C., Sec. 259.) Formerly, under the Alien Land Law, the property acquired by an alien ineligible to citizenship also escheated to the state of California.

ESCHEATS ARE NOT FAVORED

Escheats are not favored, and unless there is an express provision therefor, the right of the state to have property escheat to it does not exist. Escheat for lack of known heirs is not automatic in California.

There is a presumption that every decedent left heirs, and a proceeding is required to judicially declare the fact of escheat. (Pro. C., Sec. 1027; C.C.P., Secs. 1300–1575.)

X. Involuntary alienation

Title by involuntary alienation includes transfers effected through judicial proceedings pursuant to judgments or decrees, such as execution sales, and transfers by operation of law, under statutes such as the Bankruptcy Act (11 U.S.C.A., Secs. 1 *et seq.*). Execution sales and sales in proceedings to foreclose involuntary liens, such as federal tax liens, are considered in detail in Chapter 15. Proceedings in bankruptcy and their effect on title will now be considered.

BANKRUPTCY PROCEEDINGS

A bankruptcy proceeding is one initiated in a United States District Court under the federal statutes whereby an insolvent debtor may be adjudged bankrupt by the court, which thereupon takes possession of his property, and administers it in accordance with the provisions of the bankruptcy law, and distributes whatever assets there may be proportionately amongst the creditors in accordance with their respective rights.

Vesting of title in trustee in bankruptcy. A petition for adjudication may be filed either by the debtor or by the requisite number of creditors. The petition is referred by the court to a Referee in Bankruptcy, who is authorized to make orders and decrees, subject to a right of appeal to the court. A trustee is appointed by the referee, and upon his qualification, the trustee is vested by operation of law with all of the bankrupt's property (subject to certain exemptions), as of the date of filing of the petition.

Property that vests in trustee. As to property that vests in the bankrupt within six months after bankruptcy by bequest, devise, or inheritance, title vests in the trustee as of the date when it would become vested in the bankrupt. The property that vests in the trustee includes any property, unless exempt by law, that, prior to the filing of the petition, the bankrupt could by any means have transferred, or that might have been levied upon and sold under judicial process against him, or otherwise seized, impounded, or sequestered.

Other interests that vest in trustee. Property transferred by the bankrupt in fraud of creditors also vests in the trustee. Also included are contingent remainders, executory devises or limitations, right of entry for condition broken, rights or possibilities of reverter, and similar interests in real property, that were nonassignable prior to bankruptcy and that within six months thereafter became assignable interests in estates or give rise to powers in the bankrupt to acquire assignable interests in estates.

Property located outside the state. Title passes to the trustee by operation of law regardless of where the property is located. Thus, land located in California passes to and may be administered upon by a trustee appointed in a proceedings instituted in the state of New York or in some other state. No ancillary proceedings in California are necessary.

Property not scheduled. Property owned by the bankrupt at the time of filing the petition and not scheduled among the assets of the estate remains subject to the jurisdiction of the court, where necessary to pay debts, even after the discharge of the trustee. The proceedings may be reopened and a new trustee appointed to administer such property.

Exempt property. Title to property that is exempt by state law, such as the homestead law, remains in the bankrupt, awaiting the legal formality of having it appraised and set apart to him. Where property is properly claimed as exempt, an order is obtained setting it apart to the bankrupt, and a certified copy recorded. Title to such property thereupon vests in the bankrupt, free from the effect of the bankruptcy proceedings.

Burdensome property. The trustee is not required to take title to burdensome property, such as property subject to liens in excess of its value. An order may be made releasing such property from the jurisdiction of the court, and title thereupon revests in the bankrupt.

Valid liens not affected. Outstanding valid liens on real property of the bankrupt existing prior to the adjudication are not disturbed by the bankruptcy proceedings, and title to the property passes to the trustee subject to such liens. The trustee, however, has the right to contest their validity by appropriate proceedings. Such contest may be made on the ground that the lien was fraudulently obtained; that it involved a preference; that it was obtained within four months of bankruptcy and is void under Section 67 of the Bankruptcy Act; or the lien may be avoided on any other proper ground, such as lack of consideration.

Effect on community property. Upon adjudication of a married man as a bankrupt, all of the community property, unless exempt, passes to the possession of the trustee for the benefit of creditors of the community, and may be administered upon by the trustee in bankruptcy. Upon adjudication of a married woman, her separate estate passes to the trustee for the purpose of administration, but her interest in the community property is not accquired by the trustee in bankruptcy.

Effect on power of sale under a deed of trust. Where the power of sale under a deed of trust is to be exercised on property passing to a trustee in bankruptcy, it is necessary that leave of the bankruptcy court be first obtained in order to effect a valid sale by the trustee under the deed of trust.

Sale of property by trustee in bankruptcy. Subject to approval of the court, the trustee in bankruptcy may effect a sale of the bankrupt's property acquired by the trustee. Although the Bankruptcy Act contains no express provision conferring upon the court the power to sell property *free of liens* and to transfer such liens to the proceeds of sale, it has been held that as to property in the possession of the court, this power exists by implication (*Van Huffel* v. *Harkelrode,* 284 U.S. 225), and such sales are not uncommon.

Effect of discharge in bankruptcy. If the bankrupt obtains his discharge, this operates to release him from all of his provable debts, except taxes which became due within three years preceding bankruptcy, liabilities for obtaining money or property by false pretenses or false representations, or for wilful or malicious injuries, or for alimony or child support, or for certain types of wages earned within three months of bankruptcy, and other similar obligations.

Effect of discharge on judgments. Judgments based upon debts not within the excepted classes may be ignored for title purposes as to property acquired by the bankrupt *after* bankruptcy, if the judgments have been properly scheduled, and if the judgment debtor has been properly discharged in bankruptcy.

XI. Title by estoppel

Title to real property may pass by an equitable estoppel where justice requires that this be done. The principle of equitable estoppel sometimes applied in cases involving title to real property is this: where the true owner permits another person to appear either as the owner of the property or as having full power of disposition over it, an innocent third party who is led into dealing with the apparent owner will be protected by a court of equity against the claims of the true owner whose conduct made the fraud possible. (*Davis* v. *Davis,* 26 Cal. 23; *Butler* v. *Woodburn,* 19 Cal.2d 420).

AFTER-ACQUIRED TITLE

Another situation where title is based on estoppel involves an after-acquired title. The general rule is stated as follows: if the grantor in a conveyance of real property has no title, a defective title, or an estate less than that which he assumes to grant, but subsequently acquires the title or estate that he purported to convey, or perfects his title, such after-acquired or perfected title will inure to the grantee or his successors by way of estoppel, i.e., the grantor is estopped to deny that such after-acquired title passed by his conveyance. (*Clark* v. *Baker*, 14 Cal. 612.)

Statutory rule. This general rule, less broadly stated, has been codified in California in Section 1106 of the Civil Code, which provides:

> Where a person purports by proper instrument to grant real property in fee simple, and subsequently acquires any title, or claim of title thereto, the same passes by operation of law to the grantee, or his successors.

TYPES OF DEEDS SUFFICIENT TO RAISE AN ESTOPPEL

Under the general rule of estoppel, a grantor may be estopped even though the deed does not use the word "grant." A warranty deed or bargain and sale deed or other form of deed in which the operative words of transfer may be "bargain, sell and convey," or "sell and convey," or words of similar import that do not express or imply an intent to quitclaim merely a present interest, may be deemed sufficient to raise an estoppel. (*Estate of Wilson*, 40 C.A.2d 229.) Conversely, all grant deeds do not of necessity transfer after-acquired title; a grant deed that purports to convey merely the present interest of the grantor will not pass title afterwards acquired by the grantor. (*Emeric* v. *Alvarado*, 90 Cal. 444.)

LIMITATION ON AFTER-ACQUIRED TITLE DOCTRINE

The rule as to after-acquired title does not prevent the grantor from asserting a title subsequently acquired by him by voluntary conveyance from his grantee; or by adverse possession; or by tax deed unless the sale is for taxes that were a lien at the time of the original conveyance and not excepted from the conveyance; or by judicial sale; or by foreclosure sale under a lien created by the grantee, or a lien existing at the time of the original conveyance but excepted in such conveyance.

XII. Abandonment

Title by abandonment and title by forfeiture, strictly speaking, are not methods of transferring title from one person to another, but they do result in the extinguishment of a right or interest in favor of another and are frequently encountered in title work.

NATURE OF ABANDONMENT

Abandonment consists of a voluntary giving up of a thing by the owner because he no longer desires to possess it or to assert any right or dominion over it. It is the relinquishment of a right, the giving up of something to which one is entitled.

PROPERTY SUBJECT TO ABANDONMENT

As a general rule, personal property may be abandoned by the owner, but as to real property, a fee title cannot be divested by abandonment. However, in a unique case where a portion of a concrete foundation slid onto adjoining land as the result of an earthquake, such portion of the foundation was found to be abandoned so that the owner of the adjoining land was justified in making use of it. (*Kafka* v. *Bozio*, 191 Cal. 746.) This principle might be of importance in hilly areas where the surface of lots tends to creep downward. As to other rights in real property, the general rule is that easements, licenses, mining claims, and other rights regarded as incorporeal hereditaments may be divested by abandonment. Thus, an ordinary lease of land for years is a chattel real, which is personal property, and as such is capable of abandonment.

In 1968 the California Supreme Court, in the case of *Gerhard* v. *Stephens*, 68 A.C. 927, a case of first impression, held that the exclusive and perpetual privilege of drilling for oil and gas in California is a *profit à prendre*, an incorporeal hereditament, and is subject to abandonment. The court pointed out that the rulings in previous cases that a "fee" interest in real property cannot be abandoned are explainable upon an analysis of the particular facts involved. In these cases the court concerned itself with title to *corporeal* real property. In this latest case the court decided that incorporeal interests, as distinguished from corporeal ones, may be abandoned, whatever their life, whether limited or unlimited in time, whether "fee" or a term, and whether perpetual or restricted.

LAND CONTRACT

The interest of the vendee under a land sales contract may be abandoned. As stated in the case of *Carden* v. *Carden*, 167 C.A.2d 202, under the common law any title to an interest in land other than a fee simple estate may be abandoned, hence equitable rights in land may be abandoned.

XIII. Forfeiture

NATURE OF FORFEITURE

A forfeiture is a divestiture or loss of property without compensation in consequence of a default. A forfeiture is entirely distinct from an abandonment in that a forfeiture arises from the operation of facts and circumstances independently of any question of intent, whereas an intention to part with ownership is a necessary element of abandonment.

PROPERTY SUBJECT TO FORFEITURE

Fee title may be lost by virtue of a breach of a condition in a deed, or the leasehold estate of a lessee may be lost by breach of a condition of the lease, or the interest of a contract buyer may be extinguished by forfeiture for breach of the conditions of the land sales contract. Although a breach of a condition on which an estate is granted gives the grantor or lessor a right to terminate or forfeit the estate, the breach of condition does not alone terminate the estate. It is necessary for the grantor or lessor or his successors to enter the estate or bring an action for recovery of possession or do some other act equivalent to entry.

Questions

1. How is the word "title" defined?
2. Describe the modes of acquiring title to property as specified in the Civil Code.
3. Define a deed.
4. Explain the two forms of deed customarily used in California.
5. Discuss the essential requirements of a deed.
6. Are any warranties implied from the use of a grant deed?
7. How must the grantee be designated in the deed?
8. Give three illustrations of void deeds.
9. How may a deed be executed if the grantor is unable to write?
10. What are the main purposes of an acknowledgment on a deed?
11. Explain what is meant by "delivery" of a deed.
12. Is a transfer of title to a minor or an incompetent person valid?
13. Are aliens permitted to own land in California?
14. Does conviction of a crime result in a forfeiture of title to real property?
15. Explain the use of a general power of attorney.
16. May an attorney-in-fact execute a deed in favor of himself?
17. Describe briefly the elements of adverse possession.
18. Is title acquired by adverse possession marketable?
19. Under what conditions may title be acquired by condemnation?
20. Explain how title is acquired by dedication.
21. Illustrate how title is acquired by accession.
22. If chattels are affixed by a stranger to the realty title, under what circumstances may he remove them?
23. What do the terms "accretion" and "reliction" signify?
24. Under what circumstances does title escheat?
25. Give an example of a transfer by operation of law.
26. When is the doctrine of "title by estoppel" applicable?

8

Methods of Ownership

Summary

I. Introductory

Consideration will be given in this chapter not only to various forms of real property ownership that may be used in the acquisition of a residence, but also to ownership by entities for commercial or business purposes, and multiple ownership encountered in housing developments.

SOLE OWNERS AND CO-OWNERS

Real property may be owned by a sole owner, or it may be owned jointly by two or more persons. A person who is the sole owner of a parcel of real property is said to be the owner thereof *in severalty*. Where there are more owners than one, their ownership (referred to generally as *co-ownership*) may be in one of many ways.

TYPES OF JOINT OWNERSHIP

Under the provisions of Section 682 of the Civil Code, four types of joint ownership are recognized in California, namely, joint tenancy, tenancy in common, tenancy in partnership, and community property. Each type of co-ownership has distinct characteristics, and a knowledge of the legal effects of the different forms of ownership is essential to anyone acquiring real property in California, particularly as to the acquisition of title by husband and wife.

II. Joint tenancy ownership

A joint tenancy estate is regarded as a single estate held by two or more persons jointly, such joint tenants holding as though they collectively constituted but one person, a fictitious unity. The main characteristic of a joint tenancy is the right of survivorship. When a joint tenant dies, his interest in the land is terminated, and the estate continues in the survivor or survivors. When there is but one survivor, the estate becomes an estate in severalty, and upon the death of this last survivor, title vests in his heirs or devisees.

STATUTORY DEFINITION

A joint tenancy estate is defined in Section 683 of the Civil Code as follows:

> A joint interest is one owned by two or more persons in equal shares, by a title created by a single will or transfer, when expressly declared in the will or transfer to be a joint tenancy, or by transfer from a sole owner to himself and others, or from tenants in common or joint tenants to themselves or some of them, or to themselves or any of them and others, or from a husband and wife, when holding title as community property or otherwise to themselves or to themselves and others or to one of them and to another or others, when expressly declared in the transfer to be a joint tenancy, or when granted or devised to executors or trustees as joint tenants. . . .

CREATION OF JOINT TENANCY

The usual method of creation of a joint tenancy is by a deed describing the grantee as follows: "to *A* and *B*, *as joint tenants.*" The words "with right of survivorship" are often added, but are not a requisite, since this right is an incident of a joint tenancy, whether expressly recited or not. Although it has been held that the particular words of the statute, i.e., "in joint tenancy" or "as joint tenants," are not essential where the words used show clearly an intent to create a joint tenancy, the cases are not in agreement as to what words are sufficient. To avoid any uncertainty, it is preferable that the words "as joint tenants" be expressed in the deed or other instruments of creation. The words "to *A or B*," or "to *A* and *B*, *jointly*," are not considered sufficient to create a joint tenancy interest in real property.

Effect where conveyance is insufficient to create a joint tenancy. Where a conveyance is made purporting to create a joint tenancy in two or more persons, and the joint tenancy fails because it does not otherwise meet the requirements for creation of a joint tenancy, the conveyance, as a rule, is not wholly ineffective, but operates to pass title to the grantees as tenants in common.

Four unities essential. At common law, four unities were considered essential in the creation of a joint tenancy, namely, unity of *time, title, interest,* and *possession.* This requirement was based on the concept that joint tenants take *as one* in a fictitious *unity.* Accordingly, they must have identical interests, acquired at the same time and by the same instrument. The code definition of a joint tenancy embraces the four unities, and the courts in California have frequently stated that the four unities are essential if a joint tenancy is to exist. (*Yeoman* v. *Sawyer,* 99 C.A.2d 43.)

Unity of title. The necessity for unity of title is expressed in the code requirement that a joint tenancy be created by a "single will or transfer." If *A* conveys land to *B,* and *B* thereafter conveys to *B* and *C* as joint tenants, this would not create a valid joint tenancy at common law, because *B*'s interest in the land arises under the deed from *A,* and *C*'s interest arises under the later deed; thus, the interests do not accrue by the same and a single transfer.

Modification of rule in California. This rule has been modified in California to permit the creation of joint tenancies by direct transfer in the instances specified in Section 683 of the Civil Code. A joint tenancy conveyance may be made from a "sole owner to himself and others," or from joint owners to themselves and others as specified in the code. Formerly, where one of the proposed joint tenants already owned an interest in the property, it was necessary for the purpose of creating a valid joint tenancy that the property be conveyed to a disinterested third party (a strawman), who then conveyed the title to the ultimate grantees as joint tenants. The statute has been liberalized with the result that few situations arise today where the use of a strawman is essential.

Joint tenancy by a married person. Where a married man contributes community funds to the purchase of real property, and takes title in joint tenancy with a person other than his wife, the attempted creation of a joint tenancy may be invalid. In such a case, the essential unity of interest is lacking. The interests created under the deed are considered to be a one-half interest in the married man and his wife *as their community property,* and a one-half interest in the other grantee. This results in an inequality of interest which defeats the joint tenancy. If a married woman uses community funds to acquire title in joint tenancy with a person other than her husband, the attempted joint tenancy may also be considered ineffective.

Special recitals. Before insuring the sufficiency of joint tenancies created between a married person and another, title insurance companies usually require the written consent of the other spouse. This consent may be evidenced by the following recital in the joint tenancy deed: "John Doe and Jane Doe, husband and wife, consent to the creation of a joint tenancy in the grantees above named in the property herein described." Special recitals are also required in conveyances from a third person to husband and wife and one or more other persons as joint tenants.

Joint tenancies with persons under a disability. If one of the grantees in a joint tenancy deed is a minor or an incompetent person, and funds of the minor or incompetent person are used in the purchase of the property, the joint tenancy is questionable. An agreement by the minor or incompetent to take title in joint tenancy would be void or voidable under the usual rules governing contracts of persons under disability. Insofar as guardianship proceedings are concerned, there is no statutory provision for a guardian to take title on behalf of his ward in joint tenancy with a third party. However, if the interest of the person under disability is based on a gift, such as a gift deed from a parent to a minor child and others as joint tenants, the joint tenancy appears to be unobjectionable.

NATURE OF OWNERSHIP AS BETWEEN HUSBAND AND WIFE

Problems have frequently arisen regarding the true character of the ownership of property by husband and wife held of record as joint tenants. Frequently such property, despite the record ownership, has been treated as community property for purposes of succession, transfer, disposition in divorce, or seizure by creditors. Joint tenancy and community property are separate and distinct forms of ownership. It has been held that where husband and wife elect to take title as joint tenants, this is "tantamount to a binding agreement between them that the same shall not thereafer be held as community property but instead as a joint tenancy with all the characteristics of such an estate." (*Siberell* v. *Siberell,* 214 Cal. 767.)

Qualification of rule. The Supreme Court has qualified the application of the foregoing rule to cases where there is "an absence of any evidence to the contrary." This phrase is the foundation for a long line of decisions holding that evidence is admissible to show that husband and wife who took title as joint tenants actually intended it to be community property. This intention may be evidenced by an oral agreement at the time the property was acquired. Also, it may be shown that property taken in joint tenancy was thereafter converted into community property by either an oral or a written agreement. (*Tomaier* v. *Tomaier,* 23 Cal.2d 754.)

Effect where joint tenancy property is community property. The contention that joint tenancy property is in fact community property is often raised in divorce cases. The court does not have the power to make an award of separate property, but if it is established that joint tenancy property is in fact community property, the court may award such property to the innocent spouse. As an aid to the innocent spouse, the legislature amended Section 164 of the Civil Code in 1965 to provide that a single family residence acquired by husband and wife during marriage as joint tenants is presumed to be community property for the purpose of the division of such property upon divorce or separate maintenance.

A claim that joint tenancy property is actually community property may also be raised by creditors of the husband in appropriate proceedings. If it can be shown that joint tenancy property was acquired with community funds, a creditor may be permitted to enforce the judgment against all of the purported joint tenancy property rather than against the husband's interest alone. (*Hulse* v. *Lawson*, 212 Cal. 614.) Devisees of a deceased joint tenant may also be able to establish that the joint tenancy property is actually community property and therefore subject to testamentary disposition by the decedent. (*Huber* v. *Huber*, 27 Cal.2d 784.)

SURVIVORSHIP ASPECT

The distinguishing characteristic of joint tenancy property is the right of survivorship. When a joint tenant dies, title to the property immediately vests in the survivor or surviving joint tenant. As a consequence, joint tenancy property is not subject to testamentary disposition. Since title vests immediately upon death in the survivor, there is no estate remaining upon which the will of the deceased joint tenant can operate. The surviving joint tenant holds the whole estate free from debts and creditors' claims against the deceased joint tenant. This immunity from debts extends to liens, such as a deed of trust, created by the deceased joint tenant alone on his interest. (*Hammond* v. *McArthur*, 30 Cal.2d 512.)

Proceedings to establish fact of death. Although conventional probate proceedings are unnecessary, court proceedings may be necessary for the purpose of determining the amount of inheritance taxes due upon the death of a joint tenant (see Chapter 23). A joint tenancy does not avoid payment of inheritance taxes; in some situations it may result in an increase in taxes.

Effect of simultaneous death. The chief incident of and main reason for joint tenancy, i.e., survivorship, may be lost in a situation that sometimes occurs, namely, simultaneous death of the joint tenants. Under the provisions of the simultaneous death law, if there is no sufficient evidence that two joint tenants have died otherwise than simultaneously, the probate court may determine such fact by an order to that effect. The property is then administered upon, and distributed or otherwise dealt with, one half as if one had survived, and one half as if the other had survived. If more than two joint tenants died simultaneously, the same procedure is applicable, with each tenant's estate having an interest in proportion to the whole number of joint tenants.

EFFECT OF MURDER OR VOLUNTARY MANSLAUGHTER

It has been held that a joint tenant who has caused the wrongful death of the other joint tenant, such as by murder or voluntary manslaughter, cannot succeed to the interest of the deceased joint tenant. (*Abbey* v. *Lord*, 168 C.A.2d 499).

TRANSFERS BY A JOINT TENANT

During the lifetime of the joint tenants, either or any of them may sever the joint tenancy as to his interest by a conveyance to a third party. If there are two joint tenants, the joint tenancy is terminated by such conveyance; if there are three or more joint tenants, the joint tenancy is severed as to the interest conveyed and continues as between the other joint tenants as to the remaining interest. If title is in *A* and *B* as joint tenants, and *A* conveys to *C*, *B* and *C* then own as tenants in common. If title is in *A*, *B*, and *C* as joint tenants, and *A* conveys to *D*, then *B* and *C* continue as joint tenants as to a two-thirds interest, and *D* owns a one-third interest as tenant in common. In the case of *Clark* v. *Carter*, 265 C.A. 2d 291, a joint tenant attempted to sever the joint tenancy by a conveyance to herself. It was held that the deed was invalid, since the grantee was the same person as the grantor.

LEASE BY A JOINT TENANT

Questions sometimes arise as to whether or not an act other than a conveyance of the fee by one joint tenant will sever the joint tenancy. One joint tenant has the right to lease his interest for a term of years, but it is uncertain as to whether or not the lease effects a severance of the joint tenancy. For instance, where *A* and *B* are joint tenants, and *A* leases to *C* for a term of ten years, leaving the reversion in *A* as to his share, a question is presented as to whether such reversion vests in *B* upon *A*'s death during the leasehold term, or vests in *A*'s heirs or devisees. If the lease expires during the lifetime of *A*, a further question arises as to whether or not the joint tenancy, if severed by the lease, would revive. In the case of *Verdier* v. *Verdier*, 152 C.A.2d 348, it was held that when a joint tenant leases to a third party he confers upon the latter the same right of possession that he himself has, but the question of possible severance of the joint tenancy by the lease was not considered.

CONTRACTS OF SALE AND ENCUMBRANCES

A joint tenancy is severed by a contract of sale executed by one of the joint tenants, since the contract effects a transfer of the equitable title to the vendee. However, a contract of sale executed by all of the joint tenants in favor of a third party does not terminate the joint tenancy in the absence of such intent. (*County of Fresno* v. *Kahn,* 207 C.A.2d 213.) Also, the execution of a mortgage or deed of trust on the interest of one joint tenant creates only a lien or charge, and does not in itself effect a severance of the joint tenancy. (*People* v. *Nogarr,* 164 C.A.2d 591.) If the mortgage or deed of trust is foreclosed during the lifetime of the joint tenant executing the encumbrance, the transfer by foreclosure sale would result in a severance of the joint tenancy.

JUDGMENTS AGAINST A JOINT TENANT

The lien created by the recordation of an abstract of judgment against one of the joint tenants does not sever the joint tenancy, but an execution sale during the lifetime of the judgment debtor does effect a severance. It has been held that a judgment lien against one joint tenant ceases where the debtor dies prior to levy of a writ of execution, and the surviving joint tenant holds the property free of the lien. (*Zeigler* v. *Bonnell,* 52 C.A.2d 217.)

BANKRUPTCY OF A JOINT TENANT

If one joint tenant is adjudicated a bankrupt, the involuntary transfer of his interest to the trustee in bankruptcy operates to effect a severance of the joint tenancy, unless the interest is subject to a valid homestead.

AGREEMENTS AFFECTING JOINT TENANCY

A joint tenancy may be terminated not only by an express agreement to that effect, but also by an agreement between the joint tenants that so operates upon one or more of the elements of the joint tenancy as to cause a severance. (*Wardlow* v. *Pozzi,* 170 C.A.2d 208.) For example, an agreement "that if either joint tenant dies, the interest of that one shall go to a third party," destroys the element of survivorship, and terminates the joint tenancy. The title thereafter vests in the parties as tenants in common.

SEVERANCE BY MUTUAL WILLS

In the case of *Chase* v. *Leiter,* 96 C.A.2d 439, the court stated that where title is in husband and wife as joint tenants, they may convert the tenancy into community property or into a tenancy in common by the execution by both of them of an agreement or a deed to themselves for that express purpose, and the joint tenancy may also be severed by mutual wills.

AGREEMENTS AS TO POSSESSION

A question sometimes arises in divorce proceedings as to whether or not the provisions of a property settlement agreement under which one party is given the exclusive right of occupancy of joint tenancy property will terminate the joint tenancy. It has been held that this is primarily a question of intention. The right of possession, which must be an equal right at the time of creation of the joint tenancy, can be modified by an agreement entered into subsequent to the creation of the joint tenancy without severing the joint tenancy. (*Cole* v. *Cole*, 139 C.A.2d 691.)

ADVANTAGES AND DISADVANTAGES OF JOINT TENANCY

Joint tenancies have advantages and disadvantages, depending upon the particular circumstances. The main advantage is, of course, the incident of survivorship, eliminating the time and expense of probate proceedings. The fact that the surviving joint tenant holds title free from debts and claims against the deceased joint tenant, even when secured by deed of trust or other encumbrance, is another distinct advantage to the survivor. Disadvantages as compared with other methods of holding title include the following: (1) the possibility that the joint tenancy may be severed at any time by a transfer, voluntarily or by operation of law, of one cotenant's interest; (2) the fact that the joint tenant who dies first has no power of testamentary disposition over such property; (3) as between married joint tenants, the fact that the divorce court cannot award the true joint tenancy property to the innocent spouse; (4) the tax consequences, both as to estate and income taxes, may be unfavorable; (5) no provision exists for administering the estate of a joint tenant who has been missing for seven years and who is presumed to be dead.

III. Tenancy in common

A tenancy in common is characterized by only one unity, that of possession. The cotenants own undivided interests, but unlike a joint tenancy, these interests need not be equal in quantity or duration, and may arise from different conveyances and at different times. There is no right of survivorship; each tenant owns an interest which on his death vests in his heirs or devisees.

DEFINITION OF A TENANCY IN COMMON

A tenancy in common is defined in the code in a negative manner. Section 686 of the Civil Code provides that a tenancy in common arises whenever property, real or personal, or an interest therein, is transferred, whether by conveyance, devise, descent, or by operation of law, to several persons in their own right, unless acquired by them in partnership, for partnership purposes, or unless declared to be in joint tenancy, or unless acquired as community property.

INTEREST OF COTENANTS

Where title is acquired by two or more persons as tenants in common, the deed should recite the respective interest of each, by words such as the following: "to *A* and *B*, as tenants in common, each as to an undivided one-half interest." If the respective interests are not set forth in the instrument of acquisition or otherwise shown of record, there is a presumption that their interests are equal. This presumption is not conclusive, however, and may be overcome by evidence showing that, by virtue of unequal contributions to the purchase price or otherwise, the cotenants hold unequal interests.

RIGHT OF POSSESSION

Cotenancy, whether as joint tenants or as tenants in common, involves mutual rights and obligations. Cotenants enjoy an equal right of possession. Each tenant may occupy the whole land, or any part thereof, but he cannot exclude his cotenant from occupancy. Where one cotenant is in sole possession of land, he is not liable to a cotenant out of possession for the rental value of the land, or for the products of his labor, such as crops. However, he must account to his cotenant for a share of rents and profits received from third persons, and for profits derived from a use of the land that removes something therefrom, such as extraction of oil or minerals.

ADVERSE POSSESSION OF COTENANT

As a general rule, one cotenant cannot acquire title by adverse possession against another cotenant. Since each cotenant has a right to occupy the whole of the property owned in common, possession of one is deemed possession of all. However, one cotenant in possession may acquire title by adverse possession if there is first an "ouster" of the other cotenant, i.e., an act that manifests an intention on his part to hold exclusively for himself, and if the tenant out of possession has notice of such hostile claim.

REPAIRS AND MAINTENANCE

A right of contribution exists in favor of one cotenant who pays taxes or other liens against the entire property. If the property is income-producing, he may deduct the expenditures from rents and profits of the property. In addition, he is entitled to an equitable lien upon the shares of his cotenants for their proportional amount of such expenditures. A cotenant is also entitled to contribution for the cost of *repairs.* If one cotenant makes *improvements* upon the common property, he cannot, as a rule, assert a lien for contribution on the share of the other cotenant, unless the latter assented to the improvements.

CONFIDENTIAL RELATIONSHIP OF OWNERS

Cotenants, whether joint tenants or tenants in common, stand in a confidential relationship. One cotenant cannot take advantage of a defect in the common title by purchasing an outstanding title or encumbrance, and asserting it against his cotenants. Accordingly, where a cotenant acquires a tax title under a sale for taxes on the common property, or takes an assignment of a certificate of sale issued to the purchaser at a foreclosure sale under a mortgage or deed of trust on the common property, the title so acquired by the cotenant is deemed to be held in trust for the other cotenants if they choose within a reasonable time to claim the benefit of the purchase by contributing their share of the purchase price. (*Smith* v. *Goethe,* 159 Cal. 628.)

TRANSFER OF INTEREST OF COTENANT

As in the case of a joint tenancy, the interest of a tenant in common may be transferred, either voluntarily or by operation of law. A conveyance by a tenant in common of the undivided interest that he has, passes the identical interest of such grantor in the whole property. If title is vested of record in *A*, as to an undivided one-third interest, and in *B*, as to an undivided two-thirds interest, a deed from *A* describing an undivided one-third interest in the common property passes all of his interest in the land, and his grantee becomes a tenant in common with *B*.

LEASE BY COTENANT

One cotenant cannot execute a lease of the whole property, or of a specific portion, that will bind his cotenants and give the lessee exclusive possession of the land. Such a lease is valid, however, as to the interest of the lessor-cotenant.

IV. Community property

The husband-and-wife relationship is essential to the community-property type of co-ownership. In California, property of a married person is either separate property or community property. If separate property, it may be held in severalty, or in joint tenancy, or as tenants in common.

WHAT IS COMMUNITY PROPERTY?

Community property is defined in Section 687 of the Civil Code as property acquired by husband and wife, or either, during marriage, when not acquired as the separate property of either. Under the provisions of Sections 162 and 163 of the Civil Code, separate property is defined as property owned before marriage, and that acquired afterward by gift, bequest, devise, or descent, and the rents, issues, and profits thereof. Separate property also consists of the earnings and accumulations of the wife, and of her minor children living with her or in her custody, while she is living apart from her husband; the earnings and accumulations of each party after rendition of a judgment or decree of separate maintenance; since 1959, the earnings and accumulations of the husband after an interlocutory decree of divorce is rendered and while the husband and wife are living separate and apart; the earnings and profits of the wife from the conduct of a business as a sole trader; damages awarded to either party in a civil action for personal injuries where the cause of action arises after September 11, 1957; and property conveyed by either husband or wife to the other with the intent of making it the grantee's separate property.

BASIS OF COMMUNITY PROPERTY

The California law as to property rights of husband and wife is derived from the law of Mexico, which in turn was derived from the law of Spain. The concept of community property is that both spouses contribute to the acquisition of property during marriage, and both should have an interest in such acquisition. This concept is of Germanic origin. It was adopted in France and Spain, and thereafter transplanted to their colonies in the New World.

ORIGIN OF COMMUNITY PROPERTY IN CALIFORNIA

California owes the origin of the community property law to the Treaty of Guadalupe Hidalgo, which expressly provided that the property rights of the inhabitants of the ceded territory were to be protected. The framers of the first state constitution in 1849 preserved the Mexican law as to marital property by adopting a provision to the effect that all property of the wife owned before marriage and that acquired afterward by gift, devise, or descent shall be her separate property, and directed that laws be passed more clearly defining the rights of the wife as to property held in common with her husband. The first legislature of the state thereafter enacted a measure providing that all property acquired after marriage by either spouse, other than by gift, devise, or descent, shall be common property.

THEORY OF COMMUNITY PROPERTY

The words "common property," which have been superseded by the term "community property," express the theory of the community property system that husband and wife form, in a sense, a partnership. In this respect, then, California did not accept the basic concept of the common law, as developed in England and adopted by many of the states, that in marriage the husband and wife are merged into one. Under this latter concept the legal existence of the wife is incorporated into that of the husband, so that all property acquired after marriage belongs to the husband, subject to the wife's "dower right" to demand that a life estate in one-third of the property be given to her at his death.

STATUTORY CHANGES

The community property law in California has been changed many times by amendments to the code, usually with the object of enlarging the rights of the wife. Prior to 1923 the interest of the wife was a mere *expectancy,* but this interest has been enlarged, and today the wife's interest in community property is defined as a *present, equal,* and *existing* interest, but under the management and control of the husband. (C.C., Sec. 161a.) However, in each instance in which the rights of the wife were increased and those of the husband limited, the statute cannot be applied retroactively so as to affect vested rights of the husband in property previously acquired. Accordingly, it is necessary to consider the date of acquisition of property in order to determine fully the rights of the parties.

QUASI COMMUNITY PROPERTY

Several code changes were made in 1961 to create a classification of "quasi community property" and consequently quasi community property is treated the same as community property in divorce proceedings, under the homestead law, and for inheritance tax and other purposes. It consists basically of personal property wherever situated and of real property in California acquired while the spouses were domiciled elsewhere but which would have been community property if the spouses had been domiciled in California.

COMMUNITY RIGHTS OF A PUTATIVE SPOUSE

Although there can be no "community property" when there has been no marriage, it has been held that a woman who lives with a man as his wife in the belief in good faith that a valid marriage exists is entitled upon termination of their relationship to share in the property acquired by them during its existence. The division of the property is made in accordance with the rules for division of community property upon a divorce. A man who believes in good faith that he is the lawful husband of a woman is given the same rights. Such person believing in good faith that he or she is lawfully married is designated as a putative spouse.

DETERMINING CHARACTER OF PROPERTY

In determining whether property is separate or community, the condition of the record title is not necessarily controlling, at least as between the spouses. Property may be community property even though the record title stands in the names of the husband and wife as tenants in common or as joint tenants. Evidence may be admitted in appropriate proceedings to show that the parties intended to take property otherwise than as shown of record. Recitals in deeds do not determine the character of the property unless both spouses evidence their agreement to the truth of the recitals. For example, the recital of a deed from a third party to a married woman that the property is conveyed to her "as her sole and separate property" may be disproved by the husband. Also, it may be shown that property originally acquired as separate property was subsequently converted into community property by agreement of the spouses.

PRESUMPTIONS AS TO CHARACTER OF PROPERTY

Several presumptions as to the character of property acquired by husband or wife, or both, during marriage are provided by statute. A *presumption* is a deduction that the law expressly directs to be made from particular facts. Unless declared by law to be conclusive, a presumption may be controverted by other evidence. If not controverted, a court will find according to the presumption.

Property acquired by a married man. Real property conveyed to a married man is presumed to be community property. In an action involving the property, such as divorce proceedings, the husband may nonetheless show that the property is in fact his separate property. The burden of proof is upon him, however, and whether the evidence outweighs the presumption is a question for the court to decide.

Property acquired by a married woman. Property acquired by a married woman is presumed to be her separate property. The presumption is disputable as between the spouses, but it is declared to be *conclusive* in favor of bona fide purchasers for value from her. Evidence could not be introduced to dispute the presumption in litigation involving such purchaser's rights.

Basic presumptions. The basic presumption is that all property acquired during marriage by either husband or wife, or both, other than by gift, bequest, devise, or descent is community property. This was the only presumption under the community property law as originally adopted, but as noted above, the law has been changed from time to time, usually with the object of favoring the wife. The following summarizes the presumptions and basic rights in property acquired by a married person:

First: Property acquired by a married woman prior to May 19, 1889. This is presumptively community property, and the husband must join in all deeds of such property, but failing to do so, he or his heirs or assigns will be barred from asserting any rights after one year from the date of recording the deed. If such property in the wife's name is actually community property, the husband has complete control over it, and can mortgage or convey such property without the joinder of the wife.

Second: Property acquired by a married woman on or after May 19, 1889. This is presumed to be her separate property. This presumption applies to real property acquired on or after said date, and to personal property acquired on or after July 29, 1927. This presumption is conclusive in favor of "any person dealing in good faith and for a valuable consideration with such married woman or her legal representative or successors in interest, and regardless of any change in her marital status after acquisition of said property." (C. C., Sec. 164.)

Third: Property acquired by a married man prior to June 1, 1891. This is presumed to be community property, but can be conveyed or encumbered by the husband without the wife joining in the instrument, provided a declaration of homestead has not been recorded.

Fourth: Community property acquired by a married man on or after June 1, 1891, and prior to July 27, 1917. This can be conveyed by the husband alone, except that the husband cannot make a gift of such property, or convey the same without a valuable consideration, unless the wife consents thereto in writing.

Fifth: Community property acquired by a married man on or after July 27, 1917. As to such property, the wife, either personally or by duly authorized agent, must join with the husband in executing any instrument by which such community real property or any interest therein is leased for a longer period than one year, or is sold, conveyed, or encumbered. However, under the provisions of Section 172a of the Civil Code, "the sole lease, contract, mortgage or deed of the husband, holding the record title to community real property, to a lessee, purchaser, or encumbrancer, in good faith without knowledge of the marriage relation shall be presumed to be valid." No action to avoid any such instrument, "affecting any property standing of record in the name of the husband alone, executed by the husband alone, shall be commenced after the expiration of one year from the filing for record of such instrument in the recorder's office in the county in which the land is situate."

Sixth: Property acquired prior to September 15, 1935, by husband and wife. The wife is presumed to take an undivided one-half interest as separate property, and the husband is presumed to take the remaining half as community property.

Seventh: Property acquired on or after September 15, 1935, by husband and wife by an instrument in which they are described as husband and wife. Unless a different intention is expressed in the instrument, the presumption is that such property is community property. The presumption that property acquired after marriage is community property does not apply, however, as against the State of California under the Inheritance Tax Act (Rev. & Tax. C., Sec. 13556).

WHERE PURCHASE COMPLETED AFTER MARRIAGE

If either husband or wife owns an inchoate right to property before marriage, but completes the acquisition during marriage, the property is classified in proportion to the separate and community funds expended. For instance, if the husband is the vendee under a land contract entered into before marriage, with a balance of the purchase price paid after marriage, the property is community to the extent that community funds went into the purchase, and separate property to the extent that his separate funds were used. (*Vieux* v. *Vieux,* 80 C.A. 222.)

IMPROVEMENTS ON SEPARATE PROPERTY WITH COMMUNITY FUNDS

Where community funds are used to improve the wife's separate property, the improvements follow the title to the land, and are separate property. The husband, who has the management and control of community funds, is presumed to have intended a gift to the wife in such case, in the absence of any agreement to the contrary. He is not entitled to a lien on the property or to a right of reimbursement. However, where community funds are used by the husband to improve or pay taxes or encumbrances on his own separate property, the wife is entitled to reimbursement to the extent of her share of the community funds so used.

In the case of *Estate of Hirschberg*, 224 C.A.2d 449, it was held that separate property may become community property by the process of commingling in such manner to make segregation impossible, thus requiring application of the presumption that the property is community.

IMPORTANCE OF THE DISTINCTION BETWEEN COMMUNITY AND SEPARATE PROPERTY

Whether property of husband and wife is separate property or community property is extremely important, as different rules apply in the various actions or proceedings affecting property of a married person. Community property is not subject to a *partition* action, as is joint tenancy property or property held as tenants in common. If either the husband or wife was adjudged *incompetent,* special rules for its disposition formerly applied. Prior to 1959, community property of an incompetent spouse could be sold and conveyed or encumbered, transferred, or exchanged or otherwise disposed of only through special proceedings prescribed by the Probate Code (see Chapter 23). Rights under the *homestead* law are dependent upon whether or not property is separate or community property (see Chapter 12). The laws of *succession* distinguish between separate and community property. In *divorce* proceedings the power of the court to award property is dependent upon the character of the property. This power is limited to community property and homestead property, and does not extend to separate property.

AWARD OF COMMUNITY PROPERTY IN DIVORCE PROCEEDINGS

In California, a divorce may be granted for any of the following causes: adultery, extreme cruelty, wilful desertion, wilful neglect, habitual intemperance, conviction of a felony, or incurable insanity. Section 146 of the Civil Code provides that when adultery, extreme cruelty, or incurable insanity is the grounds for divorce, the community property shall be assigned to the respective parties in such proportions as the court deems just. This requires an award of more than one-half to the innocent spouse. However, if the divorce is granted to both parties on the grounds of extreme cruelty, the community property must be equally divided. (*DeBurgh* v. *DeBurgh*, 39 Cal.2d 858.) When the grounds are other than adultery, extreme cruelty, or incurable insanity, the community property is divided equally between the parties.

Where no disposition is made of community property. In the divorce action the parties may seek only a dissolution of marriage without a determination of property rights. In the absence of any disposition of community property, the parties hold the community property as tenants in common after the entry of a final decree.

Interlocutory and final decree. A marriage is not dissolved until a *final* decree of divorce has been entered. If the court in a divorce proceeding determines that a divorce should be granted, an *interlocutory* decree is entered declaring that the party in whose favor the court decides is entitled to a divorce. The interlocutory decree does not dissolve the marriage; it merely declares that a party has the right to a final decree of divorce *after one year.* The one-year period used to run from the date of entry of the interlocutory decree. Since 1965 it runs from the date of service of the summons. In the absence of a property agreement providing otherwise, real property acquired during the interlocutory decree is presumed to be community property to the same extent that it would be if no interlocutory decree had been entered.

LIABILITY OF COMMUNITY PROPERTY FOR DEBTS

The community property is made liable for debts of the husband and certain debts of the wife. Under the provisions of Section 168 of the Civil Code, community property is liable for all debts of the husband, whether personal or contracted for the benefit of the community, subject to an exemption of the wife's earnings from liabilities not contracted for necessities of life furnished to either spouse while they are living together. Under the provisions of Sections 167 and 170 of the Civil Code, community property, except the husband's earnings after marriage, is liable for the debts of the wife contracted before marriage, but it is not liable, except as to her earnings, for debts of the wife contracted after marriage.

Judgments against husband. A money judgment against the husband, when an abstract of the judgment is duly recorded, is a lien upon all community real property. A money judgment against the wife, however, is not a lien upon community real property. Although community property, other than the earnings of the husband, is liable for debts of the wife contracted before marriage, nevertheless, in order to obtain a judgment lien upon community real property for the wife's debts, it would be necessary for the creditor to make the husband a party defendant in the action to enforce the liability, and have judgment rendered against him.

Effect of bankruptcy. If the husband is adjudicated a bankrupt, the community property, as well as his separate property, passes to the trustee in bankruptcy for the benefit of his creditors, and may be administered upon by the trustee in bankruptcy. However, where the wife has been adjudged bankrupt, only her separate property vests in the trustee, and not her interest in the community property. It has been held that the community property does not pass to the wife's trustee in bankruptcy, nor may the trustee compel a division of community property so as to subject her interest to the payment of her debts. (*Smedberg* v. *Bevilockway,* 7 C.A.2d 578.)

DISPOSITION OF COMMUNITY PROPERTY UPON DEATH OF HUSBAND

Upon the death of the husband, one half of the community property belongs to the wife. The other half is subject to the testamentary disposition of the husband, and in the absence thereof, it all goes to the wife. However, all of the community property is subject to the husband's debts and to the administration of his estate.

DISPOSITION OF COMMUNITY PROPERTY UPON DEATH OF WIFE

As to property acquired prior to August 17, 1923, a wife's interest was an expectancy only and died with her. As to property acquired subsequent to that date, at which time the wife was given the right of testamentary disposition of one half of the community property, all of it goes to the husband without administration if the wife dies intestate. If she exercises her right to dispose of one half, that half is subject to administration in her estate. After forty days from the death of the wife, the surviving husband has power to convey, encumber, or otherwise deal with the property unless the claimants under the wife's will have recorded a notice that an interest in the property is claimed. (Pro. C., Sec. 203.) The right of the husband is dependent upon the community character of the property, and if the vesting of title does not disclose that the property is community property, a proceeding to establish the status of the property as community property may be essential.

V. Partnerships

The ownership of property by several persons, in addition to other forms such as joint tenancy and tenancy in common, may be of "partnership interests." (C.C., Sec. 682.) A partnership interest is defined in Section 684 of the Civil Code as one "owned by several persons, in partnership for partnership purposes." Since the year 1929, when the Uniform Partnership Act was adopted in California, title to real property may be taken in the name of the partnership. The partnership is considered as an entity capable of acquiring title to real property. Property so held is impressed with certain characteristics that distinguish it from property owned in other forms of cotenancy.

DEFINITION OF A PARTNERSHIP

A partnership is defined in Section 15006 of the Corporations Code as "an association of two or more persons to carry on as co-owners a business for profit." It is created by an agreement between two or more persons, either evidenced by an express contract, or implied from their acts and conduct, to carry on jointly a business and share the profits.

CERTIFICATE OF FICTITIOUS NAME

Under the provisions of Section 2466 of the Civil Code, a partnership transacting business under a fictitious name, or a designation not showing the names of the persons interested as partners in such business, is required to file with the clerk of the county in which its principal place of business is situated, a certificate stating the names in full and places of residence of all members of the partnership. The certificate also must be published once a week for four weeks. If there is a change in the members of such partnership, a new certificate is required to be filed and a new publication made. Failure of the partnership to comply with this requirement penalizes it to the extent that it cannot maintain any action on contracts or transactions made under such fictitious name until the required certificate has been filed and publication completed. The purpose of the fictitious name statute is to make public the names of the members of the partnership so that those dealing with them may at all times know the identity of the persons they are giving credit to or are becoming bound. (*Levelon Builders, Inc.* v. *Lynn,* 194 C.A.2d 657.)

STATEMENT OF PARTNERSHIP

Section 15010.5 of the Corporations Code provides that a partnership may file for record in the office of the county recorder of any county a statement of partnership that shall set forth the name of the partnership and the names of each of the partners, together with a statement that the partners named are all of the partners. Such statement must be signed, verified, and acknowledged by two or more of the partners. If this is done, it is conclusively presumed in favor of any bona fide purchaser for value of partnership property in such county, that the persons named constitute all of the partners, unless a person claiming to be a partner shall, previous to such conveyance, record a statement showing the membership to be otherwise than as set forth in the original statement. Although filing the statement is optional, title insurers—as a rule of title practice—require that this statement be recorded before insuring a conveyance by a partnership.

TITLE IN NAME OF PARTNERSHIP

Prior to the adoption of the Uniform Partnership Act, legal title could not be vested in a partnership as such, since it was not recognized as a legal entity for the purpose of acquiring land. The legal title to property acquired for partnership purposes was usually taken in the names of the individual partners. A partnership may now acquire title in the partnership name, such as "*XYZ* Company, a partnership, composed of *A* and *B*, partners." Transfers of property so acquired are made in the name of the partnership, with the name appearing in the caption of the instrument. The instrument is executed in a manner similar to an instrument of a corporation. The wives of married partners need not join in the execution of the instrument. Although one partner may bind the partnership as a matter of law, since every partner is an agent of the partnership, it is a rule of title practice that conveyances of partnership real property must be executed on behalf of the partnership by all of the partners, or by a partner, or partners less than all, who are expressly authorized, under the partnership agreement or otherwise, by all of the partners to perform the particular act.

WHEN TITLE IS IN NAMES OF PARTNERS

Partnership property may be acquired not only in the partnership name, but also in the names of one or more of the individual partners, with or without a reference to the partnership. As between the partners themselves, it may be shown that property, vested of record in an individual partner or partners, is actually partnership property. But where the rights of third parties are concerned, the record title may prevail. Thus, a purchaser in good faith from an individual record owner would be protected against the claim of the partnership that the land was actually partnership property and that the partner holding the title was not authorized to make the conveyance. It is usually considered advisable that record title to property acquired by a partnership be taken in the name of the partnership itself, rather than in individual partners.

INTEREST OF PARTNER IN PARTNERSHIP PROPERTY

The interest of a partner in specific partnership property is not subject to attachment or to levy under execution upon a judgment that is based upon a claim exclusively against the individual. A judgment against an individual partner is not a lien upon the partnership property or the partner's interest.

EFFECT OF DEATH OF A PARTNER

Upon the death of a partner, his right in specific partnership property vests in the surviving partner or partners. The representative of the estate of the deceased partner or the heirs have no interest in the property of the partnership as such. The interest of the deceased partner in the partnership is his right to an accounting and a share of the profits and surplus, which is personal property, and should be inventoried as such in the estate. The real property of the partnership is not properly inventoried in the estate of the deceased partner. The surviving partner has the title to the partnership property and the exclusive right of management of the partnership business, but only for the purpose of winding up the partnership and accounting to the estate of the deceased partner.

ADOPTION OF UNIFORM LIMITED PARTNERSHIP ACT

In the ordinary partnership, each partner is liable for all firm debts. The theory is that a person should not be allowed to share in the profits of a partnership and at the same time stipulate for a limitation of liability. A need arose, however, for some method of investment and profit sharing without partnership liability if the contributor of the capital did not permit his name to be used, and if there was absence of power or control over the business, other than a right to information and inspection of accounts. This purpose was achieved by the adoption in 1929 of the Uniform Limited Partnership Act. (Corp. C., Secs. 15501 *et seq.*)

Limited partnership. A limited partnership is defined in the code as a partnership composed of one or more general partners and one or more limited partners, the latter having no control over the business and only a limited liability for debts. The maximum liability of the limited partners for losses is fixed at the amount of their contribution to the capital of the partnership. This type of partnership is entirely the creature of statute, and all requirements of the statute must be complied with, including the recording of a certificate of partnership.

VI. Joint ventures

A joint venture (or joint adventure) results from an agreement of two or more persons to jointly conduct a business enterprise for profit. It has been defined as a joint association of persons in a single enterprise for profit but falling short of a partnership. (*Fitzgerald* v. *Provines,* 102 C.A.2d 529.) The principal difference in purpose between a joint venture and a partnership is that the former is ordinarily formed to conduct a single enterprise, whereas the latter is used to carry on a general line of business.

FORMATION

The persons who may associate to form a joint venture are considered to be the same as those who may become partners, i.e., individuals, corporations and other associations. A partnership may be a joint venturer. There are no statutory or legal requirements or authorization for filing or recording any certificate or statement to establish the existence of a joint venture.

ACQUIRING TITLE

When title or any other interest in real property is to be acquired by joint venturers, the preferred methods for title insurance purposes of naming the grantee are either (1) "*A* and *B*, doing business as the *X* Company, a joint venture," or (2) "*X* Company, a joint venture, composed of *A* and *B*." If title is acquired by other designations, such as "*X* Company, a joint venture," or merely "*X* Company," such designation does not create or describe an entity capable of acquiring title. However, if inquiry discloses that a joint venture in fact exists and that title is in fact the joint venturers' property, and their identity is established, a conveyance by the joint venturers may be considered sufficient. Conveyances should be captioned as title is held, including or adding the names of the joint venturers, together with the name of the wife of any married man who is a joint venturer and is not dealing with his separate property.

VII. Corporations

A corporation is referred to as an artificial being, existing only in contemplation of law. It has only those rights given by its charter and the laws authorizing its formation. A corporation is treated as an entity distinct from its members, with rights and liabilities of its own. A corporation, whether domestic or foreign, may own real property in its corporate name.

TYPES OF CORPORATIONS

A *domestic* corporation is one formed under the laws of California. All others are *foreign* corporations.

DISTINCTIONS BETWEEN CORPORATIONS AND PARTNERSHIPS

The chief differences between a corporation and a partnership are as follows: (1) a corporation must be organized in compliance with statutory requirements, and operates under the charter or permission of the state, whereas a partnership may be formed by mere association of the members in a business; (2) a corporation is a legal entity for all purposes, whereas a partnership is considered as a legal entity for certain purposes only; (3) a corporation, except where limited by statute, has an unlimited existence that is unaffected by change in the personnel of its shareholders or officers, whereas a partnership usually has a limited term and the death of a partner may result in a dissolution of the partnership; (4) shareholders of a corporation, as such, have practically no direct control over its affair, whereas partners are mutual agents and each can act for the firm in most matters; and (5) holders of fully paid shares in a corporation are not liable for the debts of the corporation, whereas partners are individually liable for the firm debts, with exceptions to this rule applying in the case of a limited partnership.

FORMATION OF CORPORATION

A corporation is formed by the execution of articles of incorporation by three or more persons and the filing of the articles in the office of the Secretary of State at Sacramento. The articles set forth the name of the corporation; the purpose for which it is formed, including a statement identifying the specific business in which the corporation is primarily to engage; the county where its principal office for the transaction of business is located; the number, names, and addresses of the directors, which must be not less than three; and provisions as to the amount and nature of shares. In addition, the articles may contain regulations as to the business of the corporation and the powers of the directors.

FILING ARTICLES OF INCORPORATION

A copy of the articles, certified by the Secretary of State, and bearing the indorsement of the date of filing in his office, is thereafter filed with the county clerk of the county in which the corporation has its principal place of business and with the county clerk of every county in the state in which the corporation holds real property.

POWERS OF CORPORATIONS

Every domestic corporation is given the power by law to acquire, hold, lease, encumber, convey or otherwise dispose of real and personal property; to borrow money and execute mortgages or deeds of trust; and to enter into any contracts, or do any acts incidental to the transaction of its business, or expedient for the attainment of its corporate purposes.

EXERCISE OF CORPORATE POWERS

The corporate powers of a corporation are exercised by or under the authority of its board of directors. A corporation must have as officers a president, vice president, secretary, and treasurer, chosen by the board of directors, and may have any other officers deemed expedient. Any number of offices, except those of president and secretary, may be held by the same person.

Powers of officers. Officers have only such powers as are set forth in the by-laws, and those given them by the directors, expressly or by acquiescence. For instance, the president does not have authority merely by virtue of his office to purchase, sell, encumber, or otherwise contract on behalf of the corporation with respect to property.

RESOLUTIONS OF BOARD OF DIRECTORS

The authority of an officer to execute a conveyance or contract affecting real property of a corporation must ordinarily be evidenced by a resolution of the board of directors. Evidence as to the existence of a resolution authorizing a conveyance by a corporation is required, as a general rule, by a title company for title insurance purposes, but may be waived where: (1) the instrument is executed and acknowledged on behalf of the corporation by the president or vice president, and the secretary or assistant secretary; (2) the corporate seal is affixed; (3) the act is not a conveyance of all the assets or other prohibited transaction; and (4) the certificate of acknowledgment recites that the instrument is duly executed pursuant to authority duly given by the board of directors.

CORPORATE SEAL

A corporation *may,* but is not *required to,* adopt and use a seal. The seal must show the name of the corporation and the state and date of incorporation. When an instrument executed by a corporation bears the corporate seal, such seal is prima facie evidence that such instrument is the act of the corporation, and that the instrument is executed by duly authorized officers or agents.

TRANSFER OF ALL ASSETS

A corporation may not sell, lease, convey, exchange, transfer, or otherwise dispose of all or substantially all of its property and assets unless authorized by resolution of its board of directors and with the approval by vote or written consent of the shareholders entitled to exercise a majority of the voting power of the corporation.

CERTIFICATE ANNEXED TO DEED

Under the provisions of Section 3904 of the Corporations Code, any deed or instrument conveying any assets of a corporation may have annexed to it the certificate of the secretary or an assistant secretary, setting forth the resolution of the board of directors, and (1) stating that the property described in the conveyance is less than substantially all of the assets of the corporation, if such be the case; or (2) if such property constitutes all or substantially all of the assets of the corporation, stating the fact of approval thereof by the vote or written consent of the shareholders. Such certificate is prima facie evidence of the existence of the facts authorizing such conveyance, and conclusive evidence in favor of any innocent purchaser or encumbrancer for value.

CORPORATIONS OTHER THAN PRIVATE BUSINESS CORPORATIONS

Instruments executed by corporations other than private business corporations, such as churches and other religious corporations, public utilities, mutual water companies, municipal corporations, school districts, and agencies or instrumentalities of the United States or of the state of California, are subject to various limitations, and conveyances by such types of corporations require special consideration for title insurance purposes.

FOREIGN CORPORATIONS

A foreign corporation qualified to do business in California may acquire, dispose of, or otherwise contract with respect to property in California, subject to limitations on its powers contained in its charter or articles of incorporation, and the law of the state of its incorporation. A foreign corporation is one not incorporated under the laws of California, i.e., a corporation organized under the laws of another country or of a state other than California. Its organization, existence, and dissolution are controlled by the law of the place of its incorporation. The validity and effect of corporate acts performed in California may, however, be determined by the law of this state. A foreign corporation is covered by the California law governing domestic corporations only when such law expressly so provides.

Jurisdiction over foreign corporations. Since a state, under its police power, may exclude foreign corporations, other than corporations created by an act of Congress, from the right to do intrastate business, it may, accordingly, permit them to do business within its borders only upon such conditions as it may see fit to impose. Doing "intrastate business" means entering into repeated and successive transactions in California other than in interstate or foreign commerce.

Requirements for doing business in the state. Effective September 18, 1959, Sections 6400 and 6401 of the Corporations Code, which required the filing of articles of a foreign corporation with the Secretary of State and the County Clerk, were repealed. The filing of such articles is no longer required. In lieu of such filing, a foreign corporation must secure from the Secretary of State a certificate of qualification to do intrastate business in California. Failure to obtain such certificate subjects the delinquent corporation to a fine, and until it complies with the requirement, prohibits it from maintaining any action or proceeding in any court in this state upon any intrastate business so transacted. Section 6600 of the Corporations Code was amended in 1961 to provide for the filing of incorporation papers of foreign corporations in the county clerk's office of any county in which such corporation held or holds real property, and when so filed are conclusive evidence of the incorporation and powers of the corporation in favor of any bona fide purchaser or encumbrancer of such property for value, whether or not the corporation does business in this state.

Title company requirements. A title company when insuring the acts of a foreign corporation will not only ascertain whether it has qualified to do business in California by complying with the above requirements, but also whether the corporation was in existence when it acquired title and in good standing in its own state at the date of any conveyance or encumbrance executed by it.

VIII. Unincorporated associations

As a general rule an unincorporated association cannot hold or convey property. The property of an unincorporated association is generally recognized as belonging to the members of the association, subject to the right of the trustees or governing committee or other board of control to make such use or disposition of the property as the laws of the association provide.

ASSOCIATIONS THAT MAY HOLD TITLE

As an exception to the foregoing general rule, Section 21200 of the Corporations Code provides that any unincorporated benevolent or fraternal society or association, and any labor organization, may purchase, receive, own, hold, lease, mortgage, pledge, or encumber, by deed of trust or otherwise, manage, and sell all such real estate and other property as may be necessary for its business purposes and objects. Similar powers are extended also to certain medical associations. Such society, association, or labor organization may take, by will or deed, property not necessary for its business purposes and objects, and hold it until disposed of within a period of ten years from the acquisition thereof.

CONVEYANCES BY ASSOCIATIONS

All conveyances transferring or in any manner affecting the title to real property owned or held by an unincorporated benevolent or fraternal society or association, or a labor organization, must be executed by its presiding officer and recording secretary, under its seal, pursuant to a duly adopted resolution authorizing the conveyance.

IX. Syndicates and investment trusts

The word "syndicate" is a broad term, and when applied to real estate may relate to a variety of entities or relationships under which persons, both natural and artificial, associate together to invest in real estate either for income purposes or for eventual sale at a profit. It may consist simply of a tenancy in common, or it may be a joint venture, a partnership, a trust, a corporation, or a combination of any of them. A main objective of a real estate syndicate is to operate as much like a corporation as possible without incurring double taxation, once at the corporate level and again upon distribution of income to the members of the syndicate.

INVESTMENT TRUSTS

Real estate investment trusts are not new, but because of legislation in 1961 extending tax benefits to real estate investment trusts, their use has become more prevalent. To qualify as a real estate investment trust under the tax legislation, there must be an unincorporated organization which, among other things, is managed by one or more trustees; does not hold any property primarily for sale to customers in the ordinary course of its trade or business; and its beneficial ownership is owned by one hundred or more persons. Although other forms of group ownership will still be preferred in many cases, the investment trust can be used as a vehicle through which the small investor, by direct investment in real estate holding, will be able to gain certain advantages, including income tax benefits.

X. Corporate securities act

IN GENERAL

The state Corporate Securities Act (Blue Sky Law) provides that no company shall sell or offer for sale any security of its own issue until it has secured a permit from the Commissioner of Corporations. (Corp. C., Secs. 25000–25804.) The word "company" as used in the Act includes all domestic and private corporations, associations, joint stock companies, partnerships, and also trustees and individuals. Before offering condominium or community apartment projects in California it was at one time necessary to obtain a permit from the Division of Corporations. However, by virtue of amendments in the law, effective September 17, 1965, the Corporate Securities Act is not applicable to any interest in subdivided lands or a subdivision or a real estate development except where offered for sale as part of an investment contract. The Act was completely rewritten in 1968 and is now known as the Corporate Securities Law of 1968.

DEFINITION OF SECURITY

The word "security" includes any stock, bond, note, treasury stock, debenture, evidence of indebtedness, certificates of interest or participation, certificates of interest in a profit-sharing agreement, certificates of interest in an oil, gas, or mining title or lease, collateral trust certificates, any transferable share, investment contract, or beneficial interest in title to property, profits or earnings, guarantee of a security, and any certificates of deposit for a security.

TITLE COMPANY PRACTICE

By reason of the broad definition of security, a title company may question assignments of fractional interests in oil or mining leases, deeds, or assignments conveying a series of undivided interests in oil or oil land or deeds conveying a series of oil-bearing lots, or small portions of a lot, or lots covered by a community oil lease, unless a permit covering such conveyance has been obtained from the corporation commissioner.

XI. Multiple housing developments

The enactment of a condominium statute in California in 1963 stimulated considerable interest in multifamily housing. Although a condominium plan of ownership was adaptable under existing law, the adoption of the new condominium legislation eliminated certain problems that could arise, particularly as to separate tax assessments and compliance with zoning and other governmental regulations.

CONDOMINIUM DEFINED

Condominium is defined in Section 783 of the Civil Code as an estate in real property consisting of an undivided interest in common in a portion of a parcel of real property together with a separate interest in space in a residential, industrial, or commercial building on said real property, such as an apartment, office, or store. A condominium may include, in addition, a separate interest in other portions of said real property. Such estate (as it relates to the duration of its enjoyment) may be either a fee, a life estate, or an estate for years. A "unit" is defined as being the elements of a condominium that are not owned in common with the owners of other condominiums, and the term "common areas" is defined as the entire project excepting units that are granted or reserved.

Before offering condominium or community apartment projects for sale it was at one time necessary to obtain a permit from the Division of Corporations and a public report from the Department of Real Estate. By virtue of a change in the law, effective September 17, 1965, the need to obtain the approval of the Corporations Commission to a condominium plan of development was eliminated in most cases.

The condominium statute is comprehensive, and sets forth, among other things, the requirement that a description or survey map, diagrammatic floor plan, and certificate of consent to the plan be recorded. A declaration of restrictions that shall establish equitable servitudes inuring to and binding upon the owners of all condominiums in the project must also be recorded. Such declaration may establish a management body to manage the project. If the project complies with the statutory requirements, each condominium owned in fee shall be separately assessed to the owner thereof and the tax on each condominium constitutes a lien solely thereon. A separate loan and a separate policy of title insurance are obtainable on the individual units. Although the Act may have contemplated a high-rise structure, it has been extended to cover cluster type and row housing.

OTHER METHODS OF COOPERATIVE OWNERSHIP

The condominium concept of ownership involves a "divided interest" in real property as opposed to an "undivided interest." The latter is the characteristic of the "Co-op" or "Own-your-own apartment" in use before the advent of the condominium method, under which the individual apartment owners acquired a conveyance of an undivided fractional interest in the entire property together with the exclusive right to use and occupy a designated apartment and garage, and the common right to use with others the common areas such as hallways, parkways, elevators, laundry rooms, and the like. Another method of ownership is the corporate method or stock plan under which title to the entire property is vested in a corporation, and the individual "owners" are issued shares of stock in the owner corporation, which sets forth their rights of occupancy and use. Still another method is the trust plan, under which title is vested in a trustee, and the individual "owners" are issued certificates of beneficial interest under the trust.

PLANNED RESIDENTIAL DEVELOPMENT

Sometimes called Town House Development, this program is also referred to as a "postage stamp" subdivision. Maps of such projects, to which reference is made in conveyances, usually depict a series of small lots, frequently abutting one another in the manner of the row houses that are common in some eastern cities. Because of the small size of the lots and absence of side-yard setbacks and for other reasons, special zoning ordinances or variations under existing regulations are necessary for this type of project. The lots and the improvements thereon are in separate ownership, and separate tax assessments may be available. The lot owners may also obtain undivided interests in the commonly owned "green area" lots or recreational areas.

Questions

1. Explain the meaning of the term "co-ownership."
2. Discuss the several ways in which two or more persons may own property.
3. Define a joint tenancy.
4. Describe the four unities essential to the creation of a joint tenancy.
5. What is the principal characteristic of a joint tenancy?
6. How is a tenancy in common created?
7. Discuss the main characteristics of a tenancy in common.
8. What relationship is necessary in order to have community property?
9. May separate property of a husband or wife consist of property acquired after marriage?
10. How is community property defined?
11. Can one spouse convey community real property without the joinder of the other?
12. Discuss briefly the presumptions pertaining to property acquired by a married person.
13. May a husband and wife change the character of property owned by them by a deed to themselves?
14. How is a partnership defined?

15. May a partnership acquire title to real property in the partnership name?
16. Distinguish a general partnership and a limited partnership.
17. May foreign corporations own real property in California?
18. May unincorporated associations acquire title in the name of the association?
19. Explain the application of the Corporate Securities Act to real estate transactions.
20. Compare the conventional "co-op" with condominium ownership.

9

Incidents of Ownership

Summary

I. Introductory
Permitted uses of property; Right to clear the land; Cutting trees; Discharge of offensive matter; Diversion of waters; Blasting

II. Encroachments
When an encroachment constitutes a trespass; When an encroachment constitutes a nuisance; Relief obtainable through judicial proceedings; Where encroachment intentional

III. Fences
Fencing largely a matter of discretion; Spite fences; Maintaining division fences; Interference with gates

IV. Trees and other vegetation
Overhanging branches; Control of weeds

V. Lateral and subjacent support
Statutory rule in California; Notice to adjoining owners; Duties of excavator; Support of buildings; Slide damage; Subjacent support

VI. Light and air

VII. Nuisances
Interference with use and enjoyment of property; Examples of nuisances; Acts offensive to esthetic sense; Mental and emotional factors

VIII. Liability to trespassers, licensees, and invitees
Persons outside the land; Condition of streets and sidewalks; Duty as to lightwells, driveways, and the like; Duty owned to trespassers; Duties owed to a tolerated intruder; Duties owed to licensees; Persons who are invitees; New legislation modifies rules

I. Introductory

An owner of land enjoys certain rights by virtue of his ownership; he is also subject to various duties and responsibilities, and for a breach thereof he may incur liability to third parties.

Special rules apply to owners of adjoining lands. Many rights, duties, and liabilities arise from, and are incident to, the fact that their lands are contiguous. Included in this category are such matters as encroachments, party walls and fences, lateral support, overhanging trees, and flow of surface waters. Additionally, a landowner may incur liability to third parties for maintaining a nuisance on his property, or for injuries to persons entering upon his property, or for damage to other property arising from the use of his property.

PERMITTED USES OF PROPERTY

It is a general rule that a person may make such use of his property as he chooses, provided that in so doing he does not injure others. Further, a person is not responsible for every injury that may result from the use he makes of his property, since it would be an intolerable hardship to hold an owner responsible for unavoidable accidents that may occur to his property by fire or other casualties, or acts beyond his control, even though others may in fact be injured. Accordingly, an owner may use his land for any lawful purpose, without being liable for the consequences, provided he exercises ordinary care and skill to prevent injury to adjacent owners or to other persons.

RIGHT TO CLEAR THE LAND

A landowner, as an incident to his ownership, has the right to remove trees and brush growing on his land, provided he does not act in a negligent manner. In the case of *Stewart* v. *Birchfield,* 15 C.A. 378, an owner who cleared brush from his land and thereafter failed to irrigate the land so that the wind blew sand from his land onto his neighbor's land, was held not liable for any damage done.

CUTTING TREES

An owner cannot be restrained from cutting trees on his land because it would let in the sun and cause water in an adjacent stream to evaporate more rapidly. But the felling of trees into a stream by a landowner may be restrained if as a result the water will be rendered unfit for domestic use by an adjoining owner through whose land the stream also flows.

DISCHARGE OF OFFENSIVE MATTER

An owner cannot without liability discharge offensive or injurious matter upon adjoining land. For example, a lessee of oil property who drills an oil well on the property, with knowledge of the tremendous pressure of underlying gas, is responsible for the casting of oil and debris upon adjoining premises by an explosion of the well, though he is not negligent in his drilling operations. (*Green* v. *General Petroleum Corp.*, 205 Cal. 328.)

DIVERSION OF WATERS

Prior to 1966 the cases held that an owner cannot without liability divert surface or storm waters onto the lands of another over which they would not naturally have flowed, nor accumulate surface waters upon his land and precipitate them upon a neighbor's land in larger quantities than, or in different amounts from, those which they would have taken in the course of nature. The rule as to surface waters is relaxed somewhat as to city lots, and the owner may make changes in the surface of his land, but he may not cause an accumulation of storm waters that would injure adjoining property. In the case of *Keys* v. *Romley*, 64 Cal.2d 396, the California Supreme Court modified the rule previously followed since the year 1876 regarding the liability of an upper owner for discharge of water in an unnatural manner. In reviewing the California law with respect to surface waters, the court recognized that California had followed the so-called civil law rule to the effect that there exists a "servitude" of natural drainage between adjoining parcels, so that the lower owner must accept the surface waters which naturally drain onto his land; correlatively, the rule denies to the upper owner any privilege to alter the natural system of drainage so as to increase the burden. Recognizing that the civil law rule had a tendency to discourage the improvement of land, since almost any use of property is likely to cause a change in drainage, the court abandoned the strict civil law rule and adopted what it calls a "modified civil law rule." Not every interference with natural drainage injurious to the land of another is now actionable. It must also be unreasonable. In its decision the court stated:

> What is, in any particular case, reasonable use or management has been held to be a mixed question of law and fact to be submitted to the jury under proper instructions (p. 403).
>
> Failure to exercise reasonable care may result in liability by an upper to a lower landowner. It is equally the duty of any person threatened with injury to his property by the flow of surface waters to take reasonable precautions to avoid or reduce any actual or potential injury (p. 409).

On the other hand, if both the upper and lower landowner are reasonable,

> then the injury must necessarily be borne by the upper landowner who changes a natural system of drainage, in accordance with our traditional civil law rule (p. 409).

BLASTING

Blasting by an owner on his land contiguous to a dwelling house is considered an unreasonable use of the property, and no degree of care and skill in such use will excuse the owner from liability to the adjacent owner for damages to the dwelling house proximately and naturally resulting from the act of blasting, whether caused by rocks or other substance thrown on the adjoining structure, or by concussion of the air around it. (*Colton* v. *Onderdonk,* 69 Cal. 155.)

II. Encroachments

An encroachment is described as a projection of a building or other structure on one parcel of land onto, or into the airspace of, an adjoining parcel of land. An encroachment by a building or other structure that rests in part upon the adjoining land constitutes a *trespass,* whereas an encroachment in the airspace above the land of an adjoining owner constitutes a *nuisance.* This distinction is of particular importance with respect to the time within which to maintain an action for injunction or other appropriate relief.

WHEN AN ENCROACHMENT CONSTITUTES A TRESPASS

As stated in the case of *Bertram* v. *Orlando,* 102 C.A.2d 506, the encroachment of a building obviously intended to be permanent upon the soil of another is a permanent trespass, and the cause of action based on such trespass is barred in three years under the applicable statute of limitations. [C.C.P., Sec. 338(2).] Relief against encroachments has been granted in actions of ejectment, to quiet title, and for an injunction and damages, but such actions must be commenced within the prescribed three-year period. The usual type of action is one for the removal of the encroachment and for damages.

WHEN AN ENCROACHMENT CONSTITUTES A NUISANCE

Where the encroachment is upon the space above the land, it is considered as a nuisance rather than a permanent trespass, and the cause of action is not barred by lapse of time. The maintenance of such an encroachment is considered to be a continuing trespass or nuisance, and every continuance thereof amounts to a new nuisance for which successive actions will lie until the nuisance is abated. Nuisances that consist of acts done or of particular uses of property are properly termed "continuing" when they are of such a character that they may continue indefinitely or, on the other hand, may be discontinued at any time. (*Kafka* v. *Bozio,* cited on p. 120.)

RELIEF OBTAINABLE THROUGH JUDICIAL PROCEEDINGS

A mandatory injunction will ordinarily issue at the instance of a landowner to compel the removal of the encroachment where the action is filed within the required time. However, even though the right to an injunction may be firmly established, its issuance is largely discretionary with the court, and depends upon a consideration of all of the facts, circumstances, and relative equities as between the parties. Consequently, an injunction will not be issued if the encroachment is slight, was unintentional, and if the harm to be suffered by the owner of the encroaching structure by its compulsory removal would be greatly disproportionate to the injury sustained by the owner of the land encroached upon. In such cases, damages only will be awarded in lieu of an injunction. In one case the sum of $10 damages was awarded for an encroachment of between $\frac{1}{2}$ and $\frac{5}{8}$ of an inch, with no evidence of actual damages to the owner, and in another case $200 was awarded where the encroachment was only $3\frac{5}{8}$ inches, and it would have cost $6,875 to remove the portion of the wall encroaching on the adjoining property.

WHERE ENCROACHMENT INTENTIONAL

If it appears that the encroachment was *intentional,* as distinguished from an innocent mistake, an injunction may be granted even in the absence of present damage to the land encroached upon, and even though it appears that the encroachment is slight and the cost of removal is great. This rule was recognized in the case of *Agmar* v. *Solomon,* 87 C.A. 127, involving an encroachment of $4\frac{1}{2}$ inches.

Illustrative case—unintentional encroachment. The case of *Ukhtomski* v. *Tioga Mutual Water Co.,* 12 C.A.2d 726, involved an encroachment of $^{15}/_{100}$ acre on land worth $150 an acre. The encroaching structure was a reservoir which cost $7,000 to construct, and which served five hundred people. The court awarded damages only in the sum of $762.41. In denying a mandatory injunction, the court emphasized the serious harm to the defendant if the injunction were granted, the defendant's inadvertence and innocent mistake in constructing the reservoir, the fully compensatory nature of the damage awarded, and the serious injury to the public if the reservoir were ordered removed.

III. Fences

A fence is a visible, tangible obstruction, made of wood, iron, stone, or other suitable material, interposed between two portions of land so as to separate and shut in land and set it off as private property. Fences, unless portable, are fixtures, and thus become part of the real estate to which they are attached.

FENCING LARGELY A MATTER OF DISCRETION

Except for any duty to construct and maintain fences imposed by agreement, easement, or prescription, and the duty to keep domestic animals off the land of others, and other statutory duties imposed under special circumstances, as in the case of dangerous premises, the owner of land may leave his land unfenced. On the other hand, if he so desires, he may build fences on his own property where he pleases, provided it is not in violation of the spite fence law or a nuisance, is not constructed negligently so as to cause harm, and does not violate zoning regulations.

SPITE FENCES

By statute, it is provided that a fence unnecessarily over 10 feet high, and maliciously erected or maintained for the purpose of annoying the occupant of adjoining property, is deemed a private nuisance, and may be abated as such. (C.C., Sec 841.4.)

MAINTAINING DIVISION FENCES

Under Section 841 of the Civil Code it is provided that coterminous owners (adjoining owners) are mutually bound to maintain the fences between them, unless one of them chooses to let his land lie unfenced. If he afterward incloses his land, however, he must then contribute to the other a just proportion of the value of the fence dividing their property.

INTERFERENCE WITH GATES

Under Section 602(h) of the Penal Code, it is a misdemeanor to wilfully open, tear down, or otherwise destroy or leave open the gate or bars of any fence on the inclosed lands of another.

IV. Trees and other vegetation

Trees or hedges standing partly on the land of adjoining owners belong to them in common. (C.C., Sec. 834.) Neither owner can cut or injure them, except that one owner can cut limbs that cause damage to his property if such action does not injure the other owner's windbreak.

OVERHANGING BRANCHES

Trees whose trunks stand wholly upon the land of one owner belong exclusively to him, although their roots grow into the land of another. (C.C., Sec 833.) However, the adjoining owner has the right to cut limbs or roots overhanging or extending into his property, but only to the boundary line. An adjoining landowner does not have a cause of action from the mere fact that the branches of an innoxious tree on his neighbor's land overhang his premises. He has the right to cut off the overhanging branches, which is considered a sufficient remedy. However, if the encroaching roots are noxious, an action to abate a nuisance is maintainable. (*Bonde* v. *Bishop,* 112 C.A.2d 1.)

CONTROL OF WEEDS

In the absence of a statute or ordinance, a landowner owes no duty to an adjoining proprietor to prevent seeds from vegetation naturally growing on his land from maturing and being blown by the wind onto the adjoining land. Accordingly, a landowner has been held not entitled to the abatement of arrow weeds growing on the banks of a ditch that crosses his property. (*Boarts* v. *Imperial Irr. Dist.,* 80 C.A.2d 574.) However, weeds are subject to pest control, and may also be declared a public nuisance when dangerous to public health or safety.

V. Lateral and subjacent support

Lateral support is that support which one tract of land receives from an adjoining tract separated from it by a vertical plane. At common law, an owner of land is entitled to have it supported in its natural condition by the adjoining land. Liability for infringing this right is not dependent upon any lack of care or skill by a person who removes the natural support of land, but is absolute. Although a landowner may excavate his own ground for any lawful purpose, he must do so in such a manner that the land of an adjoining owner will not, either by its own weight or through the action of the elements, fall into the excavation.

STATUTORY RULE IN CALIFORNIA

This common-law doctrine has been modified in California by statute. (C.C., Sec. 832.) This statute has been declared to be a relaxation of the rule of absolute liability. Although it restates the common-law concept that an owner of land is entitled to the lateral and subjacent support that his land receives from adjoining land, it permits a landowner to excavate his own land freed from the absolute right of lateral support in the owner of adjoining land if the conditions specified in the statute are complied with.

NOTICE TO ADJOINING OWNERS

The statute permits an owner to make proper and usual excavations on his land for purposes of construction or improvement, but requires him to give reasonable notice to adjoining owners. It also requires that ordinary care and skill be used in making an excavation, and that reasonable precaution be taken to sustain adjoining land.

DUTIES OF EXCAVATOR

With respect to support for land alone, the owner making excavations must state in the notice to the adjoining owner the time the excavation is to commence and the intended depth thereof. In actions against excavators for negligence, it is necessary to show that the negligent excavating was the proximate cause of the collapse of the adjoining land. However, heavy rainfall and saturation of soil may be a hazard reasonably foreseeable, and against which the excavator, in the exercise of ordinary care, should take due precautions. Where an excavation is carefully made and substituted support is furnished, such as a bulkhead, and the land nonetheless subsides as a result of negligence in permitting weakening of the substituted support, the excavator is liable in the same manner as if the original support had been withdrawn.

SUPPORT OF BUILDINGS

At common law, the rule of absolute liability did not extend to the support of buildings but only to the support of land. Hence, an excavator was not liable for damage to the building unless he was negligent, in which case the ordinary rules of tort liability would apply.

Statutory rule. In California, liability for support of buildings exists under general tort principles for negligence in excavation, and the requirement of notice under the statute is applicable so that the excavator is also liable for failure to give notice. In these respects the rule on damage to buildings is the same as that governing damage to the land itself. The statute additionally makes specific provision for liability where the excavation is deeper than the foundations of the adjoining building, or deeper than the standard depth of 9 feet (9 was substituted for 12 by a 1968 amendment). If the excavation is to go deeper than the walls or foundations of the adjoining building, and is to be so close as to endanger it, the excavator must give the owner of the building at least thirty days to protect it, and must for that purpose permit him to go on the land that is being excavated. If the excavation is to go to or deeper than the standard depth of foundations (defined as 9 feet below curb level), and the foundations of the adjoining structure also go to such depths, then the excavator must support the land and building or other structure, without cost to the owner. The excavator is made absolutely liable for any damage, except "minor settlement cracks," if he fails to do so.

SLIDE DAMAGE

In the case of *Rhodes* v. *San Mateo Investment Co.,* 130 C.A.2d 116, plaintiff brought an action for an injunction and for damages caused by excavation on adjoining property. Plaintiff's land was on a hillside, adjoining that of the defendant. Defendant made excavations on its property that resulted in slides creeping toward plaintiff's land. At the time of the trial this slide area was moving closer to plaintiff's property, but had not actually encroached upon it, and no physical damage had actually occurred to plaintiff's land. The court denied relief as to damages, but issued a permanent injunction, requiring the defendant to stabilize the hillside so as to prevent slides from encroaching upon or damaging plaintiff's property. Regarding damages, the court stated that if the defendant's land is stabilized so as to prevent slides from encroaching on or damaging plaintiff's property, mere buyer fear of future slides or other psychological effect on prospective buyers of the use by defendant of its property could not be the basis for an award of damages.

SUBJACENT SUPPORT

Subjacent support is that support which the surface of the earth receives from underlying strata. The general rule is that a landowner is entitled to the perpendicular support that is afforded by subjacent strata. Since the subject of subjacent support is closely related to that of lateral support, it is governed by similar rules. A city in constructing a tunnel beneath a street owes a duty similar to that imposed by statute upon coterminous owners to use ordinary care and skill and to take reasonable precautions to avoid injury to the fee owner of a part of the street. (*Porter* v. *City of Los Angeles,* 182 Cal. 515.)

VI. Light and air

The English doctrine of ancient lights under which a landowner acquires, by uninterrupted use, an easement over adjoining land for the passage of light and air was early repudiated in this state, for the reason that it is not adapted to the conditions existing in this country, and could not be applied to rapidly growing communities without working mischievous consequences to property owners. The use of light and air from adjoining premises cannot be adverse, since there is no invasion of the adjoining owner's rights of which he can complain. Thus, he cannot be presumed to have assented to that use or to have parted with a right. However, an easement for the passage of light and air over adjoining property may be created by an express grant of an interest in, or by a covenant relating to, the land over which it passes.

VII. Nuisances

Section 3479 of the Civil Code provides that anything that is injurious to health, or is indecent or offensive to the senses, or an obstruction to the free use of property, so as to interfere with the comfortable enjoyment of life or property, or unlawfully obstructs the free passage or use, in the customary manner, of any navigable lake, or river, bay, stream, canal, or basin, or any public park, square, street, or highway, is a nuisance. A public nuisance is one that affects any considerable number of persons. Any other is a private nuisance.

INTERFERENCE WITH USE AND ENJOYMENT OF PROPERTY

A nuisance consists of the unlawful interference with a person's interest in the use and enjoyment of his property. It is ordinarily immaterial whether the defendant acts intentionally, negligently, or with due care. The act or thing may affect the use of property, as in the case of an obstruction of a right of way, or it may affect the senses, as in the case of smoke or noxious odors.

EXAMPLES OF NUISANCES

Cases decided by the courts in California furnish innumerable examples of nuisances, including such things as the obstruction of an abutting owner's access to a street, which is a private as well as a public nuisance; pollution of water in a stream or an irrigation ditch; and poisonous dust, sprayed to kill plant pests, carried by the wind to adjoining land, killing the owner's bees. One case involved chickens scratching in dry dust, which sent up clouds of dust and polluted the neighbor's vineyards. (*McIntosh* v. *Brimmer,* 68 C.A. 770.)

ACTS OFFENSIVE TO ESTHETIC SENSE

Where the act complained of merely offends the esthetic sense, it has been held that it cannot be enjoined as a nuisance. (*Haehlen* v. *Wilson,* 11 C.A.2d 437.) In the cited case, plaintiff sought to compel the removal of a wooden fence, 6½ feet high, which defendant built within 3 inches of the boundary line between the property of plaintiff and defendant, but entirely on the defendant's property. Plaintiff claimed, among other things, that the fence created an ugly and untidy appearance. The court stated that in the absence of some legislative action, the courts cannot set up esthetic standards to which builders must conform. The court in quoting from another case stated:

> No case has been cited, nor are we aware of any case, which holds that a man may be deprived of his property because his tastes are not those of his neighbors. Esthetic considerations are a matter of luxury and indulgence, rather than a necessity, and it is necessity alone which justifies the exercise of police power to take private property without compensation.

MENTAL AND EMOTIONAL FACTORS

In an earlier case, decided in 1921, involving an undertaking establishment that was established in a residential district, it was held that the resulting mental depression to a property owner could not be the basis for an injunction. (*Dean* v. *Powell Undertaking Co.*, 55 C.A. 545.) However, in a later case, that of *Brown* v. *Arbuckle*, 88 C.A.2d 258, decided in 1948, the trial court held that the establishment of a mortuary and funeral parlor in a residential district should be enjoined as a nuisance, on evidence that it would be a constant mental irritant to plaintiff and his family, and would thereby cause them to suffer physical disturbances. The judgment was affirmed by the appellate court. The opinion reviewed authorities from other states, which disclosed a trend in that direction. New weight has thus been given to mental and emotional factors in determining what constitutes a nuisance, thereby accomplishing, by actions to abate a nuisance, some of the purposes of modern zoning legislation.

VII. Liability to trespassers, licensees, and invitees

An owner of land or the person in lawful possession thereof owes to persons who come on the land certain affirmative duties of care with respect to activities or conditions on the land. The extent of the duty is dependent upon the status of the person who enters upon the land. A distinction is usually made as to the duties owed to three classes of persons, namely, *trespassers, licensees,* and *invitees.* Normally, the duties do not extend to persons outside the land, e.g., on adjacent land or on the highway.

PERSONS OUTSIDE THE LAND

The owner or possessor of land is not liable to persons outside the land for harm caused by natural conditions on the land, but is under the usual liability to any person, including those outside the land, where his dangerous activities cause harm, and he is also liable for creating or maintaining dangerous artificial conditions, or for permitting a dangerous state of disrepair.

CONDITION OF STREETS AND SIDEWALKS

The doctrine that an owner is ordinarily not liable for harm resulting from conditions outside the land is illustrated by cases involving unsafe streets or sidewalks in front of the premises. As a general rule, in the absence of a statute or ordinance, the abutting owners are under no obligation to keep streets or sidewalks in safe condition for the public. Under the provisions of the Streets and Highways Code (Secs. 5610 *et seq.*), abutting owners, upon notice by the superintendent of streets, are required to repair streets or sidewalks that are in a dangerous condition, and a liability is imposed for failure to do so. However, it has been held that the liability so created is to pay for the repairs or reimburse the city therefor, but not to pay damages to an individual for injuries incurred.

DUTY AS TO LIGHT WELLS, DRIVEWAYS, AND THE LIKE

Where the owner builds something that extends into the street or highway, the situation is different. Where an owner constructs a light well in the sidewalk, or a driveway over it, he is under a duty to keep them in repair, and he may be liable to third parties who are injured as a result of his failure to make necessary repairs.

DUTY OWED TO TRESPASSERS

The least duty owed by a landowner to a person entering upon his land is the duty owed to a trespasser. A trespasser is defined as one who enters or remains upon the land of another without privilege or consent. As a general rule, a landowner or occupant is not under a duty to maintain his land in a safe condition for the reception of trespassers. It is usually said that the landowner must merely refrain from intentional harms or "wilful or wanton injury," and that no duty is owed to keep the premises in a safe condition, or to carry on activities carefully.

Exceptions to rule as to trespassers. Two exceptions to this general rule as to nonliability to trespassers for the conditions of the premises have been recognized: (1) a landowner will be liable if he sets a trap and injuries result therefrom, and (2) the attractive nuisance doctrine may apply in a case where the trespasser is a child of tender age.

Attractive nuisance doctrine. The attractive nuisance doctrine has as its origin the railroad turntable cases, and grew up as an important exception to the general rule that the landowner owes no affirmative duty of care to trespassers. The rule is stated in the case of *Cahill* v. *Stone & Co.*, 153 Cal. 571, as follows: "One who places an attractive but dangerous contrivance in a place frequented by children, and knowing, or having reason to believe, that children will be attracted to it and subjected to injury thereby, owes the duty of exercising ordinary care to prevent such injury to them, and this because he is charged with knowledge of the fact that children are likely to be attracted thereto and are usually unable to foresee, comprehend, and avoid the dangers into which he thus knowingly allures them."

Application of doctrine. The doctrine has been applied to a variety of machines, appliances, and contrivances, including an unlocked push car on the rails of a railroad track under construction; a two-wheel trailer carrying a fire box and an iron vat filled with melted tar, easily tipped over; a tunnel, dump car, and stope in an abandoned mine; and poles of an electric transmission line, containing spikes close to the ground which could be climbed by children.

Rationale of the attractive nuisance doctrine. The attractive nuisance doctrine involves what has been described as a "balancing of the opposing conveniences." The duty is to use ordinary prudence and foresight to prevent an injury to children that might be foreseeable, if it can be guarded against without placing an undue burden upon the owner of the land and his right to make a beneficial use thereof. It must be possible and practicable to install safeguards or otherwise prevent the danger without impairing the usefulness of necessary appliances. For instance, a turntable may be rendered safe by locking it, without imposing an undue burden on the owner.

Tests as to whether an attractive nuisance exists. The attraction must be an artificial contrivance, not a natural condition. Also, the attraction must be such that children do not appreciate the danger. Common and familiar dangers are excluded from the operation of the rule. The contrivance must be easily accessible, in a place where the landowner should know that children are likely to trespass. Also, the condition or contrivance must have in fact attracted the child onto the premises.

Private swimming pools. In the case of *Wilford* v. *Little,* 144 C.A.2d 477, it was held that a private swimming pool, equipped with a diving board on unfenced residential property, is not an attractive nuisance, as the term is generally used. In a later case decided by the Supreme Court in 1958, it was held that although a private swimming pool is not an attractive nuisance as a matter of law, the manner of its maintenance and use may be such as to impose the duty of ordinary care on the possessor thereof toward children of tender years, notwithstanding the children may technically occupy the position of a trespasser at the time. (*Reynolds* v. *Willson,* 51 Cal.2d 94.) Thereafter the Supreme Court did extend the attractive nuisance doctrine to swimming pools, overruling numerous earlier decisions. (*King* v. *Lenner,* 53 Cal.2d 340.)

Activities conducted on premises. With respect to activities conducted by the landowner on his property, it is a general rule that there is no duty to discover the presence of a trespasser. However, after discovering the presence of a trespasser, the landowner or occupant is under a duty to refrain from active misconduct that might result in injury to the trespasser.

DUTIES OWED TO A TOLERATED INTRUDER

A tolerated intruder, i.e., a trespasser over a well-defined area where the fact of trespass is known to the landowner who raises no objection, is owed additional duties as follows: (1) as to condition of the land, the owner is under a duty to warn of any change in the condition of the land that increases the hazard of personal injury, and (2) as to activities conducted on the land, the landowner is under a duty to discover the presence of a tolerated intruder, and to refrain from active misconduct that might result in personal injury.

DUTIES OWED TO LICENSEES

A licensee is a person who enters on the land of another by consent or permission, but usually for purposes of his own, having no relation to the business of the owner or occupant. The duty owed to a licensee is somewhat greater than that owed to a trespasser. Although a landowner is not under a duty to maintain his land in a safe condition for the use of a licensee, he is under a duty to give the licensee notice of any change in the condition of the land that increases the hazard of personal injury. With respect to activities conducted by the landowner, there is a duty to discover the presence of a licensee, and to refrain from active misconduct that might result in personal injury to the licensee.

The older cases in California have held that a licensee takes the premises as he finds them, and there was no duty to warn of obvious dangers. But in the case of *Rowland* v. *Christian,* 69 A.C. 89, decided on August 8, 1968, the California Supreme Court held that a property owner does have the duty to warn of a dangerous condition, noting that Section 1714 of the Civil Code states that everyone is responsible for an injury to another by his want of ordinary care or skill in the management of his property. The court held that the proper test to apply to the liability of the possessor of land in accordance with the section is whether in the management of his property he has acted as a reasonable man in view of the probability of injury to others.

PERSONS WHO ARE INVITEES

An invitee, or business guest, enters at the express or implied invitation of the landowner or occupant, for a purpose of common interest or mutual benefit, or in connection with the business of the owner or occupant. The term "invitee" is misleading in some respects. A social guest may be invited, and will still be only a licensee, whereas laborers coming on the property to perform work, or customers coming into a shop or store to look at goods on display, are invitees whether expressly invited or not. The distinguishing characteristic of the invitee is a mutual business interest with the occupant.

Examples of invitees. The following are examples of invitees: a customer entering a store to buy goods; children of a customer, accompanying the customer for reasons of necessity or convenience; a salesman of a wholesale house delivering goods to a retail store; employees of an independent contractor doing work on the owner's premises; employees of a tenant of a building; the guest of a hotel or inn, as well as his own invited guests; and a prospective tenant seeking an apartment.

Duties owed to invitees. The duty owed to an invitee, in addition to warning of known dangers and refraining from active negligence, is to exercise ordinary care to keep the premises in a reasonably safe condition. It has been frequently emphasized that the landowner is not an *insurer* of the personal safety of the invitee, but where the landowner knows of a dangerous condition and fails to correct it or give adequate warning, he is liable. The knowledge of the landowner's employees may be imputed to the owner, as where an employee, acting within the scope of his employment, creates the dangerous condition.

Duty to inspect premises. The fact that the landowner has no actual knowledge of the dangerous condition is not a defense; he has an affirmative duty to exercise ordinary care to keep the premises in reasonably safe condition, and therefore must inspect the premises or take other proper means to ascertain their condition.

NEW LEGISLATION MODIFIES RULES

In 1963 a new section was added to the Civil Code that removes from the legal status of licensee or invitee anyone who enters a landowner's property with his permission for such activities as hunting, fishing, and hiking. (C.C., Sec. 846.) The duty owed such persons is similar to that owed a trespasser. However if a person has been *expressly invited* on the premises, the new rule does not apply, and the landowner will owe the same duty of care owed a licensee or invitee.

Questions

1. Is an owner permitted to use his property in any way he sees fit?
2. How is an encroachment described?
3. Why is the distinction between a permanent trespass and a continuing trespass important?
4. Describe the remedies available to an owner where a building encroaches on his property.
5. Under what circumstances will an injunction be denied where a building encroaches on adjoining property?
6. Is an owner under a duty to construct a boundary fence?
7. Does an owner have the right to cut overhanging branches from his neighbor's trees?
8. May an owner cut roots that extend into his yard?
9. What duties are imposed on an owner with respect to lateral support?
10. Does an owner have any special rights with respect to light and air?
11. What remedies are available to an owner where a nuisance is created on adjoining lands?
12. Does a landowner owe any special duty to a trespasser?
13. Explain the attractive nuisance doctrine.
14. Distinguish the duties owed to a licensee and to an invitee.

10

Land: Descriptions, Surveys, Subdivisions

Summary

I. Introductory
How descriptions are obtained; Sufficiency of description; Parol or extrinsic evidence; Effect where description is insufficient

II. Descriptions by metes and bounds
Former methods of measuring land; Present-day methods; Starting point; Bearing of a line; Use of bearings and distances

III. Government surveys
Starting points for land surveys; Division of land into rectangles; Ranges and townships; Sections; Survey of public lands

VI. Rules for conveying property
Map references in deeds; Record of survey; Official maps; Assessor's maps; State plane coordinate system; Parcel maps; Assessment district maps; Unrecorded maps; Effect of reference to a map

V. Other methods of describing land
Blanket descriptions; Description of a tract by common name; Use of street address

VI. Rules for conveying property
Conveyance of fractional part of a lot; Lines of division; Descriptions in contracts and options; Option case

VII. Rules of construction
Intention must be expressed; Interpretation of a grant or reservation; Exclusion of false matters; Conflicts in numbers; Conflicts in calls; Ground marks; Visible boundaries or monuments; Reference to maps

VIII. Boundaries
Land adjoining a highway

IX. Regulation of subdivisions
Subdivided lands; Subdivision maps; Recording of subdivision maps; Conveyances in violation of Map Act; Regulations by municipalities; Other public controls; Sale of subdivided lands; Out of state lands; Federal Interstate Land Sales Act

I. Introductory

Real property is identified in ordinary day-to-day transactions by street address or popular name, which is sufficient for many purposes, such as receiving mail and directing visitors. But in conveyancing, a sufficient legal description is essential. Land is unique; no two parcels are exactly alike, since each is located in a different place on the earth. The particular location of any parcel of land may be described in such a way that it can be distinguished from all other land, and when this is accomplished, the land can be identified by what is referred to as a "good" or "sufficient" legal description.

HOW DESCRIPTIONS ARE OBTAINED

One of the essential elements of a deed is a sufficient legal description of the property conveyed. Before such a description is written, some person, usually a land surveyor, goes out and locates on the ground the exact boundaries of the tract of land in question, and then puts into words the directions for locating the lines he has traced on the ground. By this method a legal description is obtained.

SUFFICIENCY OF DESCRIPTION

Any one of several methods of describing land may be utilized, including metes and bounds descriptions, the government survey, and tract descriptions as contained in recorded maps. As a general rule, a description of land is a conveyance is sufficient if it identifies the land or furnishes the means of identifying the land. It has been held that if a competent surveyor can take the conveyance and locate the land on the ground from the description contained in the instrument, with or without the aid of extrinsic evidence, the description is legally sufficient. (*Blume* v. *MacGregor*, 64 C.A.2d 244.)

PAROL OR EXTRINSIC EVIDENCE

Parol or *extrinsic evidence* is sometimes admitted in a proper case as an aid in identifying the land. Extrinsic evidence is evidence that is not furnished by the document itself, but is obtained from outside sources. The circumstances under which an instrument was executed, statements made at the time, informal writings such as letters, memoranda, and the like would be extrinsic evidence. The word "parol" refers to oral utterances, but the term "parol evidence" within the meaning of the parol evidence rule is often used in the same sense as extrinsic evidence. Extrinsic evidence as a general rule cannot be used to explain the meaning of a written instrument, since the written instrument supersedes prior and contemporaneous negotiations. Its use is permitted, however, where the written instrument is ambiguous, and its meaning cannot be determined from the instrument itself.

EFFECT WHERE DESCRIPTION IS INSUFFICIENT

If the conveyance has an insufficient description and does not furnish the means by which the description may be made definite and certain to readily locate the land, the conveyance is void. From the standpoint of a title insurer a good description is of importance not only in determining whether the instruments describe the land with sufficient certainty to be valid and operative, but also in determining whether the successive instruments in the chain of title, which may vary greatly in form, in fact describe the same land.

II. Descriptions by metes and bounds

Land may be described by naming its boundaries in detail. These boundaries may be indicated in various ways, as follows: (1) by naming natural boundaries, such as rivers or streams, or trees, or stones, or artificial monuments, such as walls, fences, stakes, or roadways, to, from or along which the boundaries are to run; or (2) by stating the courses and distances of the boundary lines; or (3) by designating the lands of an adjoining owner as a boundary; or (4) by using two or more of these elements in the same description. All of these ways of describing land may be classed generally as descriptions by "metes and bounds," that is, so many units of measurement along a stated boundary line, "metes" meaning measurements, and "bounds" meaning boundaries. However, a metes and bounds description is more commonly thought of as a description that commences at a certain fixed point of beginning and goes on courses and distances to another point and thence following the boundary lines of the tract of land by successive causes and distances until the point of beginning is reached, with or without calls for monuments as tie points.

FORMER METHODS OF MEASURING LAND

In the period when California was principally vast, open land, it was not too material that boundaries or areas were but vaguely determined. Metes and bounds descriptions were commonly employed that by today's standards were extremely crude. Old records refer to such landmarks as "the dead oak tree with the skull of a steer set in its fork," or "the clump of sycamores springing from one root." Stones, houses, adobe walls, streams, and other such reference points were used, often with little regard for the fact that time might erase them as markers, or that their location might be changed. To measure distances from such points, the surveyors' methods varied. Two men on horseback might measure land with the aid of a rawhide thong 100 *varas* long (a *vara* being approximately 33 inches). One man would stand still while the other rode ahead with the line, then he would wait while the other rode ahead with the line. This process would continue until all the ground had been covered and the number of lengths of line required to cover the ground had been counted. Or the circumference of the wheel of a cart would be measured, and with that as a unit, and a thong tied to a spoke so that the wheel's revolution might be tallied, a driver could proceed over distant areas and report the "exact" dimensions of the land.

PRESENT-DAY METHODS

Today, of course, when land is surveyed, it is measured accurately. Competent surveyors establish exact directions of boundary lines by transits and other instruments, and with standard measuring devices precise distances are fixed, from officially registered starting points. Because of their impermanency, a description solely by reference to monuments has long been considered unsatisfactory where exactness is essential. It was discovered in ancient times by the Egyptians that some system of surveying and describing property must be used whereby boundary lines may be stabilized and identified without recourse to monuments. By developing and applying the science of geometry to land surveying, they began to describe boundaries by courses, i.e., the bearing of lines with reference to a meridian, and by distances in such manner that the land could be located and its boundaries established on the ground without the aid of monuments. This system of land survey and description is generally used today, though courses may tie to reasonably permanent and notorious monuments, such as streets, and also to adjoining lands and buildings when circumstances make it advisable.

STARTING POINT

The first requisite of a metes and bounds description is a definite and stable starting point. Sometimes this point is marked by a monument, such as an iron pipe, or quite often the point is described as the intersection of two streets, or the corner of a lot shown on a recorded map, or a point located at a specified distance from such street or lot corner. The boundary line must then be run continuously from one point to another, returning to the starting point, so as to produce a closed area. From the point of beginning the description recites the course or direction and usually the length of each succeeding boundary line. If the line runs east or west, or north or south, the course is so given. Or if the line is to run in a general course to a fixed point or monument, the direction is recited, for instance, as "thence northerly" to the point or monument. But usually the line proceeds at an angle that requires a statement of the bearing of the line.

BEARING OF A LINE

The bearing of a line is its angular deviation measured in degrees, minutes, and seconds, from any line assumed or considered as a meridian, such line usually being true north or south, or a meridian noted on some other record assumed as sufficient for the particular case, or the magnetic meridian. To illustrate, visualize a circle, whose circumference contains, as we know, 360 degrees, with each degree composed of 60 minutes and each minute composed of 60 seconds, and then divide the circle into four equal parts by a line running north and south, and a line running east and west, through the center of the circle, as illustrated in Fig. 10–1.

The north and south line has a bearing of 0 degrees; the east and west

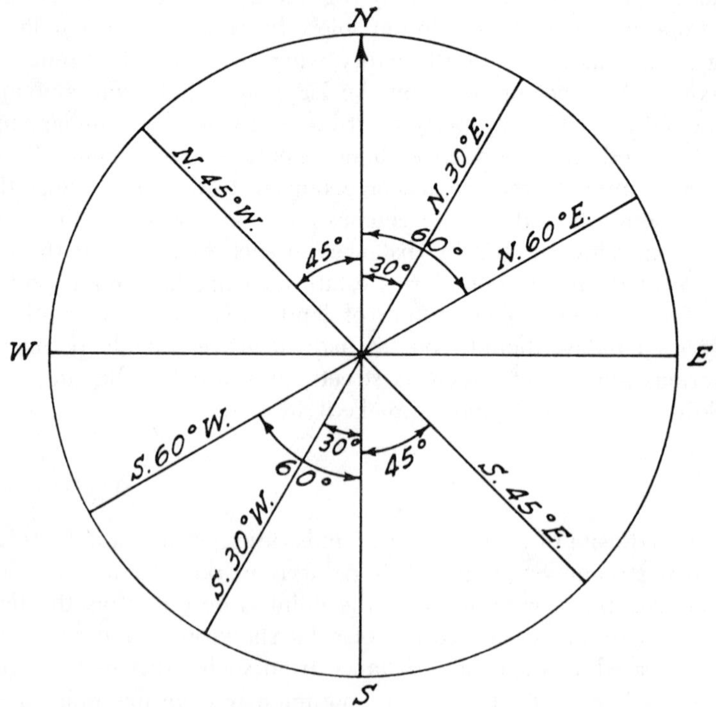

Figure 10-1

lines bear 90 degrees. With the point of beginning at the intersection of the two lines, the bearing of the course is described by measuring easterly or westerly from the north and south line to a maximum of 89° 59′ 59″. Thus, if the direction of a line measures 30 degrees from north toward east, the bearing of the line is stated as "North 30 degrees East," or merely "N 30° E." If the angular deviation is greater than 90 degrees, the measurement is not given, for instance, as 135 degrees, as in the case of a mariner's azimuth course, but as 45 degrees east of south, or "S 45° E."

USE OF BEARINGS AND DISTANCES

When the length of the line whose bearing is given is added, the descriptive details of the course are complete. From an engineer's viewpoint, bearings and distances are essential in order to check for errors, in closure. However, a statement of bearings and distances is not essential for a sufficient description. In drafting descriptions to conform to early title deeds, in the absence of a modern survey, lines are described as running to fixed points or monuments, without reciting a distance or bearing, or the distance may be given as an approximate figure followed by the words "more or less." The distance of a line, though specifically given, is controlled by any monument to which it ties.

III. Government surveys

After California became a part of the United States in 1848, public lands, consisting of lands not embraced within the boundaries of pueblos and valid Mexican or Spanish grants, were then subject to survey under the rectangular system of surveys adopted by Congress by the Ordinance of May 20, 1785. This system provided for the division of the public land into townships six miles square. By running lines north and south at one-mile intervals and east and west at right angles, the townships were then divided into 36 sections of 640 acres. This system, known as the Government Survey, had been employed previously in vast areas of the United States, such as the Northwest Territory created in 1787.

STARTING POINTS FOR LAND SURVEYS

In order to utilize this system of land description it is necessary to have some substantial landmark to serve as a starting point for the survey of a particular area of land. As we know, a ship at sea gives its position in terms of *longitude* and *latitude.* Similarly, the exact location of any point of land may be so designated, naming the north-south line and the east-west line that cross at that spot. Using such points as starting places and measuring in stated directions, descriptions of land areas of any shape and size are possible. Throughout the country, many conveniently located markers have been established on which are indicated their precise longitude and latitude.

Longitude. Longitude is measured by north-south meridians, encircling the earth through the poles, counting from the prime meridian (0°) which runs through Greenwich, England, just outside of London. West longitude extends halfway around the earth westerly from Greenwich. Each degree of longitude is 1/360 of the earth's circumference. At the equator a degree measures 69.17 miles; the distance between meridians shortens, of course, as you travel toward the poles.

Latitude. Latitude lines are called parallels. Each point of any one of them is the same distance from the equator as any other point of that parallel. North latitude is measured "up" from the equator (0°) to the North Pole (90°).

Location of California. Longitude and latitude are expressed in degrees (°), minutes (′), and seconds (″). The state of California is located between Latitude 32° North and Latitude 42° North, and Longitude 114° West and Longitude 125° West.

Base and meridian lines. Within the state three principal points have been established as starting points from which measurements are generally taken (see Fig. 10–2). The initial point in southern California, for instance, is a point on San Bernardino Mountain in San Bernardino County. From this point a line is run north and south. This line is a true meridian, and is referred to as a *principal meridian.* Through the initial point another line is run east and west on a true parallel of latitude, and this line is called a *base line.* These two lines, perpendicular to each other, are the lines of reference. The principal meridians in other areas are Mt. Diablo Meridian in central California, and the Humboldt Meridian, in northern California. The latter is located on Mt. Pierce in Humboldt County.

Reference to base and meridian lines. The reference to the meridian may also include a reference to the base line, although it is not essential. Thus a reference to the San Bernardino Meridian may be designated "San Bernardino Base & Meridian." The references are customarily abbreviated "S.B.M." or "S.B.B. & M." Reference to the meridians by local name is more convenient than would be the practice of describing the location of land always in terms of longitude and latitude.

DIVISION OF LAND INTO RECTANGLES

Starting from one of these points, the object of a government survey is to divide the land into uniform rectangular areas. This is accomplished by dividing the area being surveyed into tracts approximately 24 miles

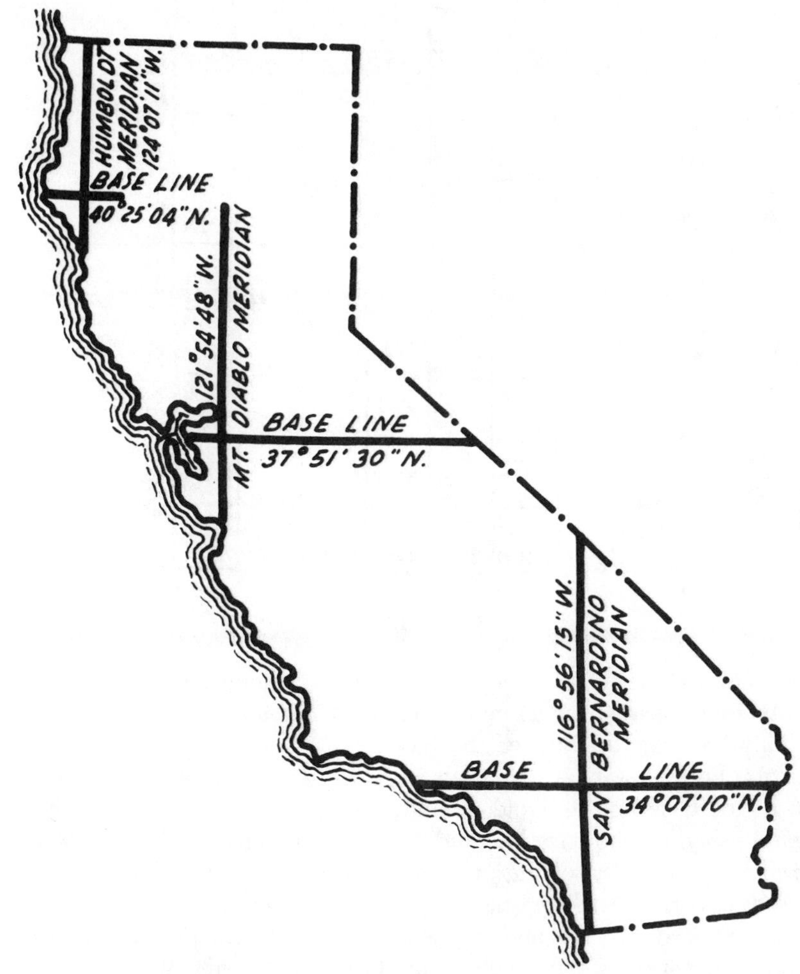

Figure 10-2. The vertical lines are California's three "principal meridians," with the horizontals base lines. Base lines "co-ordinate" with meridians; mapmakers call such lines "co-ordinates."

square. These tracts are further divided into parts that are six miles square, called townships.

Standard parallels and guide meridians. As meridians pass northward or southward from the equator, they converge toward and intersect at the poles of the earth. Thus, the true meridians of a government survey converge and cause a loss of area in the township as they are measured northward. To compensate for such loss of area, the government survey system incorporates the use of *standard parallels* and *guide meridians,* as illustrated in Fig. 10–3.

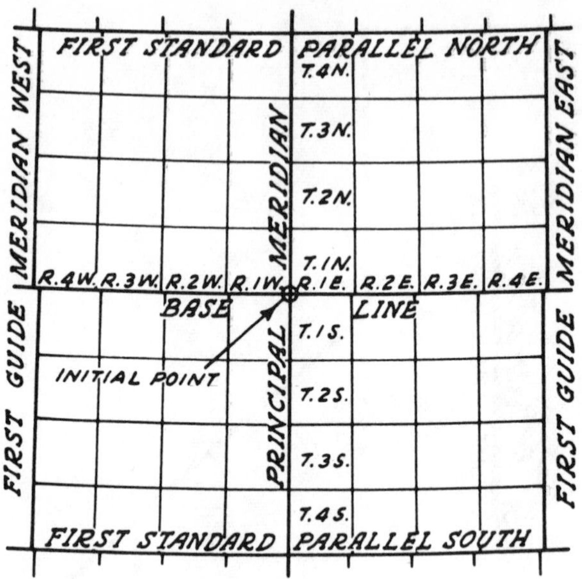

Figure 10-3

Correction lines. The standard parallels are established at points on the principal meridian at 24-mile intervals north and south of the base line. However, in the case of the San Bernardino Base and Meridian, correction lines or standard parallels were established at 30-mile intervals north of the base line to avoid mountainous areas. The guide meridians are established on the base line and on each standard parallel at 24-mile intervals east and west of the principal meridian. The standard parallels are used as correction lines; new intervals of 24 miles are measured off along a standard parallel, and a new series of guide meridians based on these new intervals is extended for another 24 miles, and so on.

RANGES AND TOWNSHIPS

From starting points six miles apart on the base line and on each of the standard parallels, lines are run north on true meridians to the standard parallel directly north of such starting points. Each of the strips of land so formed is called a *range,* and is given a number. For example, the first range east of the principal meridian is "Range 1 East," while the first range west of the principal meridian is "Range 1 West." Next, lines are run east and west at six-mile intervals, bisecting the range lines to form squares called *townships,* which are numbered similarly to ranges. The east-west rows of townships are called tiers. The first tier of townships north of the base line is "Township 1 North," and the first tier south of the base line is "Township 1 South." The townships, each ap-

SECTIONAL MAP OF A TOWNSHIP WITH ADJOINING SECTIONS

36	31	32	33	34	35	36	31
1	6	5	4	3	2	1	6
12	7	8	9	10	11	12	7
13	18	17	16	15	14	13	18
24	19	20	21	22	23	24	19
25	30	29	28	27	26	25	30
36	31	32	33	34	35	36	31
1	6	5	4	3	2	1	6

Figure 10-4

proximately six miles square, constitute the largest subdivisions of the survey. Each such township can be readily described by reference to the range and township number, as follows: "Township 2 North, Range 3 West," which is usually abbreviated to "T.2N., R.3W." As is seen in Fig. 10–3, the south corners of townships north of a standard parallel may not coincide with the north corners of townships south of the parallel.

SECTIONS

Each township is subdivided into 36 sections, each of which is theoretically one mile square and contains 640 acres (see Fig. 10–4). These sections are numbered consecutively, commencing with section 1 in the northeast corner of the township and numbering west to section 6; thence proceeding east from section 7 in the next tier to section 12 and so on, back and forth, until section 36 is reached, in the southeast corner. Sections 16 and 36 in each township were set aside for the state for school purposes.

Divisions of a section. The section corners are marked on the ground by stakes or monuments. Halfway between these corners, monuments or stakes are also set to mark what are called "quarter corners," and imaginary lines drawn from the quarter corners divide the section into four "quarter sections," each containing approximately 160 acres. Further subdivisions may be made, as illustrated by Fig. 10–5.

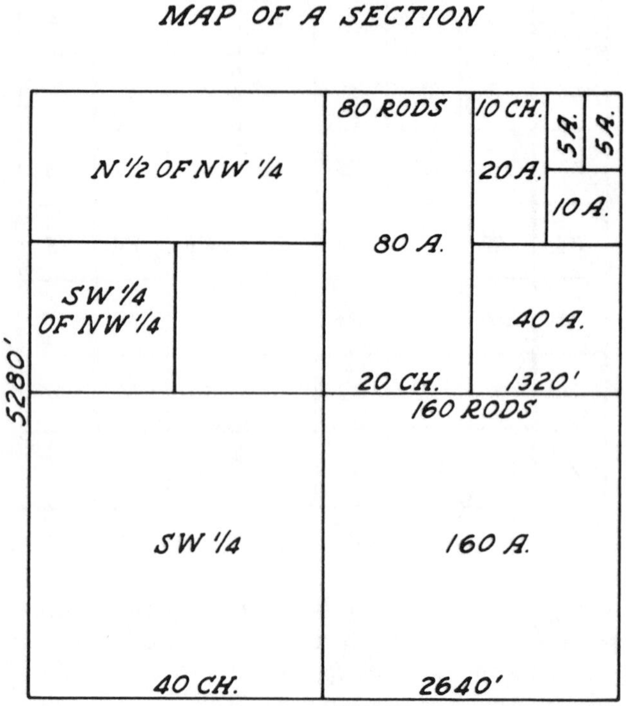

Figure 10-5

Fractional sections. The area of a section is frequently more or less than the standard of 640 acres. Because of the convergence of the meridians, a township is theoretically some 2 or 3 rods narrower across the north side than along the south side. The practice in surveying a township is to apportion any excess or deficiency to the quarter-quarter sections on the north and west sides of the townships. These irregular units are numbered as "lots," or designated as a "fractional quarter" of a quarter section. Fractional sections may also result in other cases where a section contains a shortage—if, for instance, a portion of its normal area is taken up by a body of water or by the boundaries of a Mexican grant.

Describing sectional property. A legal description of a parcel of land in a government survey identifies the land by designating the township, range, and section of the principal meridian area involved as follows:

The northwest quarter of the southwest quarter of section 10, Township 2 North, Range 3 West, San Bernardino Meridian.

Additional references in description. The names of the county and state are added customarily to the description, but omission thereof in this type of description does not make the description defective. It is desirable, especially where several government surveys have been made, to further identify the land by adding a reference to the particular government plan that controls the location of the land in question.

SURVEY OF PUBLIC LANDS

No disposition of public lands is made, as a rule, until the land in question has been officially surveyed. The survey of public lands involves the running of the lines, establishing corners, marking trees or other objects so as to identify the section on the ground, and, in addition, the preparation of field notes of the survey and a plat. The plat of the survey becomes official in most cases when duly approved or accepted and filed in the district land office of the United States.

Descriptions contained in patents. Public lands conveyed by patent from the government are described by reference to the official plat of the survey, which plat, together with the field notes, constitutes a part of the description of the land granted. The location of the land described in the patent is fixed by the position of the lines established by the last approved government survey of such land before disposition. Resurveys of public lands by the United States are authorized by law for the purpose of establishing the boundaries of public lands remaining undisposed of, but such resurveys cannot impair prior rights.

Conflicts in descriptions. Since the true corner of a section is fixed where established by the last survey before disposition by the government, a section delineated on the government plat as a perfect rectangle containing 640 acres may be shown actually to be otherwise by the monuments on the ground. This is of particular importance where subdivisions of a section are conveyed by reference to acreage, with material conflicts often resulting from such practice.

IV. Reference to maps and plats

From the earliest days of conveyancing in California, as elsewhere, it has been a recognized practice to deposit maps or plats in the office of the county recorder, and to make sales or conveyances by reference to them. A description of land by mere reference to a lot or parcel number on the map is sufficient if the map can be produced and identified, and if a surveyor by applying the rules of surveying can locate the land from the descriptive data.

MAP REFERENCES IN DEEDS

The "lot, block, and tract" method of describing property is used where land has been surveyed and subdivided into parcels, and a map of the subdivision has been recorded in the office of the county recorder. A description making reference to a map refers to a designated lot in a block of a designated tract followed by the following or similar words: "as shown on a map recorded in book ____, page ____ of Maps, in the office of the county recorder of ______________ County, State of California." The exact location of the property is shown on the recorded map of which the particular lot is a part. Various matters affecting the ownership of the lot, such as easements for street purposes, or storm drains, or dedications for parks or other public uses, may also be shown on the map.

RECORD OF SURVEY

A map showing the record of a survey by a surveyor or civil engineer may be filed with the county surveyor, and, when approved by him, it must be filed with the county recorder and placed in a book entitled "Record of Surveys." Such a map may be filed for the purpose of showing material evidence not appearing of record or material discrepancies with the record. (Bus. & Prof. C., Sec. 8762.) A description by reference to a record of survey map filed in the county recorder's offce may be sufficient if the boundaries of the land described can be identified without question from the data shown on the map. Prior to September 17, 1965, record of survey maps were also filed to establish the fact that a proposed subdivision of land did not constitute a "subdivision" under the provisions of the Subdivision Map Act. Presently parcel maps are used to establish such fact. (Bus. & Prof. C., Secs. 11535 and 11576.)

OFFICIAL MAPS

In addition to maps prepared by private individuals, official maps also may be referred to in legal descriptions. The law permits the filing with the county recorder of an "official map" of a city, town, or subdivision, showing lot and block numbers, prepared by the city engineer or county surveyor and approved by the governing body of the city or county, as the case may be. (Bus. and Prof. C., Sec. 11655.)

ASSESSOR'S MAPS

The law also permits the county assessor to prepare and file in his office maps showing parcels of land designated by number or letter. Under the provisions of Section 327 of the Revenue and Taxation Code, as amended in 1951, land may be described by a reference to such map for assessment purposes, but shall not be described in any deed or conveyance by a reference to any such map unless such map has been filed in the county recorder's office.

STATE PLANE COORDINATE SYSTEM

Another system of describing land which has been growing in use is provided for in Sections 8801 to 8816 of the Public Resources Code and is referred to as the California Coordinate System. This system is based on the theory, first advanced by Sir Isaac Newton, that the earth is an oblate spheroid (a sphere flattened at the poles) whereas it had previously been considered to be a perfect sphere. Various government offices in California have adopted this system of describing land.

PARCEL MAPS

Effective September 17, 1965, various changes were made in the Business and Professions Code to provide for the preparation, approval, and filing with the county recorder, of "parcel maps." As a rule of title practice, such a map may be used for primary reference purposes in a legal description, provided the map is complete and sufficiently definite to identify conclusively the boundaries of the land.

ASSESSMENT DISTRICT MAPS

Also effective September 17, 1965, various sections of the Streets and Highways Code were amended to provide that the map of a proposed assessment district formerly filed with the county clerk, shall be filed with the county recorder in a book of maps of Assessment Districts. The use of such descriptions may be encountered in assessments, bonds, certificates of sale and deeds on foreclosure of such liens, instead of using the usual record description. If the assessment district map as filed varies in dimensions or location from the record title and does not definitely and conclusively identify the land, remedial action may be necessary for title insurance purposes, such as a quiet title action or corrective deeds.

UNRECORDED MAPS

An unrecorded map may be sufficient for purposes of direct reference in instruments, provided the map can be introduced and properly identified, or otherwise established. But a title based on instruments containing such descriptions is not a good title of record, and is not regarded as insurable.

EFFECT OF REFERENCES TO A MAP

Where a lot conveyed by deed is described by reference to a map, such map is made a part of the deed, and the conveyance is subject to all matters shown on the map. (*Danielson* v. *Sykes*, 157 Cal. 686.)

V. Other methods of describing land

The three primary methods discussed previously are the most common ways of describing real property. However, other methods that also are legally sufficient may be employed. Thus, land may be described in a conveyance by appropriate reference to another instrument that contains a sufficient description. And a conveyance may exclude, as well as include, land by reference to another deed, as in the case where a deed describes a specified tract, excepting those portions that are described in a certain conveyance of record in a specified book and page in the recorder's office.

BLANKET DESCRIPTIONS

A conveyance of land by a blanket description, such as "all land (of the grantor) wherever the same may be situated," or "all lands belonging to the grantor in ______________ county," is sufficient to pass title to all of the grantor's land within the scope of the description.

DESCRIPTION OF A TRACT BY COMMON NAME

Another method of description sometimes used, though it was more common in the early days of conveyancing in California, is a description of a tract by a name by which it is known and may be identified. Extrinsic evidence may be admitted as an aid in locating the land and establishing its boundaries. Ordinarily a conveyance by a descriptive name is not acceptable as sufficient unless the boundaries are shown of record. A deed to the "Rancho San Vicente," a well-known Mexican grant with recognized boundaries, is considered sufficient, but a deed of the "Johnson Ranch," which has reference to sectional land owned by Johnson, is not a sufficient description for title purposes until its exterior boundaries are clearly defined by court decree or other appropriate means of record.

USE OF STREET ADDRESS

A street address may be sufficient under some circumstances; however, it use in most instruments of conveyance is not recommended.

Although it is sometimes held that a conveyance of a house and lot that designates the property by reference to an established house number, naming the street and city, is a sufficient description of the house and lot upon which it is located (*Estate of Wolf*, 128 C.A. 305), the need for parol evidence to identify the boundaries, and the uncertainty as to the extent of the land that would be determined by a court to pass by the description, usually results in a title that is unmarketable and uninsurable until the boundaries are definitely fixed. In commercial leases covering a large structure consisting of numerous store areas, a designation of a smaller area by street number is not an uncommon practice and is generally considered sufficient for such purposes. In the publication of notice of sale of real property in probate proceedings, adding the street address to the legal description by a phrase such as "which property is commonly known as 123 North Elm Street, ____________, California," has proved helpful where discrepancies or omissions in the legal description have occurred.

VI. Rules for conveying property

CONVEYANCE OF FRACTIONAL PART OF A LOT

Where a part only of a lot as shown on a recorded map, or a part of a quarter section or other subdivision of sectional land, is being conveyed, the division is sometimes made, not by a metes and bounds description, but by a description of a specific fractional part of the lot, such as the north one-half, or of a specific quantity of the lot, such as the north 50 feet or the north 10 acres. Where the lot to be divided is regular in shape, usually no problem develops, but where a lot is irregular, conflicts often arise. For instance, if a deed conveys the "north half" of an irregular lot, a question may arise as to whether it describes the north half of the lot by *area* or by *width*. Figure 10–6 illustrates but one of many problems that are encountered in lot division descriptions.

By deeds bearing the same date, assume that the owner of the lot shown in Fig. 10–6 conveyed the "north half" to *A*, and the "south half" to *B*. Two conflicting claims may thereafter arise. *B* may claim title to the portion of the lot lying south of a line extending from the middle point of the east boundary line to the middle point of the west boundary line, whereas *A* may claim title to one half of the lot bounded by a straight line drawn east and west sufficiently north of the south line to embrace one half of the lot area. Although under either contention the lot is equally divided, the location on the ground differs. This can be quite material, particularly where the frontage is affected.

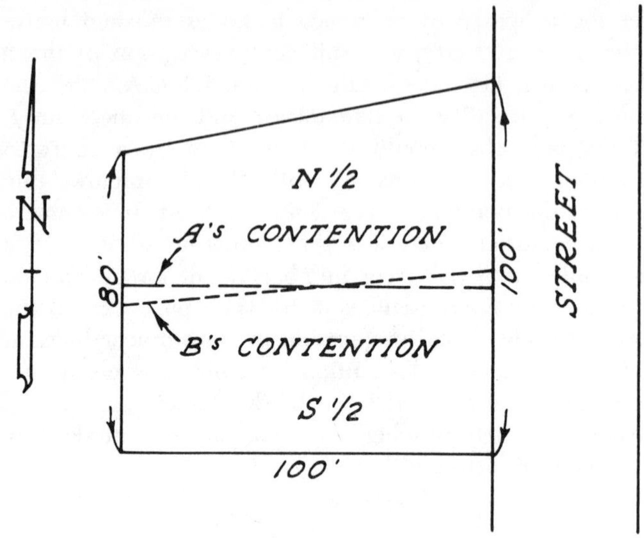

Figure 10-6

LINES OF DIVISION

The word "half" when used in a description without qualification is given its usual meaning as one of two equal parts into which anything may be divided. A conveyance of "half" of a parcel is usually construed to mean a conveyance of a half in quantity. But where the location is not indicated by the context of the conveyance, there is no fixed formula for determining the location of the line that effects the equal division. Such location depends upon the intent as shown by the surrounding circumstances, and these circumstances might be such that the division line determined will actually result in unequal portions.

DESCRIPTIONS IN CONTRACTS AND OPTIONS

Although an incomplete description in a deed of conveyance may void the deed, cases indicate a more liberal view if the questionable description is contained in a contract of sale or in an option agreement. In the case of *United Truckmen, Inc.* v. *Lorentz,* 114 C.A.2d 26, an action was brought for specific performance of a contract to purchase real property. The description contained in the contract referred to the following described property, situated in the county of Santa Clara, state of California: "The southerly portion of that certain property being under the name of Ernest Lorentz Sr. and bounded on the east by

S. 10th Street, and on the south by the Western Pacific Rd., being about 275 feet on S. 10th Street, by approximately 500 feet deep, containing about 3 acres." The whole property, of which that above described was a portion, consisted of approximately 10½ acres. A question arose as to which 3 acres was referred to. The trial court held that the description was too indefinite to compel performance of the contract, but the appellate court reversed the decision of the trial court, and held that the description was not so indefinite that parol evidence could not be offered to determine the true intent of the parties.

OPTION CASE

In the case of *Denbo* v. *Senness,* 120 C.A.2d 863, an option agreement described the property as two acres of that tip of Lot 1, Tract 9765, in the City of Torrance, facing on Pacific Coast Highway and Newton Street. In an action for specific performance of the option, the court held that the description was sufficient to identify a specific parcel, because the location and dimensions of the lot are made certain by the number of the tract, which is in effect a reference to a recorded subdivision map, and two acres of the tip of the lot would have to take in the point or apex of a triangle between the two streets because no other two acres would fit that description.

VII. Rules of construction

The cardinal rule for the construction of the description in a conveyance is to effectuate the intent of the parties if by any possibility that intent can be gathered from the language employed. In ascertaining this intention, the court will place itself as nearly as possible in the position of the parties at the time the instrument was executed, and taking it by its four corners, read the instrument. In order to determine what land was intended to be described where there is an ambiguity, as where part of the boundaries or calls are omitted, the description may be read by reversing the courses.

INTENTION MUST BE EXPRESSED

The intention must be expressed in the conveyance, not merely surmised. If the writing itself does not furnish the means whereby the description may be sufficiently definite and certain, then the instrument is considered void.

INTERPRETATION OF A GRANT OR RESERVATION

To aid in determining the probable intent of the parties where the description is ambiguous, rules of construction have been established, some of which have been enacted into statutes. Under the provisions of Section 1069 of the Civil Code, a grant, other than a grant by a public officer or body, is to be interpreted in favor of the grantee. A reservation, however, is interpreted in favor of the grantor.

EXCLUSION OF FALSE MATTERS

The rule is expressed in Section 2077(1) of the Code of Civil Procedure that where there are certain definite and ascertained particulars in the description, the addition of others that are indefinite, unknown. or false, does not frustrate the conveyance, but it is to be construed by the first-mentioned particulars. This rule is expressed in the case of *Hanlon* v. *Western Loan & Building Co.*, 46 C.A.2d 580, as follows:

> If from the description in the deed, taking into consideration all its calls, it is possible by rejecting calls which are apparently false to ascertain its application to a particular tract of land as embraced within the description, the false call will be rejected and the deed sustained.

In that case, the court rejected the false name of the county given in a description, leaving a sufficient description in the part remaining to identify the land. The same rule has been applied in the case of incorrect lot, block, tract, or map references if the description does in fact contain sufficient particulars to identify the lot intended after rejecting the false references.

CONFLICTS IN NUMBERS

If there is a conflict between a number as spelled out and as referred to in figures, the spelled-out word will prevail over the figures.

CONFLICTS IN CALLS

Where a description contains conflicting calls, the courts resort to established rules of construction, which are designed to give priority to those particulars that are most consistent with the probable intent and least likely to be mistaken. Thus, a call for a natural monument controls over a conflicting call for distance. Although a mistake might be made by the parties as to the length of a boundary line, there can be little doubt as to the extent of a boundary that ties to a natural and visible monument.

GROUND MARKS

The primary endeavor in cases of conflicting descriptions is to retrace the footsteps of the surveyor. Therefore, lines or corners actually marked on the ground usually prevail over calls for courses or distances, or any other call, provided the following conditions are met: (1) the lines were marked prior to or at the time of the grant; (2) the lines are referred to in the conveyance, either directly or indirectly, as by reference to a plat representing the survey; (3) the lines can be found or identified.

VISIBLE BOUNDARIES OR MONUMENTS

Section 2077(2) of the Code of Civil Procedure provides that when permanent and visible or ascertained boundaries or monuments are inconsistent with the measurement, either of lines, angles, or surfaces, the boundaries or monuments are paramount. As an illustration of this rule, if a call in a deed is for a line running to a specified street, such line will be carried to that point, whether the distance required to do so be more or less than named in the deed. Or, if the call in a deed is for a line running along the center of a road on a certain bearing, the true boundary is the center of the road even though such line is in conflict with the bearing given in the deed. The rule of control of monument is not absolute and inflexible, however, and like other rules is subject to qualifications and exceptions where necessary to carry out the true intention of the parties.

REFERENCE TO MAPS

Where the description refers to a map, and that reference is inconsistent with other particulars, it controls them if it appears that the parties acted with reference to the map. Otherwise the map is subordinate to other definite and ascertained particulars.

VIII. Boundaries

Where land is bounded by a monument, such as a street or other way, a conveyance of the land usually carries to the center of the monument. The monument rule in the law of boundaries is expressed in the case of *Freeman* v. *Bellegarde,* 108 Cal. 179, as follows:

> In the absence of any qualifying term the designation in a conveyance of any physical object or monument as a boundary implies the middle or central point of such boundary; as, for example, if the boundary be a

road or highway, or a stream, the thread of the road or stream will be intended; if a rock, a heap of stones, or a tree be the boundary, the central point of such tree or rock or heap of stones will be intended.

LAND ADJOINING A HIGHWAY

The rule is also expressed in the case of *Merchant* v. *Grant*, 26 C.A. 485, that a conveyance of land bounded by a highway, the fee title to which is owned by the grantor, carries the fee to the center of the highway even though the highway is not mentioned in the description.

Presumption as to ownership to street center. The law favors the ownership of abutting owners in public ways and creates a presumption that a conveyance of land adjoining a public way transfers title to the center of the way. Section 831 of the Civil Code provides that "An owner of land bounded by a road or street is presumed to own to the center of the way; but the contrary may be shown." And Section 1112 of said Code provides that "A transfer of land, bounded by a highway, passes the title of the person whose estate is transferred to the soil of the highway in front to the center thereof, unless a different intent appears from the grant." These sections of the Civil Code state a presumption of law and a rule of construction, but do not necessarily establish ownership of roads in the abutter, since ownership is dependent upon matters shown in the chain of title, which may disclose the fact of ownership of the underlying fee in a person other than the abutting owner.

Application of presumption. The application of the presumptions set forth in the Civil Code is illustrated by the case of *Brown* v. *Bachelder*, 214 Cal. 753, wherein it was held that a description of land as bounded by "the south side of Spring Street" carries the grantor's fee title to the center of the street. The court stated that the "south side of Spring Street is the south half thereof," and further stated that the presumption set forth in Section 1112 of the Civil Code is highly favored in the law.

Particular words used. The following words or terms in a description have also been held sufficient to carry title to the center of the street, providing the grantor in fact has title: "to the east line of Maple Street and thence along Maple Street"; "along Oak Street"; to or along "the street line"; to or along "the line of Elm Street." Words or terms in a description may be such, however, that the description will not carry title to the center of the street. This is true if the description reads as follows: "to the east line of Maple Street, and thence along the east line of Maple Street." The rule that such a description excludes the street has been modified to the extent that it is held inapplicable to conveyances made by a referee in partition proceedings for the purpose of dividing all the land, including streets, of the parties to the partition action. (*Machado* v. *Title Guarantee and Trust Co.*, 15 Cal.2d 180.)

Application of street center rule to subdivision map. The street center rule also applies in the case of subdivision maps. If the fee owner of a parcel of land files a subdivision map dedicating an easement for public street purposes over a street shown thereon, and thereafter conveys, by reference to the map, a lot that fronts on the street, his grantee acquires fee title to the center of the street, unless a different intent appears from the grant.

Conveyance of portions bounded by street. Another street center problem may arise in a case where the owner of a lot bounded by a street on one side conveys a fractional portion of the lot that abuts on the street. For instance, the owner may convey the east 100 feet, with 20 feet of the lot being in the street. Does the grantee thereby acquire a maximum of 100 feet, including the portion in the street, or does he acquire 100 usable feet, plus the portion in the street? In other words, is the area conveyed to be measured from the side line of the street or from the center line? It is conceded that the conveyance will pass the grantor's title to the center of the street, subject to the public easement, and that the boundary of the lot conveyed is therefore technically the center of the street. But in view of the fact that the owner of the lot has no right to the possession or occupancy of the street, it is apparent that the term "lot" as commonly used is not understood to include any portion of the street for the purposes of measuring the width. Accordingly, it is a general rule that in the absence of circumstances indicating that a more unusual or technical meaning of the word "lot" or "block" was contemplated by the grantor, a conveyance of a fractional part of a lot or block bounded by a street will be presumed to convey a fractional part of that portion of the lot or block set apart for private use and occupancy, i.e., the lot exclusive of the street area. (*Earl* v. *Dutour,* 181 Cal. 58.)

IX. Regulation of subdivisions

SUBDIVIDED LANDS

Since 1893, with the enactment of the first map act, the recording of maps of subdivisions and the making of sales or conveyances by reference to them has been regulated by the state. Today the laws governing the subdivision of real estate are contained in two different parts of the Business and Professions Code. One part, covering the sale of subdivided lands, and known as the California Real Estate Law (Bus. & Prof. C., Secs. 11000 *et seq.*), is administered by the Real Estate Commissioner. The other part, known as the Subdivision Map Act (Bus. & Prof. C., Secs. 11500 *et seq.*), regulates the filing of subdivision maps with the recorder in the county in which the land is located, and enables cities and counties to pass ordinances governing subdivisions.

SUBDIVISION MAPS

In general and with certain exceptions, a "subdivision" is defined under the Subdivision Map Act as "any real property, improved or unimproved, or portion thereof shown on the last preceding tax roll as a unit or as contiguous units, which is divided for purpose of sale or lease, or financing whether immediate or future, by any subdivider into five or more parcels." The Act contains several exceptions, including, for example, any parcel or parcels divided into lots or parcels, each of a gross area of 20 acres or more, and each of which has an approved access to a maintained public street or highway. In the enforcement of this Act, local governing bodies are primarily interested in the physical aspects of the subdivision, such as lot size and design, road improvements, water mains, sewer lines, and drainage. Under this Act, it is provided that conveyances of any part of a subdivision shall not be made by lot or block number, initial, or other designation, unless and until a final map has been recorded pursuant to the provisions of such Act.

RECORDINGS OF SUBDIVISION MAPS

The enforcement of the provisions of the Subdivision Map Act is vested in the governing body of each county and city. The enforcement of the Act in many instances is delegated to the planning commission of either city or county in which the land is located. Under the Act, the procedure for recording a subdivision map encompasses the filing of a tentative map for approval of the governing body. If the tentative map is approved, the subdivider must file a final map with the county recorder within one year, or within any extension of time that may be permitted. The final map shows lot numbers or lot and block numbers; exterior boundaries of the tract; all survey data as to monuments, and so on; street names; dedication of any public easements required by the governing body; and various certifications required by law, including a certificate signed and acknowledged by all parties having any record interest in the land subdivided, with certain exceptions, consenting to the preparation and recordation of the map. Condominium and community apartment projects are within the scope of the Act if they contain five or more condominiums or five or more parcels, respectively.

In 1965 Section 11568 was added to the Business and Professions Code to provide that when a soil report has been prepared, this fact should be noted on the final map together with the date of the report and the name of the engineer making the report. Also, Section 11590 of said Code was amended to provide that a waiver of direct access to any property dedicated for street or highway purposes may be required from the owner of an interest in abutting property as a condition precedent to the approval of any final map.

CONVEYANCES IN VIOLATION OF MAP ACT

Conveyances of any part of a subdivision are not permitted to be made by lot or block number, initial, or other designation unless and until a final map has been recorded. If a conveyance is made by lot or block number or other designation in violation of the Subdivision Map Act, the conveyance is not void, but is voidable at the sole option of the grantee, his heirs or representatives, within one year after the date of execution of such conveyance. (Bus. & Prof. C., Sec. 11540.)

REGULATIONS BY MUNICIPALITIES

City and county ordinances may also control the division of land into smaller parcels. An ordinance was adopted by the city of Los Angeles on June 25, 1962 regulating lot splits. As used in the ordinance, a lot split is defined as the division of land by separating its ownership or otherwise dividing it into two, three, or four parcels. Such a lot split is intended to control not only the shape and size of the new lots, but also to provide sufficient land for street improvements or access into the newly created lots. Sales contrary to lot split regulations are voidable to the extent and in the same manner as sales in violation of the Subdivision Map Act.

OTHER PUBLIC CONTROLS

Other public controls relate to housing and construction and may have an effect on the subdivision of land. The State Housing Law is designed to provide minimum construction and occupancy requirements for all apartment houses and hotels throughout the state and all dwellings located in cities. Additionally, any city or county may impose more stringent requirements. The State Department of Public Health has the power to control and regulate the statewide enforcement of health measures. Drainage, plumbing, and sewage disposal and water supply are all under the jurisdiction of both the local health officer and the State Department of Public Health.

In 1965 Sections 17953 *et seq.* of the Health and Safety Code were added to require that each city, county, and city and county shall enact ordinances requiring preliminary soil reports on land in subdivisions. Under certain conditions waivers can be obtained. If the preliminary report shows the soil unstable, corrective action is to be recommended by a registered civil engineer.

SALE OF SUBDIVIDED LANDS

The California Real Estate Law regulating the sale of subdivided lands defines a "subdivision," in general, as a division of lands, improved or unimproved, for purposes of sale or lease or financing into "five or more lots or parcels." (Bus. & Prof. C., Sec. 11000.) This law exempts land sold in parcels of more than 160 acres, for other than oil or gas purposes, when such parcels are described on current assessment rolls by government surveys. Section 11004.5 of the Business and Professions Code also includes as subdivisions any of the following: (1) a planned development containing five or more lots; (2) a community apartment project containing two or more apartments; (3) a condominium project containing two or more condominiums; and (4) a stock cooperative having or intending to have two or more shareholders.

The sections of the law administered by the Real Estate Commissioner are designed primarily to prevent fraud in the sale of subdivided lots. The Real Estate Commissioner investigates each tract and publishes a report on his findings, which is available to the public. In addition to matters pertaining to title, liens and encumbrances, restrictions, and method of sale, the report covers information about topography, drainage facilities, available fire protection, sanitation, public utilities (including water, gas, and telephone), streets and roads, public transportation, public schools, and shopping facilities. In 1965 the law was amended to require that a true statement on the maximum depth of fill used or proposed to be used on each lot, and a true statement on the soil conditions in the subdivision supported by engineering reports showing the soil has been or will be prepared in accordance with the recommendations of a registered civil engineer be filed with the notice of intention filed with the Real Estate Commissioner.

In 1965 the law was further amended to provide the Real Estate Commissioner with an additional ground for the denial of the public report if there is a failure to demonstrate that adequate financial arrangements have been made for any guaranty or warranty included in the offering. (Bus. and Prof. C., Secs. 11018 *et seq.*)

A copy of the public report, when issued, must be given to each purchaser prior to accepting a deposit for the execution of any agreement for the sale or lease of a subdivision lot or a unit in a community apartment, condominium, or stock cooperative project.

OUT OF STATE LANDS

The sale or lease within California of lots or parcels in a subdivision situated outside of the state are governed by the real property securities dealers section of the Real Estate Law as well as by the regular subdivision law. The out of state subdivider must obtain a real property securities permit before offering such land for sale in California in addition to the Real Estate Commissioner's public report.

FEDERAL INTERSTATE LAND SALES ACT

The federal Interstate Land Sales Full Disclosure Act (Public Law 90–448) became effective on April 28, 1969, and gives the Secretary of Housing and Urban Development the authority to require full disclosure in the sales or leases of certain undeveloped land in interstate commerce or through the mails. The Act requires developers who contemplate selling or leasing property in affected projects to file a registration statement with the Secretary of Housing and Urban Development. After the statement becomes effective, a property report must be submitted to the purchaser in advance of the signing of any contract or agreement for sale or lease. The contract or agreement for purchase or leasing is voidable at the option of the purchaser if the property report has not been given to the purchaser in advance or at the time of signing. The regulations adopted pursuant to the Act provide that a copy of the material filed with the state of California under state law shall be an effective statement under the federal law. Several exemptions apply, including "the sale or lease of lots where the offering is entirely or almost entirely intrastate." The regulations provide that a developer may obtain an advisory opinion from the Secretary of Housing and Urban Development as to whether an offering is exempt from the Act.

Questions

1. State the purpose of a legal description.
2. What test determines whether or not a description is sufficient?
3. Discuss briefly the three main types of descriptions employed today.
4. Define base and meridian lines.
5. What does "range" in a government survey represent?
6. Explain the difference between a "township" and a "range."
7. Indicate the purpose of correction lines.
8. How many sections are in a township?
9. Are all sections of a township of a uniform size?
10. What is the area of a section?
11. Explain briefly the regulations applicable to the subdivision of lands.
12. Under what circumstances may the use of street addresses be proper?
13. May land be described sufficiently by reference to another instrument?
14. In the construction or interpretation of a description, what basic rule applies?
15. Which controls–monuments or measurements–if a description is inconsistent?

16. Discuss briefly the general rule applying where land adjoining a road is transferred.
17. Does the Real Estate Commissioner have any jurisdiction over the sale in California of out of state land? Explain.

11

Recording and Constructive Notice

Summary

I. Introductory

Under the Spanish and Mexican governments there were no registry or recording laws, and one of the first acts of the California legislature, under the newly formed government following the cession of California to the United States, was to adopt a recording system. It was necessary that some device be created by which evidence of title to, or an interest in, land could be collected in a convenient and safe public place in order that persons intending to purchase or otherwise deal with land might be informed as to the ownership and condition of the title, and be protected from secret conveyances and liens. The main purpose was to make property safely transferable.

Basis of California recording system. The system adopted in California is modeled after the recording system established by the American colonies and in use in many of the eastern states at the time California became a state.

II. Purpose and effect of recording

Under the common law, if an owner of land conveyed the property to *A*, and later conveyed the same property to *B*, the latter acquired no title whatsoever. This common-law rule has been changed by the recording acts that are in force in all of the states today. The distinctive features of the recording system in California, as applied to conveyances of land, may be summarized as follows: conveyances of real property may be recorded in the office of the county recorder in the county where the property is situated, and from the time of recording impart *constructive notice* to subsequent purchasers and encumbrancers. Anyone thereafter dealing with the property is deemed to have notice of the recorded conveyance, even though he may not have inspected the public records and does not have actual notice of the conveyance.

FAILURE TO RECORD

If the conveyance is not recorded, it is considered void as against a subsequent purchaser of the same property in good faith and for a valuable consideration and without actual notice of the prior conveyance, once the subsequent purchaser records his deed. An unrecorded conveyance is valid, however, as between the parties and those who have actual notice.

SUBSEQUENT CONVEYANCE BY GRANTOR

It would seem that an owner who divested himself of his title by deed could not thereafter convey good title to another person. By virtue of the recording laws, however, the grantor retains a statutory power to defeat the first conveyance, if it is not recorded, by making a subsequent conveyance to another party. As between two innocent purchasers, the one whose conveyance is first recorded will prevail.

TIME OF RECORDING

The general purport of recording statutes is to permit rather than to require the recordation of any instrument that affects title to real property, and to penalize the person who fails to take advantage of the privilege of recording. Although the recording statutes do not specify any particular time within which an instrument must be recorded, time of recording is, of course, very important in determining whether or not a person is bound by the constructive notice that recording imparts.

RECORDING DOES NOT VALIDATE A VOID DEED

The recording system does not change the common-law rule that no title can be acquired under an invalid conveyance, such as a forged or a stolen deed. Thus, a void conveyance is not validated by recordation, even though bona fide purchasers may have relied upon the apparent record title.

NOTICE TO BUYERS AND LENDERS

The practical effect of the recording laws is that an intending purchaser of land or a prospective lender may examine the public records and ascertain whether or not the reputed owner is the owner of record, and the date when and the person from whom he acquired his interest, and whether he has encumbered his interest. This determination may be made as to each of the owners in the "chain of title" back to the original source of title. Under the provisions of Section 1215 of the Civil Code, the conveyance, which must be recorded to give notice, includes any instrument in writing by which real property is mortgaged or otherwise affected, except wills. An examination of the record title discloses the condition of the record title as well as the ownership of record.

RECORDED DOCUMENTS AS EVIDENCE

Another recognized purpose of the recording laws is to preserve the evidence of deeds and other instruments so that they may be used as proof of the matters they contain. The original record of every instrument affecting real property, or a certified copy of the record of such instrument, is admissible in evidence in judicial proceedings with the same force and effect as the original instrument. (C.C.P., Sec. 1951.)

III. Instruments that are entitled to be recorded

If the recording of a particular instrument or writing is not authorized by law, it is not entitled to be recorded, and if such an instrument is nonetheless recorded, its recordation will not impart constructive notice to third parties. It is therefore important to ascertain from the statutes what instruments may or may not be recorded.

"INSTRUMENTS" WITHIN MEANING OF RECORDING LAW

It is provided generally that any instrument or judgment affecting the title to or possession of real property may be recorded. (Govt. C., Sec. 27280.) The term "instrument" has been construed to mean some paper "signed and delivered by one person to another, transferring the title to or creating a lien on property, or giving a right to a debt or duty." (*Hoag* v. *Howard,* 55 Cal. 564.) The term includes such legal documents as deeds, mortgages, deeds of trust, leases, contracts of sale, and agreements between owners. Additionally, the recording of many other types of documents and writings that are not technically instruments within the above definition is authorized by various statutes. One class of such documents embraces involuntary liens, such as abstracts of judgments, writs of attachment, and writs of execution. Another class includes instruments transferring personal property but relating to a lien on real property, such as assignments of deeds of trust. Another class includes those giving notice of matters concerning real property, such as a "Notice of Nonresponsibility" or a "Notice of Completion" under the mechanic's lien law. Section 27289 was added to the Government Code in 1967 to provide that whenever a notice is required by law to be recorded for any purpose, it shall be *signed* by the person giving the notice or by his agent.

DOCUMENTS THAT ARE INEFFECTIVE UNLESS RECORDED

In addition to the various types of instruments that may be recorded but that do not have to be recorded to be effective, there are certain documents that have no legal effect until they are recorded. Included in this category are declarations of homestead and declarations of abandonment of homestead. Involuntary liens, such as judgment liens, are not created until recordation is effected.

IV. Manner of recordation

Section 1170 of the Civil Code provides that an instrument is deemed to be recorded when, being duly acknowledged or proved and certified, it is deposited in the recorder's office, with the proper officer, for record. Technically, an instrument is said to be "filed for record" when it is deposited with the recorder under instructions to record, and is actually not "recorded" until the recorder transcribes it into the record books. When the instrument is properly recorded, it operates to give constructive notice by relation back to the date it was filed for record.

FILING WITH COUNTY RECORDER

To record an instrument, it is deposited at the office of the county recorder in the county within which the property is located, with instructions to file for record. The recorder then indorses upon the instrument the proper filing number in the order in which it is deposited, and the year, month, day, hour, and minute of its reception, and the amount of fees for recording. Upon payment of the recording fees, the instrument is entitled to be transcribed in the records. This is done by copying the instrument and retaining the copy in a separate book or a series of books called "official records." The recorder notes at the foot of the record the instrument's filing number, the exact time of its receipt, and the name of the person at whose request it is recorded. Thereafter the recorder endorses on the instrument the book and page of the official records in which it is recorded, and then returns the instrument to the party leaving it for record. Years ago, the instruments were transcribed in the official records by longhand; thereafter typewriting replaced penmanship; and now photography is taking the place of typing as the means of reproducing the instruments. Microfilm may ultimately be used as a means of conserving space.

INDICES AND THEIR USE

The recorder is required to index the recorded instrument in alphabetically arranged grantor and grantee indices, showing the names of the parties, the title of the instrument, the date of filing, and the recording reference. These are called "name indices," and provide the only means by which the title to real property may be traced in the recorder's office. For example, if a person is purchasing land from *A*, the alleged owner, he checks back on the grantee index until he finds the recording reference to the instrument by which *A* acquired title. He then runs *A*'s grantor on the grantee index back to the instrument of acquisition, and in like manner each owner is traced to the source of original title, i.e., a government patent. In addition to a check of the grantee index, the name of each owner in the chain of title must be run on the grantor index subsequent to the date of his acquisition of ownership to determine whether or not he has executed a deed or encumbrance or other instrument, or whether he is a defendant in a court action affecting the title, or whether some other matter of record may be disclosed.

Effective November 8, 1967, the names of parties required to be indexed must be legibly signed, typed, or printed, and all parties executing or witnessing shall legibly sign or shall have the name typed or printed to the side or below the signature. (Govt. C., Sec. 27280.5.)

RECORDS OPEN TO THE PUBLIC

All documents recorded in the county recorder's office are accessible to the public. The clerks in the recorder's office do not search for documents as a general rule, but do show interested parties how to use the indices and explain the location of the various volumes making up the official records. In 1968 new sections were added to the Government Code (Secs. 6250 *et seq.*) to define public records and to provide for their inspection.

PROPERTY IN MORE THAN ONE COUNTY

Where property described in an instrument is located in more than one county, the instrument, or a certified copy of the record thereof, must be recorded in each county in which the property is located in order to impart constructive notice as to all of the property.

FOREIGN LANGUAGE INSTRUMENTS

When it is necessary to record a document written in a foreign language, such as Spanish, a certified translation must be attached to the original instrument. The original instrument and certified translation are presented to the recorder, and, upon payment of the usual fees, the recorder will accept and permanently file the instrument and record the certified translation. The recording of the certified translation gives notice and is of the same effect as the recording of an original instrument. In those counties where a photostatic or photographic method of recording is employed, the whole instrument, including the foreign language and translation, may be recorded and the original instrument returned to the party recording it after recordation has been completed. (Govt. C., Sec. 27293.)

AGENCY RELATIONSHIP OF RECORDER

The recorder is regarded as the agent of the party recording an instrument, and errors or omissions in the record are, as a matter of law, the errors and omissions of the party recording the instrument. Thus, if an instrument is actually filed for record on the first day of the month but the record erroneously shows a filing on the second day of the month or some later day, the instrument is good notice, as to subsequent purchasers, as of the filing date *shown by the record* and not the actual filing date.

V. General effect of the recording laws

An instrument entitled to be recorded and in fact recorded as prescribed by law constitutes constructive notice of its contents, in effect, "to the whole world." Notice is thereby imputed to subsequent parties dealing with the property whether or not they examine the public records, and this notice is binding upon them in the same manner and to the same extent as if they had actual notice.

PERSONS BOUND BY RECORDING

The persons who are particularly affected by the recording laws are subsequent purchasers and encumbrancers. Recording protects a buyer from the claims of subsequent purchasers and encumbrancers; conversely, a buyer's failure to record may create rights in a subsequent purchaser or encumbrancer that will have priority over the rights of the buyer. The effect of an omission or delay in the recording of an instrument affecting the title to real property is stated in Section 1214 of the Civil Code as follows:

> Every conveyance of real property, other than a lease for a term not exceeding one year, is void as against any subsequent purchaser or mortgagee of the same property, or any part thereof, in good faith and for a valuable consideration, whose conveyance is first duly recorded, and as against any judgment affecting the title, unless such conveyance shall have been duly recorded prior to the record of notice of action.

Persons included in term "purchaser." The term "purchaser" is not used in the above code section in the technical sense of purchasers of the legal title, but also includes purchasers of equitable interests in the land, such as a purchaser of land under a contract of sale. Contrary to the rule in some jurisdictions, in California the grantee under a quitclaim deed as well as under a grant deed is protected by the recording laws.

RIGHTS OF CREDITORS OF GRANTOR

A judgment creditor or an attaching creditor of the grantor is not a "subsequent purchaser or mortgagee," or one holding under an "instrument," as these terms are used in the recording law, and as a consequence, an unrecorded deed from the grantor takes precedence over a subsequent attachment or judgment against the grantor. If the conveyance, however, was in fact fraudulent as to the creditor, he may bring appropriate proceedings to have the conveyance set aside. If the judgment creditor purchases the grantor's land at an execution sale and records his certificate of sale, he is then entitled, in the same manner as any other purchaser at the sale, to assert the failure to record a prior conveyance from the grantor. (*Foorman* v. *Wallace,* 75 Cal. 552.)

PURCHASERS FOR VALUE

The subsequent purchaser or encumbrancer who asserts priority over a prior unrecorded conveyance must prove not only that he was without notice and first recorded his conveyance, but also that he parted with a valuable consideration before notice. A valuable consideration is "money or the like"; it must be more than a mere nominal consideration, although it may be less than the full value of the land. The assumption of a debt owed by the grantor or the cancellation of a preexisting indebtedness has been held to be sufficient consideration.

PURCHASERS WITH NOTICE OF UNRECORDED INSTRUMENT

Although the benefits of the recording laws are not available to a purchaser who takes with notice of a prior conveyance, there are situations where notice may not be controlling. Thus, if *A* conveys land to *B*, who is a purchaser for value and without notice of a prior unrecorded conveyance by *A*, and thereafter *B* conveys to *C*, who is a purchaser with notice of the prior conveyance, *C*'s notice will not be material. The general rule is that a bona fide purchaser can convey his interest free and clear of prior unrecorded equities even to a grantee with notice; if the rule were otherwise, the bona fide purchaser might find that he is unable to sell the property.

VI. Effect of recording defective or unauthorized instruments

All recorded instruments do not give constructive notice. Included in the types of instruments that do not impart constructive notice, even though they may have been recorded, are the following: an instrument required to be acknowledged that is unacknowledged or defectively acknowledged and not of record for a period of one year; an instrument not acknowledged by the proper party, such as the seller under a contract of sale, and not of record for a period of one year; an instrument that is made by a stranger to the title (such instrument being referred to as "wild"); an instrument recorded before the grantor or mortgagor acquired title; an instrument not in the chain of title because of a name variance; an instrument that does not describe the land it purports to affect with sufficient certainty, nor furnish the means by which the land can be identified; or an instrument that is not entitled to be recorded, such as a "Notice of Claim of Interest" under an unrecorded contract. This latter rule is illustrated by an opinion of the County Counsel of Los Angeles County, reported in the *Los Angeles Daily Journal* on January 22, 1958.

"NOTICE OF INTEREST IN REAL PROPERTY"

In the opinion of the County Counsel, it was concluded that the county recorder is not required to record a "Notice of Interest in Real Property." It was pointed out that the recordation of instruments is a matter of statutory creation, and there is no statutory provision that authorizes the recordation of such a notice. Although Section 27280 of the Government Code generally authorizes the recording of any instrument that affects the title of real property, the notice in question is not the type of instrument meant to be included within the provisions of the statute. The person executing the notice did not encumber his rights in the property, but rather attempted to give notice of some unknown claim of interest. Accordingly, the instrument was not entitled to be recorded because it had not been duly acknowledged under the meaning of the statutes that require acknowledgment by the person whose rights in the property are alienated or encumbered.

ACTUAL NOTICE OF UNAUTHORIZED INSTRUMENTS

If a prospective purchaser by running the chain of title actually sees the record of a prior instrument that is either not entitled to be recorded or is defective, he is charged with notice thereof, since he has obtained actual notice. However, if a person does not run the record, or in running the record does not see the unauthorized instrument, it is not effective as to him.

VII. "Lis pendens" (notice of action)

As a general rule, a person not a party to a court action is not affected by any judgment that might be entered in such action. An exception was recognized at common law in the case of a person purchasing or otherwise acquiring an interest in land from another person who was a party to a pending action affecting the land. Such purchaser was conclusively presumed to have notice of the pending action, regardless of his lack of actual notice, and he acquired his interest subject to the final determination of the action. This rule, known as the "doctrine of *lis pendens,*" was established to prevent a party to pending litigation relating to land from transferring his interest in the land before judgment was entered against him and thus rendering the judgment ineffectual.

MODIFICATION OF COMMON-LAW RULE BY STATUTE

This common-law rule has been modified in California by statute, under which the plaintiff in any action concerning real property or affecting the title or right of possession of real property may file for record in the recorder's office of the county where the property is located a notice of the pendency of such action. Thereafter, a purchaser or encumbrancer of the property affected by the action is deemed to have constructive notice of the pendency of the action as it relates to the real property and only of its pendency against parties designated by their real names. (C.C.P., Sec. 409.) A defendant who asks for affirmative relief may also record a notice of action. In 1959 the code was amended to allow recording of a notice of pendency of an action in the United States District Court the same as an action in a California court.

ACTIONS WHERE "LIS PENDENS" MAY BE FILED

Actions to which the statute applies include actions to quiet title, actions to foreclose a lien on real property, actions to set aside conveyances of land, actions of ejectment, actions in eminent domain, and generally all conventional actions affecting the title or possession of real property. The notice of the pendency of an action must contain the names of the parties, the object of the action, and a sufficient description of the property affected by the action.

Sometimes a *lis pendens* is recorded in an action which does not affect title or possession. In the case of *Allied Eastern Financial* v. *Goheen Enterprises*, 265 A.C.A. 148, it was held that the court was empowered to expunge such *lis pendens* from the record. In 1968 new sections were added to the Code of Civil Procedure (Secs. 409.1–409.6) to expressly provide for expungement of such a *lis pendens*.

EFFECTIVE PERIOD OF "LIS PENDENS"

A *lis pendens* is effective only during the time that the action is pending, which is the period from the time of the commencement of the action until its final determination upon appeal, or until the time for appeal has passed. Accordingly, the effect of a *lis pendens* as constructive notice ceases when the action is dismissed, or when a judgment is rendered that has become final. If the successful party to an action desires to have constructive notice of his rights continue after final judgment, he must record a certified copy of the judgment.

VIII. Notice based on possession

Where a vendee under a contract of sale or a grantee in a deed takes possession of the land, recording the instrument under which he claims his interest is not essential insofar as rights of subsequent parties are concerned. The notice resulting from possession has the same effect as the notice imparted by recording. Thus, possession of land by a person other than the owner of record is notice to an intending purchaser or lender sufficient to put him on inquiry as to the right, title, or interest of the occupant, and the intending purchaser or lender is chargeable with knowledge of all that a reasonably diligent inquiry of the occupant would have disclosed. (*Three Sixty Five Club* v. *Shostak,* 104 C.A.2d 735.) The inquiry must be made directly to the person in possession, rather than merely to the vendor or to persons living in the neighborhood.

THIRD PARTIES IN POSSESSION

The possession by the third party must be of such character as to put the purchaser on inquiry, and must exist at the time of the purchase from and conveyance by the vendor out of possession. The purchaser is not chargeable with notice if he makes a diligent inquiry in good faith and fails to discover any adverse claim, as where the occupant refuses upon inquiry to indicate the nature of his interest.

RIGHTS OF PERSONS IN POSSESSION

Inquiry of a person in possession may disclose a claim of interest inconsistent with the record based on rights under an unrecorded deed, or a contract of sale, or a lease containing an option to purchase, or the occupant may claim title based upon adverse possession. Also, the continued exclusive possession of land by a grantor after he has conveyed the title is, like the possession of any other stranger to the title regarded in California as sufficient to put a subsequent purchaser on inquiry as to any rights remaining in the grantor. For instance, if *A*, the record owner, conveys the land to *B* by a deed that is recorded, but *A* continues in possession, a purchaser from *B* is charged with notice that *A* may still have an interest, such as an interest under an unrecorded instrument, e.g., a deed back to *A* from *B,* or a possible right to avoid the deed from *A* to *B* for some reason, e.g., total failure of consideration.

POSSESSION BY TENANT

The possession of a tenant of real property charges a purchaser with notice not only of the rights of the tenant, but also of the rights of the tenant's landlord, who may be disclosed by the tenant as someone other than the record owner. Further inquiry must then be made as to the nature of the rights of the landlord. Such inquiry might disclose that the landlord was a purchaser of the land under contract, or was the grantee in an unrecorded deed.

POSSESSION BY LESSEE

The possession of a tenant under a lease is notice not only of his rights under the lease, but, also of any other rights acquired by collateral or subsequent agreement, such as an option to purchase, or a contract of sale, or an agreement for removal of the building or fixtures, or even a deed.

Questions

1. Must a conveyance be recorded to be effective?
2. Discuss the main purpose of recording.
3. Explain the words "constructive notice" as used under recording laws.
4. What types of instruments are entitled to be recorded?
5. Describe the procedure for recording an instrument.
6. Do all recorded instruments impart notice?
7. Is there any prescribed period within which instruments must be recorded to be effective?
8. What effect does the failure of a grantee to record a deed have on the rights of creditors of the grantor?
9. Explain the purpose of a *lis pendens*.
10. Can a buyer or lender rely solely upon matters disclosed of record, or is he under any additional duty regarding the property?

12

Homesteads

Summary

I. Nature of the homestead right
Object of the homestead law; Purpose of a homestead; Homestead under federal law

II. Definition and characteristics of a homestead
Effect of homestead of a married person; Limitation on number of homesteads; Off-record matters affecting validity of homestead

III. Selection of the homestead
Homestead of "head of the family"; Type of structure selected for a homestead; Property with more than one house; Extent of land area; Value of homestead; Actual residence required; Interest or estate of claimant; Selection of marital homestead; Married person's separate homestead; Filing for record

IV. Homestead exemptions
General effect of change in exemption or status; Obligations not affected by homestead; Effect of judgments; Sale of homestead; Effect of homestead on attachment; Special proceedings to reach value over exemption; Judicial proceedings to determine validity of homestead; Effect of bankruptcy on homestead; Effect of homestead on taxes; Effect of homestead on mortgages and trust deeds

V. Restraint on transfer of the homestead
Conveyance of marital homestead by separate instruments; Conveyance from one spouse to the other; Subsequent marriage of homestead declarant

VI. Divorce as affecting the homestead
Disposition where homestead selected from community property; Disposition where homestead selected from separate property; Effect of final decree of divorce

VII. Effect of incompetency of spouse

VIII. Devolution of the marital homestead on death
Homestead selected from separate property; Appraisal of home-

stead; Establishing validity of homestead; Successor in interest of homestead; Failure to assert homestead interest; Characteristics of homestead vesting in spouse

IX. Voluntary termination of the homestead
Effect of moving from the premises; Destruction of the premises; Transfers affecting homestead

X. Probate homestead
Selection of probate homestead; Title to probate homestead; Value of property set apart

I. Nature of the homestead right

The protection of the homestead was unknown at common law. In California the right to a homestead is prescribed in the state constitution. Pursuant to the constitution and as a matter of social policy, the legislature has enacted laws providing for and protecting this homestead right. (C.C., Secs. 1237–1269; Secs. 1300–1304.)

OBJECT OF THE HOMESTEAD LAW

The object, generally, of homestead legislation is expressed in the case of *Estate of Fath,* 132 Cal. 609, wherein it is stated that the homestead law is designed "to provide a place for the family and its surviving members, where they may reside and enjoy the comforts of a home, freed from any anxiety that it may be taken from them against their will, either by reason of their own necessity or improvidence, or from the importunity of their creditors."

PURPOSE OF A HOMESTEAD

More specifically, it may be stated that the purpose of the homestead law is to protect a home, up to a prescribed amount of exemption, from execution or forced sale in satisfaction of certain types of debts, and to preserve the homestead of a husband and wife by restricting its conveyance or encumbrance by one spouse without the consent of the other, and by giving one spouse special rights of survivorship in the event of the death of the other spouse.

HOMESTEAD UNDER FEDERAL LAW

The "homestead" considered in this chapter is to be distinguished from the term as it applies to filing on federal lands, whereby a person may acquire title to acreage by establishing residence or making improvements upon the land. The so-called jackrabbit homestead in desert areas, such as the Mojave and Colorado deserts, is an example of this type of homestead. It is applied for under federal laws administered by the various offices of the Bureau of Land Management, an agency of the United States government.

II. Definition and characteristics of a homestead

The homestead under state law consists of the dwelling house in which the claimant resides, together with outbuildings, and the land upon which the same are situated, selected by a *Declaration of Homestead* executed, acknowledged, and recorded as provided by law. (C.C., Sec. 1237.) Two elements must exist concurrently to give rise to a valid homestead: (1) residential property actually occupied by the claimant, and (2) a declaration of homestead properly executed, acknowledged, and recorded. When the declaration containing the required statements has been recorded, and if the statements are in fact true, the property becomes a *homestead,* protected from forced sale except as otherwise provided by law and remains so until conveyed, or until abandoned by a recorded abandonment of homestead.

EFFECT OF HOMESTEAD OF A MARRIED PERSON

To the average individual, the main purpose and effect of a homestead is to protect the declarant and his family from a forced sale of the home in satisfaction of debts owed by the homeowner. "Protection from creditors" is the usual reason given for recording a declaration of homestead. However, the effect of a marital homestead may be threefold, namely (1) exemption from forced sale; (2) restraints on transfer; and (3) vesting on death. The latter two characteristics apply only to the homestead of a husband and wife; the exemption characteristic applies to all homesteads, whether that of a single person, a married person, or the head of a household.

LIMITATION ON NUMBER OF HOMESTEADS

A person can have only one valid homestead at a time. If he attempts to acquire a second homestead while a first one is in force, the second one will have no effect. In the case of married persons, if one spouse declares a valid homestead on one parcel of land, the other spouse may not declare a valid homestead upon another parcel, unless the spouse qualifies for a married person's separate homestead under the 1959 amendment to the homestead law. (*Bullis* v. *Staniford,* 178 Cal. 40.) The foregoing rules, however, do not preclude a surviving husband, who is the owner of a homestead previously declared by himself and his deceased wife, from declaring a new homestead on the same property for the joint benefit of himself and his second wife. Also, a divorced husband owning property subject to a homestead declared during the previous marriage, undoubtedly may declare a second homestead on such property for the benefit of his second wife and family. The previously declared homestead will survive death or divorce as to the exemption rights, but a homestead for the benefit of the new community with all of the characteristics of a marital homestead would have to be newly created.

OFF-RECORD MATTERS AFFECTING VALIDITY OF HOMESTEAD

The validity of a homestead cannot be assumed solely from the recordation of a declaration of homestead, even though it is in proper form, since its validity is also dependent upon certain off-record matters. For instance, the homestead may be invalid (1) if the declarant has previously selected a valid homestead on real property in California and has not legally abandoned it; or (2) if the declarant was not actually residing on the property at the date of selection of the homestead; or (3) if the property is not in fact a proper subject of homestead; or (4) in the case of a marital homestead, if the purported husband and wife were not legally married.

III. Selection of the homestead

A homestead may be selected by any "head of a family," in which case the homestead exemption since September 20, 1963 is $15,000, or "by any other person," in which case the exemption since said date is $7,500.

HOMESTEAD OF "HEAD OF THE FAMILY"

The phrase "head of a family," includes within its meaning:

1. The husband, when the claimant is a married person.
2. Every person who has residing on the premises with him or her, and under his or her care and maintenance, either:
    a. his or her minor child, or minor grandchild, or the minor child of his or her deceased wife or husband;
    b. a minor brother or sister, or the minor child of a deceased brother or sister;
    c. a father, mother, grandfather, or grandmother;
    d. the father, mother, grandfather, or grandmother of a deceased husband or wife;
    e. an unmarried sister, or any other of the relatives mentioned in this section, who have attained the age of majority, and are unable to take care of or support themselves. [C. C., Sec. 1261.]

A wife may make the selection for the joint benefit of herself and husband where the husband has not made one. Unless the parties qualify for a married person's separate homestead, neither spouse can declare a homestead for his or her own benefit; it must be for their joint benefit.

TYPE OF STRUCTURE SELECTED FOR A HOMESTEAD

Although the Civil Code states that the homestead consists of a "dwelling house," the structure selected does not necessarily have to be a single-family residence. Valid homesteads have been declared on multiple-unit residential structures, where one unit was occupied by the claimant, and the remaining units were rented to tenants. The fact that the premises are used partially for business purposes does not prevent selection as a homestead if the property is used primarily as a home.

PROPERTY WITH MORE THAN ONE HOUSE

It has been held that a declaration of homestead covering premises in addition to those occupied as a home is nonetheless valid as to the premises properly included therein. (*Clausseneus* v. *Anderson*, 216 C.A.2d 171.) If the homestead is declared upon a residence and a lot, the subsequent erection of a second house on the lot does not destroy the homestead. Also, the transformation of a single-family residence into a duplex does not destroy the homestead. (*Oppenheim* v. *Goodley*, 148 C.A.2d 325.)

EXTENT OF LAND AREA

No statutory limit is placed on the quantity of land that may be selected as a homestead, the extent of the homestead being measured by use and occupation. A homestead of rural land might include substantial acreage. Or a homestead on a city lot could embrace an adjoining lot used as a garden in connection with the dwelling. If the homestead is declared on more land than can properly be selected, the homestead is not defective as a whole, but will be sustained on the portion that properly qualifies.

VALUE OF HOMESTEAD

A homestead may be valid regardless of the value of the property. However, creditors may reach the excess value over the homestead exemption by resorting to special proceedings.

ACTUAL RESIDENCE REQUIRED

Actual residence in good faith is a requisite to the validity of a homestead. Both the fact of physical occupancy and intention to reside on the premises selected as a homestead must concur. The provision as to residence at the time the declaration is filed is strictly construed. (*Ellsworth* v. *Marshall*, 196 C.A.2d 471.)

INTEREST OR ESTATE OF CLAIMANT

It is not necessary that the claimant be the sole owner of the homestead or that he be the owner in fee. Section 1238 of the Civil Code provides that any freehold title, interest, or estate that vests in the claimant the immediate right of possession, even though such right of possession is not exclusive, is sufficient. Thus, a homestead may be declared on property where the claimant has a life estate, or the right of possession under a contract of sale, or an interest as a joint tenant or a tenant in common with others. However, a tenant in possession under a lease for a term of years does not have the requisite freehold interest for a valid homestead.

SELECTION OF MARITAL HOMESTEAD

In the case of a marital homestead, special rules apply as to the selection of a homestead. A homestead may be selected by the husband from the community property or from his separate property, but he cannot select a homestead from his wife's separate property without her consent. However, it has been held that only the wife, and not a creditor, can assert the invalidity of a homestead declared by the husband on the wife's separate property without her consent. (*In re Miller*, 27 Fed.Supp. 999.)

Selection by wife. The wife may select a homestead from her separate property, or if the husband has not made a selection, she may select a homestead from the community property or from his separate property. As a general rule, the residence of the husband is the legal residence of the wife, and if the husband is not actually residing in the dwelling claimed as a homestead by the wife, the latter is precluded from making a valid selection. This rule has been qualified, however, by a liberal interpretation of the homestead laws to permit a declaration by the wife on the home in which she is residing in cases where the husband has deserted and abandoned the wife, or where the husband is temporarily absent from the home.

Selection from joint tenancy property. Property held by husband and wife as joint tenants may be selected as a homestead by the wife alone or by both husband and wife. Cases have also sustained the validity of a declaration by the husband alone on joint tenancy property. (*In re Miller, supra; Watson* v. *Peyton,* 10 Cal.2d 156.) In the case of *Strangman* v. *Duke,* 140 C.A.2d 185, it was held that a homestead by the husband on joint tenancy property inures to the wife's benefit and protects her interest in the joint tenancy property against her own creditors. In that case, the wife owned a half interest in the property as her separate property, and the other half was owned by the husband and wife as joint tenants. The court pointed out that the wife, after the declaration by the husband on the joint tenancy interest, would not be entitled to declare a homestead on her interest in the other half as long as her husband still had title.

Selection from property owned as tenants in common. Property owned by the husband and wife as tenants in common may be selected as a homestead by the wife, or by the husband and wife together, but insofar as the wife's separate interest in such property is concerned, a declaration by the husband is ineffectual as to her interest without her joinder.

MARRIED PERSON'S SEPARATE HOMESTEAD

In 1959 the legislature amended the homestead law to provide that, following the entry of a decree of separate maintenance or an interlocutory decree of divorce, each spouse may declare a homestead from such spouse's separate property or any property awarded by the decree, such homestead being designated as a "married person's separate homestead." (C.C., Secs. 1300–1304.) Unlike a marital homestead, such homestead is for the benefit solely of the spouse declaring the same. Prior to 1959, neither spouse, during the period of the interlocutory decree of divorce (one year), could declare a valid homestead on his or her property for the sole benefit of such spouse; a valid homestead could be declared only for their joint benefit.

Effect of married person's separate homestead. Such a homestead is excepted from the requirement that both spouses join in the conveyance or encumbrance of the homestead of a married person, and may be abandoned by the one spouse alone. Such homestead is also excepted from the rule providing for a right of survivorship as to homestead property between spouses, and from the provisions for setting aside the homestead to a surviving spouse and minor children by the Probate Court.

FILING FOR RECORD

The declaration of homestead is not effective until it is executed in proper form, acknowledged, and filed for record in the office of the county recorder of the county in which the land is situated. Both execution and acknowledgment must be done personally; it cannot be done by an agent.

Contents of declaration. The declaration of homestead by the husband or other head of a family, or by the wife, must contain the following: (1) a statement showing that the person making it is the head of a family, and if the claimant is married, the name of the spouse; or, when the declaration is made by the wife, showing that the husband has not made such declaration and that she therefore makes the declaration for their joint benefit; (2) a statement that the person making it is residing on the premises, and claims them as a homestead; (3) a description of the premises claimed as a homestead; and (4) an estimate of the "actual cash value" of the homestead premises. A declaration by a person other than the head of a family must contain everything required in the homestead of a head of a family except the statement relating to head of family and marital status.

Declaration of married person's separate homestead. The declaration of a married person's separate homestead must contain a statement that the declarant is a married person, and that there is in existence a decree of separate maintenance or an interlocutory decree of divorce between the declarant and his or her spouse, a statement showing the declarant is the head of a family, if such is the case, and certain other nonconflicting statements, including the optional verified information referred to below.

Optional statement. The declaration may also contain a statement and affidavit, optional with the declarant, in accordance with Section 1263(5) of the Civil Code, which provides as follows:

> Such declaration of homestead may further contain a statement of the character of the property sought to be homesteaded, showing the improvement or improvements which have been affixed thereto, with sufficient detail to show that it is a proper subject of homestead, and that no former declaration has been made, or, if made, that it has been abandoned and if it contains such further statement and the declaration is supported by the affidavit of the declarant, annexed thereto, that the matters therein stated are true of his or her own knowledge, such declaration, when properly recorded, shall be prima facie evidence of the facts therein stated, and conclusive evidence thereof in favor of a purchaser or encumbrancer in good faith and for a valuable consideration.

Sufficiency of statements. A statement that the claimant is "the head of a family" is sufficient without recitation of the facts that give him this status, i.e., the identity of the members of the family need not be disclosed. If the declaration shows the claimant to be a male, married person, this is a sufficient showing of "head of family." A declaration by the wife that does not recite that it is made for the "joint benefit" of herself and her husband is defective. However, the courts have not always required strict compliance with this provision. Whether the court will require strict compliance or a substantial compliance with this requirement appears to be dependent upon the nature of the proceedings in which the question is raised. Thus, in the case of *Johnson* v. *Brauner,* 131 C.A.2d 713, the court followed the substantial compliance rule where a creditor questioned the validity of the homestead declaration, whereas in the case of *Godfrey* v. *Witten,* 138 C.A.2d 610, strict compliance was held to be essential where the issue was raised by the representative of the husband's estate after the death of the wife. The courts are inclined to adopt a liberal construction where the exemption feature of the homestead is material, but not where it is a question of devolution on death.

Description of premises. A correct description of the premises is important, although the courts have sometimes been liberal in this respect. The description should be one that is considered sufficient for the purpose of a conveyance of land. The case of *Oktanski* v. *Burn*, 138 C.A.2d 419, presented a problem where the declaration described the property correctly by street address, but incorrectly as to legal description, the latter designating property in an entirely different tract. The court held that the street address controlled and sustained the validity of the homestead.

Estimate of value. Regarding the estimate of actual cash value, it is considered sufficient if the estimate states a determinable sum, such as "cash value is $3,000" or "value about $4,000," or "does not exceed in value the sum of $5,000." A statement that "the actual cash value is $5,000 and over" has been held insufficient. (*Ames* v. *Eldred*, 55 Cal. 136.) It has been stated that where the valuation is in excess of the statutory limit, that fact is of significance to creditors, and claimants are held to greater strictness in the estimate in such cases than in cases where the value is less than the limit. (*Schuyler* v. *Broughton*, 76 Cal. 524.)

Effect of failure to show value. A case in bankruptcy, *Lynch* v. *Stotler*, 215 F.2d 776, involved a declaration of homestead in which the value of the property was left blank. The property was subsequently listed in the bankruptcy schedules as having "no value beyond encumbrances and homestead." The district court construed the declaration to mean that it could affect only so much of the property's value as was unencumbered, stating that it was logical to assume that the declarants meant to say in their declaration, when they left the value of the property blank, that in their opinion the property had no value or no value above encumbrances. The appellate court reversed this decision, holding that the declaration failed to comply with the requirement that it contain an estimate of the actual cash value of the realty; accordingly, there was no valid homestead exemption.

Statement of equity. A statement of a declarant's equity in the property, as distinguished from the "actual cash value," has been held to be substantial compliance with the code. (*Samuels* v. *Delucchi*, 286 Fed.2d 503.)

IV. Homestead exemptions

With certain exceptions, the homestead is exempt from execution or forced sale up to the amount of the exemption in effect at the time credit was extended. The amount of the homestead exemption was originally

$5,000 for the head of a family, and $1,000 for other persons. In 1945 the exemption was increased to $6,000 and $2,000, and in 1947 was increased to $7,500 and $3,000. Effective September 9, 1953, the exemption was increased to $12,500 and $5,000, and effective September 20, 1963 the amounts were raised to $15,000 and $7,500, which are the amounts presently in effect. It has been held in the state courts that the controlling exemption is the one in effect *at the time the debt was incurred,* which makes a distinction between old creditors and new creditors, their rights being dependent upon whether a debt was incurred *before* or *after* a statutory change in the exemption amount. However, this distinction is not made in bankruptcy proceedings. All of the creditors are considered to be in the same category, and if one can claim under a lower exemption, all of the creditors are given the same privilege. (*England* v. *Sanderson,* 236 Fed.2d 641.)

GENERAL EFFECT OF CHANGE IN EXEMPTION OR STATUS

In the absence of any intervening rights of third parties, it is probable that the exemption of existing homesteads is automatically increased by statutory amendments increasing the amount of the homestead exemption. Whether the amount of the homestead would automatically be reduced if the status of a person selecting a homestead as the head of a family is subsequently changed to the status of a single person, has not been definitely decided by the courts, but such reduction would probably follow.

OBLIGATIONS NOT AFFECTED BY HOMESTEAD

The homestead does not exempt the property from all forced sales. Under the provisions of Section 1241 of the Civil Code, the homestead is subject to execution or forced sale in satisfaction of judgment obtained: (1) before the declaration of homestead was filed for record, and which constitute liens upon the premises; (2) on debts secured by mechanics, contractors, subcontractors, artisans, architects, builders, laborers of every class, materialmen's or vendor's liens upon the premises; (3) on debts secured by encumbrances on the premises executed and acknowledged by husband and wife, or by an unmarried claimant; and (4) on debts secured by encumbrances on the premises, executed and recorded before the declaration of homestead was filed for record.

EFFECT OF JUDGMENTS

As a general rule, the homestead is not subject to execution and sale in satisfaction of a money judgment where an abstract of the judgment is not recorded until after an effective declaration of homestead has been filed for record. Recordation of the declaration exempts the premises from execution, and the judgment, as a consequence, does not become a lien upon the homestead premises, regardless of the value of the homestead.

SALE OF HOMESTEAD

There is one situation where the judgment lien may appear of record ahead of the homestead, but the subsequently declared homestead can have priority over the judgment lien. This situation arises where a homestead is sold and the proceeds are used to acquire another home. Under the provisions of Section 1265a of the Civil Code, if the homestead is sold by the owner, the proceeds from such sale, to the extent of the value allowed for a homestead exemption, are exempt for a period of six months following the sale. Real property purchased with these proceeds within the six-month period may be selected as a homestead and such selection, when a new declaration has been filed for record, has the same force and effect as if it had been created at the time the prior declaration of homestead was filed. Under such circumstances, the new homestead is given a retroactive effect.

EFFECT OF HOMESTEAD ON ATTACHMENT

An attachment lien may be defeated by a homestead. If an attachment is levied upon the premises *before* the recording of a declaration of homestead, but an abstract of judgment in such action is not recorded until *after* the homestead, the judgment does not relate back to the date when the attachment was levied, and the judgment will not constitute a lien. Accordingly, a valid declaration of homestead recorded during the pendency of the litigation will defeat an attachment. (*Johnson* v. *Brauner*, 131 C.A.2d 713.) However, the attachment may accomplish one purpose. Even though no judgment lien is acquired, the attachment suffices to hold the property for the purpose of proceedings to reach the excess if the value of the debtor's interest (equity) in the property exceeds the homestead exemption. (*Marelli* v. *Keating*, 208 Cal. 528.)

SPECIAL PROCEEDINGS TO REACH VALUE OVER EXEMPTION

Although a judgment creditor does not have a lien on property subjected to a homestead before a judgment lien could attach, he may resort to special proceedings to reach the excess value, if any, over the exemption. These special proceedings are provided for in Section 1245 of the Civil Code. Under these proceedings, the judgment creditor causes execution to be levied on the homestead property, and within sixty days thereafter he must file a petition with the court for the appointment of an appraiser. If the appraised value is in excess of the encumbrances and the amount of the homestead exemption, the property may be sold under execution and the excess applied toward the satisfaction of the judgment. The failure of a creditor to comply with the provisions of Section 1245 extinguishes the lien of the execution, and precludes a subsequent levy against the homestead property based upon the same judgment. (*Arighi* v. *Rule & Sons, Inc.*, 41 C.A.2d 852.)

JUDICIAL PROCEEDINGS TO DETERMINE VALIDITY OF HOMESTEAD

As a general rule, a money judgment against a homestead declarant, even though it may not be a lien by virtue of the homestead, is not automatically disregarded for title insurance purposes. It is usually necessary that the validity of the homestead be judicially determined in appropriate court proceedings, such as an action for declaratory relief or to quiet title against the judgment creditor. This rule is based upon the fact that the validity of a homestead is dependent upon off-record matters.

EFFECT OF BANKRUPTCY ON HOMESTEAD

Where the owner of the homestead is adjudicated a bankrupt, the homestead, if valid, is not affected by the bankruptcy proceedings, i.e., title to such property does not vest in the trustee in bankruptcy. However, it is necessary that an order be obtained in the bankruptcy proceedings setting apart the property as exempt. The declaration of homestead must be filed *before* the filing of a voluntary petition in bankruptcy in order that the property may be set apart to the bankrupt as exempt. (*Sampsell* v. *Straub*, 194 Fed.2d 228.) In one case the declaration of homestead was filed approximately ten minutes after the filing of a petition in bankruptcy, and this was held to be insufficient.

EFFECT OF HOMESTEAD ON TAXES

Tax obligations as a general rule are not defeated by a homestead. Where a state, county, or city tax is a basis for a direct lien against the property homesteaded, such property is not exempt from execution and sale in satisfaction of such tax. Various types of state taxes, such as the sales and use tax, become a lien on real property of the taxpayer when an abstract of judgment or certificate of tax is recorded in the office of the county recorder of the county in which the land is situated, which lien is declared to have "the force, effect and priority of a judgment lien." It would appear that such liens, although based on a tax, would not be a lien on homestead property to the same extent that a judgment lien in favor of a private individual would not be a lien. However, there is no decision of the appellate courts in this state directly deciding this point.

Federal taxes. As to federal tax liens, the question of whether such liens attach to real property exempt under state law is determined by federal laws, and it may be generally concluded that homestead property is not exempt from federal tax liens. (*U.S.* v. *Heffron*, 158 Fed.2d 657; *U. S.* v. *Heasley*, 283 Fed.2d 422.)

EFFECT OF HOMESTEAD ON MORTGAGES AND TRUST DEEDS

A mortgage or deed of trust of record is not impaired by a declaration of homestead *subsequently* recorded, and the homestead is subject to forced sale in satisfaction of a judgment obtained on the debt secured by such prior encumbrance. A mortgage or deed of trust executed and acknowledged by both husband and wife (if a marital homestead), or by an unmarried claimant, takes priority over an *existing* homestead.

V. Restraint on transfer of the homestead

Except as to a married person's separate homestead, the homestead of a married person cannot be conveyed or encumbered by one spouse alone; both spouses must execute a conveyance or encumbrance on homestead property. This is generally true even though the record title is held by one of the spouses as his or her separate property.

CONVEYANCE OF MARITAL HOMESTEAD BY SEPARATE INSTRUMENTS

Prior to September 22, 1951, it was the rule that a marital homestead could not be conveyed or encumbered except by a single instrument jointly and concurrently executed and acknowledged personally by both husband and wife. Subsequent to that date, the marital homestead can be conveyed or encumbered by the separate instrument of each spouse in favor of the same party or his successor in interest. (C.C., Sec. 1242.)

CONVEYANCE FROM ONE SPOUSE TO THE OTHER

The requirement prior to the above-mentioned date that a conveyance of a homestead must be jointly executed by married persons did not prevent one spouse from conveying his interest in the homestead property to the other spouse. Although the effect of such a conveyance was to vest title in the grantee as his or her separate property, it remained subject to all of the homestead characteristics. Thus, a subsequent encumbrance or conveyance to a third person required a jointly executed instrument. This rule is still applicable to all such conveyances made before this date. Since that date, however, one spouse can convey the homestead property to the other by an instrument executed by the grantor spouse alone, and unless the one conveying expressly reserves his homestead rights, the grantee spouse may convey or encumber the homestead property in the same manner and to the same extent as though no homestead had been declared. The homestead characteristic of exemption from execution or forced sale in satisfaction of debts is not affected by such a conveyance from one spouse to the other. The exemption characteristic remains, but the restraint-on-transfer and the devolution-on-death characteristics are no longer in effect.

SUBSEQUENT MARRIAGE OF HOMESTEAD DECLARANT

A situation sometimes encountered is one where a widow, widower, or a single person declares a homestead as "head of a family" and thereafter marries. This raises a question as to whether the new spouse is required to join in the execution of instruments conveying or encumbering the homestead. In the case of *Vieth* v. *Klett,* 88 C.A.2d 23, the court stated that the homestead would continue "for the benefit of the second community," inferring that all of the characteristics of a marital homestead would apply. As a rule of title practice, both spouses are required to join in an abandonment or transfer of such a homestead.

VI. Divorce as affecting the homestead

Section 146 of the Civil Code provides for the disposition of the homestead in case there is a dissolution of the marriage, or where there is a decree for separate maintenance without dissolution of the marriage.

DISPOSITION WHERE HOMESTEAD SELECTED FROM COMMUNITY PROPERTY

If the homestead has been selected from the community property, it may be assigned to the party *to whom* the divorce or decree of separate maintenance is granted, or in cases where the divorce or decree of separate maintenance is granted on the ground of incurable insanity, it may be assigned to the party *against whom* the divorce or decree of separate maintenance is granted. The assignment may be either absolute or for a limited period, or the homestead may in the discretion of the court be divided, or be sold and the proceeds divided.

DISPOSITION WHERE HOMESTEAD SELECTED FROM SEPARATE PROPERTY

If the homestead has been selected from the separate property of either, it shall be assigned to the owner, i.e., the spouse holding title as separate property, but subject to the power of the court to assign it for a limited period to the party *to whom* the divorce or decree of separate maintenance is granted. However, where the decree is rendered on the ground of incurable insanity, it shall be assigned to the owner, subject to the power of the court to assign it to the party *against whom* the divorce or decree of separate maintenance is granted for a term of years not to exceed the life of such party.

EFFECT OF FINAL DECREE OF DIVORCE

When a final decree of divorce is entered, the homestead rights of the spouse not in title are terminated as a general rule, but the final decree of divorce does not necessarily terminate the right of exemption of the spouse in title. The exemption characteristics would remain, but the other aspects of a marital homestead—restraint on transfer and devolution on death—would no longer exist. (*City Store* v. *Cofer*, 111 Cal. 482.) In the case of *Calif. Bank* v. *Schlessinger*, 159 C.A.2d Supp. 854, it was held that a homestead on joint tenancy property continues after entry of a final decree of divorce.

VII. Effect of incompetency of spouse

Where property is subject to a marital homestead and one of the spouses is insane or incompetent, special judicial proceedings may be utilized to effect a sale, exchange, lease, or encumbrance on such property. (Pro. C., Secs. 1435.1 *et seq.*) The procedure is the same as prescribed for a disposition of community property where one of the spouses is insane or incompetent. Prior to 1959 this was an exclusive procedure, but since 1959 the Probate Code provides for an alternative procedure to be followed in a guardianship or conservatorship proceeding for dealing with homestead property (see Chapter 23).

VIII. Devolution of the marital homestead on death

It is sometimes stated that the effect of a marital homestead is to create an involuntary joint tenancy in property that otherwise would be subject to the testamentary disposition of the spouse in title. The result arises by virtue of the provisions of Section 663 of the Probate Code. Under this section, if the homestead selected by the husband and wife, or either of them, during their coverture, and recorded while both were living, was selected from the community property, or from the separate property of the person selecting or joining in the selection of the same, and if the surviving spouse has not conveyed the homestead to the other spouse by a conveyance that failed to expressly reserve his homestead rights, *the homestead vests,* on the death of either spouse, *absolutely in the survivor.*

HOMESTEAD SELECTED FROM SEPARATE PROPERTY

If the homestead was selected from the separate property of the decedent without his consent, or if the surviving spouse has conveyed the homestead to the other spouse by a conveyance that failed to expressly reserve his homestead rights, the homestead vests, on death, in the heirs or devisees of the decedent, subject to the power of the court to set it apart for a limited period to the family of the decedent.

APPRAISAL OF HOMESTEAD

If the homestead selected and recorded prior to the death of the deceased spouse is appraised at not over the amount of the homestead exemption, the court in the probate proceedings will order it set apart to the persons in whom title is vested by Section 663 of the Probate Code. If the inventory amount exceeds the homestead exemption, the appraisers must determine whether the homestead premises can be divided without material injury, and if this can be done, they must set apart to the parties entitled thereto such portion of the premises, including the dwelling house, as will amount in value to the homestead exemption. (Pro. C., Sec. 664.) If the value of the premises at the time of their selection exceeded the amount of the homestead exemption, and the property cannot be divided without material injury, the court may order a sale of the premises and a distribution of the proceeds to the persons entitled thereto.

ESTABLISHING VALIDITY OF HOMESTEAD

These statutory provisions as to the devolution of the homestead upon the death of either spouse supersede the usual rules of succession, and prevail over any attempted testamentary disposition by the decedent. If the record title to the homestead was in the deceased spouse, or in both spouses other than as joint tenants, it is necessary that the validity of the homestead be judicially determined before title is insurable in the surviving spouse. This is accomplished by obtaining an order of the court in the probate proceedings setting apart the homestead to the surviving spouse. If the title to the homestead was held in joint tenancy, or the record title was not in the name of the deceased spouse, all that is necessary is to establish the fact of death of record, since the only rights that the deceased spouse had would terminate upon his death.

SUCCESSOR IN INTEREST OF HOMESTEAD

A person succeeding by purchase or otherwise to the interest of a surviving spouse in a homestead that has been declared in the lifetime of the decedent has the same right to apply for an order setting aside the homestead to him as is conferred by law on the person whose interest he had acquired.

FAILURE TO ASSERT HOMESTEAD INTEREST

Sometimes the surviving spouse in whom a recorded homestead vests will fail to assert his or her ownership, through either lack of knowledge of the legal effect of the homestead, or lack of knowledge that a homestead exists, and proceedings are undertaken in the administration of the deceased spouse's estate whereby a probate sale of the land is undertaken or a decree of distribution is made to persons other than, or in addition to, the surviving spouse. As a general rule, the title of the survivor, which vests by operation of law, is not divested or otherwise affected by subsequent orders of the probate court, subject, of course to proceedings under Section 664 of the Probate Code where the value of the homestead exceeds the exemption. However, situations may arise where the surviving spouse is estopped by his or her conduct from claiming the homestead. For example, estoppel was applied where the survivor was the representative of the estate and received the benefit of the proceeds of a probate sale. (*Ions* v. *Harbison,* 112 Cal. 260.) Also a surviving spouse may be precluded from asserting a homestead interest where such spouse elects to relinquish homestead rights and take under the decedent's will.

CHARACTERISTICS OF HOMESTEAD VESTING IN SPOUSE

Homestead property vesting in the surviving spouse retains its homestead characteristics of exemption, but the homestead characteristics of restraint and devolution cease when title passes to the surviving spouse. If a surviving husband remarries, the homestead characteristic of exemption continues to protect the property, but he may convey or encumber the property without the consent of his new wife, and upon his death title vests in his heirs or devisees and not in the second wife as survivor. (*Estate of Clavo,* 6 C.A. 774.) The husband could, of course, impress the property with all of the attributes of a marital homestead by declaring a new homestead after his remarriage.

IX. Voluntary termination of the homestead

A homestead can be abandoned by a declaration of abandonment or by a conveyance. Where the homestead is for the benefit of husband and wife, each must execute, jointly or by separate instruments, the declaration of abandonment or the conveyance. (C.C., Sec. 1243, as amended in 1959.) A declaration of abandonment is effectual only from the time it is recorded in the office in which the homestead was recorded. (C.C. Sec. 1244.) Also, a homestead, like other property, may be lost by adverse possession.

EFFECT OF MOVING FROM THE PREMISES

Removal from the homestead premises, with or without the intent of not returning to them, does not constitute an abandonment of the homestead. Nor does abandonment result from the declaration of a new homestead, unless the second declaration by its terms expressly abandons the former homestead.

DESTRUCTION OF THE PREMISES

The destruction of the original home and placing of a second house on homesteaded property has been held not to be an abandonment. (*Rey* v. *Valdez,* 175 C.A.2d 502.)

TRANSFERS AFFECTING HOMESTEAD

The term "grant," as used in the code prescribing the method of abandonment of a homestead, includes various types of transfers, such as a grant deed made upon a condition subsequent, a quitclaim deed, or a transfer by operation of law such as a commissioner's deed upon foreclosure of a mortgage on the homestead. But a grant of a limited nature is not effective as an abandonment, such as a deed of the fee title reserving a life estate, in which case the homestead still attaches to the life estate. A deed to and from a "strawman" for the purpose of creating a joint tenancy in the homestead property has been held not to abandon the homestead. (*Vieth* v. *Klett,* 88 C.A.2d 23.)

X. Probate homestead

If a homestead was not recorded on property of a decedent before his death, or if a homestead was declared on decedent's separate property and the decedent had not joined in the declaration, the probate court is empowered to designate and set apart a probate homestead from suitable property of the estate, for the benefit of the surviving spouse and/or minor children.

SELECTION OF PROBATE HOMESTEAD

Section 661 of the Probate Code authorizes such a homestead by providing that if no marital homestead has been recorded, or in case the homestead was selected by the surviving spouse out of the separate property of the decedent without his consent, the probate court *must* select, designate, set apart, and cause to be recorded a homestead for the use of the surviving spouse and minor children, or if there be no surviving spouse then for the use of the minor child or children, out of the community property or property owned in common, or if no such property, out of the separate property of the decedent.

TITLE TO PROBATE HOMESTEAD

If the homestead is selected from the decedent's separate property, it may be set apart for a limited time only, which may not exceed the lifetime of the surviving spouse or minority of a child. If the homestead is selected from community property, or quasi community property, the court order passes the ownership in fee of the homestead as follows: if there are no minor children, the title vests in the surviving spouse; if there is no surviving spouse, the title vests in the minor children; and if there are both a surviving spouse and a minor child (or children) the title vests one half in the surviving spouse, and one half in the minor child or children. This probate homestead vests free from creditors' claims and the rights of heirs and devisees.

VALUE OF PROPERTY SET APART

The statute does not place a limit on the value of the property set apart as a probate homestead. The rule is set forth in the case of *Estate of Raymond*, 137 C.A.2d 134, as follows:

> In selecting a probate homestead, the probate court has wide discretion, and its order will not be disturbed unless there has been an abuse of discretion. The court will give the family a homestead of as great a value as possible, considering the amount and condition of the estate. It is the court's duty to provide a place for the family and its surviving members where they may reside and enjoy the comforts of a home, freed from any anxiety that it may be taken from them against their will, either by reason of their own necessity or improvidence or from the importunity of their creditors. . . . There is no absolute rule to control the court in the selection of a homestead. But while it must be governed by a

sound discretion, yet it must consider the value of the homestead, the estate's financial status, and the rights of creditors.

In a case decided in 1964, that of *Estate of Nelson*, 224 C.A.2d 138, a 30-unit apartment house was set apart to the surviving spouse as a probate homestead.

Questions

1. Discuss the main purpose of a homestead.
2. What property may be the subject of a homestead?
3. Explain the three characteristics of a marital homestead.
4. Describe briefly the procedure that must be followed to obtain the benefits of a homestead.
5. May a homestead be declared by a married person for his or her own benefit?
6. Who is permitted to make a homestead selection?
7. May a homestead be declared on a multiple unit?
8. Is the homestead exempt from forced sale as to all types of obligations?
9. What are the amounts of homestead exemption?
10. May a divorce court dispose of a homestead interest?
11. Will a homestead be effective if recorded immediately after a bankruptcy petition is filed?
12. Is an attachment affected by a subsequently recorded homestead?
13. May homestead property of an incompetent spouse be sold in ordinary guardianship proceedings?
14. When a married person dies, what is the effect on the homestead?
15. How may a homestead be terminated?
16. Explain briefly a probate homestead.

13

Contracts for the Sale of Land

Summary

I. Introductory—types of contracts

The types of contracts commonly used in real estate transactions include the following: listing agreement; sales deposit receipt; escrow instructions; purchase and sale agreement used in lieu of or in addition to escrow instructions; and the long-term land contract or installment contract.

NATURE OF AGREEMENTS

The *listing agreement* is a contract between a real estate broker and a prospective buyer or seller of land; it gives rise to rights, duties, and obligations as between the broker and client, but in itself it does not give enforceable contract rights in a third party. The *sales deposit receipt,* when executed by both buyer and seller, constitutes a contract for the sale and purchase of land, and is used to bind the bargain pending the opening of an escrow. *Escrow instructions* may then be executed by the parties, which, even though separately executed, constitute a valid contract of sale. The escrow instructions may, but do not necessarily, supersede the provisions of the deposit receipt. Many real estate transactions involve the execution of a *formal agreement* by the buyer and seller, prepared by an attorney, to be used in lieu of the printed form of escrow instructions commonly in use, or to supplement the escrow instructions. Such an agreement covers, additionally, various items with which the escrow is usually not concerned.

INSTALLMENT CONTRACT

Another type of contract is the long-term or installment contract entered into between a buyer and seller, where payments are to be made over a protracted period, with the deed to be given either on the final payment of the purchase price, or when a specified amount has been paid at which time the seller agrees to execute and deliver a deed, and obtains a deed of trust from the buyer to secure payment of the balance of the purchase price. It is this type of contract that will be considered in detail in this chapter.

II. Essential elements of a land contract

Land contracts wherein the seller of the land, called the vendor, agrees to convey the land to a purchaser, called the vendee, upon payment of the purchase price or performance of some other act, are variously designated as "installment sales contracts," or "contracts of sale," or "agreements to convey," or "agreements for purchase and sale," or may be given some other similar caption. There is no prescribed form for a contract for the sale of land, nor is the name by which the parties choose to call the contract controlling as to its true character. Thus, where an instrument was called a "lease" but recited no term, and referred to "interest," "payments," and "purchase," and contained other provisions showing its true character to be a contract for the sale and purchase of real property, it was so construed by the court. (*Losson* v. *Blodgett*, 1 C.A.2d 13.)

REQUISITES OF CONTRACT

The essential elements of a contract for the sale of land are those of any contract, namely parties capable of contracting, mutual consent, a lawful object, and sufficient consideration. When these elements are present, the general rules of contract law apply. In addition, there are certain specific requisites for this type of contract, which are as follows: (1) written agreement or note or memorandum thereof; (2) names and signatures of both parties; (3) sufficient description of the land; (4) a designated purchase price; and (5) the time and manner of payment.

In 1965 a new section was added to the Civil Code (Sec. 2985.5) which provides that every real property sales contract entered into after January 1, 1966, shall contain a statement of (1) the number of years required to complete payment in accordance with the terms of the contract, and (2) the basis upon which the tax estimate is made. Such contract is defined as one which does not require conveyance of title within one year from the date of formation of the contract.

Where the contract of sale contains a subordination clause, it has been held that such a clause must be "just and reasonable" in order that the contract be enforceable, and that such clause must contain terms that will define and minimize the risk that the subordinating liens will impair or destroy the seller's security. (*Handy* v. *Gordon*, 65 Cal.2d 578.)

Rules as to the enforceability of a real estate agreement are also considered at length in the case of *Loeb* v. *Wilson*, 253 C.A.2d 383, which deals with the effect of the following in determining the rights of the parties: (1) inadequacy of consideration, where property worth $80,000 was sold for $59,000; uncertainty in a subordination clause, where the number of units in the apartment house to be constructed on the property by the buyer was not set out; and mistake of fact as to ownership, where the seller thought she could sell her niece's one-half interest as a joint tenant.

Mutuality of obligation. Numerous cases have arisen in the last few years regarding the enforceability of a contract where performance was made subject to the buyer's approval of specified items, the seller contending that such a provision rendered the contract illusory or lacking in mutuality and therefore unenforceable. Although the tendency of earlier cases was to deny enforceability, later cases have upheld such contracts. Thus, a contract was held to be enforceable where the buyer conditioned his performance upon his obtaining satisfactory leases (*Mattei* v. *Hopper*, 51 Cal.2d 119); where the purchaser's performance was conditioned on their satisfaction with a subdivision map to be obtained by them (*Rodriquez* v. *Barnett*, 52 Cal.2d 154); where the purchaser reserved the right to have a well tested by a reliable pump company to determine the amount of water available (*Lyon* v. *Giannoni*, 168 C.A.2d 336); and where the sale was contingent on obtaining a construction loan in a specified amount (*Pease* v. *Brown*, 186 C.A.2d 425).

Requirement that contracts must be written. The requirement that contracts must be written is set forth in Section 1624 of the Civil Code, which section is referred to as the Statute of Frauds. Such a statute was first passed in England in 1676 for the purpose of preventing fraud and perjury, and required certain contracts to be in writing to be enforceable. (*Burge* v. *Krug*, 160 C.A.2d 201.)

Exceptions to this requirement have been applied in the case of an oral contract that has been partially performed by the vendee's taking possession and making improvements, or where the seller's fraud has prevented the contract from being put in writing.

Signature of the parties. The vendor's signature alone has been held sufficient in some cases, although the contract, as a rule, should be signed by both parties. It is a mandatory requirement that the contract be signed by the party against whom the contract is sought to be enforced, i.e., the vendor, or by his agent duly authorized in writing.

Description of the property. The subject matter of the contract is the land, which must be described with certainty. However, contracts of sale are not held to the same degree of certainty in the description as are deeds. In the case of *Coleman* v. *Dawson*, 110 C.A. 201, the following description in a contract was considered sufficient: "My land consisting of 94$\frac{6}{10}$ acres located about 4 miles northwest from Porterville, Cal." It was held in that case that oral evidence was admissible to complete the description.

Prepayment privilege. Section 2985.6 was added to the Civil Code in 1968 to require that real estate contracts of sale affecting land subdivided into residential lots, or lots which contain a dwelling for not more than four families, must have a provision permitting the contract vendee to prepay all or part of the contract balance. The new law applies to contracts executed on or after January 1, 1969.

III. Option as a contract right in land

An option is defined as a contract by which the owner of property invests another person with the *right* to purchase such property at a stipulated sum within a specified period of time, but without imposing any *obligation* to purchase. The distinguishing characteristic of an option is the initial lack of mutuality in the obligation created. The owner of the land, called the optionor, binds himself to sell if the purchaser, called the optionee, elects to accept the offer, but the optionee is not bound to buy, and may reject the offer contained in the option. However, the exercise of the right to purchase by the optionee does give rise to a mutually binding contract of sale, and the interest acquired is said to relate back to the time of giving the option so as to cut off intervening rights acquired with knowledge of the existence of the option. A purchaser from the optionor with notice of the option would take title subject to the right of the optionee to exercise his right and require a conveyance of the land.

ASSIGNMENT OF OPTION

Generally, the rights of the optionee under an option to purchase are assignable. Options to purchase are often contained in a lease, and such an option ordinarily passes with an assignment of the lease, even though the option is not specifically mentioned in the assignment.

TERMINATION OF OPTION

An option terminates upon expiration of the specified time within which the optionee may accept or exercise his right to purchase. However, for title insurance purposes a recorded option is not ignored solely on the basis of the expiration of the specified time, as the option may have been extended, or its exercise may have been prevented by acts of the optionor.

In 1965 a new section was added to the Civil Code (Sec. 1213.5), operative January 1, 1967, providing that a recorded instrument creating an option to purchase real property ceases to be constructive notice within one year after the option has expired by its terms or by operation of law, when no conveyance, contract, or other instrument has been recorded showing that the option has been exercised or extended.

RIGHT TO REVOKE AN OPTION

An option to purchase, unless supported by a sufficient consideration, is revocable by the optionor at any time before the optionee exercises his right to purchase, but an option to purchase that is supported by a sufficient consideration is irrevocable for its duration. In the latter case, the death of the optionor does not impair the right of the optionee to exercise his right to purchase within the period allowed, unless the death of the optionor renders impossible the performance of a condition precedent to the right to purchase.

NECESSITY FOR WRITING

The California Supreme Court has held that a contract between a contemplated purchaser and a broker, employing the broker to obtain an option for the purchase of real property, comes within the Statute of Frauds and must be in writing. (*Pacific Southwest Development Corp.* v. *Western Pacific Rd. Co.*, 47 Cal.2d 62.)

IV. Title or interest of vendor

A contract for the purchase and sale of real property passes to the purchaser the *equitable* ownership, leaving the legal title in the vendor for the purpose of securing the payments under the contract and the performance of the other conditions of the contract by the buyer.

CONVEYANCES BY VENDOR

The vendor may convey the land to a third party, and such conveyance passes all of the vendor's rights, which include the legal title to the land and the right to receive the unpaid purchase price. The grantee in the deed from the vendor holds the legal title in trust for the purchaser under the contract, and will be bound to convey the title upon completion of the terms of the contract by the buyer. The grantee from the vendor is under a duty to notify the contract buyer that the vendor has conveyed the legal title to him, otherwise the contract buyer may continue to make payments to the original vendor. The contract buyer can compel a conveyance from the grantee when the contract has been paid in full.

ASSIGNMENT OF CONTRACT INTEREST BY VENDOR

Prior to 1961 the vendor could assign his interest under the contract to a third party and retain the legal title to the land. In 1961 the Legislature enacted Section 2985.1 of the Civil Code, which prohibits a transfer of the sales contract without a transfer of the real property; also, it prohibits a transfer of the fee without an assignment of the contract. This section was amended in 1963 to permit the assignment of the contract for collection or to the holder of a first lien as additional security or a transfer of the fee in trust without the assignment of the contract. An opinion of the Attorney General in 1962 concluded that the vendor need not transfer the contract when placing a deed of trust on the property. (40 Ops. Cal. Atty. Gen. 159.)

ENCUMBRANCE BY VENDOR

The vendor may encumber his interest by mortgage or deed of trust. A deed of trust executed by the vendor, describing the land that is the subject of the contract, operates to transfer as security all of the vendor's interest in the property, including his interest under the contract. In such cases, arrangements may be made whereby the purchaser under the contract, after notice, will make payments to the lender, to be applied on the indebtedness. Abuses in the use of land sales contracts resulted in legislation in 1960 designed to give the purchaser a measure of protection from encumbrances by the vendor. The law was further amended in 1963 to provide that a person is guilty of a public offense punishable by not more than $5,000 or five years in jail if he sells a parcel of land under a sales contract that is not recorded and thereafter causes the total encumbrances to exceed the amount due under the sales contract, or causes the aggregate amount in any periodic payment to exceed the periodic payment due under a sales contract excluding the *pro rata* amount of insurance and taxes. A seller or his assignee is guilty of a public offense with the same fine or imprisonment if he appropriates a payment from the buyer that is due to the seller, except to the extent that the payment received from the buyer exceeds the amount on such encumbrances. (C.C., Secs. 2985.2 and 2985.3.) In the definition of a sales contract an exception is made for those contracts that require the conveyance of title within a year from the date of formation of the contract. (C.C., Sec. 2985.)

Other provisions to protect buyer. Section 2985.4 of the Civil Code, enacted in 1963, provides that when a seller of real property under a sales contract receives a *pro rata* payment for insurance and taxes, he must hold these amounts in trust for that purpose. Section 2954 of the Civil Code was also amended in 1963 to provide that upon a written request by the vendee, the vendor shall furnish an itemized statement of the monies applied and disbursed by him.

JUDGMENTS AGAINST VENDOR

A money judgment against the vendor is a lien on the legal title and the vendor's interest in the payments due under the contract. If the vendor has been paid the full purchase price by the contract buyer, a subsequent judgment against the vendor creates no lien since the vendor would have no real interest to which a judgment lien could attach. If there is an execution sale under a judgment against the vendor prior to payment of the contract in full, the execution purchaser stands in the place of the original vendor, and will be obligated to convey title to the vendee upon full performance of the contract by the vendee.

EASEMENTS BY VENDOR

A vendor, even though he may transfer his title or create lien on the property, in subordination of the vendee's interest, cannot burden or charge the land with an easement or similar encumbrance that would be effective as against the purchaser when he fulfills his contract.

EFFECT OF DEATH OF VENDOR

The death of the vendor will not terminate the contract of sale. An order may be obtained in probate proceedings authorizing and directing the representative of the deceased vendor's estate to complete the terms of the contract by the execution and delivery of a deed upon payment of the balance due under the contract.

LIABILITY OF VENDOR FOR CONDITION OF PREMISES

The liability of a vendor was expanded in 1965 whereby a vendor may be subjected to liability to the vendee and to others on the land with the vendee's consent for physical harm caused by a dangerous condition after the vendee has taken possession if the vendor knows *or has reason to know* of an undisclosed dangerous condition, whether natural or artificial, and realizes *or should realize* the risk involved to those persons and has concealed or failed to disclose the condition to his vendee. Previously, liability was imposed only where the vendor actually knew of the condition and realized the risk involved.

As to persons outside the land who are physically harmed as a result of a dangerous condition of the premises, such as a structure in a state of disrepair, a vendor was previously liable where he had *created*, prior to the transfer of possession, such dangerous condition on the land. The liability has been expanded in scope by imposing liability where the vendor negligently permits such a structure or condition to remain on the land.

V. Title or interest of vendee

The vendee is the equitable owner of the property, and has many rights incident to the ownership of the fee. He may transfer his interest in the contract, either by an assignment of the contract or by a deed. Even though the contract contains a covenant against assignment without the vendor's consent, an assignment would nonetheless be valid as between the parties thereto, and passes the vendee's interest. A covenant against assignment is for the benefit of the vendor alone, which he may waive either expressly or by conduct, such as by accepting payments from the assignee.

POSSESSION USUALLY DETERMINES RISK OF LOSS

The purchaser is not entitled to possession of the land unless he is given the right of possession under the contract, or unless the vendor places him in possession. The question of risk of loss is usually dependent upon right of possession. The problem as to who should bear the loss if the property is materially damaged, as by fire, without fault on the part of either party, after the execution of the contract of sale but before execution of the deed, was for many years a perplexing one in California. However, in 1947 there was enacted the Uniform Vendor and Purchaser Risk Act (C.C., Sec. 1662), which provides in effect that transfer of possession is determinative of the question of risk of loss, "unless the contract expressly provides otherwise." Under this code provision, if the possession has been transferred, the risk of loss is upon the purchaser; if possession has not been transferred, the risk of loss is upon the seller. In the case of *Tinker* v. *McLellan,* 165 C.A.2d 291, it was held that under the terms of the contract, the buyer must stand the loss where the property was severely damaged by flood after the deposit receipt constituting an agreement of sale was fully executed and delivered.

HOMESTEAD BY VENDEE

The purchaser may declare a homestead on his interest if he is in possession and if other conditions of the homestead law are complied with. The homestead on the purchaser's equitable interest under the contract rides through and protects the fee title acquired by the purchaser upon fulfillment of the contract. (*Belieu* v. *Power,* 54 C.A. 244.)

CONTRACTS BY VENDEE

The purchaser may execute a contract of sale in favor of another purchaser, but such subcontract is not an assignment and creates no relationship between the original vendor and the second purchaser.

ENCUMBRANCE BY VENDEE

The purchaser may mortgage or otherwise encumber his contract interest in the same manner as an encumbrance on real property, but the lien covers only the interest under the contract, which is generally considered not attractive security from a lender's viewpoint.

JUDGMENTS AGAINST VENDEE

The equitable title of the purchaser is not subject to the lien of a money judgment against him. However, his interest is subject to sale by the levy of a writ of execution pursuant to the judgment.

No deficiency judgment against vendee. As in the case of a purchase money mortgage or deed of trust, there can be no deficiency judgment against the purchaser in proceedings to foreclose his interest if a default occurs.

EFFECT OF DEATH OF VENDEE

The death of the purchaser will not terminate the contract of sale. If the purchaser dies, his executor or administrator has the right and the duty to perform the contract in accordance with its terms if it is for the best interests of the estate.

RECORDING THE CONTRACT

The purchaser is not entitled to record the contract unless it is acknowledged *by the vendor.* The latter normally prefers that the contract not be recorded in order to avoid the necessity of obtaining a quitclaim deed from the buyer or a decree quieting title against him if the contract is not performed. A provision in the contract of sale that the contract is not to be recorded would doubtless be void. (*Resh* v. *Pillsbury,* 12 C.A.2d 226.)

CONTRACT INTEREST DISCLOSED BY OTHER MATTERS

In cases where the vendee does not take possession, it may be desirable for his protection that his contract interest appear of record. Although the contract itself may not be entitled to be recorded because it has not been acknowledged by the vendor, the effect of the contract often is disclosed of record indirectly. This may be accomplished by the recordation of various types of instruments executed and acknowledged by the vendee, such as a deed or assignment of his interest, a subcontract, a mortgage, a lease, or a property agreement. An action to prove an instrument or other types of litigation may disclose the contract interest. If either the vendor or the vendee dies, is adjudged an incompetent, or becomes a bankrupt, the contract interest will usually be disclosed in the estate proceedings.

RECORDATION FOR PURPOSES OF VETERAN'S EXEMPTION

For the purpose of qualifying the property for the veteran's tax exemption, it has been ruled that the contract creating the buyer's interest must be recorded. (30 Ops. Cal. Atty. Gen. 201.) The mere reference to a contract in a recorded document is insufficient if the actual contract is not of record, either in an integrated form or by reference. Subsequent to this opinion, the Revenue and Taxation Code was amended in 1961 to permit a veteran who has an unrecorded interest in real property, consisting of a contract of sale, to qualify for exemption by filing a claim of specified exemption (Rev. & Tax. C., Sec. 261.)

VI. Conveyance in fulfillment of the contract

When the purchaser has fulfilled his obligations under the contract, he is entitled to a conveyance in a form sufficient to pass the title, subject only to such encumbrances on the title as may have been provided for by the contract. Most contracts of sale contain stipulations regarding the condition of title and provide for a policy of title insurance showing title as required. In the absence of any express provisions as to title or encumbrances, there is an implied condition that the vendor will convey an unencumbered and marketable title. Section 1114 of the Civil Code defines the term "encumbrances" as including taxes, assessments, and all liens upon real property. However, this enumeration is not all-inclusive, and matters such as the following have been held to constitute encumbrances: building restrictions, encroachments, easements, and pending actions. On the other hand, the following matters have been held not to constitute encumbrances: zoning ordinances, existing and obvious easements, and proposed assessments.

In 1965 a new section was added to the Civil Code (Sec. 1097) which restricts to $10 the fee that may be contracted for or charged by a vendor or lessor of a single-family residence property for signing or delivering a document in connection with the transfer, cancellation, or reconveyance of any title or instrument when the buyer or lessee exercises an option to buy or completes performance of the contract.

CHAIN OF TITLE TO VENDEE'S INTEREST

Problems of title are frequently encountered in connection with the issuance of a deed by the original vendor. For instance, the deed may not be in favor of the original vendee or his assignee of record, and the chain of title to the vendee's interest is thus broken, often because of an intervening assignment not being recorded. This omission may be corrected either by recording the assignments not of record when they are presently available for recordation, or by obtaining and recording a quitclaim deed from the original vendee or the last assignee of record. Otherwise, a quiet title action may be necessary.

DEEDS VARYING FROM CONTRACT INTEREST

Another problem that may arise results from the issuance of a deed to the vendee in a tenure different from that expressed in the contract. For instance, the contract may name the purchasers as "*A* and *B*, as joint tenants," whereas the deed may be in favor of "*A* and *B*, as tenants in common." As a general rule, the provisions of the deed, if clear and unambiguous, will prevail over an inconsistent provision in the contract.

RESTRICTIONS AND RESERVATIONS

A further problem may arise where the contract is made subject to certain restrictions or reservations, but the deed is silent as to these matters. Generally, a deed executed in consummation of a contract merges all prior agreements, and in the absence of fraud or mistake, the deed is the sole guide for measuring the rights of the parties. Where restrictions in the contract have created rights in third parties—a general plan of restrictions, for instance—the mutual assent of the vendor and vendee eliminating such restrictions from the deed will not be effective insofar as the rights of third parties are concerned.

VII. Remedies for breach of contract

Where a purchaser defaults under the contract, several remedies are available to the vendor, including the following:

First: he may sue for specific performance of the contract to compel payment and acceptance of a deed;

Second: he may stand upon the terms of the contract, offer to perform, and sue for damages;

Third: he may agree with the purchaser for a mutual abandonment and rescission, in which event the purchaser normally is entitled to a refund of the payments made under the contract;

Fourth: he may waive his security and sue for the balance of the purchase price due under the contract;

Fifth: he may bring an action to require the vendee either to pay the monies due under the contract or be foreclosed of all his rights thereunder, in which case the court may render a decree, interlocutory in nature, declaring that a default has occurred in a specified amount, fix a time in the court's discretion within which the purchaser must cure the default, and if the purchaser fails to pay the amount within the prescribed time, enter a final decree, foreclosing all of his rights under the contract;

Sixth: he may bring an action to quiet title against the vendee; or

Seventh: he may declare a forfeiture pursuant to the terms of the contract.

EFFECT OF FORFEITURE

The effect of a proper forfeiture is to terminate the contract, and the vendor may, in a proper case, retain the monies paid under the contract and thereafter deal with the land as if the contract had never been made. However, a purchaser in default may be relieved from a forfeiture upon making full compensation to the vendor, except in the case of a grossly negligent, wilful, or fraudulent default.

REFUND OF PURCHASE PRICE

It was formerly the rule in this state that the vendor had a right to declare the buyer's rights forfeited without refunding to the buyer any part of the purchase price paid. (*Glock* v.*Howard & Wilson Colony Co.*, 123 Cal. 1.) However, later decisions have modified this rule, and the courts now permit even a wilful defaulter to recover such portions of the payments as are in excess of the vendor's actual damages. (*Freedman* v. *The Rector*, 37 Cal.2d 16.) The basis of the decision in the later case is that to enforce a forfeiture would result in the unjust enrichment of the vendor. Also, the opinion has frequently been expressed that the courts "abhor a forfeiture."

REQUIREMENTS FOR TITLE INSURANCE PURPOSES

Where the contract is disclosed of record, it normally cannot be ignored for title insurance purposes on the basis of an asserted breach and forfeiture of the vendee's interest in accordance with the terms of the contract. A quiet title action is the customary and appropriate remedy to establish the fact of forfeiture and to eliminate the contract interest of record. A deed from the purchaser or a cancellation agreement between the vendor and the purchaser will of course be sufficient to eliminate the contract interest of the vendee. An election of a remedy by the buyer, such as an action of rescission and for damages, that is inconsistent with a further claim of interest under the contract, may be sufficient to eliminate the vendee's interest. Occasionally contracts of sale may be disregarded for title insurance purposes on the basis of factors such as lapse of time, purchaser out of possession, small value of land, long continued breach, relatively small equity, and similar considerations indicating little or no risk.

BUYER'S REMEDIES

Where a breach of the contract by the vendor occurs, the purchaser not in default has several available remedies, including the following:

First: he may sue for specific performance to compel a conveyance by the vendor;

Second: he may stand upon the terms of the contract and sue for damages for the breach; or

Third: he may rescind and sue to recover the monies paid under the contract, together with the value of any services rendered or improvements made, and any special damages.

ELECTION OF REMEDIES

As a general rule, the election by the vendor or vendee of any one of the available remedies is a waiver of another and inconsistent remedy. This rule is illustrated by the case of *Buckmaster* v. *Bertram,* 186 Cal. 673, where the purchaser sued the vendor for damages, and the vendor, relying upon the purchaser's election of remedy, sold the land to another purchaser, who also relied upon the election. An amendment of the complaint thereafter to seek specific performance of the contract was not permitted, as the original purchaser was deemed to have abandoned any remedy except his action for damages.

VIII. Advantages and disadvantages of land contracts

The installment contract for the purchase of land has certain advantages, particularly from the vendor's viewpoint, but it does have many disadvantages.

USE OF LAND CONTRACTS

The main purpose in using a land contract is to effect a sale to a buyer who can make only a small down payment, plus small monthly payments over an extended period of time. The sale of real property under installment contracts where the vendor is a responsible corporation, such as a trust company, is a sound and recognized practice, especially in the disposal of unimproved lots held by a corporate trustee under a subdivision trust. The main disadvantage of the land contract from the buyer's viewpoint exists largely in case of sales by individual vendors or entities that do not prove to be financially sound.

ADVANTAGES TO VENDOR

The advantages of such a contract from the standpoint of the vendor are the facility and economy in eliminating the purchaser's interest in the event of a default, provided that the contract interest is not disclosed of record. When a default occurs, the vendor may elect to forfeit the purchaser's interest in accordance with the terms of the contract, a notice of forfeiture often being all that is required. Less time may be consumed to regain possession after forfeiture than in the case of foreclosure of a mortgage or deed of trust.

DISADVANTAGES TO VENDOR

The disadvantages from a vendor's standpoint arise if the contract is disclosed of record. The process of clearing the record title, such as by quiet title or other court action, may be involved, prolonged, and expensive, particularly if the purchaser or any of his assigns is under a legal disability, i.e., is a minor or an incompetent person, or is a nonresident or cannot be located, or is a bankrupt. Difficulties can also arise if the purchaser has suffered or created liens, subcontracts, or other encumbrances or interests in favor of third persons whose rights must be adjudicated in a court action.

DISADVANTAGES TO VENDEE

There are many disadvantages in the use of a land contract from the vendee's viewpoint including the following:

First: transfers of the vendee's interest may be restricted or impeded because of covenants against assignment;

Second: the vendee's interest is not considered an attractive security to lenders;

Third: unless the vendee is in possession, or the contract interest is disclosed of record, rights in third parties may be created by the vendor and obtain priority over the interest of the contract purchaser;

Fourth: the purchaser's rights might be prejudiced by liens against the vendor arising after the contract is made. For instance, installment payments made to the vendor after the vendee has notice of a judgment lien against the vendor may be at the vendee's peril;

Fifth: there is a risk of loss of title by a declaration of forfeiture without redemption rights;

Sixth: there is uncertainty that the purchaser, upon completion of the terms of the contract, will get the title contracted for. Many forms of contracts provide for a policy of title insurance showing title as required, but not until the contract is performed. Prior to the time for performance, the vendor is not obligated to have good title, and the purchaser does not have the right to rescind for that reason alone, in the absence of fraud or incurable defects. The purchaser must continue to make installment payments in the hope that he can compel specific performance in accordance with the terms of the contract when he has paid the contract in full. If the vendor has no title or a defective title when the contract has been performed by the purchaser, the latter's sole remedy may be an action for damages against the vendor; or

Seventh: regardless of the status of the title and the good intentions of the vendor at the time the contract is entered into, there is no assurance that the vendee will be able to obtain a deed without unanticipated court proceedings, arising, for instance, in cases where the vendor dies, becomes incompetent, or is adjudged a bankrupt.

IX. Liability for misrepresentation (fraud and deceit)

Litigation based on alleged misrepresentations of the seller has frequently arisen in connection with contracts for the sale of real property. Litigation results where the buyer discovers that he obtained substantially less than he bargained for and seeks redress against the seller and the seller's agent, contending that he was the victim of fraud and deceit. Fraud and deceit are actionable wrongs under Section 1709 of the Civil Code, which provides that one who wilfully deceives another person with intent to induce him to alter his position to his injury or risk, is liable for any damages that he thereby suffers.

SELLER'S DUTIES

Although as a general rule a vendor not in a confidential relation to the buyer is not under a duty to make a full and complete disclosure concerning the object that he is offering to sell, it is a well-recognized exception that if he undertakes to do so he is bound not only to tell the truth, but he is equally obligated not to suppress or conceal facts within his knowledge that materially qualify those facts stated. Concealment or suppression of facts may constitute actionable fraud to the same extent that affirmative statements that are untrue may give rise to an action in fraud and deceit.

RIGHT OF BUYER

A vendee who is induced to purchase property through fraud and deceit may, upon discovery, repudiate and rescind the contract, or he may allow the contract to stand and sue for damages.

DUTIES OF BUYER

In the ordinary situation, a buyer is under a duty to satisfy himself to the extent possible that the property being sold is in fact what it purports to be. The rule of "*caveat emptor*" or "let the buyer beware" still applies in most transactions. Thus, where the means of knowledge are at hand and equally available to both parties and the subject matter is alike open to their inspection, a person who fails to avail himself of these opportunities will not be heard to say that he was deceived by the other party's misrepresentations. However, in the case of *Lingsch* v. *Savage,* 213 C.A.2d 729, where the property was sold "as is," the seller was nonetheless liable for failing to disclose that the property was in a state of disrepair and had been placed for condemnation by the city. The court stated that where a seller knows of facts materially affecting the value or desirability of the property, which are known or accessible only to him, and also knows that such facts are not known to, or within the reach of the diligent attention and observation of the buyer, the seller is under a duty to disclose them to the buyer. The fact that the buyer agreed to take "as is" will not be a complete defense. In its decision the court stated:

> Under particular circumstances, the use of an "as is" provision seems to convey the implication that the property is in some way defective and that the buyer must take it at his own risk. . . . We are of the opinion that, generally speaking, such a provision means that the buyer takes the property in the condition visible to or observable by him. Where the seller actively misrepresents the then condition of the property, or fails to disclose true facts of its condition not within the buyer's reach and affecting the value or desirability of the property, an "as is" provision is ineffective to relieve the seller of fraud. . . . An "as is" provision may be effective as to a dilapidated stairway, but not as to a missing structural member, a subterranean creek in the backyard, or an unexploded bomb buried in the basement, all being known to the seller.

MISREPRESENTATIONS AS TO QUANTITY

The foregoing rule has not been applied in California to representations as to land quantities, and there are many cases where the courts have held that misrepresentations as to the amount of the land being sold constituted fraud, including the following: *Morey* v. *Bovee,* 218 Cal. 780 (18 acres of orange trees represented as 23 acres); *Nathanson* v. *Murphy,* 132 C.A.2d 363; *Richard* v. *Baker,* 141 C.A.2d 857; and *Piazzini* v. *Jessup,* 153 C.A.2d 58. The court in the case of *Quarg* v. *Scher,* 136 Cal. 406, expressed the rule as follows:

> As a general rule, the owner of real estate, in the absence of facts showing the contrary, is presumed to know the boundaries and area of his land, and a buyer is warranted in relying upon his representations in respect to such facts. The acreage of land is a thing that cannot be seen with the eye at a glance, but can only be ascertained with accuracy by scientific measurement, and when a vendor states to a vendee the amount of land in the tract which is the subject of the sale, such vendor will not thereafter be heard to say in a court of equity, the vendee had no right to believe him.

RELIANCE ON VENDOR'S DESCRIPTION

In the case of *Richard* v. *Baker,* cited above, it was pointed out that although a recorded map referred to in a deed becomes incorporated in the deed, and the recorded map may disclose areas, this rule does not preclude the vendee from proving by parol evidence that he bought in reliance on the vendor's description of the area and boundaries, rather than in reliance on the map.

FILLED-IN LAND

In California there is an affirmative duty on the part of a seller to disclose whether or not the land is filled-in land. The rule as expressed in the case of *Rothstein* v. *Janss Investment Corp.*, 45 C.A.2d 64, may be stated as follows: "A personal inspection of property by a purchaser is no defense to an action for fraud where the conditions are not visible and are known only to the seller. Where material facts are accessible to the vendor only and he knows them not to be within the reach of the diligent attention and observation of the vendee, the vendor is bound to disclose such facts to the vendee. This rule applies where the property sold is filled in to a considerable depth." Other recent cases applying this rule are the following: *Worthen* v. *Jackson,* 139 C.A.2d 615; *Kruse* v. *Miller,* 143 C.A.2d 656; and *Burkett* v. *J. A. Thompson & Son,* 150 C.A.2d 523. The case of *Kruse* v. *Miller* involved a misrepresentation by the broker that the residence sold was not built on a filled lot. The seller was held responsible for this false representation, since the seller's broker is the seller's agent, and a misrepresentation made by the broker is treated as if it had been made by the seller personally. In that case the seller obtained a judgment against the broker for the amount of damages sustained by the seller in a previous action against him by the buyer.

OTHER TYPES OF MISREPRESENTATION

Other types of false representation that have been held actionable include the following: representations as to freedom of a building from termites (*Wice* v. *Schilling*, 124 C.A.2d 735); misrepresentations as to deed restrictions (*Evans* v. *Rancho Royale Hotel Co.*, 114 C.A.2d 503); misrepresentations as to tenantable condition of residential property (*Unger* v. *Campau*, 142 C.A.2d 722); misrepresentations as to income or that the business was profitable (*Leary* v. *Baker*, 119 C.A.2d 106; *Eatwell* v. *Beck*, 41 Cal.2d 128); concealment of the fact that there was an encroachment on a state right-of-way (*Kallgren* v. *Steele*, 131 C.A.2d 43); failure to disclose an engineer's report on hillside property (*Gilbert* v. *Corlett*, 171 C.A.2d 116); misrepresentations as to the water supply (*Crawford* v. *Nastos*, 182 C.A.2d 659); and misrepresentations as to compliance with building code requirements (*Curren* v. *Heslop*, 115 C.A.2d 476; *Milmoe* v. *Dixon*, 101 C.A.2d 257). As stated by the court in the last-cited case, a party who makes an inspection of the property does not forfeit his right to rely on the representations or concealment of the seller as to matters of a technical nature, or as to facts not ascertainable by the exercise of reasonable diligence in the inspection.

Questions

1. Discuss briefly the common types of contracts used in real estate transactions.
2. Describe the essential elements of a contract for the sale of land.
3. May the vendor convey the land to a third party after the execution of a land contract?
4. Explain the effect of a judgment lien against the seller.
5. Discuss briefly the nature and extent of the buyer's interest in the land.
6. What remedies are available to the seller in the event of default by the buyer?
7. What action can the buyer take if the seller refuses to perform?
8. Discuss the advantages of a land contract.
9. Discuss the disadvantages of a land contract.
10. Describe the main characteristics of an option.
11. Is the seller under any duty to disclose that land is filled-in land?
12. If misrepresentations are made by the seller as to the area of the land, does the buyer have any remedy?
13. Does a vendor owe a duty with respect to condition of the premises?

14

Mortages and Trust Deeds

Summary

I. Introductory
Comparison with contract of sale; Trust deeds prevalent in California; Historical development of mortgages; Present-day characteristics of a mortgage

II. Mortgages and trust deeds compared
Trust deed defined; Distinguishing characteristics; Title of debtor; Statute of limitations; Remedies; Redemption rights; Deficiency judgments

III. Essential characteristics of a mortgage
Application of recording laws; Priority of mortgage; Debt or obligation; Obligation evidenced by promissory note; Nature of obligation; Effect of payments; Future advances; Optional advances; When junior lien holders should give notice; Agreements affecting priority; Chattel mortgages; Obligations secured by real and personal property; After-acquired title; Priority as to after-acquired property; Priority of purchase money mortgage; More than one purchase money encumbrance may exist; Obligations of mortgagor; Other provisions; Assignment-of-rents provision; Extension agreements; Beneficiary statements; Assignment of obligation; Assumption of obligation; Release of mortgage; Partial release of mortgage; Extinguishment of lien; Mortgages with power of sale; Regulation of small loans; Federal Truth in Lending Act

IV. Mortgage foreclosures
Nature of the action; Right to reinstate; Judicial sale; Deficiency judgment; Right of redemption; Period of redemption

V. Essential characteristics of a deed of trust
Trust deeds similar to mortgages; Distinguishing feature of trust deed; Form of trust deed; Trustee cannot be compelled to act; "All-inclusive" deed of trust; Substitution of trustee; Judicial foreclosure of trust deed; Mortgage rules applicable

VI. Trustee's sale proceedings
Evidence of default; Contents of notice of default; Mailing copies

I. Introductory

In California three principle types of instruments are employed to create a lien on real property as security for the payment of money or for the performance of some other obligation, namely a *mortgage, a mortgage with power of sale,* and a *deed of trust* (or trust deed, as commonly referred to).

COMPARISON WITH CONTRACT OF SALE

The contract of sale is sometimes used in real estate transactions, but strictly speaking it is not a security instrument in the conventional sense. Where a contract of sale is used, legal title to the real property is retained by the seller until the buyer (debtor) has paid the purchase price in accordance with the terms of the contract, at which time he is entitled to a conveyance of the property by deed. In the case of a security transaction involving either a mortgage or a deed of trust, the legal title vests in the debtor, subject to the effect of the trust deed or mortgage in favor of the creditor.

TRUST DEEDS PREVALENT IN CALIFORNIA

The trust deed is the most widely used type of real estate security transaction in this state, the real estate mortgage being but little used by comparison. This is aptly demonstrated by the fact that during the year 1963, for example, the number of trust deeds recorded in the office of the county recorder of Los Angeles county totaled 323,121, whereas only 87 mortgages were recorded during the same period. Nonetheless, consideration should be given to the nature and characteristics of mortgages, since the courts, in passing upon the validity and effect of trust deeds, have drawn upon the principles of law applying to mortgages, as well as the principles applying to trusts, and features of each are contained in a deed of trust.

HISTORICAL DEVELOPMENT OF MORTGAGES

The mortgage as developed in early English law was a conveyance of land by the debtor to the creditor on condition that, upon payment of the obligation on or before a specified day, the mortgage would become void and the creditor would reconvey the land to the debtor. If the debtor did not perform on or before the day specified, known as the "law day," the creditor would then become the absolute owner of the land. Legal title to the mortgaged land passed to the creditor, subject to being divested by payment of the obligation secured by the mortgage within the prescribed time. The creditor was also entitled to possession of the land and the rents and issues thereof. The land was thus considered as "dead" in the sense that it gave no return to the debtor, a meaning that refers to the origin of the word *mortgage,* which in Old French meant "dead pledge."

Equity of redemption. The English courts of equity in time viewed with disfavor the strict rule of absolute forfeiture of property upon nonpayment of a debt. Accordingly, they established a doctrine that the debtor should have a right to repay the debt within a reasonable time after breach of the condition and thereby reacquire or redeem the mortgaged land. This equitable right to save the property after a forfeiture at law was called the "equity of redemption." This placed the creditor somewhat at a disadvantage, as there was no longer any certain time at which he would either receive payment or retain the security. As a solution, a procedure for foreclosure of the debtor's rights was evolved, whereby upon a petition by the creditor, the courts of equity would enter a decree requiring the debtor to repay the debt by a fixed date, and providing that upon default in such payment the debtor's equity of redemption would be barred and foreclosed.

Waiver of right of redemption. Once this right of the debtor to redeem was established, lenders then attempted to destroy it by requiring that the debtor at the time of executing the mortgage agree in writing not to exercise such right, i.e., to waive this right of redemption. However, the courts refused to enforce such waivers, holding that such advance waivers of redemption rights were contrary to public policy and therefore void.

PRESENT-DAY CHARACTERISTICS OF A MORTGAGE

The English theory of mortgage laws was generally adopted in the United States in the early days, but has been modified considerably by statutes and court decisions. In California, the mortgage, by force of statute, creates merely a lien, with the legal title and right to possession remaining in the debtor until divested by foreclosure proceedings. The equitable right of redemption has been supplanted by a statutory right of redemption for a fixed period after sale of the mortgaged land under foreclosure proceedings. The rule denying validity to advance waivers of the right of redemption has been codified in Section 2953 of the Civil Code.

II. Mortgages and trust deeds compared

A mortgage is defined as a contract by which specific property is hypothecated for the performance of an act, without the necessity for a change of possession. (C.C., Sec. 2920.) To *hypothecate* means to pledge a thing without delivering the possession of it to the pledgee. Hypothecation is a term of the civil law, and as contrasted with a pawn, is that kind of pledge in which the possession of the thing pledged remains with the debtor.

TRUST DEED DEFINED

A trust deed is defined as a conveyance of property to an individual or a corporation as trustee, for the purpose of securing a debt or other obligation, with a power of sale in the trustee, exercisable upon default, with the proceeds of the sale to be applied in payment of the obligation.

DISTINGUISHING CHARACTERISTICS

Basically, both mortgages and trust deeds are forms of transactions involving land as security, but there are several distinguishing characteristics of each. As to *parties,* in a mortgage there are two parties, whereas in the deed of trust there are usually three parties. The parties to a mortgage are the mortgagor (debtor) and the mortgagee (creditor). The parties to a trust deed are the trustor (debtor), the trustee, and the beneficiary (creditor).

TITLE OF DEBTOR

In the case of a mortgage, title to the mortgaged property remains in the mortgagor, but subject to the lien in favor of the mortgagee. The mortgagor's title may be divested by foreclosure proceedings if the debt is not paid, but until such event occurs, the mortgagor has title. In the case of a deed of trust, legal title passes to the trustee and remains there until the debt is paid or until transferred by the trustee to a purchaser under a sale based on a default. The trustee, however, takes only such title as is necessary to the execution of the trust; until the necessity of a sale actually arises, the trustee's title lies dormant. In the meantime, the trustor, like a mortgagor, may convey or encumber the property and exercise all of the other usual rights of an owner, subject, of course, to the effect of the encumbrance.

STATUTE OF LIMITATIONS

As to the statute of limitations, different rules are applicable to mortgages and to deeds of trust. An action to foreclose a mortgage is barred when the statute of limitations has run on the obligation secured. In the case of a deed of trust the statute of limitations is not a bar to a trustee's sale proceedings, which may be undertaken regardless of whether or not the statute has run on the principal obligation. The trustee has title and can always sell, with no limitation on the time when a default must be declared.

REMEDIES

As to applicable remedies, there are material differences. Foreclosure by court proceedings is the only remedy for enforcement of the terms of an ordinary mortgage. Under a deed of trust alternative remedies are available: either foreclosure by court proceedings, or trustee's sale proceedings.

REDEMPTION RIGHTS

There are also differences with respect to the right of redemption, and as to deficiency judgments. After foreclosure sale under a mortgage, the mortgagor, has a statutory right to redeem within a prescribed period of time. Although the owner has a right of reinstatement for a prescribed period prior to the sale, he has no right of redemption after a trustee's sale under a deed of trust.

DEFICIENCY JUDGMENTS

When a mortgage is foreclosed, a deficiency judgment may be entered unless the mortgage is a purchase money mortgage and the limitations of Section 580b of the Code of Civil Procedure do not apply (see p. 265). There is no provision for a deficiency judgment after a trustee's sale under a deed of trust. If a deficiency judgment is desired, it is necessary to foreclose the deed of trust as a mortgage. An exception to this rule might apply, however, in the event of waste or conversion by the trustor which impairs the security. (*Weaver* v. *Bay*, 216 C.A.2d 559.) However, a deficiency judgment can be had even if it is a purchase money deed of trust if the rights of the United States are affected where, for instance, an FHA or VA loan is involved. (*McKnight* v. *United States*, 259 Fed.2d 540.)

III. Essential characteristics of a mortgage

A mortgage can be created, renewed, or extended only in writing, executed with the formalities required in the case of a grant of real property. (C.C., Sec. 2922.) Any interest in real property that is capable of being transferred may be mortgaged. (C.C., Sec. 2947.) Under the provisions of Section 2948 of the Civil Code a mortgage of real property may be made in substantially the following form:

> This mortgage made this ________ day of ______________, 19____ by *A.B. of* ______________________________, California, mortgagor, to *C.D.*, of ______________________, California, mortgagee, witnesseth: That the mortgagor mortgages to the mortgagee the following property [description], as security for the payment to him of $__________ on (or before) the ________ day of ______________, 19____, with interest thereon [or as security for the payment of an obligation, describing it, etc.]
>
> *A. B.*
>
> ________________________
>
> Mortgagor

APPLICATION OF RECORDING LAWS

The recording statutes apply to a mortgage the same as to a conveyance by deed. Before a mortgage can be recorded, it must be executed by the mortgagor and acknowledged by him or proved as required by law, and it must describe the property with common certainty. A mortgage, like a deed, should be filed for record with the recorder of the county in which the property is situated. Upon recordation, it obtains the same priority and protection from recording as a deed.

In 1968 a new section was added to the Business and Professions Code (Sec. 10141.5) which imposes a duty on a real estate broker in connection with recording a deed of trust. The section provides that within one week after the closing of a transaction negotiated by a real estate broker in which title to real property is conveyed from a seller to a purchaser and a deed of trust secured by real property is executed, such broker shall cause such deed of trust to be recorded with the county recorder of the county in which the real property is located, or cause it to be delivered to the beneficiary with a written recommendation that it be recorded forthwith, unless instructions not to record are received from the beneficiary. If the transaction is closed through escrow and the deed of trust is delivered to the escrow holder within the time prescribed, that shall be deemed compliance. Nothing in the section shall effect the validity of a transfer of title to real property.

PRIORITY OF MORTGAGE

As a general rule, a mortgage, when duly recorded, is prior to any interest or lien subsequently attaching. It is also prior to any interest or lien previously created but not then of record unless the mortgagee had knowledge thereof at the time his mortgage was recorded. A mortgage does not have priority over the lien of federal, state, or local taxes or assessments if by statute such liens are accorded preference over private rights. Also, under some circumstances a mortgage may be inferior to a subsequently recorded mechanic's lien. (See Chapter 15 for a discussion of mechanics' liens and their priority.)

DEBT OR OBLIGATION

The mortgage is an incident of the debt or obligation secured, and there can be no mortgage without such debt or obligation. When the obligation is satisfied, the mortgage ceases to be more than a cloud on the title, and the discharge of the mortgage of record can be compelled.

OBLIGATION EVIDENCED BY PROMISSORY NOTE

The obligation secured by a mortgage, when consisting of a debt of fixed amount, ordinarily is evidenced by a promissory note or notes, payable to the lender or order. The note or notes are usually negotiable in form; they are not rendered nonnegotiable by virtue of the fact that they are secured by a mortgage or deed of trust. (C.C., Sec. 3265.) If negotiable, they gain certain adventages under the Negotiable Instruments Law. The main advantage of negotiability is to afford protection to "holders in due course," who take free of certain defects that may be inherent in the original transaction, such as undue influence, duress, fraud in the inducement, lack of delivery, or absence or failure of consideration.

NATURE OF OBLIGATION

It is not essential that the mortgage itself contain a description of the obligation; it is necessary only that there be an obligation in fact, and that this be referred to in the mortgage sufficiently to put third persons upon inquiry. The obligation may be a debt of fixed amount then owing to the mortgagee, or all existing indebtedness of the mortgagor to the mortgagee, or either of these and additionally all sums afterward advanced by the mortgagee to the mortgagor, either under an optional advance clause (open-end mortgage), or under an obligatory advance clause.

EFFECT OF PAYMENTS

Unless the mortgage is expressly made security for future indebtedness or advances, it secures only the existing obligation, and once the obligation so secured is reduced, a further loan may not be made on the security of the mortgage, although within the amount of such reduction. As payments are made on the obligation, the security of the mortgage is automatically satisfied *pro tanto,* and cannot be revived or extended to cover additional loans unless the original agreement so provides, or unless the agreement is so amended. Intervening encumbrancers, however, are not bound by a subsequent amendment unless they consent thereto.

FUTURE ADVANCES

If a mortgage contains a future advance clause, the priority of the mortgage as to additional advances is dependent upon whether or not the advances are *obligatory* or *optional.* As a general rule, to the extent that the mortgage secures future advances, it takes the priority of its original date of recording as against liens arising between such date and the date of the additional advance. This general rule applies if such advances are obligatory, i.e., if the mortgagee cannot properly refuse to make them on demand of the mortgagor. In this category are successive advances under a building loan that the mortgagee has agreed to make as the building progresses. (*Fickling* v. *Jackman,* 203 Cal. 657.) This rule now applies in the case of intervening United States tax liens. By statutory amendment in 1966, the lien of a previously recorded deed of trust securing a construction loan may extend its priority to additional advances made subsequent to the filing of a federal tax lien.

OPTIONAL ADVANCES

Except as to a United States tax lien, the general rule as to priority also applies where the advances are optional, i.e., discretionary with the mortgagee, provided the mortgagee does not have *actual knowledge* of intervening rights of third parties at the time when he makes an additional advance. This knowledge of intervening rights is something more than the constructive notice afforded by the recording laws; it must be actual notice, or knowledge of facts sufficient to put a prudent person on inquiry. (*Atkinson* v. *Foote,* 44 C.A. 149.)

WHEN JUNIOR LIEN HOLDERS SHOULD GIVE NOTICE

A junior encumbrancer, before making a loan, should make inquiry of the mortgagee under a prior mortgage containing an optional advance as to whether or not additional advances have been made. If advances have not been made and a loan is thereupon made by the new lender, he should immediately give notice to the mortgagee under the prior mortgage of the fact that he has made a loan and holds a junior lien on the property. Thereafter, any further optional advances under the prior mortgage will be junior to the rights of such intervening lender.

AGREEMENTS AFFECTING PRIORITY

The relative priorities of mortgages over other liens and charges may be altered in various ways, as by recitals of priority contained in the mortgage, or by the execution and recordation of a subordination agreement, or by provisions in the mortgage that a prior encumbrance may be renewed in a specified way and that the renewal instrument will then be prior and superior thereto. Subordination agreements were the subject of new legislation in 1963 requiring that subordination documents be so entitled and that notices of subordination be included in prescribed type size in those instruments, including mortgages and deeds of trust, coming within the scope of the act. (C.C., Secs. 2953.1 *et seq.*)

CHATTEL MORTGAGES

Personal property as well as real property may be mortgaged. Prior to January 1, 1965, a mortgage of personal property was called a chattel mortgage, and for the protection of creditors of the mortgagor, certain statutory requirements peculiar thereto had to be observed. Such mortgage had to be in writing, executed and acknowledged in like manner as a grant of real property; had to be clearly entitled, on its face, and apart from and preceding all other terms of the mortgage, *"a mortgage of crops and/or chattels,"* as the case may be; had to be promptly recorded; and had to be rerecorded within four years of the original recording or a subsequent rerecording. (C.C., Sec. 2957.) After January 1, 1965 a personal property security agreement is used instead of chattel mortgage, with a financing statement to be recorded or filed (see p. 31 for a further discussion).

OBLIGATIONS SECURED BY REAL AND PERSONAL PROPERTY

Sometimes an obligation is secured by both real and personal property, in which case the lender should take a mortgage (or deed of trust) on the real property, and a security instrument on the personal property, with a recital in each that it is also secured by the other; that in the event of default, the mortgagee may resort to both, concurrently or in such order or manner as he may elect; and that the application of the proceeds of enforcement of one will not cure existing defaults or impair any pending proceedings for the enforcement of the other.

AFTER-ACQUIRED TITLE

After-acquired title of a mortgagor inures to the benefit of the mortgagee as security for the debt. (C.C., Sec. 2930.) Thus, a mortgage of realty will cover permanent improvements constructed afterward on the mortgaged property. Also, a mortgage by its terms may be made to cover after-acquired property as well as that specifically described. The so-called county indigent mortgages offer an example of a mortgage expressly covering after-acquired property.

PRIORITY AS TO AFTER-ACQUIRED PROPERTY

Although a provision extending the lien of the mortgage to after-acquired property is valid and binding on the mortgagor and on third parties dealing with the property, after its acquisition by the mortgagor, with knowledge of such mortgage, the recordation of such a mortgage prior to the date of acquisition of title by the mortgagor will not constitute constructive notice to innocent purchasers or lenders dealing with the mortgagor in good faith and for value, since the mortgage is not in the mortgagor's chain of title. Persons dealing on the strength of the record title are not obligated to run the records as to the party they are dealing with prior to the date of acquisition of title by the latter on the chance that he might have encumbered the property prior to the date he acquired it. (*Dobbins* v. *Economic Gas Co.*, 182 Cal. 616.)

PRIORITY OF PURCHASE MONEY MORTGAGE

Under the provisions of Section 2898 of the Civil Code, a mortgage given by the purchaser of real property to secure any portion of the purchase price of the property covered thereby obtains a special priority, i.e., it is superior to all other liens created against the purchaser, subject to the operation of the recording laws. The deed and the mortgage back are considered as contemporaneous acts, and no lien or charge then existing against the purchaser can be prior to the rights of the vendor under his purchase money mortgage. Thus, the lien of a previously recorded abstract of judgment against the purchaser is subordinate to a purchase money mortgage. (*Walley* v. *P. M. C. Investment Co., Inc.*, 262 A.C.A. 244.) Also, where a third party advances the purchase money with the understanding that the advance will be secured by the property, his security comes within the rule and will be accorded the same priority. (*Van Loben Sels* v. *Bunnell*, 120 Cal. 680; *Stockton Savings & Loan Bank* v. *Massanet*, 18 Cal.2d 200.)

MORE THAN ONE PURCHASE MONEY ENCUMBRANCE MAY EXIST

There may be more than one purchase money encumbrance on the same property at the same time. This may occur in cases where a third party advances funds to the buyer for the purpose of completing the purchase and obtains a first deed of trust or mortgage, and the seller takes back a second encumbrance. It has been held that with purchase money encumbrances, the character of the transaction must be determined at the time the encumbrance is executed, and its nature is then fixed for all time. (*Brown* v. *Jensen*, 41 Cal.2d 193.) In the case of *Bargioni* v. *Hill*, 59 Cal.2d 121, a deed of trust in favor of the broker was considered to be purchase money and a personal judgment against the borrower after foreclosure was not obtainable.

OBLIGATIONS OF MORTGAGOR

A mortgage usually includes numerous provisions that, although not essential to the validity or enforceability of the mortgage, have been developed as necessary or proper to afford adequate protection to the lender. These include covenants to maintain and repair the property; to comply with health laws and police regulations; to keep the property insured against fire and other hazards; to pay taxes, assessments, and encumbrances having priority, and authorizing the mortgagee to pay them if they become delinquent; also to prosecute or defend proceedings where necessary to safeguard the security.

OTHER PROVISIONS

Additionally, provisions are included authorizing the mortgagee to take protective or defensive measures if the mortgagor neglects them, and to add the costs to the debt; also, provision is made for disposition of condemnation awards; for partial releases; for subordination agreements and the grant of easements and execution of subdivision maps, and so on. In some cases provision is made for periodic payments into an impounded fund maintained and to be used by the mortgagee to pay taxes, assessments, and insurance premiums as they become due.

ASSIGNMENT-OF-RENTS PROVISION

The mortgage may also contain an assignment-of-rents provision, assigning the rents then due or thereafter to accrue, either absolutely or effective upon the happening of some future event, such as a default in payment or performance of the obligations secured by the mortgage. As an aid to the enforcement of such provision, a receiver may be appointed by the court to collect the rents. A receiver may also be appointed upon a showing of waste or inadequacy of the security.

EXTENSION AGREEMENTS

Parties to a mortgage may agree upon an extension of the maturity date, or the alteration or modification of the terms of the mortgage or the obligation secured by the mortgage, provided the rights of third parties are not prejudiced. A junior encumbrancer is not bound by an extension or modification to which he does not consent, and that would operate to the prejudice of his right.

BENEFICIARY STATEMENTS

In 1961 and 1963 new sections of the Civil Code were enacted dealing with the furnishing of information by a lender to the borrower on a real estate loan. As amended in 1963, Section 2943 of the Civil Code requires the lender, upon the written request of the borrower made before foreclosure proceedings have been commenced, to furnish a written statement showing, among other things, (a) the amount of the unpaid balance of the obligation secured by the mortgage or deed of trust and the interest rate; (b) the amounts of periodic payments, if any; and (c) the date on which the obligation is due in whole or in part. The statement is required to be mailed within twenty-one days after the receipt of the request, and a lender who for a period of twenty-one days wilfully fails to prepare and deliver such statement is liable for any actual damages sustained and in any case for the sum of $100. The lender may make a charge of not to exceed $15 for furnishing the statement, providing that the provision for such charge is contained in the deed of trust. However, the charge may be made in the case of FHA or VA loans whether or not there is any such provision in the deed of trust. The amended section applies only to loans made on or after January 1, 1964. It is intended primarily to assist the owner of the property in obtaining information needed for the purpose of a sale or refinancing.

The section was amended in 1968 to enlarge the group of persons entitled to a statement to include, in addition to the mortgagor or trustor or a successor in interest to all of the property, the successor in interest as to any part of the mortgaged property, and any beneficiary under a subordinate deed of trust and any other person having a subordinate lien or encumbrance of record. The amendment also added the following to the information previously required in the statement: (a) the total amount of all overdue installments of principal or interest, or both, and (b) the nature and amount of any additional charges, costs or expenses paid or incurred by the beneficiary which have become a lien on the property. Also, the time within which the demand could be made was changed to any time before or within two months after the recording of the notice of default in the case of a power-of sale foreclosure, or more than thirty days prior to entry of the decree in the case of a judicial foreclosure. The amendment further provides that the twenty-one day grace period allowed for compliance with the demand begins upon beneficiary's receipt of reasonable proof that the person making the demand is entitled to the statement, and that the liability for the $100 penalty for noncompliance is to the person entitled to the statement rather than to the trustor or mortgagor as in the previous provisions.

Section 2954 of the Civil Code, added in 1961, requires a beneficiary or mortgagee, upon the written request of the trustor or mortgagor, to render an annual accounting of funds received from the borrower. This section is intended primarily to inform the owner of the property of the status of the impound account.

ASSIGNMENT OF OBLIGATION

An assignment of the obligation secured by a mortgage carries the mortgage with it, whereas an assignment of the mortgage apart from the obligation is ineffective and transfers nothing. The obligation may be assigned by an indorsement on the note or on the mortgage, or by a separate instrument. In order to obtain the benefit of the recording laws, the assignment must be executed in form sufficient to entitle it to be recorded. Also, notice of the assignment should be given to the obligor. If the obligor does not have actual notice of the assignment, payment to the assignor may discharge the obligation, and the assignee will then be compelled to look to his assignor for payment.

ASSUMPTION OF OBLIGATION

When a purchaser of mortgaged property expressly assumes the mortgage, he becomes primarily liable on the obligation, and the maker of the note becomes a surety for the debt. However, if a purchaser, instead of assuming the obligation merely takes "subject to" the mortgage, the property becomes primarily liable and the maker becomes a surety. Under the provisions of Section 1624 of the Civil Code, an assumption agreement to be effective must be in writing. It is not essential to the validity or enforceability of a mortgage that anyone in fact be personally liable for payment of the obligation secured by the mortgage. All recourse against the maker of the note may be waived. Also, when the maker of the note dies, recourse beyond the security is lost by failure to file a claim against the estate. Recourse against the maker is restricted in the case of a purchase money encumbrance.

RELEASE OF MORTGAGE

Payment or satisfaction of the obligation extinguishes the mortgage, which thereupon ceases to be a lien. The record thereafter reflects a mere cloud on the title, and the mortgagee can be compelled to execute and deliver, in form sufficient to entitle it to be recorded, a certificate that the mortgage has been paid, satisfied, or discharged, or cause satisfaction to be entered of record. The mortgagee is liable for all damages occasioned by a failure to effect a discharge after payment, and he may also be subject to a penalty of $300 under the provisions of Section 2941 of the Civil Code. Also, under Section 2941.5 of the Civil Code, it is a misdemeanor to refuse to release the mortgage after payment.

PARTIAL RELEASE OF MORTGAGE

In the absence of a provision requiring the mortgagee to release a portion of the mortgaged property, the obligation must be paid in full before the mortgagee can be compelled to release any part of his security. Provision is often made in the mortgage for the release of portions of the security upon payment of release prices as therein provided, in which case the mortgagor or his successors in ownership of such portion of the security can compel the mortgagee to effect releases in accordance with the release clauses.

EXTINGUISHMENT OF LIEN

Pursuant to the provisions of Section 2911 of the Civil Code, the lien of a mortgage is extinguished by lapse of the time within which an action can be brought on the obligation. The only action that can be brought upon an obligation secured by a mortgage is an action for foreclosure of the mortgage (C.C.P., Sec. 726), and when recourse to judicial foreclosure is barred by lapse of time, the lien ceases. However, it is still a matter of record until released, and ordinarily will not be ignored by a title company until a release is recorded or a decree quieting title is obtained and recorded. The fact that the debt is outlawed will not necessarily entitle the mortgagor or his successor to a quiet title decree against the holder of the obligation. A quiet title action is a proceeding in equity, and it is a principle of equity that the obligor or his successors in interest cannot obtain relief by clearing the property of such "outlawed" mortgage without "doing equity," i.e., paying the debt as a condition for obtaining a decree quieting title.

MORTGAGES WITH POWER OF SALE

The addition to a conventional mortgage of a power of sale whereby, on default, the mortgagee may effect a sale of the property without the necessity of judicial proceedings, does not change its essential character from that of a lien. This power of sale in the mortgagee is similar to the exercise of a power of attorney, and in the absence of express provision in the mortgage, the mortgagee must execute his deed to the purchaser, after sale under the power, in the name of the mortgagor by himself as attorney-in-fact or as donee of the power. When the debt is outlawed by lapse of time, the power of sale under a mortgage is lost. This is a major difference between a mortgage with power of sale and a deed of trust, since under the latter the power of sale never outlaws, and can be undertaken in spite of the fact that judicial enforcement of the debt and security is barred.

REGULATION OF SMALL LOANS

In 1955 a new chapter was added to the Civil Code (Secs. 3081.1–3081.93) pertaining to the regulation of loans secured by real property, the aim being to stop objectionable practices under which persons of small means were compelled periodically to renew or refinance loans and incur additional brokerage fees and expenses in substantial amounts. This resulted mainly from the inclusion of balloon payment provisions in short-term installment notes secured by mortgages or trust deeds on real property. The new law (known as the Small Loan Act) requires that installment loans with a maturity date of less than three years provide for substantially equal payments over the period of the loan, with no installment, including the last, to be greater than twice the amount of the smallest installment. As enacted in 1955, this provision was applicable to direct transactions between borrower and lender as well as loan brokers, and was interpreted to include purchase money loans. (27 Ops. Cal. Atty. Gen. 374.) By amendment, effective September 11, 1957, purchase money loans are exempt from the balloon payment provision.

Other provision of Small Loan Act. The Act also was designed to limit the fees, charges, and commission imposed by persons negotiating loans on real property, and brought loan brokers under the jurisdiction of the Real Estate Commissioner (see Chapter 20). The Act does not apply to several classifications of lenders, including banks, nor does it apply to loans secured by a first mortgage or trust deed, the principal sum of which amounts to $12,000 or more, or to loans secured by a second mortgage or trust deed, the principal sum of which amounts to $6,000 or more (before November 13, 1968, the amounts were $10,000 and $5,000 respectively.) In 1961 the Small Loan Act was transferred to the Business and Professions Code, and in 1963 building loans were excluded from the balloon payment provision under specified conditions. (Bus. & Prof. C., Sec. 10244.)

FEDERAL TRUTH IN LENDING ACT

The federal Truth in Lending Act which became effective on July 1, 1969, as a portion of the Federal Consumer Credit Protection Act (Public Law 90–321), together with Regulation Z issued pursuant to the Act, may apply in transactions involving a real estate security instrument executed by a natural person encumbering a dwelling or agricultural land.

The application of the Act is limited to the extension or arranging of credit to a natural person where the money, property, or service that is the subject of the transaction is primarily for personal, family, household, or agricultural purposes. In general, the Act requires creditors to disclose the cost of credit in a statement to the consumer prior to the consummation of a loan transaction.

Additionally, the Act includes a right of rescission applicable in certain situations. The Act and regulations provide that if a security interest is or will be retained or acquired in any real property transaction that is used or is expected to be used as the principal residence of the customer, the latter shall have the right to rescind the transaction until midnight of the third business day following the date of consummation of the transaction to extend credit or the date of delivery of the disclosures required by the Act, whichever is later, by notifying the creditor of his intention to rescind. Exceptions apply in the case of a purchase money first mortgage or construction loan on a home. Upon rescission the customer is not liable for any finance or other charge, and any security interest taken by the creditor becomes void.

IV. Mortgage foreclosures

There is only one form of action that may be brought for the recovery of any obligation secured by a mortgage or deed of trust, and that is an action to foreclose the mortgage. (C.C.P., Secs. 725a and 726.) This is an action in equity by the mortgagee or his successor in interest against the record owner of the property and the record holders of all interests and encumbrances that are junior or subordinate to the mortgage under foreclosure. It is unnecessary, insofar as resort to the security is concerned, to join as defendants the mortgagor or others personally liable but no longer having an interest in the mortgaged property. However, to the extent that enforcement of their liability for any deficiency is sought, they must be made parties to the action. The United States, as the holder of a subsequent federal tax lien against the property, may be joined as a party defendant and a judgment obtained against it. In such case the United States is given a one-year period within which to redeem. (28 U.S.C.A. 2410.)

NATURE OF THE ACTION

The object of the foreclosure action is to sell the right, title, and interest that the mortgagor had in the property at the time of the execution of the mortgage, or that he thereafter acquired. The action must be brought in the Superior Court in the county in which the property or some part thereof is situated, within four years after the maturity of the obligation secured by the mortgage or after the last payment where payments have been made after maturity. The action is commenced by the filing of a *complaint.* A *notice of action* (*lis pendens*) should then be recorded in the office of the county recorder. This will bind persons acquiring interests or liens during the pendency of the action. After jurisdiction has been obtained over the defendants, either by service of process or by their voluntary appearance, a trial is held, and a judgment entered. The judgment is called a *decree of foreclosure and order of sale.*

RIGHT TO REINSTATE

The mortgagor or his successor in interest has the right to reinstate the mortgage, the maturity of which has been accelerated by reason of default in payment of an installment or other money obligation, by paying the mortgagee, at any time *prior to the entry of the decree of foreclosure,* the entire amount that would then be due had there been no default, plus attorney's fees not exceeding $100 or ½ of 1 per cent of the entire unpaid principal sum secured, whichever is greater. (C.C., Sec. 2924c, as amended in 1957.)

JUDICIAL SALE

The judgment in the foreclosure action establishes the existence and validity of the mortgage, the amount due thereon, including interest together with costs and attorney's fees, and directs the sale of the property, either by the sheriff or by a commissioner named therein, in the manner provided by law. The sheriff or commissioner, as the case may be, holds a public auction sale of the property after giving notice of the time, place, and purpose of the sale by posting and publication. Upon receipt of the amount bid, the officer conducting the sale issues a *certificate of sale* to the purchaser, which certificate operates as a conveyance of title to the property, subject to redemption as provided by law. If no redemption is made within the time allowed, a *deed* is issued in favor of the purchaser or his assignee.

DEFICIENCY JUDGMENT

Unless the mortgage is a purchase money encumbrance, the judgment creditor may obtain a deficiency judgment against the defendants personally liable on the indebtedness, in the event the sale does not bring sufficient funds to satisfy the judgment in full. In 1963 the Code of Civil Procedure was amended to limit the application of the prohibition against deficiency judgments to two classes: (1) a deed of trust or mortgage or contract of sale given to a *vendor* to secure payment of the balance of the purchase price of real property, and (2) a deed of trust or mortgage or contract of sale on a dwelling for not more than four families given to a lender to secure repayment of a loan that was in fact used to pay all or part of the purchase price "of such dwelling occupied entirely or in part by the owner." (C.C.P., Sec. 580b.)

RIGHT OF REDEMPTION

Although the certificate of sale on foreclosure passes title to the purchaser, it is a conditional title, subject to being defeated by redemption, and does not carry the right of possession prior to expiration of the period of redemption. The purchaser, however, does have the right to rents or the value of the use and occupation, unless the mortgagor later redeems. If redemption is made, rents collected by the purchaser are credited upon the amount of redemption to be paid.

Who may redeem. The right to redeem property sold under decree of foreclosure is now purely statutory. There are two distinct classes who may redeem, and two different results flow from a redemption, depending upon who redeems. One class consists of the judgment debtor or his successor in interest. The other class consists of creditors having subsequent liens on the property. The latter class is termed "redemptioners." For anyone to be able to enforce a right to redeem, he must bring himself within one or the other of these two classes.

Effect of redemption by judgment debtor. Upon redemption by the judgment debtor or his successor in interest, the effect of the sale is terminated, and he is restored to his estate. (C.C.P., Sec. 703.) By paying to the purchaser or to the officer making the sale the purchase price, plus the statutory percentage (1 per cent per month) and any interim advances made by the purchaser for taxes, assessments, insurance, or upkeep upon the property, and since 1963, any sum paid on a prior obligation secured by the property to the extent such payment was necessary for the protection of his interest, he "redeems" the property and thereby terminates the sale, regaining the title to the property for all purposes as fully as though he had paid the mortgage without foreclosure. However, if a deficiency judgment was entered against him and an abstract of the judgment recorded, the lien of the judgment attaches to the title so regained by him upon redemption.

Redemption by a creditor. A redemptioner, on the other hand, by "redeeming," i.e., by paying the purchase price, statutory percentages, and advances, if any, becomes the assignee of the certificate of sale, and in the absence of a redemption from him becomes entitled to a deed to the property upon expiration of the period allowed for such further redemption.

PERIOD OF REDEMPTION

Redemption by the judgment debtor or his successor in interest must be effected within twelve months after the sale. This twelve-month period is shortened to three months if a deed of trust or a mortgage with power of sale is foreclosed, and if the full amount of the judgment is bid at the sale. (C.C.P., Sec. 725a.)

V. Essential characteristics of a deed of trust

The deed of trust is considered to be somewhat of an anomaly in the California legal system. Although California, at an early date, adopted the "lien" theory as to mortgages, it adopted the "title" theory as to deeds of trust. The "title" theory in reference to deeds of trust is that title to the property actually is conveyed to the trustee, who retains title until the debt is satisfied or the property is sold to enforce payment of the obligation secured thereby. Most states regard deeds of trust simply as mortgages with power of sale.

TRUST DEEDS SIMILAR TO MORTGAGES

Several distinctions between mortgages and trust deeds have already been noted. In numerous situations, however, they are regarded as the same. A number of cases, while adhering to the title theory of deeds of trust, have emphasized the identical function of trust deeds and mortgages and have applied similar rules. Thus, it has been held that the execution of a deed of trust does not effect an abandonment of homestead (*MacLeod* v. *Moran*, 153 Cal. 97), and that a deed of trust is merely an encumbrance under the mechanic's lien law (*Ficking* v. *Jackman,* 203 Cal. 657).

DISTINGUISHING FEATURE OF TRUST DEED

A distinguishing feature of a deed of trust is that it is a three-party instrument. The owner of the property is called the trustor; the grantee is called the trustee; and the lender or creditor is called the beneficiary. The latter is usually the payee of the note or other obligation secured by the deed of trust. By the execution of a trust, the trustor grants the property to the trustee "in trust, with power of sale."

FORM OF TRUST DEED

There is no standard form of trust deed prescribed by statute in California, but through the efforts of the large lending institutions, basic forms have been adopted that are more or less standardized and are in general use by lenders. These printed forms contain substantially the same general provisions that the laws of this state, court decisions, and experience have shown to be essential for the creation of a valid and a practical deed of trust. The forms used consist of two classifications, termed the *accepted form* and the *automatic form.*

Accepted form. The accepted form, which provides for the express acceptance by the trustee of its appointment, requires presentation to the trustee before the instrument is recorded. It is used today only in exceptional situations. It has the advantage that the trustee considers it prior to acceptance and determines that all of its provisions are acceptable. Also, a positive identification of the note that it secures is made at the time of the acceptance, eliminating any uncertainty in this respect in the future. A main objection to the use of this form is the delay in obtaining an express acceptance on each deed of trust prior to recordation.

Automatic form. The automatic form, in widespread use, contains a provision that the trustee therein named accepts the trust created when the deed of trust is duly executed, acknowledged, and recorded. There is no requirement that the trustee be notified of its appointment, and as a general rule the trustee is not aware of its appointment until it is called upon to perform some act under the instrument, either to reconvey the property covered by the instrument when the debt or obligation has been paid or performed, or to proceed under the power of sale when a default occurs.

TRUSTEE CANNOT BE COMPELLED TO ACT

Although the acceptance of the appointment as trustee is automatic under this latter form, the trustee nonetheless has the right to decline to act at the time it is called upon to perform. A refusal to act might be based upon an objectionable provision in the deed of trust that is contrary to the policy or practices of the trustee, or a trustee may refuse to act because the beneficiary fails to furnish sufficient evidence of a default, or where the obligation secured by the trust deed is usurious or otherwise illegal.

"ALL-INCLUSIVE" DEED OF TRUST

A form of deed of trust that has become more prevalent throughout the state is the all-inclusive or overriding deed of trust. This is a junior deed of trust, given back to a seller, that includes the amount of the first encumbrance as well as the second, with a provision that the seller will pay off the first under its terms from monies he is paid by the buyer. It is sometimes used instead of an installment type sales contract in the sale of real property.

SUBSTITUTION OF TRUSTEE

Another trustee may be substituted for the trustee named in a deed of trust. Depending upon the special circumstances, the substitution may be accomplished in several ways, including the following: (1) in the manner, if any, provided in the instrument, where practicable; (2) in the manner provided by Section 2934a of the Civil Code; (3) by agreement of the trustor and the beneficiary, or their respective successors in interest; and (4) by the Superior Court in proceedings pursuant to Section 2287 *et seq.* of the Civil Code.

Section 2934a of the Civil Code was amended in 1967 to specify that the statutory method for the substitution of a trustee under a deed of trust authorized by this section shall be effective and operative notwithstanding any contrary provisions in any deed of trust executed on or after January 1, 1968.

The enactment of such change had the effect as to such deeds of trust of overruling the holding in the case of *Mutual Bldg. and Loan* v. *Wyborg*, 59 C.A.2d 325, which held that where a deed of trust contained a provision for substitution of the trustee and provided that such method was exclusive of all other provisions for substitution, statutory or otherwise, then the provisions of the Civil Code relating to substitution of a trustee under a deed of trust were inapplicable.

JUDICIAL FORECLOSURE OF TRUST DEED

Until 1933 judicial foreclosure of deeds of trust was not permitted in the absence of special grounds for resort to equity. Since August 21, 1933, however, foreclosure by court action has been allowed by law. (C.C.P., Sec. 725a.) Where court foreclosure is sought, all of the mortgage rules apply. Thus, such an action must be instituted within the applicable period of the statute of limitations; and the sale is subject to the right of redemption. Institution of proceedings for enforcement of a deed of trust by one method is not an irrevocable waiver of the right to resort to the other at any time prior to the decree of foreclosure or the sale by the trustee. (*Flack* v. *Boland*, 11 Cal.2d 103.)

MORTGAGES RULES APPLICABLE

The rules discussed under mortgages, such as recordation, priority, after-acquired property, future advances, and so on, (see pp. 253–263), are substantially the same under deeds of trust. A main distinction is that the power of sale under a deed of trust does not outlaw. Also, satisfaction or release of a deed of trust is evidenced by a *reconveyance* executed by the trustee pursuant to the request of the beneficiary, rather than a release by the beneficiary.

VI. Trustee's sale proceedings

The power of sale in a deed of trust is largely a matter of contract. Until regulated by statute, it depended entirely upon the terms of the instrument conferring the power. The first statute regulating such sales became effective in California on July 27, 1917, and since that date the procedure has been increasingly regulated by statutory enactments. Nonetheless, regard must be had for the terms of the instrument as well as the requirements of law, for the reason that the contract provisions will also apply to the extent that they do not conflict with legal requirements.

EVIDENCE OF DEFAULT

When the trustee is called upon to act after a default has occurred, the trustee as a usual practice obtains from the beneficiary the trust deed and note, together with receipts evidencing advances made by the beneficiary for the protection of the security, such as taxes, fire insurance, and payments due under prior encumbrances. The trustee also obtains a statement of the account between the trustor and the beneficiary, including a statement showing the date of the original default, the date to which interest has been credited, and the unpaid balance of the obligation secured. It is then essential for the purpose of effecting a sale that a notice of default be recorded. Section 2924 of the Civil Code provides that, before the power of sale in the deed of trust is exercised, a notice of default must be recorded in the county where the property is situated at least three months before notice of sale is given.

The case of *Manning* v. *Queen*, 263 A.C.A. 754, decided in July, 1968, raised a question as to the right of the beneficiary under a second trust deed to declare a default where taxes were not paid by the trustor but were paid by the beneficiary under the first trust deed. Both trust deeds obligated the trustor to pay taxes, insurance, and other items. The court held that the beneficiary under the second trust deed had the right to declare a default since there could be an impairment of his security, pointing out that a beneficiary under a second trust deed should not be required to sit idly by while the first encumbrance is enlarged by the failure of the trustor to make required payments.

CONTENTS OF NOTICE OF DEFAULT

The notice of default must be executed by the trustee or beneficiary; it must identify the deed of trust by giving the recording data or the legal description of the property affected, and it must recite the name of the trustor and that a breach of the obligation has occurred and the nature thereof, and that the person executing the notice of default has elected to sell or cause a sale of the property to satisfy the obligation secured. Many forms of trust deeds require that such notice of default be executed by the beneficiary and delivered to the trustee with a declaration of default and demand for sale, also executed by the beneficiary, the trustee then attending to the recordation of the notice of default. In order to properly exercise the power of sale, all of these requirements must be complied with.

MAILING COPIES OF NOTICE OF DEFAULT

Within ten days after the recordation of the notice of default, a copy must be mailed to each person who has requested notice of default pursuant to the provisions of Section 2924b of the Civil Code. If a request for notice of default is not contained in the deed of trust or has not been subsequently recorded by the trustor, the notice of default must be published once a week for four weeks, the first publication being within ten days after recordation, or must be personally served on the trustor.

RIGHT OF REINSTATEMENT

During the three-month period following the recordation of the notice of default, the trustor or his successor in interest or any junior lien holder has the right under Section 2924c of the Civil Code to reinstate the obligation by paying to the beneficiary or his successor in interest all sums then due, including costs, also trustee's fees not exceeding $50 or ½ of 1 per cent of the entire unpaid principal sum secured, whichever is greater. This cures the default, compels a discontinuance of the sale proceedings, and restores the obligation and security to their former position.

WHEN PAYMENT IN FULL REQUIRED

After the expiration of the three-month period, the right of reinstatement is gone, and the beneficiary or his successor in interest is entitled to payment of the full amount of the obligation, plus costs and fees, and, if not paid, the property may be sold.

NOTICE OF SALE

If reinstatement has not occurred and the beneficiary or his successor in interest desires to proceed with the foreclosure, the trustee executes a notice of sale, stating the time and place of sale, describing the property to be sold, and, ordinarily, stating the occasion for such sale. The sale date, usually twenty-two or twenty-three days hence, is scheduled to allow sufficient time for the required publication and posting of notice.

PUBLISHING AND POSTING NOTICE OF SALE

The notice of sale must be published in a newspaper of general circulation printed and published in the city in which the property, or any portion thereof, lies, if there is such a newspaper, otherwise in the judicial district or in the county, and must be published once a week for twenty days, i.e., three publications not more than seven days apart. The notice must also be posted for the same period in at least one public place in the city or judicial district where the sale is to be made, and also in some conspicuous place on the property. A copy of the notice of sale must be mailed to the persons requesting notice of default under Section 2924b of the Civil Code.

PLACE OF SALE

The sale must be held in the county in which the property, or some part thereof, is situated; it should be held on a weekday, during business hours, and in a place sufficiently public so that all intending bidders may attend.

POSTPONEMENT OF SALE

The sale may be postponed, from time to time, if permitted by the terms of the deed of trust, at the time and place fixed by the notice of sale or by a previous postponement. Such postponements may be made by oral announcement, if so provided; otherwise, reasonable notice of the new date of sale should be given. The person conducting the sale may postpone the sale even over the objections of interested parties if he is of the opinion that the substantial interests of the parties will be protected by such postponement.

Postponement based on a consideration. Where the postponement of the sale is made in consideration of a partial payment by the trustor, a formal agreement should be executed by the parties setting forth the trustor's consent to the postponement, which will overcome any subsequent claim by the trustor that acceptance of part payment constituted a waiver of the default necessitating a new notice of default. (*Bechtel* v. *Wilson,* 18 C.A.2d 331.)

CONDUCT OF SALE

The sale should be so conducted that the best cash price for the property will be obtained. At the designated time and place the person conducting the sale announces the purpose of the sale and identifies the property, and then the sale is open to bidding. Any person, including the debtor and the creditor, may bid. Bids must be in cash or the equivalent. Only the holder of the debt under foreclosure can offset the amount owing to him. He can bid, without a tender of cash, up to the amount of the debt. The holder of a junior encumbrance may not offset his encumbrance. When the highest responsible bid is announced, the property is declared sold to such bidder, who pays the amount bid, and a trustee's deed is thereafter issued to him.

TRUSTEE'S DEED

The trustee's deed, under the power of sale, passes to the purchaser the title to the property held by the maker of the deed of trust on the date he executed the same, and any title acquired afterward. It is free from any right or period of redemption, except in favor of the United States under prescribed conditions where there is junior federal tax lien, and entitles the purchaser to immediate possession. Pursuant to provisions usually contained in deeds of trust making recitals in the trustee's deed conclusive, the deed should contain full recitals of the several steps and proceedings leading up to and including the sale. Title insurance companies usually rely upon the truth of such recitals appearing in deeds made by responsible trustees under deeds of trusts.

Under the provisions of Section 580d of the Code of Civil Procedure there can be no deficiency judgment following a trustee's sale. In the case of *Union Bank* v. *Gradsky*, 265 A.C.A. 48, this rule was extended in favor of a guarantor, the court holding that there could be no deficiency against a guarantor following the creditor's *nonjudicial* sale of the security.

DEFECTS IN PROCEEDINGS

It is important, of course, that all of the steps leading up to the issuance of the trustee's deed be complied with, as irregularities in the proceedings, such as a failure to publish or post properly, will invalidate the sale. It has been held that a material misdescription of the property in the notice of sale invalidates the sale. (*Crist* v. *House & Osmonson, Inc.*, 7 Cal.2d 556.) A misstatement of the amount due is not necessarily fatal. It has been held that a sale under a power of sale specifying a larger sum than the amount actually due is valid in the absence of proof of fraud, or if property rights of the debtor were not injuriously affected, or if bidders were not deterred from attending the sale. (*Savings and Loan Society* v. *Burnett*, 106 Cal. 514.)

STATUS OF TRUSTOR

The power of sale in a deed of trust is not extinguished by the death, subsequent incompetency, or bankruptcy of the trustor. However, in the case of bankruptcy of the trustor or his successor in interest, the consent of the bankruptcy court must be obtained prior to the sale, otherwise the sale may be held to be void or at least subject to the right of the trustee in bankruptcy to pay the indebtedness and take the property as an asset of the bankrupt's estate. (*Cohen* v. *Nixon & Wright*, 236 F. 407.)

EFFECT OF SALE ON JUNIOR LIENS

Most junior liens are eliminated by a trustee's sale and may be ignored for title insurance purposes, and include state tax liens having the "force, effect, and priority of a judgment lien." (*Wayland* v. *State of California*, 161 C.A.2d 679.) However, certain junior liens are not automatically eliminated, and in the absence of a specific release, a judicial proceeding may be necessary before such liens will be eliminated from a title report. Included in this category are mechanics' liens, even though recorded *after* the recordation of the deed of trust. Prior to 1960 federal tax liens were also included in this category.

FEDERAL TAX LIENS

The reason for the former rule that a federal tax lien could not be eliminated after a trustee's sale under a prior deed of trust was based on the decision in the case of *Metropolitan Life Ins. Co.* v. *United States,* 107 F.2d 311, holding in effect that Congress had not sanctioned a trustee's sale under a trust deed as a procedure for cutting off the government's lien, and the federal tax lien was not affected by such a sale. This rule was followed for years. In 1960 the United States Supreme Court, in the case of *Bank of America* v. *United States* 363 U.S. 237, held that a junior tax lien was extinguished as a lien against real property by the exercise of a power of sale by the trustee under a prior deed of trust. Then in 1966 a new law was enacted by Congress that changed the rule. The Federal Tax Lien Act of 1966 (Public Law 89–719) provides, among other things, that written notice of a nonjudicial sale be given to the Secretary of the Treasury or his delegate as a requirement for the discharge of a federal tax lien recorded more than 30 days before the sale or the divestment of any title of the United States, and establishes a right in the United States to redeem the property within a period of 120 days from the date of such sale.

When a federal tax lien inferior to the deed of trust being foreclosed has been recorded more than 30 days before the sale date, notice must be given to the federal government in order that the lien be eliminated by the sale. If the lien was recorded 30 days or less before the sale, no notice is required. Although the trustee's sale will eliminate such lien, the right of redemption must still be considered.

MECHANICS' LIENS

Mechanics' liens are not automatically eliminated for the reason that such liens, although recorded after the recordation of the deed of trust under foreclosure, may in fact be prior to the lien of the deed of trust. A mechanic's lien will have priority if the work of improvement commenced prior to the date the deed of trust was recorded.

TAXES AND ASSESSMENTS

Real property taxes and assessments against the property are not affected by the trustee's sale or by a judicial foreclosure of the deed of trust, nor are liens under the provisions of the Health and Safety Code subsequently arising in connection with the removal of substandard or unsafe structures, which liens are on a parity with state, county, and city taxes.

DISPOSITION OF SURPLUS FUNDS

After a trustee's sale there may be surplus funds on hand. This occurs where the amount bid is in excess of the debt due on the obligation under foreclosure. The proceeds of the sale are applied, first, in payment of the costs, fees, and expenses of the sale, and then in satisfaction, *pro tanto,* of the obligation under the deed of trust that was foreclosed. If the net proceeds are more than sufficient to fully satisfy such obligation, the balance is called surplus, and subordinate liens and rights that were cut off by the sale attach to these surplus funds in their order of priority, and are immediately payable therefrom, whether matured or not. (*Dockrey* v. *Gray,* 172 C.A.2d 388.) If there is a dispute concerning disposition of the surplus funds, the trustee may bring an action in interpleader, and the court will then determine the issue.

VII. Some practical aspects of trust deeds

In order to save the expense and delay of foreclosure proceedings, a beneficiary under a deed of trust sometimes will obtain a *deed in lieu of foreclosure* from the trustor or his successor in interest. Although it is contrary to law to stipulate in the deed of trust that upon default the property shall be forfeited to the beneficiary without the necessity of foreclosure (C.C., Sec. 2889), it is nonetheless permissible at any subsequent time and upon a sufficient consideration to transfer the property to the beneficiary in satisfaction of the obligation so secured. Because of the superior economic position of the lender, however, such transactions are scrutinized by the courts with great care to be sure that the subsequent conveyance by the trustor or his successor in interest represents a bona fide sale, for an adequate price, and without any advantage being taken by the lender.

CONSIDERATION FOR A DEED IN LIEU OF FORECLOSURE

Although no additional consideration may be necessary where the grantor is personally liable for the debt and it approximates the reasonable value of the property, some additional consideration is required where a deed in lieu of foreclosure is given by a person who is not personally liable. This is true because such person would lose nothing by the foreclosure and normally would have the value of the use of the property during foreclosure.

SPECIAL RECITALS IN A DEED IN LIEU OF FORECLOSURE

As a consequence of the foregoing, title insurers usually require special recitals in a deed in lieu of foreclosure, or special assurances by way of affidavit, before undertaking to pass such deeds as sufficient to eliminate the interest of the trustor or his successor in interest. These special recitals provide substantially as follows:

If the grantor is personally liable:

> This deed is an absolute conveyance, the grantor having sold said land to the grantee for a fair and adequate consideration, such consideration, in addition to the sum above described, being full satisfaction of all obligations secured by the deed of trust executed by ________________ to ________________, recorded in book _____, page _____, Official Records of ________________ county.
>
> Grantor declares that this conveyance is freely and fairly made, and that there are no agreements, oral or written, other than this deed between grantor and grantee with respect to said land.

If the grantor is not personally liable:

> Grantor declares that this conveyance is freely and fairly made, grantor having sold said land to the grantee for a consideration equal to the fair value of grantor's interest in said land; and grantor further declares that there are no agreements, oral or written, other than this deed between grantor and grantee with respect to said land.

CONTINUED POSSESSION BY TRUSTOR

Where the grantor is permitted to remain in possession either under a lease or an option to purchase or otherwise, this circumstance casts doubt on the sufficiency of the deed in lieu of foreclosure, and it may deter a title insurer from treating such deed as an effective satisfaction of the deed of trust.

EFFECT OF JUNIOR LIENS

A deed in lieu of foreclosure is usually undesirable where there are junior liens. When such a deed is given, a merger of the legal title with the equitable interest under such deed of trust ordinarily results, and junior liens and encumbrances are not eliminated.

OBTAINING RECONVEYANCE

When the trustor or his successor in interest has paid the amount due on the obligation, he is entitled to a full reconveyance of the deed of trust. Upon making the final payment, the trustor or his successor in interest should obtain the note and the deed of trust from the beneficiary or his assignee, together with a request for full reconveyance. These instruments should then be presented to the trustee and a reconveyance obtained upon payment of the trustee's fees. The reconveyance should then be recorded.

Necessity that note be preserved. The original note should not be destroyed after payment, as it must be surrendered to the trustee before a reconveyance can be issued; otherwise, a surety bond may have to be obtained and filed with the trustee to take the place of the note. If the note becomes lost, a surety bond will also be required.

Partial reconveyances. It is common practice to provide for partial reconveyances of property covered by a deed of trust, particularly where the instrument covers several lots or separate parcels of land, or where the property is to be subdivided and developed as separate parcels. Where partial reconveyances are to be made, the deed of trust should contain an express provision to that effect, and the exact terms and conditions should be specified with certainty. When executing a partial reconveyance, the trustee normally requires that the note be submitted to it for the purpose of noting on it the fact that a partial reconveyance has been issued.

REQUEST FOR NOTICE OF DEFAULT

The holder of an inferior deed of trust or other lien should record a *request for notice of default* pursuant to the provisions of Section 2924b of the Civil Code. When a notice of default is recorded under a prior deed of trust, the holder of the junior lien will then be entitled to notice. When a notice of default is received by the holder of a junior lien, the latter may elect to cure the default, and then proceed to foreclose his own lien, adding the amount paid to cure the default to the amount due under his junior deed of trust. If the holder of the junior lien does not cure the default under a prior deed of trust, but seeks to protect his interest by bidding at the foreclosure sale under such prior deed of trust, he must be able to bid at the trustee's sale the full amount *in cash or the equivalent,* and he does not get credit during the bidding for the amount due him on the obligation held by him.

EFFECT OF PURCHASE MONEY TRUST DEEDS

A person taking a purchase money deed of trust assumes the risk that the security may become inadequate, especially where he takes a purchase money second deed of trust. This is illustrated by the case of *Brown* v. *Jensen,* cited on p. 258, wherein the holder of a second deed of trust (a purchase money second) brought an action on the note after the first trust deed had been foreclosed, the beneficiary under the first having become the purchaser at a sale that brought only enough to pay off the first trust deed. The trial court held that the beneficiary under the second could maintain an action on the note, since the security was lost on foreclosure of the first. The judgment was reversed on appeal, however, the Supreme Court expressing the opinion that since this was a purchase money deed of trust, there could be no deficiency, even though the security later became valueless. The security alone might be looked to for payment of a debt secured by a purchase money trust deed. The effect of the 1963 amendment to Section 580b of the Code of Civil Procedure on the foregoing rule has as yet not been judicially determined (see p. 265.)

Questions

1. Identify the various types of instruments creating liens on real property.
2. Discuss briefly some of the characteristics of a mortgage in early English law.
3. Define a mortgage.
4. Define a trust deed.
5. Explain the distinctions between mortgages and deeds of trust.
6. May a mortgage cover after-acquired title?
7. May a mortgage be made security for future indebtedness?
8. Explain the difference between an optional advance and an obligatory advance.
9. Is there a difference between "taking subject to" and "assuming" an obligation of record?
10. How is a mortgage discharged of record?
11. Identify the parties to a trust deed.
12. May a deed of trust be foreclosed by court proceedings?
13. Discuss briefly the right of redemption.
14. May a deficiency judgment be obtained upon foreclosure of a deed of trust?
15. Describe briefly the main steps in a trustee's sale proceedings.
16. May a deed of trust be reinstated after a default has been declared?
17. Are subsequent tax liens and mechanics' liens automatically eliminated by a trustee's sale?
18. Who is entitled to surplus funds, if any, after a trustee's sale?
19. What is the main purpose of a request for notice of default?
20. Explain the use of a deed in lieu of foreclosure.
21. Discuss the procedure to be followed in obtaining a reconveyance of a trust deed.
22. Is it advisable to destroy the note secured by a trust deed after it is paid in full?

15

Involuntary Liens on Property

Summary

I. Introductory
Creation of liens; Effect of lien on rights of landowner; Right to discharge the lien; Priority of liens; Expiration of lien; Main types of liens; Enforcement of equitable lien

II. Judgment liens
Recording an abstract of judgment; Duration of lien; Requisites of a judgment lien; Exempt property; Property subject to lien; Ownership of record; Effect of death of debtor; Interest of heirs or devisees; Lien on joint tenancy interest; Effect of bankruptcy of debtor; Priority of judgment lien; Assignment of judgment; Extinguishment of lien

III. Attachment liens
Actions in which attachment is available; Attachment procedure; Property subject to attachment; Interest of debtor in property; Property in name of third party; Sale of property; Priority of attachment; Duration of lien; Release of lien

IV. Execution liens
Creation of lien; Time when writ may issue; Levy of writ; Execution sale; Right of redemption; Issuance of deed

V. Mechanics' liens
Constitutional provision; Applicable statutes; Public property; Basis of claim; Performance of contract; Persons who may claim liens; Work of improvement; Lien on land as well as improvements; Classes of claimants; Lien on improvements; Notice of nonresponsibility; Effect of filing contract; Filing contract and recording bond; Recording claim of lien; When liens may be filed; Time within which to file action; Nature of foreclosure action; Parity of liens; Bond to release lien; Priority of mechanics' liens; Offsite improvements; Priority not dependent upon time of recording lien; Prerequisite to priority of mortgage or trust deed; What constitutes commencement of work; Insuring priority of deed of trust; Stop notices; Equitable liens; Title company practices

I. Introductory

A lien is defined as a charge imposed upon specific property by which it is made security for the performance of an act, usually the payment of money.

CREATION OF LIENS

Liens on real property may be created by voluntary act of the landowner, such as the execution of a mortgage or deed of trust, or may be created by operation of law, such as tax liens or judgment liens recorded by the creditor of the landowner.

EFFECT OF LIEN ON RIGHTS OF LANDOWNER

A lien does not operate at the outset to transfer any title to, or estate in, the property subject to the lien. When a lien is created on real property, the ownership of the property, with the incidents of possession and right of transfer, remains in the landowner, subject, however, to the right of the lienholder to force a sale of the property, under judicial process or other prescribed methods, to satisfy the performance of the obligation secured by the lien. Upon a forced sale of the property, title then passes to the purchaser at the sale. Ordinarily such transfer of title will relate back to the time when the lien arose and thereby convey the title held by the debtor at the date the lien attached, cutting off rights of third persons that accrued subsequent to the creation of the lien.

RIGHT TO DISCHARGE THE LIEN

The owner of the property subject to the lien, or any person having an interest in the property, has the right, at any time after the claim is due and before the right of redemption has expired, to discharge the lien by satisfying the claim. Statutory provisions for enforcement of liens by judicial sale usually grant the owner of the property and other persons having interests under inferior liens the right to redeem the property within a specified time after the forced sale.

PRIORITY OF LIENS

As to priority of liens, Section 2897 of the Civil Code provides that other things being equal, different liens on the same property have priority according to their time of creation, subject to the operation of the recording laws and subject to the effect of statutes according special priority, as in the case of taxes and mechanics' liens.

EXPIRATION OF LIEN

Liens usually cease or become unenforceable after a lapse of time. The lien period of judgment liens and most statutory liens is fixed by the statute authorizing the lien.

MAIN TYPES OF LIENS

The foregoing are general principles of law underlying all liens. Special rules apply as to each type of lien, and in this chapter consideration will be given to these rules as they relate to four main types of liens, i.e., judgment liens, attachment liens, execution liens, and mechanics' liens. Voluntary liens created by mortgage or deed of trust are considered in Chapter 14, and tax liens and assessments are considered in Chapter 16.

Equitable liens. Before considering in detail the rules applicable to the particular types of liens referred to above, mention should be made of equitable liens, which the courts have sometimes declared under special circumstances. Without regard to any expressed intent of the parties to create a specific lien, the courts in equity, when circumstances warrant, may declare a lien on real property "to do justice and equity and prevent unfair results." This type of lien may be based upon a written agreement, which by itself is insufficient to create a lien (*Higgins* v. *Manson,* 126 Cal. 467), or an equitable lien may arise by implication of law from the conduct and dealings of the parties. (*Wagner* v. *Sariotti,* 56 C.A.2d 693.)

Vendor's lien. A vendor's lien is traditionally regarded as an equitable lien. In California this lien is recognized by statute. Section 3046 of the Civil Code provides that upon a conveyance of land, a lien on the land arises by implication of law in favor of the grantor for "so much of the purchase price as remains unpaid and unsecured otherwise than by the personal obligation of the buyer." The vendor's lien need not be expressly declared or reserved in the deed; it arises from the nature of the transaction without express agreement. It is waived, however, by taking a purchase money mortgage or other security for the obligation.

Liens under a contract of sale. A purchaser of real property under a contract of sale is also given a special lien upon the property for such part of the amount paid as he may be entitled to recover back in case of failure of consideration. (C.C., Sec. 3050.)

Liens in favor of a co-owner. An owner of an undivided interest in real property, such as a joint tenant or a tenant in common, who pays off an encumbrance on the property, or who makes expenditures in good faith for necessary repairs and maintenance for the benefit of the property owned in common, is entitled to contribution from his cotenants for such expenses, and is given an equitable lien on their interest.

ENFORCEMENT OF EQUITABLE LIEN

Equitable liens on real property are enforced by proceedings in court similar to the procedure prescribed for the foreclosure of a mortgage. An equitable lien is dependent upon a judgment for its recognition, but it relates back to the time of its creation by the acts or conduct of the parties. Although it would not be effective as against a purchaser or encumbrancer in good faith, for value and without notice, a subsequent purchaser with notice either actual or constructive, would take subject to the rights of a third party under such type of lien.

II. Judgment liens

A judgment is defined in Section 577 of the Code of Civil Procedure as the "final determination of the rights of the parties in an action or proceedings." Judgments that may result in a lien upon real property are of several types: (1) judgments (or decrees) that foreclose liens upon specific property, ordering the sale of such property and the application of the proceeds of the sale to the amount found due in the judgment; (2) judgments that award money and impose a lien upon specific property of the judgment debtor to secure payment of the award, a not uncommon practice in divorce proceedings; and (3) judgments for money against a debtor that do not involve the imposition of a lien on specific property of the debtor, but that may result in a general lien on all property of the judgment debtor not exempt from execution when an abstract of the judgment is duly recorded. It is the latter type that will be considered in this chapter.

RECORDING AN ABSTRACT OF JUDGMENT

Under the provisions of Section 674 of the Code of Civil Procedure, an abstract of judgment may be recorded in the office of the recorder of any county, and from such recording the judgment or decree becomes a lien upon all the real property of the judgment debtor, not exempt from execution, in such county.

DURATION OF LIEN

Such lien continues for *ten years* from the date of entry of the judgment or decree, unless enforcement of the judgment or decree is stayed on appeal, or unless the judgment or decree is previously satisfied, or the lien otherwise discharged.

REQUISITES OF A JUDGMENT LIEN

For a judgment to constitute a lien it must meet certain prerequisites, including the following: (1) it must be a judgment that money is owed; (2) it must establish a personal liability of the debtor for a definite specified sum; (3) it must be a valid judgment based upon jurisdiction of the subject matter and the parties; (4) it must be a judgment rendered by a lawfully constituted court; (5) it must be an enforceable judgment, i.e., its enforcement has not been stayed on appeal; and (6) an abstract of the judgment or a certified copy must be recorded in the county in which the real property is situated.

Judgment for alimony. Prior to 1959 a judgment for alimony or for maintenance and support became a lien when recorded only to the extent that it was for the payment of a definite and certain sum of money, i.e., a fixed amount, even though payable in installments. In 1959 a new section was added to the Code of Civil Procedure (Sec. 674.5) to provide that a certified copy of any judgment or order for alimony or child support, when recorded, shall become a lien upon all real property of the judgment debtor not exempt from execution, in the county where recorded for the respective amounts and installments as they mature. The lien is effective for ten years from date of recording. A certificate of the judgment debtor that all amounts and installments that have matured prior to the date of the certificate have been fully paid may be recorded to effect a release of the judgment as to a bona fide purchaser.

EXEMPT PROPERTY

The lien of a judgment does not attach to real property that is exempt from execution. If a valid declaration of homestead has been recorded prior to the recordation of an abstract of judgment, the judgment will not be a lien on the property subject to the homestead.

PROPERTY SUBJECT TO LIEN

The lien attaches only to real property actually owned by the judgment debtor, i.e., property in which he has a vested legal interest. It does not attach to real property where the only interest of the debtor is an equitable interest, such as the vendee's interest under a contract of sale, or where the debtor has the bare legal title, such as title held by him as trustee for another. An equitable interest of a debtor, although not subject to a judgment lien, may be reached by levy of a writ of attachment or execution.

OWNERSHIP OF RECORD

The existence of the judgment lien does not depend upon ownership of record. Thus, if the record title to a parcel of property is in the debtor at the time the abstract of judgment is recorded, but the debtor previously executed and delivered a deed to a third party, the judgment is not a lien, since the judgment debtor is not in title. Conversely, if the judgment debtor owns a parcel of property under an unrecorded deed, the judgment lien attaches to such interest.

EFFECT OF DEATH OF DEBTOR

If the judgment debtor dies after an abstract of judgment has been recorded, the lien is not thereby terminated. Although execution cannot issue after the death of the judgment debtor, the lien of the judgment continues, and such lien may be foreclosed in an action in equity. A judgment against an executor or administrator of a decedent's estate is not a lien on property of the estate, but is payable in the course of administration.

INTEREST OF HEIRS OR DEVISEES

The lien of a judgment against an heir or devisee attaches to his interest in real property in the estate, which interest vests in him immediately upon the death of the decedent, and such lien is not defeated by a subsequent assignment or renunciation by the heir or devisee of his interest. The interest of the heir or devisee is subject to administration, however, and a probate sale of property of the estate to a third party would eliminate the lien from the property so sold.

LIEN ON JOINT TENANCY INTEREST

Where title to real property is held in joint tenancy, the lien of a judgment against one of the joint tenants attaches to his interest. If such interest is sold at an execution sale, the joint tenancy is severed, and the purchaser and the other joint tenant become tenants in common. But if the judgment debtor dies prior to levy of execution, the surviving joint tenant takes the entire property free of the judgment lien.

EFFECT OF BANKRUPTCY OF DEBTOR

Judgments against a debtor who obtains his discharge in bankruptcy and thereafter acquires real property are not liens on this after-acquired property, provided (1) the judgments were properly scheduled in the bankruptcy proceedings, or the creditors had notice thereof; and (2) the judgments were of the type that are dischargeable in bankruptcy. Judgments that attached as liens on property owned by the bankrupt prior to bankruptcy are not eliminated by the bankruptcy proceedings.

PRIORITY OF JUDGMENT LIEN

The lien of a judgment is subject to prior liens and conveyances, including those created by bona fide transfers that are unrecorded, and it takes precedence over all subsequent liens and conveyances, subject to exceptions where other liens are given preference by statute, such as taxes and assessments. As to real property already owned by the judgment debtor, judgment liens rank in order of their creation, i.e., according to the time of the recording of the respective abstracts. As to property acquired by the judgment debtor *after* the recording of the abstracts of two or more judgments, the judgment liens attach simultaneously at the moment of acquisition of title, and the liens all have equal rank. However, the creditor who first levies a writ of execution on specific property will obtain a superior lien. (*Hertweck* v. *Fearon,* 180 Cal. 71.)

ASSIGNMENT OF JUDGMENT

A judgment is a property right that can be assigned or otherwise transferred. Unlike transfers of real property, there are no requirements that the assignment be in writing or that it be filed or recorded. To fully protect his rights, the assignee must notify the judgment debtor of the fact of assignment.

EXTINGUISHMENT OF LIEN

A judgment lien may be extinguished in several ways besides by lapse of time. The lien terminates upon *full satisfaction* of the judgment, either by an acknowledgment of satisfaction, or by an execution returned fully satisfied. The judgment lien may also be released by the judgment creditor as to specific property by a *partial release* executed and acknowledged by him.

Demand for satisfaction of judgment. In 1963 the Code of Civil Procedure was amended to provide that if a judgment creditor or his assignee of record, without just cause, refuses to acknowledge a written demand for acknowledgment of satisfaction within fifteen days after receipt, he is liable for damages plus $100. (C.C.P., Sec. 675.) This is comparable to the right given an owner of real property to obtain a full reconveyance of a deed of trust when the obligation has been paid. (C.C., Sec. 2941).

III. Attachment liens

An attachment is defined as a seizure under legal process, called a "writ of attachment," of the defendant's property as security for any judgment that the plaintiff may recover in the action. It is a proceeding auxiliary to the main action, and it enables the plaintiff to acquire a lien for the security of his claim by levy of process made *before*, instead of after, the entry of a judgment. The main purpose of an attachment is to hold property of the defendant for eventual sale under execution when the action has proceeded to judgment, thus assuring the plaintiff that he will have something tangible to levy on in satisfaction of his claim.

ACTION IN WHICH ATTACHMENT IS AVAILABLE

An attachment is not available in all types of actions. Under the provisions of Section 537 of the Code of Civil Procedure, the plaintiff may have the property of the defendant attached if the action is brought upon a contract, express or implied, for the direct payment of money, where the contract is made or is payable in this state, and is not secured. Also, an attachment is available in certain types of actions including personal injury actions, where the defendant does not reside in the state or has left the state or is in hiding; also, in unlawful detainer actions in certain instances; and in actions by the state of California or its political subdivisions for collection of taxes and similar obligations.

In 1965 Section 537 of the Code of Civil Procedure was amended to permit attachment for out-of-state claims if in excess of $5,000.

ATTACHMENT PROCEDURE

The procedure for obtaining an attachment is summarized as follows: After the complaint has been filed and at the time of issuing the summons, or at any time thereafter and prior to judgment, an affidavit may be filed with the clerk of the court showing the facts that entitle the plaintiff to an attachment. A sufficient undertaking (bond) must be filed to the effect that if the defendant recovers judgment or the attachment is discharged, the plaintiff will pay costs and damages due the defendant. A writ of attachment is then issued directed to the sheriff or other officer requiring him to attach all property of the defendant not exempt from execution unless the defendant gives a sufficient undertaking or deposit of money in lieu of the property. If no undertaking is given by the defendant, the sheriff or other officer to whom the writ is directed levies on real property by: (1) filing for record with the county recorder a copy of the writ, together with a description of the property and a notice that is attached, and (2) serving the occupant of the land with a copy of such writ, description, and notice, or posting the same if there is no occupant.

PROPERTY SUBJECT TO ATTACHMENT

Under Section 540 of the Code of Civil Procedure, the sheriff or other officer to whom the writ is directed must attach "all the property of such defendant within his county not exempt from execution, or so much thereof as may be sufficient to satisfy the plaintiff's demand." Real property not subject to attachment includes the homestead of the debtor to the extent that the equity of the debtor does not exceed the homestead exemption, and property in the custody of the law under bankruptcy or receivership. If a declaration of homestead is recorded *after* levy of a writ of attachment but *before* the recordation of an abstract of judgment, the attachment is defeated to the extent of the homestead exemption value, but holds the property for the purpose of reaching any excess value over the homestead exemption.

INTEREST OF DEBTOR IN PROPERTY

An attachment lien reaches only such right, title, or interest as the debtor has in the real property at the time of the levy. If he has no interest in fact, the creditor gets nothing by the levy. An attaching creditor is not protected by the recording laws as a bona fide purchaser for value; his lien is subject to all rights and equities that accrued against the debtor prior to levy of the writ of attachment, even though not disclosed by the records and not known to the creditor.

PROPERTY IN NAME OF THIRD PARTY

Real property that may be attached includes not only property owned of record by the debtor, but also property belonging to the debtor and standing of record in the name of another person. In the latter case the notice of attachment must state the name of the record owner of the property in which the debtor's interest is attached, and a copy of the writ, description, and notice must be served on such record owner. The notice in such case recites that the property attached is "all right, title and interest of *A* (the debtor) standing of record in the name of *B*."

SALE OF PROPERTY

A sale of the property cannot be had pursuant to a writ of attachment; the attachment merely holds the property until a judgment is entered, at which time a sale of the property may be had under a writ of execution.

PRIORITY OF ATTACHMENT

The general rule as to priority between different liens on the same parcel of property applies in the case of attachments. Attachment liens rank in order of their date of creation, i.e., the dates of the respective levies. A valid attachment lien on real property is prior to other liens accruing or conveyances made subsequent to the levy of attachment, except as to certain liens that are accorded priority by statute, such as property taxes and federal tax liens.

DURATION OF LIEN

An attachment lien continues for a period of three years after the date of levy unless sooner released or discharged, and it may be extended by the court for an additional period of two years.

RELEASE OF LIEN

An attachment may be released or discharged in various ways, such as: (1) by a release signed by the plaintiff or his attorney or by the officer who levied the writ, acknowledged and recorded in like manner as a grant of real property; or (2) by a dismissal of the action; or (3) by an order of court discharging the attachment; or (4) by a satisfaction of judgment if a judgment is entered in favor of the plaintiff; or (5) by judgment for defendant, but the discharge of the attachment may be postponed either by an appeal or by a motion to vacate judgment or for judgment notwithstanding the verdict or for a new trial. If an appeal is perfected or one of the foregoing motions is made, the attachment will remain in effect only if the plaintiff files the necessary undertaking (bond).

IV. Execution liens

A *writ of execution* is a means of enforcing a judgment. In the case of the ordinary money judgment, an execution is defined as a writ issued by the court directed to the sheriff or other officer to enforce the judgment against the property of a judgment debtor. (C.C.P., Sec. 682.) By its issuance, a sale of the property of the judgment debtor may be accomplished.

CREATION OF LIEN

Where a judgment is a lien on the debtor's real property, an execution does not extend the judgment lien or create a new lien. It is the method of enforcing such lien. However, where a judgment is not already a lien on the debtor's real property, the execution when levied not only provides the means for enforcement of the judgment, but it also creates a new and distinct lien as of the date of levy. An execution lien continues for a period of one year unless sooner terminated.

TIME WHEN WRIT MAY ISSUE

A writ of execution may be issued by the clerk of the court at any time within ten years from entry of the judgment, and thereafter by leave of court. A motion for issuance of a writ of execution after the lapse of ten years must be supported by an affidavit setting forth the reasons for failure to have the execution issued within the ten-year period. It has been held that a creditor must show due diligence in pursuing a debtor's property within the period prescribed by statute, and that the debtor may show circumstances from which the court may conclude that the creditor is not entitled to collect the judgment. (*Butcher* v. *Brouwer,* 21 Cal.2d 354.)

LEVY OF WRIT

An execution is levied in the same manner as an attachment, that is. real property belonging to the debtor and not exempt from execution is seized by filing for record with the county recorder a copy of the writ of execution, together with a description of the property and a notice of the levy, and by serving similar documents on the occupant of the property, or if there is no occupant, by posting notice on the property.

EXECUTION SALE

Before a sale of real property on execution can be had, notice must be given by: (1) *posting* written notice showing the time and place of the sale and describing the property, at least twenty days before the date of sale, in a prescribed public place and in some conspicuous place on the property to be sold; and (2) *publishing* a copy of the notice once a week for the same period in a prescribed newspaper of general circulation. Notice of sale must also be given by *mailing* to any person who has filed a request for notice with the clerk of the court pursuant to Section 692a of the Code of Civil Procedure.

Time and place of sale. The sale must be held in the county where the property or some part thereof is situated, and must be made at public auction, to the highest bidder, at a designated time between the hours of 9:00 A.M. and 5:00 P.M.

Certificate of sale. The purchaser at the sale receives a *certificate of sale* from the officer conducting the sale, and a duplicate is filed for record in the office of the county recorder. The certificate of sale is assignable. By the certificate of sale the purchaser acquires legal title to the interest of the judgment debtor in the property sold, but this title is subject to being defeated by a redemption within a prescribed period. It is also subject to the debtor's right to remain in possession during the redemption period.

RIGHT OF REDEMPTION

Under the provisions of Section 700a of the Code of Civil Procedure, real property sold on execution is subject to redemption at any time within twelve months after the sale. Generally, a redemption cannot be made after expiration of this statutory period. However, the time for redemption may be extended by agreement of the parties. A redemption may be effected either by the judgment debtor, or by his successor in interest, or by a creditor having a junior lien. Redemption is made by paying the redemption money to the holder of the certificate of sale, or to the officer who made the sale.

Amount necessary to redeem. The redemption amount includes the sale price together with interest, plus any reasonable sums advanced by the purchaser for taxes, assessments, fire insurance, maintenance and repair, and, since 1963, any sum paid on a prior obligation secured by the property to the extent such payment was necessary for the protection of his interest. Thereupon, the person to whom redemption is made must execute, acknowledge, and deliver a *certificate of redemption,* which is then recorded in the county recorder's office.

Redemption by debtor. Upon redemption by the debtor or his successor in interest, it is provided that "the effect of the sale is terminated and he is restored to his estate." (C.C.P., Sec. 703; *Bateman* v. *Kellogg,* 59 C.A. 464.) The title upon such redemption vests in the same manner and subject to the same liens and encumbrances (including junior liens and encumbrances, which would have been eliminated had no redemption occurred), as though no sale had taken place.

Redemption by junior creditor. A redemption by a creditor having a junior lien, rather than by the judgment debtor or his successor in interest, does not terminate the sale. It operates as an assignment of the certificate of sale, and a subsequent redemption may thereafter be made within the time prescribed.

ISSUANCE OF DEED

If no redemption is effected within the statutory period, the officer making the sale executes and delivers a *deed* to the purchaser or his assignee. This deed does not convey a new title, but evidences the fact that the sale has become absolute, and that the title by the certificate is no longer qualified by any rights of the judgment debtor.

V. Mechanics' liens

A mechanic's lien is a statutory lien upon real property to secure the compensation of persons whose labor or materials have contributed to the improvement of such property. The lien was unknown at common law or in equity. In California the lien right is based upon a provision of the constitution.

CONSTITUTIONAL PROVISION

Article XX, Section 15 of the California constitution provides as follows:

> Mechanics, materialmen, artisans, and laborers of every class, shall have a lien upon the property upon which they have bestowed labor or furnished material for the value of such labor done and material furnished; and the Legislature shall provide, by law, for the speedy and efficient enforcement of such liens.

APPLICABLE STATUTES

The mechanic's lien law is contained in Sections 1181–1203.1 of the Code of Civil Procedure. These sections provide a means for the enforcement of the right accorded by the constitution. Mechanics' liens are favored in the law, and the statutes are liberally construed in favor of a mechanic's lien claimant.

PUBLIC PROPERTY

Public property or public buildings are not subject to a mechanic's lien. In such cases a claimant's security is by way of a bond required by statute on public construction work. Also, a stop notice can be filed with the public agency concerned and thereby cause the withholding of payment from the contractor for the public work.

BASIS OF CLAIM

A mechanic's lien must be founded upon a *valid contract,* express or implied. It is not essential, however, that the owner of the property personally enter into a binding contract for work or materials. A lien may arise from work done or materials furnished not only at the instance of the owner, but also at the instance of any person acting by his authority or under him as contractor, subcontractor, architect, or otherwise. It may also attach to the owner's interest where the work of improvement is contracted for by a lessee or a vendee, unless a notice of nonresponsibility is filed as required by statute.

PERFORMANCE OF CONTRACT

A lien claimant must substantially perform under the contract for his services before he is entitled to a lien. However, failure of the original contractor to perform his contract with the owner does not affect the lien rights of a subcontractor, materialman, or any claimant other than the original contractor.

PERSONS WHO MAY CLAIM LIEN

A mechanic's lien exists in favor of every person who contributes to a work of improvement—from the architect to the landscape gardener. Section 1181 of the Code of Civil Procedure provides specifically for a lien in favor of "mechanics, materialmen, contractors, subcontractors, artisans, architects, machinists, builders, teamsters, and draymen, together with all persons and laborers of every class performing labor upon or bestowing skill or other necessary services on, or furnishing materials to be used or consumed in, or furnishing appliances, teams, or power contributing to, the construction, alteration, addition to, or repair, either in whole or in part, of, any building, structure, or other work of improvement." By amendment effective September 11, 1957, registered engineers and licensed land surveyors are also expressly included among those who may claim a lien.

WORK OF IMPROVEMENT

A work of improvement, as defined in Section 1182a of the Code of Civil Procedure, includes "seeding, sodding, or planting of any lot or tract of land for landscaping purposes, the filling, leveling, or grading of any lot or tract of land, the demolition of buildings, and the removal of buildings." In the case of *Nolte* v. *Smith,* 189 C.A.2d 140, decided in 1961, it was held that the setting of permanent monuments by a civil engineer constituted a "work of improvement" even though nothing further was done on the subdivision.

In the case of an architect, it has been held that there must be work of a structural character in order for the architect to be entitled to a lien. (*McDonald* v. *Filice,* 252 C.A.2d 613, citing *Design Associates, Inc.* v. *Welch,* 224 C.A.2d 165.) And in the case of *Tracy Price Associates* v.

Hebard, 226 C.A. 2d 778, it was held that a trust deed has priority over a mechanic's lien for architectural services where no work had commenced on the ground prior to the recordation of the trust deed.

LIEN ON LAND AS WELL AS IMPROVEMENTS

Lien rights are given not only in buildings or other improvements upon land, but also are given to any person who performs certain types of work upon an unimproved lot, such as grading or filling, or who improves the street or sidewalk adjoining such lot, or installs public utilities therein.

CLASSES OF CLAIMANTS

Mechanic's lien claimants fall within certain classes—contractor, subcontractor, laborer, or materialman—and it is important to ascertain in a given case the particular classification of the claimant, as this will determine not only whether he is entitled to a lien, but also the time within which he must file a claim of lien.

Materialmen. A materialman is one who *furnishes materials only* to the owner, or contractor, or subcontractor, to be used and that are used in a building or other work of improvement. A person who merely sells materials to a materialman is not within the classification of those entitled to a lien. The following case is illustrative of this principle: *A* furnished water softeners to *B* at an agreed price. *B* installed the water softeners in *C*'s building under contract with *C*, and was paid the cost of the fixtures and installation by *C*. *A* was not paid, and claimed a lien, asserting that he was a materialman who furnished materials to *B* as contractor. In the trial of the case it was held that *B* was a materialman, and hence *A*, who furnished materials to a materialman, was not entitled to a mechanic's lien against *C*'s building. (*Harris & Stunston, Inc., Ltd.* v. *Yorba Linda Citrus Assn.*, 135 C.A. 154.)

Laborers. A laborer is one who *performs labor only* upon a building or other work of improvement. One who performs labor for a materialman is ordinarily not entitled to a lien.

Contractors. A contractor, or "original contractor" as the term is used in the mechanic's lien law, is one who undertakes to furnish labor, materials, and superintendence under a direct contract with the owner or his agent, for all or some specific portion of the work of improvement. An original contract is not limited to a contract for the entire work or improvement. For instance, an owner might enter into different original contracts for different phases of the work involved in the construction of a building. If he enters into a contract with *A* for all construction work except painting, and a contract with *B* for painting, both *A* and *B* are classified as original contractors.

Subcontractor. A subcontractor is one who agrees with the original contractor to furnish similar services for some part of the original contract.

LIEN ON IMPROVEMENTS

A mechanic's lien attaches primarily to the structure or other improvement. Secondarily and as an incident to the lien on the structure, it attaches to the land on which the structure stands. If a structure is destroyed without fault of the owner prior to the recordation of a lien, no lien attaches to the land. (*Humboldt Lumber Mill* v. *Crisp*, 146 Cal. 686.)

NOTICE OF NONRESPONSIBILITY

If the person who causes a building or other work of improvement to be constructed, altered, or repaired is not the owner in fee of the land, but has a lesser interest, such as a lessee's interest under a lease, or a vendee's interest under a contract of sale, the fee owner may relieve his interest in the land from liability for liens attaching to the structure by giving a notice of nonresponsibility as provided by law.

When notice must be given. To relieve an owner of responsibility, a notice that the owner will not be responsible for the cost of construction, alterations, or repairs must be given *within ten days* after the owner obtains knowledge of the actual commencing of the work. Notice is given by posting such notice in some conspicuous place on the property, and by filing a verified copy of such notice in the office of the county recorder of the county in which the land or some part thereof is situated. The notice must contain a description of the property sufficient for identification, together with the name and nature of the title or interest of the person giving the same, the name of the purchaser under contract, if any, or of the lessee if known.

Notice must relate to specific work of improvement. The notice must refer to a work of improvement that has actually commenced. The law does not contemplate the giving of a general notice of nonresponsibility to be applied indiscriminately to all future improvements.

When notice ineffective. There are some circumstances under which the giving of a notice of nonresponsibility will not relieve the noncontracting owner's interest from liability. Thus, if by the terms of a lease a lessee is *obligated* to make the improvements, the entire interest or property will be subject to the lien for improvements by the lessee, despite a notice of nonresponsibility by the owner. In such case, the lessee is regarded as the owner's agent in making the improvements. (*Ott Hardware Co., Inc.* v. *Yost,* 69 C.A.2d 593.)

EFFECT OF FILING CONTRACT

An owner who is contemplating improvements on real property usually enters into a contract with a general contractor for the work of improvement as a whole, or into separate contracts for different phases of the work. Although the owner is not required to file the contract in the office of the county recorder, nor to furnish any bond for the protection of lien claimants, he receives certain benefits if he does file the contract, or files the contract and records the bond. If he files the contract before commencement of work, claims are limited to the items of material and labor embraced in the contract. However, no limitation is placed on the amount of the claim, nor is the owner's liability absolved by payment of the contract price to the general contractor.

FILING CONTRACT AND RECORDING BOND

If the original contract is filed before work is commenced and a bond of the contractor recorded, referred to as a "statutory labor and material bond," in an amount not less than 50 per cent of the contract price, conditioned for payment in full of all lien claimants, the liability of the owner for payment of liens becomes limited to the amount equal to what he may owe to the contractor at the time the liens are claimed. Judgment is then rendered against the contractor and sureties for any excess of such liens over such amount. The owner may deposit in court the sum owing by him to the contractor, and the court may make an order freeing the property of the liens. (C.C.P., Sec. 1185.1.)

RECORDING CLAIM OF LIEN

A mechanic's lien is not enforceable unless a *claim of lien* is recorded within the time and in the manner provided by law. This requirement has several purposes: first, it gives notice of the claim to third parties dealing with the property; second, it informs the owner of the amount of the claim, thus enabling him to protect himself against double payment by withholding from the contractor a sufficient amount to satisfy the claim; and third, it fixes the time within which the claimant must sue to enforce the lien.

Notice of lien. By amendment in 1959, the requirement was added that a notice of claim of lien be given by a mechanic's lien claimant to the owner and general contractor at least fifteen days prior to filing the lien; this was not required, however, of claimants who have a direct contract with the owner and persons performing labor for wages. (C.C.P., Sec. 1193a.) The amendment was tested in court as to its validity, and the constitutionality eventually upheld by the Supreme Court in the case of *Borchers Bros.* v. *Buckeye Incubator Co.*, 59 Cal.2d 234.

In 1967 the Mechanic's Lien Law was amended extensively and now provides that anyone entitled to assert a mechanic's lien claim or stop-notice right, except one under direct contract with the owner or one performing actual labor for wages, as a condition to filing a valid claim of lien and giving a stop notice, must give a preliminary written notice to the owner, to the original contractor, and to the construction lender not later than twenty days after the claimant has first furnished labor, services, equipment, or materials to the jobsite. If a claimant fails to give such notice within twenty days after he has first furnished labor, services, or material, he is not precluded from giving such a notice at a later date, but is then entitled to claim a lien and assert a stop-notice right only for such labor, services, or materials furnished within twenty days prior to giving such notice and at any time thereafter.

WHEN LIENS MAY BE FILED

If a valid *notice of completion* is recorded, a mechanic's lien may be recorded within the following times: (*a*) by the original contractor within sixty days after the date of filing for record such notice; (*b*) by any claimant, other than the original contractor, within thirty days after the date of filing for record such notice. However, in case a notice of completion is not recorded by the owner, then all persons have ninety days after the completion of the work of improvement within which to file a lien. (C.C.P., Sec. 1193.1c.)

Separate structures. "Work of improvement" means the entire structure or scheme of improvement as a whole. However, where the work consists in the construction of two or more separate residential units, each separate residential unit is considered a separate work of improvement, and the time for filing claims of lien commences to run upon the completion of each unit.

Effect of recording notice of completion. The effect of the recording by an owner of a valid notice of completion is to shorten the time for filing liens from ninety days to thirty days by claimants other than the original contractor, or sixty days by the original contractor. The notice of completion to be effective must be recorded within ten days after the completion of the work of improvement. Actual completion of a work of improvement means a substantial completion sufficient to enable the contractor to recover the contract price if he sued. Minor imperfections do not prevent completion. Occupation or use of a work of improvement by the owner or his agent, accompanied by cessation of labor thereon, constitutes completion. The acceptance by the owner or his agent of the work of improvement is equivalent to actual completion.

Effect of failure to record notice of completion. Although the code provides that the "owner or his successor in interest shall within ten days after completion of the work of improvement file for record a notice of completion," the only penalty for failure to do so is that the lien period is not shortened. A notice filed before the date of completion or more than ten days after such date is a defective notice, and will not shorten the lien period.

Cessation of labor. A cessation of labor may occur after commencement of a work of improvement, which cessation may be tantamount to completion for the purpose of filing liens. Under the provisions of Section 1193.1 of the Code of Civil Procedure, a cessation of labor for a continuous period of sixty days is declared to be equivalent to a completion, and starts the lien period running just as actual completion sets it in motion. Thus, if work has ceased for a period of sixty days, all claimants have ninety days thereafter within which to file a lien. However, the owner may record a notice of cessation within the time prescribed, in which event the original contractor has sixty days within which to file a lien, and all others have thirty days.

TIME WITHIN WHICH TO FILE ACTION

After a lien is duly recorded, the claimant has a limited time within which to bring an action to foreclose his lien. Under the provisions of Section 1198.1 of the Code of Civil Procedure, a mechanic's lien does not bind any property for a longer period than ninety days after the filing of the lien, or ninety days after expiration of a credit, unless foreclosure proceedings are commenced in a proper court within that time. If a credit is given, it can extend for no longer than one year from the time work was completed, and a notice of credit must be filed for record before the expiration of the ninety-day lien period.

NATURE OF FORECLOSURE ACTION

An action for the foreclosure of a mechanic's lien is a proceeding in equity, and resembles an action to foreclose a mortgage. A complaint is filed, summons issued, a foreclosure decree entered, a sale thereafter made by the sheriff or other officer pursuant to a writ of enforcement, and a certificate of sale issued to the purchaser at the sale, followed by a deed if no redemption is made within one year from the date of sale. In an action to foreclose a mechanic's lien, all parties claiming or having a subordinate interest in the property, whether an owner, mortgagee, lien claimant, or otherwise, are necessary parties defendant.

PARITY OF LIENS

All mechanics' liens arising out of the same work of improvement are on a parity with each other, regardless of the time when the respective claimants performed labor or furnished materials. Such claimants are entitled to share pro rata in the proceeds of the foreclosure of the property under a mechanic's lien foreclosure decree.

BOND TO RELEASE LIEN

Section 1193.1 of the Code of Civil Procedure authorizes the filing of a bond by the owner of the property or by the contractor or a subcontractor to effect a release of a mechanic's lien. Upon the recording of such bond, the real property described in the bond is freed from the claim of lien and any action brought to foreclose the lien.

PRIORITY OF MECHANICS' LIENS

Questions of priority are frequently encountered as between deeds of trust and mechanics' liens. A mechanic's lien attaches as of the time the work of improvement first commenced, and not at the time the lien was recorded or the time when the lien claimant performed his work or furnished materials. A mechanic's lien is declared to be superior to any mortgage, deed of trust, or other lien or encumbrance, that may have attached to the property *subsequent* to the time of commencement of the work of improvement in connection with which the lien claimant has done his work or furnished his materials. In the case of *Rheem Mfg. Co.* v. *United States,* 57 Cal.2d 621, it was held that obligatory advances under a loan agreement have priority over a mechanic's lien where the deed of trust was recorded ahead of the mechanic's lien.

OFFSITE IMPROVEMENTS

Section 1184.1 of the Code of Civil Procedure relates to offsite improvements and provides that any person who, at the instance or request of the owner of any lot or tract of land, demolishes or removes any improvement, trees, or other vegetation located thereon, or drills test holes, or grades, fills in, or otherwise improves the same, or the street, highway, or sidewalk in front of or adjoining the same, or constructs or installs sewers or other public utilities, or other such improvements, has a lien upon the lot or tract of land for his work done and materials furnished. Under prescribed conditions, a claimant who furnishes labor, equipment, or material for the offsite improvements may have priority over the construction lender. (C.C.P., Sec. 1189.1.)

PRIORITY NOT DEPENDENT UPON TIME OF RECORDING LIEN

The time of recording does not necessarily determine priority; the mechanic's lien may be recorded after a deed of trust, but have priority by virtue of the earlier date of commencement of the work of improvement. Furthermore, a mechanic's lien is superior to a mortgage or deed of trust or other lien of which the mechanic's lien claimant had no notice and which, although executed and delivered, was not recorded at the time of commencement of work. However, a mortgage or deed of trust that is inferior to mechanics' liens because recorded subsequent to the commencement of work, or for any other reason, may attain priority over such liens if a statutory bond is filed to protect lien claimants. Such bond must be an amount not less than 75 per cent of the principal amount of the mortgage or deed of trust.

PREREQUISITE TO PRIORITY OF MORTGAGE OR TRUST DEED

Generally, a mortgage or deed of trust that is executed and recorded prior to the commencement of a work of improvement is superior to any mechanics' liens arising out of the work, and the priority thus attained extends to the building or other improvements as well as to the land. However, there are certain prerequisites to priority besides recording the mortgage or deed of trust. There must be a valid and existing debt or obligation in existence prior to commencement of the work of improvement. The proceeds of the loan evidenced by the mortgage or deed of trust and the note secured thereby either must be paid to the borrower before commencement of the work, or the lender must be obligated to advance the funds. If the mortgagor or trustor does not acquire title until *after* the commencement of work, the mortgage or deed of trust, even though recorded before commencement of work, is subordinate to mechanics' liens arising out of the work. Where optional rather than obligatory advances are made by the construction lender, there may be a priority of the mechanics' liens over the deed of trust of the construction lender to the extent of the optional payments if such optional payments were not used to pay labor and material claims on the project. (C.C.P., Sec. 1188.1.)

WHAT CONSTITUTES COMMENCEMENT OF WORK

The question of what constitutes commencement of work for the pupose of determining relative priorities is a mixed question of law and fact. Commencement of work of improvement has been described as "some work and labor on the ground, the effects of which are apparent

—easily seen by everybody; such as beginning to dig the foundation, or work of like description, which everyone can readily see and recognize as the commencement of a building." (*Simons Brick Co.* v. *Hetzel*, 72 C.A. 1.) The most difficult commencement problems concern operations that are preparatory to actual construction. The following evidence is usually regarded as commencement of work: building materials or equipment deposited, whether on the property in question or on other property in the immediate vicinity, if intended for use on the property in question; foundation stakes set by a surveyor; test holes dug; load of dirt deposited; trees and weeds removed; water meter set in parking place by contractor; preliminary landscaping; installation of sprinkling system; and demolition of old buildings.

INSURING PRIORITY OF DEED OF TRUST

Where a title company is requested to insure a deed of trust ahead of possible mechanics' liens, it will have an inspection made of the property on the morning that the deed of trust is to be recorded to determine that none of the foregoing acts is apparent, or that there is no other evidence of a work of improvement having commenced.

STOP NOTICES

The Mechanic's Lien Law also permits the filing of a stop notice as an additional remedy. Customarily, there is a construction lender on a private work of improvement who loans money to the owner of the project to finance the development and who retains the money loaned in order to insure that such funds will be used for construction purposes under an agreed pay-out plan. A notice to withhold may be given to the construction lender by a person who furnishes labor, equipment, or material to the project. Such notice must be accompanied by a bond one and one-quarter times the claim. Such notice catches whatever funds are on hand at the time the notice is received, but no more than the amount of the demand. The general contractor may not file such a notice. (C.C.P., Sec. 1190.1h.)

Effective November 8, 1967, a notice to withhold may be given only for labor, equipment, or material already furnished. Such notice may be filed at any time prior to the expiration of the lien period. Further, a preliminary notice must be given to the construction lender within twenty days of first furnishing labor, equipment, or material.

As pointed out in the case of *Idaco Lumber Co.* v. *Northwestern S. & L. Assn.*, 265 A.C.A. 537, the provisions for filing of stop-notice claims is an additional remedy afforded to mechanics and materialmen, which reaches the construction fund directly, whereas the mechanic's lien is against the property and could be extinguished by foreclosure of the construction lender's first trust deed which has obtained priority.

EQUITABLE LIENS

Under the law prior to November 8, 1967, a claimant on a construction project who did not have a valid notice to withhold could nevertheless look to the unexpended construction funds under certain circumstances, and his claim against such funds could have priority over the claim of the lender or the owner-borrower. Such a claim was called an equitable lien claim and was held to be second in priority to a valid notice to withhold. (*Miller* v. *Mountain View Sav. & Loan*, 238 C.A.2d 644.) However, the 1967 amendments to the Mechanic's Lien Law abolished the equitable lien doctrine.

TITLE COMPANY PRACTICES

Although a mechanic's lien terminates by the expiration of the period prescribed for foreclosure, i.e., ninety days after the lien is filed or after expiration of a credit, the lien is not automatically eliminated for title insurance purposes. As a general rule of title practice, a recorded mechanic's lien must be shown as an exception in a policy of title insurance unless all of the following conditions are present: (1) the lien has been of record for more than ninety days, or more than ninety days have elapsed since the date to which the lien has been extended or credit has been given as shown by a recorded notice; (2) no action is pending in which foreclosure of the lien is sought; (3) the period for foreclosure has not been extended by the bankruptcy of the owner, or by the fact that either the owner or the claimant was in the military service during the ninety-day period; and (4) the insured is a purchaser or encumbrancer for value and in good faith whose rights were acquired subsequent to the expiration of the ninety-day period. If the insured is not a purchaser or encumbrancer but is the owner at the time the lien was filed, it is considered safe to ignore the lien if: (1) more than one year has elapsed since the date of recording of the lien or the date to which credit was given as shown by a recorded notice, and (2) no foreclosure action is pending.

Questions

1. How is a lien defined?
2. In what ways are liens created?
3. Explain briefly the nature of an equitable lien.

4. How may a judgment lien be created?
5. What is the duration of a judgment lien?
6. Discuss the prerequisites of a valid judgment.
7. Does a judgment lien attach to the buyer's interest under a land contract?
8. Explain the purpose of an attachment lien.
9. May property be sold under an attachment lien?
10. How may an execution lien be obtained?
11. Explain the purpose of an execution lien.
12. Distinguish a marshal's certificate of sale and marshal's deed.
13. Discuss the basis of the mechanic's lien law.
14. Is there any limitation on who may record a mechanic's lien?
15. Does a mechanic's lien have priority only from the date it is recorded?
16. Explain the purpose of a notice of nonresponsibility.
17. Is there a limitation on the time during which a mechanic's lien may be recorded?
18. Does the filing of a notice of completion afford any advantage to an owner?
19. After a mechanic's lien is recorded, are any further steps necessary to effect payment?
20. Describe briefly the ways that a mechanic's lien may be released.

16

Taxes and Assessments

Summary

I. Introductory
Land as a basis of taxation; Requisites of a valid tax; Property subject to tax; Exempt property; Modes of taxation

II. Annual property taxes
Veterans' exemptions; Property sold under contract; Annual levy; System of taxation–cities and counties

III. Assessment and levy of property tax
Property statements; Assessment roll; Assessed value; Equalization of assessments; Levy of tax; Due date of taxes; Delinquent tax list; Payment of tax on wrong property; Property escaping assessment; Segregation of taxes

IV. Lien of tax
Lien date

V. Sale for delinquent taxes
First tax sale; Second tax sale; Effect of sale to the state; Tax sales to the public; Tax deed; Relative priorities of taxes and assessments; Parity rule

VI. Redemption from tax sale
Segregation for redemption purposes; Installment plan of payment; Privilege of redemption; Effect of redemption

VII. Tax titles
Need for tax title stability; Curative acts; Conclusive presumption statutes; Statutes of limitation; Insurance of tax titles

VIII. Special assessments
Types of special assessments; Notice of special assessment proceedings; Cost of the improvement; Improvement districts; Special improvement districts; Improvement bonds

IX. Other types of taxes
Federal taxes

I. Introductory

A tax is defined as a burden or charge imposed on persons or property, or a proportional contribution levied by the sovereign, to raise money for the support of the government and to enable it to discharge its appropriate functions. It is not a debt as that term is ordinarily used, but is a *levy,* under authority of law, for governmental purposes. It is the principal source of revenue for most government functions, such as police and fire protection, schools, roads, parks, and playgrounds. It is ordinarily paramount to all other claims and liens.

LAND AS A BASIS OF TAXATION

Land as a basis of taxation first drew the eyes of the tax assessor in England over six hundred years ago, based upon the assumption that taxes should be assessed in accordance with a man's ability to pay. In those times, the extent and quality of an individual's agricultural holdings were a dependable index of his ability to pay taxes, since his income was derived almost entirely from agricultural products. It therefore followed that land that a person owned became a surface guide for determining the amount of tax to be levied. Another basis for taxation of land is the fact that it is so easily assessable and cannot be concealed from the tax collector.

REQUISITES OF A VALID TAX

The exercise of the taxing power has long been a source of concern. "Taxation without representation" was a primary complaint in colonial times and a moving factor in the Revolutionary War. Today, the validity of a tax is dependent upon certain jurisdictional requirements that must be present to sustain the exercise of the tax power. The jurisdictional requisites of a valid tax are set forth in the case of *Miller* v. *McKenna,* 23 Cal.2d 774, as follows: (1) a duly constituted *taxing authority;* (2) *property* to be taxed within the territorial jurisdiction of the taxing body; (3) property or subject matter legally subject to the tax, i.e., property which is *not exempt;* (4) sufficient notice and opportunity for hearing to constitute compliance with *due process of law.*

PROPERTY SUBJECT TO TAX

As a general rule, all property within the jurisdiction of the taxing power is taxable, unless specially exempt, and exemption statutes are strictly construed. The Constitution of the State of California (Art. XIII,

Sec. 1) provides that all property in the state except as therein otherwise provided, not exempt under the laws of the United States, shall be taxed in proportion to its value. The word "property" is declared to include monies, credits, bonds, stocks, dues, franchises, and all other matters and things, real, personal, and mixed, capable of private ownership, except a mortgage, deed of trust, or other security transaction affecting land.

EXEMPT PROPERTY

The state constitution specifically exempts property used for free public libraries and free museums, growing crops, property used for public schools, church or parochial schools, and property belonging to the state, or to any county, city and county, or municipal corporation owning the same that was subject to taxation at the time of acquisition. Other provisions allow additional exemptions, including burial grounds not used or held for profit; property used for religious, hospital, and charitable purposes; and exemptions based on military service.

Section 218 was added to the Revenue and Taxation code in 1968 relating to the homeowner's property tax exemption approved by the voters in 1968 by the passage of Senate Constitutional Amendment No. 1 of the 1968 Extra Session of the legislature. The section is operative on the 1969 lien date.

MODES OF TAXATION

Four basic modes of taxation apply today, namely, property taxes; income or use taxes; franchise taxes; and gift, inheritance, and estate taxes. In this chapter main consideration will be given to property taxes.

II. Annual property taxes

One of the most important sources of revenue is the tax on property located in the state. Under the provisions of Section 201 of the Revenue and Taxation Code, all property in California not exempt under the laws either of the United States or of the state is subject to taxation in the manner provided in said code. The State Board of Equalization prescribes the procedure and forms required to carry into effect the various exemptions. The welfare exemption, which applies to property used exclusively for religious, hospital, scientific, or charitable purposes, owned and operated on a nonprofit basis by community chests, funds, and foundations, or corporations organized and operated for such purposes, must be claimed annually by filing the prescribed affidavit on or before March 15 of each year with the tax assessor, supported by the required financial statements of the owner and operator.

VETERANS' EXEMPTIONS

As to the veterans' exemption, the state constitution provides for a property exemption to the amount of $1,000 to persons who have served in the Armed Forces, or to certain of their relatives, and who are legal residents of the state of California. This exemption is not allowable to a veteran who owns property of the value of $5,000 or more, or whose spouse owns property of the value of $5,000 or more, or $10,000 community property. The assessed value of real and personal property and the market value of nontaxable property as of the first day in March are used to determine this limitation.

Property must be owned and the conveyance of ownership recorded before the first day in March of the year for which the exemption is claimed. A statement of property owned with the exemption certificate attached must be filed with the assessor between the first day in March and April 15 in each year that the exemption is claimed.

PROPERTY SOLD UNDER CONTRACT

Title to property that the State Department of Veterans Affairs sells under contract to a veteran is held in the name of the department as an agency of the state. Prior to 1948 it was treated as state property not subject to general taxes, but the purchaser was considered to have a taxable "possessory interest." In that year the State Supreme Court, in the case of *Eisley* v. *Mohan*, 31 Cal.2d 637, recognized the purchaser as the real owner, and such property is now taxable to him, at full value, like other property. Such property may be subject, of course, to the veteran's exemption. Prior to September 15, 1961, the contract of purchase was required to be recorded in order to obtain the exemption. By amendment effective that date, a veteran who has an unrecorded interest in real property, consisting of a contract of sale, is permitted to qualify for the veterans' tax exemption by filing a claim of specified exemption.

ANNUAL LEVY

Property taxes are levied annually by each county on the taxable property within its borders, and by each city on the taxable property within such city, except that most cities take advantage of the provisions of Section 51500, *et seq*., of the Government Code permitting cities to delegate the levy and collection of their taxes to the county. For example, as of March 1, 1968, Los Angeles county serves as assessing and collecting agent for 74 of the 76 incorporated cities in the county.

SYSTEM OF TAXATION—CITIES AND COUNTIES

The procedure set forth below is that followed by the counties. Cities that collect their own taxes follow substantially the same general system, although the due dates, delinquency dates, sale dates, penalties, and redemption periods vary in the different cities.

III. Assessment and levy of property tax

The first step in the taxing of property is the determination of its value, in relation to the value of all other property to be taxed, so that no substantial inequality or unfairness will result. This job is performed by the county tax assessor, an elected official whose legal responsibility requires him each year to discover, appraise, and list all taxable property in his jurisdiction. This assessment is made annually to the person owning, claiming, possessing, or controlling the same on the lien date (March 1). All requests for changes in property description or property divisions must be made to the assessor prior to the lien date for entry on the assessment roll for the ensuing year. The assessor is not the tax collector and has nothing to do with the total amount of taxes collected. His primary function is to ascertain the fair market value of taxable property.

PROPERTY STATEMENTS

Section 441 of the Revenue and Taxation Code provides that every person owning taxable personal property having an aggregate cost of $30,000 or more, other than household furnishings and personal effects, shall file a written property statement reporting such property. Every person owning personal property which does not require the filing of a written property statement or real property shall upon request of the assessor file a written property statement. The property statement shall be filed under oath with the assessor between March 1 and 5:00 P.M. on the last Monday in May, annually, or within such time as the assessor may appoint. If the assessor appoints a time other than the last Monday in May, it shall be no earlier than April 1. The property statement, in addition to identifying the person, must show all taxable property owned, claimed, possessed, controlled, or managed by him, the county and any city or revenue district in which it is situated, a particular description of the property, and any debts claimed as a deduction from a solvent credit. A person having no record interest is entitled to have property assessed to him if he so desires. (33 Ops. Cal. Atty. Gen. 118.)

ASSESSMENT ROLL

The assessment roll is the listing and assessed value of all taxable property within the assessor's jurisdiction. From all available data with respect to the property, the assessor prepares the assessment roll, establishing the values as determined by him, in detail and under the appropriate divisions, e.g., the land and improvements are separately assessed. Title to mineral interests, when the ownership has been separated from that of the surface estate, may be separately assessed to the persons owning, claiming, possessing, or controlling them. Thus, the interest of the lessee under an oil and gas lease, including community oil and gas leases, can be separately assessed to the lessee.

ASSESSED VALUE

As part of an extensive property tax reform in 1966, Section 401 of the Revenue and Taxation Code was rewritten to provide that every assessor should assess all property subject to general property taxation from the lien date for the 1967–68 fiscal year through the 1970–71 fiscal year at a publicly announced ratio of his own choosing which shall be between 20 per cent and 25 per cent of full cash value. Beginning with the lien date for the 1971–72 fiscal year, he shall assess all such property at 25 per cent of its full cash value. In implementation of this statute the State Board of Equalization promulgated a regulation requiring each county assessor to announce his chosen ratio on or before the third Monday in January each year. The constitutionality of this statute was sustained in the case of *County of Sacramento* v. *Hickman*, 66 Cal.2d 841.

EQUALIZATION OF ASSESSMENTS

The yardstick by which the assessed value is determined is not as important as is the *equalization* of the assessment, i.e., the application to each assessment of an effective method of determining that no parcel is assessed on a different basis than any other parcel similarly situated. This is the function of each county board of supervisors, sitting as a *Board of Equalization*, and as such, vested with the power and authority to adjust manifest inequalities in the assessments. The board of supervisors meets annually for this purpose on the first Monday in July, and continues in session until finished, but not later than the third Monday in July. Acting as such Board of Equalization, it may increase or lower any assessment, but not the entire roll, and it may not lower any assessment unless the owner files an application for such reduction. The *State Board of Equalization* performs a similar function respecting property subject to taxation by the state. Adjustment of valuations cannot be made after adjournment of the board.

For counties having a population of four million or more, which presently is limited to Los Angeles, the State Legislature in 1963 authorized the formation of tax appeals boards for the purpose of equalizing assessments. The designation now used is the Assessment Appeals Board.

LEVY OF TAX

After all of the taxable property has been assessed, the assessments equalized, the amount of revenue to be raised determined, and the tax rate established, the board of supervisors "levies the tax," i.e., formally determines that the taxes be collected and enforced. The county auditor thereupon extends the tax against each parcel or item subject to taxation by applying the rate fixed by the board against the assessed value of each such property. The assessment roll is then delivered for collection to the tax collector, who prepares and mails the tax bills.

The *tax base* is the total assessed value in a given taxing district. The sum of the monies needed each year by all the taxing agencies, as well as by the county, determines what is called the *tax rate*. This tax rate is a levy per each $100 of assessed value.

Following is a brief explanation of how the tax determination works: If the assessor has determined the market value of property to be $20,000, this would mean it has been assessed at $5,000, using 25 per cent of value. If the tax rate in your area has been set by the taxing agencies at $8.00, that represents $8.00 per $100 of assessed value. By dividing the assessed value of the property by $100, we get the figure 50, which is then multiplied by $8.00 to get $400 as the amount of the tax.

DUE DATE OF TAXES

Tax levies cover a fiscal-year period from July 1 to the following June 30. All taxes on personal property secured by specific real property and one half the tax on real property are due November 1, and are delinquent on December 10 at 5:00 P.M., after which a penalty of 6 per cent attaches. The second half of the tax on real property is due on February 1, but may be paid sooner if desired, either with payment of the first half or thereafter. The second half of real property taxes is delinquent after April 10, and a penalty of 6 per cent then attaches.

DELINQUENT TAX LIST

The delinquent tax list is published on or before the 8th day of September each year in the daily newspaper that is awarded the contract for county printing. The publication states the date when the delinquent property will be sold to the state for nonpayment of taxes (on or before June 30), and the amount for which each parcel is to be sold. On or before June 8 each year, there is a publication of a list of properties upon which any portion of the taxes for a period of five years or more has been delinquent, and which will be deeded to the state (on or about July 1 of each year), unless they are redeemed in full or have installment payments initiated prior to July 1. All properties that have been deeded to the state for delinquent taxes may be sold by the county tax collector at any time after the issuance of the deed to the state unless previously redeemed.

PAYMENT OF TAX ON WRONG PROPERTY

Payment of taxes on the wrong property sometimes occurs. If a property owner by mistake pays the tax on other than the property intended, and by substantial evidence convinces the tax collector that the payment was intended for another property, the tax collector shall cancel the credit on the unintended property and transfer the payment to the property intended at any time before a guaranty or certificate of title issues respecting the unintended property, and before two years have elapsed since the date of payment. (Rev. & Tax. C., Sec. 4911.) If the amount paid is greater than necessary, a refund will be made in the same manner as for an overcollection of tax. A refund on overcollection of taxes may be made upon presentation of both tax receipts together with an affidavit, or one receipt and a waiver. Application for such refund must be made within three years.

PROPERTY ESCAPING ASSESSMENT

If any property belonging on the local roll has escaped assessment, the assessor is required to assess the property on discovery at its value on the lien date for the year for which it escaped assessment. Except as otherwise provided, it shall be subject to the tax rate in effect in the year of its escape. (Rev. & Tax. C., Sec. 531.)

SEGREGATION OF TAXES

Where a purchaser or other person acquires an interest in a portion only of a larger area that is assessed as one parcel on the tax rolls, a procedure is set forth in Section 2821 *et seq*., of the Revenue and Taxation Code for segregating the taxes. Under these provisions, any person showing evidence, by presentation of a duly executed and recorded deed, purchase contract, deed of trust, mortgage, or final decree of court, of an interest in any parcel of real property, except possessory interests, that does not have a separate valuation on the roll, and who is not the owner or contract purchaser of the entire parcel as assessed, may apply to the tax collector to have the parcel separately valued on the roll for the purpose of paying current taxes. Application shall be made during the current fiscal year. Section 2822 of said code, added in 1968, permits the acceptance of payment of the tax on an undivided interest under prescribed conditions.

IV. Lien of tax

Every tax on real property is a lien thereon, and every tax on personal property is a lien on the real property of the owner. The owner of personal property may, in his property statement filed with the assessor, designate the particular land that shall secure his personal property tax. Prior to September 11, 1957, the owner could designate a parcel of real property as to which the lien of personal property taxes would attach, regardless of the location of the personal property. Subsequent removal or change of ownership did not relieve such lien against the real property. As a consequence of this provision, buyers of real property not obtaining a tax statement through escrow sometimes found that they were obligated to pay personal property taxes, in many instances, on such items as the seller's yacht or other craft. This situation was remedied to a certain extent by the amendment of Section 2189 of the Revenue and Taxation Code, which now provides that a tax on personal property is a lien on any real property on the secured roll also belonging to the owner of the personal property, *if the personal property is located upon such real property on the lien date,* and if the fact of the lien is shown on the secured roll opposite the description of the real property.

LIEN DATE

As amended in 1967, Section 2192 of the Revenue and Taxation Code provides that the tax lien attaches annually as of 12:01 A.M. on the first day of March preceding the beginning of the fiscal year (July 1 to the following June 30). Such lien has the effect of an execution duly levied against the property subject to the lien, and continues until the tax is paid, or until the expiration of thirty years unless enforced by a tax sale in the interim. The lien is prior to all private interests and rights, except certain easement, water rights, and restrictions of record.

Taxes are levied on both real and personal property as it exists on the lien date. The lien against real estate or the tax on personal property is not relieved by subsequent removal or change of ownership, and the tax collector cannot accept payment for taxes on real property unless the personal property tax indicated on the tax bill has been paid or is tendered.

V. Sale for delinquent taxes

Real property taxes, also secured personal property taxes, are enforced by a sale of the property at a tax sale if payments become delinquent. The procedure involves two sales, one at the end of the fiscal year, and another at the end of the fifth year thereafter.

FIRST TAX SALE

On or before the end of the fiscal year, i.e., June 30, real property upon which the tax for the year or either installment is delinquent is sold to the state at the time fixed in the publication of the notice of intent to sell to the state. Although referred to as the first tax sale, this is not a sale in the conventional sense, but is a so-called "book transaction," with the fact of sale being noted on the tax rolls. It establishes the commencement of the statutory five-year period of redemption during which the owner has a right to redeem from the sale by paying all delinquent taxes together with the prescribed penalties. Taxes for ensuing years continue to be assessed, but no subsequent "sale" is entered on the tax rolls while a prior "sale" is still in effect.

SECOND TAX SALE

At the end of the fifth year following the initial "sale" to the state, the property for the first time becomes available for sale to the state of California. This is an actual sale, and in the absence of any fatal defects in the tax sale proceedings, the state acquires an absolute title, i.e., title freed from all private rights, interests, encumbrances, and claims, except easements burdening the property, water rights held separately, and restrictions. (Rev. & Tax. C., Sec. 3712.) It is not free, however, from special assessments or improvement bonds that are on a parity, nor from municipal taxes separately assessed by a municipality and not included in the delinquent taxes satisfied by the sale.

EFFECT OF SALE TO THE STATE

Once sold and conveyed to the state, the property is off the tax rolls. It belongs to the state, although actually held in trust for the county and other taxing authorities whose levies were included in the delinquent taxes for which sold.

TAX SALES TO THE PUBLIC

Sales of tax-deeded property to the public are made at public auction by the county tax collector, upon authorization of the board of supervisors and with the approval of the State Controller, after notice by publication and mailing. Such sales may be at the request of prospective purchasers or on the initiative of the tax collector. A minimum bid usually is established, at least sufficient to cover expenses. Any person, including the former owner, may be a purchaser at such tax sale. Formerly, no resale of tax-deeded property by the state could be made for less than the amount required to redeem, thus assuring ultimate payment of all delinquent taxes. However, since 1933, sales may be made for less, i.e., to the highest bidder. A tax deed is issued upon payment of the amount of the bid, and the proceeds of the sale distributed pro rata among the taxing agencies having an interest in the delinquent taxes that were the basis of such sale. If any such taxing agency objects to the sale, it must elect to purchase in accordance with a prescribed procedure.

TAX DEED

The deed issued by the tax collector upon completion of the sale of tax-deeded land should be promptly recorded by the purchaser in the office of the county recorder. In the absence of fraud this deed is declared to be conclusive evidence of the regularity of all prior proceedings.

RELATIVE PRIORITIES OF TAXES AND ASSESSMENTS

A problem with which the taxing authorities and the court frequently have had to deal in the past has been the relative priorities of taxes and special assessments. The rule now followed in this state is that they are on a parity, i.e., of equal rank, so that the enforcement of either one does not extinguish the other. This rule is stated in the case of *La Mesa Lemon Grove & Spring Valley Irrigation District* v. *Hornbeck*, 216 Cal. 730, as follows: "We may now safely conclude that under our system of taxation, liens, in favor of county and municipal corporations, and special assessments, under the authority of state agencies for public purposes, are all on an equality. By this is meant that, in case of delinquency, a deed to any one of these agencies for such taxes will not obliterate the existing liens on the property in favor of any or all of the others." However, the parity rule does not apply when a tax deed is based upon a tax levied at a time when the property was not subject to other taxes or assessments. (*Elbert, Ltd.* v. *Barnes*, 107 C.A.2d 659.) Liens created by Section 17829, Health and Safety Code, relating to the cost of removal of substandard structures, or created by comparable ordinances, are also on a parity with the lien of State, county, and municipal taxes.

PARITY RULE

Where the title acquired by a purchaser of a tax title by deed from the state or other taxing agency, and the title acquired by a purchaser at a street bond foreclosure or by treasurer's deed pursuant to a sale for delinquent assessments, are on a parity, such purchasers become tenants in common, each owning an undivided one-half interest in the property, irrespective of the time when the liens upon which their respective titles are based arose. The time when their respective deeds were executed with reference to each other is immaterial. Each party has an equitable lien against the property to the extent of the amount paid by him. In the event of a subsequent sale of the property, which may be effected through partition proceedings, each cotenant is entitled to reimbursement for the amount paid by him, and after such payments the parties are entitled to an equal division of the excess. The parity rule does not apply, however, as between successive special assessments and improvement bonds themselves, numerous decisions by the courts having established intricate rules for determining their relative priority.

VI. Redemption from tax sale

Real property that is "sold to the state" at the end of the fiscal year may be redeemed by paying the delinquent taxes that led to such sale, all similar taxes subsequently assessed thereon, and statutory penalties. This is an absolute *right* which continues for five years. (Rev. & Tax. C., Secs. 4101 *et seq.*)

SEGREGATION FOR REDEMPTION PURPOSES

Under the provisions of Section 4151 of the Revenue and Taxation Code, any person claiming an interest, evidenced by presentation of a duly executed and recorded deed, purchase contract, deed of trust, mortgage or final decree of court, in any parcel of tax-sold or tax-deeded property that does not have a separate valuation on the roll for the year for which it became tax delinquent or on any subsequent roll, and who is not the owner or contract purchaser of the entire parcel as assessed, may apply to the redemption officer to have the parcel separately valued in order that it may be redeemed.

In the case of *Smith* v. *Anderson*, 67 Cal.2d 635, decided in 1967, it was held that upon the request of an owner of an *undivided* interest in real property sold and deeded to the state for delinquent taxes, the redemption officer and assessor are required under Section 4153 and 4154 to separately value the owner's undivided interest in the property in order that he might separately redeem his interest. Then in 1968 Section 4152 of said code was added to provide in part that when the application is made for the purpose of paying the tax on an undivided interest, the redemption officer shall accept an amount that bears the same proportion to the tax as the undivided interest bears to the interest as assessed.

INSTALLMENT PLAN OF PAYMENT

Under prescribed conditions, delinquent taxes may be paid and redemption effected on the installment plan. (Rev. & Tax. C., Secs. 4216 *et seq.*) These sections provide for a permanent five-year installment plan, under which delinquent taxes may be paid in annual installments. The installment plan of payment may be employed at any time prior to the deed to the state.

PRIVILEGE OF REDEMPTION

Real property deeded to the state *after* five years from the first sale may also be redeemed by paying all delinquencies and statutory penalties at any time prior to the disposition of such property by the state. This is a *privilege,* however, and not a right, and can be curtailed by subsequent legislation.

EFFECT OF REDEMPTION

Upon redemption the effect of the sale and deed to the state is terminated; the title is restored to the former owner or his successor in interest, and the sale and deed are cancelled.

VII. Tax titles

The hazard of error in proceedings for the collection and enforcement of taxes has prevented the insurance of tax titles until quite recently. Heretofore, the courts regarded purchases of tax titles as speculative, and it was tantamount to buying a lawsuit. Tax titles were invalidated upon slight grounds.

NEED FOR TAX TITLE STABILITY

Economic conditions during the depression years resulted in wholesale delinquencies, and with thousands of parcels off the tax rolls, counties and cities began to suffer from the impact of dwindling revenues. Faced with the necessity of realizing revenue from tax-sold lands, hard-pressed taxing agencies soon realized the need of greater stability to tax titles, since selling a lawsuit, rather than a marketable title, made a great deal of difference to them financially. The aid of the legislature was sought, with the result that three general types of remedial legislation were enacted, namely, curative acts; conclusive presumptions; and short statutes of limitations.

CURATIVE ACTS

A curative act provides, in substance, that every act and proceeding taken by county officials in fixing the budget or tax rate, in assessing or equalizing the assessment of property, or in the resultant levy of taxes, tax sales, and tax deeds, is confirmed, validated, and declared legally effective, so far as can be done under constitutional limitations, thereby correcting defects, irregularities, and ministerial error which the legislature could have omitted from statutory requirements under which such acts were taken. The courts have held such acts to be valid, applicable to prior proceedings, and effective to cure all but jurisdictional defects. (*Miller* v. *McKenna,* 23 Cal.2d 774.)

CONCLUSIVE PRESUMPTION STATUTES

A conclusive presumption statute, such as Section 3711 of the Revenue and Taxation Code, provides in effect that, except as against actual fraud, a tax deed is conclusive evidence of the regularity of all proceedings culminating in such deed. It has been held, however, that defects that go to jurisdiction and make the action taken void cannot be cured by either a curative act or a conclusive presumption clause. In the case of *Ramish* v. *Hartwell,* 126 Cal. 443, the court stated that the legislature may make a tax deed conclusive evidence of a compliance with all provisions of the statute that are merely directory of the mode in which the power of taxation may be exercised, but that it cannot make it conclusive evidence of those matters that are essential to the exercise of the power. As to those steps that are jurisdictional in their nature, and without which the power of taxation cannot be called into exercise, the legislature cannot deprive the owner of the right to show want of compliance.

STATUTES OF LIMITATION

The third method devised to bolster tax titles and the one that far excels the others in its effectiveness is the provision that any attack upon the tax title is barred unless commenced within a limited period of time after the issuance of the tax deed. Several such statutes have been enacted in this state, and their validity has been sustained by the courts. (*Tannhauser* v. *Adams,* 31 Cal.2d 169; *Devault* v. *Essig,* 80 C.A.2d 970.) In the latter case it was held that the legislature has the right to fix some reasonable limitation upon the time within which a constitutional right may be exercised, and therefore has the right to fix a statutory limitation of time in which to attack the validity of a tax deed to the state.

Effect of statutes of limitation. Cases based upon statutes of limitation go a long way toward validating all defects, however basic, in tax sale proceedings, and constitute the principal basis for title companies, under certain conditions, now insuring tax titles without the necessity of bringing judicial proceedings against the former owner.

INSURANCE OF TAX TITLES

Most title insurance companies now insure tax titles under prescribed conditions. If one year has elapsed since the date of the state's deed to the purchaser, the deed may be insured, provided the former owner is not in possession, current taxes have been paid, and no serious defects are shown in the title company's examination of all the proceedings leading up to the deed from the state.

Necessity for quiet title action. If there are serious defects in the proceedings, or unusual circumstances, such as legal disabilities, oil possibility, or valuable improvements in existence or contemplated on the property, the tax title is usually considered to be uninsurable. In such case it is necessary that the tax deed purchaser proceed with a quiet title action against the former owner, which action may be undertaken pursuant to special proceedings contained in the Revenue and Taxation Code.

VIII. Special assessments

In addition to annual taxes levied for the general support of state or local government, there are several ways in which property is assessed for its share of special levies, such as for the support of schools, flood control, irrigation, drainage, and similar purposes; for the cost of local improvements such as streets, sewers, and other public conveniences; or for maintenance of publicly owned utilities, such as street lighting.

TYPES OF SPECIAL ASSESSMENTS

Special assessments are of three general types, as follows: (1) assessments at rates fixed annually and collected at the same time as the annual local taxes; (2) assessments for the maintenance of districts, such as irrigation districts, levied annually but collected separately and in the manner specified in the laws governing such districts; and (3) nonrecurring assessments, levied at the inception of work of special benefit to property in a limited area, called a special improvement district, and designed to cover the costs of installation of a particular local improvement, such as streets, sidewalks, sewers. An adjunct of the latter are subsequent annual maintenance assessments to cover the cost of maintenance, such as of street lighting.

COST OF THE IMPROVEMENT

In the case of *City of Los Angeles* v. *Offner,* 55 Cal.2d 103, it was held that the legislature cannot properly authorize a special assessment for a local improvement in an amount that exceeds the actual cost of the improvement and necessary incidental expenses. The theory of special assessments for local improvements is that the improvement must confer a special benefit on the property assessed. Thus, sewer connection charges, which were not measured by the actual cost of the improvement but were in excess thereof, were held invalid.

IMPROVEMENT DISTRICTS

Various districts have been formed in California, pursuant to statutory provisions, for the purpose of providing necessary works of improvement or development, such as dams, ditches, canals, and drainage. These usually require periodic outlays of large sums, necessitating the creation of a bonded indebtedness, secured by both the district's fixed assets and its future revenues. The amounts needed annually to service its bonds and pay its current operations are estimated and spread over the lands included in and served by the district on an ad valorem basis. Such assessments are liens on the lands so assessed, have fixed due and delinquent dates, and on default in payment are enforced by sale of the lands as to which the assessments are not paid, in a manner somewhat similar to, but independent of, the enforcement of county taxes.

SPECIAL IMPROVEMENT DISTRICTS

"Special improvement districts" is the designation given to areas deemed benefited by a particular local improvement. The procedure is prescribed by state laws and administered by designated officials of the county or city in which the land lies. The cost of a work of improvement having been determined and the benefited area established, assessments are levied on the property in the district, which assessments become a lien upon the respective parcels, usually upon acceptance of the work of improvement and completion of the assessment. Such assessments are payable, initially, to the contractor making the improvements; but, after a short period, they are payable to a designated city or county official.

NOTICE OF SPECIAL ASSESSMENT PROCEEDINGS

Legislation was passed in 1963 designed to give more adequate notice of special assessment proceedings and the lien of special assessments. Prior to the time a special assessment district is formed, there must be filed with the County Clerk a map showing the boundaries of the district. Then, before assessments levied under the proposed district can become a lien, a prescribed notice of assessment must be recorded in the office of the county recorder.

IMPROVEMENT BONDS

Assessments exceeding a stated amount (usually $25) may be allowed to "go to bond," i.e., to stand as security for the amount due, which is made payable over a period of years, in equal annual installments with interest, and evidenced by negotiable bonds, issued by the local government and sold, either to the contractor or to the investing public. Such bonds are not, ordinarily, a general obligation of the local government, but are payable only out of collections, on the underlying assessments, by the city or county officials.

Bond foreclosures. Upon or at any time after default in the payment of an installment of principal or interest of an assessment securing a particular bond, and before the expiration of four years after the due date of the last installment, the holder of that bond may enforce the bond in either of two ways: (1) by treasurer's sale, or (2) by judicial foreclosure, provided such right existed at the date of issuance of the bond. Rights subsequently accorded bondholders by law do not extend to bonds then outstanding, because so to apply the law would be an unconstitutional impairment of the contract deemed to exist between bondholder and property owner.

IX. Other types of taxes

Various types of state taxes may become liens on real property when a certificate of tax or an abstract of judgment is recorded in the office of the county recorder of the county where the property is situated. Such certificate or abstract creates a lien having the effect and priority of an ordinary money judgment. Included in such taxes are the sales tax, the use tax, the income tax, and the unemployment tax. Other taxes, such as the inheritance tax, become a lien on real property without the necessity of recording notice thereof in the county recorder's office.

FEDERAL TAXES

There are also a host of federal taxes imposed to meet the needs of the federal government for revenue, and under the provisions of a general tax lien statute (26 U.S.C.A., Sec. 6321, 1954 Code), many of these taxes constitute a lien in favor of the United States upon all property and rights to property belonging to the taxpayer. Such liens as a general rule are not valid as against purchasers or encumbrancers of real property unless a notice of lien is recorded in the county where the property is situated. The federal income tax is the most frequently encountered tax of this nature.

In 1967 the law was amended by the enactment of the Uniform Federal Tax Lien Registration Act to provide for procedures and standards believed consistent with the Federal Tax Lien Act of 1966 pursuant to which the federal government may file of record notices of liens and other notices or certificates relating thereto with the Secretary of State as well as with county recorders, which conform, as to personal property, with procedures established by the Uniform Commercial Code for the filing of various other liens. (Govt. C., Secs. 7200 *et seq.*)

Some federal taxes, such as the estate tax, attach as liens to specific property of the taxpayer under the provisions of the particular statute imposing the tax and without reliance upon the general tax lien statute mentioned above. Such liens are not dependent upon the filing or recording of any notice in the recorder's office. They are subordinate to prior valid liens, such as a deed of trust, but are superior to other liens subsequently accruing, despite lack of record notice.

Enforcement of federal tax liens. Federal tax liens may be enforced by seizure and sale of the property subject thereto (distraint proceedings), or the lien may be enforced by judicial sale under proceedings initiated by the District Director of Internal Revenue in the United States District Court.

Questions

1. Describe briefly the nature of a tax.
2. Discuss the jurisdictional requisites of a valid tax.
3. Is all property subject to tax?
4. Explain the principal exemptions from real property taxes.
5. How is the amount of a tax on real property determined?
6. Discuss briefly the priority of a property tax.
7. Explain the procedure followed in a tax sale.
8. Are tax titles considered insurable?
9. Explain the meaning of the parity rule.
10. Discuss the principal types of special assessments.
11. List some of the common types of state tax liens.
12. What procedures may be employed to enforce a federal tax lien?

17

Covenants, Conditions, and Restrictions

Summary

I. Introductory
Permissible restrictions; Distinctions between covenants, conditions, and restrictions

II. Creation and validity of restrictions
Covenants and conditions construed; Creation of covenant; Creation of condition; When a covenant will be implied; Implied reversions; Validity of restrictions; Racial restrictions

III. Covenants
Rights of assignee of covenantee; Obligations of assignee of covenantor; Enforcement against subsequent parties; Covenants running with the land; Covenants created by agreement; Covenants creating easements; Equitable servitudes

IV. Conditions
Characteristics of a condition; Reversion of title; Forfeitures not favored; Lien subordination clauses

V. General plan restrictions
Subdivision restrictions; Creation of general plan restrictions; Rights acquired under general plan restrictions; When enforcement may be denied; Declaration of covenants, conditions, and restrictions; Necessity of incorporating restrictions in deed; Variations permitted; Waiver by less than all lot owners; Condominium requirements

VI. Interpretation of particular restrictions
Residential purposes; Garages and outbuildings; Front line provisions; Use of the word "street"; Cost of buildings; Approval of plans and specifications

VII. Termination of restrictions
Expiration date; Voluntary cancellation or modification; Termination by merger; Enforcement may be denied on equitable principles; Acts of public authorities; Effect of foreclosure of a lien

I. Introductory

Restrictions on the use of land fall into two general classifications, namely, private restrictions and public restrictions. The latter type are exemplified by zoning ordinances, discussed in Chapter 18. Private restrictions are those voluntarily imposed on land by the landowners, and usually constitute both a benefit and a burden. To the extent that a landowner is restricted in the use that he may make of his land, the restriction is considered to be a burden, but to the extent that he has a right of enforcement against other landowners, he obtains a benefit.

PERMISSIBLE RESTRICTIONS

Deeds or other instruments may impose restrictions on the use of property for any legitimate purpose. The right to acquire and possess property includes the right to dispose of all or any part of, and to impose upon the grant whatever reservations or restrictions the grantor may see fit, provided that it is not contrary to prohibitions prescribed by law. Section 712 of the Civil Code, added in 1965, is illustrative of a void restriction. That section declares void any restrictions upon a fee owner of real property that would prohibit the display on the property of a sign of suitable dimensions advertising the property for sale, lease, or rent.

In contrast to zoning ordinances, private restrictions need not be promotive of public health, safety, morals, or public welfare; they may be intended to create a particular type of neighborhood deemed desirable to the individual tract owner, and may be based solely on esthetic considerations.

DISTINCTIONS BETWEEN COVENANTS, CONDITIONS, AND RESTRICTIONS

Private restrictions are classified generally as covenants and conditions. The distinction in those terms is based primarily upon the *right of enforcement* in the event of a breach. Historically, restrictive provisions in deeds, if they did not fall into the category of conditions, were called *covenants, i.e.*, a promise or agreement to do or not to do certain things; the grantor could enforce the covenant only by suing for damages if the covenant was violated. Commencing about a hundred years ago, the courts began to enforce restrictive provisions in another method by enjoining or forbidding their violation. Injunction is now a customary method of enforcing *restrictions*.

A *condition* is defined as a qualification annexed to an estate, upon the happening of which the estate is enlarged or defeated. The outstanding characteristic of a condition in a deed is that the grantor has the power to terminate the interest conveyed in the event a violation of the condition occurs. The term "restriction" is employed today as a general classification, embracing both covenants, where the enforcement may be by way of injunction or damages, and conditions, where the right of enforcement may additionally result in a loss of title.

II. Creation and validity of restrictions

Several methods may be used for the purpose of placing restrictions on property, including the following: (1) covenants or conditions imposed in a deed of a single parcel of land; (2) covenants contained in an agreement between two or more landowners; (3) covenants and conditions set forth in a recorded declaration of restrictions describing a general plan of restrictions for a tract, and thereafter imposed in deeds by reference to the recorded declaration; and (4) covenants and conditions imposed as a part of a general plan for a tract by inclusion in the deed for each lot of the tract.

COVENANTS AND CONDITIONS CONSTRUED

Covenants and conditions differ in two material respects: first, in regard to the relief afforded; and second, as to the persons by or against whom they may be enforced. Since a failure to comply with a condition may result in a loss of title, which is a harsh result, the courts will construe the restrictive provisions of a deed as covenants only, unless the intent to create a condition is plainly expressed. The mere use of the words "condition" or "covenant" is not always controlling; the real test is whether the intention is expressed clearly that the enjoyment of the estate conveyed is dependent upon the performance of the condition specified, otherwise the limitation in use will be construed as a covenant only.

CREATION OF COVENANT

A covenant may be created by a deed as follows: *A*, the owner of adjoining lots 1 and 2, conveys lot 2 to *B* upon *B*'s agreement, contained in the deed, that he will not keep horses on any part of lot 2. If *B* breaches the agreement, *A* may sue *B* for damages or bring an action in equity to enjoin the violation.

CREATION OF CONDITION

A condition may be created by deed as follows: *C* conveys land to *D* upon the express condition that *D* will not sell intoxicating liquors thereon, and further providing "that a breach of the foregoing condition shall cause said premises to revert to the grantor, his heirs, successors or assigns, who shall have the right of immediate reentry upon said premises in the event of such a breach." If *D* breaches the condition, *C* may bring an action against *D* to have the title revert to *C*.

WHEN A COVENANT WILL BE IMPLIED

A deed, as in the first illustration, merely reciting that it is given upon the agreement of the grantee to do or not to do certain things, implies a covenant only and not a condition. Also, a recital in a deed that the land conveyed is or is not to be used for certain purposes, such as a clause "to be used for church purposes," or "that a schoolhouse be erected thereon," implies a covenant rather than a condition.

IMPLIED REVERSIONS

Although an express reentry or forfeiture clause is not essential if a condition in a deed is clearly expressed, it is the better practice to include such a clause, so the intention will be plain. If the deed does not contain such a clause, but it is clear that a condition was created, the deed will be construed as containing an implied reversion.

VALIDITY OF RESTRICTIONS

Regarding the legality of restrictions, it is a general rule that an owner of land can dispose of it as he sees fit, imposing such restrictions as he chooses, this right being limited, however, to the extent that the restrictions must not be unlawful or contrary to public policy. A condition in a deed that the grantee shall not marry is void, but a condition under which a party is to enjoy the use of property until he or she marries is not invalid.

Invalid restrictions. A restriction is invalid if it is repugnant to the estate granted, such as a restriction, in a conveyance of the fee, against alienation of the land to persons of a specified race or class, or against a sale of the land by the grantee without the grantor's consent or at a price to be fixed by the grantor. A restriction is void if it calls for the commission of an unlawful act or an illegal use of the land, such as the commission of a crime or the use of the land for immoral purposes.

Other types of invalid restrictions. A restriction that is unreasonable or capricious and not calculated to benefit any individual, such as a condition that there shall be no windows in a house to be constructed on the property, is of no effect. Although a grantor may lawfully impose restrictions forbidding certain types of activity on the property conveyed, such as a restriction against the sale of intoxicating liquors, such a restriction is void if the grantor imposed it solely for the purpose of reserving to himself a monopoly of such business. (*Burdell* v. *Grandi,* 152 Cal. 376.) A restriction is invalid if it is impossible of performance when created, such as a condition that title shall revert to the grantor if the grantee does not construct a perpetual motion machine within five years.

Conditions precedent. If the condition that is impossible of performance is a condition precedent, i.e., a condition that must be performed before title vests in the grantee, the condition is not void, but operates to prevent the estate from vesting in the grantee. (*City of Stockton* v. *Weber,* 98 Cal. 433.) In the other situations mentioned, where the condition is invalid, title nonetheless passes to the grantee, free of the restriction.

Effect of invalidity. Even though a restriction imposed in a deed may appear to be void because unlawful or contrary to public policy, the effect of such a restriction is generally shown for title insurance purposes since it is a matter of record, and generally can be eliminated only by a quitclaim deed from the grantor or a decree quieting title.

RACIAL RESTRICTIONS

The enforcement of racial restrictions has been the subject of considerable litigation. Although it was determined by the courts in this state that restrictions against the *sale* of property to persons not of the Caucasian race were void as an unlawful restraint on alienation, no such decision was made with respect to restrictions that limited *occupancy and use,* and the latter types of racial restrictions were for a number of years considered to be valid and enforceable. (*Los Angeles Investment Co.* v. *Gary,* 181 Cal. 680.)

Racial restrictions unenforceable. In 1948 the Supreme Court of the United States held that race restrictions were unenforceable. In its decision the Court declared that the judicial enforcement by state courts of covenants restricting the use or occupancy of real property to persons of the Caucasian race violated the equal protection clause of the Fourteenth Amendment. (*Shelley* v. *Kraemer,* cited on p. 12) Following the decision in that case, the California courts have uniformly held that state court injunctive enforcement of a private racial restrictive covenant or condition as to occupancy of land is state action that denies persons of the excluded race their right to equal protection of the laws, and therefore violates the Fourteenth Amendment. (*Coleman* v. *Stewart*, 33 Cal.2d 703.)

Damages not recoverable for breach of racial restriction. Heretofore the courts have declared that such a covenant is not itself invalid; no one would be punished for making it, and no one's constitutional rights are violated by the covenantor's voluntary adherence thereto, inasmuch as such voluntary adherence would constitute individual action only, as distinguished from state action. In a case decided in 1953 it was held that a property owner who is entitled to the benefit of a covenant restricting the use of land to Caucasians cannot recover damages from a vendor who sells real property subject to the restriction to a Negro purchaser, since an award of damages would result in the judicial enforcement of a discriminatory covenant by state action in violation of the equal protection clause of the Fourteenth Amendment. (*Barrows* v. *Jackson*, 112 C.A.2d 534; *affirmed* by the United States Supreme Court, 346 U.S. 249.)

Open-Housing Law. In April 1968 Congress enacted the Civil Rights Act of 1968 containing broad fair housing provisions. (Public Law 90–284.) As expressed in the Act, it is the policy of the United States to provide, within constitutional limitations, for fair housing throughout the United States. It affects all those connected with residential real estate—brokers, builders, lenders, buyers, sellers, and investors. It became effective on the date of enactment (April 11, 1968) and banned discrimination because of race, color, religion, or national origin, in the sale or rental of housing insured or guaranteed by the federal government and certain other housing. Effective January 1, 1969, the ban applies to all dwelling units, no matter how financed, with two exceptions: (a) single family houses, provided the owner does not own more than three single-family houses at one time, and (b) one-to-four family dwellings if the owner occupies one of the units. Banks, savings and loan associations, and other lenders are forbidden to discriminate in making loans on apartment buildings or houses, whether for purchase, repair, or construction. Also forbidden is discrimination in setting the terms of the loans. Also, real estate organizations and multiple listing services cannot discriminate in their membership rules.

Effective January 1, 1970, the single-family homes will no longer get an exemption if they are sold or rented through a real estate broker or his agent. In other words, under the Act, the owner is permitted to choose any buyer he wishes only if he sells or rents the house himself. In addition, the owner loses his exemption if his advertising of the home for sale or rent has any discriminatory words or references.

The sale of vacant land is also covered if the land is offered for sale or lease for the construction of a dwelling.

The impact of a 1968 decision of the United States Supreme Court will need to be considered in any subsequent litigation relating to the Civil Rights Act of 1968. This is the case of *Jones* v. *Mayer Co.*, 20 L.Ed.2d 1189 decided on June 17, 1968, shortly after the new federal law was passed. An effect of the decision may be to eliminate the exemptions from the Act as they relate to racial discrimination. In that case the plaintiff, suing for injunctive and other relief in the United States District Court for the Eastern District of Missouri, alleged that defendants had refused to sell him a home solely because he was a Negro, and that such refusal violated the provisions of an 1866 federal statute (42 U.S.C., Sec. 1982) that all citizens shall have the same rights as are enjoyed by white citizens to purchase real property. The District Court denied relief and the Court of Appeals for the Eighth Circuit affirmed, holding that Section 1982 applied only to state action and did not reach private refusals to sell.

On certiorari, the Supreme Court reversed, holding that Section 1982 was intended to bar all racial discrimination, private as well as public, in the sale or rental of property, and that the statute, thus construed, was a valid exercise of the power of Congress to enforce the Thirteenth Amendment prohibiting slavery and involuntary servitude.

The court held that the 1866 statute stands independently of the Civil Rights Act of 1968, and it cannot be assumed that Congress, in enacting the 1968 Act, intended to effect any change, either substantive or procedural, in the prior statute.

It was pointed out in the decision that the 1866 Act was not a comprehensive open housing law. In sharp contrast to the Fair Housing provisions of the 1968 Act, the 1866 statute deals only with racial discrimination and does not address itself to discrimination on the grounds of religion or national origin, nor does it deal with many other facets of a comprehensive open housing law. The court stated that the enactment of the 1968 Act had no effect upon the 1866 Act, and no effect upon this litigation, but it underscored the vast difference between, on the one hand, a general statute applicable only to racial discrimination in the rental and sale of property and enforceable only by private parties acting on their own initiative and, on the other hand, a detailed housing law, applicable to a broad range of discriminating practices and enforceable "by a complete arsenal of federal authority."

Race restrictions void in California. Section 782 of the Civil Code, added in 1961, provides that any provision in any deed of real property in California, whether executed before or after the effective date of the new act, which purports to restrict the right of any person to sell, lease, rent, use, or occupy the property to persons of a particular racial, national, or ethnic group by providing for payment of a penalty, forfeiture, reverter, or otherwise, is void. Section 53 was also added to the Civil Code with comparable provisions.

FHA and VA regulations re racial restrictions. On and after February 15, 1950, the insurance by the Federal Housing Administration or by the Veterans Administration of loans secured by mortgages or deeds of trust was made subject to regulations designed to discourage the practice of restricting real property against sale or occupancy on the ground of race, color, or creed.

Title company practices. It has been the practice of title companies to show race restrictions as an encumbrance affecting the property, but insurance against loss or damage resulting from the judicial enforcement of such restrictions could be given. However, if they are the only restrictions, they can be omitted from a report or policy of title insurance.

III. Covenants

A covenant is defined as a promise respecting the use of land. The party making the promise is the *covenantor;* the one to whom the promise is made is the *covenantee.* A covenant is binding on the covenantor and persons who may assume his obligations; it benefits the covenantee and persons to whom the benefits may be assigned. The original parties, or their assigns, are said to be "in privity of contract," and their rights and obligations arise out of the contractual relationship. If the covenant is breached, the legal remedy of the persons entitled to enforce it is an action for damages (money), or where the circumstances justify equitable relief, an injunction may be granted by the court to restrain or prevent the violation.

RIGHTS OF ASSIGNEE OF COVENANTEE

The case of *Pedro* v. *County of Humboldt,* 217 Cal. 493, is illustrative of the rights of the assignee of a covenantee. In that case, *A,* the owner of Blackacre, conveyed a 40-foot strip to the county for road purposes. The deed contained a provision as follows: "It is understood and agreed that the grantee is to maintain and keep open a ditch along the east side of said right of way." *A* conveyed the remaining portion of Blackacre to *B,* and expressly assigned the benefit of the covenant to *B.* The county breached the covenant, whereupon *B* sued the county for damages. The county contended that the covenant was personal in favor of *A,* but the court held that *B* was entitled to enforce the covenant as assignee of the covenantee.

OBLIGATIONS OF ASSIGNEE OF COVENANTOR

Another problem arises where the covenantor conveys the property to a third party who does not expressly assume the obligations of the covenant. Can the original grantor or his successor enforce the burdensome covenant as against the successor to the interest of the covenantor? Or suppose it is *A*, the grantor, who makes a promise for the benefit of the land conveyed to *B*—a promise to refrain from a particular use of adjoining land owned by *A*, for instance—and then *A* conveys his remaining land to *C*. Can *B* enforce the covenant as against *C* as successor to the covenantor?

ENFORCEMENT AGAINST SUBSEQUENT PARTIES

As a general rule, a transferee or successor to the estate or interest in land of one of the original parties to a covenant is not bound by the covenant nor entitled to its benefits unless the covenant meets the legal requirements for "a covenant running with the land," or unless the covenant is construed to create a lien upon or an easement in the land. Also, an exception may be applied where the covenant is enforceable on equitable grounds.

COVENANTS RUNNING WITH THE LAND

The Civil Code provides in effect that the only covenants contained in a grant of an estate in real property that run with the land are those which are made for the *direct benefit of the land.* (C.C., Secs. 1461 and 1462.) This rule carries out the policy favoring free use and alienability of land. Thus, where the fee title to land is conveyed subject to a covenant by the grantee restricting the use of the land, the burden of the covenant does not run with the land so as to bind transferees of the grantee. The case of *Marra* v. *Aetna Construction Co.*, 15 Cal.2d 375, is illustrative of this rule. *A* conveyed Blackacre to *B* by a deed which recited that *B* agreed that for a period of forty years no structure other than a one-family residence costing at least $8,000 would be built on the land, which provision was recited to be a "covenant running with the land," and at all times binding on *B*, his successors and assigns. *B* thereafter conveyed Blackacre to *C*. It was held that the covenant, being one that burdened but did not benefit Blackacre, was not enforceable at law against *C*. Such covenants may, however, be enforceable in equity against successors of the covenantor, depending upon special circumstances.

COVENANTS CREATED BY AGREEMENT

Under the provisions of Section 1468 of the Civil Code, as originally enacted, two landowners by agreement (as distinguished from a grant in a deed) may create burdens on land by covenants that will run with the land so as to bind subsequent grantees. This section was amended in 1968 to provide that covenants between landowners and covenants by a grantor with his grantee to do or to refrain from doing some act on his own land, and which is expressed to benefit the land of the covenantee, may run with the land owned by the covenantor and the land owned by or granted to the covenantee, provided that the requirements of said Section are complied with.

COVENANTS CREATING EASEMENTS

A covenant, although lacking the technical requirements for a covenant running with the land, may be given effect as creating a lien upon or an easement in land, which lien or easement can be enforced against the land in the hands of subsequent grantees. The case of *Relovich* v. *Stuart*, cited on p. 49, is illustrative of this principle. *A*, the owner of Blackacre, conveyed a portion to *B* and agreed to furnish water for irrigation of *B*'s land from the water system on *A*'s remaining land. *A* conveyed the remaining portion of Blackacre to *C*, a purchaser with notice of the agreement to supply water. It was held that *A*'s covenant in effect created an easement appurtenant to *B*'s land and constituted a servitude binding on *A*'s successor.

EQUITABLE SERVITUDES

Although a covenant may not fulfill the technical requirements of a covenant running with the land or may not in effect create a lien or legal easement, it may still be binding on successors of the covenantor under recognized rules of equity. A burden created in such manner is referred to as an "equitable servitude" or "equitable easement." The principle is expressed in the case of *Richardson* v. *Callahan*, 213 Cal. 683, as follows:

> The marked tendency of our decisions seems to be to disregard the question of whether the covenant does or does not run with the land and to place the conclusion upon the broad ground that the assignee took with knowledge of the covenant and it was of such nature that when the intention of the parties coupled with the result of a failure to enforce it was considered, equity could not in conscience withhold relief.

IV. Conditions

As noted, restrictions upon the use of land may also be imposed by conditions subsequent, which are often employed as a means of restricting the use of land in preference to a covenant, presumably because the harsh penalty exacted for a breach, i.e., loss of title, is thought to have a greater tendency to promote observance of the restrictions imposed by a condition.

CHARACTERISTICS OF A CONDITION

A condition is distinguished from a covenant in the following way: (1) a covenant may be created by an agreement, but a condition can only be imposed as a qualification of an estate granted in a conveyance; (2) upon breach of a covenant, the remedy is an action for damages or injunctive relief, whereas the consequences of a breach of a condition may be reversion of the title to the land to the creator of the condition; (3) a covenant does not bind successors in the ownership of the restricted land unless it is a covenant running with the land or otherwise regarded as binding, whereas a condition runs with the land restricted regardless of circumstances; a breach by a subsequent owner will empower the grantor or his successors to terminate the estate.

REVERSION OF TITLE

A breach of a condition subsequent does not automatically effect a reversion of title. If the grantor who imposed the condition or his successor desires to exercise the power to terminate the estate, he must take proper steps to effect a forfeiture of the title. An action to quiet title against the grantee or his successors is an appropriate type of proceedings. In such action all other persons having liens or other interests in the land subsequent to the creation of the condition are named as defendants.

FORFEITURES NOT FAVORED

The law does not favor forfeitures of title, and in most cases the courts have strictly construed a condition subsequent in order to prevent a forfeiture. However, where the language of the deed, construed in the light of the surrounding circumstances and of the valid purpose for which the restrictions were imposed, is clear and unambiguous, the courts in many cases have enforced provisions for forfeiture of title when a breach of condition has occurred.

LIEN SUBORDINATION CLAUSES

When the grantor or his successor properly terminates the estate granted for breach of condition, title revests in him free from all rights, interests, and liens suffered or created by owners of the land after the creation of the condition, other than such paramount liens as taxes and assessments, unless the deed provides otherwise. Because of the drastic results that might occur, most lenders refuse to make loans to be secured by liens on land subject to a condition subsequent unless the deed imposing the condition contains a "lien subordination" clause, preserving the lien of a lender in good faith and for value from the effect of any future reversion. It is common practice, then, for the instrument creating the condition to include a clause such as the following:

> Provided, also, that a breach of any of the foregoing conditions, or any reentry by reason of such breach, shall not defeat or render invalid the lien of any mortgage or deed of trust made in good faith and for value as to said property or any part thereof; but said conditions shall be binding upon and effective against any owner of said property whose title is acquired by foreclosure, trustee's sale, or otherwise.

V. General plan restrictions

Modern subdivisions generally establish uniform restrictions as to the use and occupancy of all the lots and as to the character, cost, and location of structures to be built on the lots. It is desirable that each lot owner be able to protect his investment by having the power to enforce the restrictions as against every other lot owner in the tract. A deed from an owner imposing conditions or covenants in favor of the grantor does not give the grantee any right recognized at law to enforce the restrictions as against other land owned by the grantor or conveyed to other owners. But if the deeds from the subdivider properly express an intention that the tract restrictions are for the benefit of all lot owners, the restrictions then become enforceable by the grantees as between themselves.

SUBDIVISION RESTRICTIONS

Most subdivision restrictions today are drafted in the form of covenants and conditions that are enforceable by the grantor and by all of the purchasers of lots in the subdivision as between themselves. These are known as general plan restrictions, as distinguished from single plan restrictions. The latter are in favor of the grantor alone or his successors, and are not for the benefit of other lot owners.

CREATION OF GENERAL PLAN RESTRICTIONS

The intention to create general plan restrictions must be expressed in the first deed of each lot in the tract. The existence of surrounding circumstances showing that the grantor actually intended the restrictions to be for the benefit of all lot owners is sufficient in some jurisdictions, but not in California. And the first deed of each lot must expressly declare that the restrictions are for the benefit of lots in a designated area. (*Werner* v. *Graham,* 181 Cal. 174; *Martin* v. *Ray,* 76 C.A.2d 471.)

RIGHTS ACQUIRED UNDER GENERAL PLAN RESTRICTIONS

The mutual servitudes created by general plan restrictions spring into existence at the time of the first conveyance by the tract owner. The grantee at that time acquires the right to enforce the restrictions against the grantor's remaining lots and the purchasers to whom the grantor later conveys such lots, and the grantee takes title to his lot subject to the right of enforcement in favor of the grantor and the subsequent purchasers.

WHEN ENFORCEMENT MAY BE DENIED

If some of the deeds of lots in a tract are silent as to restrictions, or if some deeds contain restrictions that differ in many respects from the restrictions contained in other deeds, such circumstances may be considered as showing a lack of a sufficiently uniform scheme of improvement to justify enforcement between the lot owners.

DECLARATION OF COVENANTS, CONDITIONS, AND RESTRICTIONS

When a new subdivision map is recorded, the procedure is often followed of recording a "Declaration of Covenants, Conditions, and Restrictions" prior to the first deed out, and thereafter incorporating these restrictions in each of the deeds in language substantially as follows:

> This deed is made and accepted upon the covenants and conditions set forth in "Declaration of Establishment of Restrictions" recorded [recording reference], all of which are incorporated herein by reference to said declaration with the same effect as though fully set forth herein.

Deed provisions. This practice has the advantages of reducing the recording fee for each deed and assuring that the restrictions in the deeds will be uniform. The deeds should use language specifically incorporating the recorded restrictions; the mere use of the words "subject to covenants, conditions and restrictions," may be considered to be insufficient. The latter statement may be construed as no more than a recital of what the tract owner intends, and is not of itself an operative act of imposition of restrictions. The deed is the "final and exclusive memorial" of the rights of the parties. (*Beran* v. *Harris,* 91 C.A.2d 562.)

NECESSITY OF INCORPORATING RESTRICTIONS IN DEED

The case of *Murry* v. *Lovell,* 132 C.A.2d 30, illustrates the importance of incorporating restrictions in a deed. In that case an action was brought against the owners of a lot in a subdivision to enjoin them from violating certain use restrictions. Plaintiff and defendants were the owners of adjoining lots in the subdivision and claimed under a common grantor. Certain restrictions stated as to all lots in the subdivision that "no noxious or offensive trade or activity shall be carried on upon any lot, nor shall anything be done thereon which may be or become an annoyance or nuisance to the neighborhood." When the defendants began conducting a trucking business upon their lot and on an adjacent lot, the noise was found to be offensive, and this action was brought.

The facts in the above case disclosed that the original subdivider had prepared a map of the subdivision and recorded it, and at the same time recorded a document that described the entire parcel, and recited that the owners were declaring and establishing restrictions upon the property and each part thereof. The document contained a list of the use restrictions, including the one quoted above. It stated that the tract should be known as a residential tract, prescribed limitations upon the type of residences that could be built, and upon the location of such residences upon the lots with respect to front and side lines. It appeared that the owners had in mind a uniform plan of restrictions. When the lots were sold, the seller told the buyers about the restrictions and read to them a copy of the restrictions. However, the deeds did not incorporate the restrictions. The trial court rendered judgment in favor of the plaintiff, enjoining the defendants from violating the restrictions. The defendants appealed and the appellate court reversed the trial court, holding that it was essential to incorporate the restrictions in the deed, by reference or otherwise, and this not being done, the restrictions sought to be imposed were therefore not enforceable.

VARIATIONS PERMITTED

Although a general plan restriction implies uniformity, some variation is permissible. There must, of course, be a general plan of restrictions imposed upon all of the lots in the tract, but it is not essential that all lots be restricted to the same uses or that all lot owners be given rights of enforcement as to each and every lot. The restrictive plan may provide that certain designated lots shall be used for residential purposes, and other lots for business purposes. Rights of enforcement with respect to violations of restrictions in a specified area may be limited to the owners of lots in such area, e.g., a specified block in the tract. Or the right to enforce restrictions as to any particular lot in the tract may be limited to the owners of lots immediately adjoining.

WAIVER BY LESS THAN ALL LOT OWNERS

The right to waive, modify, or cancel the restrictions may be conferred on less than all of the lot owners, for instance, a stated percentage of the owners, or the owners in a specified area. And a provision giving the grantor alone the right to modify the restrictions at any time may not in itself defeat the restrictive plan, although the exercise of such right might render the original restrictions unenforceable as between the lot owners. (*Burkhardt* v. *Lofton,* 63 C.A.2d 230.)

CONDOMINIUM REQUIREMENTS

The Condominium Act requires that, prior to the conveyance of any condominium, a declaration of restrictions relating to the project must be recorded. Although considerable latitude in the selection of appropriate language is permitted, the Act also establishes certain rights, benefits, and easements as statutory matters for the benefit and protection of all of the condominium owners. The Act provides that such restrictions shall be enforceable equitable servitudes and shall inure to and bind all owners of condominiums in the project.

VI. Interpretation of particular restrictions

Problems of interpretation of the exact meaning of provisions contained in deed restrictions have often arisen. They illustrate the importance of using precise language in order that the intent and purpose of deed restrictions be fully accomplished.

RESIDENTIAL PURPOSES

A restriction that land "shall be used for residential purposes only" relates to the use or mode of occupancy to which a building may be put, and not to a type of building. Thus, the restriction does not prohibit the construction of an apartment house, duplex, flat, or any building used for residential purposes only, whether occupied by one family or a number of families. On the other hand, a restriction providing that "no buildings other than a first-class private residence shall be built" on the land relates to the type of structure and excludes any multiple residence as well as any business structure.

GARAGES AND OUTBUILDINGS

A restriction limiting the use of land to "residential purposes," or prohibiting the erection of any structure other than "a residence" or "dwelling house," does not, as a rule, prohibit the erection of a private garage, whether or not attached to the main residence. Where the restrictions provide that outbuildings must be in the rear of the premises or located on a specified portion of the lot, it is probable that a garage constructed as an integral part of a residence and in architectural harmony therewith is not an outbuilding, and would not violate the restriction. In the case of *Howard Homes, Inc.* v. *Guttman,* 190 C.A.2d 526, it was held that a pad on which a house was to be built, consisting of 20,000 cubic yards of dirt, was not a "structure" separate from the house within a deed provision restricting construction to two one-story houses and garages and prohibiting "other structures." It was further held that the restriction did not require the buildings to be erected on the existing grade, slope, or level.

FRONT LINE PROVISIONS

The application to a corner lot of a restriction that a building shall "face the front line," or shall be not nearer than a specified distance from the "front line," frequently involves the question of which is the front and which is the side of the lot. Restrictions that regulate the distance at which buildings shall be placed from the street or property lines, which restrictions are intended to secure unobstructed light, air, and vision for the benefit of adjoining lots and to preserve uniformity in the appearance of a tract, involve a problem as to what is meant by the term "building," and whether or not it includes eaves, steps, bay windows, awnings, and so forth.

USE OF THE WORD "STREET"

Where the restriction prohibits the construction of a building within a specified distance from a "street," a problem arises in the event the line of the street is changed by widening of the street. It is probable that the line of the street as it exists at the date of the imposition of restrictions fixes the point.

COST OF BUILDINGS

Restrictions against buildings costing less than a specified minimum price are enforceable, but where such restrictions are imposed in terms of fixed amounts without regard to the fluctuating purchasing power of the dollar, the purpose may be defeated. Thus, a $10,000 cost restriction imposed in 1930 would be complied with in 1955 by the construction of a residence far below the standard of a residence built at the date of the deed—a technical but not a realistic compliance.

APPROVAL OF PLANS AND SPECIFICATIONS

Most modern tract restrictions provide that no structure shall be erected until the plans and specifications have been approved by an individual, usually the tract owner who imposed the restrictions, or by a group of persons, such as an architectural committee composed of representatives of the lot owners. Enforcement of such restriction is permitted where the refusal to approve plans is a reasonable determination made in good faith. (*Hannula* v. *Hacienda Homes, Inc.*, 34 Cal.2d 442.) Where the architectural committee has ceased to function or cannot be located, the lack of approval of plans by the committee may be unobjectionable if the improvements in fact comply with the restrictions in all other respects and are in harmony with other improvements in the tract.

VII. Termination of restrictions

Restrictions may be terminated in the following ways: (1) expiration of their prescribed period of duration; (2) voluntary cancellation; (3) merger of ownership; (4) change of conditions or other circumstances that cause the courts to deny enforcement; and (5) act of public authorities.

EXPIRATION DATE

Instruments creating restrictions usually provide for a date on which the restrictions will automatically expire. An expiration date is not essential, however, and there is no statutory provision limiting the duration of restrictions. Where the duration is not expressly limited by the parties, it will usually be implied that the duration is such period as is reasonable under the particular circumstances.

VOLUNTARY CANCELLATION OR MODIFICATION

A covenant or condition may be modified, waived, or released by mutual agreement between the parties affected, or by an instrument, such as a quitclaim deed, executed by the party entitled to enforce the restriction. Where general plan restrictions are involved, the necessary parties to a completely effective modification or cancellation of the restrictions are all parties having a right to enforce the restrictions as to the land in question, which usually are all of the lot owners in the tract. The restrictions may provide for a right of cancellation by less than all, however, and if the terms of the instrument establishing tract restrictions provide for modification or abrogation of the restrictions by specified persons or in a specified manner, such provisions are controlling. (*Sharp* v. *Quinn*, 214 Cal. 194.)

Effect of general plan restrictions on voluntary cancellation. General plan restrictions often create two separate rights that may be enforced independently. Thus, where *A*, the tract owner, conveys all lots in the tract by general plan deeds that impose covenants and conditions giving a right of reentry to the grantor for breach of conditions, and mutual rights of enforcement in favor of all lot owners, *A*, as owner of the right of reentry, is the only person who can forfeit the title, but each of the lot owners has a right to enjoin a violation. The rights of *A* and of the lot owners are independent; either may enforce or release the restrictions as to his interest without affecting the legal rights of the other. A complete cancellation and termination of the restrictions can be accomplished by unison of action by all of these holders of the right of enforcement.

TERMINATION BY MERGER

Termination by merger is effected when the ownership of the land benefited by a covenant and the ownership of the land burdened by the covenant come into a single ownership. Where restrictions have been extinguished by merger, they do not revive upon a subsequent severance of ownership. If the restrictions are to be effective upon a subsequent severance of ownership, they must be newly created. Merger also results where the grantor in a deed containing a condition subsequent reacquires the ownership of the restricted land. However, merger of the right of reentry with the ownership of a parcel of land that is subject also to a general plan of restrictions will not affect the rights existing in favor of the other lot owners.

ENFORCEMENT MAY BE DENIED ON EQUITABLE PRINCIPLES

Courts sometimes will deny enforcement of restrictions on the ground that it would be inequitable or oppressive under the circumstances to give effect to the restrictions. Change in the character of the neighborhood; acts indicating an abandonment of the right of enforcement; prior violation of the restrictions by the party presently seeking to enforce the restriction—these and other circumstances may present hardships or unfairness that would justify denial of enforcement in a court of equity. Not only are equitable defenses available to the lot owner against whom enforcement of the restrictions is sought, but in a proper case the lot owner may obtain affirmative relief in an action for a declaration of rights and to quiet title as against persons claiming a right of enforcement. (*Downs* v. *Kroeger*, 200 Cal. 743.)

Effect of violations by party seeking enforcement. It appears to be well settled that an owner cannot enforce general plan restrictions if he himself is guilty of a substantial breach of the same restrictions. The breach must have been something more than trivial; it must be sufficiently material and of an adverse effect on the purposes sought to be achieved by the restriction. Thus, an owner who builds a few inches beyond the prescribed setback line may not be precluded from enjoining another lot owner from building several feet beyond the line. And a previous violation by the complaining party of one type of restriction will not necessarily preclude him from seeking relief to compel the observance of another restriction that is beneficial to his property. Thus, a violation of setback lines will not estop the party from obtaining enforcement of another restriction limiting structures to private residences. (*Robertson* v. *Nichols*, 92 C.A.2d 201.)

Effect of acquiescence in violation. Acquiescence by the complainant, whether he is the common grantor or an individual lot owner, in a substantial violation of general plan restrictions by one or more lot owners may preclude him from enforcing the restrictions as against others. But the complainant's failure to object to minor violations, or to violations of which he has no actual knowledge or that do not affect or injure him, such as a violation in a distant part of the tract, does not prevent him from objecting to violations that do cause him to be damaged. Also, acquiescence in the violation of one of several restrictions does not necessarily operate as a waiver of the right to object to a violation of other separate and distinct restrictions that are material and beneficial to him.

Where uniform observance is lacking. The rule is set forth in the case of *Bryant* v. *Whitney*, 178 Cal. 640, that where there has been no uniform observance of a general plan of restrictions, and substantially all of the owners have so conducted themselves as to indicate an abandonment of the right to have the tract kept to the standard established by the original plan, and where enforcement will not tend materially to restore to the tract the character imposed upon it by the general scheme, and the infraction complained of does not diminish the value of other estates, then it will be deemed to be inequitable and oppressive to compel at considerable loss compliance with the restrictions by another owner.

Time limitations on right of enforcement. The law does not look with favor upon persons who sleep on their rights. A failure to proceed with reasonable promptness to secure relief against a violation of restrictions has the effect of precluding the one guilty of such neglect from securing relief. Thus, in the case of *Hanna* v. *Rodeo-Vallejo Ferry Co.*, 89 C.A. 462, a delay of more than one year after a breach occurred, with knowledge that the owners of the restricted land were making valuable improvements thereon, was regarded as one of the factors barring relief. Apart from the period of time within which a court might hold that relief is barred because of laches or unwarranted delay in commencing an action, a statute of limitations (C.C.P., Sec. 320) bars an action for forfeiture for breach of condition unless the action is brought within five years from the time the right accrued.

Change of conditions in area. The rule as to change of conditions is frequently applied. Under this rule, injunctive relief against violation of restrictions cannot be obtained if conditions in the area have so changed since the establishment of the restrictions that it is not possible any longer to secure in a substantial degree the benefits intended to have been secured by observance of the restrictions. Forfeiture for breach of a condition may likewise be denied upon a showing of change of conditions.

Changes affecting residential and minimum area requirements. Enforcement of residential restrictions has been denied where the character of the surrounding territory has changed to a business or commercial district. (*Wolff* v. *Fallon,* 44 Cal. 2d 695.) And restrictions in the minimum area of parcels in a subdivision, often an acre or more, imposed twenty or twenty-five years ago when land was more plentiful, have been held unenforceable based on changed conditions. (*Hirsch* v. *Hancock,* 173 C.A.2d 745; *Key* v. *McCabe,* 54 Cal.2d 736.) The principle is stated in the case of *Hurd* v. *Albert,* 214 Cal. 15, as follows:

> Equity courts will not enforce restrictive covenants by injunction in a case where, by reason of a change in the character of the surrounding neighborhood, not resulting from a breach of the covenants, it would be oppressive and inequitable to give the restriction effect, as when the enforcement of the covenant would have no other result than to harass or injure the defendant, without benefiting the plaintiff.

When denial of enforcement is not warranted. The fact alone that the land subject to the restriction would be more valuable if used for a purpose not permitted, such as a use for business instead of residential purposes, does not warrant denial of enforcement where the original purpose of the restrictions can yet be realized.

Change of zoning. Although change of zoning by the city is not decisive, it has been recognized in many cases as evidence. (*Bard* v. *Rose,* 203 C.A.2d 232.) Also, some courts have declined to grant relief based upon a change in the neighborhood unless zoning ordinances permit the contemplated use.

ACTS OF PUBLIC AUTHORITIES

Lands acquired for public uses are released from private restrictions at least during the time the property is in public ownership. The state or any of its subdivisions may acquire land for public purposes by gift, purchase, or condemnation, and use it in violation of restrictions that are inconsistent with use for the public purpose. Thus, land restricted to residence has been acquired by school districts for school and playground purposes, free of the restriction. (*Sackett* v. *Los Angeles City School District,* 118 C.A. 254.)

Condemnation of land subject to condition subsequent. Where land that is subject to a condition subsequent is taken by condemnation prior to a breach of the conditions or even after a breach but prior to the exercise of the right to forfeit, the owner of the reversionary interest is not entitled to compensation, unless the owner of the right of re-entry has a special value in the land, as where the lands are shown to be mineral bearing or otherwise of value separate from the surface use of the land.

Effect of zoning ordinances. As a general rule, zoning ordinances do not affect private restrictions, and both may be effective with respect to the same land at the same time, with the private restrictions usually imposing additional limitations in the use. (*Wilkman* v. *Banks,* 124 C.A.2d 451.) However, where the private restrictions permit a use forbidden by zoning regulations, the latter will control.

EFFECT OF FORECLOSURE OF A LIEN

As a general rule, the foreclosure of a lien that is superior to the burden of restrictions will eliminate the restrictions. If the restrictions are part of a general plan, and only some of the restricted lots are released from a prior lien, the effect of the foreclosure as to the remaning lots is somewhat uncertain. There is no California case directly in point, but in other jurisdictions it has been held that if through foreclosure under a prior lien, portions of the tract subject to the general plan of restrictions are sold free thereof, and if the effect of such sale is to render the enforcement of the restrictions unjust or inequitable as to the remainder of the tract, the restrictions will not be enforced as between the owners of such remaining portion.

Questions

1. Discuss briefly the meaning of the phrase "covenants, conditions, and restrictions."
2. Distinguish between a "covenant" and a "condition."
3. In what manner are restrictions customarily created?
4. May a landowner impose any type of restriction he chooses?
5. List various types of restrictions that are considered valid.
6. How are covenants enforced?
7. Explain the meaning of the phrase "covenant running with the land."
8. May a successor in interest enforce a condition?
9. Describe the characteristics of a general plan restriction.
10. Who has a right to enforce general plan restrictions?
11. How is the following phrase interpreted: "used for residential purposes only"?
12. Describe five ways that restrictions may be terminated.
13. Does the foreclosure of a deed of trust have any effect on deed restrictions?
14. Do zoning ordinances supersede deed restrictions?

18

Zoning Ordinances

Summary

I. Nature and purpose of zoning
Types of zoning; Historical background; Constitutional provisions as basis for zoning; Statutory authority for zoning; Charter provisions; Master plans for zoning; Scope of city planning; Justification for zoning

II. Operation of zoning laws
Review by the courts; Basis for attack on zoning laws; When zoning ordinances will be held invalid; Retroactive application; Right to change zoning; Illustrative cases; Limitations on size of lots; Effect of zoning on deed restrictions; Effect of deed violating minimum area requirements

III. Spot zoning
Creation of "islands"; Zoning should attain reasonable uniformity; When spot zoning is justified; Illustrative case–spot zoning; Alteration of boundaries

VI. Nonconforming use
Elimination of nonconforming use; Discontinuance of nonconforming use; Use of amortization schemes; Prohibitions against extension of nonconforming use; Illustrative case–nonconforming use

V. Variances or exceptions
Conditions may be imposed; Procedure to obtain variances; Exceptions relating to size of lots; Variances a matter of discretion

VI. Conditional use permits
Uses of public concern

VII. Title insurance covering zoning

VIII. Other governmental regulations affecting use
Ordinances regulating construction; Building codes; Enforcement of building ordinances; State Housing Law; Restrictions on construction deemed valid; Building regulations not inconsistent with zoning; Abating nuisances; Removal of offensive matter; Encroachments on sidewalks and streets

I. Nature and purpose of zoning

Zoning is described briefly as the governmental regulation of the use of land and buildings. It consists of the division of land into areas called zones, and the designation and control of the use made of the land in each of the zones. Zoning laws are enacted in the exercise of the police power, and ordinarily they do not constitute a taking of property for public use for which compensation must be paid.

TYPES OF ZONING

Zoning is *comprehensive* where it is governed by a single plan for an entire municipality. It is *partial* or *limited* where it is applicable only to a certain part of the municipality or to certain uses. Fire, height, and building regulations are forms of partial or limited zoning, which are antecedents of modern comprehensive zoning.

HISTORICAL BACKGROUND

Partial or limited zoning and use regulations have long been governmental activities of American municipalities. Use zoning to control the location of certain industries, potentially if not actually nuisances, such as distilleries, slaughterhouses, kilns, and the like, was established in the American colonies as early as the last decade of the seventeenth century.

CONSTITUTIONAL AUTHORITY FOR ZONING

In California, local police regulations are authorized by the state constitution. Article XI, Section 11 provides that any county, city, town, or township may make and enforce within its limits all such local, police, sanitary, and other regulations as are not in conflict with general laws.

STATUTORY AUTHORITY FOR ZONING

Zoning regulations are specifically authorized by the Government Code. Section 65800 provides that pursuant to the provisions of said code, the legislative body of any county or city may by ordinance: (*a*) regulate the use of buildings, structures, and land as between agriculture, industry, business, residence, and other purposes; (*b*) regulate location, height, bulk, number of stories, and size of buildings and structures; the size of yards, courts, and other open spaces; and the percentage of a lot which may be occupied by a building or structure; (*c*) establish and maintain building setback lines along any street, highway, freeway, road, or alley; and (*d*) create civic districts around civic centers, public parks, and public buildings and grounds for the purpose of enabling a planning commission to review all plans for buildings or structures within the district prior to the issuance of a building permit in order to assure an orderly development in the vicinity of such public sites and buildings.

CHARTER PROVISIONS

Zoning may also be subject to provisions of city charters, and many cities have adopted various plans pursuant to their charters, rather than under the statutory authorization.

MASTER PLANS FOR ZONING

As elsewhere in the United States, master plans for zoning have been developed for many communities in California, covering the ultimate pattern for such things as freeways and recreational, airport, and shoreline development. These master plans—or comprehensive zoning laws—are of relatively modern origin, but their enactment has become widespread. The modern tendency is in the direction of extending the power of restriction in aid of city planning.

Comprehensive zoning plan for a city. The "Comprehensive Zoning Plan of the City of Los Angeles" is an example of a master plan for a city. Prior to June 1, 1946, the city of Los Angeles had no comprehensive zoning ordinance. There existed a series of heterogeneous zoning ordinances applicable to various parts of the municipality, which were considered as stop-gap ordinances eventually to be absorbed by a single comprehensive zoning ordinance. The first such ordinance (Ordinance No. 90500), applying to every part of the city, was adopted and became effective on June 1, 1946. The ordinance designates, regulates, and restricts the location and use of buildings, structures, and land for agriculture, residence, commerce, trade, industry, or other purposes. It regulates the height and size of buildings, regulates the open spaces, and limits the density of population. This comprehensive zoning ordinance has been held constitutional as a legitimate exercise of the police power. (*Beverly Oil Co.* v. *City of Los Angeles,* 40 Cal.2d 552; *Zahn* v. *Board of Public Works of the City of Los Angeles,* 195 Cal. 497.)

SCOPE OF CITY PLANNING

Zoning obviously is a phase of city planning. Strictly speaking, however, zoning is exclusively concerned with use regulation, whereas planning is broader and connotes a systematic development of a municipality with the purpose of promoting the common interest not only with respect to uses of land and buildings, but also with respect to other matters of general concern, such as streets, parks, residential developments, industrial and commercial enterprises, civic beauty, public convenience, and the like. Urban renewal through redevelopment projects is another phase of governmental planning designed to reclaim blighted and deteriorating areas.

JUSTIFICATION FOR ZONING

The justification for zoning ordinances is that they promote public health, safety, comfort, convenience, and general welfare. Like other laws of similar character, they must be reasonable and not discriminatory or oppressive. It has been held that a regulation for an esthetic purpose only is not a reasonable exercise of the police power. (*Varney & Green* v. *Williams,* 155 Cal. 318.) However, if it also has for its purpose the protection of the public health, safety, or welfare, incidental esthetic considerations will not cause it to be invalid. (*Brougher* v. *City and County of San Francisco,* 107 C.A. 15.)

II. Operation of zoning laws

As noted previously, the power of a municipality to enact zoning ordinances is expressly authorized by statutory and charter provisions, and by the general provision contained in the state constitution. Zoning laws and ordinances, both for cities and for counties, usually provide for a zoning board or commission to administer the law, and usually require public notice for a specified length of time and the holding of a public hearing, either by the board or commission, prior to the submission of its report, or by the city council or other municipal legislative body prior to the adoption of the zoning ordinance, or a public hearing by both. Parties objecting have the right to appeal to the courts. However, every intendment is in favor of a zoning ordinance. The enactment of such an ordinance by a city is deemed to be a proper exercise of the police power and adopted to promote the public welfare. (*Willett & Crane* v. *City of Palo Verdes Estates,* 96 C.A.2d 757.)

REVIEW BY THE COURTS

When a case is taken to court, the courts will inquire as to whether or not the scheme of classification and districting under a zoning ordinance is arbitrary or unreasonable, but a decision of the zoning authorities as to matters of opinion and policy will not be set aside unless the regulations have no reasonable relation to the public welfare, or unless the physical facts show that there has been an unreasonable, oppressive, or unwarranted interference with property rights and abuse in the exercise of the police power. (*Lockard* v. *City of Los Angeles,* 33 Cal.2d 453.)

BASIS FOR ATTACK ON ZONING LAWS

The usual attack on zoning laws is on the ground of discrimination, i.e., a denial of the right of equal protection. Although occasionally an ordinance has been held void in its application to a property owner by reason of arbitrary inclusions or exclusions, in most cases it is recognized that zoning necessarily results in some inequalities, particularly to persons on the boundaries of a zoned district. However, if the general scheme is reasonable and fair, individual hardship is not a basis for a constitutional attack on the legislative or administrative determination.

WHEN ZONING ORDINANCES WILL BE HELD INVALID

The cases in which zoning ordinances have been held invalid and unreasonable as applied to particular property fall roughly into four categories: (1) where the zoning ordinance attempts to exclude and prohibit existing and established uses or businesses that are not nuisances; (2) where the restrictions create a monopoly; (3) where the use of the adjacent property renders the land entirely unsuited to or unusable for the only purpose permitted by the ordinance; and (4) where a small parcel is restricted and given less rights than the surrounding property—where, for instance, a lot or parcel in the center of a business or commercial district is limited to use for residential purposes, thereby creating an "island" in the middle of a larger area devoted to other uses. (*Wilkins* v. *City of San Bernardino,* 29 Cal.2d 332; *Kissinger* v. *City of Los Angeles,* 161 C.A.2d 454.) It has also been held that the location of school sites is not subject to municipal zoning ordinances. (*Town of Atherton* v. *Superior Court,* 159 C.A.2d 417.)

RETROACTIVE APPLICATION

Zoning ordinances have generally been prospective in their application, i.e., they have not attempted to eradicate existing nonconforming uses immediately, but have sought to eliminate them gradually by prohibiting alteration or repair of nonconforming structures. A retroactive application may render the ordinance invalid. This rule is illustrated by the case of *Jones* v. *City of Los Angeles,* 211 Cal. 304, involving the validity of an ordinance restricting sanitariums to certain districts, which ordinance was expressly made retroactive. An action was brought to enjoin its enforcement, and the court held that nonconforming uses could not be summarily eliminated by a retroactive ordinance unless the uses were such as to amount to a nuisance.

RIGHT TO CHANGE ZONING

The case of *Robinson* v. *City of Los Angeles,* 146 C.A.2d 810, involved the validity of an ordinance amending the comprehensive zoning ordinance by rezoning vacant land in San Fernando Valley for light industrial in place of agricultural uses. Objections were made by owners of other property in the area, but the amendment was held to be valid, the court pointing out that an owner has no vested right to continuity of zoning for the general area in which he may reside.

ILLUSTRATIVE CASES

In the case of *County of San Diego* v. *McClurken,* 37 Cal.2d 683, the court pointed out that a landowner's purpose in purchasing land must yield to the public interest in the enforcement of a comprehensive zoning plan. In the case of *Hart* v. *Beverly Hills,* 11 Cal.2d 343, the court upheld an ordinance prohibiting auction sales in a residential district on the theory that the assembling of curious crowds attracted by auctions furnished an opportunity for petty frauds and other crimes to be perpetrated. The case of *City of South San Francisco* v. *Berry,* 120 C.A.2d 252, presented a question relative to the effect of annexation on a zoning ordinance. It was held that where land, which was subject to a county ordinance zoning it for single-family residences was thereafter annexed by a city having no such ordinance, the land left the territorial jurisdiction of the county and thereupon ceased to be subject to its zoning ordinance and was no longer limited to single-family residences.

LIMITATIONS ON SIZE OF LOTS

An ordinance limiting the size of city lots to a minimum of 50 feet in average width and 5,000 square feet in area was held to be valid in the case of *Clemons* v. *City of Los Angeles,* 36 Cal.2d 95. However, in a later case, that of *Morris* v. *City of Los Angeles,* 116 C.A.2d 856, it was pointed out that such an ordinance may be valid in its general aspects and as to some properties, but invalid as to others, and that whether a zoning ordinance is unreasonable, arbitrary, and discriminatory is dependent upon its application to the particular property involved. In the latter case, a provision of the Municipal Code forbidding a separation in ownership of certain nonconforming lots, which were excepted from certain minimum area requirements of the code, was held to be invalid and unenforceable as to the sale of part of a lot in Brooklyn Heights, or as to the ownership of the remainder, where it appeared that the owner had done nothing out of conformity with general neighborhood conditions, where the separation of ownership would not affect the health, safety, or welfare of the community, and where the enforcement of the code provision would constitute an unreasonable oppression.

EFFECT OF ZONING OF DEED RESTRICTIONS

Deed restrictions are ordinarily not affected by zoning regulations. If a zoning law permits a use to be made of property that is restricted by construction and use limitations contained in a deed, the deed provisions will control. A zoning law cannot relieve land within the district covered by it from lawful restrictions affecting the use of the land imposed by deed or by a recorded declaration of covenants, conditions, and restrictions.

EFFECT OF DEED VIOLATING MINIMUM AREA REQUIREMENTS

If a deed is executed and delivered that is violative of a zoning ordinance prescribing a minimum area, a question arises as to the effect of such a deed and the rights of the grantee thereunder. Section 11540.1 was added to the Business and Professions Code in 1949, providing that any conveyance made contrary to the provision of an ordinance prescribing the area or dimensions of lots or parcels, or prohibiting the reduction in area or the separation in ownership of land, or requiring the filing of a map of any land to be divided, shall not be invalid, but that such ordinance may provide that any deed of conveyance, sale, or contract to sell made contrary to its provisions is voidable to the extent and in the same manner as a deed in violation of the Subdivision Map Act. Any deed of conveyance, sale, or contract to sell made contrary to the provisions of the Subdivisions Map Act is voidable at the sole option of the grantee, buyer, or person contracting to purchase, *within one year* after the date of execution of the deed, sale, or contract of sale.

III. Spot zoning

The problem of spot zoning is encountered where a large area, such as a zoning district for residential purposes, has small zones, sometimes no larger than a city lot, created within its confines permitting other uses, usually commercial in nature. By spot zoning, a specified parcel of property is thus placed in a different zone from that of neighboring property. This situation is usually accomplished by the amendment of a general zoning ordinance.

CREATION OF "ISLANDS"

Spot zoning may result in the creation of two types of "islands." The legally objectionable type arises when the zoning authority improperly limits the use that may be made of a small parcel located in the center of an unrestricted area. The second type of "island" results when most of a large district is devoted to a limited or restricted use, but additional uses are permitted in one or more "spots" in the district. The validity of the latter type is dependent upon the basis for the difference in use.

ZONING SHOULD ATTAIN REASONABLE UNIFORMITY

It is a fundamental rule that zoning in a haphazard manner is legally objectionable. The courts have often stated that zoning should proceed in accordance with a definite and reasonable policy. The legislative intention in authorizing comprehensive zoning is reasonable uniformity within districts having in fact the same general characteristics, and not the marking off of small districts for peculiar uses or restrictions when the districts are essentially similar to the general area in which they are situated. Thus, in the case of *Hamer* v. *Town of Ross,* 59 Cal.2d 776, it was held that a one-acre limitation was invalid as applied to the plaintiff, the court stating that an isolated area had thereby become an "island" of one-acre minimum lot size zoning "in a residential ocean" of substantially less restrictive zoning.

WHEN SPOT ZONING IS JUSTIFIED

Spot zoning is justified where it is in fact germane to an objective within the valid exercise of the police power; no hard and fast rule can be made that such zoning is or is not illegal. The question is dependent upon what is reasonable under all of the circumstances. The zoning of shopping and business districts at convenient places within residential districts generally is sustainable as reasonable and valid.

ILLUSTRATIVE CASE—SPOT ZONING

The case of *Wilkins* v. *City of San Bernardino,* 29 Cal.2d 332, involved a typical spot zoning situation. In that case a property owner brought an action for declaratory relief, claiming that the zoning ordinance of the city of San Bernardino was unreasonable and invalid as applied to the portion of his property that was placed in a single-family dwelling zone. The remainder of his property was located in a small business zone situated in the center of a large residential district zoned for single-family dwellings (see Fig. 18–1).

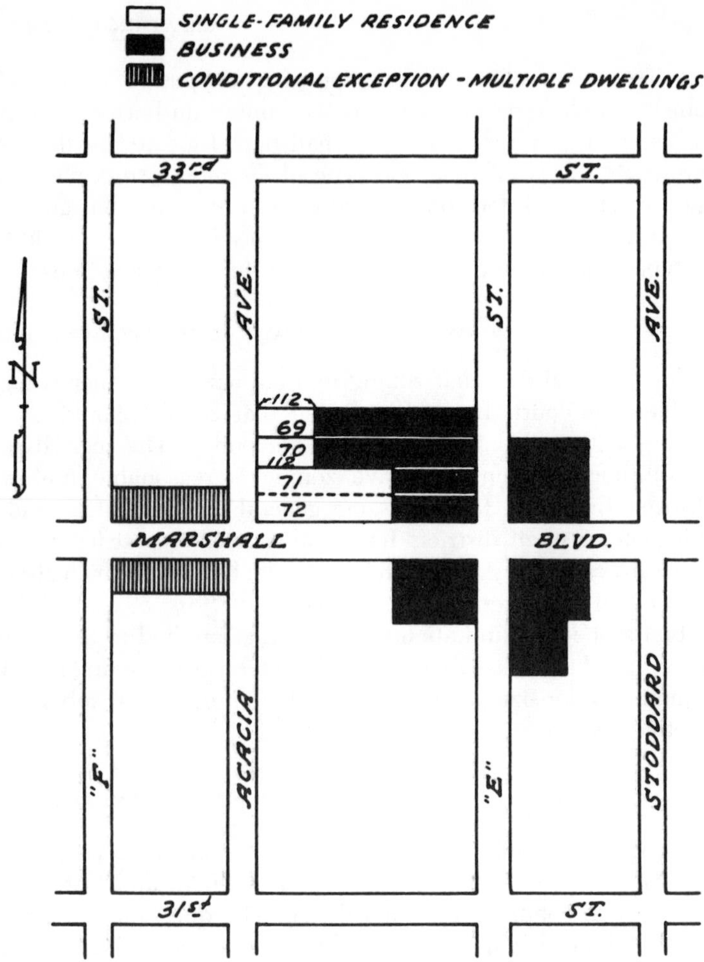

Figure 18-1

In denying relief to the plaintiff, the court stated that where a large zoning area is devoted to a limited or restricted use, but additional uses are permitted in a "spot" or an "island," it is within the discretion of the legislative body of the city to determine whether such an "island" should be enlarged. The mere fact that the owner may enjoy greater benefits, or that his property will be enhanced in value, if the size of the "island" is increased, does not give him the right to compel the allowance of such increase in size.

ALTERATION OF BOUNDARIES

The court in the above-mentioned case stated that zoning necessarily involves boundary problems, and that where spot zoning is permitted in a residential district, the legislative body must determine where the boundary is to be placed, attempting, as far as possible, to minimize the resulting inconvenience. This is essentially a legislative and not a judicial problem, and the determination may be attacked only if there is no reasonable basis for it. Often there may be little difference in the character of the property on either side of the zone line, but such a showing will not justify a judicial alteration or extension of the boundaries. If an owner could compel the extension of the boundaries of the "island" by any such showing, then the next adjoining owner in turn could likewise make the same kind of showing and obtain another extension of the "island" to his property, and in a short time there would be an end to the effectiveness of all zoning legislation.

IV. Nonconforming use

As noted previously, a comprehensive zoning ordinance places limitations upon the use of land within certain areas in accordance with a general policy that has been adopted. Such ordinances ordinarily except from their operation any existing lawful uses that are in conflict (generally referred to as nonconforming uses), primarily because of the hardship or unusual difficulties as to certain properties, and also because of the questionable constitutionality of legislation that would terminate such uses immediately. Zoning legislation looks to the future; and it may effect the eventual liquidation of nonconforming uses. As stated in the case of *Orange County* v. *Goldring*, 121 C.A.2d 442, it is the purpose of zoning to crystallize present uses and conditions and to eliminate nonconforming uses as rapidly as is consistent with proper safeguards for those affected. To this end, provisions that preclude the extension or enlargement of such uses, forbid resumption of a use when terminated, or provide a reasonable time within which the use must cease, have been sustained as a valid exercise of the police power.

ELIMINATION OF NONCONFORMING USE

When the nonconforming use relates to the existence of a type of structure, provisions that look to the elimination thereof through obsolescence or destruction have been approved. (*Rehfeld* v. *San Francisco*, 218 Cal. 83.) There is also a growing tendency to guard against the indefinite continuance of nonconforming uses by providing for their liquidation within a prescribed time. (*County of San Diego* v. *McClurken*, cited on p. 347.) The view was expressed in the case of *Consolidated Rock Prod. Co.* v. *City of Los Angeles*, 57 Cal.2d 515, that the adoption of a comprehensive plan of community development looking toward the containment and eventual elimination of nonconforming uses, including rock and gravel operations, accords with recognized zoning objectives under settled legal principles.

DISCONTINUANCE OF NONCONFORMING USE

In the case of *City of Los Angeles* v. *Gage*, 127 C.A.2d 442, it was held that a city zoning ordinance requiring the discontinuance of a nonconforming use of land in the city within a five-year period, and the discontinuance of nonconforming commercial and industrial use of residential buildings in residential zones within the same five-year period, was a constitutional exercise of the police power insofar as it required the discontinuance of a wholesale and retail plumbing business that had been established in a residence district prior to the enactment of the ordinance. The court stated further that such zoning ordinance was not arbitrary or unreasonable and did not constitutionally impair property rights of the owners.

USE OF AMORTIZATION SCHEMES

The courts have held that the use of a reasonable amortization scheme provides an equitable means of reconciliation of the conflicting interests in satisfaction of the due process of law requirement. As a method of eliminating existing nonconforming uses, it allows the owner of the nonconforming use, by according him an opportunity to make new plans, at least partially to offset any loss he might suffer. The loss he suffers, if any, is spread out over a period of years, and he enjoys a monopolistic position by virtue of the zoning ordinance as long as he remains. If the amortization period is reasonable, the loss to the owner may be small when compared with the benefit to the public. Under such a plan, nonconforming uses will eventually be eliminated. A legislative body may well conclude that the beneficial effect on the community of the eventual elimination of all nonconforming uses by a reasonable amortization plan more than offsets individual losses.

PROHIBITIONS AGAINST EXTENSION OF NONCONFORMING USE

Sometimes a zoning ordinance will permit a nonconforming use to continue indefinitely, but the courts generally follow a strict policy against the subsequent extension or enlargement of property uses not in conformity with zoning ordinances. In the case of *Dienelt* v. *County of Monterey,* 113 C.A.2d 128, the court refused to permit the enlargement of a resort, operating in a residence zone, by the addition of 1,562 feet of heated floor space.

ILLUSTRATIVE CASES—NONCONFORMING USE

In the case of *Beverly Oil Co.* v. *City of Los Angeles,* cited on p. 344, an ordinance was held to be valid that allegedly would restrict and eventually terminate a property owner's nonconforming use of land for oil development. The court stated that the very essence of the police power as differentiated from the power of eminent domain is that the deprivation of individual rights and property cannot prevent its operation once it is shown that its exercise is proper, and that the method of its exercise is reasonably within the meaning of due process of law. This rule was aptly illustrated in the case of *Hadacheck* v. *Sebastian,* 239 U.S. 394, affirming the California Supreme Court in upholding a zoning ordinance of the city of Los Angeles in a similar case.

In the last-mentioned case, Hadacheck had erected his brickyard and kiln in an almost uninhabited locality several miles outside the city on an 8-acre tract of land with soil peculiarly valuable for brickmaking. Thereafter the city boundaries were extended to include the locality, and later a zoning ordinance was enacted that operated retroactively to require the removal of the industry. In its opinion the Supreme Court of the United States said:

> It is to be remembered that we are dealing with one of the most essential powers of the government, one that is the least limitable. It may, indeed, seem harsh in its exercise, usually is on some individual, but the imperative necessity for its existence precludes any limitation upon it when not exerted arbitrarily. A vested interest cannot be asserted against it because of conditions once obtaining. . . . To so hold would preclude development and fix a city forever in its primitive conditions. There must be progress, and if in its march private interests are in the way they must yield to the good of the community.

V. Variances or exceptions

Zoning ordinances generally provide for variances or exceptions from the strict rule or literal enforcement of zoning laws. Such provisions are designed to introduce a measure of elasticity in the administration of zoning, and are based on exceptional circumstances or hardships. The case of *Ames* v. *City of Pasadena,* 167 C.A.2d 510, is illustrative, where the granting of a variance for the construction of a swimming pool was held to be valid; also, the case of *Flagstad* v. *City of San Mateo,* 156

C.A.2d 138, where a variance was granted for the installation of a service station.

CONDITIONS MAY BE IMPOSED

In granting a variance, the administrative body may attach conditions controlling the excepted use in accordance with the spirit and purpose of the general zoning plan. Unlike spot zoning, which is accomplished by an amendment of the general zoning ordinance, a variance or exception sanctions a deviation from a particular provision of a zoning requirement that pertains to the area. (*Rubin* v. *Board of Directors,* 16 Cal.2d 119.)

PROCEDURE TO OBTAIN VARIANCES

A zoning ordinance usually provides that the owner of any property located within a zone established by ordinance may petition to have his property excepted from some particular restriction or restrictions applicable to the zone in which the property is located. After notice and a hearing, the petition may be granted if it is determined that the exception is necessary for the preservation of a substantial property right of the petitioner, and such exception will not be materially detrimental to the public welfare nor to the property of other persons located in the vicinity. An exception may also be granted where there are practical difficulties or unnecessary hardships in the way of carrying out the strict letter of the ordinance, and if in the granting of such exception the spirit of the ordinance will be observed, public safety secured, and substantial justice done. (*Patterson* v. *Los Angeles County,* 79 C.A.2d 670.)

EXCEPTIONS RELATING TO SIZE OF LOTS

A variance or exception is sometimes granted where an owner of a parcel that is slightly less than the area required for two standard-size lots wishes to divide the parcel for purposes of sale. For instance, the owner's parcel may consist of 19,500 square feet, and the minimum area requirement may be 10,000 square feet per lot. Under a strict enforcement of the zoning laws the owner could not divide the parcel into two lots. To alleviate this situation, an exception may be granted upon a proper showing.

VARIANCES A MATTER OF DISCRETION

The granting or denial of petitions for variances from certain requirements of a zoning ordinance rests largely in the discretion of the administrative body designated by ordinance for such purpose. Once an exception has been granted, it cannot be summarily revoked. As stated in the case of *Ricciardi* v. *County of Los Angeles,* 115 C.A.2d 569, an exception under a zoning ordinance represents a valuable property right that cannot be revoked except on grounds and through procedure prescribed by the ordinance.

VI. Conditional use permits

Zoning ordinances usually authorize the administrative board or commission to grant a conditional use permit upon a finding of the existence of certain facts justifying the issuance of the permit, such as a finding that the permitted uses of the property are essential or desirable to the public convenience or welfare, and are in harmony with the various elements or objectives of the master plan. This principle is illustrated by the case of *Wheeler* v. *Gregg,* 90 C.A.2d 348, where a conditional use permit was granted to the defendant to excavate for the commercial production of rock, sand, and gravel in an area of land containing 105 acres in the San Fernando Valley area of the city of Los Angeles. The owners of properties within 3,000 feet of the defendant's property brought an action to have the permit declared void. The court denied relief to the adjoining property owners and sustained the action of the city in issuing the permit, but did impose additional conditions to the permit.

USES OF PUBLIC CONCERN

In the above case, defendant's property had been classified in an R-A zone, which permitted residential and agricultural uses only, and excluded the excavation of rock, sand, or gravel. However, the ordinance provided for the granting of variances from its existing provisions, and also provided for the granting of conditional use permits by the planning commission or the city council to permit certain uses, of public concern, including "the development of natural resources," in zones from which such uses would otherwise be excluded, "when it is found that such uses are deemed essential or desirable to the public convenience or welfare."

Basis of court's decision. In its decision the court pointed out that the exclusion of ordinary business enterprises does not destroy any inherent property right, and if not discriminatory will be held reasonable and valid, since most such businesses can be conducted at another place. But rock and gravel, like any other natural resource, can be obtained only in those particular areas where the deposit has been lodged by nature. Therefore, it follows that to absolutely prohibit the removal of rock, sand, and gravel from a person's own land in an instance where such land is primarily valuable only by reason of the existence of rock, sand, and gravel might be regarded as an unreasonable exercise of the police power. The same conclusion applies in the case of other natural resources, such as oil and gas. (*Trans-Oceanic Oil Corp.* v. *City of Santa Barbara,* 85 C.A.2d 776.)

Denial of use permit. In the case of *Floresta, Inc.* v. *City Council,* 190 C.A.2d 599, the denial of a use permit authorizing the establishment of a cocktail bar or lounge in a shopping center was upheld by the court.

VII. Title insurance covering zoning

Policies of title insurance specifically exclude zoning and other governmental regulations from their coverage. Under its conditions and stipulations, a policy of title insurance does not insure against loss or damage by reason of any law, ordinance, or governmental regulation, including building and zoning ordinances, restricting or regulating or prohibiting the occupancy, use or enjoyment of the land, or regulating the character, dimensions, or location of any improvements on the land. However, assurances with respect to zoning may be given to a lender by special endorsement, respecting (1) the zone in which the land is situated, (2) the type of structure that may be erected, and (3) the minimum area measurements for a building site.

Zoning reports. Letter reports on zoning are also obtainable from title companies, which furnish information that the land may be used for a certain purpose, or that a certain type of building may be constructed thereon, or that the land is situated within a particular zone.

VIII. Other governmental regulations affecting use

In addition to zoning ordinances, many other ordinances and laws restrict, prohibit, or affect the use that may be made of property. In many areas, building line ordinances have been enacted, under which setback lines are established on certain streets. The general purpose of such ordinances is to keep buildings a required distance from streets, thereby affording more light and air, reducing the danger of the spread of fire, keeping dwellings farther from the dust, noise, and fumes of the street, and affording a better view at street intersections in order to lessen the risk of accidents.

ORDINANCES REGULATING CONSTRUCTION

A municipality in the exercise of its police powers may also enact ordinances regulating the construction, repair, or alteration of buildings. (H.& S.C., Sec. 15153.) It may provide for the summary abatement, destruction, or removal of unsafe structures and of unsightly or partially destroyed buildings. It may regulate the location and construction of drains and sewers, the materials used in wiring structures for electricity and piping them for water, gas, or electric supply, and may prohibit structures not conforming to such regulations. (Govt. C., Sec. 38660.)

BUILDING CODES

Building codes have been adopted pursuant to the foregoing and other statutory authority, specifying in detail the various requirements as to the construction of buildings. Permits are required before construction can commence on a work of improvement. An application for a building permit, with its accompanying plans and specifications, is examined not only for possible zoning ordinance violations, but also for possible violations of the building code.

ENFORCEMENT OF BUILDING ORDINANCES

Departments of Building and Safety have been created in larger communities to enforce the city's building ordinance, which departments issue permits for the building of new structures, and inspect existing structures for all factors of safety, including plumbing, electrical, and heating installations.

STATE HOUSING LAW

In 1961 the Legislature enacted a new State Housing Law (H.& S.C., Secs. 17910–95) under which apartment houses, hotels, and dwellings in all parts of the state are subject to state building requirements. Under this law, minimum requirements are established administratively by rules and regulations enacted by the Department of Industrial Relations through the Division of Housing. Cities and counties retain the power to enact building ordinances and regulations pertaining to hotels, apartments, houses, and dwellings, which ordinances may impose building standards equal to or greater than those prescribed by the state's zoning ordinances.

RESTRICTIONS ON CONSTRUCTION DEEMED VALID

It has been held that a regulation is not unreasonable, even though it may disturb the rights of an owner in the use of his property, that places a restriction on the construction or repair of certain wooden buildings on his property (*In re Fisk*, 72 Cal. 125), or because it distinguishes between buildings in existence and those to be erected in the future (*In re Stoltenberg*, 165 Cal. 789).

BUILDING REGULATIONS NOT INCONSISTENT WITH ZONING

Municipal building regulations are not necessarily inconsistent with zoning regulations, and both sets of regulations may remain in force at the same time. (*Brougher* v. *City and County of San Francisco*, cited on p. 345.)

ABATING NUISANCES

A municipality, in the exercise of its police powers, may also enact ordinances designed to prevent or abate nuisances. The legislative body may declare by ordinance what constitutes a nuisance, and may provide for its summary abatement at the expense of the persons creating or maintaining it, and may make the expense of abatement a lien against the property. Ordinances have been enacted in the past prohibiting various types of activities as nuisances, such as slaughter houses (*In re Shrader*, 33 Cal. 279; *In re Heilbron,* 65 Cal. 609); dairies (*In re Linehan,* 72 Cal. 114); carpet beating establishments (*In re Lacey,* 108 Cal. 326), and many other similar activities.

REMOVAL OF OFFENSIVE MATTER

A city's legislative body may compel the owner, lessee, or occupant of property in the city to remove dirt, rubbish, weeds, and the like from the property and adjacent sidewalk. In the event of default after notice, it may authorize the removal or destruction of such matters by a city officer at the owner's expense, may prescribe a procedure for its removal or destruction, and may make the expense thereof a lien on the property. (Govt. C., Sec. 39501.)

ENCROACHMENTS ON SIDEWALKS AND STREETS

A city is also authorized to prohibit and prevent encroachments or obstructions on any sidewalk, street, or similar public place, and may provide for removal of any such encroachment or obstruction. (Govt. C., Sec. 38775.)

Questions

1. Briefly describe the nature of zoning.
2. Under what power are zoning laws enacted?
3. Identify two types of zoning ordinances.
4. Explain the essential requirement of a valid zoning ordinance.
5. Under what circumstances have zoning ordinances been held to be invalid?

6. Give an illustration of "spot zoning."
7. How are present uses affected by a newly enacted zoning ordinance?
8. Under what circumstances are variances made?
9. When is a conditional use permit justified?
10. Discuss briefly other governmental regulations affecting the use of property.

19

Leases and the Landlord-Tenant Relationship

Summary

I. Relationship of landlord and tenant

The relationship of landlord and tenant arises when there is a hiring of real property. Section 1925 of the Civil Code defines a hiring as a contract by which one person gives to another the temporary possession and use of property, other than money, for reward, with an agreement that it shall be returned at a future time. The person who lets real property is known as the "landlord" or "lessor," and the person who receives possession of the property is designated the "tenant' or "lessee." The landlord-tenant relationship may exist without a formal lease, and usually does where the term is only of short duration.

NATURE OF A LEASE

Although the terms "landlord" and "lessor," or "tenant" and "lessee," are often used interchangeably without any distinction, in the strict sense the words "lessor" and "lessee" are more properly used to designate the parties to a formal lease. A "lease" is the designation given to the contract by which the possession and profits of land are exchanged for rent. It conveys an interest in the land to the lessee for a period of time, measured by the life of a party or for years or at will. The word "term" designates the time and period of the enjoyment of the estate. "Rent" is the return or compensation for the use of property. Standard forms of leases are in common use, both as to residential and commercial properties; their formal preparation, however, should be entrusted to an attorney.

TENANT AND LICENSEE DISTINGUISHED

The question as to whether or not an occupant of real property is a *tenant* or a *licensee* is an important one, since widely varying results may follow. A fundamental distinction between a tenant and a licensee is that the tenant has a legal interest in the possession or right to possession of property, whereas a licensee merely has permission to do certain acts on property in the possession of another, which acts, without the license, would constitute trespass. A license, being a right personal to the licensee, rather than a property interest, is *not assignable,* whereas the interest of a tenant is assignable. As a general rule, a license is *revocable* at any time.

Other distinctions. The distinction between a tenant and a licensee is of primary concern with respect to the *duty owed to the person in possession.* A person who engages a room at a hotel is a licensee, whereas a person who rents an apartment is a tenant. The owner of a hotel may be liable to the lodger or transient guest for injuries suffered by the guest, since the owner owes a duty, at all times, to maintain the premises in a reasonably safe condition. On the other hand, the proprietor of a furnished apartment is not liable to a tenant for injuries caused by the condition of the property leased, in the absence of fraud, concealment, or a covenant in the lease.

Illustrative case—injuries to a lodger. In the case of *Stowe* v. *Fritzie Hotels, Inc.,* 44 Cal.2d 416, a question was raised as to whether or not the owner of premises was liable for injuries sustained by an occupant as the result of the fall of a top-heavy lamp. The question of liability was dependent upon whether or not the occupant was a "tenant" or a "lodger." The court held that the occupant was a "lodger," where the evidence showed that the premises were under the direct control and supervision of the owner, the rooms being furnished and attended to by him, and he or his servants retaining the keys. The court emphasized that the chief distinction between a tenant and a lodger lies in the *character of possession.* A "tenant" has exclusive possession of premises, and is responsible for their care and condition. A "lodger" has only a right to use the premises, subject to the landlord's retention of control and right of access to them.

CONCESSIONS IN COMMERCIAL ESTABLISHMENTS

The distinction between a licensee and a tenant is also important in the case of concessions in commercial establishments. In retail merchandising houses, concessionaires are usually considered to be licensees rather than tenants. However, such a status does not of necessity follow from the occupancy of but a single department in a store or other place of business. The basic question is one of *possession,* to be determined from an examination of the contract between the parties and their actions under it. In the case of *Wukaloff* v. *Malibou Lake Mountain Club,* 96 C.A.2d 147, a concessionaire of the dining facilities in defendant's private club was held to be a licensee and not a tenant. But an occupant in a store who is given a definite space for a fixed period for which he pays a prescribed rental, whether measured in percentage of sales or otherwise, is usually regarded as a tenant. (*Beckett* v. *City of Paris Dry Goods Co.,* 14 Cal.2d 633.)

RELATIONSHIP OF LANDLORD-TENANT IS BASED ON CONTRACT

A tenancy may be created without a formal agreement. A person may become a tenant by mere occupancy with the consent of the owner, such as a tenant at will or a periodic tenant. However, the relationship of landlord and tenant presupposes a contract, express or implied, from which the intention to create the relationship must appear. There must be a permission to occupy, conferring on the permittee a legal estate and the right of possession. The relationship may be created by, or implied from, the promise of the occupant to pay rent, and the acceptance of the promise by the owner.

TYPES OF TENANCIES

Various types of tenancies may be created, including a tenancy at sufferance, a tenancy at will, a periodic tenancy, and a tenancy for a fixed term.

TENANT AT SUFFERANCE

Although not a trespasser, a tenant at sufferance lacks much of the protection afforded other classes of tenants. The relationship is not by express consent of the landlord, but arises by implication, hence the difference in the rights of the tenant. A tenant by sufferance is one who goes into possession lawfully, but whose right to remain in possession has expired, such as a tenant holding over after the expiration of a lease, or a tenant at will whose right to possession has expired by virtue of the death of the landlord.

Status of tenant at sufferance. Technically, a tenant at sufferance is not a tenant of anyone, but is an occupant against the reversioner; the phrase is used merely for convenience. The landlord may elect to treat him as a trespasser, or, after demand of possession, recover treble rent under the provisions of Section 3345 of the Civil Code. A tenant at sufferance is not entitled to notice prior to ejection by the owner, and is liable for the reasonable value of the use and occupation of the property until the tenancy is terminated. If the owner of the property elects to treat him as a tenant, as by accepting rent at the rate previously paid during the term, the tenancy at sufferance ceases and the occupant becomes a tenant at will or a periodic tenant.

TENANCY AT WILL

A tenancy at will is created by agreement of the parties, but has no fixed term, and is terminable at the will of either party. Tenancies at will are now uncommon because of their conversion to periodic tenancies through acceptance of periodic rents as provided by Section 1945 of the Civil Code. Although the tenancy is terminable at the will of either party, the landlord is required to give 30 days' notice. (C.C., Sec. 789.) At common law, the tenancy was terminable without advance notice by either party.

Creation of tenancy at will. A tenancy at will is created when a person goes into possession with the consent of the owner to remain for a specified purpose without payment of rental, or when a tenant enters, with permission of the landlord, under an invalid lease or contract. In the case of *Covina Manor, Inc.* v. *Hatch,* 133 C.A.2d Supp. 790, the court pointed out that a person who enters on land by permission of the owner under a void parol contract, or a void lease, or pending negotiations for a written lease, is a tenant at will. A tenant at will has no transferable interest, and an attempted assignment will terminate the tenancy. Upon acceptance of a periodic rental by the owner of the property, the tenant at will becomes a periodic tenant.

PERIODIC TENANCY

A periodic tenancy is created by the parties to continue for successive periods of the same length, unless sooner terminated by notice. Examples are tenancies from year to year and tenancies from month to month. This type of tenancy does not terminate by mere lapse of time. It is deemed to be renewed at the end of each of the periods by which the payment of rent is determined, unless terminated by notice.

Tenancy may be created by implication. A periodic tenancy may be created by implication where a tenant under a lease for a fixed term holds over after expiration of the term, and pays rent periodically thereafter. In such a case the tenancy is not renewed for a term equal to the term of the original lease, but a periodic tenancy is created, either from month to month or from year to year, whichever mode of payment of rent is adopted. It is presumed in such cases that the parties have renewed the hiring on the same terms and for the same time, not exceeding one month when the rent is payable monthly, and in any case not exceeding one year. (C.C., Sec. 1945.)

Tenancy for an indefinite period. A tenancy for an indefinite period under which the rent is payable or is paid monthly is a tenancy from month to month. A tenancy of property other than a lodging or dwelling house, in the absence of contrary local usage, and unless a contrary intention is expressed in writing, is presumed to be a month-to-month tenancy. In the case of property used for agricultural or grazing purposes, the tenancy is presumed to be for one year. (C.C., Sec. 1943.) Where the possession under such a tenancy is continued beyond the year and rent is accepted monthly, the hiring is presumed to have been continued on a month-to-month basis on the same terms as before. A hiring of lodgings or a dwelling house for an unspecified length of time is presumed to be for such period as the parties adopt for the estimation of rent. Thus, a hiring at a monthly rate of rent is presumed to be for one month, and a hiring at a weekly rate is presumed to be for one week. In the absence of an agreement respecting the length of time or the rent, the hiring is presumed to be monthly (C.C., Sec. 1944.)

Termination of periodic tenancy. A periodic tenancy may be terminated by giving 30 days' notice as provided by Section 1946 of the Civil Code. Such notice in a month-to-month tenancy may be given at any time; it need not be given or expire only upon the anniversary of the hiring. In the case of *Kingston* v. *Colburn,* 139 C.A.2d 623, it was held that a notice of termination of a tenancy from month to month that is insufficient under Section 1946 of the Civil Code to terminate the tenancy as of the stated date because it is within the 30-day period, is not necessarily ineffective as a notice of termination after the lapse of 30 days from the date of the notice.

TENANCY FOR A FIXED TERM

A tenancy for a fixed term is the most common type of leasehold estate in commercial properties. Such an interest is possessed by a tenant having the right to the exclusive possession for a fixed period, whether for more or less than one year. The estate is often referred to as an estate for years, although as long as the period is definite, it may be for years, for a single year, or for a fixed period shorter than a year, e.g., for specified months or specified weeks.

RIGHTS OF POSSESSION

When a tenant's term commences, he succeeds to all of the rights of the landlord with respect to possession and enjoyment of the premises unless special reservations are made. As a general rule, everything that belongs to the demised premises or is used with or appurtenant to them, and is reasonably essential to their enjoyment, passes as incident to them unless specifically reserved.

USE OF PREMISES

Unless restricted by agreement, the tenant can make use of the premises for any lawful purpose for which they were let, or for any purpose not materially different from that for which they are usually employed, are adapted, or were constructed. Under this rule, the tenant of a building or part thereof for business purposes has the exclusive right, in the absense of an agreement providing otherwise, to use for advertising purposes that portion of the outside walls included in the rental agreement, and may enjoin others from interfering with that right.

PAYMENT OF RENT—LANDLORD'S LIEN

Rent is payable at the termination of the successive periods of the holding, either weekly, monthly, or yearly as the case may be, in the absence of usage or an agreement to the contrary. Generally, a landlord does not have a lien for the rent, unless provided for by agreement. However, innkeepers, hotel and motel proprietors, and keepers of boarding houses, lodging houses, furnished apartments, and bungalow courts have statutory liens upon the baggage and other property of the tenant or lodger for rents and charges. In 1953 the law was broadened to include owners of unfurnished apartment houses, apartments, cottages, or bungalow courts, within the lien provisions, with certain items of property exempt. (C.C., Sec. 1861a.) Subsequent amendments broadened the right to enforce such lien.

II. Characteristics of a lease

A lease, as it pertains to real property, is a *grant* or *conveyance* by the owner of an estate to another person of a portion of his interest therein for a term less than his own. A lease is not only a grant or conveyance of an interest in land, but is also a *contract* between the parties. Upon a breach of any covenant contained in the lease, the injured party has a right of action the same as he has with respect to other contracts.

TWO SETS OF RIGHTS

A lease has two sets of rights and obligations, one comprising those growing out of the relation of landlord and tenant and based on the *privity of estate*, and the other comprising those growing out of the express stipulations of the lease and based on *privity of contract.*

REVERSIONARY INTEREST

It is essential to the relationship of landlord and tenant, whether created by lease or otherwise, that the occupancy of the tenant be in subordination of the rights of the landlord, and that a reversionary interest, referred to as the "reversion," remain in the landlord.

NATURE OF ESTATE

The interest or estate of the lessee under a lease is called a "leasehold" or "leasehold estate." Leases for a definite period are considered to be personal property, whereas leases for an indefinite period, as are most oil and gas leases, are regarded as real property.

III. Statutory restrictions on term of lease

At common law there was no limitation on the term for which a leasehold estate could be created. Whether the fixed term was for one year or for 500 years, the interest created was considered to be personal property and legally inferior to a life estate or other freehold estate. The incongruity of a lease for 500 years being less as a matter of law than a life estate led to the enactment of a statute in Massachusetts at an early date that converted every lease for 100 years or more into a fee simple ownership. The use of the 99-year lease in many areas is probably based upon the practice in Massachusetts of drafting leases for no longer than that period. Several states, including California, now have statutes providing that a lease for a term longer than 99 years is invalid.

DURATION OF ESTATES

There are several limitations on the duration of leasehold estates in California. Prior to 1963, land for agricultural and horticultural purposes could not be leased for a term in excess of 15 years (C.C., Sec. 717); in 1963 the time was extended to 51 years. Town or city lots may not be leased for a period in excess of 99 years. (C.C., Sec. 718.) A lease of a city lot for a permissible term, but with an option for renewal that, if exercised, would extend the lease beyond the term allowed, has been held to be in violation of the statute. (*Epstein* v. *Zahloute,* 99 C.A.2d 738.) In the case of *Coruccini* v. *Lambert,* 113 C.A.2d 486, the court held invalid a 15-year lease of agricultural lands containing an option to extend indefinitely the same for additional terms of one year each.

Illustrative case. The case of *Kendall* v. *Southward,* 149 C.A.2d 827, also involved the validity of a lease for agricultural purposes. In that case the plaintiff leased certain lands to the defendant on April 10, 1946, at a specified rental *for the term of the natural life of the plaintiff.* The effective date of the lease was September 1, 1946. In May of 1955 the plaintiff brought an action for declaratory relief, contending that the lease was void on the ground that it was in violation of Section 717 of the Civil Code. The court held that the lease was valid for a period of 15 years from its effective date or until the death of the lessor, if she died before the end of that period.

Rule against perpetuities. The case of *Haggerty* v. *City of Oakland,* 161 C.A.2d 407, decided in 1958, illustrates the unlikely circumstance in which the rule against perpetuities was applied and a lease thereby rendered void. The City of Oakland executed a 10-year lease to begin on completion of a building to be constructed on the premises. It was held that since completion might take longer than 21 years, and since the lease was to commence only when the building was constructed, the lease was void. However, in a later case the Supreme Court decided to the contrary, holding that although a lease of a building under construction which provided that the term of the lease was to commence on the recording of a notice of completion, did contain a minor possible ground of future uncertainty which might postpone completion of the building beyond the period of the rule against perpetuities, the agreement will, if feasible, be interpreted to avoid a conclusion that it violates the rule. (*Wong* v. *DiGrazia*, 60 Cal.2d 525.)

MINERAL LEASES

A lease of land for the purpose of effecting the production of oil, gas, or other minerals from other parcels may be made for a period certain or determinable by any future event prescribed by the parties, but no such lease is enforceable after 99 years from the commencement of the term thereof. (C.C., Sec. 718f.) This section was added to the code in 1953 to cover drill site agreements (slant drilling).

LEASES IN PROBATE PROCEEDINGS

The real property of a decedent may not be lèased for a term in excess of ten years, except in the case of mineral leases or for the growing of asparagus. (Pro.C., Sec. 842.) The maximum term of a lease of real property of a minor or incompetent person is not so limited.

GOVERNMENT LEASES

With respect to leases by governmental bodies, such as the state, a county, or a city, there are various limitations on the permitted terms. The statutes must be examined to determine the particular limitation that applies, both as to the purpose of the lease and the lawful term. In the case of chartered cities, the provisions of the charter must also be examined to determine the authority of the city to enter into a lease. Statutory provisions limiting the lawful term of a lease of city property include limitations of 55 years for general purposes, with other periods permitted for certain designated purposes, such as 99 years for recreational purposes, 66 years for tide and submerged lands for waterfront and harbor development, and 35 years for mineral leases.

IV. Requisites of a valid lease

A lease for a term exceeding one year must be in writing; must contain the names of the parties; must include a sufficient description of the property leased; must contain an agreement for the rental to be paid, and the time and manner of such payment; and must state the term of the lease. As in the case of contracts, there must also be a meeting of the minds, i.e., *mutual assent* of the parties to the creation of a binding lease, and a *consideration,* which is usually the undertaking to pay rent. The rent may consist of either a fixed rental, or a percentage of the business done by the lessee, or a combination of both a fixed rental and a percentage.

In 1965 a new section was added to the Civil Code (Sec. 1945.5) which provides that printed lease provisions for automatic renewal or extension of a residence lease (if the lessee remains in possession after the expiration of the lease, or fails to give notice of intention not to renew or extend the lease) are required to be in 8-point bold type. There must also be reference to such provisions in 8-point bold type above the place for the lessee's signature.

OPERATIVE WORDS

Leases usually contain operative words, such as "let," "lease," or "demise," but no particular form of words is necessary. Any agreement whereby one party obtains the right of enjoyment of the property of another, with the latter's consent and in subordination to his right, may create the relation of landlord and tenant.

SIGNATURE OF PARTIES

It is essential that the lessor sign the lease, but the lessee need not sign provided he accepts the lease and acts thereunder. Taking possession and paying rent is sufficient evidence of acceptance by the lessee. It is, of course, better practice to require the lessee's signature in order to be certain that he will be bound under the covenants contained in the lease.

RECORDATION

If the lease is to be recorded, it must be acknowledged by the lessor. It is sometimes the practice of lessees, particularly under oil and gas leases, to record a so-called *short form of lease* in lieu of the original lease with its many terms, conditions, and provisions and to incorporate the terms and conditions of the unrecorded lease by reference. Such short-form lease should give the names of the lessor and lessee, contain the necessary operative words to create a lease, and include a description of the property leased. If the short-form lease includes a provision that it is made "subject to the terms, conditions and provisions of that certain unrecorded instrument between the parties hereto, dated ________," it may be considered sufficient without the necessity of setting forth any other provisions of the lease, including the term and rental.

NECESSITY FOR WRITTEN INSTRUMENT

It is required by statute that an estate in real property, other than an estate at will or for a term not exceeding one year, may be created only by an instrument in writing signed by the lessor or his agent having written authorization. (C.C., Sec. 1091.) Statutes also provide that an agreement to lease for longer than one year is invalid unless in writing signed by the party sought to be charged. (C.C., Sec. 1624.4.) This section has been construed to require that a one-year lease to commence at a future date must be in writing. An oral lease for one year to commence one day after the agreement is made has been held to be invalid. (*Wickson* v. *Monarch Cycle Mfg. Co.*, 128 Cal. 156.)

DESCRIPTION OF PREMISES

The requirement that a deed must describe the premises with certainty applies equally to leases. A street address may meet minimum requirements in many cases, but a careful draftsman will also describe the premises by a sufficient legal description. This requirement is of particular importance if a parking lot adjacent to a restaurant or store is involved. In such case the use of a street address alone should be avoided. Where part only of a building other than an entire floor is being leased, blueprints or other suitable sketches attached as exhibits to the lease may be used to show the exact spaces to be leased.

STATUS OF PARTIES

In the preparation of a lease it is important to have not only the correct names of the lessor and lessee, but also an accurate statement in the lease of the capacities of the parties and the nature of their equities. The marital status of the parties is of particular concern. Under the provisions of Section 172a of the Civil Code, a wife must join in the execution of a lease where the husband seeks to lease community real property for a period longer than one year. Where a married woman is a lessee, her husband should be joined as a lessee if it is intended to hold the community property liable on the contract obligations of the lease.

PARTIES ACTING IN A REPRESENTATIVE CAPACITY

If either party to a lease is acting in a representative or fiduciary capacity, the power to act should be ascertained by both parties; as to the one, to avoid breach of implied warranty of authority, and as to the other, to make certain of a valid lease. In the case of a trustee, the power to lease is not necessarily implied from the power to sell or the power to dispose of land. However, even though the trust instrument does not expressly authorize a lease, such power is sometimes regarded as implied from the purpose of the trust, or as justified by the trustee's duty to keep the land productive. For title insurance purposes, though, the power to lease must be specifically conferred, or appropriate proceedings undertaken to raise a power or to determine that such power exists.

LEASES BEYOND TERM OF A TRUST

Unless otherwise authorized under the terms of the trust, it has been held that a trustee cannot make a lease that will be effective after the termination of the trust. However, Section 2272 of the Civil Code now provides that a lease for a reasonable period is not impaired by termination of the trust where: (1) the term of the trust is of uncertain or indefinite duration, or is terminable at the death of one or more persons; (2) the trustee has power to lease; and (3) the instrument creating the trust contains no provision to the contrary. In the case of a testamentary trust, an order of the probate court is required to establish the reasonableness of the term of such lease.

SECURITY DEPOSITS

It is common practice in the preparation of leases to require a security deposit or to provide for advance rental payments of a sufficient amount to insure compensation to the lessor in the event he is unable to collect from the tenant. The common characterization of all such payments as "security deposits" is often misleading. The courts have broken down such deposits or advance payments into four categories as follows: (1) advance payment of rent, usually for the last month of the term; (2) payment that is expressly stipulated to be a bonus or consideration for the execution of the lease; (3) payment of an amount as liquidated damages; and (4) payment as a deposit to secure faithful performance of the terms of the lease. If the deposit under the lease falls within the first two classes, it may be retained by the lessor; if it falls within the third class, it is a penalty, results in a forfeiture, and is invalid as such and may be recovered by the lessee; and if it falls within the fourth class, it may be retained by the lessor only to the extent of the amount of damages actually suffered by him. (*Warming* v. *Shapiro,* 118 C.A.2d 72.)

EXECUTION AND DELIVERY OF LEASE

As in the case of a deed, in order to have the lease operative it must be executed by the lessor and delivered to the lessee. The instrument must pass into the control of the lessee to constitute an effective delivery. Under some circumstances acceptance of the leased premises by the lessee may be regarded as delivery.

INTERPRETATION OF LEASES

In the interpretation of the provisions of a lease, the instrument must be construed according to the intent of the parties, which intent is gathered from the language of the lease and in accordance with the rules of interpretation of contracts generally.

ALTERATION OF THE LEASE

Any alteration of the lease must be in writing, and the lease cannot be changed by mutual oral agreement, unless these agreements have been fully performed and thereby become an executed modification of the lease. In the case of *Cirimele* v. *Shinazy,* 124 C.A.2d 46, it was held that where the lessor accepts monthly rental payments less than called for by a written lease, in accordance with an oral agreement between the parties reducing rental, such payments constitute an executed oral agreement, but as to monthly payments subsequently due and unpaid, the oral agreement is not executed and the lessor is entitled to the amount named in the written lease.

RESTRICTIVE COVENANTS

Under the provisions of Section 1470 of the Civil Code, a lessor may covenant not to use land contiguous to leased property contrary to the terms of the lease (negative covenant). This agreement is binding on the lessor's successors in interest when, among other things, the lease is recorded. Frequently, only a memorandum of the lease is recorded which may not contain a description of the contiguous property. Section 1470 was amended in 1963 to require that the recorded lease include a description of any contiguous land described in an unrecorded instrument incorporated by reference in said lease.

Under the provisions of Section 1469 of the Civil Code, as amended in 1965, relating to affirmative covenants, i.e., covenants of a lessor to do any act or acts on other real property which is owned by the lessor and is contiguous to the leased property, the recorded lease, in order for the convenants to bind successive owners, must include a description of the contiguous land described in any unrecorded instrument incorporated by reference in said lease.

V. Transfer by lessor

As a general rule, the landlord may sell the land during an unexpired leasehold term, in which event the vendee becomes the landlord by operation of law. The vendee succeeds to all of the rights of the original lessor and in the absence of a contrary stipulation, is entitled to all of the rents that fall due on the next rent day. Exceptions to this rule apply, as in the case where the lease contains a provision that a sale of the land prior to the expiration of the leasehold term shall terminate the lease.

ASSIGNMENT OF RENTS

The owner of leased premises may convey the reversion and retain the rents, or he may assign the rents and the covenant for rent under the lease without conveying the reversion or the lease itself. When the rent is assigned, the assignee becomes chargeable with notice of any express or implied covenants of the lease. The right to receive future rents is an interest in land, called an incorporeal hereditament, and a grant of such right is a conveyance within the statutory definition.

VI. Transfers by lessee

A lessee may assign or sublease all or a part of the leased premises, subject to any restrictions in the lease against assignment or subletting. Whether a transfer by a lessee is an assignment or a sublease is of importance, since the respective rights and liabilities of the parties are dependent upon the nature of the instrument of transfer.

ASSIGNMENT OF LEASE

If there is to be an assignment of a lease, the assignee must take precisely the same estate that the assignor has in the property. A lessee who has not obligated himself personally to pay rent is relieved of any further obligation to pay rent where he transfers his interest to an assignee with the consent of the lessor. Such obligation is thereafter upon the assignee, who has come into privity of estate with the landlord. However, where the lessee has expressly agreed to pay rent, his liability under his contract remains, notwithstanding an assignment with the consent of the lessor. He is liable as surety in the event the assignee fails to perform the covenant to pay rent.

OBLIGATION OF ASSIGNEE

Where the assignee takes possession under an assignment and pays rent without an express assumption of the obligation of the lessee and thereafter abandons the premises, his liability, based only on privity of estate, is limited solely to the period of his occupancy and does not continue after his abandonment of the premises. Where the assignee by express terms in writing covenants and agrees to pay the rent reserved in the lease, there result two sets of obligations and rights, one comprising those due to the relation of landlord and tenant based on privity of estate, and the other due to privity of contract. The obligation of the assignee is identical with that of the original lessee upon his express covenants. If the assignee repudiates the lease and abandons the premises, the lessor may sue to recover the rent to the same extent as though the assignee had been the original lessee.

OPTION TO PURCHASE

An option to purchase contained in a lease is a covenant running with the land, and in the absence of restrictive language in the lease, an assignment of the lease includes the option. The general consideration of the lease, such as the covenant to pay rent or do other acts, supports the option to purchase, but such option does not normally exist beyond the fixed term of the lease. In the absence of a provision making the exercise of the option personal to the lessee, the option to purchase is severable from the other provisions of the lease and may be transferred without assigning the lease. (*Mott* v. *Cline,* 200 Cal. 434.)

EFFECT OF ASSIGNMENT WITHOUT LESSOR'S CONSENT

An assignment of the lessee's interest made without the consent of the lessor, where the lease provides that his consent is necessary, does not of itself terminate the lease or render the assignment void, but merely gives the lessor certain rights provided by law, such as an election to declare a forfeiture of the lease or to sue for breach of the covenant. If the lessor ignores the breach, the lease is valid and subsisting as to all other parties. Acceptance of rent from the assignee constitutes a waiver of the lessor's right to declare a forfeiture.

DISTINCTION BETWEEN ASSIGNMENT AND SUBLEASE

The generally stated distinction between an assignment and a sublease is that an assignment transfers the entire unexpired term, whereas a sublease transfers only a part of such term. A lease that contains a provision against assignment but none against subletting does not prevent a sublease. A sublessee ordinarily is liable only to the sublessor and not to the original lessor, since he does not acquire the whole estate but only a portion of the unexpired term.

RIGHTS OF SUBLESSOR

Where a lease does not prohibit a sublease, and a tenant is in possession under a valid sublease, a voluntary surrender by the original lessee to the original lessor does not affect the right of the sublessee in possession, and the anomalous situation may arise where the sublessee may legally remain in possession without paying rent. The lessor can protect himself against such contingency, either by refusing to consent to such cancellation unless it is accompanied by a surrender of possession by the sublessee, or by taking an assignment of the rentals under the sublease. (*Buttner* v. *Kasser,* 19 C.A. 755; *Bailey* v. *Richardson,* 66 Cal. 416.)

VII. Termination of the lease

The expiration of the express term of the lease will, of course, effect a termination. Additionally, a lease may be lawfully terminated prior to the expiration of the term on several grounds. A lease may be terminated by the tenant for violation of the landlord's duty to place him in quiet possession, or for violation of the landlord's duty to repair, or upon eviction by the landlord. The lease may be terminated by the landlord if the premises are used by the tenant for an unauthorized or illegal purpose. Either party may terminate the lease upon breach of a condition of the lease by the other party, or upon the destruction of the premises if there is no covenant to repair.

SURRENDER OF PREMISES

A lease may also be terminated by the surrender of the leased premises by the lessee and the unqualified acceptance thereof by the lessor. In such case the lessee is released from all further liabilities under the lease.

REMEDIES WHERE LESSEE ABANDONS POSSESSION

Upon abandonment of possession by a lessee before the expiration of the term of the lease, the lessor has three remedies: (1) he may consider the lease as still in effect and sue for the unpaid rent as it becomes due for the unexpired portion of the term; (2) he may treat the lease as terminated and retake possession for his own account; or (3) he may retake possession for the lessee's account and relet the premises, holding the lessee for the difference between the lease rentals and what he is able to procure by reletting in good faith. (*Kulawitz* v. *Pacific Woodenware & Paper Co.*, 25 Cal.2d 664.) In the third alternative, the lessor must notify the lessee of the election in order to avoid a surrender by operation of law.

COVENANT OF QUIET ENJOYMENT

In every lease there is an implied covenant by the lessor of quiet enjoyment and possession by the lessee during the term of the lease. This warranty is breached by an eviction, whether actual or constructive. An eviction occurs, of course, when the landlord ousts the tenant or allows him to be ousted by a person with paramount title. There does not have to be an actual ouster, however, to have an eviction. As a general rule, any disturbance of the tenant's possession whereby the premises are rendered unfit or unsuitable for occupancy, in whole or in a major part, for the purposes for which they were leased, or any interference with the beneficial enjoyment of the premises, such as threats of expulsion or an attempt to lease to others, may amount to a constructive eviction. When this occurs, the tenant has the right, if he so elects, to abandon the premises and pay no further rent. The courts have held that the tenant must actually surrender possession; if he stays on, there is no eviction and he cannot escape the obligation to pay rent.

EFFECT OF CONDEMNATION ACTION

If the entire premises are condemned in eminent domain proceedings, the lessee is released from his obligation to pay rent. However, if only a portion of the premises is taken by the condemnation proceedings, the lessee must pay the rent in full, but he, rather than the lessor, will be entitled to damages in the condemnation action.

DESTRUCTION OF THE PREMISES

In the event of destruction of the premises, if the lease does not provide for an apportionment of rent, the tenant who has paid rent in advance cannot recover it.

DOCTRINE OF COMMERCIAL FRUSTRATION

The doctrine of commercial frustration is sometimes invoked to allow a termination of a lease by the tenant where the premises are leased for a specific purpose, and thereafter it becomes unlawful or impossible to use the premises for such purpose. A change in the laws forbidding the sale of liquor is an example. The doctrine has been approved in California, although some jurisdictions have refused to allow a termination of a lease on this theory because of the dual character of a lease as a conveyance of real property as well as a contract. If the premises may be used for other purposes to which the owner has consented either in the lease or subsequently, the tenant will not be relieved of his obligations.

Illustrative case. In the case of *Lloyd* v. *Murphy,* 25 Cal.2d 48, it was held that the doctrine of commercial frustration was not applicable to a lease of property in Los Angeles for five years commencing September 15, 1941, for the purpose of conducting the sale of new automobiles, where the sale of new automobiles was subsequently prohibited by government wartime regulations adopted after the commencement of the term. The court stated that the doctrine is inapplicable where the frustrating event was *reasonably foreseeable* at the time of the execution of the lease.

FORFEITURE OF LEASE

A breach of a *condition* by the tenant gives the landlord a right of forfeiture of the estate, whereas a breach of a *covenant* ordinarily gives only an action for damages. However, if the lease provides for forfeiture for violation of conditions or covenants, the lessor may terminate the tenancy upon either violation. A provision for forfeiture must be clear, and the courts will attempt to avoid it by judicial construction or interpretation if enforcement will lead to inequitable results.

FAILURE TO PAY RENT

Failure to pay rent does not ordinarily justify a forfeiture forthwith; a demand for payment is necessary and is usually made a part of a three-day notice to quit, required by Section 791 of the Civil Code. In the case of *Igauye* v. *Howard,* 114 C.A.2d 122, it was held that where a lease does not *ipso facto* work a forfeiture of the leasehold for failure of the lessee to pay rent, but only gives the lessor the right at his option to terminate, this amounts to no more than the right to terminate the lease in the manner provided by law and does not justify the lessor in reentering and dispossessing the lessee until he has been given the required three days' written notice to pay the rent or quit possession. This rule was again expressed in the case of *Jordan* v. *Talbot,* 55 Cal.2d 597, where the court held that no immediate right to possession of property can be obtained under a right of reentry until a proper three-day notice has been served on the lessee. It has also been held that the notice required to be given to a delinquent tenant, where the condition or covenant assertedly violated is capable of being performed, must be framed in the alternative, that is "pay the rent or quit" or "perform the covenant or quit"; a notice that merely directs the tenant to quit is insufficient. (*Hinman* v. *Wagnon*, 172 C.A.2d 24.)

UNLAWFUL DETAINER

The remedy of unlawful detainer is available against a tenant who continues in possession after default in the payment of rent, or continues in possession after neglect or failure to perform other conditions or covenants of the lease, or holds over after the expiration of the term. This type of action is entitled to priority on the court's calendar. Such an action where the rental value is $600 or less per month and the total claim does not exceed $5,000 may be brought in the Municipal Court.

TITLE COMPANY PRACTICES

Where a lease is terminated prior to the expiration of the term set forth in the lease, other than by judicial proceedings, and a title company is asked to ignore the effect of the lease for title insurance purposes, the company ordinarily will require either a cancellation agreement executed by both the lessor and the lessee, or a quitclaim deed by the lessee with evidence of acceptance by the lessor as a cancellation of the lease.

VIII. Liability of lessor for condition of premises

As a general rule, a lessor of land is not liable for injuries resulting from a defective condition of the land. The rule is stated in *Jones* v. *Regan*, 169 C.A.2d 635, that in the absence of fraud, concealment, or a covenant in the lease, a landlord is not liable to a tenant or his invitee for defective conditions or faulty construction on leased property. Liability for injuries is placed upon the one who is in control of the land, which is the lessee. Several exceptions to this rule are applicable. Where injuries result from a defective condition of that part of the land over which the lessor retains control—stairs, common hallways, and the like—the lessor and not the lessee is liable. However, a liability does not arise where the structural defects are obvious. Also, in such cases the only duty of the lessor is to use reasonable care. Another exception to the above general rule applies where injuries result from a latent defect that was not capable of discovery by a reasonable inspection made by the tenant, provided the lessor knew or should have known of the condition. A lessor is also liable for personal injuries resulting from a defective condition if he undertakes to make repairs and does so in a negligent manner.

DUTY OF LESSOR WITH RESPECT TO A DWELLING

Where the premises let to a tenant are a dwelling house, there is a statutory duty placed upon the landlord to keep it fit for human occupation, by repairing such dilapidations as render the premises untenantable, except such as are caused by the tenant's negligence. (C.C., Sec. 1941.) The landlord cannot be forced to perform this duty, and his default merely permits the tenant to take certain limited steps in his own behalf. The tenant may give notice to the landlord to repair, and if the landlord fails to do so, the tenant may either spend one month's rent in repairs or abandon the premises and be discharged from payment of rent or performance of other conditions.

IX. Oil and gas leases

California is one of the large oil producing states, and the use of oil and gas leases has been widespread. Oil and gas leases differ from the surface leases heretofore discussed; they are in effect something in addition to an ordinary lease. In a surface lease the lessee generally has only the right to use the property; in an oil and gas lease he has, in addition, the right to take something from the property, i.e., oil and gas. A surface lease generally runs for a definite period of time, whereas the usual form of oil and gas lease runs for a specified period of years and for an indefinite period thereafter, expressed as follows: "and so long thereafter as oil is produced."

NATURE OF INTEREST OF LESSEE

In a lease for a definite period, the interest of the lessee is a chattel real and as such is personal property. (*Dabney* v. *Edwards,* 5 Cal.2d 1.) The interest of a lessee in an oil lease for an indefinite period is an interest in real property in the nature of a *profit à prendre.* (*Callahan* v. *Martin,* 3 Cal.2d 110.) This interest is an incorporeal hereditament, and has been held to be real property. Accordingly, a judgment lien attaches to the interest of the lessee under an oil and gas lease for an indefinite period.

STATUS AND CAPACITY OF PARTIES

As in the case of other leases, it is important to ascertain the status and capacity of the lessor and any limitations on his authority to execute an oil and gas lease. Under the provision of the Probate Code, an executor, administrator, or guardian may enter into an oil and gas lease, subject to approval by the court. Whether a trustee or an attorney-in-fact is empowered to execute an oil and gas lease is dependent upon the provisions of the instrument under which he acts. It has been held that the object of an oil and gas lease "is to effect, if not technically a sale and conveyance of a substantial and specific part of the land, at least a disposition and transfer thereof." (*Stone* v. *City of Los Angeles*, 114 C.A. 192.) Accordingly, a power to "lease," without an unrestricted power to sell or to execute oil and gas leases, probably does not authorize the execution of an oil and gas lease. The power to enter into a *community* oil and gas lease also requires specific authorization.

LEASE BY CO-OWNER

A co-owner can lease property for oil and gas purposes, and if he produces oil, he is entitled to charge the interests of nonproducing co-owners for their proportionate share of drilling and operating expense. (*Little* v. *Mountain View Dairies, Inc.*, 35 Cal.2d 232.) If a lease is executed by one co-owner alone, the other co-owners may either recognize the lease and receive their share of the royalty thereunder or reject the lease and receive their fractional part of the oil produced, less their proportionate part of the cost of discovery and production.

INTEREST OF LANDOWNER

An owner of land, when he leases it for oil and gas purposes, is vested with three separate and distinct interests: (1) the fee simple title to the surface estate; (2) the reserved royalty interest under the lease; and (3) the possibility of a reverter of the minerals. Each of these interests is an alienable interest in real property which may be conveyed separately and independently of the others. In addition to the right of the lessor to receive rent or a royalty, he has a reversionary interest in the right to drill for and produce oil after the termination of the existing lease.

ROYALTY INTERESTS

The term "landowner's royalty" (or "royalty") is generally applied to fractional interests in the production of oil and gas created by the owner of the land, either by reservation when an oil and gas lease is entered into, or by a direct grant to a third person. When a lessor assigns to third persons the fractional interests in the royalties that he has reserved to himself, such persons acquire estates in real property and become tenants in common with the lessor. Such estates continue beyond the termination of the lease unless the assignments specifically limit such estates to the term of the lease.

COMMUNITY OIL AND GAS LEASES

In a community oil and gas lease, several owners of parcels of land join in the execution of a single lease for the development of oil from all of their land, each owner to receive a percentage of the oil produced, measured by the ownership of the surface. In such a lease, each lessor in effect assigns or conveys to his colessors a percentage interest in all oil produced on his land during the continuance of the lease. This gives rise to *reciprocal rights* in the lands of each other.

ROYALTY INTEREST UNDER COMMUNITY OIL AND GAS LEASE

The royalty interest so transferred by each landowner to his colessors is an incorporeal hereditament in gross, and each lessor's interest in the oil produced upon the property of one of the colessors is entirely separate and distinct from the royalty interest retained by him in oil that might be produced from his own premises. Although the percentage of the royalty reserved by a lessor in oil produced from *his* land passes to a grantee of the fee as an incident of the conveyance, except as such rights may be reserved by the deed, the interest owned by the grantor in the oil produced from the land of the colessors, existing in gross, does not pass with the conveyance of the lessor's land, but can only be conveyed by a specific transfer of that interest (*Tanner* v. *Title Insurance and Trust Co.*, 20 Cal.2d 814), unless the lease contains a special clause providing that a conveyance by the lessor will transfer all interest under such leases.

OVERRIDING ROYALTY INTERESTS

A lessee under an oil and gas lease may assign his lease in its entirety, or he may assign it and reserve to himself a portion of the oil and gas to be produced, which reserved interest is called an "overriding royalty." If the lessee makes no reservation of a right to enter the premises for the purpose of drilling for oil and gas, such drilling rights pass to the assignee. Although the overriding royalties constitute interests in real property, such interests are not unlimited, but are determinable interests limited to the duration of the existing lease. If the lease provides for its termination (by a quitclaim deed, for instance), a quitclaim by the assignee to the lessor ordinarily terminates the lease and eliminates the overriding royalty interest without the joinder or consent of the holders of such interests. (*La Laguna Ranch Co.* v. *Dodge,* 18 Cal.2d 132.) A lessee may retain his lease and drilling rights and sell and transfer fractional interests in the oil and gas to be produced, which interests are also called overriding royalty interests, and are also limited to the duration of the existing lease.

CORPORATE SECURITIES ACT

The word "security" as defined in the Corporate Securities Act includes not only stocks, bonds, and evidences of indebtedness, but also any "certificate of interest or participation in an oil, gas, or mining title or lease." Transactions that may be within the definition of a "security" include a conveyance by the landowner of a royalty interest, or an assignment of a fractional interest in an oil and gas lease, or in the oil and gas in land that is subject to a lease, and in other interests in oil-bearing lands.

TERMINATION OF OIL LEASES

Termination by abandonment will more readily occur in the case of oil and gas leases than in other types of leases. The courts have declared that the rule that forfeitures are not favored in law does not apply to oil and gas leases. (*Wallace* v. *Imbertson,* 197 C.A.2d 392.) However, an abandonment will not be inferred unless it can be shown that *nonuser* by the lessee is coupled with an intent to relinquish all rights in the premises.

DISTINCTION BETWEEN "UNLESS" AND "DRILL OR PAY" LEASES

Oil and gas leases are sometimes referred to as "unless" leases, and "drill or pay" leases. An "unless" lease is one that automatically terminates if the lessee does not commence drilling prior to a specified time, *unless* he pays a specified rental for the privileges of delaying commencement of drilling. Failure to drill or to pay the rent in the specified period terminates all rights of the lessee. A "drill or pay" lease, on the other hand, is one in which the lessee agrees to drill or, in lieu of drilling, to pay rental. Under such a lease, even when it contains a surrender clause, the payment of rentals is not necessary to keep it alive, nor does it automatically terminate.

TERMINATION BY CANCELLATION

A lease may be terminated by cancellation. A problem may then arise as to whether or not all necessary parties have consented to the cancellation. In the case of single-property leases, as distinguished from community leases, a quitclaim deed by the lessee, which contains no reservations and is accepted by the owner, can be treated as a full cancellation. In the case of a community oil and gas lease, the usual form of lease provides in effect that the lessee may at any time quitclaim the lease in full, and thereupon the reciprocal rights of the lessors under the pooling agreement shall cease. If the lease does not contain such provisions, a cancellation of the lease and termination of the reciprocal rights requires consent of all of the landowners.

Questions

1. Explain briefly the relationship of landlord and tenant.
2. What is the main distinction between a tenant and a licensee?
3. Why are the distinctions between a tenant and a licensee important?
4. Define a tenancy at sufferance.
5. Give an illustration of a tenancy at will.
6. What is meant by a periodic tenancy?
7. How is a lease defined?
8. Explain the two sets of rights existing under a lease.
9. Are there any limitations on the term or period of lease?
10. Describe briefly the requisites of a valid lease.
11. Is it important to know the status of a person executing a lease? Explain.
12. Discuss the rules applicable to security deposits.
13. May a written lease be changed by oral agreement?
14. Are the interests of a lessor and a lessee transferable?
15. Discuss the difference between an assignment and a sublease.
16. Describe the ways in which a lease may be terminated.
17. Does a lessor of premises owe a duty with respect to condition of the premises?
18. In what respects do oil and gas leases differ from other types of leases?
19. What are royalty interests?

20

Real Estate Brokers

Summary

I. Introductory
Distinguishing characteristics of an agency; Broker defined; Real estate broker defined; Business opportunity; Mineral, oil, and gas brokers; Exception from license requirement; Realty loan brokers; Application of Corporate Securities Act

II. Regulation of brokers
Department of Real Estate; Real Estate Commissioner; Real estate licenses; Activities of Department of Real Estate in aid of licensees; Real Estate Education, Research and Recovery Fund

III. Employment and authority
Commission dependent upon written agreement; Authority to take listing; Contract of employment; Disposition of deposit

IV. Types of listing
Open listing; Exclusive agency listing; Exclusive right to sell listing; Termination date; Net listing; Option listing; Multiple listing.

V. Deposit receipt
Contract rules apply; Deposit receipt should evidence all terms of contract; All conditions should be specified; Deposit receipt forms

VI. Right to compensation
Computation of commission; Written contract and license essential; When commission is earned; Asking price; Procuring cause; Where sale consummated after termination of employment; Revocation of authority; Extension of time limit by oral agreement; "No deal—no commission" agreements; Payment of commission from escrow funds; Agreement for commission contained in a deposit receipt; Agreement for commission evidenced by escrow instructions; Forfeiture of deposit; Commission payable though seller not obligated to perform

VII. Duties and responsibilities
Agent owes utmost good faith; Duty to disclose best offer; Confidential relationship; False representations; Agent must use care and skill; Duty as to condition of premises; High standards of real estate practice required; Real Estate Boards; "Realtor" a mark of distinction; California Real Estate Association

I. Introductory

Most real estate transactions today utilize the services of a real estate broker. The real estate broker is ordinarily an *agent,* and the relationship between him and the person he represents is governed by substantially the same general legal principles that apply to any agency relationship.

DISTINGUISHING CHARACTERISTICS OF AN AGENCY

An agent is one who represents another, called a principal, in dealing with third persons; such a relationship is called an agency. An agent acts for and in the place of the principal for the purpose of bringing him into legal relations with third persons. An agent is distinguished from a servant or an employee, the latter being defined as persons who are employed to render personal services to the employer and who, in such service, remain entirely under the control and direction of the employer or master. An agent is also distinguished from an independent contractor, the latter being defined as a person who, in rendering services for another, exercises an independent employment or occupation and is responsible to the one hiring him only as to the results of his work. The main characteristic of this relationship is that the person hiring an independent contractor has no right of control as to the mode or method of doing the work contracted for.

Importance of distinctions. The distinctions between an agent and an employee and an independent contractor are of primary concern in connection with the following: (1) where liability is sought to be imposed on the principal for the wrongful act of the person hired, in which case it must be shown that the wrongdoer was an agent or employee; (2) where claims for injuries to the person hired are made, which presents a question of the application of workman's compensation laws; and (3) where contributions and benefits under Social Security laws are affected.

BROKER DEFINED

Although a broker is an agent, the term "broker" is somewhat less inclusive than the term "agent." The term "broker" generally applies to an agent who, for a commission or brokerage fee, acts as a negotiator or intermediary between his principal and third persons in connection with the acquisition of contractual rights, or the sale or purchase of property, real or personal, where the custody of the property is not intrusted to him for the purpose of discharging his agency. A broker is commonly regarded as a middleman whose duty is to bring a buyer and a seller together.

REAL ESTATE BROKER DEFINED

A real estate broker as defined in the code is a person who, for a compensation or in expectation of a compensation, does any of the following: sells or offers to sell; buys or offers to buy; solicits prospective sellers or purchasers; or negotiates the purchase, sale, or exchange of real property or of a business opportunity; or negotiates loans on real estate; or leases or offers to lease or negotiates the sale, purchase, or exchange of leases; or rents or places for rent or collects rent from real property or improvements thereon. (Bus. & Prof. C., Sec. 10131.) Sections 10131.1 and 10131.2 extend the definition of a broker to include additional transactions relating to real property sales contracts or promissory notes secured by lien on real property, or relating to advance fee listings.

Real estate salesman. A real estate salesman is a person who, for compensation, is employed by a real estate broker to perform any of the above-mentioned acts. (Bus. and Prof. C., Sec. 10132).

Real estate brokers and salesmen must be licensed. Under the provisions of the Real Estate Law (Bus. & Prof. C., Secs. 10000 *et seq.*), it is unlawful for any person to engage in the business, act in the capacity of, or advertise or assume to act as a real estate broker or salesman without first obtaining a license from the Department of Real Estate.

BUSINESS OPPORTUNITY

Prior to January 2, 1966, business opportunity brokers and salesmen were also required to be licensed. (Bus. & Prof. C., Secs. 10250 *et seq.*) Such persons are defined in terms of acts similar to those performed by real estate brokers, but with reference to *business opportunities.* This term means and includes business, business opportunity, and goodwill of an existing business. The primary distinction between the business of real estate brokerage and that of business opportunity brokerage lies in the respective subject matters. The term "real estate" as used in the Real Estate Law is regarded as synonymous with "real property." Thus, an equity in real estate under a contract of purchase is included within the scope of real estate brokerage. The sale of a business opportunity, however, involves the sale of personal property, and the rules and laws governing the transfer of chattels generally apply.

Effective January 2, 1966, real estate and business opportunity licenses were merged by statute. A real estate license is now required for a person to engage in the sale of business opportunities, and the special classification of business opportunity license no longer exists.

MINERAL, OIL, AND GAS BROKERS

Mineral, oil, and gas brokers are also subject to regulations under the Real Estate Law. (Bus. & Prof. C., Secs. 10500 *et seq.*) Since 1943, persons engaging in the business, acting in the capacity of, or advertising or assuming to act as a mineral, oil, and gas broker or a mineral, oil, and gas salesman within this state were required to obtain a mineral, oil, and gas license from the Division of Real Estate.

In 1967 the mineral, oil and gas salesman license designation was deleted. Any person, subject to certain exceptions, who now acts as a mineral, oil, and gas broker dealing with mineral, oil, or gas lands or leases is required to have a mineral, oil, and gas broker license. The law defines mineral, oil, and gas property as land used for, intended to be used for, or concerning which representations are made with respect to, the mining of minerals or the extraction of oil and gas therefrom. This law differs from the law affecting real estate brokers in one important respect, namely it has a special provision requiring that each licensee maintain with the Real Estate Commissioner a bond in the penal sum of $5,000.

EXCEPTION FROM LICENSE REQUIREMENT

The sections of the code requiring mineral, oil, and gas operators to obtain a license make an exception of licensed real estate brokers who engage in the sale, lease, or exchange of real property or an interest therein, in those cases where the transfer of mineral, oil, or gas property is *purely incidental* to the sale, lease, or exchange of real property. For instance, if the property to be conveyed, leased, or exchanged is primarily of agricultural value, the fact that it may have some incidental oil and gas or mineral value does not require the broker to hold a mineral, oil, and gas license. As an illustration, many real estate brokers specialize in the sale of orchards and other types of agricultural property in the San Joaquin and Sacramento Valleys. This property may also have some mineral value. If the latter is incidental to the agricultural value, the broker is regarded as engaged in a real estate transaction rather than in a transaction in mineral, gas, or oil property. Further, the law provides that a real estate broker who occasionally makes a transfer of mineral, oil, or gas property as an incident to his real estate business may secure a permit for such transaction from the Real Estate Commissioner without having to obtain a license. No more than ten such permits may be issued by the commissioner in any fiscal year to any one licensee.

REALTY LOAN BROKERS

Realty loan brokers are subject to regulations of the Real Estate Commissioner under the provisions of Section 10131 and other sections of the Business and Professions Code. It has been a long time requirement of the Real Estate Law that the person who negotiates a loan on real property for another and for a compensation must be licensed as a real estate broker or salesman. In 1955, because of complaints of hidden charges and excessive commissions exacted by some brokers, the legislature passed the Real Property Loan Brokerage Law. This law was made part of the Civil Code rather than the Business and Professions Code. This law became inadequate to cope with objectionable practices, however, and in 1961 the legislature enacted a new law to supersede the former one. The new law is regarded as the most comprehensive and stringent mortgage loan legislation in California history. It lifted most of the old mortgage loan brokerage provisions from the Civil Code, making them part of the Real Estate Law contained in the Business and Professions Code; it established a new classification for real estate brokers engaged in the sale of real estate securities, namely "Real Property Securities Dealers" (Bus. & Prof.C., Sec. 10237), and established controls on such dealers' operations.

In 1963 additional provisions were added, extending the coverage to conservatorship and liquidation proceedings and to the treatment of merchandising of out-of-state subdivision properties under the securities sections of the Real Estate Law. (Bus. and Prof. C., Sec. 10249.2.)

APPLICATION OF CORPORATE SECURITIES ACT

In 1955 the law was also amended to clarify the uncertain situation with respect to jurisdiction of the Division of Real Estate and the Division of Corporations over persons selling promissory notes secured by a lien on real property. It is now specifically provided that the Corporate Securities Law does not apply to the sale of any security (other than an interest in a real estate development) the issuance of which is subject to authorization by the Real Estate Commissioner, or of a promissory note secured by a lien on real property that is not one of a series of notes secured by interests in the same real property. (Corp.C., Sec. 25100.)

II. Regulation of brokers

The real estate business is regulated by the provisions of the Real

Estate Law for the purpose, among others, of raising the standards of the profession and requiring its members to act fairly and ethically with their clients. A primary function of the law is to allow only those persons who are honest, truthful, and reputable to operate as brokers or salesmen. The enactment of the Real Estate Law is within the general power of the state to regulate any occupation whose members should be specially qualified. Good moral character on the part of persons engaged in the real estate business may reasonably be required as a safeguard to the public.

DEPARTMENT OF REAL ESTATE

The State Division of Real Estate, now designated as the California Department of Real Estate, was created by legislative act in 1917. It was the first act of this nature to become law in the United States and has served as a pattern for similar legislation in many other states. The enactment was sponsored by real estate brokers who felt that reasonable regulation of persons engaged in the business of real estate would benefit the public and assist in creating and maintaining higher professional and ethical standards. Although the first law was declared unconstitutional, another law was enacted in 1919 which, with subsequent amendments, has been in force since that date. The jurisdiction of the Department of Real Estate extends not only to the issuance of licenses, but also to their suspension or revocation, and also includes the regulation of the sale of subdivisions in addition to other activities.

REAL ESTATE COMMISSIONER

The Real Estate Commissioner, appointed by the Governor for a four-year term, is the chief officer of the Department of Real Estate, and is chairman of the State Real Estate Commission, comprised of the commissioner and until 1968 six other members, three from the northern part of the state and three from the southern part. The commission members and the commissioner are required by law to be experienced in the real estate business. The commission is authorized to inquire into the needs of the real estate licensees, to confer and advise with the Governor and other state officers on real estate matters, and since 1949 has also been charged with the duty of passing on certain experience and educational claims made by broker license applicants.

In 1968 the law was amended to add two "public members" to the Real Estate Commission; one must be an attorney, the other a public planning official. Now four of the members have to be residents of northern California, and the other four, residents of southern California.

Duties of Real Estate Commissioner. The Real Estate Commissioner is charged with the enforcement of the Real Estate Law, and in this connection has full power to regulate and control the issuance, suspension, and revocation of all licenses under that law, and to perform all other acts and duties provided in the law and necessary for its enforcement. He is empowered to promulgate necessary rules and regulations for the administration and enforcement of the law and for the conduct of his office.

REAL ESTATE LICENSES

Licenses are issued to qualified applicants, either as a broker or a salesman. The date October 1, 1955, is considered an important date in the history of real estate licensing in California. Previous to 1955 all licenses issued by the Real Estate Commissioner were for a term of one year. In 1955 the legislature approved a change under which existing licenses would be renewed for a four-year term, rather than for one year. However, the new legislation drew a sharp line of distinction between real estate licenses issued and in good standing prior to that date and licenses thereafter issued. Licenses in good standing as of September 30, 1955, remained as *renewable licenses*, i.e., eligible for renewal periodically upon proper application and payment of the required fee, unless such licenses were revoked as a disciplinary measure. Licenses issued on October 1, 1955, and thereafter were referred to as *original licenses*, and did not become permanent, renewable licenses until the holders thereof met certain further examination requirements. The law was again amended in 1965, and the provisions for issuance of the original one-year license were eliminated effective January 2, 1966. The candidate for a real estate broker license, upon passing the required test or tests, is now entitled to apply for a four-year broker license, renewable every four years. The applicant for a real estate salesman license, if successful, is also entitled to apply for a four-year salesman license, renewable every four years unless revoked.

Qualifications of applicants for a license. Applicants for a real estate license must be able to establish qualifications of "honesty, truthfulness, and good reputation." Also, they must show, by written examination, an appropriate knowledge of the English language, including reading, writing, and spelling, and of arithmetic common to real estate and business opportunity practices; an understanding of the principles of real estate conveyancing, the general purposes and general legal effect of deeds, mortgages, land contracts of sale and leases, and of the elementary principles of land economics and appraisals; and a general and fair understanding of the obligations between principal and agent, of the principles of real estate practice and the canons of business ethics pertaining thereto, as well as pertinent provisions of the California Real Estate Law, including the regulation of subdivided lands. (Bus. & Prof. C., Sec. 10153.)

The examination consists of an all-day test, plus two special tests of not more than one and a half hours' duration each covering "legal aspects of real estate" and "real estate practice." However, the broker license candidate who has satisfactorily completed a three-unit course in one or both of these subjects at an accredited institution of higher learning is excused, accordingly, from one or both of these specialized tests.

New legislation was enacted in 1968 that makes it mandatory, as of January 2, 1970, that these two courses be completed in order to qualify for the broker license examination. After that date, the applicant must have completed three-unit college-level courses in real estate finance and real estate appraisal or be required to take special tests in these subjects. Starting in January, 1972, completion of all four of these courses will be a prerequisite for the real estate broker license examination.

Licensing of corporations and partnerships. The provision of the law requiring brokers to be licensed has applied to corporations and partnerships as well as to individuals. However, the law was amended in 1968 to eliminate a partnership license. Partnerships can continue to exist in the real estate business, and all members of a partnership performing activities calling for a license must be licensed individually as brokers.

A corporation can be licensed as a real estate broker but only if at least one officer is a duly qualified real estate broker. A corporation licensed as a real estate broker may include among its officers any of the licensed real estate salesmen employed by it, provided its chief executive officer primarily responsible for its management and operations has a real estate broker's license.

Fictitious firm names. If a broker is to engage in the real estate business under a fictitious firm name, that fictitious name must appear on his license in accordance with the rules and regulations of the Real Estate Commissioner. Other rules and regulations pertain to branch offices, signs and license display, and many other related matters.

ACTIVITIES OF DEPARTMENT IN AID OF LICENSEES

Although the service of the Department of Real Estate is basically that of protecting the public as a licensing and law enforcement agent, it endeavors to conduct its affairs in such a manner as to be of material assistance to its licensees and to encourage a high level of ethical and professional standards. The commissioner publishes a Real Estate Reference Book, and issues periodical bulletins to all licensed brokers and salesmen to keep them informed of the latest administrative provisions and also of current practices in real estate and allied activities. The Reference Book sets forth the requirements to be met in obtaining a license, and contains valuable study suggestions for the real estate license requirments.

REAL ESTATE EDUCATION, RESEARCH AND RECOVERY FUND

In 1956 the Real Estate Education and Research Fund was established to further education and research in real estate at the University of California, state colleges, and junior colleges. In 1963 the law was amended to change the name of this fund to the Real Estate Research, Education and Recovery Fund, and sections were added to the code for the creation and administration of a new concept in license law, whereby a minimum reserve of $400,000 is created and maintained to underwrite the payment of otherwise uncollectible court judgments obtained against licensees on the basis of fraud, misrepresentation, and deceit. One-fourth of the amount of license fees in excess of the first $10 collected by the Real Estate Commissioner shall be paid into the treasury of the state to the credit of this fund. (Bus. & Prof. C., Sec. 10450.6) Money credited to the fund shall be allocated as follows: 80 per cent for education and research and 20 per cent for recovery purposes. Under a 1965 amendment specific real estate research projects may be undertaken by private California universities with assistance from the fund.

III. Employment and authority

A contract of employment is essential to the creation of the broker-client relationship. Such a contract must be in writing. By virtue of the provisions of the Statute of Frauds (C.C., Sec. 1624), most contracts affecting any right, title, or interest in real property are required to be in writing, otherwise they are unenforceable. Under this code provision, an agreement authorizing or employing an agent or broker to purchase or sell real estate for compensation or a commission is unenforceable unless the same, or some note or memorandum thereof, is in writing and subscribed by the party to be charged. It has been held that the Statute of Frauds does not apply to a contract between brokers for the sharing of commissions. (*Holland* v. *Morgan & Peacock Properties*, 168 C.A.2d 206.)

COMMISSION DEPENDENT UPON WRITTEN AGREEMENT

As a general rule, unless a property owner gives the broker a written employment contract duly signed by the owner, showing the intention that the property owner is to be charged with payment of a commission in the event a buyer is procured by the broker, the latter cannot enforce a claim for his commission. A verbal agreement to pay a commission is considered *unenforceable,* although some of the earlier cases use the words "void" or "invalid" and "unenforceable" indiscriminately.

Exception to rule. An exception to the above rule may apply if the broker has changed his position to his detriment in reliance on the oral promise. In the case of *Le Blond* v. *Wolfe,* 83 C.A.2d 282, the broker cancelled a contract with the seller upon the oral promise of the purchaser that the latter would pay the commission. The buyer refused to pay, and an action was brought to recover the commission. The buyer raised as a defense the Statute of Frauds, but it was held that the broker changed his position to his own detriment by releasing the seller from any obligation to pay him a commission, and such change of position created an equitable estoppel against the purchaser from setting up the Statute of Frauds as a defense.

Contract to obtain an option to purchase. In the case of *Pacific Southwest Development Corp.* v. *Western Pacific Rd. Co.*, cited on p. 234, a question arose as to whether or not a contract employing a real estate broker to obtain an option for the purchase of real property was within the Statute of Frauds and must be in writing. The broker, pursuant to an oral contract, performed services on connection with the procurement of an option to purchase real property. Upon the client's refusal to pay a commission, the broker brought an action to recover his commission. The trial court held that he was not entitled to recover, since the contract was not in writing. The District Court of Appeal reversed the trial court, stating that an option to purchase real property conveys no interest in land to the optionee, but vests in the optionee only a right to buy; that an option contract relating to the sale of land is not a sale of property but of a right to purchase; and therefore a contract employing a broker to obtain an option does not fall within the Statute of Frauds. However, on appeal to the Supreme Court it was held by a four-to-three decision that such a contract must be in writing.

AUTHORITY TO TAKE LISTING

In the case of *Oaks* v. *Brahs,* 132 C.A.2d 182, a question arose as to whether or not a salesman who took a listing from the seller was required to have written authority from the broker to take such a listing. The court held that written authority was not essential in such cases.

CONTRACT OF EMPLOYMENT

The authority given the broker is governed by the terms of his contract. Most contracts are evidenced by a printed form of *listing agreement.*

The form customarily used is one approved by the California Real Estate Association. A listing is defined briefly as a contract of employment between a principal and an agent. The agent holding a listing is bound by the rules of law applying to the agency relationship and owes certain obligations to his principal. Although the written agreement employing a broker to sell real estate is usually called a listing, it need not be entitled as a "Listing." The most commonly used form is captioned "Authorization to Sell."

Essential requirements of contract of employment. It is essential that the contract, whatever its designation, be complete in all of its terms. Being a contract, it must have all of the essential elements of a valid contract, i.e., competent parties, a lawful object, a meeting of the minds, a sufficient consideration, and a proper description of the property involved. An approved form of listing agreement, when properly filled out and duly executed by the person employing the broker, accomplishes the purpose and is sufficient evidence in writing of the contract of employment.

Principal entitled to copy of contract. In all cases, whatever the form of the contract of employment, whether a listing agreement or some other agreement, the broker must deliver to his customer or client a copy of the document that the latter has signed. (Bus. & Prof. C., Sec. 10142.)

Listing agreement does not compel a sale. The usual contract creating the relationship of brokerage authorizes the broker to find a purchaser, but this does not obligate the owner to sell. The language employed may recite that the broker is authorized to sell, but this means that he is authorized only to find a purchaser. It does not bind the owner to sell and convey.

DISPOSITION OF DEPOSIT

The listing agreement may authorize the broker to accept a deposit from the purchaser. The seller becomes entitled to the deposit when he accepts the purchaser procured by the broker. The deposit money does not belong to the broker, and he is not entitled to retain custody of it. Normally, the authority of the broker is only to produce a purchaser who is willing to contract with the seller upon the prescribed terms. The broker, solely by virtue of his employment as a broker, has no authority to accept a deposit. If the purchaser pays money to the broker who is not authorized to accept a deposit, the broker holds the deposit as the agent of the purchaser and not the seller, and the risk of loss is upon the purchaser. However, if the listing agreement gives the broker the authority to accept a deposit, as it often does, he holds it as the agent of the seller.

Deposit money must be kept separate. Since the deposit money does not belong to the broker in any event, it is a basic rule that he must not commingle it with his own funds. This is not only a general principle of agency, but a violation of this rule subjects the broker to disciplinary action by the Real Estate Commissioner.

IV. Types of listing

Various kinds of listing agreements are in common use, the ones most frequently encountered being the *open listing,* the *exclusive agency listing,* and the *exclusive right to sell listing.* Other types that may be encountered are the *net listing,* the *option listing,* and the *multiple listing.*

OPEN LISTING

An open listing is a written memorandum signed by the party to be charged—in most cases the seller of the property—authorizing the broker to act as agent for the sale of designated property. Usually there is no time limit to the employment. By the use of an open listing, the seller may employ a number of brokers, each of whom will have an equal opportunity to earn a commission. Under such listing, a commission is payable only to the broker who first procures a buyer who is ready, willing, and able to buy pursuant to the terms of the listing or pursuant to other terms acceptable to the seller. The sale of the property by any one of the brokers, or by the seller himself, terminates the open listing of all other brokers. The seller is not obligated to notify the other brokers of the sale and of the termination of their agency.

EXCLUSIVE AGENCY LISTING

In an exclusive agency listing the broker is designated as the "exclusive agent," and the broker named in the listing is entitled to a commission even if the property is sold by another broker. However, since such a listing refers only to sales by "agents," the owner may sell the property himself without being liable for payment of a commission.

EXCLUSIVE RIGHT TO SELL LISTING

The exclusive right to sell listing goes one step further than the exclusive agency listing. It not only makes the broker the sole agent of the owner for the sale of the property, but provides that the broker will receive a commission if the property is sold by the named broker, by the seller, or by anyone else within the prescribed time. Even if the owner makes a sale through his own efforts, he must pay a commission to the broker. In such case the broker need not show that he was the procuring cause of the sale.

TERMINATION DATE

The "exclusive right" and the "exclusive agency" type of listing must be for a definite term and must contain a specified date of termination. If the contract does not provide for a definite termination date, the broker is subject to a penalty of revocation or suspension of his license, as provided for in Section 10176f of the Business and Professions Code. Moreover, a violation of this section by a broker renders the listing void, and the broker cannot recover a commission. (*Dale* v. *Palmer,* 106 C.A.2d 663.)

Illustrative case on termination date. In the case of *Summers* v. *Freeman,* 128 C.A.2d 828, one of the defenses raised to an action by a broker for his commission was the contention that the contract was an exclusive agency and therefore void because it lacked a definite termination date. The contract, written on the back of a map of the defendant's property, was dated July 24, 1951, and recited that the owner agreed to sell the property "as outlined in red on the map, consisting of 8.8 acres, more or less," through the agency of the plaintiff. The court held that the agreement was not exclusive, and that plaintiff was entitled to his commission. The court stated that a real estate broker's authority to sell real property is not exclusive unless it is made so in unequivocal terms or by necessary implication. To construe the agreement as exclusive in this case would disregard the rule "a contract must receive such an interpretation as will make it lawful if it can be done without violating the intention of the parties."

NET LISTING

In a net listing the compensation to the broker is not definitely stated. Such a listing entitles the broker to receive as compensation all proceeds acquired from the sale in excess of the selling price fixed by the seller. If the property is sold for the sum specified for the seller's account or for less, the broker does not receive any compensation. If the property sells for more than the price fixed by the seller, the broker is entitled to retain the surplus. Although net listings are legal and have been held enforceable, their use is generally frowned upon, as they often give rise to a claim of unfairness.

Duty to disclose selling price. Section 10176g of the Business and Professions Code makes it a cause of revocation or suspension of a license if the broker fails to disclose the amount of his compensation in connection with a net listing. This must be done prior to or at the time the principal binds himself to the transaction.

OPTION LISTING

An option listing gives the broker himself an option to purchase the property. When exercising the option, the broker is in a fiduciary position and must make disclosure of all outstanding offers and other material information in his possession. As stated in the case of *Curry* v. *King*, 6 C.A. 568, where a broker is employed to find a purchaser for the property of a principal and is given an option, running concurrently with the agency, to purchase the property, he cannot, when pursuing his own interests, ignore those of the principal, and he will not be permitted to enjoy the fruits of an advantage taken of a fiduciary relation, whose dominant characteristic is the confidence reposed by one person in another. Were the rule otherwise, the broker would be tempted to wait until he had arranged for a profitable resale of the property to a third party, and then exercise the option.

Duty to disclose amount of profit. Under Section 10176h of the Business and Professions Code, a license may be revoked or suspended if the broker fails to disclose the full amount of the profit before exercising the option. This disclosure must be in writing, and the written consent of the seller must be obtained approving the amount of the profit.

MULTIPLE LISTING

A multiple listing is not, technically, a legal term for a type of listing, but is the name commonly applied to a service by realty boards to their members. A multiple listing service is defined as an organized real estate listing service conducted by a group of brokers, usually members of a real estate board. The brokers pool their exclusive-right-to-sell listings by furnishing such listings to the multiple organization, which distributes the listing to all members of the group who then have an equal opportunity to sell the listed properties. In the event of a sale, the brokerage commission is divided in agreed proportions between the listing broker and the member of the board who effected the sale. If the listing broker himself sells the property, he is entitled to the commission in its entirety.

Action to recover commission under multiple listing. Where an action is brought against the owner to recover a commission on a sale through a multiple listing service, it has been held that a member of the realty board, other than the broker named in a listing agreement, is without right to maintain an action for the stipulated commission against the owner, where such agreement constituted the broker the owner's exclusive agent vested with the exclusive right to sell. (*Goodwin* v. *Glick*, 139 C.A.2d Supp. 936.) The court pointed out that although the listing agreement permitted a referral to a multiple realty board, which could rightfully refer the listing to the broker effecting the sale, such broker, being a subagent, could not maintain an action for the commission. The action would have to be brought by the broker named in the listing agreement. This case must be considered, of course, in the light of the particular wording of the listing agreement upon which the decision is based. It is undoubtedly possible to draft a listing agreement permitting the use of multiple listing services so as to specifically enable the selling broker as well as the listing broker to maintain a cause of action for a commission.

V. Deposit receipt

It is a general practice in California for brokers to use a deposit receipt when accepting "earnest money" to bind an offer for the purchase of property. This deposit receipt is one of the most important instruments used in a real estate transaction. A deposit receipt not only constitutes a receipt for a deposit by the prospective purchaser, but when duly executed by the buyer and seller constitutes a *contract* for the purchase and sale of real property. In addition to being a contract between the seller and buyer, a deposit receipt also evidences the agreement between the seller and the broker for the payment of a specified sum as a commission.

CONTRACT RULES APPLY

Since a deposit receipt is a contract, the elementary concepts of contract law are applicable. Of particular significance are the elements of offer and acceptance. In the ordinary transaction, when the buyer signs the deposit receipt, this constitutes an offer by the buyer. This offer may be revoked at any time prior to communication to him of the seller's acceptance. If the seller accepts the buyer's offer and communicates his acceptance to the buyer, a binding contract arises, provided of course, that all other elements of a lawful contract are present. If the seller makes a counteroffer, a binding contract does not come into being until the buyer's subsequent acceptance is communicated to the seller. For an acceptance to result in the formation of a binding contract, it must be made in the exact terms set forth in the offer.

DEPOSIT RECEIPT SHOULD EVIDENCE ALL TERMS OF CONTRACT

In the preparation of a deposit receipt, it is desirable that all of the basic provisions of the contract of sale and purchase be set forth, and that nothing be left for further determination in the escrow agreement or otherwise, including arrangements for financing. If the buyer must obtain financing before he is unconditionally obligated to purchase the seller's property, the deposit receipt should so state. It should further specify the amount of the loan the buyer needs, the duration of the loan, the rate of interest, the amount of monthly payments, including principal and interest, the conditions of prepayment, if any, and the total loan charges and fees that the buyer is willing to incur. Provision should be made as to the disposition of the matter if the buyer is unable to obtain such a loan.

ALL CONDITIONS SHOULD BE SPECIFIED

If the purchase and sale are contingent upon the happening of some other event or condition, the deposit receipt should spell out the contingency with certainty and clarity. If the buyer must sell property that he presently owns before he is obligated to purchase the seller's property, the deposit receipt should so recite. It should specify what is to happen to the deposit money in the event the buyer is unable to sell his property at the designated terms within the specified time. The deposit receipt should contain further a complete understanding between the buyer, the seller, and the broker as to the return of the deposit in the event the buyer's offer is not accepted, and as to the forfeiture provisions and disposition of the deposit money if the buyer should fail to complete the purchase.

DEPOSIT RECEIPT FORMS

Some of the foregoing provisions are incorporated in printed forms of deposit receipts, but obviously the form must be filled out completely and carefully by the broker or salesman. The California Real Estate Association standard deposit receipt form is set up in such a manner that if it is properly filled in, it can become a completed contract of sale when accepted by the seller. A new form was approved by the California Real Estate Association and the State Bar of California in 1967. The new form is entitled "Real Estate Purchase Contract and Receipt for Deposit" and contains several major changes intended to aid enforceability.

VI. Right to compensation

Brokers customarily are paid on a commission basis. A commission is defined as an agent's compensation for performing the duties of his agency. In real estate practice, this is a percentage of the selling price, or a percentage of rentals, or the like. The amount or rate of the commission that a broker may charge is not fixed by law, but is a matter of contract between the parties, and may be an amount that they agree upon. For many years 5 per cent was the prevailing rate of commission payable to a broker upon a sale of residential property, but an increase to 6 per cent is in effect in most areas. If no amount has been fixed in the agreement, it will be presumed that the customary commission payable in the area was intended.

COMPUTATION OF COMMISSION

In determining the amount of commission due a broker on a sale of real property, the computation is based upon the total price paid disregarding the amount of the encumbrances on the property. If property is listed at a given amount but sold at a greater price, the broker will be entitled to the same rate of commission on the higher price as provided for at the lower price.

WRITTEN CONTRACT AND LICENSE ESSENTIAL

Before a broker can maintain an action to recover a commission for selling land, he must allege and prove that he was a duly licensed real estate broker at the time of the transaction, and that he was employed under a contract in writing.

WHEN COMMISSION IS EARNED

As a general rule, a broker has earned his commission when he has procured a buyer who is ready, willing, and able to buy the property on the exact terms of the listing agreement or any other terms acceptable to the seller. When this has been accomplished, the broker is usually entitled to his commission regardless of whether the sale is ever consummated.

The following two cases are illustrative of the rights of the parties where the contract of sale is subject to a contingency. In the case of *Wesley N. Taylor Co.* v. *Russell*, 194 C.A.2d 816, an action was brought by the broker to recover a commission in the sum of $5,500. The contract of sale was contingent on the buyer's ability to obtain a loan. which provision was inserted at the buyer's request. Before the time for closing of the escrow the seller repudiated the contract. In the meantime the buyer waived the condition. In this resulting action, the seller contended that he was not liable because the buyer's obligation to perform was not *unconditional.* However, the court held that since the condition had been inserted at the request of and for the protection of the buyer, who had waived the requirement, the condition was accordingly fulfilled, and the broker was entitled to his commission. Judgment for the broker was confirmed on appeal.

In the case of *Kopf* v. *Milan*, 60 Cal.2d 600, an action was brought to recover a real estate commission on a sale of a parcel of property in Marin county for $87,000. The deposit receipt contained the following provision:

> Balance of the purchase price is to be paid as follows: Subject to buyers assuming an existing loan of approximately $58,000 secured by a First Trust Deed bearing 6% interest.

The buyers deposited cash in the escrow for the difference between the first trust deed and the amount of the sale. It was thereafter discovered that the first trust deed contained a "due on sale" clause. The beneficiary was unwilling to waive his right to declare the entire balance due on a transfer of the property, so the escrow failed to close. The court held that no commission was payable, stating that when a contract for the sale of real property is conditional, the broker's commission is not earned if the condition is not performed.

The court stated:

> When a vendor enters into a valid *unconditional* contract of sale with a purchaser procured by a broker, the purchaser's acceptability is conclusively presumed because the vendor is estopped to deny the qualifications of a purchaser with whom he is willing to contract. . . . When the contract is *conditional*, however, the broker's commission is not earned if the condition is not performed.

ASKING PRICE

Ordinarily, the price at which a broker is authorized to sell property is considered merely an asking price to guide the broker in his negotiations with prospective purchasers. If the broker procures a purchaser willing to pay a lower price, the owner cannot deprive the broker of his commission by conducting the final negotiations himself, and selling at a lower figure to the purchaser procured by the broker.

PROCURING CAUSE

The broker must be the *procuring cause* of the sale. Procuring cause is defined as the cause originating a series of events that, without break in their continuity, result in the accomplishment of the prime object of the employment. (*Rose* v. *Hunter*, 155 C.A.2d 319.) The word "procure" does not necessarily imply the formal consummation of an agreement. In its broadest sense, the word means to prevail upon, induce, or persuade a person to do something. The originating cause, which ultimately leads to the conclusion of the transaction, is held to be the procuring cause.

Determination as to procuring cause. Open listings have frequently given rise to disputes over who was the procuring cause of a sale. To entitle the broker to a commission, the sale must of course be the direct or proximate result of the acts performed by the broker. However, the broker personally is not obliged to bring the buyer and the seller to an agreement. Whether the broker was the motivating force that caused his principal to execute a sales agreement with the buyer is a question of fact, to be determined from all of the circumstances of the case. This rule is illustrated by the case of *Oaks* v. *Brahs* (cited on p. 393), in which it was held on appeal that a finding by the trial court that the broker was the procuring cause of the sale of ranch property was sustained by evidence that the buyer had no thought of buying the ranch before the broker's salesman contacted him; that his interest was so much aroused that he promised "to look at it"; and that such interest did not subside, although the sale was consummated directly between the seller and buyer after the buyer had gone out to look at the property by himself.

WHERE SALE CONSUMMATED AFTER TERMINATION OF EMPLOYMENT

The case of *Delbon* v. *Brazil,* 134 C.A.2d 461, involved a question as to the broker's right to a commission on a sale consummated after termination of his employment. The contract gave the broker an exclusive right to sell certain real property during a specified term (June 16 to July 16, 1952), or within 30 days thereafter to a person with whom the broker had "negotiated for a sale" during the specified term. A salesman employed by the broker held an interview with a prospective buyer in the broker's office on July 11, 1952. During the conference and for an hour or more the salesman discussed the property with the prospect, informing him that the property would be good clover ground, was easily leveled, and so forth. The salesman offered to show the property to the prospect, but the latter said he preferred to go alone. The salesman thereupon made a diagram showing the location of the property. Three days later the salesman phoned the prospect. The latter said he wanted more information regarding the description, water, taxes, and so on. The next day the salesman went to Merced, obtained the information, telephoned the information to the prospect, and gave him the name of the owner. The prospect stated he was debating between this property and another parcel. Within a week the salesman telephoned the prospect, who said he was still waiting to make up his mind. Within the 30-day period the prospect purchased the property through another broker with whom the owner had listed the property. The original broker claimed he was entitled to a commission, but the seller refused to pay. An action was filed and recovery allowed. The main question raised pertained to the meaning of the words "negotiated for a sale." The court stated that "negotiation" when used in a contract such as the one in question means that "the efforts of the broker to interest a prospect must have proceeded to the point where the prospect would be considered a likely purchaser."

In the case of *E. A. Strout Western Realty Agency, Inc.* v. *Lewis*, 255 C.A.2d 254, it was held that a real estate broker was the primary procuring cause of the sale of real property and thus entitled to a commission where, although the sale was made after the seller's contract with the broker had been terminated, the listing agreement provided that the commission would be paid if the property was sold within one year after the termination to a prospect procured by the broker prior to such termination, and the buyer, although not procured by the broker, was the brother of the person procured by the broker, and the evidence showed that the property was actually purchased for the benefit of such person.

REVOCATION OF AUTHORITY

In the absence of a contract to the contrary, a broker is not entitled to compensation for his services where his principal in good faith revokes his authority before he has earned his commission by procuring a purchaser. Accordingly, if the principal's agreement to pay a commission is unilateral, or if he has not contracted to employ the broker for any particular length of time, the principal can, without liability, terminate the employment at any time before the broker fully performs. The broker is not entitled to reimbursement for expenditures made or expenses incurred in attempting to make a sale unless he is expressly authorized to do so by the principal.

When revocation of employment not permitted. If the broker has expended time and effort to sell the property and is in the midst of negotiations that are approaching success, the principal cannot, without incurring liability, terminate the broker's employment with the purpose of enjoying the fruits of the broker's efforts and thereby avoid the payment of a commission. In such a case, performance may be said to be prevented by the principal's wrongful acts, and the broker will be entitled to his commission.

EXTENSION OF TIME LIMIT BY ORAL AGREEMENT

In the case of *Filante* v. *Kikendall,* 134 C.A.2d 695, a question was raised as to the right to a commission where a sale was effected after the listing agreement had expired. It was held that where an owner of realty, after expiration of the time limit in a listing contract within which a broker was to sell the property, encouraged the broker to continue his efforts to find a purchaser, and the broker did so with the owner's knowledge and approval with the result that a purchaser was produced to whom the owner sold the property, the time limit in the contract was waived, and the broker was entitled to his commission. The owner raised as a defense the fact that the agreement extending the time was not in writing and was therefore unenforceable, but the court held that a provision in a written agreement limiting time for performance may be waived orally.

"NO DEAL—NO COMMISSION" AGREEMENTS

Contracts may expressly provide that no commission is payable unless a completed sale is made. This is known as a "no deal—no commission" arrangement. The right of the broker to recover a commission must be measured of necessity by the terms of his contract. If the seller and broker contract that no commission shall be considered earned until the happening of a specified event or contingency, or upon certain terms and conditions being complied with, the commission will not be deemed earned unless the event, contingency, or condition occurs. Such contracts are not the usual ones between a seller and broker, however, and to create such a contract the courts have held that the terms must be clear and unequivocal. It has also been held in such cases that if the seller's refusal to complete the transaction is arbitrary and without legal cause, or in bad faith, the broker will be entitled to his commission. (*Swanson* v. *Thurber,* 132 C.A.2d 171.)

PAYMENT OF COMMISSION FROM ESCROW FUNDS

Sometimes a broker, who will have earned a commission pursuant to the listing agreement, is the motivating cause in setting up escrow instructions that provide for payment of commissions out of the "escrow proceeds" or at the "close of escrow." If the sale is not consummated, there will, of course, be no "escrow proceeds" or "close of escrow," and therefore no commission. In such a case the broker may be estopped from relying on the listing agreement because of his acquiescence in the subsequent agreement for payment of commission in the escrow. (*Cochran* v. *Ellsworth,* 126 C.A.2d 429.)

AGREEMENT FOR COMMISSION CONTAINED IN A DEPOSIT RECEIPT

Where the only agreement to pay a broker a commission is contained in a deposit receipt between the buyer and seller, it has been held that the broker's right to a commission is dependent upon performance of the provisions contained in the deposit receipt. If the buyer refuses to perform, or if the agreement is cancelled or rescinded, the broker is not entitled to recover his commission. (*Lawrence Block Co.* v. *Palston,* 123 C.A.2d 300.) This case was cited by the Supreme Court in the case of *Collins* v. *Vickter Manor, Inc.,* 47 Cal.2d 875, which held that where the broker's right to a commission is based solely upon a deposit receipt executed by the seller, the prospective purchaser, and the broker (the broker having been employed under an oral agreement), the right to a commission is not defeated *as a matter of law* by the failure of the parties to actually consummate the sale. This is a *question of fact* in each case. The court stated: "Such a three-party writing may unequivocably specify, or where uncertain may be construed or shown by extrinsic evidence to mean, that the broker has fully performed the duties of his employment and earned his commission by having obtained a buyer ready, able, and willing to proceed with a purchase in accord with those terms of the writing." Where the deposit-receipt agreement can be so interpreted, the sale itself need never be consummated to entitle the broker to his commission.

AGREEMENT FOR COMMISSION EVIDENCED BY ESCROW INSTRUCTIONS

In the case of *Martin* v. *Chernabaeff,* 124 C.A.2d 648, it was held that the requirement that a contract with a broker to sell real property be in writing is satisfied by evidence that the buyers signed escrow instructions providing for payment of a commission out of monies deposited in escrow, and that the sellers signed similar instructions.

FORFEITURE OF DEPOSIT

Deposit receipts often have provided for a forfeiture of the deposit if the buyer defaults. Where the deposit receipt provides that the seller shall pay to the broker one half (or some other proportion, not exceeding the full amount of the commission) of the buyer's deposit in the event of a default by the buyer, the broker is of course entitled to his share of such deposit if the buyer refuses to perform and the seller elects to declare a forfeiture, and the clause is not declared to be unenforceable.

The new form mentioned on p. 399 has substituted a "liquidated damage clause" for a forfeiture provision permitting the retention of the deposit as consideration for executing the agreement. Forfeiture clauses have almost uniformly been held invalid by the courts. However, a liquidated damage clause, wherein the parties agree to a specified amount where it would be impractical or extremely difficult to fix actual damage accruing to the seller as a result of the buyer's breach, may be enforceable, depending on the facts in the particular case.

COMMISSION PAYABLE THOUGH SELLER NOT OBLIGATED TO PERFORM

The case of *Austin* v. *Richards,* 146 C.A.2d 436, raised a question as to whether or not the broker was entitled to a commission where the seller was not obligated to perform because of inadequacy of consideration. The seller had entered into a contract with a buyer obtained by the broker, based upon the terms of the seller. The seller thereafter decided not to go through with the deal because the selling price was considered inadequate. The buyer brought an action against the seller for specific performance, but because the purchase price was in fact inadequate, the court refused to compel the seller to perform. The seller in turn refused to pay the broker his commission. In this resulting action by the broker, the court held that the seller was still liable to the broker for the commission, even though the seller could not be compelled to perform the contract with the buyer.

VII. Duties and responsibilities

The relationship between a broker and his principal is *fiduciary* in nature, and imposes upon the broker the duty of acting in the highest good faith toward his principal. (*Wells Fargo Bank* v. *Dowd,* 139 C.A.2d 561.) This fiduciary character with which the broker is clothed throughout the course of his dealings with his client is the most important phase of the relationship. The courts have regarded this relationship in the same general manner and in virtually the same strictness as that of a trustee and beneficiary. It is a fundamental rule that in all matters connected with his trust, a trustee is bound to act in the highest regard toward his beneficiary, and may not obtain any advantage over the latter by the slightest misrepresentation, concealment, duress, or adverse pressure of any kind.

AGENT OWES UTMOST GOOD FAITH

An agent may not unite his personal and his representative character in the same transaction. The agent owes to his principal the utmost good faith, and he must so circumscribe his conduct that he not only does what is in the best interests of his principal, but must make no personal profit out of the subject matter of the agency in conflict with the rights of the principal. (*Crogan* v. *Metz,* 47 Cal.2d 398.) An agent is forbidden to make a secret profit out of the transaction he is handling for his principal, and commits actionable fraud where, for instance, in a net-listing situation he represents to his principal that he is selling property at a certain price but is in fact obtaining a greater price.

DUTY TO DISCLOSE BEST OFFER

In the case of *Simone* v. *McKee*, 142 C.A.2d 307, judgment was obtained against a broker where a $17,000 offer was not disclosed in preference to a $13,000 offer. The court stated that it is obviously a breach of a real estate broker's duty if he fails to disclose to his client an offer to buy the client's property listed for sale with the broker.

CONFIDENTIAL RELATIONSHIP

In the case of *Devers* v. *Greenwood*, 139 C.A.2d 345, involving loose practices in connection with loan transactions, a judgment was obtained against the broker based on constructive fraud. The court stated the rule as follows: "One who holds a confidential relation toward another will not be permitted to take advantage of such relation in favor of himself or deal with the other party to that relation upon terms of his own making."

FALSE REPRESENTATIONS

In the case of *Kruse* v. *Miller*, 143 C.A.2d 656, the sellers of real property brought an action based on fraud against the real estate broker where the broker, in showing the property to prospective purchasers, represented that the residence was not built on a filled lot, which representation was false. The purchasers bought in reliance on such representation, and later brought an action against the sellers for rescission. The purchasers prevailed in the rescission action. The sellers then brought this action against the broker and recovered judgment for $4,857.98 as follows: $3,191.97 for damages recovered against the sellers in the rescission action; $575 for broker's commission; $60.50 for escrow charges; $800 for attorney's fees in the rescission action; $113.35 for court costs in the rescission action; and $111.16 for loss of earnings in time spent in defending the rescission action. It was held that the broker violated his duty to his principals by not informing them of the representations he had made to the purchasers that the lot was not a filled lot, and thereby perpetrated a fraud upon the confidence bestowed upon him by the sellers.

AGENT MUST USE CARE AND SKILL

A broker is under a duty to use care and skill in the performance of his duties. He is required at all times to exercise reasonable care and diligence in the transactions in which he is employed. A broker is liable for negligence in the performance of his duties. This is illustrated by the case of *Wilson* v. *Hisey*, 147 C.A.2d 433, where a judgment was obtained against a broker in an action by a buyer to rescind a lease and option-to-purchase agreement, and for damages against the broker who had prepared the lease. The court held that the real estate salesman representing the plaintiff in the real estate transaction was negligent in reporting, without sufficient information as to the true facts, that there was only one trust deed against the property, and that the monthly payments included interest, whereas the facts disclosed a second trust deed, and interest was not included in the monthly payment. The court indicated further that the salesman might have been negligent in failing to recommend a title search on the property.

DUTY AS TO CONDITION OF PREMISES

In the case of *Merrill* v. *Buck*, 58 Cal.2d 552, which was an action for personal injuries sustained by a lessee of a dwelling house as the result of a fall down a flight of basement stairs, a judgment for $65,700 in favor of plaintiff was affirmed by the California Supreme Court against all defendants, namely: (1) the owner of the real property (lessor); (2) the real estate saleswoman who showed the house to plaintiff and negotiated the lease; (3) the real estate broker.

Plaintiff had assumed the door was a closet door; it actually led directly to the basement. Plaintiff had not been cautioned about the door, which was one of several leading from an entry hall. Plaintiff sued the owners upon the basis of common-law principles of landlord and tenant negligence law; that they were liable for failure to warn plaintiff of the known *latent* danger (concealed hazard) behind the basement door, the precipitous stairway becoming a veritable trap causing plaintiff's injuries. Plaintiff's claim against the realtors rested on their voluntary undertaking to show her the house and on their negligence, as business volunteers, in failing to warn her of the existence of the doorway, the stairs, and the basement.

The court stated that the case as far as the real estate agents were concerned was one admittedly without exact precedent, but the court was satisfied that, having affirmatively undertaken to show the house to plaintiff in the regular course of their business, with the purpose of earning a commission if she decided to rent it, these defendants were under a duty of care to warn her of a concealed danger in the premises of which they were aware and from which her injury might be reasonably foreseen if she did become a tenant.

HIGH STANDARDS OF REAL ESTATE PRACTICE REQUIRED

As in other professions, those engaged in real estate activities should have regard for more than the law as contained in statutes, rules, and regulations; professional courtesy and ethics require additional consideration. It is said that the man who tries only to stay on the border of the law will at some time step across. The course of conduct set forth in the Real Estate Law and the rules and regulations prescribed pursuant thereto *must* be followed by a broker; other things should also be observed as a rule of conduct in order to maintain the high standards of real estate practice and the respect that the public has for any profession requiring the exercise of the highest degree of skill, competency, honesty, and integrity.

REAL ESTATE BOARDS

A National Association of Real Estate Boards was formed in 1908. The national association and its constituent boards and state associations form a composite organization of brokers whose object has been to forward the interests of brokers, disseminate education, and raise the standards of real estate practice and the esteem in which brokers are held in the community. To this end a Code of Ethics was formulated and adopted, which, as recommended by the Real Estate Commissioner, should be scrupulously observed.

"REALTOR" A MARK OF DISTINCTION

The Code of Ethics uses the word "Realtor." "Realtor" is not a synonym for "real estate broker." It is the distinctive and exclusive designation for those within the membership of the national association, and its exclusive use has been upheld by the courts. Every Realtor has pledged that he will observe and abide by the Code of Ethics, promulgated by the national association and adopted by his own board to govern real estate practice of members of the board, and has manifested that he is of good business character.

CALIFORNIA REAL ESTATE ASSOCIATION

The pioneer real estate organizations in California were the San Diego Realty Board organized in 1887 and the San Jose Real Estate Board in 1890. Others followed in the 1900's. In 1905 the California Real Estate Association was formed at Los Angeles; it is now composed of over 160 local real estate boards throughout the state and also of individual members from communities that do not have a local board. The objects and purposes of the California Real Estate Association are set forth in its constitution as follows:

1. To unite its members.
2. To promote high standards.

3. To safeguard the land-buying public.
4. To foster legislation for the benefit and protection of real estate.
5. To cooperate in the economic growth and development of the State.

The objectives and ideals of the Association have accomplished a great deal in the advancement of the real estate profession and the service afforded by it to the public.

Questions

1. How is the term "broker" defined?
2. Distinguish an agent, an employee, and an independent contractor.
3. Are real estate brokers and salesmen required to be licensed?
4. Discuss the various types of licenses provided for in the Real Estate Law.
5. Explain the use of the term "original license."
6. Describe briefly the duties of the Real Estate Commissioner's office.
7. Must an agreement employing a broker to sell real estate be in writing?
8. Discuss the common types of listing agreements in general use.
9. Must an "exclusive listing" have a definite termination date?
10. Is the use of "net listings" permitted?
11. Describe the purpose and effect of a deposit receipt.
12. At what time has a broker earned his commission?
13. Explain the meaning of the term "procuring cause."
14. Discuss briefly the duties owed by a broker to his principal.
15. Are the terms "Realtor" and "real estate broker" synonymous?

21

Escrows

Summary

I. Nature of an escrow
Definition of an escrow; Origin of the word "escrow"; Contract an essential requirement; Code definition; Common meaning of escrow; Scope of escrow; Escrow as a "stakeholder"

II. Requisites of a valid escrow
Escrow contract; Contract prior to escrow; Rules of construction

III. Status of the escrow holder
Regulation of escrow agents; Deposit of funds; Real estate brokers; Agency status of escrow holder; Nature of agency

IV. Duties and responsibilities of the escrow holder
Documents on deposit; Conflicting demands; Instructions are confidential; Forfeitures

V. Title and possession during escrow
Incidents of relationship; Fire insurance policies

VI. Performance of conditions
Waiver of conditions; Effect of unauthorized delivery; When title passes; Particular provisions; Doctrine of relation back

VII. Cancellation or revocation of the escrow
Payment of broker's commission; Right of cancellation by one party; Notice of cancellation; Where neither party has performed; Performance during extension; Reasonable time for performance; Effect of death or incompetency

VIII. Practical considerations
Southern California practice; Northern California practice; Initial steps in a sale; Preparation of escrow instructions; Procedural steps; Manner of taking title; Description of the property; Adjustments in escrow; Termite reports; Possession

I. Nature of an escrow

Most transactions in California affecting title to real property are closed through the instrumentality of an escrow. Sales escrows are of common occurrence, but the use of an escrow is not limited solely to the sale of real property. Other types of escrows, such as loan escrows and exchange escrows, are also frequently utilized.

DEFINITION OF AN ESCROW

An escrow is generally defined as a deed, bond, or other type of written obligation, delivered to a third person, to be delivered by him to the grantee only upon the performance or fulfillment of some condition. The deposit of the escrow places it beyond the control of the grantor, but no title passes until the fulfillment of the condition.

ORIGIN OF THE WORD "ESCROW"

The word "escrow" is derived from the French word *escroue,* meaning a scroll or a roll of writing. Where an owner of real property executed an instrument in the form of a deed conveying land to *X*, and delivered the deed to a third person with instructions that the instrument should be delivered to *X* and take effect as a deed upon the performance of an act or the occurrence of an event, some legal term for the document while held in abeyance was necessary. It could not be called a "deed," since a deed is an instrument that in legal contemplation is immediately operative. For this reason the instrument in the form of a deed was designated an "escrow."

CONTRACT AN ESSENTIAL REQUIREMENT

The common-law concept of an escrow required a deed alone, and a contract was not essential. In California and many other jurisdictions there must be a valid contract between the parties in addition to an instrument of conveyance.

CODE DEFINITION

The common-law definition of an escrow has been codified in California in Section 1057 of the Civil Code, which provides: "A grant may be deposited by the grantor with a third person, to be delivered on performance of a condition, and, on delivery by the depositary, it will take effect. While in the possession of the third person, and subject to condition, it is called an escrow." It has been held that the word "grant" as used in the code definition is not confined to deeds, but includes other instruments as well. (*Rockefeller* v. *Smith,* 104 C.A. 544.)

COMMON MEANING OF ESCROW

The technical definition of an escrow as denoting the instrument that is conditionally delivered does not entirely reflect its meaning in modern usage. Thus, when parties speak of "an escrow," or "going into escrow," they generally regard the "escrow" as a transaction wherein one party, for the purpose of effecting a sale, transfer, or lease of real property, or an encumbrance upon real property, in favor of another party, delivers a written instrument, money, or other thing of value to a third person, called an escrow agent or escrow holder, to be held by such third person for further delivery upon the happening of a specified event or the performance of a prescribed condition.

SCOPE OF ESCROW

In California the escrow has developed into an expedient instrumentality in all real property transactions, sales or otherwise. It is an effective means of providing (1) a *custodian* who holds the funds and documents and makes concurrent delivery thereof at the exact moment when all of the terms and conditions of the transaction have been performed; (2) a *clearing house* for the payment of all demands; (3) an *agency* that provides the clerical details in making prorations and adjustments for settlement of accounts between the parties; and (4) a method that can be and often is used to achieve a binding *contract* between the parties during the period of abeyance.

ESCROW AS A "STAKEHOLDER"

The word "stakeholder" is sometimes used to designate the escrow holder. He is considered as the *agent* of the respective parties until such time as the escrow is closed, and then he becomes a *trustee* for the money and documents until they are distributed in accordance with the escrow instructions.

II. Requisites of a valid escrow

In order for an instrument to operate as an escrow, there must be a valid and enforceable contract between the parties. A contract sufficient to support an escrow must comply with the requirements of any valid contract, i.e., competent parties, a valid consideration, a proper subject matter, and mutual assent as to the terms and conditions of the contract.

It must be in writing where required under the Statute of Frauds, which rule applies in all cases involving the sale of land. Usually the contract is evidenced by the escrow instructions prepared by the escrow holder pursuant to the directions of the parties.

Additional requirements. The escrow must also comply with the following requirements: (1) the escrow agreement must contain a condition; (2) the deed deposited in escrow must be a sufficient and valid deed; and (3) the escrow holder must be a stranger to the transaction.

ESCROW CONTRACT

The escrow contract, which is the basis of a delivery in an escrow for the sale of land, may be either a conventional *contract* for the sale and purchase of land, or an *option* to purchase exercised by the optionee, or *mutual instructions* given to the escrow holder by the seller and the purchaser. Even separately executed escrow instructions are regarded as sufficient if they are consistent and contain all of the necessary elements to make a contract. Until both parties execute the instructions, the instructions executed by one party constitute merely an offer to perform and can be revoked, but when the other party gives the escrow holder instructions that coincide with the offer and operate as an unconditional acceptance, the escrow contract is complete. It is not essential that the separate instructions be executed on the same day provided they are otherwise in agreement.

CONTRACT PRIOR TO ESCROW

Although a seller and a buyer may evidence their contract of sale and purchase solely by the mutual instructions given to the escrow holder, they frequently bind the bargain at the outset by a written agreement, such as a "sales deposit receipt," signed by both parties, and thereafter execute escrow instructions. Usually the prior contract and the escrow instructions will match as to the terms and conditions of the sale, but occasionally the two will vary, either by way of a conflict in the terms of the two instruments, or by the omission in the escrow instructions of provisions contained in the prior contract. A problem is then encountered as to whether the subsequent contract supersedes the prior contract.

RULES OF CONSTRUCTION

It is an established rule of construction that two contracts relating to the same matters, between the same parties, and made as parts of substantially one transaction, are to be read together to ascertain the entire contract between the parties. (C.C., Sec. 1642.) If the escrow instructions are merely supplemental to the prior agreement, then both contracts will be given effect. The parties to an agreement for sale may execute escrow instructions providing for delivery of the deed upon payment of the purchase price, and leave other matters, such as adjustment of rentals or interest, to be settled according to the prior agreement. But if the two contracts are in conflict on the same subject matter, the general rule applies that the subsequent contract rescinds a prior inconsistent one relating to the same subject matter, and the provisions of the later instrument will control.

III. Status of the escrow holder

The depositary of the deed and other instruments, called the "escrow holder" or "escrow agent," must be a disinterested third party. An instrument in the form of a deed cannot be delivered to the grantee of an escrow. A conditional deposit of a deed with the grantee may pass an absolute title, free of the condition, or it may fail to pass any title, depending upon the intent of the grantor. In either event the instrument cannot be held by the grantee as an escrow.

REGULATION OF ESCROW AGENTS

Since 1947, escrow agencies have been regulated by state law. (Fin. C., Secs. 17000–17614.) An escrow agent is defined in the code as "any person engaged in the business of receiving escrows for deposit or delivery for compensation." (Fin. C., Sec. 17004.) The regulations originally provided that any person engaging in the business of an escrow agent must be licensed as such by the Commissioner of Corporations. Since September 9, 1953, individuals cannot be licensed as escrow holders; the license must now be held by a corporation duly organized for the purpose of conducting an escrow business. (Fin. C., Sec. 17200.) The regulations do not apply, however, to banks, trust companies, building and loan associations, savings and loan associations, insurance companies, title companies, attorneys-at-law not actively engaged in conducting an escrow agency, brokers or others subject to the jurisdiction of the Real Estate Commissioner while performing acts in the course of or incidental to their real estate business, or to any transaction wherein a joint control agent disburses funds in payment for labor, materials, and other items of expense incurred in the construction of improvements upon real property.

DEPOSIT OF FUNDS

Escrow regulations as prescribed in the code require that all escrow funds must be deposited in a bank and kept separate, distinct, and apart from funds belonging to the escrow agent, and such funds when deposited are to be designated "trust funds," or "escrow accounts," or some other appropriate name showing that the funds are not the funds of the escrow agent. Escrow funds are not subject to execution or attachment on any claim against the escrow agent individually. All officers and employees of an escrow agent having access to funds and having certain other responsibilities must be covered by a fidelity bond in such amount and form as the Corporation Commissioner shall prescribe.

REAL ESTATE BROKERS

The exemption permitting real estate brokers to handle escrows has been interpreted to mean that they may not hold them except in connection with some transaction wherein they are acting as a real estate broker, and that they may not hold escrows for compensation in connection with transactions by other brokers. Also, a real estate licensee who acts as an escrow holder under this exemption provision of the escrow law must maintain all escrow funds in a trust account, subject to inspection by the Real Estate Commissioner, and must keep proper records.

AGENCY STATUS OF ESCROW HOLDER

The status of the escrow holder is that of an agent or trustee for *both* parties at the inception of the escrow and until the conditions have been performed. For example, if a deed is deposited in escrow, under a valid escrow contract for delivery to the grantee upon payment by him of a specified sum of money, and the grantee deposits the funds in escrow for payment to the grantor in exchange for the deed when a policy of title insurance can be issued showing title as called for in the agreement, the escrow holder, as to the deed and money, is an agent or trustee for both parties. However, when the conditions of the escrow have been performed, the nature of the dual agency changes to an agency, not for both, but for *each* of the parties respecting those things placed in escrow which each is entitled to, i.e., the escrow holder becomes the agent or trustee for the seller as to the money, and the agent or trustee of the buyer as to the deed.

Importance of distinction in agency status of escrow holder. The foregoing distinction is of particular importance if there is a loss of funds through the defalcation of the escrow holder. By way of illustration, if the escrow holder embezzles the purchase money before the time when, under the terms of the escrow, the seller is entitled to it, the loss falls on the buyer, but if the money is embezzled after the time when the seller has become entitled to the money, the loss falls on the seller, since it is now considered to be his. (*Crum* v. *City of Los Angeles,* 110 C.A. 508.)

Time when dual agency changes. The exact moment at which the dual agency changes to an agency for each party depends upon the language of the particular escrow instructions. Under most instructions the change occurs when all money called for is in escrow and when, in addition to performance of any other conditions, the deed or other instrument can be or has been recorded and a policy of title insurance will be issued as required.

Effect of embezzlement of funds. The case of *Burnett* v. *Vestermark*, 145 C.A.2d 374, illustrates the importance of the provisions of the escrow instructions in determining whether or not funds on deposit belong to the buyer or the seller at the time when the defalcation of the escrow agent occurs, and consequently upon which party the loss must fall. In that case the escrow instructions provided that the escrow would close "provided instruments have been filed for record entitling you to procure assurance of title." A trust deed existed against the property being sold, which was to be paid from funds accruing to the seller's account. Funds were obtained by the buyer through a loan transaction covering other property owned by the buyer. From these funds the deed of trust was paid, and the balance forwarded to the escrow. The escrow thereupon closed, although the trust deed had not actually been reconveyed at the time. This, however, was to have been effected within a few days, which was not an unusual procedure and presented a typical delayed reconveyance situation.

The escrow agent embezzled these and other funds within a day or two of the closing date of this particular escrow, and the seller never got his money. He brought an action against the buyer to recover the property and prevailed in the action, the court holding that the escrow was not in fact in a condition to close since the reconveyance had not been *filed for record* at the time, even though all arrangements had been made to obtain and record the reconveyance and it was in fact recorded within a short time after the escrow closed. Consequently, the risk of loss fell on the buyer rather than the seller. A different result would have followed if the escrow had contained a provision, often used, to the effect that the event of closing is dependent upon the following: "When you hold instruments, duly executed, upon the recordation of which (if recordation thereof is necessary) you can obtain a policy of title insurance."

NATURE OF AGENCY

Although an escrow holder is an agent for the parties to a transaction, it is generally considered to be a limited agency rather than a general agency. Since an escrow holder is an agent, it might seem to follow under the general rules of agency that it would be his duty to communicate to his principals any knowledge that he has or acquires concerning the subject matter of the escrow, and that any such knowledge would be imputed to each of the parties to the escrow. This broad application of the rules of agency has been made in some cases.

Cases of general agency. In the case of *Ryder* v. *Young,* 9 C.A.2d 545, it was stated that the knowledge of the escrow holder of a defect in the record title was to be imputed to the purchaser. However, in that case the court found that the purchaser also had knowledge of facts sufficient to place him on inquiry. In the case of *Early* v. *Owens,* 109 C.A. 489, it was held that the seller was charged with constructive notice, through the escrow holder as his agent, of the fact that his broker was making a secret profit on a resale.

Limited agency. It has been recognized in other cases that a general agency is not created, and that the agency is a limited agency only, under which the obligations of the escrow holder to each party in the escrow are limited to those set forth in the instructions. (*Lee* v. *Title Ins. & Trust Co.*, 264 A.C.A. 194.) In the case of *Blackburn* v. *McCoy*, 1 C.A.2d 648, it was held that an escrow holder in an escrow for the sale of land was under no duty to disclose to the buyer the fact that his seller was purchasing the land from the record owner in the same escrow and reselling it to the buyer at a profit, where the buyer's escrow instructions did not include any demand for such information. The doctrine of a limited agency appears to be the rational view of an escrow holder's status, but it is nonetheless generally concluded that an escrow holder, regardless of the absence of legal liability, should decline to handle an escrow involving a secret profit by a person, such as the broker, standing in a fiduciary relationship to a principal to the escrow.

IV. Duties and responsibilities of the escrow holder

The duties and responsibilities of an escrow holder are many and varied. A fundamental rule is that the escrow holder may not deliver funds or documents unless there has been a full compliance with the conditions of the escrow. It is the duty of the escrow holder to see that funds or documents remain in its possession until the expiration of the time fixed by the instructions for performance. After the time limit has expired, the escrow holder does not have the authority to permit one of the parties to perform unless the escrow instructions contain appropriate extension provisions.

DOCUMENTS ON DEPOSIT

Where parties to an escrow deposit documents to be held for further instructions, the escrow holder may not return to one party a document deposited by him, without the consent of the other party. (*Karras* v. *Title Insurance & Guaranty Co.*, 118 C.A.2d 659.)

CONFLICTING DEMANDS

If the escrow holder receives conflicting demands from the parties, it is not required to assume the responsibility of deciding the controversy. Such a conflict may arise, for instance, where a purchaser demands an immediate closing of the escrow, and the seller serves notice on the escrow holder to return his deed claiming the escrow is terminated. In such case the escrow holder may bring an action in interpleader against the conflicting claimants and compel them to litigate their claims in court.

INSTRUCTIONS ARE CONFIDENTIAL

Escrow instructions are confidential. It is a primary rule that information concerning the existence or terms of an escrow should not be given to persons who are not parties to the escrow. Each of the principals to an escrow has the right to see the instructions of the other party, which, when matched against his, constitute the escrow contract. This does not mean, however, that everyone in an escrow has the right to see all of the instructions of every other person. Where the escrow additionally covers a resale by the original purchaser to a third party, the original seller is not entitled to see the instructions with respect to the resale, assuming, of course, that the original instructions do not expressly demand such information. Where the escrow involves a resale, a responsible escrow holder will decline to act if it is apparent that the resale involves a breach of a fiduciary relationship. This problem sometimes arises, for instance, where a broker has procured a "dummy" as purchaser, and is making a secret profit on the resale.

FORFEITURES

Problems in connection with forfeitures frequently arise in escrow transactions. If there is a breach by the purchaser of a contract for the sale of real property, the seller may have the right to retain the amount paid on the purchase price. This does not justify the escrow holder in paying forthwith to the seller the funds deposited by the purchaser upon an apparent breach of the escrow agreement by the purchaser. It is possible that the breach may be excusable, or that a court might grant relief from the forfeiture. If the escrow holder is confronted with conflicting demands for the money deposited, his safest procedure is to resort to an interpleader action.

Provisions regarding forfeiture. Prudent escrow agents recognize the hazards in determining the merits of a claimed right of forfeiture, and usually refuse to handle an escrow that specifically calls for payment to the seller of a purchase money deposit in escrow, either as a forfeiture or as liquidated damages. As a consequence, it is a customary practice in real estate sales to have the initial deposit paid directly to the seller or his agent under a sales agreement providing for retention by the seller of such deposit as liquidated damages upon breach by the purchaser. The remainder of the purchase money is then deposited in escrow as called for without provision for forfeiture.

V. Title and possession during escrow

Where a deed is placed in escrow for delivery to the grantee upon payment of the purchase price, it has been stated that "the grantee does not acquire any title to the land" prior to the performance of the conditions. (*Los Angeles City High School District* v. *Quinn,* 195 Cal. 377.) However, if the escrow is supported by a valid contract of sale, whether created by the escrow instructions or by a separate instrument, a more accurate statement is that the grantor holds the legal title, and the grantee has the equitable title conditioned upon performance of the contract. (*Estate of Erskine,* 84 C.A.2d 323.)

INCIDENTS OF RELATIONSHIP

Included in the important incidents arising from the relationship of the parties during the pendency of the escrow are the following:

First: Right to possession remains in the grantor, unless the grantee is given possession by the terms of the contract.

Second: The title of either grantor or grantee is transferable or descendible. A purchaser from the grantor with notice of the escrow takes subject to the equitable interest of the grantee.

Third: The grantor's legal title is undoubtedly subject to the lien of attachments or judgments obtained against him before performance of the escrow conditions. Upon execution sale, it is probable that the grantor's title passes to the execution purchaser as of the date the attachment or judgment lien attached, subject to the interest of the grantee under the escrow if the execution purchaser had notice thereof. There is no clear-cut decision in California on this point, but the foregoing expresses the general rule that has been adopted elsewhere.

Fourth: The grantor is liable for property taxes accruing while the deed is in escrow, unless otherwise provided in the escrow agreement.

Fifth: Risk of loss upon damage or destruction of the property appears to be governed by the rules applicable to the vendor-vendee relationship in general. Unless the agreement provides otherwise, risk of loss is upon the person who has the right of possession.

FIRE INSURANCE POLICIES

A question sometimes arises as to whether an escrow for the sale of improved property operates to cancel or suspend a fire insurance policy in favor of the vendor, where the policy contains a provision to the effect that it shall be void in the event of a change of interest, title, or possession without the consent of the insurer. Where the vendor and purchaser have executed escrow instructions, and thereafter the improvements are destroyed or damaged by fire prior to the close of escrow, the question arises as to whether or not the vendor can recover on the policy. It has been held that the execution of a contract of sale under which the purchaser acquires the equitable title and the right of possession voids the policy unless the insurer consents to the contract of sale. (*Brickell* v. *Atlas Assurance Co., Ltd.,* 10 C.A. 17.) If the escrow instructions do not give the purchaser the right to possession, so that the risk of loss still falls on the seller, it is possible that the policy is not voided by the execution of the escrow instructions. To cover this situation, some escrow holders have blanket contracts with insurers that preserve the policy protection during escrow and until notification of a transfer after close of escrow.

VI. Performance of conditions

Where an instrument is deposited in escrow for delivery upon compliance with agreed conditions, the escrow holder is not authorized to make delivery, and the instrument cannot become operative until the conditions have been fully performed. Strict compliance with all of the terms and conditions of the escrow is ordinarily essential. Performance must be made within the time limited by the terms of the agreement, unless a waiver is obtained. If the last day for performance falls on a Sunday or holiday, the time is extended to include the following day. Conditions imposed by escrow instructions are satisfied by compliance outside of escrow, such as payment of a trust deed outside of escrow.

WAIVER OF CONDITIONS

Performance of a condition may be waived by the party imposing the condition. By way of illustration, if the terms of an escrow for the sale of real property are complied with except for the obligation of the grantor to furnish a marketable title, the grantee could authorize a closing of the escrow by waiving this requirement.

EFFECT OF UNAUTHORIZED DELIVERY

An attempted delivery of an instrument by the escrow holder before the performance of the conditions of the escrow is not a valid delivery; no title passes, nor does title pass where the escrow holder delivers a deed that contains a description of the property in excess of that called for in the escrow instructions. Thus, in the case of *Montgomery* v. *Bank of America*, 85 C.A.2d 559, it was held that title did not pass where the escrow holder delivered a deed covering an entire lot, contrary to instructions designating the property to be conveyed as half of such lot. The rule also applies to an instrument fraudulently procured from the escrow holder by the grantee. The same result follows where the escrow holder embezzles the purchase money before performance of the conditions, and then makes an unauthorized delivery of the deed. No title passes to the grantee, and the burden of loss of the purchase money falls upon him. It is probable that a deed delivered in violation of escrow instructions is ineffective even as to bona fide purchasers.

WHEN TITLE PASSES

When the conditions of an escrow have been performed, a question may arise as to the time when title is deemed to have passed to the purchaser. It has been broadly stated that an instrument in the form of a deed deposited in escrow becomes effective to pass title as soon as the conditions of the escrow are so far performed that the grantee is entitled to possession of the deed, although it is not then actually delivered to him. (*Hagge* v. *Drew*, 27 Cal.2d 368.) However, this broad statement is subject to qualification, inasmuch as the moment at which the conditions of the escrow are performed and the title passes is determined in a given case by the provisions of the particular escrow instructions, which vary according to the diverse forms in use by escrow holders.

PARTICULAR PROVISIONS

The escrow instructions may provide that the conditions of the escrow are performed when the escrow holder has received funds and an instrument "by the use" or "delivery" of which title will vest in a stated manner. In such case title has been held to pass when the escrow holder holds the funds and instruments, although the instrument is neither manually delivered nor recorded, and clerical functions, such as adjustment of taxes, are yet to be performed. (*Law* v. *Title Guarantee & Trust Co.*,

91 C.A. 621.) In other instances the instruments may authorize the use of funds when the escrow holder can obtain or secure a policy of title insurance showing title vested in the grantee. In such case it has been held that title does not pass until a deed has been recorded, which will then enable the title company to issue its policy. (*Hildebrand* v. *Beck*, 196 Cal. 141.) Other instructions, as in the case of *Burnett* v. *Vestermark*, discussed on p. 417, leave no doubt as to the event of closing; they may expressly authorize use of the funds when a deed or other instrument has been "filed for record," enabling a title company to issue a policy showing title in the grantee.

DOCTRINE OF RELATION BACK

The doctrine of relation back is sometimes applied where an escrow has in fact closed in accordance with the conditions. Under this doctrine, in order to avoid hardship or to effectuate the intention of the parties, the delivery of the instrument to the grantee upon performance of the conditions, i.e., the second delivery of the deed, is considered to operate retroactively and to pass title by relation back to the date the instrument was delivered to the escrow holder, i.e., the first delivery. (*Miller & Lux, Inc.* v. *Sparkman*, 128 C.A. 449.) The fiction of relation back has been applied to protect a purchaser in an escrow against an intervening grantee who took a conveyance from the grantor with knowledge of the pending escrow. In other cases the doctrine has afforded protection to the buyer where an abstract of judgment was recorded against the grantor, prior to close of escrow, but not until after the escrow was in fact ready to close.

VII. Cancellation or revocation of the escrow

An escrow may be cancelled voluntarily by the consent of all of the parties. Ordinarily the only necessary parties to the cancellation are the principals. Occasionally, however, third parties may have acquired rights that must be considered. If the seller has assigned in escrow all or a portion of the purchase price as evidenced by an order to the escrow holder to pay the proceeds or a portion thereof to the third party upon close of escrow, an escrow holder usually will require that the assignee consent to the cancellation. If the assignment or order to pay is contingent upon the closing of the escrow, the consent of the assignee is not essential.

PAYMENT OF BROKER'S COMMISSION

Where the escrow instructions constitute an enforceable contract of sale and provide for payment of a commission to a real estate broker for the seller on "close of escrow," it has been held that the broker is entitled to recover the commission from his principal if the escrow is voluntarily cancelled by the parties, but the broker cannot recover a commission if the escrow fails through no fault of the seller. (*Wilson* v. *Security-First National Bank,* 84 C.A.2d 427.)

RIGHT OF CANCELLATION BY ONE PARTY

The right of one party to an escrow to revoke or withdraw without the consent of the other party is normally controlled by the provisions of the particular escrow instructions. A form of instructions in common use provides that the conditions of the escrow are to be performed on or before a specified date, usually thirty days from the inception of the escrow, but that in the absence of a written demand for cancellation by either party the escrow may be closed as soon thereafter as possible. The instructions also contain a clause that time is of the essence. Under such instructions, neither party has a right to withdraw during the time fixed for performance without the consent of the other party. The mere fact that one party attempts to revoke the escrow during this period does not excuse performance by the other, or authorize the other to withdraw. An initial repudiation by one party is ineffectual and cannot as a rule be treated as an anticipatory breach that relieves the other party of his obligations.

NOTICE OF CANCELLATION

If at the expiration of the specified time limit under the escrow, one party has performed, but the other has not, the party not in default may withdraw, subject, however, to compliance with any provisions in the escrow agreement requiring that notice of the revocation be given to the other party, or with any other provision restricting the right of termination. If the party seeking to withdraw does not act promptly after his right accrues, it may be contended that he has thereby waived the "time is of the essence" provision. Consequently, many escrow holders will not return documents or money, on a demand not seasonably made, until after at least a five-day notice has been given to the other party. (*Chan* v. *Title Ins. & Trust Co.,* 39 Cal.2d 253.)

WHERE NEITHER PARTY HAS PERFORMED

If at the expiration of the time limit neither party has performed, either one may withdraw, subject, however, to any special requirements of the escrow instructions relating to the right or method of cancellation.

PERFORMANCE DURING EXTENSION

If the escrow instructions contain a so-called "open end" time limit, i.e., if they authorize completion of the escrow as soon as possible after expiration of the specified time limit if no demand for revocation is made, and one party performs before an attempted withdrawal by the other party, but after the specified time limit date, the other party cannot cancel the escrow.

REASONABLE TIME FOR PERFORMANCE

Where an escrow does not express a definite time limit for performance, a reasonable time will be implied. The question as to what is a reasonable time is dependent upon the facts and circumstances of the particular case. In the case of *First National Bank of La Habra* v. *Caldwell,* 84 C.A. 438, it was held that 3½ months was unreasonable under the facts.

EFFECT OF DEATH OR INCOMPETENCY

Where one party to an escrow dies or becomes incompetent, the general rule is that when a legal escrow has been established, i.e., an instrument has been deposited with an escrow holder for delivery under a valid contract, it is not revoked by the death or incapacity of either party during the time fixed for performance. If the party entitled to the benefits of the instrument fully performs within the time limit of the escrow, he is entitled to receive delivery of the instrument.

Where seller dies before contract executed. Where *A,* the owner, deposits a deed with an escrow holder for delivery to *B* upon payment of a specified purchase price, but no contract of sale is executed, and *A* dies before payment of the price by *B,* the instructions of *A* merely constitute an offer, and the death of *A* terminates the agency. The offer cannot thereafter be accepted, and *B* has no enforceable rights.

Where seller dies before deed deposited. Where *A* as seller and *B* as buyer sign escrow instructions that result in a binding contract of sale, but *A* does not deposit a deed for delivery to *B* upon performance of the condition, i.e., payment of the purchase price, and *A* thereafter dies, *B* cannot acquire title through the purported escrow. If *B* is not in default under the contract, he may seek to acquire title by an action for specific performance against the representative of *A*'s estate, or by obtaining an appropriate order in the probate proceedings, authorizing the representative of *A*'s estate to execute a deed upon payment by *B* of the purchase price.

Where seller dies after deed deposited. The true escrow situation is illustrated by the following facts: *A* as seller and *B* as buyer execute escrow instructions that are sufficient as a contract for the sale of land. *A* deposits a deed with the escrow holder for delivery to *B* "within 30 days if the purchase price is paid by *B*." *A* dies prior to the expiration of the 30-day period. *B* thereafter deposits the purchase price and otherwise fully performs the contract within the prescribed time. It has been held that *B* is entitled to the deed as a matter of law. (*Brunoni* v. *Brunoni*, 93 C.A.2d 215.) However, practical considerations usually necessitate probate proceedings. First of all, a qualified representative of the decedent's estate is usually needed for the purpose of receiving payment of the purchase price. Also, a release from the state inheritance tax office is essential before the money can be disbursed. It is usually required that an order from the probate court authorizing a deed by the representative of the decendent's estate be obtained.

VIII. Practical considerations

Most title transactions in California are closed through the instrumentality of an escrow. There is some diversity of practice throughout the state, based largely on local custom and experience, as to the form of escrow instructions, the division of charges, and the particular escrow holders whose services are utilized in the transaction. However, in all parts of the state it is a recognized practice to make the closing of a real estate transaction conditional upon the issuance of a policy of title insurance.

SOUTHERN CALIFORNIA PRACTICE

Throughout southern California the prevailing practice is to draft more or less formal escrow instructions; the escrow is an independent transaction from the issuance of a title policy, with a separate fee for each service; the escrow holder may or may not be a title company; and the seller usually pays the fees for a title policy, with the escrow fees being divided equally.

NORTHERN CALIFORNIA PRACTICE

In northern California, generally, the escrow instructions tend to be less formal; the handling of an escrow and the issuance of a title policy are part of the same services furnished by title companies for a single fee; and the buyer customarily pays the policy fee.

INITIAL STEPS IN A SALE

In the case of a sale of real property, the initial agreement to buy and sell is customarily evidenced by a sales deposit receipt, with a deposit by the buyer being made to the real estate broker. The escrow holder is usually a bank, or a corporation formed to handle escrows, or a title company.

PREPARATION OF ESCROW INSTRUCTIONS

Escrow instructions are usually prepared on the escrow holder's printed form. Although an escrow holder cannot advise the parties as to their legal rights and obligations, he can and should ask such questions as are appropriate and essential to ascertain their intention concerning the terms and conditions of the sale, as a basis for drafting the escrow instructions.

PROCEDURAL STEPS

Following the signing of the escrow instructions by both parties, the procedural steps that culminate in closing the escrow may be briefly described as follows:

First: A search of title is ordered and a preliminary report of title thereafter forwarded to the escrow office by the title company.

Second: A Beneficiary's Statement is requested from the beneficiary under a deed of trust shown on the title report. This is a statement as to the unpaid balance and condition of the indebtedness.

Third: Matters disclosed by the preliminary report of title that are not approved by the escrow instructions are reported to the seller for clearance, or to the buyer for approval.

Fourth: When all documents and funds are in the hands of the escrow officer and the escrow is in a condition to close, the necessary adjustments and prorations between the parties are made on a settlement sheet, and the instruments are forwarded to the title company with recording instructions.

Fifth: The search of title is "run to date" as of the close of business of the escrow completion date, and if no change of title is found, the deed is recorded the next morning at 8:00 A.M., i.e., at the moment the county recorder's office is open for business. By filing papers in the recorder's office at that time, it is possible to issue a title policy and disburse funds in escrow with assurance that there are no intervening matters.

Sixth: Immediately after the filing of the documents in the recorder's office, the escrow holder disburses the funds to the parties entitled thereto, causes any fire insurance policies to be transferred or amended, and presents a closing statement to the parties. The title policy is issued within a reasonable time thereafter.

MANNER OF TAKING TITLE

Numerous details need to be worked out in escrow, and many problems require special consideration. Of primary concern is the manner in which the buyer is to take title. This is particularly true if the buyers are husband and wife. Many such persons automatically take title in joint tenancy without having a complete understanding of the nature of joint tenancy and the possible disadvantages with respect to taxes and other matters. Although the escrow agent must ascertain the proper names of all of the parties to the escrow and must find out how the purchasers wish to take title, the manner in which the title is to be vested in the purchasers cannot be decided or suggested by the escrow agent. This is a matter for determination by the purchasers or their attorney.

DESCRIPTION OF THE PROPERTY

A sufficient legal description of the property is essential. Also, if any personal property is to be included in the transaction, such as furniture and furnishings, the escrow may include instructions for obtaining a bill of sale. If stock in a mutual water company is to be transferred to the buyer, it should be ascertained whether or not there are any unpaid assessments that would in any way interfere with the transfer of the water stock.

ADJUSTMENT IN ESCROW

Adjustments in escrows are usually made with respect to taxes, interest, rents, and fire insurance premiums. The theory upon which adjustments are made in escrow is that the seller is the owner of the property and entitled to possession until the conditions of the escrow have been performed and title has passed to the purchaser. Accordingly, the seller should receive or be credited with the benefits of his ownership, and he also should bear the burden of the obligations of ownership. The purchaser assumes the benefits and burdens of ownership as of the close of escrow. The parties in the escrow instructions may agree, of course, to adjustment on any basis they desire, or they may waive any adjustments.

Taxes. The adjustment of taxes is determined by the date upon which the escrow is closed, an event usually defined as the date escrow instruments are recorded in the office of the county recorder. It is the general custom to prorate taxes on the basis of the taxes for a fiscal year. County taxes become a lien on the first day in March of each year, when the tax year begins, and are referred to as taxes of the current year. However, the fiscal year—the period in which the tax funds are expended—is from the first day of July to midnight of June 30 of the next year. A fiscal year for proration purposes is divided into two periods, the first installment of taxes for the period from July 1 to midnight of December 31, and the second installment of taxes for the period from January 1 to midnight of June 30.

Adjustment of taxes. As an illustration of adjustment of taxes, assume that an escrow is closed on December 1, and that the taxes for the fiscal year are $240, and that no portion of the taxes has been paid. The purchaser is entitled to receive through escrow an adjustment equal to the prorated amount of taxes for the period from July 1 to December 1, and therefore will be credited with five-twelfths of $240, or $100. The seller is debited with this amount, which will be deducted, at the close of escrow, from the purchase price paid to him. If the seller in this case had paid the first half of the taxes, the taxes then would be paid to December 31, and the seller would receive as an adjustment the prorated amount of the taxes from December 1 to December 31, being one-twelfth of $240, or $20, which amount is debited to the buyer and credited to the seller. If all of the year's taxes have been paid by the seller, he would be entitled to receive a rebate through escrow for the period from the close of escrow to June 30 following, being in this case seven-twelfths of $240, or $140.

When amount of taxes unavailable. In the event an escrow is to be closed at a time when the amount of the current taxes is not available, the proration of taxes is usually based upon the amount of the taxes for the previous year. Personal property taxes assessed with real property are payable with the first half of the real property tax, but the tax covers payment for the entire year. Unless the chattels upon which the personal property tax is assessed are being transferred, it is customary to prorate taxes on the real property only.

Fire insurance. The seller in an escrow may cancel existing fire insurance policies and be entitled to any rebate on the premiums paid, in which event the purchaser will undertake to purchase any new fire insurance he may desire. However, if the existing fire insurance policies are transferable, it is customary to assign the seller's interest in such policies to the buyer. In such case the seller is entitled to have his account credited with the unearned premium for the period from the close of escrow until the end of the term of the policy, and the purchaser is debited with the amount of such unearned premium. By way of illustration, assume that the premium paid by the seller for a three-year policy is $72, and that the escrow closed one year and four months before the end of the three-year term. Since the purchaser is obligated to pay the premium for the unexpired term of the policy, representing sixteen months in this case, the purchaser's account is debited with $32, and the seller's account is credited with this amount.

Proration of rents. The general principles of proration apply to rents in cases where the premises being sold are occupied by tenants. As a basis for making adjustments of rents, the escrow holder is usually authorized to adjust rents as shown on a statement submitted by the seller and approved by the buyer. This statement should give the name of the tenant, the house or apartment number, the monthly rental rate, the date on which rents are due, the date to which rentals have been paid, and the amount of any advance payments that may have been collected. The statement may provide that all rentals due have been collected, and that the buyer may be credited with any advance payments collected by the seller. A prudent purchaser will examine the lessor's copy of any leases, verify the fact as to tenancies, and require that the rent statement include any amounts collected by the seller as security money or in payment of the rent for the last month of the lease.

Interest on encumbrances. A purchaser of real property should receive credit for any interest payments on encumbrances that he thereafter must make covering the period of ownership of the seller, and should be charged with the amount of payments made by the seller that accrue to his benefit. For example, assume that the buyer is purchasing land subject to a deed of trust securing a note with interest payable on the first day of each third month, and the last interest payment was made on January 1, with the next interest payment being due on April 1, covering the interest due from January 1 to April 1. The agreed adjustment date is March 1, which is the date of transfer of title. In such case the purchaser will become the owner one month before interest is due, but when he does pay the interest installment due on April 1, he will be paying for the months of January and February, during which time the seller was the owner of the property. Accordingly, the buyer should receive as a credit through escrow the amount of interest for January and February. If, however, interest had been paid in advance by the seller, then the buyer would be debited with the March interest, and the seller would receive a credit for this amount.

Interest on purchase money encumbrance. If the purchaser is delivering a purchase money encumbrance through escrow, the note and deed of trust are usually executed many days prior to the close of escrow. It is then customary to endorse interest on the note as paid to the close of escrow, on the theory that no interest should be paid on the encumbrance until title has been acquired by the purchaser.

Existing encumbrances. Where the title to property is conveyed subject to an existing loan, it is the usual practice for the purchaser to require that a statement be secured from the lender as to the unpaid balance and the condition of the loan, which statement is to be subject to the buyer's approval. If the statement shows that an installment falls due during the pendency of the escrow, the escrow agent will usually check with the lender prior to close of escrow to determine whether or not the installment has been paid. If the installment payment has been made, a corrected statement must be obtained from the lender showing the date to which the interest has been paid and the exact amount of the unpaid balance.

Terms of loan. When the statement is received from the lender it must be carefully checked against the terms of the loan as approved by the buyer in the escrow instructions. Difficulties are sometimes encountered where the note secured by the encumbrance of record does not permit the payment of the note in full at any time, or where there are provisions for conditional prepayment, or where the note contains provisions affecting the due date, such as an "alienation clause," or an "automatic acceleration of due date provision" providing as follows: "Upon conveyance by the trustor of the real property described in this deed of trust, or upon the divestment in any manner of his title thereto, all sums secured hereby shall become due and payable immediately at the option of the beneficiary." Such provisions are of vital concern to the buyer. In the case of *Whiteman* v. *Leonard Realty Co.,* 189 C.A.2d 373, an escrow agent was held liable in damages to the buyer for failure to comply with *oral* instructions regarding a prepayment penalty.

Taking "subject to" or "assuming" encumbrance. Where an existing encumbrance is to remain on the property, it must be ascertained through the escrow whether the buyer is to take *subject* to the encumbrance, or is to *assume* the obligation. In the latter case, the lender's approval is essential if the seller, as maker of the note secured by the encumbrance of record, is to be relieved of any further obligation under the note.

Closing contingent on buyer obtaining loan. If the buyer's instructions state that he is obtaining a loan for the purpose of obtaining the necessary funds to purchase the property, the escrow instructions should state whether or not the escrow is contingent upon the buyer's obtaining the loan in a specified amount and upon designated terms. The following form of recital in the buyer's instructions is often used:

> The closing of this escrow is contingent upon my obtaining a loan in the sum of $__________ upon the following terms: [quote terms]. My

execution of loan papers in connection with this escrow is to be deemed my waiver of said contingency, provided the loan to which such papers relate is consummated.

TERMITE REPORTS

Termite reports can cause as much difficulty as anything else in escrow. They may be called many different names, such as "termite clearance," or "termite statements," or some other similar designation. Actually, a "termite clearance" as such is not possible, since termite companies do not purport to furnish a clearance. It is their necessary practice to use qualifying words in their reports, such as "visible" or "accessible areas," and the like. To obtain a report showing the premises entirely clear of termites would necessitate taking the building apart and examining each timber, piece by piece. An acceptable way for the escrow holder to cover the matter where the parties themselves have raised the question of termites is to prepare instructions providing that a termite report be furnished at the expense of either the buyer or the seller, and that it is to be approved by the purchaser prior to close of escrow. Or a provision may be inserted that the escrow is not to be closed until the buyer has satisfied himself as to the question of termites and has so notified the escrow agent in writing.

Legislation regarding termite reports. In 1961 a requirement was added that an escrow holder or real estate broker must obtain a pest control report from the Pest Control Board whenever such an inspection report was requested by any party to a real estate transaction. In 1963 this requirement was modified to provide that any person has a right on payment of the required fee to obtain from the Pest Control Board a certified copy of all inspection reports and completion notices filed with the Board by any pest control operator during the preceding two years. When any party to a real estate transaction requests a "wood destroying organism inspection report," it is the duty of the real estate broker to advise him in writing of his right to obtain inspection reports and completion notices from the Pest Control Board. (Bus. & Prof. C., Sec. 8616.)

Provision for termite statement. A suggested provision for inclusion in escrow instructions is the following: "The seller is to furnish a statement by a licensed Pest Control Operator, certifying the premises at [address of property] to be free from visible evidence of infestation by termites, dry rot, and fungi."

Instructions for payment of corrective work. Where the termite statement shows corrective work to be necessary, it is not safe for the escrow holder to assume that payment of the cost will automatically be borne by the seller. Specific instructions covering this obligation must be obtained. For instance, in a recent case a purchaser called for a termite report subject to his approval. The report thereafter received by the escrow stated that several hundred dollars worth of work should be done before the issuance of a clearance. The purchaser approved the report, with a proviso that the escrow *hold* the amount of money set forth in the report to do the necessary work. The seller then authorized the escrow to *hold* the amount necessary to do the work. Several days after the escrow closed, the seller demanded the money held by the escrow for his account, contending that he authorized the *holding* of funds but never authorized *payment* of the termite bill. The escrow holder was obligated to return the funds to the seller, and paid the bill itself.

POSSESSION

Problems sometimes arise during the pendency of an escrow with which the escrow holder cannot be concerned. Caution must be exercised to avoid inclusion in the escrow instructions of any items for which the escrow agent cannot assume any responsibility. Possession of the property is an example of such an item. If the escrow is not to be concerned with possession, a statement such as the following should be included in the escrow instructions: "As a memorandum with which the escrow holder is in no way concerned, it is understood that possession is to be given as of [date]." If, however, the escrow is to be concerned with possession of the property, a clause such as the following should be added in the buyer's instructions: "You are not to close this escrow until I notify you in writing that the property is now vacant, or that I have received possession." Obviously, this is a condition of the escrow, and the escrow holder cannot close the escrow until the buyer has given notice of compliance with the condition.

Questions

1. Explain the nature of an escrow at common law.
2. In California, is any instrument in addition to a deed required in order to have a valid escrow?
3. Discuss briefly four functions accomplished by an escrow.
4. Describe five requisites of a valid escrow.
5. Are separately executed escrow instructions sufficient basis for a contract?
6. If the escrow instructions are inconsistent with the prior contract of the parties, which is controlling?
7. Is there any limitation as to parties who may act as escrow agents?
8. Explain the status of the escrow holder after all conditions of the escrow have been met.

9. Explain the distinction between a limited agency and a general agency.
10. Discuss briefly the primary duties and responsibilities of an escrow holder.
11. Who has the right of possession during the pendency of a sales escrow?
12. Discuss the effect on title after parties have entered into a sales escrow.
13. Does an unauthorized delivery before performance of conditions of an escrow have any effect?
14. If the vendor dies during the pendency of an escrow, what rights does the buyer have?
15. Explain the doctrine of "relation back."
16. Describe briefly the usual adjustments made in escrow.
17. Why is it important to ascertain the terms of an existing encumbrance?
18. Discuss the legal effect of a closing "contingent on buyer's obtaining a loan."

22

Title Insurance

Summary

I. Introductory
Policy forms; Statutory definition; Regulation of title insurance companies

II. Development of title insurance
Necessity for recording laws; Reliance on public records; Specialists in title searching; Formation of abstract companies; Interpretation of abstracts; Need for further change; Certificate of title; Guarantee of title; Liability limited to matters disclosed of record; Coverage of a policy of title insurance

III. Basic coverage of title insurance
Elements of risk; Coverage of matters disclosed of record; Examination of public records; Interpretation of instruments; Examination of court proceedings; Taxes and assessments; Insuring ownership of record; Insuring against encumbrances; Unmarketability of title

IV. Coverage against off-record risks
Forged deeds; Competency of parties; Status of parties; Powers of agents and others; Delivery of instruments; Estate tax liens; Other factors

V. Standard coverage policy
Coverage of standard policy; Matters excluded from coverage; Special indorsements

VI. Extended coverage policy
A.L.T.A. policy; Priority of liens; Defects disclosed by an inspection or a survey; Extended coverage policies for owners

VII. Other types of policies
Insuring contract interests; Other title company services

VIII. The title insurer
Need for title plant; Facilities of a title plant

I. Introductory

The use of policies of title insurance in this state is widespread. In general, a policy of title insurance insures the ownership of an estate or interest in land, or the priority and validity of an encumbrance on land. It is a contract to indemnify against loss through defects in the title, or against liens or encumbrances that may affect the title at the time the policy is issued.

POLICY FORMS

The usual form is a *standard coverage* policy, but an *extended coverage* type of policy is also available that insures against loss or damage from additional matters not included within the scope of coverage of the standard form. Although neither form of policy provides "full" coverage, the matters insured against afford invaluable protection to a buyer or lender, and it is considered essential in most types of real estate transactions that title insurance be obtained.

STATUTORY DEFINITION

A title insurance policy is defined in Section 12340 of the Insurance Code as follows: "Any written instrument purporting to show the title to real or personal property or any interest therein or encumbrance thereon, or to furnish such information relative to real property, which in express terms purports to insure or guarantee such title or the correctness of such information, is a title policy."

REGULATION OF TITLE INSURANCE COMPANIES

Under the provisions of the Insurance Code (Secs. 12340 *et seq.*), each title insurance company organized under the laws of this state is required to make an initial deposit of $100,000 in cash or approved securities with the state treasurer. It must also set apart annually, as a "title insurance surplus fund," a sum equal to 10 per cent of its premiums collected during the year until this fund equals 25 per cent of the subscribed capital stock of the company. This fund, which is very substantial in the case of larger and older companies, is maintained constantly as a security to the owners of policies of title insurance. Title insurance companies are subject to various other provisions of the state insurance laws. Companies issuing policies of title insurance in substantial numbers and large amounts, and upon the strength of which vast sums of money change hands, must necessarily be subjected to the same supervision and compliance with regulatory laws as other insurance companies.

II. Development of title insurance

In a small community, where land holdings are personal and become matters of common knowledge, the possession of real property by a family, passed on from generation to generation, usually constitutes sufficient proof of ownership, and will seldom be disputed. This was particularly true in olden times. With the growth of communities, however, holdings are divided and contracted; strangers with no background of long and continuous occupancy acquire ownership; exact boundaries become important as land values rise. Documentary title becomes an essential proof of ownership, by which an owner can trace his right to the property in an unbroken chain of conveyance dating back to the original source of title; i.e., a land patent issued by the government.

NECESSITY FOR RECORDING LAWS

The danger, as time goes on, that important documents will be lost or destroyed, and the voluminous accumulation of documents resulting from a need to keep the originals over a long period of time, led to the establishment of a public repository for them—the county recorder's office—where authentic copies are preserved and may be examined. Documents are deposited with the recorder long enough for the recorder to make copies and index them. Preservation of the originals, after recordation, becomes of minor importance.

RELIANCE ON PUBLIC RECORDS

Formerly, the information readily available from the recorder's office, when considered with the known fact of occupancy, could be regarded as sufficient in most real estate transactions. Anyone dealing with a person who was recognized by his fellow citizens as the owner, and who had a good record chain of title, usually could rely with safety upon such title. As time went on, more and more reliance came to be placed upon the record title.

SPECIALISTS IN TITLE SEARCHING

The increase in the number of documents affecting a particular parcel, and their distribution among various public offices, made it more difficult for the average person to search the public records for necessary information regarding property. As a result, he enlisted the help of persons who began to specialize in title searching. From merely helping to find the records relating to the property in question, these persons soon developed the business of furnishing summaries, called *"abstracts,"* of the pertinent documents. These searchers of title became known as *"abstracters."*

FORMATION OF ABSTRACT COMPANIES

As the business of abstracters grew, it became important and valuable to them to preserve all of their previous abstracts, since thereafter, when another search covering the same parcel of property was requested, they could fix a date behind which they need not retrace their search of the title. They would need only to copy the previous work down to the point where a separation of ownership occurred and new instruments appeared of record, then search the records from that point forward. This effected a considerable saving in time and energy, which would be augmented if the abstracter could have access to the abstracts of other persons engaged in the business of searching titles. However, each one guarded his own abstracts as his principal stock-in-trade, and would permit their use by others only upon payment of a consideration. Because of this and for other reasons such as speed, economy, and efficiency, abstracters with comparable stocks of completed abstracts pooled their resources to form an abstract company.

INTERPRETATION OF ABSTRACTS

The work of the abstracter related only to the compilation of the "chain of title." It did not involve the *construction, interpretation,* or *legal significance* of the various items comprising such chain. This work called for the services of a lawyer versed in the intricacies of land law, and having a knowledge of the laws relating to other matters affecting titles, such as corporation, probate, bankruptcy, and divorce laws. Only a qualified lawyer could construe authoritatively the instruments in the chain of title and form a conclusion, or "opinion," as to the current condition of the title. This system of an abstract of title and an attorney's opinion developed to a high point of perfection and has afforded and still affords a reasonably satisfactory method of establishing a merchantable title in many areas of the United States.

NEED FOR FURTHER CHANGE

Before the turn of the century, experience showed that the abstract-opinion system of establishing title failed in many instances to meet the ever-increasing demand for a fast and reliable evidence of title. Such system proved to be too slow in a time of rapid movement in the field of real estate, and was too costly when the instruments in the chain of title were numerous, resulting in an extensive and consequently expensive abstract. Of particular concern, also, was the fact that the liability of the abstracter and of the attorney was limited. Liability did not arise as to every mistake; it was limited to those types of omissions and errors of judgment that a qualified person should not have made; i.e., mistakes based on negligence. Liability was limited also to the actual loss occasioned by the error, and then only to the person for whom the work was done. As a practical matter, recourse was limited further to the financial responsibility of the abstracter or attorney.

CERTIFICATE OF TITLE

The next important development was the issuance of a "certificate of title." Instead of preparing a formal abstract of title, supported by the opinion of an attorney, the abstract company compiled a search of title sufficient for the purposes of its examiners of title and its attorneys. Upon reaching an opinion as to the current condition of title, the abstract company would furnish the customer a "certificate of title." In it the company certified that from its examination of the title, it found the title to be vested in the owner as shown, subject only to the encumbrances or other matters noted. This took the place of the abstract, and could be done much quicker and cheaper, and with equal satisfaction to the average customer. However, the protection afforded was essentially no different under the certificate of title than under the abstract-opinion method.

Liability under a certificate of title. The liability under a certificate of title is limited and in many cases uncertain. The responsibility of the company issuing it is contractual. It assures that it has made a careful study of the records and has exercised the requisite skill in reaching its conclusions. The measure of its care and skill in this respect is that commonly exercised by other competent members of the same profession. In claiming damages based on a mistake in a certificate, the burden is upon the injured party to show that the error is based on negligence amounting to a lack of the requisite knowledge and skill.

GUARANTEE OF TITLE

The next development that occurred is reflected by the decision of the abstract companies to *guarantee* the title, rather than merely certify the correctness of the examination. For such guarantee to mean much, it was necessary, of course, for the issuing company to show its ability to respond to any losses that might occur. Companies therefore increased their capitalization and set aside reserves to protect the interests of the customers.

Liability under a guarantee of title. By the issuance of a guarantee of title, the company guarantees that the title is vested as shown. It is more than a guarantee of careful search and skillful analysis; it is a guarantee of the title of the owner. Although it will show the title subject to any exceptions noted of record, as would a certificate, it is an *undertaking* to pay any loss the customer sustains in the event the record title proves to be otherwise than as shown. It in effect places an absolute guarantee behind the work of the company. Whereas under the certificate it is necessary to establish that an error was made negligently, under a guarantee of title the fact that an omission or error occurred, plus proof of loss, establishes the liability of the company, regardless of any lack of skill.

LIABILITY LIMITED TO MATTERS DISCLOSED OF RECORD

All of the practices so far considered have one thing in common, i.e., such protection as they afford is limited to those matters that are disclosed by an examination of the public records. These records, particularly those in the county recorder's office, are merely transcribed copies of original instruments no longer available for inspection. Hidden defects that cannot be determined by an examination or study of such records alone may in fact exist. A deed may be forged, for instance, but this would not be detected solely by an examination of the recorded instruments. Defects arising from fraud, incompetency, identity, status, limitation of power, lack of delivery, or failure to comply with the law would not be detected from the record alone. None of the practices considered up to now—the abstract, the opinion, the certificate, or the guarantee of title—affords any protection against such matters. They are regarded as "off-record" risks, and as such are not within the contemplation of such evidences of title. Yet these off-record risks may result in a total failure of title.

COVERAGE OF A POLICY OF TITLE INSURANCE

The policy of title insurance extends protection against the abovementioned off-record risks. Its coverage may also be extended to other types of risks that are disclosed, not from the public records, but from an inspection of the property. The scope of this coverage is continually expanding.

Need for greater coverage. The demand for wider coverage than that afforded by abstracts, certificates, and guarantees was first felt in the larger centers of population where the rise of corporate ownership of land, the intensive improvement of land, and the use of land and improvements as security for the safe investment of trust funds and life insurance company reserves necessitated greater concern for and protection of the underlying title. The rapidly growing use of land in urban areas had created greater complexity in titles, including such things as complicated trusts, ground leases, new and novel easements above and below the surface, complete utilization of the surface necessitating close attention to boundaries, encroachments, party wall agreements, building restrictions, zoning laws, and police and fire regulations. Moreover, many substantial investors required additional protection at a time when the examination of titles was becoming increasingly complex. Title companies with extensive financial reserves and adequate facilities were called upon to give such increased protection. The insurance of title to land has now become centered in established and progressive organizations.

III. Basic coverage of title insurance

A title insurance policy represents the final result of three successive processes: namely, an examination or investigation of the title; a determination of the amount of insurance required; and the protection of the insured against possible title losses.

ELEMENTS OF RISK

The elements of risk or chance in title insurance arise from three principal sources: (1) errors in searching the record; (2) errors in interpreting the legal effect of instruments found in the chain of title; and (3) facts external to the record. A title insurer meets the first two of these matters in much the same way as an abstract company. A title insurance company will have at its disposal a title plant from which most of the examination of the record title can be made, and will also have a corps of trained and experienced searchers and examiners, and in addition will have competent legal assistance available. The added element of hazard, i.e., the risks that lie outside the public records, which is the distinctive coverage of the policy of title insurance, requires additional cautions.

COVERAGE OF MATTERS DISCLOSED OF RECORD

The policy of title insurance affords the same protection as the guarantee of title insofar as coverage of the public records is concerned. The policy of title insurance provides that the public records so covered are those which impart constructive notice of matters relating to the land insured. These include not only the records in the county recorder's office, but additional public records as well, including the following: (1) federal land office records, both local and in Washington, D.C.; (2)

records of the state of California located in Sacramento; (3) tax records of every taxing agency whose levies constitute a lien on real property—cities, counties, and the state, as well as numerous districts, such as irrigation, reclamation, and drainage districts; (4) records of special assessment districts, which are filed in city and county treasurers' offices; (5) records of city and county clerks where governmental action relating to land is recorded; and (6) records in the office of the county clerk.

Court records. Other records are found in the offices of the clerks of the various courts, both state and federal. In these offices are maintained innumerable files of cases affecting titles to real property, or the status of persons having interests in real property. These actions include foreclosure, quiet title, partition, guardianship, divorce, bankruptcy, and many other types of proceedings.

EXAMINATION OF PUBLIC RECORDS

The files and records referred to above are examined, summarized, and classified by the title company at the time of filing, and a record made in the title company's plant. Absolute accuracy is essential to the proper performance of this function. Thereafter, when the title company is requested to issue a policy of title insurance, a search of title can be made from the records in its own title plant.

INTERPRETATION OF INSTRUMENTS

After the title search is completed, the next important function in the examination of title is the interpretation of the instruments in the chain of title. Knowledge and experience are indispensable prerequisites in construing the validity and effect of the instruments in the chain of title. It must be ascertained that all necessary parties have joined in the execution of the instruments. Not only must they have signed their names, but they must have been correctly designated in the instrument, and must have properly acknowledged its execution. The instrument to be effective must be legally sufficient to accomplish its intended purpose, must identify the property correctly, and must be consistent with the prior title. If it is a lease or a declaration of trust, it must have a valid term and purpose. If it is a deed creating or reserving immediate or future interests, such interests must conform to the laws governing their nature and extent.

EXAMINATION OF COURT PROCEEDINGS

An examination of the file in judicial proceedings affecting title, and an analysis of the legal effect and sufficiency of such proceedings are essential. The examination of such proceedings must take into consideration the nature of the action, the necessary parties thereto, the jurisdiction of the court both as to the parties and the subject matter, any limitations upon the power of the court to render specific relief in the proceedings, and whether or not the judgment is final.

TAXES AND ASSESSMENTS

Due consideration of all data pertaining to unpaid taxes and assessments is also of extreme importance. Such examination can involve many problems, since tax records are scattered in many offices, tax descriptions often vary materially from record descriptions, and tax deeds are not always issued or recorded. Protest and invalidity suits and bond foreclosure or treasurer's sales may be outstanding. Overlapping assessments may occur, or assessments and bonds may be issued under more than one of the many improvements and bond acts. All of these matters must be considered in making a complete examination of the record title, and a proper determination then made as to the legal effect of such matters.

Illustrative case involving taxes. In the case of *National Holding Co. v. Title Ins. and Trust Co.*, 45 C.A.2d 215, the insurer did not refer to taxes that had been paid under protest and that in subsequent proceedings were set aside and held void. After the policy was issued, the property was reassessed and taxes again levied for the year in question. The insurer was held liable to idemnify the insured against such reassessment.

INSURING OWNERSHIP OF RECORD

A policy of title insurance shows title to the estate or interest covered by the policy as vested in the record owner, and insures against loss that the insured may sustain by reason of the land being vested otherwise than as stated in the policy. The insured is also protected against any defect in, or lien or encumbrance on, the title that exists at the date of the policy and is not shown. Title may be defective for a number of reasons, such as lack of capacity or power of a grantor to execute an instrument, or failure of a wife to join in the conveyance of community property, or defective judicial proceedings affecting the title, or unauthorized acts of corporate officials. One of the most valuable features of a policy of title insurance is the assurance and insurance that the insurer has made a complete examination and correct evaluation of every instrument properly recorded that affects the title to the land described in the policy.

INSURING AGAINST ENCUMBRANCES

The policy affords protection not only from defects in the title, but also gives assurances that there are no recorded encumbrances other than those shown. The word "encumbrance" has a broad meaning and includes taxes, assessments, and liens (C.C., Sec. 1114); also, whatever charges, burdens, obstructs, or impairs the use of the land, or impedes its transfer. Easements, overlaps, encroachments, and covenants, conditions, and restrictions have been held to be encumbrances. Where the policy fails to disclose a recorded easement, it has been held that the liability of the insurer is the difference in value of the property with and without the easement. (*Overholtzer* v. *Northern Counties Title Ins. Co.*, 116 C.A.2d 113.)

UNMARKETABILITY OF TITLE

Title insurance policies insure against loss or damage arising from *unmarketability* of the title. Marketability of title is a legal concept and denotes a title that is ascertainable from the public records and not dependent upon proof of off-record matters. An insurable title may not always be a perfect record title. A claim of loss on this ground is unusual, however, since a buyer will almost always accept a title that a title insurer will insure, without regard to technical questions of marketability. (*Hocking* v. *Title Ins. and Trust Co.*, 37 Cal.2d 644.)

IV. Coverage against off-record risks

As mentioned above, the distinctive coverage of a policy of title insurance, as compared with a guarantee of title, is the extension of the coverage to certain off-record risks. These hazards, which the policy of title insurance primarily was developed to cover, relate to the *identity* and *capacity* of the parties. A policy of title insurance protects a bona fide purchaser or encumbrancer against forgery or false personation. Similar protection is afforded against loss due to lack of capacity on the part of any party to any transaction involving the title to the property.

FORGED DEEDS

A forged deed, or a deed not executed by the real owner even though signed by a person of the same name, is ineffective to pass title. It is a *void* deed, and has no legal effect whatever. Yet such a deed will have the appearance, on the records, of being just as effective as one executed by the true owner. The hazard of forgery or false personation somewhere in the chain of title is a serious off-record risk, and insurance against such risk is a substantial contribution to persons requiring title insurance.

Statement of information. The "statement of information" usually required by title insurers is one means of guarding against the possibility of a forgery. Most insurers require that in every transaction the parties personally sign "statement of information," or "statements of identity," containing essential personal data about themselves. These statements are preserved in the files for future reference and afford a ready reference for comparison of signatures, ascertainment of marital status, alienage, and the like. Many cases of forgery have been detected as a result of information contained in such a statement. As an illustration, one deal appeared to be in order, but in the identity statement furnished by the purported seller it was stated that he had lived in "Stokton" for many years. The misspelling of the name of the California town in which he was supposed to have lived for at least ten years, along with other factors, aroused suspicion. An investigation followed, which led to arrest, conviction, and imprisonment.

COMPETENCY OF PARTIES

The *competency* of parties to transactions involving land is also a matter of vital concern, and the public records may offer no clue as to this important aspect. Competency involves questions of minority, insanity, death, or presumed death. Dealings with a person under 18 years of age or dispositions of land by such a person are void. A deed by a person wholly without understanding is void, as is a deed by a person who has been adjudged an incompetent. Guardianship proceedings may be pending in another county or another state, but may not be evidenced in the records of the county where the property is located. An owner of property may have been missing for over seven years; there is a presumption that he is dead, but that presumption will not support the conventional probate of a decedent's estate, and will not bind him if he reappears.

STATUS OF PARTIES

The status of each person involved in the chain of title is of considerable importance in passing on titles. This is readily appreciated with reference to marital status and the obvious necessity of the joinder of the wife in the disposition of community property. It also arises in cases of bankruptcy. For example, property inherited by a bankrupt within six months after bankruptcy becomes a part of the estate in bankruptcy. It therefore is essential to know whether or not an owner was previously adjudicated a bankrupt.

POWERS OF AGENTS AND OTHERS

Particular attention must also be given to the powers conferred upon agents and fiduciaries under powers of attorney, trusts, and the like, and to the powers of governmental agencies, corporations, partnerships, and other associations. The powers of a domestic or foreign corporation may be incapable of exercise through expiration, suspension, or forfeiture of its charter, although this may not appear in the public records of the county where its property is situated.

DELIVERY OF INSTRUMENTS

Delivery is an essential element of the validity of any instrument affecting the title to real property, yet this vital act cannot be established by the public records alone. Recordation of an instrument is presumptive of delivery, but this presumption is rebuttable. A deed executed in blank is invalid, yet this will seldom appear of record. A stolen deed is void, and this again would not appear from the public records.

ESTATE TAX LIENS

The possible lien of federal estate taxes, which arises at the instant of death, requires no notice to anyone and is only released by payment or through such arrangements with the Commissioner of Internal Revenue as are authorized by the revenue laws. The title of even a good-faith purchaser, under probate proceedings or otherwise, is subject to the lien of federal estate taxes, although such lien may not be ascertainable from an examination of the public records.

OTHER FACTORS

Many other laws, federal, state, and local, have a direct bearing upon title to real property and require constant study and attention in order to protect persons dealing with land, since the effect of such laws may be included in the off-record risks covered by a policy of title insurance.

V. Standard coverage policy

Two basic forms of policies of title insurance exist—the standard coverage and the extended coverage. The standard coverage policy is the form customarily used by buyers and many lenders throughout California. This form is designated as the "California Land Title Association Standard Coverage Policy Form," which is the approved form used by members of the California Land Title Association, the trade organization of the title companies doing business in the state of California. It is an *"Owner's Policy"* if the owner only is insured; a *"Loan Policy"* if the lender only is insured; and a *"Joint Protection Policy"* when both an owner and a lender are insured. Land value is the basis of the charge for an owner's policy. The amount of the loan is the basis for a lender's policy.

COVERAGE OF STANDARD POLICY

The standard coverage policy insures the ownership of the land and the priority and validity of the insured mortgage or deed of trust. In general, it insures the correctness of the information obtained from an examination of the public records, in addition to the off-record risks discussed above. It does not insure against types of off-record risks that are ascertainable only from an inspection of the land or by making inquiry of persons in possession of the land. Nor does it necessarily insure that the property has access to a public street.

MATTERS EXCLUDED FROM COVERAGE

The standard coverage policy can be best explained by a consideration of risks that are not insured against. The matters that are specifically excluded from the coverage of this type of policy are mainly such matters as may be disclosed from an inspection of the land. Since the insuring company does not ordinarily make an inspection or survey of the land or premises involved in a standard coverage policy, the reasons for most of these general exceptions are largely self-explanatory. For the average buyer or lender who is personally familiar with the land with which he is dealing, this form of policy is usually sufficient.

Taxes and assessments not shown as liens. The standard policy excepts from coverage taxes and assessments that are not shown as existing liens by the records of any taxing authority that levies taxes or assessments on real property or by the public records. A *proposed* assessment is not insured against if it has not become a lien at the date of the policy. These assessments, however, are referred to in the preliminary report of title by a statement to the effect that a designated assessment has been noted in the examination of the records, but unless it becomes a lien prior to the issuance of the policy, will not be shown in such policy. Certain charges that might be assessed against the land are also excluded. For example, various cities have installed sewer mains with funds other than those raised by assessments against lands to be serviced by such mains. It is their practice to make a substantial charge, which they sometimes call an assessment, when permits for connection are requested. Such charges do not constitute a lien upon the property and, accordingly, are not shown in the policy. It is the practice, however, to disclose available information in the preliminary report of title.

Easements and encumbrances not disclosed of record. Also excluded from the coverage of the standard policy are easements, claims, or encumbrances that are not shown by the public records. This exception refers generally to previously executed instruments that are not recorded. This exclusion is based upon the fact that a good-faith purchaser or lender will be protected in any event. Persons dealing with property are entitled to rely on the public records, and title acquired in good faith and for value and without knowledge of off-record interests and liens will be superior. A *vendor's lien* is also a type of lien excluded from the coverage of the policy because not disclosed of record, but this lien would not be valid against a subsequent purchaser or encumbrancer in good faith and for value.

Instruments not in chain of title. A problem sometimes arises where the policy fails to disclose a mortgage that shows of record, but that was made and recorded *prior* to the time the mortgagor acquired title to the property. Although recorded, it is not in the chain of title of the mortgagor, since it precedes acquisition of title. A recorded instrument that is not in the chain of title is "wild" and does not, in law, impart notice to those dealing with the maker after he acquires title.

Rights of persons in possession. Another exclusion from coverage is the following: "Rights or claims of persons in possession of said land which are not shown by the public records." This exception is based on the fact that the insurer does not make an inspection of the property or inquiry of person in possession. A prospective purchaser or lender is under such a duty, however, and in many cases is willing to assume this risk, since he will have inspected the property as a normal incident of the transaction. Rights of persons in possession are, from the fact of possession alone, just as effective against persons dealing with the land as are rights evidenced by the public records. Such possessory rights might exist under an unrecorded lease or license, an unrecorded deed or contract of sale, an unrecorded lease with option to purchase, or might depend entirely upon adverse possession against the interests of the record owner. If there is a billboard on the land, for instance, inquiry of the owner of the billboard may disclose that he is paying rent to a stranger of the record title, and inquiry of such stranger might disclose that he holds an unrecorded contract of sale from the record owner.

Other matters disclosed by an inspection. The standard policy also excludes "Any facts, rights, interests, or claims which are not shown by the public records but which could be ascertained by an inspection of said land, or by making inquiry of persons in possession thereof or by a correct survey." Many off-record matters in addition to claims of ownership are ascertainable from an inspection of the land. The telephone company or the light and power company may have poles upon the land or wires crossing the property. Inquiry may disclose that they have an unrecorded agreement with the owner, or they may have entered without hindrance and erected their facilities with the tacit consent of the owner. The public use having intervened, they cannot be ousted. Their visible possession is notice to the world of their interest in the land. Or there may be a community driveway, used in common with the owner of the adjoining parcel. Again, the visible location of the driveway, straddling the common boundary, is notice sufficient to put an intending purchaser or encumbrancer on notice of the reciprocal rights of the adjoining owners. Also, the possibilities of mechanics' liens, which can be anticipated by observation of construction in progress upon inspection of the premises, fall within this exception.

Physical characteristics of the land. Hidden defects in boundaries, in surveys, in encroachments and overlaps, and other such matters are not insured against in the standard policy. These matters relate to the physical characteristics of the land. If the property being purchased is a lot in a subdivision or a parcel in a built-up neighborhood, the new owner is not too much concerned with such possible defects; he can ordinarily buy or build with reasonable assurance, as a practical matter, that his possession will not be disturbed. If, however, he contemplates a use or enjoyment of the property that will require substantially the entire parcel, such as an apartment house or office building that will be built to the exact boundaries, he may require further assurances as to the true location of the boundaries and that buildings on adjoining property do not encroach on his. This necessitates an accurate survey.

Errors on recorded maps. Recorded maps, especially the older ones, are sometimes unreliable. A title insurer who examines the record chain of instruments finds that they all refer to a recorded map, but whether it is an accurate map or not would not be ascertainable from the record alone. By way of illustration, a recorded map, by reference to which a lot in the tract shown on such map has passed through successive ownerships over a period of years, may show that a certain block is divided into 20 lots, each having a stated frontage of 50 feet, the two tiers of lots having a common rear line, with 10 lots facing each of the two streets bounding the block. A correct survey now shows that there is an excess of land in the block, 5 feet along the frontage of the lots. On the basis of apportionment each lot will have a true frontage of 50.5 feet, and the third lot will be located 101 feet from the corner, rather than 100 feet as shown on the public records.

Discrepancies in patents. Resurveys of old government subdivisions often disclose very substantial discrepancies, and the exact location on the ground of patented land becomes a somewhat difficult problem. Unless a correct survey is made by a competent surveyor, a title insurer must reflect ownership as it appears on the public records, without undertaking to establish precisely where the land lies on the ground.

Mining claims. The standard policy does not cover unpatented mining claims; reservations or exceptions in patents; water rights or claims of title to water, whether or not of record. The mining claims exception deals primarily with unpatented claims made under the federal mining laws. Claimants may have monumented their claims, given them distinctive names, and filed notice of the claim in a mining district where the records are now incomplete or unavailable. Often these claims are described by natural landmarks, with the result that they cannot be located with reference to data in the public records. Claimants are required to do annual assessment work on their claims, but unless someone else sought to claim the same ground, the old claim is not lost by failure to work it. As a consequence, the standard coverage policy excepts mining claims from its protection. This can make no difference respecting property comprising part of a Mexican grant, for such land was never open to entry under the mining laws. It makes little difference in dealing with improved urban property. The danger increases, however, in rural areas, particularly in the foothills and mountains, and especially where it is known that mining has been or is being conducted in the vicinity.

Reservations or exceptions in patents. Patents issued by the government often include reservations. These may be reservations of minerals, of easements and rights of way, and of water rights. The exclusion of such matters from the standard coverage policy is dictated by several considerations. One reason is that the rights reserved belong to the government and cannot ordinarily be removed. Another is that considerable delay would result if each patent had to be examined and the nature and effect of the reservation shown in the policy. A third is that here, again, such reservations are not important in many cases, e.g., in highly improved urban areas. Also, since no such reservations were contained in titles acquired under confirmed Mexican grants, this exclusion from coverage becomes unimportant in areas once covered by those grants.

Water rights. Water rights are excluded, as such rights do not necessarily appear in the public records. The water right appurtenant to riparian land originated from its location on the stream, not from any conveyance of record. There have been widespread dealings with water rights, and many of these may appear on the records, but since they do not originate in a recorded title, a complete chain of ownership of a given right often does not exist and cannot be insured.

Governmental acts and regulations relating to use. A policy of title insurance excludes from its coverage any law, ordinance, or governmental regulation, including zoning ordinances, that restrict, regulate, or prohibit the occupancy, use, or enjoyment of the property, or any zoning ordinance prohibiting a reduction in the dimensions or area, or separation in ownership, of any lot or parcel of land. Although important in relation to the use of property in many cases, and therefore having a bearing upon the title and binding an owner the same as other laws, it has not been found practical to attempt to extend the coverage of title insurance to the inclusion of such regulations. Comprehensive zoning ordinances and building codes of large cities have become so complex and detailed, are modified so often, and exceptions are made with such regularity, title insurers have found it impossible to attempt to cover them. With respect to a particular piece of property, a statement of what such ordinances provide at the date of the policy would be good for that day only and could give the customer no assurance that the ordinances would not be changed the next day. In the case of improved property that has not been altered recently, it may be assumed, ordinarily, that it complies with applicable regulations. In the case of unimproved property, anyone contemplating building needs to know more about the zoning and building requirements of the locality than could be reflected in a policy of title insurance.

Defects known to the insured. Another exclusion in a policy of title insurance, which applies to both types of policies, extended coverage as well as standard coverage, relates to any loss arising from defects or other matters concerning the title *known to the insured to exist* at the date of the policy and not theretofore communicated in writing to the insurer. No one could undertake to protect a person against facts with which that person is familiar and which he fails to disclose. Thus, if the grantor is a minor, and that fact is not ascertainable from an examination of the public records, but is known to the insured, any loss sustained by the insured would not be recoverable from the insurer. The failure of the insured to communicate to the insurer other essential facts pertaining to the transaction relieves the insurer of liability for loss attributable thereto. This is true where the transaction was induced by the fraud, duress, undue influence, or mistake of the insured. It would be true where the insured dealt with a person knowing him to be married, where such person held title of record and purported to deal with it as a single man, or where the insured knew that the person he dealt with was under some disability unknown and undisclosed to the insurer.

SPECIAL INDORSEMENTS

Many of the risks that are not covered by the standard policy of title insurance can be insured against by a title insurer, either by the insertion in the standard policy of a special indorsement undertaking such extended coverage, or by the employment of special forms of policy. Special indorsements are furnished, in proper cases, for various situations, such as protection to lenders against the assertion of priority by a mechanic's lien claimant; protection of the insured against forced removal of encroachments upon adjoining land; and insurance against loss by reason of an existing violation of private building restrictions. The special indorsements can be adapted to numerous situations where the insured desires special insurance against a particular risk, whether based on off-record matters or otherwise. Such an indorsement is especially appropriate when a defect in the title appears of record and is known to the parties, but the insurer is reasonably satisfied that the defect will not result in a loss. Such defect is noted in the policy, but an indorsement is added, protecting the insured from any loss occasioned thereby. Following are two typical illustrations: (1) restrictions upon the use of land, unlimited in duration, but which are known or believed to be unenforceable; and (2) easements of record, but long in disuse and unlikely to be claimed in the future.

VI. Extended coverage policy

The protection afforded by the standard policy is limited by the several exceptions discussed above, but these risks are primarily matters that the insured can assume as a result of his own inspection of and familiarity with the property. Occasions arise, however, where the standard policy is not suited to the needs of the particular customer, and special extra-coverage, extra-premium policies have been devised to assume many of these risks. These policies are known as extended coverage policies. Most of the general exceptions contained in the standard coverage policy may be eliminated, provided, of course, that the title company's on-the-ground investigation of the title discloses no serious defect. Because of the additional work involved in making an inspection of the premises and the additional risks assumed, the cost of such policies is proportionately greater. Extended coverage policies are available to both owners and lenders, although the most prevalent use is by lenders in connection with loans made on recently completed structures.

A.L.T.A. POLICY

The most common form of extended coverage policy is the American Land Title Association form of lender's policy (A.L.T.A. policy), for many years referred to as an A.T.A. policy. This policy, which is used on a national basis, originated in the requirements of institutional lenders, such as the large eastern life insurance companies, which were not in a position to make local inspections of the land upon which a loan was being requested. This policy, in addition to the usual coverage of the standard policy, eliminates where possible the standard exceptions pertaining to off-record easements and liens, rights of persons in possession, rights and claims that an inspection of the land or a correct survey would show, and mining claims, reservations in patents, and water rights. This extended coverage is made possible by obtaining correct surveys and by the insurer's acceptance of the responsibility of inspecting the property in each case and determining whether any such rights or claims exist, and if so, their nature and extent. This form of policy also includes assurances that the property has access to a public street.

PRIORITY OF LIENS

In the extended coverage policy, insurance is given that the lender has an enforceable lien that is valid and prior to defects, liens, and encumbrances on the title at the date of the policy. In addition, the policy insures against mechanics' liens and street assessments for work completed or under construction that may be recorded after the date of the policy and gain priority over the insured mortgage or deed of trust.

DEFECTS DISCLOSED BY AN INSPECTION OR A SURVEY

Inspection or survey often discloses numerous defects, including a variety of encroachments, either the building itself or architectural details thereof, such as cornices, flag poles, fire escapes, hydrants, and signs; party walls, boundary fences, and trees; community driveways; easements by prescription; streets improperly centered so that they do not conform with record easements; and shortages or excesses on the ground so that physical improvements occupy parcels differing from those appearing of record. A title company does not invariably cover such defects by the issuance of an extended coverage policy. Such defects are disclosed when ascertained, and in cases where it is considered reasonably safe to insure that no loss or damage will result from the defects noted, appropriate assurances are given to that effect, usually by an indorsement on the policy of title insurance.

EXTENDED COVERAGE POLICIES FOR OWNERS

The California Land Title Association extended coverage policy provides the same protection to owners that the A.L.T.A. form affords to lenders. Both the A.L.T.A. and other extended coverage policies lend themselves more readily to urban and subdivided land although they can, of course, be written on rural property. Unimproved land may be covered, but the policies are more in demand where improvements have been made.

VII. Other types of policies

In addition to policies for owners and lenders, numerous types of policies are available insuring other interests in real property. An easement policy insures the owner of a right of way or easement in land, such as might be required by an oil company or a public utility. In another type of policy the fee title to the land and the easement appurtenant to the land are both insured. There are several types of policies available in which the owner of a leasehold or the holder of a mortgage or deed of trust on the leasehold is given assurance of title, both as to commercial leases and oil leases.

INSURING CONTRACT INTEREST

Insurance of the title under a recorded contract of sale may also be obtained. The title is shown in the policy to be vested in the vendee as to the equitable title created by the specific contract of sale and purchase, and in the vendor as to the legal title.

OTHER TITLE COMPANY SERVICES

Additionally, many other types of policies and special indorsements to expand or supplement the coverage of standard form policies are available, plus special reports, litigation guarantees, and other services where the records of the title company can be profitably utilized. One of the most important services in connection with land subdivisions is the issuance of a subdivision guarantee.

VIII. The title insurer

To enable it to furnish the many services offered, a title insurance company maintains a title plant in which it keeps a classified and summarized history of all real estate transactions in the county, and of every type of document and court action that affects or might affect the ownership of land.

NEED FOR TITLE PLANT

An adequate title plant is essential, because the work of examining and reporting the title to land cannot be done effectively, economically, and speedily without an up-to-date title plant. If the insurer does not have its own, it must rely upon another company that has such a plant for the actual work of examination and report, predicating its policies upon the work of such a company. The latter need not be a title insurance company; it may be, and often is, an "abstract" or "title" company capable of turning out its own abstracts or certificates of title. Traditionally, almost all of the title insurers in California are corporations maintaining plants of their own in one or more counties of the state. In many instances they also issue policies covering land in other counties based upon the title work of a local abstract or title company.

FACILITIES OF A TITLE PLANT

A title plant has many facilities, but begins with the establishment of four principal sets of books, the *lot books,* the *general indices,* the *map books,* and the *books of abstracts* or photo copies of recorded instruments. An up-to-date plant usually will include a complete set of tax records, gathered from all of the taxing offices and agencies in the county. Because tax descriptions often vary from record descriptions, these tax records may be completely separate from the conventional lot books. The use of computers and other electronic equipment has been adopted by title companies resulting in better and faster service.

Lot books. The lot books constitute the heart of the title plant. They reflect every instrument describing real property that has been recorded in the county in which the land lies. Instruments when recorded in the county recorder's office are indexed by the recorder by the names of the parties, not by description of the land. These instruments in the recorder's office are then copied into permanent books, one after another, based generally on time of recording. The only way in which the recorded instruments can thereafter be located in these books is by first ascertaining the names of the parties and then scanning the indices of names. Lot books, however, are prepared by a title company to furnish a ready means of ascertaining what transactions have been recorded affecting a particular parcel of real property. In the lot books every parcel of property in separate ownership is given a separate space or column, and each instrument on the records affecting that particular parcel is entered in its space or column, so that the title thereto can be traced from the earliest to the latest instrument by examining that column alone. A geographic system may also be employed, where recording information on each parcel is kept in separate folders.

Abstracts or photo copies of recorded instruments. In the compilation, as well as in the maintenance of these lot books, an abstract is made of each recorded instrument at the recorder's office on the date of recordation of the instrument. This abstract, called a "daily slip," shows the date of the instrument, the date of recording and instrument number, the nature of the instrument, whether deed, lease, deed of trust, or whatever, the parties thereto, and the property affected. A notation of the date and nature of each instrument is posted to the respective parcels in the lot books, starting with the earliest, until each instrument in the chain of title of every parcel has been entered in the lot book. These daily slips are then bound into books labeled by date and chronologically arranged for ready reference. The abstracts of each day's recordings are posted as promptly as possible, often on the same day, and then bound up, so that the title plant is strictly up to date. In lieu of abstracts, photo copies of the documents may be made and retained on file.

General index. Many of the recorded instruments do not relate to or indicate any particular parcel of land. They may be powers of attorney; declarations of trust; court decrees affecting status, such as adjudications of bankruptcy, or of divorce, or incompetency, or change of name; and judgments creating liens on all property of the judgment debtor, or income tax liens. Abstracts or daily slips of such matters obviously cannot be posted to any particular parcel of real property on the lot book, so they are noted in another set of books, alphabetically arranged, according to the names of the persons affected. These books are known as the general index, or "G.I."

Map books. Every parcel of land must be identified by a "description" —a delineation thereof by established calls from which it can be identified and located on the ground. Initially, surveys were made by the government, identifying land by a legal method of subdivision; private grants were identified by name, supplemented by calls for monuments crudely or obscurely identified. In patents, in proceedings to establish private grants, and in civil actions for partition, these descriptions were supplemented by maps and surveys, often crudely drawn. From these beginnings, resurveys, subdivisions, and public and private maps have been made, retraced, revised, and recorded until the accumulated data comprise an imposing collection, particularly in the more populous counties. A title company must necessarily maintain a complete collection of official maps, but its files will not stop there. It should have available for ready reference as many of the private maps and surveys as possible, in order to facilitate the interpretation of the instruments in the chain of title that refer to such maps and surveys. The title company will keep on file, also, so far as necessary, copies of maps and plats for insertion in its policies as an aid to the insured. An incident of this part of the title plant is the compilation of "arbitrary" maps by the title company's engineering staff to facilitate the posting of recorded data to portions of larger holdings not identified by a separate lot number or designation, such as a parcel consisting of acreage described by metes and bounds.

End result of plant facilities. Having adequate plant facilities, a title company is then able to search the title with considerable speed. The ultimate purpose is, of course, the furnishing of accurate reports of title and policies of title insurance that can be relied upon with safety.

Questions

1. Define a policy of title insurance.
2. Are title companies subject to provisions of the Insurance Code?
3. Explain briefly the basis of liability under an abstract of title.
4. Does a guarantee of title have any advantage over a certificate of title?
5. Does a policy of title insurance cover risks not included in a guarantee of title?
6. Discuss briefly the basic coverage of a standard coverage policy.
7. Describe briefly the items that are excepted from the coverage of a standard policy.
8. Explain the additional protection afforded by an extended coverage policy.
9. Can an owner as well as a lender obtain an extended coverage policy?
10. May title policies be issued in favor of persons other than owners and lenders?
11. Describe briefly the sets of books maintained in a title plant.
12. Explain briefly the advantages of the lot book system.

23

Probate Proceedings and Their Effect on Title

Summary

Termination of guardianship of an incompetent; Community or homestead property—special proceedings where spouse is incompetent

VII. Miscellaneous proceedings
Procedure in simultaneous death cases; Missing persons; Administration of estate of missing person; Proceedings to establish fact of death of joint tenant or life tenant; Proceedings to establish identity

I. Introductory

The law of real property is governed by the laws of the state where the real property is located. Where an owner of real property in California is deceased, is missing, or is an incompetent or a minor, California law applies, even though the owner's residence is in another state. Questions often arise as to the applicable procedure to effect a sale or other disposition of such a person's property. The procedure is covered by various provisions of the Probate Code. This chapter will include a discussion of the procedural aspects of probate proceedings, with particular reference to real estate transactions.

II. Jurisdiction and nature of probate proceedings

The Superior Courts in California are given jurisdiction by the state constitution over all matters of probate and administration of estates, in like manner as they are given jurisdiction of cases at law and in equity, and this jurisdiction is part of the general jurisdiction of the Superior Court. The "probate court" is no more than the department of the Superior Court that exercises this jurisdiction. There is a Superior Court for each county in the state, with the large counties, such as Los Angeles, having several departments of the Superior Court.

JURISDICTION BASED ON STATUTORY AUTHORITY

The jurisdiction of the court in probate is entirely statutory. The power of the court to order a particular thing done in probate proceedings is circumscribed by the statutes governing probate administration, and may not be exercised in a manner essentially different from that provided.

JURISDICTIONAL REQUISITES

The administration of the estate of a decedent is dependent upon three jurisdictional requisites, as follows:

First: The fact of death, which is an essential element of the court's jurisdiction of the estate proceedings; for the court's authority extends only over the property of deceased persons. Proceedings based upon an erroneous assumption of death are always subject to attack. (*Scott* v. *McNeal,* 154 U.S. 34.) A decree purporting to distribute the estate of a living person is void, and may be annulled at any time.

Second: Property to be administered. There can be no administration proceedings unless the decedent leaves property to administer or an interest in property.

Third: Residence or property in the state or county. The California courts have jurisdiction if the decedent was either a *resident* of this state, or if a nonresident left *property* in this state. Section 301 of the Probate Code specifies the county in which the proceedings must be had.

DOMICILIARY AND ANCILLARY PROCEEDINGS

The proceedings may be either *domiciliary* or *ancillary.* If a decedent leaves property in more than one state, administration proceedings may be necessary in each state. The original proceedings are usually brought in the state of the decedent's domicile, and accordingly are known as *domiciliary* proceedings. The proceedings in other states where property is found are known as *ancillary* administration proceedings.

PROCEEDINGS "IN REM"

Probate proceedings are designated as proceedings *in rem,* as distinguished from proceedings *in personam.* In the ordinary civil action, jurisdiction of the court attaches with the filing of a complaint and either *service* of the summons on the defendants or their *voluntary appearance.* In probate proceedings, jurisdiction attaches upon the filing of a petition and the giving of such notice as the statute may require, usually by posting at the court house, by mailing notice to interested persons, or by publication in a newspaper. Personal service as in civil actions is not required. "Proceedings *in rem*" is a technical term used to designate proceedings or actions instituted against some thing, such as property, in contradistinction to personal actions.

Notice requirements must be strictly observed. Since probate proceedings are *in rem,* and the notice of the proceedings is usually *constructive* rather than *actual* notice, strict compliance with the notice provisions of the Probate Code is essential. This is of particular importance for title insurance purposes. Whenever title to real property is affected by probate proceedings, a title company will ordinarily require that an examination of the proceedings be made to determine whether or not the proceedings are regular. Of foremost concern is whether or not the court has jurisdiction in the particular proceedings. If it does, then inquiry is made to determine that all of the prescribed steps have been taken in accordance with the statutory requirements.

III. Wills and succession

When a person dies, title to his real property vests in his *heirs* or *devisees*. The law permits a person to make a will disposing of his estate to other persons upon his death (i.e., to make testamentary disposition). In the absence of a will, his estate passes by succession to his heirs as designated by the laws of succession in effect at the time of his death.

CHARACTERISTICS OF A VALID WILL

A will is an instrument by which a person disposes of his property, effective upon his death. An essential characteristic of a will is that it operates only upon the death of the maker of the will; up to the time of death the will is said to be *ambulatory*, and no rights of the maker in his property are divested by execution of the will, and no rights vest in the beneficiaries under the will until the death of the maker. The maker of the will, if a man, is called the *testator;* if a woman, the maker is called the *testatrix*. When a person dies leaving a will, he is said to die *testate;* if he dies without leaving a will, he is said to die *intestate*. A will may be amended or changed by a *codicil*.

GIFTS BY WILL

A *devise* is a gift of real property by will. The one who takes such property is called a *devisee*. A *bequest* is a gift of personal property by will. A *legacy* is also a gift of personal property by will, but it usually denotes a gift of money. The recipient of a gift of personal property by will is called a *legatee*.

REPRESENTATIVE OF AN ESTATE

The person named in the will to act as representative of the decedent's estate is called the *executor;* or if a woman, such person is called the *executrix*. If a person dies without leaving a will, the representative of his estate is called the *administrator;* or if a woman, such person is called the *administratrix*. If a person leaves a will, but fails to name an executor, or the person designated as executor is unable or unwilling to act, then the person appointed to act as representative is called the *administrator with-the-will-annexed* (administrator *cum testamento annexo*), usually abbreviated to read "Administrator c.t.a." Properly, one should refer to the *executor of the will* of a person dying testate, and to the *administrator of the estate* of a decedent who dies intestate. The word "representative" applies to either executor or administrator.

Duties of representative. In general, there is little difference between the authority and powers of an executor and an administrator. Both are charged with the duty of administering the estate of a deceased person in accordance with the law, and both have the same responsibility to all persons interested in the estate.

TYPES OF WILL

Three types of wills are valid in California, namely, a *witnessed will*, a *holographic will*, and a *nuncupative will*.

Witnessed will. The witnessed will, sometimes designated as a "formal will," is one in writing, signed at the end thereof by the testator, and witnessed by at least two attesting witnesses, who must sign at the testator's request and in his presence and to whom the testator declares the instrument to be his will. (Pro.C., Sec. 50.)

Holographic will. A holographic will is one entirely written, dated, and signed by the testator, and need not be witnessed. (Pro.C., Sec. 53.) Its use is recommended only where the time factor or other circumstances do not permit the execution of a formal will. The principal objection to such wills is that they often fail to carry out the testator's intention and are more apt to result in litigation than a formal will.

Nuncupative will. A nuncupative will, sometimes designated as an "oral will," is a will that requires no writing, but can be made only by persons in military service in actual contemplation, fear, or peril of death, or by persons in expectation of immediate death from an injury received the same day. Such type of will can dispose of personal property only, and not exceeding $1,000 in value. (Pro.C., Secs. 54 and 55.) It must be offered for probate within six months, and the words reduced to writing by a witness within thirty days. (Pro.C., Sec. 325.)

WHO CAN MAKE A WILL

By statutory provision, every person of sound mind, over the age of 18 years, may dispose of his or her property by will. (Pro.C., Sec. 20.) The right to dispose of property by will is entirely statutory. Such right is actually a statutory privilege that may be enlarged, diminished, or abolished by the legislature, subject to rights that may have become vested prior to legislative changes.

LIMITATIONS ON RIGHT TO DISPOSE OF PROPERTY BY WILL

Several limitations have been placed on the right of disposition of property by will, including limitations of gifts to charity, rights of pretermitted heirs, rights arising from a subsequent marriage, special rights of the family, and restrictions on subscribing witnesses, nonresident aliens, and murderers.

Gifts to charity. The law limits gifts to a charity by prescribing time periods before death that must elapse after the making of the charitable gift, and by providing a maximum percentage of the estate that may be given to charity if the decedent leaves immediate relatives. (Pro.C., Secs. 40–43.)

Pretermitted heirs (forgotten children). A testator is not required to leave any part of his estate to his children, but he must have them in mind when he makes his will. If a testator omits to provide in his will for any of his children, or the issue of any deceased child, such child or issue succeeds to the same share in the estate of the testator as if he (the testator) had died intestate, unless it appears from the will that the omission was intentional, or provision has been made for such child or issue by settlement or advancement. (Pro.C., Secs. 90–91.)

Marriage after will executed. The spouse of a testator who marries after making a will is protected in much the same way as pretermitted heirs. If a person marries after making a will, and the spouse or issue of the marriage survives the testator, the will is revoked as to such spouse or issue unless they are provided for in the will or marriage contract (as to the spouse) or some settlement (as to issue), or unless they are mentioned in such a way in the will as to show an intention not to provide for them. (Pro.C., Secs. 70–71.)

Nonresident aliens. An alien not residing in the United States or its territories cannot take real or personal property by testamentary disposition or under the laws of succession unless citizens of the United States can take property in such alien's country upon the same terms and conditions. This is commonly known as *reciprocal rights.* (Pro.C., Sec 259.)

Subscribing witness to will. A gift to a subscribing witness to a will is void unless there are two other witnesses who are disinterested. However, if the witness to whom the property is left by will would have taken a share of the estate if the decedent had died intestate, such witness may take under the will up to the amount of the intestate share. (Pro.C., Sec. 51.)

Murderer. A person convicted of murder of the decedent cannot succeed to any portion of the estate. The Probate Code was amended in 1955 to disqualify in a similar manner a person convicted of voluntary manslaughter of the decedent. (Pro.C., Sec. 258.) The code was further amended in 1963 to provide that no person shall be entitled to the estate who has wilfully and intentionally caused the death of the decedent or has caused such death in perpetration of certain crimes, including arson, robbery, rape, or mayhem.

SPECIAL RIGHTS OF SPOUSE AND CHILDREN

Superior to the rights of heirs or devisees are certain special rights in the estate of the decedent that are given to his family, including homestead rights, family allowance, and the rights to estates not exceeding $5,000 in value.

Declared homestead. Under prescribed conditions, where a homestead was recorded on property of a decedent during his lifetime, the probate court must set the homestead apart to the surviving spouse in accordance with special rules that supersede the usual rules of succession and prevail over any attempted testamentary disposition by the decedent. (Pro.C., Sec. 663.)

Probate homestead. If no homestead was recorded on property of the decedent before his death, the court must, upon petition, designate and set apart a probate homestead from suitable property of the estate, for the benefit of the surviving spouse and minor children. This probate homestead vests free from creditors' claims and the rights of heirs or devisees. (Pro.C., Secs. 660 *et seq.*)

Family allowance. The surviving spouse and children are entitled to such reasonable allowance out of the estate of a decedent as may be necessary for their maintenance during probate administration, which right is superior to rights of heirs, devisees, or creditors. (Pro.C., Secs. 680 *et seq.*)

Estates not exceeding $5,000 in value. A further exemption in favor of the surviving spouse or minor children is contained in the Probate Code provisions that authorize the probate court to set aside to them the whole estate if its net value does not exceed $5,000 (formerly $2,500), subject to limitations as to the value of other estate owned by them. (Pro.C., Secs. 640 *et seq.*)

LAWS OF SUCCESSION

Where a person dies without leaving a will, his estate is distributed to his heirs at law. The Probate Code designates the persons to whom the court shall order distribution of the property of such decedent, which code provisions are known as the *statutes of succession.* Where the decedent was a married person, it is necessary to determine whether or not the property is *separate* or *community,* as different rules are applicable.

Community property. Upon the death of one of the spouses, one half of the community property belongs to the surviving spouse, and the other half is subject to testamentary disposition. If there is no will, all of the community property goes to the surviving spouse.

Separate property. If the decedent left a surviving spouse and one child, the estate goes one-half to each. If he left more than one child, the estate goes one-third to the surviving spouse and two-thirds to the children. If the decedent left a child or children and no surviving spouse, all of the estate goes to the child or children. If any of the children are deceased and left lawful issue, then the share of the deceased child goes to his lawful issue. If the decedent left a surviving spouse but no issue, the estate goes one-half to the surviving spouse and one-half to the parents of the deceased spouse. Various other contingencies are provided for, including disposition to next of kin in the absence of relatives of the designated classes. If the decedent leaves no relative entitled to take the estate under the laws of succession, then the estate escheats to the state of California.

IV. Steps in the administration of a decedent's estate

Although title to property of a decedent vests immediately upon his death in his heirs or devisees, it is subject to administration in appropriate judicial proceedings. As a general rule, all estates consisting of any interest in real property must be administered. Where an estate does not exceed $2,000 (formerly $1,000) in value, consisting solely of money, shares of stock, and other personal property, relatives of a designated class or a sole devisee may collect the estate upon proof by affidavit to the custodian of the personal property of their rights as heirs or devisees.

PURPOSE OF PROBATE PROCEEDINGS

The main purpose of probate proceedings is to collect the assets of the estate, pay the debts and taxes, and determine the persons to whom the balance of the estate is to be distributed. Further, it provides for the management of the property during the period the estate is being administered. By virtue of the proceedings, title to property is properly transmitted of record. The heirs or devisees do not have a marketable title until administration proceedings have been had.

PETITION FOR PROBATE OF WILL

If the decedent died testate, the custodian of the will, within thirty days after learning of the testator's death, should deliver the will to the clerk of the probate court or to the executor named in the will. A petition for probate of the will is filed by the executor, or by a devisee or legatee named in the will, or by any person interested in the estate. Probate of a will means proof of the will in court as provided by law.

PETITION FOR LETTERS OF ADMINISTRATION

If the decedent died intestate, a petition for letters of administration is filed by an heir or other interested person. The petitions referred to above must include a statement of the jurisdictional facts (i.e., death, residence, and property to be administered), and the names, ages, and residences of the heirs, devisees, and legatees, so far as known to the petitioner. If a charitable trust is involved, notice may also have to be given to the Attorney General (Pro.C., Sec. 328, as amended in 1963).

ISSUANCE OF LETTERS

Notice of hearing is given as required by law, and at the hearing, an order is made admitting the will to probate (in the absence of a successful will contest), and directing the issuance of *letters testamentary* to the person named as executor, or *letters of administration with-the-will-annexed* to another person if the executor named in the will is unable or unwilling to act. If the decedent died intestate, the order directs the issuance of *letters of administration.* Letters testamentary or of administration, as the case may be, are signed by the clerk of the court, under seal of the court, and issued when the executor or administrator takes the oath of office and also furnishes a sufficient bond if such is required.

SPECIAL ADMINISTRATOR

Pending the appointment of an executor or administrator, a *special administrator* may be appointed where the circumstances require the immediate appointment of a personal representative. A necessity would arise, for instance, where the assets of the estate include perishable personal property. Ordinarily, the appointment of a special administrator may be made without notice. The special administrator must take possession of and preserve all property of the decedent, and must collect all claims, rents, and income belonging to the estate.

Special administrator with general powers. When a special administrator is appointed pending determination of a contest of a will or pending an appeal from an order appointing, suspending, or removing an executor or administrator, the special administrator may be given the same powers, duties, and obligations as a general administrator. He may then exercise whatever powers are necessary for administration of the estate up to the point where distribution is requested.

NOTICE TO CREDITORS

The representative must cause a notice to creditors to be published, requiring all persons having claims against the estate to file them either with the clerk of the court or with the representative within four months after first publication of the notice to creditors. The time for filing used to be six months, but in 1968 this was shortened to four months. The representative is required to either allow or reject the claim in writing. If a claim is allowed by the representative and approved by the court, it is a debt of the estate to be paid in the course of administration, in a prescribed order of priority. If a claim is rejected, the claimant may bring an action against the representative to determine the validity of the claim.

INVENTORY AND APPRAISEMENT

Within three months after his appointment, the representative must file with the clerk of the court an inventory and appraisement of the estate. The appraisal is made by an inheritance tax appraiser appointed by the court. The condition of the estate regarding availability of funds for costs and expenses and debts, including taxes, must be ascertained, and consideration given to the need to sell, exchange, lease, or otherwise deal with the property of the estate.

DISPOSITION OF ESTATE PROPERTY

During the course of estate proceedings, it may be necessary or advisable to dispose of property of the estate, by either a sale, exchange, or conveyance in fulfillment of a contract, or it may be necessary to borrow money and to execute a deed of trust on estate property, or it may be beneficial to lease property of the estate. The Probate Code expressly authorizes these and many other types of transactions upon compliance with prescribed procedures.

PETITION FOR INSTRUCTIONS

For practical reasons, every situation that might arise in a probate proceeding cannot be anticipated and provided for. Accordingly, there is also included in the Probate Code a section providing that in cases where no other or different procedure is provided by statute, the court on petition of the representative may *instruct and direct him* as to the administration of the estate and the disposition, management, operation, care, protection, or preservation of the estate or any property thereof. (Pro.C., Sec. 588.) This section affords a procedure for acts not otherwise specifically provided for by statute but necessary for the preservation of the estate—for example, an order authorizing the representative to subordinate a second deed of trust owned by the estate to a renewal of a first lien in default, as to which foreclosure is threatened if an effective renewal cannot be had.

SALE OF ESTATE PROPERTY

Proceedings to effect a sale of real property occur most frequently. When a sale of property of the estate is necessary for the purpose of paying debts, legacies, family allowance, or expenses of administration, or when it is to the advantage, benefit, and best interests of the estate and those interested therein that any property of the estate be sold, the representative may sell the same, either at public auction or private sale, using his discretion as to which property to sell first, subject to a prescribed order of resort where the decedent died testate.

Contract with real estate broker. Prior to proceeding with a sale, the representative may enter into a contract with a real estate broker or multiple group of agents or brokers in order to secure a purchaser for the estate; this contract may provide for the payment of a commission out of the proceeds of the sale. When the sale is confirmed to such purchaser, the contract with the broker is binding and valid as against the estate for an amount to be allowed by the court. The code provides that no personal liability shall attach to the representative, and no liability shall be incurred by the estate unless an actual sale is made and confirmed by the court. An exclusive agency agreement would not be enforceable against the estate unless the broker was the procuring cause of a sale.

Notice of sale. Unless notice of sale is waived in the will, it is necessary to give notice of sale for the period and in the manner prescribed. By advertising property for sale, the representative is not bound to accept the highest bid received, since the advertising for bids is not an offer but rather an invitation to make an offer. The representative may call for higher bids or may postpone the sale from time to time. The price offered at a private sale must be at least 90 per cent of the appraised value of the real property to be sold.

Confirmation by the court. When a bid is accepted it is subject to confirmation by the court. A return of sale and petition for confirmation is filed and set for hearing. At the hearing, if it appears to the court that good reason existed for the sale and that the sale was legally made and fairly conducted and that the sum bid is not disproportionate to the value, the court may confirm the sale and direct the execution of a conveyance. Before confirming the sale the court asks if there are any higher bids. If an increased bid in the requisite amount (at least 10 per cent on the first $10,000 and 5 per cent on the balance) is made in open court, the court in its discretion may accept such bid and confirm the sale to the new bidder, or it may order a new sale. The court may also postpone the hearing, at which time it may receive additional bids and accept a higher bid.

Broker's commission. If a commission is payable, the order of confirmation must so provide; if this is not done, a commission cannot be recovered. In the case of *Estate of Efird,* 130 C.A.2d 227, an order confirming sale was amended to provide for the commission, but the heirs appealed, questioning the jurisdiction of the court to amend the order. The appellate court held that the probate court has exclusive jurisdiction to adjust brokers' claims, and ruled in favor of the broker.

Commission payable to original broker. The Probate Code provides that in the case of a sale on an increased bid in open court made to a purchaser not procured by the broker holding the listing, the court shall allow a commission on the full amount for which the sale is confirmed, with one half the commission on the original bid to be paid to the broker whose bid is returned to the court for confirmation, and the balance of the commission payable to the broker who obtains the new purchaser to whom the sale is confirmed. The Probate Code was amended in 1955 to provide that if the successful bidder is not produced by a bona fide agent, then the broker holding the listing shall be allowed a full commission on the amount of the original bid.

Determining compensation to broker on increased bid. If the sale is confirmed to a new bidder on a sale in open court, the court is empowered to fix a reasonable compensation for the services of the broker procuring the successful bidder. However, the compensation of the broker producing the successful bidder shall not exceed one half of the difference between the amount of bid in the original return and the amount of the successful bid. For the purposes of the section authorizing a sale on an increased bid, the court determines the amount of the bid without regard to any commission to which a broker may be entitled. Prior to the code amendement in 1955, there was a conflict in the cases as to whether or not the increased bid should take into consideration a broker's commission payable on the increased bid.

Deed by representative. After confirmation of the sale, a deed is executed by the representative, which deed must refer to the order confirming sale, and a certified copy of the order is recorded in the office of the county recorder together with the deed.

Necessity that sale comply with code requirements. It is essential for title insurance purposes that the sale proceedings comply with the statutory requirements. If there is a defect in the proceedings, the title company may not be able to insure the transaction. For instance, the description in the published notice of sale of real estate may be erroneous. If the error is material, the proceedings will be ineffective, since prospective bidders would not receive sufficient notice of sale, and the highest possible bid may not have been obtained. Or the terms of the sale as authorized may not have been complied with by the representative, or the property may have been subject to a recorded homestead. The right of a surviving spouse to a recorded homestead usually prevails over any attempted probate sale or distribution in disregard of such rights.

Sale to representative prohibited. Except where the will of the decedent or a contract in writing made during the lifetime of the decedent so permits, the representative is prohibited from purchasing any property of the estate, or any claim against the estate, or being interested in any such purchase, directly or indirectly. (Pro.C., Sec. 583.) A transaction in violation of this rule is voidable at the instance of the heirs or other parties interested in the estate. The rule applies regardless of adequacy of consideration, lack of actual fraudulent intent, or apparent regularity of the proceedings. If a prohibited sale is made to a person who is acting for the representative and the property is resold to a bona fide purchaser for value and without notice of the representative's interest, it is probable that such purchaser's title would not be set aside. But if the interest of the representative is disclosed by the record chain of title, as where the probate sale is made to a third party who then, or shortly thereafter, conveys to the representative individually, or to the wife of the representative, it would appear that a subsequent purchaser would be charged with notice of the possible invalidity of the sale.

ENCUMBERING ESTATE PROPERTY

In many cases it is necessary to encumber real property of the estate. The representative cannot encumber the property of the estate without an order of court. The Probate Code defines the circumstances when property of the estate may be encumbered. The procedure to obtain an order authorizing the encumbrance requires a verified petition, notice of hearing on the petition, and an order of the court authorizing the loan. A certified copy of the order must be recorded in the office of the county recorder. Where the estate owns an undivided interest in real property, a joint encumbrance may be authorized for the special purposes set forth in the Probate Code.

EXCHANGE OF ESTATE PROPERTY

Exchanges of estate property are authorized, but are of less frequent occurrence than sales and encumbrances. Exchanges of estate property for other property were first authorized in 1929. The authority was then limited to the exchange of *real* property for other property. In 1935 the code was amended to authorize the exchange of *any* property of the estate for other property. In 1939 the code was again amended to permit the exchange to be made upon such terms as the court may prescribe, which may include the payment or receipt of part cash by the executor or administrator. The law to apply in a given case is the law in effect at the date of death of the decedent.

LEASING ESTATE PROPERTY

Orders authorizing leases are of frequent occurrence during the course of probate proceedings. Whenever it appears to the advantage of the estate to lease any real property of the decedent, the court may authorize the representative to execute such lease upon petition and after hearing on notice. An alteration or modification of a lease made by the decedent in his lifetime is in effect a new lease and requires authorization of the probate court. The representative may, however, lease real property of the estate without court authorization when the tenancy is from month to month, or for a term not to exceed one year, and the rental does not exceed $250 a month. By amendment in 1957, the court, in hearing the petition for authority to lease estate property, may consider any other offer made, in good faith, to lease the property on more favorable terms.

Period of lease. The period of the lease that the court may authorize cannot exceed ten years, except as to leases for the production of minerals, oil, gas, or other hydrocarbon substances (referred to generally as mineral leases), or a lease to grow asparagus. The law with respect to mineral leases has been changed from time to time, and it is necessary to check the former law as to the estates of decedents dying prior to the enactment of the law presently in effect.

CONVEYANCES IN FULFILLMENT OF CONTRACT

Where the decedent was bound by a contract in writing to convey real or personal property, a conveyance in fulfillment of such contract may be authorized. The procedure set forth in the Probate Code is not exclusive, but rather an alternative remedy to an action for specific performance. The code procedure provides an effective means of completing a sale of real property in accordance with an escrow agreement executed by the decedent as vendor but not consummated before his death. The Probate Code was amended in 1955 to broaden the statutory procedure by providing that the court may order such conveyance or transfer even though the obligation may not have arisen until *at* or *after* the death of the decedent. The amendment makes possible the enforcement of contracts where the decedent's obligation did not arise until his death, as in the case of an agreement for the purchase of a partnership interest where the right of the surviving partners to make the purchase does not aris until the death of the partner whose interest is to be purchased.

THIRD-PARTY CLAIMS

In 1965 a new procedure was adopted (Pro.C., Sec. 851.5) whereby the representative may petition for, and the court may grant, authority for the representative to transfer to a third person the estate's interest in real or personal property claimed by the third person. Prior to the enactment of the new law, the probate court had very limited jurisdiction to determine questions of title.

OPTION TO PURCHASE

Sometimes an option to purchase real property is given to a devisee in a decedent's will. Prior to 1963 no specific procedure was prescribed in this situation, but effective September 20, 1963, Section 854 was added to the Probate Code to establish the procedure for the exercise of an option given in the will. The optionee petitions the court for an order authorizing the representative to transfer or convey such property upon compliance with the terms and conditions stated in the will. The matter is set for hearing after notice is given. A maximum time limitation for exercise of the option is six months after issuance of letters.

ACTIONS BY OR AGAINST THE ESTATE

Actions by or against representatives are not infrequent. In this connection it should be observed that an "estate" is not an entity capable of suing or being sued. Actions by or against an estate must, as a rule, be brought by or against the administrator or executor in his representative capacity. The right of a representative to sue or be sued is dependent upon statutory authority. In any case the statutes must be examined to determine whether or not the particular type of action by or against the representative is authorized. The heirs or devisees are not necessary parties defendant in an action that the representative has the power to defend, and they are bound by a judgment against the representative.

PAYMENT OF TAXES

The estate is not in a condition to be closed until taxes have been paid as required. The tax problems arising in estate administration are often many and varied. An estate has all of the tax problems of an individual, plus those resulting from the transfer of property because of death, i.e., state inheritance and federal estate taxes. The representative must pay all taxes promptly, and make certain before closing the estate that all tax obligations have been paid or that the estate has been released from liability therefrom.

State inheritance tax. The California state inheritance tax is a tax on the right of each beneficiary as heir to succeed to the share of the estate left to him. The tax may also attach as a lien to property acquired by the survivor in the case of a joint tenancy, or to property acquired by the remainderman in the case of the death of the holder of a life estate created by deed in which the grantor in conveying the land reserves a life estate to himself, or to property transferred in contemplation of death or intended to take effect at or after such death. The law permits a certain amount of property to be given to each donee free from the tax, but beyond this exemption, each gift is subject to payment of an inheritance tax, the amount of tax depending upon (1) the value of the property given, and (2) the relationship of the recipient.

Amount of exemption. Effective July 29, 1967, the exemptions range from $12,000 in favor of a minor child to $300 for a stranger. Prior to September 15, 1961 a widow was allowed an exemption of $24,000; also, her half of the community property was not subject to tax. A surviving husband, however, was allowed a 100 per cent exemption as to community property and a $5,000 exemption as to separate property. Effective on and after the last mentioned date, the community property is exempt as to both spouses, and each is entitled to a $5,000 exemption as to separate property. Various *deductions* also apply, including debts of the decedent owing at date of death, expenses of last illness, funeral expenses, and various taxes and expenses of administration.

Duration of lien. The tax is a lien on the property, and except where otherwise provided, the lien remains until the tax—plus interest, if any, is due—is paid in full.

Federal estate tax. The federal estate tax is imposed by the federal government upon the right to dispose of property at death. Unlike the California inheritance tax, it is computed on the net value of the estate without regard to the number or relationship of the persons to whom the estate is distributed. It attaches to property transferred within three years of death without adequate consideration, also to trusts and transfers made in contemplation of death, interests in joint tenancies, and assets generally.

Amount of exemption. A flat exemption of $60,000 is presently allowed to the estate (including life insurance) of a resident of the United States. A marital deduction in the same amount is also allowed in the case of a husband or wife. In addition to the exemption, *deductions* are allowed for funeral and administration expenses, claims against the estate, and other similar charges.

Duration of lien. The lien of the estate tax attaches immediately upon death, and is effective without the recording of any notice in the office of the county recorder. It is subordinate, however, to a bona fide encumbrance on the property existing at the time of death, but is superior to any encumbrance later placed upon the property. Unless paid in full sooner, the lien continues for a period of ten years from date of death.

FINAL ACCOUNT AND PETITION FOR DISTRIBUTION

After the time for filing claims has expired and when the debts and taxes have been paid and the estate is in a proper condition to be closed, the representative renders his final account and asks that the estate be distributed to the persons entitled thereto. Where desirable, a proceeding for the determination of heirship may be had in advance of distribution. If the estate is not in a condition to be closed, but distribution of some of the assets can be made without prejudice to the estate and those interested therein, the court may order *preliminary distribution.* The present law permits filing a petition for preliminary distribution after three months have elapsed from the first publication of notice to creditors. Prior to September 20, 1963 the time was four months. When the estate is ready to be closed, *final distribution* is had. This is done by an order or decree settling the final account and distributing the estate. A certified copy of the decree should be recorded in the office of the county recorder if real property is included in the decree.

DISCHARGE OF REPRESENTATIVE

Upon a showing that all property has been distributed as ordered, the court makes an order discharging the representative. Estate proceedings usually take at least one year to fifteen months, with the minimum time being approximately nine months.

PERSONS ENTITLED TO DISTRIBUTION

The decree of distribution must name the persons and the proportions or parts of the estate to which each is entitled. Ordinarily, the distributees named in the decree are those heirs or devisees who are entitled to the estate under the laws of succession or under the will, as the case may be. However, the heirs or devisees may have entered into a compromise agreement as to their distributive shares, in which case the court may distribute the property in accordance with the agreement. Or distribution may be made in accordance with a partition of the property by the probate court under partition proceedings had before distribution. Or distribution may be made to an assignee or other transferee of an heir or devisee.

ASSIGNMENTS AND AGREEMENTS FOR DISTRIBUTION

Where distribution is made pursuant to an agreement for distribution or pursuant to assignments between heirs or devisees, special consideration is required for title insurance purposes. Ordinarily, property acquired by a decree of distribution is the separate property of the distributee and may thereafter be conveyed by him without the joinder of his spouse. This, however, is not always the case where distribution is pursuant to an assignment. The distributee to whom the property in question is distributed may have purchased the interest of the other heirs with community funds, and to that extent the property would be community property rather than separate property. Therefore, the usual practice in title work when the decree is made pursuant to an assignment is not to treat the interest of the distributee as separate property, and to require the spouse of the distributee to join in a conveyance of the property.

OMNIBUS CLAUSE

An omnibus clause in a decree of distribution is frequently helpful in title work in cases where, through inadvertence or otherwise, the decree fails to describe a parcel of property owned by the decedent, or the property is incorrectly described. In such case it would be necessary, if there were no omnibus clause in the decree, that the proceedings be reopened or that the decree be amended to correctly describe the property. The usual language of an omnibus clause reads as follows: "The following described property, *and all other property of the estate, whether described herein or not,* is distributed to ________ ."

FINALITY OF DECREE OF DISTRIBUTION

A decree of distribution when it becomes final is conclusive as to the rights of heirs, devisees, and legatees. It is a final determination as to the persons entitled to take the estate, and as to the property or shares that each distributee takes. It is conclusive against minors or persons under a legal disability, as well as against adults. It is conclusive as to persons who assert a right or interest in the estate whether they appear in the proceedings or not. However, the decree is not conclusive as to title claims of third parties adverse to the decedent or to the estate, since the decree of distribution gives the distributee only that title owned by the decedent or acquired by the estate subsequent to his death. It is binding only upon those claiming *from* the estate, and not upon those claiming *against* the estate. The property passes to the distributees subject to whatever rights might have been asserted by adverse claimants against the decedent or his estate.

EFFECT OF DISCOVERY OF LATER WILL

If a later will than that probated is discovered, the old proceedings are not reopened. The new will may be offered for probate, and the prior decree of distribution will not be a bar to the new proceedings. When the new will is admitted to probate, the rights of the beneficiaries thereunder may be determined in an appropriate equity action, e.g., an action to impress a trust against the distributees of the property in the previous proceedings.

V. Testamentary trusts

When a trust is created by will, a special jurisdiction, created and limited by statute, arises in the probate court. Section 1120 of the Probate Code confers jurisdiction on the probate court to administer testamentary trusts. Without such a statute, jurisdiction to administer testamentary trusts would remain exclusively in the superior court, sitting as a court of equity.

DETERMINATION OF VALIDITY OF TRUST

A decree of distribution distributing property to a trustee, when such decree has become final, is a conclusive determination of the terms and validity of a testamentary trust and of the rights of all persons thereunder.

JURISDICTION OF THE COURT

The probate court has jurisdiction over controversies between the trustee and the beneficiaries and is empowered to settle the accounts of the trustee and pass upon the acts of the trustee. Jurisdiction of the probate court includes instruction as to the administration of the trust. Jurisdiction is also retained to determine the interests of assignees of beneficiary interests in the trust estate. Upon termination of the trust according to its terms, the court may settle the final account of the trustee, find that the trust has terminated, and determine to whom the property passes to the extent that such matters were not concluded by the decree of distribution.

STATUS OF TRUSTEE

A trustee is a distributee, and generally anyone who is legally entitled to take property on distribution may be a trustee, if, in addition, he is qualified to act in the fiduciary capacity required to carry out the terms of the trust. A trustee cannot, then, be a minor or other person under a legal disability, or a corporation that has no power to act as a trustee. A nonresident individual who is otherwise qualified is not barred by reason of his nonresidence, although the court may hesitate to make such an appointment because of the difficulties in maintaining supervision over trust property.

TRANSACTIONS BY THE TRUSTEE

Upon distribution, title passes to the trustee, and he may deal with the property as authorized by the trust. If real property is being sold by the trustee, it is necessary to examine the probate proceedings to determine that the trustee has the power of sale. This also applies to other transactions the trustee may enter into, including mortgages, deeds of trust, leases, exchanges, and so forth. Also, it is necessary to determine from the proceedings that the trust by its terms has not terminated. An examination of the file may disclose that the trustee is still acting of record, but this may not be relied upon because of an event actually occurring that would terminate the trust—the death of the beneficiary, for instance, or a child attaining a designated age that entitles him to the trust estate. Often off-record proof is required to establish that the event of termination has not in fact occurred, and that the trust is still legally in effect.

PETITION FOR INSTRUCTIONS

Under the provisions of Section 1120 of the Probate Code, the trustee may petition the court for instructions in the administration of the trust, and if the circumstances are such that it is necessary to exercise a power not expressly conferred upon the trustee—a power of sale, for instance—a petition for instructions is the proper procedure. In such case the petition must set forth the particulars of and the necessity for the action sought to be taken, and a copy of the petition must be sent to all of the beneficiaries. The court in such proceedings must appoint a guardian *ad litem* to appear for the minor or incompetent beneficiaries and for any persons of a designated class not yet ascertained.

DUTIES OF TRUSTEE

In all matters connected with the trust, the trustee is bound to act in the highest good faith toward his beneficiary, and may not obtain any advantage over the latter by the slightest misrepresentation, concealment, threat, or adverse pressure of any kind. He must not use or deal with the trust property for his own profit, or for any other purpose not connected with the trust.

Prudent man rule. California has adopted a standard for investments made by fiduciaries that is commonly called the "prudent man rule." In making investments a trustee is expected to exercise the judgment and care, under the circumstances then prevailing, that men of prudence, discretion, and intelligence exercise in the management of their own affairs, not in regard to speculation, but in regard to the permanent disposition of their funds considering the probable income as well as the probable safety of their capital.

SUCCESSOR TRUSTEES

Regarding successor trustees, the Probate Code provides that if a vacancy is created in a testamentary trust by reason of death, resignation, removal, or by any other cause, the court has the power to appoint a new trustee to fill the vacancy. Anyone interested in the trust may file a petition for the appointment of a successor trustee, which petition is heard by the court after notice is given to all interested parties.

DISTRIBUTION OF TRUST PROPERTY

Upon a final or partial termination of the trust, the probate court is given jurisdiction to determine to whom the property shall pass and be delivered to. In making this determination it is, of course, bound by the provisions of the decree of distribution at the time the property passed from the hands of the executor to the testamentary trustee. Testamentary trusts contain varying provisions for termination, usually at indefinite dates, such as the death of the widow, or the youngest child's attaining the age of 21. When such event occurs, the authority of the trustee ceases, except as to matters incidental to the closing of the estate.

TERMINATION OF THE PROCEEDINGS

When the trust has terminated, the property must be distributed to the beneficiaries entitled thereto. Often the trust does not specify by name the persons entitled to receive the property, but merely refers to a class, such as "the children of the decedent, and if any are deceased then to the issue of such deceased child." Upon the trustee's filing his final account and request for distribution, the matter is set for hearing after notice, and the court makes its decree approving the final account, determining who is entitled to distribution of the property, and directing that the property be delivered accordingly. Instruments are then executed by the trustee conveying the legal title to the beneficiaries in accordance with the decree.

VI. Guardianship proceedings

When a person is under a legal disability of minority or incompetency so that he cannot act for himself to protect his property or his person, the probate court may appoint someone to act for him. Such person may be appointed as guardian of the estate, or guardian of the person, or both. The person for whom the guardian acts is known as the *ward.* Jurisdiction to supervise the acts of the guardian is in the probate court.

MINORS

Minors are all persons under 21 years of age, provided, however, that any person who has contracted a lawful marriage and is of the age of 18 years or older is deemed to be an adult person for the purpose of entering into any property transactions or contract. Also, veterans under the age of 21 are deemed to be adults for the purpose of purchasing a home or farm from the California Department of Veterans Affairs.

Contracts of minors. Contracts of minors under 18 years of age relating to real property, or personal property not in the minor's immediate possession or control, are *void.* Contracts of minors between 18 and 21 years of age are *voidable* and may be disaffirmed by the minor either before attaining his majority, or within a reasonable time thereafter, upon restoring the consideration or paying its equivalent.

When guardianship proceedings necessary. A minor may acquire title to real property, such as by gift deed, without the necessity for guardianship proceedings. But guardianship proceedings are essential for the purpose of obtaining a valid conveyance from the minor, or in connection with other transactions affecting the title, such as leases or encumbrances.

Procedure for appointment of guardian of minor. Proceedings are begun for the appointment of a guardian for a minor by the filing of a petition, which must allege the residence or temporary domicile of the minor in the county, or the existence of property of the minor in the county if the minor is a nonresident. Notice must be given to the persons having custody of the minor and to the parents of the minor, unless they are the petitioners. The court may also require notice to other relatives, but this is not mandatory. If the minor is 14 years of age or over, he may nominate a guardian.

Appointment of guardian. If the court is satisfied at the hearing that a guardian is required, the court may appoint either the petitioner or any other qualified person. The person appointed must give the required bond and take the oath of office. *Letters of guardianship* are then issued to him.

INCOMPETENT PERSONS

Incompetent persons having an estate also need to act through a guardian. A conveyance or other contract of a person of unsound mind but not entirely without understanding, made before his incapacity has been judicially determined, is *voidable* and is subject to being rescinded. After his incapacity has been judicially determined, a person of unsound mind can make no valid conveyance or other contract. A person entirely without understanding, even though there has been no adjudication to this effect, likewise cannot make a valid contract or conveyance, but he is liable for the reasonable value of necessities furnished for his support.

Acquisition of property. An insane or incompetent person may, notwithstanding the rules governing his contracts, acquire title to property without a guardian.

Adjudication of incompetency. In proceedings for the appointment of a guardian of an alleged incompetent there must be an adjudication of incompetence. As defined in the Probate Code, incompetence is not the same as insanity. A person may be incompetent by virtue of old age or failure of memory and be unable, unassisted, to properly manage and take care of himself or his property, and by reason thereof is likely to be deceived and imposed upon by artful and designing persons. This is the usual reason given for the appointment of the guardian.

Procedure for appointment of guardian of incompetent. After the petition for the appointment of a guardian is filed, a citation must be issued, which must be served personally on the alleged incompetent, together with a copy of the petition. The Probate Code also requires notice by mail to all relatives within the second degree who reside outside as well as in California. The alleged incompetent must be produced at the hearing, or evidence of his inability to attend or evidence that his attendance would retard or impair his recovery or increase his mental debility, must be shown. If an objection to the petition is filed on behalf of the alleged incompetent, it raises issues of fact that are triable by a jury. If the court finds that the person is incompetent and that other facts justify a guardianship, a guardian is ordered appointed. The person appointed qualifies by giving the required bond and taking the oath of office. He is then entitled to have *letters of guardianship* issued to him.

CONSERVATORSHIP

In 1957 new sections were added to the Probate Code (Secs. 1701–2207) authorizing the appointment of a conservator instead of a guardian in proper cases. The court is authorized to appoint a conservator of the person and property of any adult person who because of advanced age, illness, injury, mental weakness, intemperance, addiction to drugs, or other disability, or other cause, is unable properly to care for himself or his property, or who for said cause is likely to be deceived or imposed upon by artful or designing persons. The conservator has powers similar to those granted to a guardian of an estate, or of the person and estate of an incompetent person. A conservator may be appointed to succeed an existing guardian, and an existing guardian may be appointed by the court as a conservator and new letters issued.

ADMINISTRATION OF A GUARDIANSHIP ESTATE

The administration of a guardianship estate, whether of a minor or of an incompetent, differs from that of a decedent's estate insofar as the main purpose of the proceedings is concerned. The problems that arise in the handling of guardianship estates are more similar to those found in trust estates, that is, problems of property management and the use of income for the benefit of the ward. Though they seldom occur in the administration of decedents' estates, investment and production of income are duties of the guardian.

Powers of the guardian. Procedurally, however, the guardian is like the representative in decedents' estates in that he find his powers, duties, and limitations in the Probate Code. He may sell, borrow, exchange, lease, or do all things necessary to properly conduct the affairs of the guardianship, but he must be authorized by the court in performing these acts. The procedures for notice, confirmation, obtaining authority, and the like, must conform as nearly as possible to the provisions of the Probate Code covering similar proceedings by executors and administrators. Unless special procedures are prescribed in the code relating to guardianship, then the procedural sections of the code dealing with estates of decedents are made applicable.

TERMINATION OF GUARDIANSHIP OF A MINOR

In the case of a minor, the guardianship terminates when the ward reaches his majority, which is 21 years of age, or between 18 and 21 if the ward marries before attaining 21. When a minor attains the age of majority, the authority of the guardian ceases except for the purpose of filing his final account. However, in title work it is still necessary to show the effect of the guardianship proceedings until an order approving the final account has been entered, or a release of any claims for fees by the guardian and his attorney is obtained, because such claims might be imposed as liens on the ward's property by the order settling the guardian's final account. Similar consideration must be given where the estate of an incompetent is terminated.

TERMINATION OF GUARDIANSHIP OF AN INCOMPETENT

Guardianship of an estate of an incompetent continues until death of the ward, until his restoration to capacity, or until the estate is exhausted. A proceeding for restoration to capacity is initiated by filing a verified petition with the court. This may be filed by or on behalf of the ward by the guardian or by any relative or friend of the ward. Notice of the hearing must be given in the manner prescribed by the code. A jury trial is provided for. If the court finds that the ward is competent, it must so order, and the guardianship proceedings must then cease. The guardianship proceedings may also be terminated for the reason that the estate of the ward has become depleted prior to a termination by death or restoration to capacity. There must be estate to be administered upon, otherwise there is no basis for a guardianship continuing.

COMMUNITY OR HOMESTEAD PROPERTY—SPECIAL PROCEEDINGS WHERE SPOUSE IS INCOMPETENT

Prior to September 18, 1959, where either the husband or wife was, or both were, incompetent, and community or homesteaded property was involved, the conventional guardianship proceedings to effect a sale, transfer, or other disposition of such property were not applicable. A special type of proceedings applied which was exclusive. Under such procedures, the sane spouse (or if both spouses are incompetent, the guardian of the husband's estate) may petition the court for an order permitting him or her to sell and convey, exchange, mortgage, lease, or execute a deed of trust on the homestead or community property, or for an order permitting him or her to transfer such property in compromise, composition, or settlement of a mortgage or deed of trust thereon. (Pro. C., Secs. 1435.1 *et seq.*) In 1959 such procedure was made an alternative one.

VII. Miscellaneous proceedings

Special rules apply in the case of *simultaneous death* of two or more persons owning or having interests in property. Prior to 1945, certain presumptions governed the order of death when two persons died in the same calamity and there were no circumstances from which the order of death could be determined. In 1945 a Uniform Simultaneous Death Act was enacted, which provides that where there is no sufficient evidence that persons have died otherwise than at the same time (simultaneously), the property of each person shall be disposed of as if he had survived. (Pro. C., Secs. 296 *et seq.*) Joint tenancy property as well as community property is affected by these proceedings.

PROCEDURE IN SIMULTANEOUS DEATH CASES

The representative of the estate of a person who has died under circumstances where there is not sufficient evidence that such person and another person or persons have died otherwise than simultaneously, files a petition to have the court establish the order of death, and the petition is set for hearing, with notice of hearing to be given as prescribed. At the hearing the court makes a decree that death was simultaneous, or if the evidence shows the deaths not to have been simultaneous, the court makes a decree in which it sets forth the order of death. Such decree, when it becomes final, is a binding determination of the facts therein set forth, and is conclusive as against the representatives of the estate of the deceased persons named in the decree, and against all persons claiming by, through, or under such deceased person.

MISSING PERSONS

Special code sections apply in the case of missing persons. Where a person is missing for a long period of time and leaves an estate, a problem arises with respect to the disposition of such estate. Statutes permitting the administration of the estate of a missing person similar to the administration of the estate of a deceased person have been enacted in many jurisdictions, including California.

Presumption of death from long absence. In California, there is a rebuttable presumption of death from seven years' absence without tidings. (Evid. C. Sec. 667.) This rebuttable presumption, however, will not support conventional proceedings for probate of the estate of such person as a deceased person, or a finding of the date of death.

ADMINISTRATION OF ESTATE OF MISSING PERSON

Although proceedings brought under general state statutes dealing with the administration of the estates of deceased persons, based upon the presumption of death arising from long absence, are absolutely *void* if the missing person is in fact not dead, a state has the power to provide for *special proceedings* for the administration of estates of persons missing and unheard from for a considerable length of time, irrespective of the fact of death. The validity of such proceedings is not dependent upon whether or not the missing person is in fact dead, but rather upon whether the statutes providing for such proceedings violate the principles of due process. The United States Supreme Court has indicated that the essentials of due process are present if the proceedings provide for a reasonable period of absence on which to base a presumption of death, ample notice of the proceedings, and adequate safeguards for the protection of the missing person's rights if he reappears. (*Cunnius* v. *Reading School District,* 198 U.S. 458.) It has been held that if the requirements of due notice are met, and there is a statute of limitations protecting against an attack on the proceedings, distribution is conclusive. (*Blinn* v. *Nelson,* 222 U.S. 1.)

Two procedures prescribed. Two main procedures are prescribed by the Probate Code with respect to the estates of missing persons, one where a person has been missing over ninety days (Pro. C., Secs. 260–72), and one where a person has been missing over seven years (Pro. C., Secs. 280–94).

Persons missing over ninety days. Where a resident of California owning property in this state is missing for at least ninety days, the Superior Court of the county of the missing person's residence, on verified petition of his wife or any of his family or friends alleging that his whereabouts have been for such time and still are unknown, and that his property requires attention, supervision, and care, and that a trustee should be appointed to take charge and possession of such estate and to manage and control it under the direction of the court, holds a hearing after notice. If the court is satisfied that the allegations of the petition are true, it appoints a trustee to take charge of the missing person's property. The trustee, after the elapse of eight months from his appointment and qualification, may sell, mortgage, or give a deed of trust on the property pursuant to an order of the court. There is doubt as to the constitutionality of such procedure, however, and such proceedings are not regarded as sufficient for title insurance purposes.

Persons missing over seven years. If a person has been missing over seven years, his last will and testament may be probated, and his property may be administered as though he were in fact dead. Except to pay taxes, assessments, liens, or insurance premiums, to allow claims for debts contracted by or to specifically perform contracts made by the missing person before his disappearance, or to prevent depreciation of property, a sale, mortgage, or other disposition of the property may not be made until one year after appointment and qualification of the executor or administrator. No distribution may be made until one year after appointment and qualification of the representative, nor until three years after such appointment and qualification unless the distributee gives a surety bond for the return of the property or its value in case the missing person be adjudicated to be still living since the beginning of the seven-year period.

Time within which estate may be claimed. Within the three-year period after appointment and qualification of the representative, any person claiming to be the missing person may have such claim determined by the court. If it is determined that the missing person is living, all proceedings are vacated, except those providing for payment of taxes, assessments, liens, insurance premiums, allowed claims, specific performance of contracts, preservation of property, and any sale, encumbrance, or other disposition of property made in compliance with court order; the residue, less expenses, is delivered to the claimant.

Final distribution of estate. If no claim is made within the three-year period mentioned, it is conclusively presumed that the missing person died prior to the filing of the petition for probate of the will or for administration, and his estate may be finally distributed and the liabilities of the parties ended. If the period of absence exceeds ten years when the petition for letters is filed, final distribution without bond can be had one year after the appointment and qualification of the representative. After the expiration of the periods of time provided for and the final distribution of the estate, and after the missing person has been missing for the ten-year period, the statute of limitations is deemed to have run against all claimants. Except as otherwise provided, the estate of a missing person is administered in the same manner as the estate of a deceased person.

PROCEEDINGS TO ESTABLISH FACT OF DEATH OF JOINT TENANT OR LIFE TENANT

Another special proceeding relates to joint tenants and life tenants. Where a decedent was a joint tenant or a life tenant, it is often necessary to obtain a judicial determination of the fact of death. The Probate Code provides for such a proceeding. (Pro. C., Sec. 1170.) This section originally related to real property interests only, but in 1965 was amended to include personal property, such as a note secured by a deed of trust. The main purpose is to obtain a determination of the amount of inheritance tax payable by virtue of the death of the joint tenant or life tenant.

Procedure prescribed. Proceedings are instituted by the filing of a petition to establish the fact of death. An inheritance tax appraiser is appointed by the court, who renders a report after appraising the property. If in his report he finds that no inheritance tax is due, he issues a certificate to that effect, and the petition may then be set for hearing. If he finds that a tax is due, he makes his report and the court thereafter determines the amount of inheritance tax due. Upon payment of the tax, the petition is set for hearing and a decree obtained establishing the fact of death. A certified copy of the decree should be filed in the office of the county recorder.

Affidavit method of establishing fact of death. Where no inheritance tax is payable, the affidavit method of establishing the fact of death of record is used in many areas in the state. An affidavit of death of the joint tenant or life tenant, with certified copy of the death certificate attached, is recorded in the office of the county recorder in lieu of a decree establishing the fact of death.

PROCEEDINGS TO ESTABLISH IDENTITY

Sometimes the record title to real property is vested in the decedent under a name substantially different from the name under which probate proceedings are had. An example is that of a married woman who acquired title in her maiden name but whose estate was administered under her married name. Under such circumstances the title of a purchaser at a probate sale or of a distributee or his successor in interest is technically unmarketable. If an investigation satisfactorily establishes that title is vested in a deceased person whose estate has been or is being probated under a different name from that in which title is vested of record, title may be insured upon compliance with one of the following requirements: (*a*) if the transaction is a sale out of the estate and the representative's deed, pursuant to order confirming sale, refers in the caption to the name under which the decedent held record title; or (*b*) in the event the probate proceeding is still pending, upon the entry of an order of the probate court adding to the title of the proceeding the name by which title was acquired; or (*c*) in the event the probate proceeding has been closed, a decree is obtained in a civil action establishing identity under the provisions of Section 751a, Code of Civil Procedure.

Questions

1. Which courts have jurisdiction over probate proceedings?
2. Describe the three jurisdictional requisites of probate proceedings.
3. What happens to a person's property when he dies?
4. List the types of wills valid in California and explain their use.
5. Who may make a will?
6. Discuss briefly the main characteristics of a will.
7. Who are the principal heirs of a decedent in California?
8. Explain the necessary steps to effect a sale of real property in probate proceedings.
9. Are real estate commissions payable in a probate sale?
10. Discuss the principal powers and duties of a testamentary trustee.
11. Are minors all persons under 21?
12. Explain the powers and duties of a guardian.
13. May community property of an incompetent spouse be sold by the guardian?
14. Discuss the effect of simultaneous death of joint owners of property.
15. Are any special proceedings available where an owner of property is missing?
16. Discuss the proceedings that are required when a joint tenant or a life tenant dies.

Index